'The 8th edition of *An Introduction to Global Financial Markets* is a concise and insightful introduction to the workings of financial markets, products and institutions. This book is essential reading for students and finance professionals who wish to familiarise themselves with the workings of financial markets and institutions in an intuitive and yet comprehensive manner.'

Jens Hagendorff, Martin Currie Professor of Finance & Investment,
University of Edinburgh Business School, University of Edinburgh, UK

'This 8th edition of *An Introduction to Global Financial Markets* by Valdez and Molyneux is a much appreciated guide to better understand contemporary financial markets, institutions and regulators around the globe. Its clear and concise language makes it a valuable asset for both students and practitioners alike. Anyone embarking on an analysis of finance and financial markets against the backdrop of recent and ongoing crises and regulatory responses should resort to this comprehensive yet to-the-point book.'

Michael Koetter, Professor of Banking and Finance,
Frankfurt School of Finance and Management, Frankfurt, Germany

'We are limited as to how many books we can read, but we do have the privilege of the right choice. Presenting the vocational aspects of modern financial markets, without sacrificing the academic rigour is an art that most aim to strike. When this is combined with a very insightful way of the mechanics of global finance, then this becomes a masterpiece that everyone should read. This is what the latest edition of the book *An Introduction to Global Financial Markets* is all about.'

Dr Sotiris K. Staikouras, Cass Business School,
City University London, UK

'I welcome this well-revised edition of this highly successful book. Its authors combine world-class scholarship with the highest level of real-world knowledge and experience. Their book not surprisingly therefore continues to be a most reliable guide for students that dare to venture into the bewildering (and at times bewitching) landscape of global financial markets.'

Steven Ongena, Professor of Banking, University of Zurich,
Swiss Finance Institute, Switzerland and CEPR, UK

'This is an excellent introductory text, full of information, written with great clarity and in a style that will make it readily accessible and understandable for students.'

Graham Partington, Chair of the Finance Discipline,
University of Sydney, Australia

'The eighth edition of *An Introduction to Global Financial Markets* is a must-read for those beginning to study finance and an essential reference for advanced students of the topic. The coverage of the recent financial crisis is fantastic and provides a thorough update of all the data, markets, institutions and financial instruments that played a role in the crisis.'

Allen N. Berger, H. Montague Osteen, Jr., Professor in Banking and Finance,
Carolina Distinguished Professor, Moore School of Business,
University of South Carolina, US

AN INTRODUCTION TO

GLOBAL FINANCIAL MARKETS

8th edition

Stephen Valdez

& Philip Molyneux

First edition published 1993 as
An Introduction to Western Financial Markets
Second edition 1997
Third edition 2000
Fourth edition 2003
Fifth edition 2007
Sixth edition 2010
Seventh edition 2013
This edition 2016

Published by
PALGRAVE

Palgrave in the UK is an imprint of Macmillan Publishers Limited, registered in England, company number 785998, of 4 Crinan Street, London N1 9XW.

Palgrave Macmillan in the US is a division of St Martin's Press LLC, 175 Fifth Avenue, New York, NY 10010.

Palgrave is a global imprint of the above companies and is represented throughout the world.

Palgrave® and Macmillan® are registered trademarks in the United States, the United Kingdom, Europe and other countries.

ISBN 978–1–137–49755–0

This book is printed on paper suitable for recycling and made from fully managed and sustained forest sources. Logging, pulping and manufacturing processes are expected to conform to the environmental regulations of the country of origin.

A catalogue record for this book is available from the British Library.

Printed in China

Short Contents

Contents

List of Figures

List of Tables

List of Boxes

Preface

Originally, the idea of a book on global financial markets came to Stephen Valdez when he hit the problem of recommended reading for candidates coming from Continental Europe to one of the courses run by his former company, Valdez Financial Training. Because the courses in question were about the markets in general, books called *How the City of London Works* (or similar titles) did not exactly answer the problem. This was particularly true when they found themselves facing audiences from the former Russian republics and Eastern Europe.

It seemed to Stephen that there was a need for a more general book about global markets as a whole, as opposed to one about markets in one particular country such as the US or the UK. In any case, the financial world is becoming more integrated and global in its operations. A parochial knowledge of just one country is proving less and less satisfactory. This book seeks to answer this need.

Having said that, the book does not attempt a systematic coverage of the markets in all countries. Such a book would be far bulkier than this one and probably unreadable. Instead, he usually concentrates on examples from the US, the UK, Germany, France and Japan, with the inclusion in the fifth edition of a chapter on the new tiger economies of China and India. From time to time, illustrations have also been given from markets such as the Netherlands, Spain, Italy and Switzerland. The aim is not only to give a basic idea of how the markets work but also to show the diversity of customs and practices within a common theme.

The book should prove useful for those preparing for a variety of examinations (MBA, banking, finance, economics and business studies), those working in banking and financial institutions in a support role (computer staff, accountants, personnel, public relations, back office and settlement) and, finally, staff in the many suppliers of information and computer services to the financial markets (computer manufacturers and software houses, Thomson Reuters and so on).

The first edition came out in 1993, and although each subsequent edition has been brought up to date, it has sometimes seemed appropriate to add completely new chapters. Thus, the third edition added a chapter on European Economic and Monetary Union and the fifth edition, as mentioned, a chapter on China and India. In view of their growing influence, a chapter on hedge funds and private equity was also included. Apart from these new chapters, the fifth edition had new or expanded sections on credit derivatives, Islamic banking, the Sarbanes-Oxley legislation and hybrid bonds. The situation in the European Union (EU) following the rejection of the constitution was discussed, as well as recent directives such as the Markets in Financial Instruments Directive (MiFID). The last chapter reviewed current trends. Finally, for that edition, the companion website was introduced (see below).

It was a great pleasure to be asked to collaborate with Stephen Valdez on the sixth, seventh and eighth editions of his text. Global financial markets have been in turmoil since the onset of the mid-2007 credit crisis. Liquidity in interbank and other markets has dried up, and a collapse in global bank lending has resulted in a global economic downturn. Over the past decade or so, banks' involvement in markets has increased dramatically, partially as a reflection of the trend towards universal banking and also because technological advances have made it easier to price and trade an increasingly broad array of complex financial products. Banks have experienced an increasing dependence on financial markets not only as a funding source but also for risk management (hedging) purposes. What has emerged is a complex web of interdependence between banks and markets for their well-being. Banks rely on the interbank markets for funding (to supplement traditional retail and corporate deposits) and have also increasingly used securitization techniques, not only to move credit off their balance sheets but also to fund a lending explosion, particularly in mortgage markets. As we have seen since the start of the credit crunch, when interbank and securitized markets collapse, failure in banks and other financial institutions soon follows.

In light of these momentous events, it was a challenge to revise the sixth edition, which attempted to capture many of the trends relating to the global financial crisis of 2008. Major changes were made throughout the text, reflecting rapid developments in markets as well as the crisis. Chapter 5 on investment banking was substantially revised in light of the failure of Bear Stearns and Lehman Brothers and the problems faced by Merrill Lynch and other bulge bracket firms. Chapters 6–8 (on hedge funds and private equity) were significantly altered. There was a new Chapter 9 on the crisis and its consequences. Chapters 10 and 16 on trade finance and insurance, respectively, were removed, although updated versions are now found on the text's companion website, details of which are given below. Chapter 11 had emphasized the historical features of the European Union, whereas in the sixth edition various contemporary issues associated with Europe and the single currency were emphasized. Chapters 12–14 were updated to highlight recent trends in derivatives markets. The booming Chinese and Indian economies were again highlighted in Chapter 15, and the book ended by looking at key trends in Chapter 16. Here, the focus was on lessons learned from the credit crisis, deleverage, regulation of OTC derivative markets, precious metals, hedge fund prospects and various 'new' economic paradigms. The credit crisis dramatically changed the financial and economic landscape and the regulatory framework under which financial firms and markets operate. All tables and figures were updated to cover the crisis period.

A big thanks to Dr Jo Wells for checking through our discussion of derivatives products in the seventh edition and for the excellent insights provided. The previous edition also included revision questions at the end of each chapter and offered a brief summary of the content of the references and the suggested readings. This aimed at providing students with a good guide to the readings provided.

This eighth edition provides another substantial update and major re-design compared to previous editions. We have done our best to make all the information provided as contemporary as possible. A major innovation has been to try to make the book less 'text dense' and more user-friendly with a substantial number of illustrative Boxes that highlight key concepts as well as topical developments. In terms of content, the main differences are that substantial attention has been paid to the many regulatory developments that were only new proposals when we were writing the seventh edition; now that they have become reality, these are documented throughout the text. These cover issues like the impact and implementation of the US Dodd-Frank legislation, the EU's Capital Requirements Directive IV (that incorporates Basel III into EU law) as well as the European Market Infrastructure Regulation (EMIR) that plans to move much OTC derivatives business back onto exchanges. We cover the regulatory trend for banks to hold more capital and liquidity, the tougher requirements placed on systemically important banks (and other financial institutions) and the regulation of credit rating agencies (CRAs). Chapter 8, in particular, has updates on the major regulatory reforms that have taken place in European securities markets. Chapter 12 covers the new European Banking Union. Chapter 16 highlights the (short-term at least) reversal in fortune of some of the emerging economies that were booming a couple of years. We also note the downturn of global commodities markets.

We very much hope you enjoy the new substantially revised and re-designed text and hope it helps you obtain a contemporary insight into the key features of the trends and developments in global financial markets.

Stephen Valdez
Philip Molyneux

Companion Website

www.palgrave.com/business/valdez8

Books on financial markets usually involve a large number of mathematical formulae. In this case, we have had the non-numerate reader in mind, and though there are references to formulae from time to time, no equations or Greek letters are given (to the relief of many). On the other hand, those readers who are quite happy with mathematics may find this a little limiting.

For this reason, the eighth edition is supplemented with a companion website, which contains analytical material on the following topics:

Chapter 7	The Money and Bond Markets
	– Theories of the yield curve
	– Bond price calculation and duration
Chapter 8	Equity Markets
	– Portfolio theory (the capital asset pricing model)
Chapter 13	Traded Options
	– Option pricing

These examples are all taken from the excellent *Finance and Financial Markets* (2010) by Keith Pilbeam (Basingstoke: Palgrave Macmillan) and we are grateful for his cooperation. Indeed, those who are happy with mathematics might consider using this book in association with our own.

In addition to this mathematical content, the website also offers:

- bonus chapters on trade finance and insurance;
- PowerPoint slides for lecturers with all figures, tables and boxes from this edition included; and
- additional revision questions.

Stephen Valdez
Philip Molyneux

Acknowledgements

The authors and publishers wish to thank the following for permission to reproduce copyright material:

Advfn.com for Figure 8.2 SETS screen and Figure 8.3 SEAQ screen, originally published online at http://www.advfn.com/Help/the-sets-screen-64.html and http://www.advfn.com/Help/what-does-the-seaq-aim-window-show-59.html, respectively.

Association for Financial Markets in Europe and Oxford University Press for Figure 10.1: The securitization process; The Bank for International Settlements for Figure 2.3 Capital requirements under Basel III; Table 4.1 Number of ATMs, EFT-POS terminals and credit cards, end 2012; Table 7.2 International commercial paper issuance, March 2014; Table 10.1 Stages of the crisis; Table 10.2 Timeline of key events; Table 11.5 Central bank foreign exchange surveys: Daily foreign exchange dealings; Appendix Foreign exchange turnover by currency pairs; Table 15.1 Notional amounts outstanding of OTC derivatives by risk category and instrument; and Table 15.2 Derivative instruments traded on organized exchanges. All source data is available on the BIS website free of charge: www.bis.org.

The Banker July 2014, 2012, 2011, 2010 and 2009 for Table 2.4 Top 20 world banks by assets, 2013; Table 2.5 Nationality of top 20 banks by assets, 2008, 2010 and 2013; Table 2.6 Global structure: Share of global tier 1 capital, 2009, 2010 and 2013; Table 2.7 Top 20 world banks by tier 1 capital, 2013; Table 2.8 Nationality of top 20 banks by tier 1 capital, 2008 and 2013; Table 16.3 Top 20 Chinese banks by tier 1 capital and assets 2013; and Table 16.6 Top 10 Indian banks by assets (2013).

Bankscope for Table 2.1 Top European savings banks, 2013; Table 2.2 Cooperative banks' share of deposits, 2013; Table 16.3 Top 20 Chinese banks by tier 1 capital, 2013; and Table 16.4 Top 20 Chinese banksby total assets, 2013.

BBVA Research (Alicia Garcia-Herrero, Chief Economist for Emerging Markets) for Figure 16.1 Contribution to world economic growth and current GDP size 2013 and 2023; and Figure 16.2 Contributions of regions to world economic growth over next 10 years 2013–2023.

Bloomberg *L.P.* for Figure 5.4 Major global M&A deals in 2013 and Table 5.1 Top M&A advisers: Global announced deals in 2012 and 2013, both from *Global Financial Advisory Mergers and Acquisitions Rankings*; Table 7.3 US Corporate bond market in 2013 and Table 7.5 Top underwriters in international debt, 2013 – both from *Global Fixed Income League Tables*; and Box 16.4: Bank Non-performing Loans in China.

Board of Governors of the Federal Reserve System (US) for Figure 6.2 Borrowing from the US Federal Reserve, 1919–2014.

British Venture Capital Association for Table 9.7 UK private equity returns, 3-, 5- and 10-year average.

Credit Suisse for material from the *Credit Suisse Global Wealth Report (2013)* for Table 1.2 Size of global financial assets and Table 1.3 The world's financial assets, by market.

DBS Bank Limited for Table 16.2 Size and ownership of China's equitized commercial banks.

Euromoney for Table 11.1 Top 5 traders by % share of foreign exchange market 2013.

The European Commission for table: Parliamentary approved amounts of state aid in the period 2008 to 1 October 2014, in Box 10.5.

The Federal Trust for Table 8.3 Age dependence ratio, persons over 65 as a percentage of persons aged 15–64. Federation of European Securities Exchanges, Online statistical database for information in Table 13.6 Main stock index, options and futures markets in Europe.

The Financial Services Industry Regulator for Box 8.4 Block Trades and Dark Pool Trading ©2015 FINRA. All rights reserved. FINRA is a registered trademark of the Financial Industry Regulatory Authority, Inc. Reprinted with permission from FINRA.

FTSE for the figures of stock market performance in the UK and US in Chapter 17. 'FTSE®' is a trade mark of the London Stock Exchange Group companies and is used by FTSE International Limited (FTSE) under licence. All information is provided for information purposes only. No responsibility or liability can be accepted by FTSE or its licensors for any errors or for any loss from use of this publication. Neither FTSE nor any of its licensors makes any claim, prediction, warranty or representation whatsoever, expressly or impliedly, either as to the results to be obtained from the use of any index or the fitness or suitability of an index for any particular purpose to which it might be put. FTSE makes no representation regarding the advisability of investing in any asset. A decision to invest in any such asset should not be made in reliance on any information herein. Indices cannot be invested in directly. Inclusion of an asset in an index is not a recommendation to buy, sell or hold that asset. Distribution of FTSE index values requires a licence with FTSE and/ or its licensors.

Futures Industry Association *Annual Volume Survey* for Table 14.2 Top 30 derivatives exchanges, 2013 Investment Company Institute, www.ici.org, for Table 8.5 Worldwide total net assets of mutual funds, $m.

Alicia Garcia-Herrero, Chief Economist for Emerging Markets, BBVA Research, for permission to reproduce Figures 16.1 and 16.2.

ICE Benchmark Administration Limited for Table 7.1, 3-month LIBOR, 4 August 2014.

The International Monetary Fund for Chart 5.1 Size of shadow banking using alternative measures and Chart 5.2 Who does shadow banking in Box 5.2; Table 6.2 Haircuts on repo agreements; Table 6.5 Systemically important banks (2012); and the table Banking Crises Outcomes, 1970–2011 in Box 10.5.

Investment Company Institute and International Investment Funds Association for Table 8.5 Worldwide total net assets of mutual funds, $m.

PricewaterhouseCoopers, HK, *Foreign Banks in China Report*, 2014, for Table 16.5, Peer ranking summary of foreign banks in China.

St Louis Federal Reserve Bank, stlouisfed.org, for data in Table 11.2 Sterling/dollar exchange rates, 1972–2014; and Figure 11.1 US dollar/UK pound rates,1971–2014; and Table 11.3 Sterling/deutschmark exchange rates, 1960–2002; Figure 11.2 US dollar/euro rates, 1999–2014.

© *Telegraph Media Group Limited*, 23 September 2008, for Table 9.5 Most shorted banks.

TheCityUK www.thecityuk.com for Table 9.1 Regional breakdown of private equity activity, 2001 and 2011, % share; Table 9.2 World's largest hedge funds 2012 and Table 9.3 Global hedge fund returns 2002–12, both from *Hedge Funds*, 2013; Table 9.4 Largest private equity firms total funds raised, 2006–11; and Table 9.6 Largest private equity transactions – all from *Private Equity*, 2012.

Towers Watson for Table 8.2 Global pension assets (2014); and Table 8.4 Pension fund asset allocation, 2014.

The United Nations for Figure 8.1 Ageing populations: Proportion of the population aged 60 years or over. World and Development Regions 1950–2050.

The World Federation of Exchanges Ltd for Table 8.1 International stock market comparisons, equity turnover, market capitalization and number of companies listed, January 2014.

Figure 3.1 New approach to UK financial regulation and Figure 7.2 UK gilts yield curve, March 2015, are reproduced under terms of the Open Government License: http://www.nationalarchives.gov.uk/doc/open-government-licence/version/3/.

Every effort has been made to trace copyright holders, but if any have been inadvertently overlooked, the publishers will be pleased to make the necessary arrangements at the first opportunity.

We have found the staff of the BIS to be exceedingly helpful and courteous in pointing us in the right direction for certain answers. Other individuals who were very helpful include Steve Kelly of Thomson Financial Ltd for details from the annual Thomson Extel Survey; Sandie Deane of UBS Global Asset Management for pension fund statistics; Stuart Drew for useful comments on insurance; Ashmita Chhabra of Eurohedge for hedge fund figures; Ian Tabor of Euronext.liffe for the FTSE 100 EDSP calculation; Richard Stevens of the same organization for an explanation of swapnotes; John Ward of Dealogic on various matters; and Lisa Clifton of Swiss Re for pointing out sources in the sigma publications. The China British Council website includes a useful summary of Chinese banking. In other cases, we have extracted figures from magazines like *The Banker, Euromoney*, the *Financial Times* and *Futures Industry* as well as the *GTNewsletter*.

For the seventh and eighth editions, a wide range of sources of information was used to update and revise chapters. The various contemporary reports provided by TheCityUK are particularly useful for an excellent insight into contemporary capital and financial market issues. For gauging the cause and influence of the credit crisis on a whole range of areas, a number of key resources were used. The Bank for International Settlements (2009) *79th Annual Report* (1 April 2008 to 31 March 2009) was particularly useful in providing a detailed account of the crisis and its impact, and the 80th to the 83rd Annual Reports also helped with updates. Other useful studies included M. Bailey, D. Elmendorf and R. Litan (2008) *The Great Credit Squeeze: How it Happened, How to Prevent Another* (Brooking Institution, Washington, DC), and M.K. Brunnermeier (2009) 'Deciphering the liquidity and credit crunch 2007–08', *Journal of Economic Perspectives*, 23: 77–100. Wilhelm Buiter's piece on regulating the financial sector at www.voxeu.org/index.php?q=node/3232 was also insightful. A. Berger, P. Molyneux and J.O.S Wilson (eds) (2014) *The Oxford Handbook of Banking* (2nd edn) (OUP, Oxford) was of use, as it has a large number of review articles covering key themes in banking. G. Caprio and P. Honohan's chapter on banking crises was also useful. For the policy response to the crisis, essential reading included de Larosière (2009) *The High-level Group on Financial Supervision in the EU Report*, and J. Goddard, P. Molyneux and J.O.S Wilson (2012) 'The financial crisis in Europe: Evolution, policy responses and lessons for the future', *Journal of Financial Regulation and Compliance*, 17(4): 362–80. Also helpful were R. Litan and M. Bailey's (2009) *Fixing Finance: A Road Map for Reform* (Brooking Institution, Washington, DC), and the IMF's (2009) *Global Financial Stability Report: Responding to the Financial Crisis and Measuring Systemic Risks* (IMF, Washington, DC). Features of the sovereign debt crisis in the eurozone and its impact are also neatly covered in European Central Bank *Financial Stability Review* for 2011, and further developments are reviewed up to 2014 (ECB, Frankfurt). Also see the BIS (2011) *The Impact of Sovereign Credit Risk on Bank Funding Conditions* (Committee on the Global Financial System, Basel, July) and Barbara Casu, Claudia Girardone and Philip Molyneux's (2015) *Introduction to Banking*, that provide a good summary of the impact of many recent events on bank operations.

Stephen Valdez
Philip Molyneux

Abbreviations

ABCP	asset-backed commercial paper
ABS	asset-backed security
ACH	Automated Clearing House (US)
ADR	American Depository Receipt
ADV	average daily volume
AGM	annual general meeting
AIDA	attention, interest, desire, action [model]
AIFMD	Alternative Investment Fund Managers Directive (EU)
AIM	Alternative Investment Market (UK)
AMEX	American Stock Exchange
APR	annual percentage rate
APS	asset protection scheme
ATM	automated teller machine
ATV	average trading volume
Aum	assets under management
BaFin	Federal Supervisory Authority (Germany)
BBA	British Bankers Association
BBVA	Banco Bilbao Vizcaya Argentari
BENELUX	Belgium, Netherlands, Luxembourg
BIS	Bank for International Settlements
bp	basis point
BRIC	Brazil, Russia, India and China
BSE	Bombay Stock Exchange
BTAN	*bons du Trésor à intérêt annuel*
BTF	*bons du Trésor à taux fixe*
BTP	*Buoni del Tesoro poliennali*
BVCA	British Venture Capital Association
CAC	Cotation Assistée en Continu (Continuous Assisted Quotation)
CAC	collective action clause
CAD	Capital Adequacy Directive (EU)
CATS	Computer-Assisted Trading System
CBO	collateralized bond obligation
CBOE	Chicago Board Options Exchange
CBOT	Chicago Board of Trade
CBRC	China Banking Regulatory Commission
CCB	China Construction Bank
CCP	central counterparty
CCT	*certificati credito del Tesoro*
CD	certificate of deposit
CDO	collateralized debt obligation
CDS	credit default swap
CET1	Common Equity Tier 1
CFETS	China Foreign Exchange Trade System

CFTC	Commodity Futures Trading Commission
CGT	capital gains tax
CHAPS	Clearing House Automated Payments (UK)
CHIPS	Clearing House Interbank Payments (US)
CLO	collateralized loan obligation
CMBS	commercial mortgage-backed securities
CME	Chicago Mercantile Exchange
CP	commercial paper; also *pagares de empresa*
CPI	Consumer Price Index
CRA	Credit Rating Agency
CRD	Capital Requirement Directive (EU)
CRR/CRD IV	Capital Requirements Regulation and Directive
CSR	corporate social responsibility
CSRC	China Securities Regulatory Commission
CTO	*certificati del Tesoro con opzione*
DAX	Deutscher Aktienindex
DM	deutsche mark
DMO	Debt Management Office
DOT	Designated Order Turnaround
DTB	Deutsche Terminbörse
DTC	Depository Trust Corporation
EAGLEs	emerging and growth-leading economies
EASDAQ	European Association of Securities Dealers Automated Quotations
EBA	European Banking Authority
EBITDA	earnings before interest, tax, depreciation and amortization
EBS	Electronic Broking Services
EBU	European Banking Union
EC	European Community
ECB	European Central Bank
ECDs	eurocertificates of deposit
ECHO	Electronic Clearing House, Inc.
ECN	electronic communications network
Ecofin	European Council of Finance
ECP	Eurocommercial paper
ECSC	European Coal and Steel Community
EDR	European depository receipt
EDSP	exchange delivery settlement price
EEA	European Economic Area
EEC	European Economic Community
EFAMA	European Fund and Asset Management Association
EFSF	European Financial Stability Fund
EFSM	European Financial Stabilization Mechanism
EFTA	European Free Trade Act
EFT-POS	electronic funds transfer at point of sale
EIB	European Investment Bank
EIOPA	European Insurance and Occupational Pensions Authority
EMH	efficient market hypothesis
EMIR	European Market Infrastructure Regulation
EMS	European Monetary System

EMU	Economic Monetary Union
EONIA	Euro Overnight Indexed Average
ERM	Exchange Rate Mechanism (EU)
ESAs	European supranational authorities
ESCB	European System of Central Banks
ESFS	European System of Financial Supervisors (EU)
ESM	European Stability Mechanism (EU)
ESMA	European Securities and Markets Authority (EU)
ESRB	European Systemic Risk Board (EU)
ETFs	exchange traded funds
EU	European Union
EUR	euro
EURIBOR	European Interbank Bid Rate
EURONIA	Euro Overnight Index Average
Fannie Mae	Federal National Mortgage Association (US)
FAZ	*Frankfurter Allgemeine Zeitung*
FCA	Financial Conduct Authority (UK)
FCP	*fonds communs de placement*
FDIC	Federal Deposit Insurance Corporation (US)
FICC	fixed income, currency and commodities
FINRA	Financial Industry Regulating Authority
FPC	Financial Policy Committee (UK)
FRA	forward rate agreement
Freddie Mac	Federal Home Loan Mortgage Corporation (US)
FRN	floating rate note
FSA	Financial Services Authority (UK)
FSAP	Financial Services Action Plan (EU)
FTSE	Financial Times Stock Exchange
FX	foreign exchange
G7	Group of Seven [countries]
GAI	Greenwich Alternative Investments
GAO	Government Accounting Office
GBP	pound sterling
GDP	gross domestic product
GDR	global depository receipt
GKO	Gosudarstvennoye Kratkosrochnoye Obyazatyelstvo (government short-term commitments)
GNMA	Government National Mortgage Association
GSE	government-sponsored enterprise (US)
G-SIFI	global systemically important financial institution
HBOS	Halifax and Bank of Scotland
HFTs	high-frequency traders
HICP	Harmonized Index of Consumer Prices
HSBC	Hong Kong and Shanghai Banking Corporation
HY	high yield
IASB	International Accounting Standards Board
IBA	ICE Benchmark Administration
IBRD	International Bank for Reconstruction and Development (World Bank)
ICBC	Industrial and Commercial Bank of China

ICE	Intercontinental Exchange (US)
ICICI	Industrial Credit and Investment Corporation of India
IDA	International Development Association
IDB	interdealer broker
IFC	International Finance Corporation
IFSL	International Financial Services London
IG	investment grade
IMF	International Monetary Fund
IOSCO	International Organization of Securities Commissions
IPE	International Petroleum Exchange
IPO	initial public offering
IRB	internal rating–based
ISD	Investment Services Directive
IT	information technology
JPY	Japanese yen
KfW	Kreditanstalt für Wiederaufbau
KKR	Kohlberg Kravis Roberts
LBBW	Landesbank Baden-Württemberg
L-DAX	late DAX
LDC	less developed country
LIBID	London Interbank Bid Rate
LIBOR	London Interbank Offered Rate
LLR	lender of last resort
LME	London Metal Exchange
LSE	London Stock Exchange
LTCM	Long-Term Capital Management
LTRO	long term refinancing operation
M&A	mergers and acquisitions
MBO	management buyout
MBS	mortgage-backed security
MDAX	Mid-Cap DAX
MEFF	*Mercado Español de Futuros Financieros*
MEPC	Metropolitan Estates and Property Corporation
MiFID	Markets in Financial Instruments Directive (EU)
MOF	Ministry of Finance
MOF	multiple option facility
MONEP	*Marché des Options Négociables de Paris*
MPC	Monetary Policy Committee (UK)
MSCI	Morgan Stanley Capital International
MTFS	mutualized trading facilities
MTN	medium-term note
NASDQ	National Association of Securities Dealers' Automated Quotations
NCA	national competent authority
NIF	note issuance facility
NMS	normal market size
NPL	non-performing loan
NSC	Nouveau Système de Cotation
NSE	National Stock Exchange
NYSE	New York Stock Exchange

OATS	*obligations assimilables du Trésor*
OCC	Office of the Comptroller of the Currency
OECD	Organisation of Economic Co-operation and Development
OFC	offshore financial centre
OFEX	off exchange
OTC	over the counter
p.a.	per annum
PBOC	People's Bank of China
PC	personal computer
P/E	price earnings [ratio]
PHLX	Philadelphia Stock Exchange
PIN	personal identification number
PNS	Paris Net Settlement
POPS	Pankkien On-line Pikasiirrot ja Sekit-järjestelmä
POS	point of sale
PPIP	Public-Private Investment Program
PPP	purchasing power parity
PRA	Prudential Regulatory Authority (UK)
PSBR	public sector borrowing requirements
QE	quantitative easing
RAFT	revolving acceptance facility by tender
RAROC	risk-adjusted return on capital
RBI	Reserve Bank of India
RBS	Royal Bank of Scotland
RELIT	*règlement livraison de titres*
RMB	renminbi
RMBS	residential mortgage-backed securities
ROE	return on equity
RONIA	Repurchase Overnight Index Average
ROSE	repeat offering securitized entity
RPI	Retail Price Index
RTGS	real-time gross settlement
RUFs	revolving underwriting facilities
RWA	risk-weighted asset
S&Ls	savings and loans
SAFE	State Administration of Foreign Exchange
SDRs	special drawing rights
SEA	Single European Act
SEAQ	Stock Exchange Automated Quotations
SEC	Securities and Exchange Commission
SEET	social, environmental, ethical and trust
SENSEX	Bombay Stock Exchange Sensitive Index
SETS	Stock Exchange Electronic Trading Service
SETSqx	Stock Exchange Electronic Trading Service – quotes and crosse
SEPA	Single Euro Payments Area
SGP	Stability and Growth Pact
SICAV	*Société d'Investissement à Capital Variable*
SIFIs	strategically important financial institutions
SIMEX	Singapore Monetary Exchange

SIT	Système Interbancaire de Télécompensation
SIV	structured investment vehicle
SMP	Securities Market Program
SNB	Swiss National Bank
SOFFEX	Switzerland's Swiss Options and Financial Futures Exchange
soFFin	Financial Market Stabilization Fund
SONIA	Sterling Overnight Indexed Average
SPV	special purpose vehicle
SRB	Single Resolution Board
SRF	Single Bank Resolution Fund
SRI	socially responsible investing
SRM	Single Resolution Mechanism (EU)
SSM	Single Supervisory Mechanism (EU)
TAF	Term Auction Facility
TARGET	Trans-European Automated Real-time Gross settlement Transfer System
TARP	Troubled Asset Relief Program
TBTF	too big to fail
TCS	Tata Consulting Services
TIBOR	Tokyo Interbank Offered Rate
TIPANET	Transferts Interbancaires de Paiements Automatisés
TIPS	Treasury inflation-protected securities
TOPIX	Tokyo Stock Exchange Price Index
TVA	Tennessee Valley Authority
UCITS	undertakings for collective investment in transferable securities
UK	United Kingdom
US	United States
US SIF	US Forum for Sustainable and Responsible Investment
VaR	value at risk
VAT	value-added tax
VRN	variable rate note
XD	ex-dividend
XR	ex rights

1 Introduction

The Money Merry-go-round

RAISON D'ÊTRE OF THE MARKETS

The beginning is always a good place to start. Let's go straight to the heart of the matter and ask the most fundamental question of all: What are financial markets *for*? What is their purpose? What is their raison d'être?

Financial markets are all about raising capital and matching those who want capital (borrowers) with those who have it (lenders). How do borrowers find lenders? With difficulty, clearly, but for the presence of intermediaries such as banks. Banks take deposits from those who have money to save and bundle the money up in various ways so that it can be lent to those who wish to borrow.

More complex transactions than a simple bank deposit require markets in which borrowers and their agents can meet lenders and their agents, and existing commitments to borrow or lend can be resold to other people. Stock exchanges are a good example. Companies raise money by selling shares to investors, and existing shares are freely bought and sold.

The money goes round and round, just like a carousel on a fairground (Table 1.1).

Lenders

Let's have a look at some of those who might be lenders.

Individuals

People may have savings in banks of various kinds. Individuals may not think of themselves as conscious savers but nevertheless pay monthly premiums to insurance companies and contributions to pensions. Regarding pensions, there are different traditions. The United States, the United Kingdom, the Netherlands, Switzerland and Japan have a strong tradition of pension funds and invest the money paid into either private pension plans or employers' pension schemes. In France, the state takes care of most pensions and pays them out of current taxation, not out of a fund. In Germany, company pensions are important, but the company decides on the investment, which may be in the company itself. Where pension funds exist, these funds, along with those of insurance companies, are key determinants of movements in the markets. Pension and insurance companies have to look ahead to long-term liabilities and will assist the borrowers of capital by buying government bonds (otherwise known as sovereign bonds), corporate bonds, corporate equities and so on. The shortage of such funds in many of the newly emerging economies was an important reason for the relatively slow growth of local securities markets in earlier years.

▼ **Table 1.1** *The money merry-go-round*

Lenders	Intermediaries	Markets	Borrowers
Individuals	Banks	Interbank	Individuals
Companies	Insurance companies	Equity market	Companies
	Pension funds	Money market	Central government
	Mutual funds	Bond market	Municipalities
		Foreign exchange	Public corporations

Companies

We think of commercial companies as borrowers of capital. However, even if a company is a borrower, if some of the money is not needed for a short period of time, the company will seek to make money by lending in the short-term markets, called money markets, that is, transactions of up to 1 year in duration.

There are also companies whose cash flow is strong and who tend to be lenders rather than borrowers.

Borrowers

Who, then, are the borrowers of capital?

Individuals

Individuals may have bank loans for domestic purchases or longer term mortgages to fund house purchases.

Companies

Companies need short-term money to fund cash flow. They need money for a longer term for growth and expansion.

Governments

Governments are typically voracious borrowers. Their expenditures exceed their receipts from taxes, so they borrow to make up the deficit. They may also borrow on behalf of municipalities, federal states, nationalized industries and public sector bodies, generally. The total is usually called the 'public sector borrowing requirement' (PSBR). The cumulative total for all the borrowing since a government started borrowing is called the 'national debt'. The first surprise for many of us is that governments don't pay off the national debt; it just gets bigger. If there are doubts about a country's abilities to pay its debts – as in the case of Greece in 2011 – this can lead to a crisis. Of this, more in Chapters 3 and 10.

Municipalities and similar bodies

Apart from a government borrowing on behalf of various local authorities, these bodies may borrow in their own name. This would cover municipalities like Barcelona, counties in the UK, or federal states like Hesse in Germany.

Public corporations

These might include nationalized industries, like SNCF in France or the German railways and post office authorities, or general public sector bodies like Crédit Local de France or the German Unity Fund.

Within an economy, many of the above (individuals, companies and public corporations) will not be nationals, but foreigners, and therefore may need to borrow in foreign currency – this has implications for the foreign exchange market.

Securities

When the money is lent, it may simply be a deposit with a bank. Most of the time, however, the borrower will issue a receipt for the money, a promise to pay back. These pieces of paper are, in the most general sense, what we call 'securities'. Unfortunately for the beginner, these have many different names – Treasury bills (T-bills), certificates of deposits (CDs), commercial paper (CP), bills of exchange, bonds, convertibles, debentures, preference shares, Eurobonds, floating rate notes (FRNs) and so on. At least we can console ourselves with the thought that they are essentially all the same – promises to pay back, which show key information:

- how much is owed,
- when it will be paid and
- the rate of interest to reward the lender.

A major characteristic of the markets is that these securities are typically freely bought and sold. This makes life easier for the lender and helps the borrower to raise the money more easily.

For example, a young American wanting to save for old age spends $5,000 on a 30-year government bond that has just been issued. After 5 years, he decides that this was not such a good idea and wants the money now. What does he do? He simply sells the bond to someone else. This is crucially important, as it means that he is more willing to put the money up in the first place, knowing that there is this escape clause. It also gives great velocity to the 'money merry-go-round', as the same security is bought and sold many times.

Let's tackle the market jargon here. The first time the money is lent and changes hands, the first time the security is issued, is the *primary market*. All the buying and selling that takes place thereafter we call the *secondary market*. The secondary market is significant as the flexibility it gives makes the primary market work better – it's the oil that helps the wheels turn round.

Let's look at other terminology used (see Figure 1.1).

Suppose the government announces a new bond. We can say the government is *issuing* a new bond. We could just as easily say that the government is *selling* a new bond. We might see it as a sign of the government's need to *borrow* more money. If you hear of the new bond, you may tell a friend that you've decided to *invest* in it. Alternatively, you might say that you've decided to *buy* the new bond. You probably won't think of it that way, but you are effectively the *lender* of money to a government.

▼ Figure 1.1 *Market terminology*

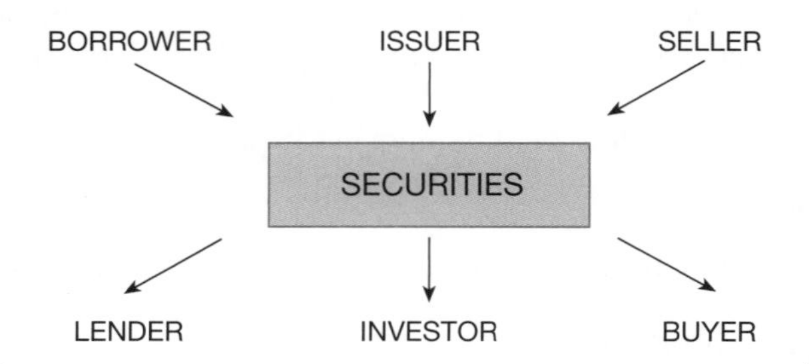

It may seem an obvious point, but all these terms might be used. Sometimes, newcomers need to be reminded that whoever buys a security is directly or indirectly lending money, unless it is equity.

RAISING CAPITAL

Let's look at an example outline in Box 1.1.

BOX 1.1

Examples of Raising Capital

Suppose a commercial company needs $200m to finance building a new factory. We have just explained that the financial markets are all about the raising of money. What, then, are the choices?

Bank Loans

One obvious source of money when we need it is the bank. These days, when large sums of money are required, it may be a syndicate of banks in order to spread the risk. The banks take deposits lent to them and relend the money to the commercial company. It's their classic role as an intermediary. In the international syndicated bank lending market, based in London, the money will not be lent at a fixed rate, but at a variable rate, which changes from time to time according to market rates. This is called the floating rate. The banks may lend at a basic rate, such as the prime rate in the US or the interbank rate in Europe, plus a given margin, such as 0.75%. The bank will readjust the rate, say, every 3 months. The rate is fixed for 3 months but then changes for the next 3 months. Note that this creates *risk*. If rates fall, the lender loses income. If rates rise, the borrower pays more. Note, however, that in many European domestic markets, the banks' tradition is to lend to corporates at a fixed rate.

Bonds

Another choice would be to issue a bond. A bond is just a piece of paper stating the terms on which the money will be paid back. For example, it may be a 10-year bond, paying interest at 7% in two instalments per year. The word 'bond' implies that the rate of interest is fixed. If it's floating, then we have to find another name, such as floating rate note. The bond may be bought by a bank as another use for depositors' money, or it might be bought directly by an investor who sees the bond notice in the paper and instructs his agent to buy.

There is a strong obligation to meet the interest payments on the bond. If an interest payment is missed, the bondholders acquire certain rights and might even be able to put the company into liquidation.

Equity

A final choice would be to raise the money by selling shares in the company. Shares are called *equity*. If it's the first time the company has done this, we call it a 'new issue'. If the company already has shareholders, it may approach them with the opportunity to buy more shares in the company, called a *rights issue*. This is because, under most but not

Examples of Raising Capital (*continued*)

all EU law, the existing shareholders must be approached first if any new shares are to be offered for cash. These rights are not protected as strongly in the US or in Germany.

The reward for the shareholders by way of income is the dividend. However, the income is usually poorer than that paid on a bond, and the shareholders look to capital gains as well, believing that the share price will go up as time goes by.

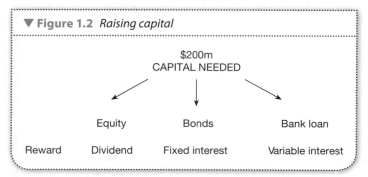

▼ **Figure 1.2** *Raising capital*

$200m
CAPITAL NEEDED

Equity	Bonds	Bank loan
Reward	Dividend	Fixed interest	Variable interest

The three means of raising capital are shown in Figure 1.2. The way the world's financial assets have shifted between these methods over time is shown in Table 1.2, and the world's financial assets by market are shown in Table 1.3.

We must recognize that raising capital through equity is fundamentally different from the other two methods. The shareholder is part-owner along with the other shareholders. There is, therefore, no date for paying the money back (the shares may be sold on a stock exchange to someone else, but that's quite different). The shareholders accept risk – they could prosper if the firm prospers, or lose some or all of their money if the firm goes into liquidation. If the latter sad event happens, the shareholders are the last to receive a share of any money left. In addition, if the firm hits trouble, the dividend can be cut or even missed altogether. However, if the company does this, the share price will usually fall – a reminder that, in issuing shares, the company generates a claim on its future earnings.

We should also note that capital raised by bank loans or issuing bonds is *loan* capital. That raised by issuing equity is known as share (or *equity*) capital.

In the case of bonds and bank loans, the money must eventually be paid back, and there are strong legal obligations to meet the interest payments – they are *debt*, not *equity*.

Gearing/Leverage

There's nothing wrong in principle with borrowed money. It enables the company to do more trading than it could on the shareholders' equity alone. The danger comes when too much money is borrowed, especially if boom times are followed (as they usually are) by recession. The firm may be unable to pay the interest out of its reduced profits, quite apart from the problem of repaying the principal sum itself.

Stock market analysts, therefore, look at firms' balance sheets and look at the ratio of long-term debt to equity. However, let's note here that when we say 'equity', we don't just mean the money raised by selling shares originally and by subsequent rights issues.

▼ **Table 1.2** *Size of global financial assets*

	World $ trillion	
	2001	**2013**
1) Bank deposits	79.0	93.2
2) Equities	29.0	49.3
3) Bonds	42.0	98.3
Total (=1+2+3)	150.0	240.8

Source: Data from Credit Suisse (2013) *Global Wealth Report* and own estimates.

▼ **Table 1.3** *The world's financial assets, by market*

Market	Mid-2013 %
Africa	1.1
Asia Pacific	20.0
China	9.2
Europe	31.7
India	1.5
Latin America	3.8
North America	32.8
WORLD	100

Source: Data from Credit Suisse (2013) *Global Wealth Report*.

The firm (we hope) will make profits. Out of the profits, it will pay tax to the government and dividends to the shareholders. The remaining profit is retained for growth and expansion. This money also belongs to the shareholders. As a result, the term 'shareholders' funds' is used for the total equity of the shareholders:

Original equity + Rights issues + Retained profit = Shareholders' funds

Analysts, then, look at the ratio between the long-term debt and the shareholders' funds. This relationship is called *gearing* ('leverage' is the US term). The metaphor is from mechanics. A gear enables more work to be done with a given force. The lever is a similar idea. Remember Archimedes's saying 'Give me a fulcrum and I will lever the world'? The shareholders are doing more trading than they could with their money alone. How? By borrowing other people's money. The general idea behind gearing or leverage is to make a given sum of money go further. It can be summarized by the popular American expression 'more bang for your buck'. In this context, we do it by borrowing someone else's money. We shall also meet other contexts in this book.

The ratio between long-term debt and shareholders' funds is thus the gearing ratio. What ratio is safe? Frankly, this has become a matter of some controversy. Generally, people worry if the ratio reaches 100%, but that's only a crude guideline. For example, if the business is cyclical, analysts will worry more than if it is a steady business from one year to the next. They will also worry less if there are assets that can easily be realized rather than assets that may not be easy to dispose of, especially during a recession, for example property. In a low-interest-rate environment, corporate gearing will tend to increase – 2008 saw some companies flush with cash and not borrowing much (for instance, the FTSE 100 companies amassed £180bn in cash that year), although some firms availed themselves of the low interest rates, borrowing substantial amounts, especially for takeovers and private equity deals. At the end of 2008, the overall average gearing for the UK's top 100 companies was 38%. Of course, it is important to remember that since the onset of the credit crunch in 2007, the banks' ability to lend has been substantially curtailed, and markets have generally suffered a downturn.

Having looked at the three key choices for new capital – equity, bonds and bank loans – we should also be aware that, in Western financial markets generally, probably 50% of the money needed for growth and expansion comes from retained profits. 'Profit' can be a sensitive topic and, in some people's eyes, a pejorative term, for example 'they are only in it for the profit'. However, profit provides not only rewards for shareholders and taxes for governments, but funds for expansion, which create further employment and a more secure environment for the employees.

We shall look at the concept of international markets in Chapter 7. Briefly, we are talking about equity raised across national boundaries; bonds issued in, say, London in dollars and sold to international investors; and international banks getting together to syndicate a large loan. In addition to this, there is capital raised in purely domestic markets. Equity, bonds and large syndicated loans usually refer to long-term capital. There is also the raising of short-term capital for meeting cash flow needs rather than growth and expansion. Equity is not applicable here, but there are various securities and types of bank loan that meet this need.

International figures can be misleading, as the emphasis may be quite different in domestic markets. Each country has its own traditions. The US is a big market for company bonds, as well as a large equity market. German companies, however, have a long tradition of close relationships with banks and the use of bank finance. Equity finance is strong in the UK, with a higher proportion of companies publicly quoted than in most other European countries.

CONCLUSION

We have seen that the raison d'être of the financial markets is the raising of capital. Our examination of the choices for finding capital shows us the financial markets in action and also the themes we study in this book, as shown in Box 1.2:

BOX 1.2

Book Content – What Is Ahead

Banking: In Chapters 2–5, we look at banking in all its aspects.

Regulation: Chapter 6 examines the role for regulation of the banking and financial sector, and highlights recent developments, particularly the reregulation of strategically important financial institutions (SIFIs).

Money and bond markets: In Chapter 7, we examine the domestic and international markets. We look at raising money for short term (money markets) and long term (bond markets).

Equities: Stock markets, brokers, market makers and institutions are explained in Chapter 8.

Hedge funds and private equity: Enormous funds are being invested in the markets today by these organizations, which is explained in Chapter 9.

Credit crisis: The credit crisis, which started with defaults in the US subprime market and culminated in the collapse of Lehman Brothers, the failure of large swathes of US, UK and other banking markets, and the resulting major state bailouts, are covered in detail in Chapter 10. We outline the causes of the crisis and the key events that occurred, noting features of the recent sovereign debt crisis and the ongoing policy response.

Foreign exchange: The international character of the markets today and gradual deregulation create strong demand for foreign currencies. This is considered in Chapter 11.

EMU: European Economic and Monetary Union and the introduction of the euro started on 1 January 1999 for 11 countries. This key development is discussed in Chapter 12, along with an overview of the role of the euro and characteristics of the recent eurozone crisis.

Derivative products: Interest rates, currency rates, bond prices and share prices fluctuate, creating risk. There are financial products that are, paradoxically, used to both exploit risk and control risk. These are called 'derivative products' and are, possibly, the fastest growing sector of the financial markets today. This complex but fascinating subject is looked at in Chapters 13–15.

Emerging and growth-leading economies: The role of various booming emerging economies is considered in Chapter 16. Particular focus is placed on the role of China and India, together with the increased influence of other emerging markets.

Key trends: Finally, in Chapter 17, we analyse the key trends in the financial markets today.

SUMMARY

- The purpose of the markets is to facilitate the raising of capital and match those who want capital (borrowers) with those who have it (lenders).
- Typically, the borrower issues a receipt promising to pay the lender back – these are *securities* and may be freely bought and sold.

- Money may be raised by a bank loan (commercial banking) or by the issue of a bond or equity (the capital markets). The first two represent debt. The relationship between debt and equity on a balance sheet is known as *gearing / leverage*.
- There are domestic markets and international (cross-border) markets.

REVISION QUESTIONS/ASSIGNMENTS

1 Discuss the difference between primary and secondary markets.
2 Outline the main differences between bonds and equity.

3 Can governments borrow indefinitely? Are government bonds different from corporate bonds?
4 How do firms increase their gearing / leverage? Is there a level of gearing / leverage that is considered excessive?

FURTHER READING

Arnold, G. (2011) *Modern Financial Markets & Institutions: A Practical Perspective Financial Times*, Prentice Hall, London. Undergraduate text covering the role of markets and institutions.

Chisholm, A.M. (2009) *An Introduction to International Capital Markets: Products, Strategies, Participants* (2nd edn), Wiley Finance, Chichester. Undergraduate text providing an introductory insight into the role and functions of capital markets.

Pilbeam, K. (2010) *Finance and Financial Markets* (3rd edn), Palgrave Macmillan, Basingstoke. Introductory text discussing the institutional features of financial markets.

PART

2

Banking

Banking Background

....

HISTORY

Money, and the use of metal coins as money, has a long history, going back at least 10 centuries. Banking, certainly in today's sense, is rather more modern.

In many ways, the origins of capitalism as we see it today lie in the operations of Italian merchanting and banking groups in the 13th, 14th and 15th centuries. Italian states, like Lombardy and Florence, were dominant economic powers. The merchants had trading links across borders and used their cash resources for banking purposes.

The bankers sat at formal benches, often in the open air. The Italian word for bench is *banco*, giving us the modern word for bank. (If you happen to be in Prato, Italy, look in the Convent of San Francesco for a fresco showing the moneychangers' *banco*, or counter.) If a bank went into liquidation, the bench would be solemnly broken, giving us the word *bancarotta*, or 'bankrupt' as we say today. The early associations were partnerships, as shareholding companies did not begin until 1550. As a result, people might have written to the *Medici e compagni*, the 'Medici and their partners'. It gives us the modern word – the 'company'. It is the Italians who claim the oldest bank in the world, the Monte dei Paschi of Siena, founded in 1472.

For a long period, Florence was a major centre. As a result, many coins ended up with names based on Florence: the UK had a 'florin' until the coinage was decimalized in 1971; the former Dutch guilder had the abbreviation FL – florin; and the Hungarian currency is the 'forint'. We also read that in 1826, Schubert sold his D major piano sonata for '120 florins'. As a result of all this, at the European Council summit in Madrid in December 1996, John Major put forward the florin as the proposed name for Europe's single currency. The meeting finally decided on the rather more boring name, the euro.

Italian bankers had a long relationship with the British crown. The first bankers to lend money in London came from Lombardy, and until the 1980s, most UK-based banks had their head offices in Lombard Street. Bankers lent money to Edward I, Edward II and Edward III (to finance their various wars). Edward III, however, defaulted on the loan in 1345, and the proud Bardi and Peruzzi families in Florence crashed into liquidation as a consequence. Presumably this was the world's first (but not last) international banking crisis.

Those bankers were very advanced for their time. They used bills of exchange (to be explained in Chapter 7), letters of credit, book entry for money (instead of physically transporting it) and double-entry bookkeeping. The first textbook on double-entry bookkeeping was published in 1494 by a Franciscan monk, Luca Pacioli. The early Italian bankers experimented with marine insurance and evolved a body of mercantile law. The Bardi operated 30 branches in Italy and overseas and employed more than 350 people.

In *The Rise of Merchant Banking* (1984), Chapman shows how the Medici bank helped an Italian firm in Venice to sell goods to a firm in London, using a bill of exchange. The Medici bank in London would collect the money, and the bank would take care of the foreign exchange conversion and risk. The goods were invoiced at £97.18s.4d (in old pounds, shillings and pence). This was the equivalent of about 535 ducats. The Medici branch in Venice paid the local firm 500 ducats on the bill of exchange, making 7% on money it would not receive for 6 months, that is, about 14% p.a. The date? 20 July 1463.

The bill above was not 'discounted' in the modern sense, because this would imply charging interest on money, which was forbidden by the Roman Catholic Church as 'usury'. The bill represented a service to facilitate trade and change foreign money – it could not appear to involve the lending of money. On the deposit side, no formal interest could be paid for the same reason. Depositors received a share of profits paid at discretion; thus the liabilities side of the balance sheet was headed *Discrezione*. Islamic banking faces similar problems due to the Koran's rejection of the concept of interest as such. Today there are over 500 Islamic banks (with assets exceeding $1.3 trillion) which follow the principle that the reward for deposits is not fixed, but based on the profit from the use of the money (we return to this later in this chapter).

The one thing the Italians didn't invent was banknotes. For this, we look to goldsmiths in the United Kingdom (UK). There, merchants would hold money for safe keeping in the Royal Mint. Charles I had many arguments with Parliament about money and solved one of them in 1640 by marching down to the Royal Mint and stealing £130,000. Although the money was replaced later, confidence in the Royal Mint had gone. This was good news for goldsmiths who had secure vaults for gold and silver coins and thus began an era of goldsmiths as bankers, which lasted for some 150 years. Coutts Bank, still going today, began in 1692 as a goldsmith bank. The goldsmiths found it convenient to give out receipts for a deposit of gold coins made out to 'the bearer' and to issue 10 receipts for a deposit of 10 coins. In this way, if the bearer owed someone else 3 gold coins, he could pass on 3 bearer receipts. Even better, if someone wanted to borrow 5 gold coins, the goldsmiths could lend him 5 of these nice pieces of paper and not give gold coins. We are now very much into modern banking traditions, except that today the notes aren't backed by gold or silver. By the end of the 17th century, the goldsmiths' receipts had become banknotes in a formal sense, the first being issued by the Bank of Sweden in 1661.

Internationally, the emphasis in banking, which had been in Florence, moved to Genoa as gold and silver flooded in from the New World. Outside Italy, the Fugger family of Augsburg created a financial dynasty comparable to the Italians'. Originally, they were wool merchants but turned to precious metals and banking. They had gold, silver and copper mines in Hungary and Austria and became principal financiers to the Hapsburg Empire in Germany, the Low Countries and Spain (see Green, 1989).

Later still, we have the rise of the two great rivals, the Dutch and British Empires and Amsterdam and London as rival financial centres. The Amsterdam Stock Exchange, for example, is the oldest in the world.

We also see merchant banking (or investment banking) in the modern sense as illustrated in Box 2.1.

From the 1750s up to the 1900s, Europe's population grew, rising from 180 million in 1800 to 450 million by 1914. This period also saw the growth of industrialization and urbanization, which was followed by the spread of banking. Although in many cases private banks continued to flourish, the gradual change in legislation to allow joint stock banks (that is, banks with shareholders) paved the way for the growth of larger commercial banks with many branches and a strong deposit-taking function.

BOX 2.1

Origins of Investment Banking – Early Merchant Banking

Francis Baring, a textile merchant from Exeter in the UK, started Baring Brothers in 1762.

In 1804, Nathan Mayer Rothschild opened up for banking business in London, after a brief spell in textiles in Manchester.

In Holland, Mees & Hope opened in 1702, and later, Pierson, Heldring & Pierson, which are both still in business today as subsidiaries of the Fortis Group under the name Mees Pierson. (In 2008, the Fortis Group was saved by the Belgium state and BNP Paribas as a result of the credit crisis and eventually broken up, although Mees Pierson remained intact. To be a personal customer of Mees Pierson, individuals need investable assets exceeding €1m.)

Merchant bankers had two key activities – financing trade, by using bills of exchange, and raising money for governments by selling bonds.

Baring Brothers financed the huge reparations imposed on France after the Napoleonic Wars with a large international bond issue. As a consequence, the Duc de Richelieu dubbed them 'Europe's sixth superpower'. In 1818, the Rothschilds raised a large loan for Prussia, to be redeemed after 36 years. They arranged to pay dividends to bondholders in their local currency. The bonds were sold to merchants, private subscribers and the aristocracy. Prussia paid 7.5%, of which 5% was paid to bondholders and 2.5% was used to create a 'sinking fund' to redeem the bond after 36 years (see Chapman, 1984).

The Dutch bank Hope & Co., together with Baring Bros, helped the American states to finance the purchase of Louisiana from Napoleon in 1803. Later, corporate finance emerged as another investment banking business.

In 1886, Baring Bros floated Guinness, which created a scandal because most of the shares were allocated to 'friends' of Baring Bros – police had to hold back the crowds.

In the United States (US), the Bank of New York and the Bank of Boston (later First National Bank of Boston) opened in 1800. The water company, the Manhattan Company, became a bank around about the same time, becoming Chase Manhattan in 1955. The City Bank opened in 1812, becoming the National City Bank later and merging in 1955 with First National Bank to form today's Citibank (now Citigroup after further acquisitions – another casualty of the credit crisis saved in November 2008 by the US government in a massive bailout).

In Europe, the Société Générale of Belgium formed in 1822; the Bayerische Hypotheken und Wechsel Bank in 1822; Creditanstalt in Austria in 1856; Credit Suisse also in 1856; UBS in 1862; Crédit Lyonnais in 1863 and the Société Générale (France) in 1864 (by 1900, they had 200 and 350 branches, respectively); Deutsche Bank in 1870 and Banca Commerciale Italiana in 1894 (which became part of Banca Intesa in 2001).

In the UK, the Bank of England's monopoly of joint stock banking ended in 1826. There were 1,700 bank branches in 1850, 3,300 by 1875 and nearly 7,000 by 1900. The Midland Bank opened in 1836, and the forerunners of National Westminster, in 1833–36. Private banks, threatened by the greater resources of the new joint stock banks, were either bought out or merged. One such merger formed the Barclays we know today. One of the earliest of such private banks was Child & Co., at No. 1 Fleet Street since 1673 and nowadays part of the Royal Bank of Scotland. By 1884, the London Clearing House was clearing cheques worth £6bn.

There is one interesting point about the UK. Although on the Continent Rothschild had a hand in setting up some of the commercial banks (Creditanstalt and Société Générale of France are examples), in the UK the merchant banks ignored the new developments and stuck to that which they knew and did best (international bonds and trade finance). As a result, the British tradition has been one of looking at two types of bank – the 'merchant' bank and the 'commercial' bank (we examine the differences later in this chapter). It was only in the 1960s and later that the large commercial banks thought it necessary to open merchant bank subsidiaries or buy one (for example Midland Bank buying Samuel Montagu).

In Europe, especially Germany, Austria and Switzerland, the pattern became that of banks who did all types of banking – both 'merchant' and 'commercial'. This is the universal bank tradition – banks like Deutsche Bank and UBS.

These developments take us into this century and the age of computers, communications, ATMs (automated teller machines), credit cards, bank mergers, EFT-POS (electronic funds transfer at point of sale) and banking via the Internet or even mobile phones.

BANKING SUPERVISION

Let's start with the question: Who is in charge of the banks? If you were in the Netherlands or Italy, you might reply, 'The central bank', and you would be correct. However, this is by no means always the case. Indeed, it is more common to find that the supervisory body is separate. In Germany, the Bundesbank is not legally responsible for supervision; that is the task of the Federal Supervisory Authority (BaFin), which, in April 2002, combined the supervisory roles of the three previously separate authorities for banking, insurance and securities. It does, of course, consult the Bundesbank, and the latter collects detailed reports from all the country's banks. However, if any action is to be taken, it will be taken by BaFin.

There is a Banking Commission in France and Belgium and a Federal Banking Commission in Switzerland. In Japan, the Financial Services Agency is in charge.

In the US, the picture is very mixed, with differing roles played by the Federal Reserve, individual states, the Federal Deposit Insurance Corporation (FDIC), and the Office of the Comptroller of Currency and savings and loan associations (S&Ls) reporting to the Federal Home Loan Bank System. For example, when Chicago's Continental Illinois Bank hit trouble in 1984, it was rescued by the FDIC and not the Federal Reserve. Although the US system of regulation is relatively complex, it is easy to remember that the Federal Reserve is responsible for regulating all the largest US domestic and foreign banks. (The largest US banks operate as financial or bank holding companies, and the foreign banks as subsidiaries.) Even prior to the 2007 credit crisis, the US Congress had been promising to simplify confusion over regulatory responsibility for different types of bank. By the end of 2014, the system is slowly adapting to the changes encompassed under the 2010 Dodd-Frank Act (see Chapter 6).

In the UK, the Bank of England used to be the supervisory body, but in mid-1998, the Labour government transferred powers to the new Financial Services Authority (FSA). Since the near collapse of the UK banking system, as a result of the credit crisis and the rescues of Northern Rock, Lloyds Group (including HBOS) and Royal Bank of Scotland (RBS), there has been much policy debate as to whether the regulatory framework should be changed. The Conservative Party said it would bring regulatory responsibility for the banking system back to the Bank of England when elected and, true to its word, in June 2010 announced plans to abolish the FSA and separate its responsibilities between a number of new agencies and the Bank of England. The June 2011 draft Financial Services Bill outlined that a Financial Conduct Authority will be responsible for policing the City and the banking system. In addition, a new Prudential Regulatory Authority will carry out the prudential regulation of financial firms, including banks, investment banks, building societies and insurance companies. All other responsibilities will be assumed by the Bank of England, which will establish a Financial Policy Committee. The transition was completed during 2012 (see Chapter 3).

In China, banking supervision is in the hands of the People's Bank of China, the central bank, and in India, too, the central bank, the Reserve Bank of India, is in charge. The central bank is responsible for bank regulation in both Brazil (Banco Central do Brasil) and Russia (Bank of Russia).

Having decided who is in charge, what general rules will they lay down? Usually, the following are included:

- Conditions of entry (who obtains a banking licence or not)
- Capital ratios
- Liquidity rules
- Large exposure rules
- Foreign exchange control
- Rights of inspection

The meaning of the more technical terms here is explained within the banking chapters.

TYPES OF BANK: DEFINITIONS

There are many different terms used, not all mutually exclusive. Let's examine the following:

- Central banks
- Commercial banks
- Merchant/Investment banks
- Savings banks
- Cooperative banks
- Mortgage banks
- Giro banks and National Savings banks
- Credit unions
- Islamic banks

Central Banks

Typically, an economy will have a central bank, like the Federal Reserve in the US, the Bundesbank in Germany or the Bank of England in the UK. The role of the central bank is examined in detail in Chapter 3.

Commercial Banks

Commercial banks are in the classic business of taking deposits and lending money. There are two further relevant terms here – 'retail banking' and 'wholesale banking'. Retail banking involves high-street branches, which deal with the general public, shops and very small businesses. The use of cheques and plastic cards is normally of crucial importance; for example, 876 million cheques were written in the UK in 2012 (as opposed to 3,800 million in 1991). At the same time, some 10,300 million card-based transactions took place at point of sale, of which around 76% by value were debit cards. We are talking here of high volume but low value. Wholesale banking involves low volume and high value. It covers dealings with other banks, the central bank, corporates, pension funds and other investment institutions. Cheques and cards are not so important here, but electronic settlement and clearance is – with systems like CHIPS (Clearing House Interbank Payments System) in New York, CHAPS (Clearing House Automated Payments System) in the UK, SIT (Système Interbancaire de Télécompensation) in France, EAF2 in Germany and TARGET (Trans-European Automated Real-time Gross Settlement Express Transfer) for the euro. The dealings in the money markets that we describe in Chapter 7 are wholesale banking activities. Retail banking and other wholesale activities like corporate loans are discussed in Chapter 4. Foreign exchange may be retail (a member of the public going on holiday) or wholesale (a French corporate wants SFr10m to buy Swiss imports). Foreign exchange is discussed in Chapter 11.

A special subset of retail banking is private banking. This involves handling the needs of high-net-worth individuals – deposits, loans, fund management, investment advice and so on, as detailed in Box 2.2.

BOX 2.2

What Is Private Banking?

Private banking, often referred to as 'wealth management', primarily involves advising high-net-worth individuals on how to invest their wealth.

Historically, it is a key Swiss speciality, and the most select independent banks are based in Geneva, including Banque Pictet & Cie (founded in 1805) and Bank Lombard Odier & Co (1796). Both are members of the Association of Swiss Private Banks. Other members include Bordier & Cie, E. Gutzwiller & Cie, Gonet & Cie, Bank La Roche & Co Ltd., Mirabaud & Cie SA, Mourgue d'Algue & Cie, Rahn & Bodmer Co. and Reichmuth & Co.

In the US, the oldest private bank is the New York–based Brown Brothers Harriman. In the UK, C. Hoare & Co. (1672) is the longest established independent private bank.

Many large banks also offer private banking services, the largest being UBS, Credit Suisse, HSBC Private Bank, Citi Private Bank, Barclays Wealth and Deutsche Private Bank.

According to the RBC/Capgemini/*World Wealth Report 2013*, the size of the global private banking market amounted to $46 trillion.

Merchant/Investment Banks

'Merchant bank' is the classic UK term, whereas 'investment bank' is the US equivalent and perhaps the more general and modern term. We use them interchangeably (but beware of the use of the term 'merchant banking' in the US, where it is applied to taking an active part with the bank's own capital in takeover/merger activities). If commercial banking is about lending money, merchant banking can be summarized as 'helping people to find the money'. For example, in Chapter 1, we examined three choices for raising capital – bank loan, bond issue or equity. Sometimes the choice depends on the ability of banks and markets to provide the different types of financing. For instance, in July 2009, an article in the *Investors Chronicle* noted that corporate bond issues had become the preferred route for raising finance, as investors were 'showing increasing signs of rights issue fatigue'. Merchant or investment banks will give advice on raising finance. If the choice is bonds or equities, they will help the issuer to price them, assist in selling them and, with other associates, 'underwrite' the issue, that is, they will buy the securities if the investors do not. The other activities of merchant or investment banks will be covered in Chapter 5.

Savings Banks

In many European countries, such as France, Germany, Italy, Austria, the Netherlands and Spain, there are banks that do not have outside shareholders but are 'mutually' owned in some way. These are the savings banks and cooperative banks. What we have to distinguish here is the historical, traditional role of savings banks and their more modern role today. In the modern world, they look more and more like ordinary commercial banks because of growing mergers of previously autonomous savings banks and deregulation, removing restrictions on their activities and giving them powers to act like commercial banks. In spite of this, what might still make them a little different is their ownership structure – usually they are mutuals, that is, owned by the members.

There are strong savings bank movements right across Europe, with terms like these:

- Sparkasse   Germany/Austria
- Cassa di Risparmio Italy
- Caja de Ahorros   Spain
- Caisses d'Epargne   France/Belgium

In the US, they are known as 'S&Ls' or 'thrifts', and in the UK (historically, but not today), as 'trustee savings banks'.

There are 418 savings banks in Germany, with some 14,000 branches and 50 million customers holding over €1 trillion of deposits. As it is a federal republic, each federal state or county within a state guarantees the deposits, and there is a central bank for the savings banks called the 'Landesbank'. There is also an overall central authority to coordinate activities, the Dekabank, which is owned by the savings banks and the Landesbanks. It distributes products via the branches of the savings banks, which themselves account for close to 40% of retail deposits and 30% of the consumer lending market. Dekabank also operates wholesale banking and is one of largest fund managers in Germany, with over €145bn under management at the start of 2013. Federal guarantees given to Landesbanks used to enable them to raise capital cheaply. Other German banks argued that this was unfair competition, and the European Commission ended this in 2005.

Having some form of central bank for savings banks is not uncommon. In Austria, it is the Girozentrale Vienna – later called GiroCredit Bank and now part of Bank Austria. In Finland, prior to its financial collapse in September 1991, it was the Skopbank, which was reorganized as the Savings Bank of Finland. Widespread mergers are taking place in Spain and Italy, and even mergers with other banks. For example, in Italy, the Cassa di Risparmio di Roma has merged with Banco di Roma and Banco di Santo Spirito to form a large bank called (curiously) Banca di Roma, which merged with other banks to create Capitalia in 2002, eventually becoming part of Unicredit. In addition, the largest Italian savings bank, Cariplo, has merged with Banco Ambrovenuto and changed its name to Banca Intesa. A major force in Spain is the Catalan 'la Caixa', which has formed alliances with other savings banks. It has invested heavily in industry, and in 2012 its portfolio was worth around €25bn, approximately 3% of Spain's stock market. However, there have been big changes in Spain since the downturn in the domestic economy. In 2010, the 45 regionally based *cajas*, accounting for over 40% of the nation's retail banking activity, were forced to merge into 15 regional groups to bolster their financial strength. The *cajas* had experienced a substantial decline in performance from 2007 onwards, and some needed government support to keep them afloat. They were overexposed to corporate and commercial property lending and continued to suffer losses as a consequence of the rapid downturn in the Spanish economy heralded by the property market crash. The culmination of this crisis situation was this forced reorganization in 2010.

In the UK, the savings bank movement was started in 1810 in order to accept small deposits, as the minimum deposit for a normal bank was quite large. In 1817, the government passed a law that the banks must be run by trustees to protect the depositors, hence 'trustee savings banks'. In 1976, they were deregulated and given normal banking powers. From a large number of distinct, autonomous banks, the movement eventually came together as one bank, simply known as 'TSB Bank'. In 1986, the government sold shares to the general public and lost its mutual status. Finally, in 1996, it was taken over by Lloyds Bank.

In France, too, the movement is coming together and up until 2008 sold and marketed its services as Caisse Nationale des Caisses d'Epargne et de Prévoyance (CNCE). At the time the bank was France's fifth largest by asset size (and the 25th largest in the world) and coordinated the activities of 22 local savings banks with over 25 million customers. In October 2008, however, Groupe Caisse d'Epargne announced plans to merge with the fellow mutual Groupe Banque Populaire, and this marriage took place in July 2009, creating the country's fourth largest banking group by assets size in 2014. The new bank, known as Groupe BPCE, has normal banking powers, and has expanded into bancassurance (see Chapter 4), lending to local authorities, leasing, venture capital, property investment and collective investment sales. Groupe BPCE has over €500bn in savings deposits (over 27% of the domestic market) and is allowed to run special tax-exempt accounts (as is the National Savings Bank). As in Germany, the other banks are complaining that this is unfair competition.

In the US, the deregulation of the S&Ls in 1981 was a total disaster, leading to a mixture of fraud and mismanagement. It created one of America's biggest banking crises, which culminated in the collapse of the system in 1986 and major reforms.

Japan has a broad range of mutual banks, including Shinkin banks, cooperative banks and some second-tier regional banks (*sogo*). They are numerous and typically restricted in their operations to specific localities. They take retail deposits and are important lenders to small businesses.

▼ Table 2.1 *Top European savings banks, 2013*

Bank	Assets $mn
Caja de Ahorros y Pensiones de Barcelona-LA CAIXA (Spain)	484,442
Sparkassen-Finanzgruppe Hessen-Thuringen (Germany)	372,691
Banco Financiero y de Ahorros SA-Bankia (Spain)	371,203
Swedbank AB (Sweden)	283,447
Catalunya Banc SA (Spain)	86,971
Cassa di Risparmio di Parma e Piacenza SpA	69,180
Powszechna Kasa Oszczednosci Bank Polski SA – PKO BP SA	66,145
Banco Mare Nostrum SA-BMN (Spain)	65,534
Liberbank SA (Spain)	61,435
Banque et Caisse d'Epargne de l'Etat Luxembourg (Luxembourg)	56,150

Source: Bankscope (December 2014). Note the French bank BPCE is not in this ranking as it is defined by Bankscope as a commercial bank.

▼ Table 2.2 *Cooperative banks' share of deposits, 2013*

Country	%
France	46.4
Netherlands	39.0
Austria	37.0
Italy	34.3
Finland	34.1
Germany	19.8
Luxembourg	12.0
Poland	9.4
Hungary	8.7
Spain	8.7
United Kingdom	4.2
Portugal	4.5
Sweden	2.1
Denmark	4.4

Source: Bankscope (2014) and own estimates.

A list of Europe's top savings banks is shown in Table 2.1, which shows that the majority of large savings banks are from Spain – a result of the recent forced consolidation.

Cooperative Banks

Cooperative banks are owned by the members, with maximum profit not necessarily the main objective; for example, they may aim to give low-cost loans to members.

Usually, the membership derives from a trade or profession, the most common being agriculture, which gives us Crédit Agricole in France (in asset terms, France's second biggest bank and the world's ninth largest in 2014), the Rabobank Group in the Netherlands and the Norinchukin Bank in Japan. Table 2.2 shows the share of deposits in the European Union (EU) accounted for by cooperatives. From this we see that they are significant in France, the Netherlands, Finland, Austria, Italy and Germany.

Crédit Agricole has 39 regional banks and is the largest high-street banking group, handling some 24% of the domestic retail banking market. In 1996, it bought Banque Indosuez, and in 2003, the troubled Crédit Lyonnais. At the start of 2013, Crédit Agricole had a 22% share of deposits, over 7,000 branches and assets over €2 trillion. In addition to this business in France, it has operations outside France that generate just under 30% of its turnover. There is one stand-alone cooperative organization in France – Crédit Mutuel – and the merged savings bank/cooperative bank Groupe BPCE.

Germany also has a strong cooperative tradition drawn from all sorts of trades and professions. There is, for example, the 'Chemists and Doctors' Bank' (Apotheker und Ärztebank). There are over 1,100 regional cooperative banks with around 30 million customers. There is a single central bank, the DZ Bank, which acts as a clearing house and uses central funds wholesale and for international activities. DZ Bank has access to the customers of the cooperative banks and the investment books of the banks themselves. They are not obliged to use the DZ Bank, but 90% do. Cooperative banks take around 17% of all deposits in Germany.

In the Netherlands, Rabobank Nederland is the name for the central body that acts for some 129 plus independent local agricultural cooperative banks – the Rabobanks. It is the second biggest bank in Holland in terms of total assets and used to be the only bank in the world with AAA credit rating – or, to put another way, it used to be considered the safest bank in the world. Its rating has fallen recently (to AA–) but it still remains one of the worlds safest banks (it has the same rating in 2014 as HSBC). Rabobank offers a wide range of banking facilities, is the market leader for savings products, and has over 26% share of the mortgage market and 38% of the savings market (and also has more retail branches than any other bank), and even operates retail branches in the US and Australia.

In Japan, there are cooperative banks in agriculture, fishery and forestry. The Norin-chukin Bank (ranked 33rd in the world in total assets size in 2014) is the central cooperative bank for over 5,600 agriculture, fishing and forestry cooperatives. There are also a large number of commercial credit cooperative banks.

The Agricultural Bank of China is the country's third largest in asset terms, and there are 33,000 plus rural credit cooperatives and around 1,000 urban credit cooperatives offering finance to farmers.

India has over 1,600 urban cooperative banks and around 90,000 rural cooperative credit institutions that lend to farmers and small local businesses.

In the UK, there is only one cooperative bank, the Co-operative Bank, part of the Co-operative Group. It works closely with the general retail cooperative movement and has normal banking facilities. Its share of total UK bank deposits increased to 5.0% in 2011 – an increase on the lowly 2.0% in 2008. However, it experienced financial difficulties in 2013, positing major losses and a big capital shortfall that resulted in major restructuring; the Co-operative Group lost majority control of the Bank.

Finland has over 200 cooperative banks, with their own central bank, the Okobank, which has joined with the Pohjola Bank for insurance.

Mortgage Banks

Some economies have a special sector dealing with mortgages, and some do not. The most obvious example of a special sector is the UK's building societies. Originally, they were associations that came together to build houses and then disbanded. Gradually, they became permanent mutual organizations, collecting small high-street savings and using the money to fund domestic mortgages.

There were over 2,000 in 1900, but today there are only 45 in a movement dominated by the larger societies. Nationwide is by far the largest, with group assets over £189bn, followed by the Yorkshire Building Society which has £35bn in assets (the top five societies account for 88% of sector assets). The building societies have around 1,600 branches, with a 20% retail deposit market share, plus 3 million borrowers (about a 30% market share).

The Building Societies Act 1986 deregulated them to the extent of allowing them to offer cheque accounts and unsecured loans as well as a variety of other services. However, the amount of such business that they can do is strictly limited. The Act also allowed them to become public limited companies if the members agreed. Abbey National took advantage of this and went public in 1989, becoming the UK's fifth biggest bank in asset terms. By 1995–6, the movement underwent considerable change. Lloyds Bank acquired the Cheltenham & Gloucester; Abbey National acquired National & Provincial; and the merged Halifax/Leeds Societies, along with the Alliance & Leicester, the Woolwich and Northern Rock, all revealed plans to go public and become banks. Others, like the Britannia, defended the 'mutual' principle and announced loyalty bonuses for their longer-term members. However, in late April 1999, Bradford & Bingley, one of the largest remaining mutual societies, announced its intention to convert to a bank after a vote by its members. This rekindled the debate, and many believed that the remaining large mutuals would end up as banks. By 2014, by far the largest – Nationwide – maintains its strategy of following the mutual path.

Germany has 35 mortgage banks (*Hypothekenbanken*), often subsidiaries of other banks, and a few building societies (*Bausparkassen*). The largest mortgage bank is Eurohypo, owned by Commerzbank. The mortgage banks fund the mortgages with a special bond – the *Pfandbrief*. The Netherlands has several mortgage banks that are subsidiaries of other banks (for example Rabobank) or insurance companies. Denmark has a small number of mortgage credit associations which sell bonds on the stock exchange and hand the proceeds to the borrower whose property is security for the bond.

The specialists in mortgages in the US are the S&Ls, which were deregulated in 1981. Unlike the UK's 1986 Building Societies Act, however, prudent restrictions on new powers were not imposed, and the movement hit serious trouble in the mid-1980s, as mentioned earlier.

Giro Banks

Let's start by considering this word 'giro'. It comes from the Greek *guros*, meaning a wheel or circle. The circle in finance is the passing round of payments between counterparties. We find references to this term in early Italian banking. In the Middle Ages, there were important trade fairs for the cloth industries of France and Flanders. Merchants would incur debts, and if they were not settled, they could be carried forward to the next fair. Gradually, the merchants who were bankers began to offer a clearing system. One can imagine the circle of debt as trader A owes B who owes C who owes D who also owes A (Figure 2.1).

The bankers set up a clearing system known as *giro di partita* – the giro of ledger entries. In 1619, the state of Venice set up the Banco del Giro to speed up payments to the state's creditors. The bank also issued interest-bearing bonds to creditors, and a secondary market gradually developed.

In the modern age, the word 'giro' crops up in two connections. In the first, it simply refers to money transfers by which an individual sends a giro slip to her bank instructing it to pay a sum of money to, say, the electricity or gas company. In Germany and Holland, this is far more likely than sending a cheque directly to the company.

The second use is in the term 'giro bank' and the use of post offices to help those without a bank account to pay their bills. The idea began in Austria in 1883. Those without bank accounts could pay a variety of bills at post offices, and the money was then transferred to the payee. There is a Post Office Giro in Belgium, and the UK set up the Girobank in 1968, which was sold to a building society in 1990. It is difficult to separate out postal giro from the general concept of a postal bank,

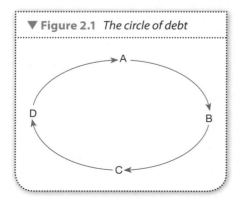

▼ **Figure 2.1** *The circle of debt*

which may be known instead as the national savings bank. In the UK, the Post Office Savings Bank, which was set up in 1861, became the National Savings Bank in 1969. The general idea is to encourage small savings rather than letting the bank engage in lending. France has a Caisse Nationale d'Epargne; Ireland has a Post Office Savings Bank; Finland has the important Postipankki, which handles much of the government's finances; and Spain has a Post Office Savings Bank. In the Netherlands, the Post Office Bank and the National Savings Bank merged to become Postbank, which later merged with the NMB Bank and is now known as ING Bank.

The Belgian Bankers' Association has claimed that the post offices' financial activities are subsidized, and in France the opening of Banque Postale on 1 January 2006 met with furious opposition from the major banks. They are angry at its duopoly of a big savings account, Livret A (26 million customers), which is tax free. Spain's Caja Postal has gone into leasing, asset management and property consulting. It was drawn together with other state-owned financial institutions into a single body called Argentaria and later merged with the BBVA bank.

Germany's Deutsche Post was owned by the government until early in 2005, when it was part-privatized and Deutsche Bank took a 30% stake in the Postbank subsidiary, increasing this to majority ownership in 2012. It is now part of Deutsche's retail banking operations. Japan's post office is the largest deposit-taking financial organization in the world, operating through 24,000 branches nationwide (and nearly 11,000 more than the total for domestically licensed banks). It delivers pensions, offers government-backed life insurance, and a range of investment products. At the start of 2012, it held $2.2 trillion in low-yielding savings accounts and over $500bn in life insurance business. It offers cheap, easy finance to the government (it is estimated to hold around 20% of the country's national debt in the form of government bonds), which many believe has led to wasteful spending. Postal savings represents around 21% of total banking sector deposits. The Japanese parliament voted to privatize the bank in July 2005 and also agreed that its savings and insurance business would have to be sold by 2017.

In both China and India, the government is unhappy about the inefficiencies of the post office movement. Savings are collected and handed over to the government, with little attempt to sell other services or provide loans to small businesses. China has now set up a formal Post Office Savings Bank and in mid-2006 decided to turn it into China's fifth largest bank. It has no less than 1,000 million renminbi deposited with the government. India has over 155,000 post offices, many in rural areas. The investment in technology has been poor, but banks like ICICI and others are forming links with post offices to do money transfers and to sell other banks' products.

Credit Unions

The idea of credit unions goes back to 1849 in Germany, when a local mayor formed a union to help people cope with debt and poverty. By the early 1900s, the idea had spread to Australia, Canada, New Zealand, Ireland, the UK and the US. The general idea is that a local credit union has some common bond – possibly place of work or membership in a church. The members save money and are allowed to borrow a sum of money, usually a multiple of the money saved. There may be tax privileges.

In the US, for example, credit unions don't pay federal income tax. There are 6,557 credit unions in that country, with over $1 trillion in assets serving over 100 million members. Navy Federal, the largest, with assets of $58.1bn and over 4.8 million members, is bigger than many regional banks. The commercial banks complain of unfair competition and are pursuing a case through the Supreme Court, claiming that the 'common bond' idea is being ignored in some cases.

In the UK, there are 375 credit unions with 1.2 million members, including British Airways and the London Taxi Drivers, and also community credit unions in economically deprived areas like Toxteth (Liverpool), Clerkenwell (London) and Strathclyde (Glasgow). The number has reduced over time, as many unions are small and are struggling to comply with new regulations introduced by the FSA in 2002. The Association of British Credit Unions expects further consolidation over the coming years.

In Ireland, the 508 credit unions have over 20% of the population as members but have recently been under review as result of the austerity measures imposed by the International Monetary Fund/EU as a consequence of the country's bailout in 2010. Major consolidation is expected. In Japan, there are over 420 credit associations, which also enjoy tax privileges.

Islamic Banks

Over 550 institutions globally manage money in accordance with sharia (Islamic) law, that is, they are sharia compliant. Paying or receiving interest (*riba*) is not allowed, but depositors are paid a share of profit on a range of permitted investments in companies – excluding those involved with gambling, liquor or tobacco. This is because, in the Koran, *riba* is forbidden. Money must not earn interest but can be put to use in trade or entrepreneurial activity, although, to be fair, a minority of Muslim experts interpret *riba* as usury, or excessive interest.

The rise in Muslim consciousness since 9/11 and the massive flow of funds into the Gulf Cooperation Council region due to the high oil price have led to an enormous increase in Islamic finance, both banking and bonds (which we discuss in Chapter 7). Current forecasts suggest the industry is growing at more than 15% plus, and Islamic banks have also been less affected by the credit crunch compared to Western banks, as the former were not engaged in securitization activity or holding mortgage-backed securities, which collapsed in value when property prices fell and borrowers defaulted (the credit crunch is discussed later).

The first Islamic bank is thought to be Mitshamr in Egypt in 1963. Today, there are many Islamic banks and HSBC, Citigroup, UBS, Lloyds TSB, Barclays, Deutsche Bank, BNP Paribas and Standard Chartered operate in this market.

Islamic banks are now into sale and leaseback to provide domestic mortgages and finance aircraft and equipment purchases, for instance the $240m funding of Pakistan's purchase of two Boeing 777s. For mortgages, the banks either buy the property outright, rent it to the mortgage holder and hand over legal ownership when the contract ends (*ijara*), or they resell the property to the customer at a fixed mark-up price and are paid in monthly instalments (*murabaha*). Another version of *murabaha* is used for trade finance deals, like that offered in April 2006 for BXP, one of Australia's largest electronic retailers and valued at A$80m (US$55m, £33m). This was the first Islamic finance deal arranged for an Australian company.

Naturally, there is great interest in East and Southeast Asia. Singapore is promoting Islamic finance, and Malaysia is probably the most proactive country in the world in advancing Islamic banking. Maybank Islamic Bank, the Malaysian bank, was awarded Global Islamic Bank of the Year in The Banker's Investment Banking Awards, 2014.

In the UK, there is increasing interest, as illustrated in Box 2.3.

London as a Major Islamic Finance Centre

In June 2006, the Muslim Council of Britain organized a conference on Islamic finance and trade. This was addressed by, among others, Gordon Brown, the then UK chancellor. He announced his intention to make London a global centre for Islamic finance, at that time said to be worth up to $400bn (£240bn) worldwide (by 2014 it was worth over $1.3 trillion). He had already made a change in the 2006 Finance Act to ease the *murabaha* technique for mortgages, mentioned above. Because this involves the bank buying the property and then selling it to the customer, in theory stamp duty would be paid twice.

The Finance Act abolished the double stamp duty on such transactions and also resolved anomalies in the tax treatment of *ijara* rental and leasing transactions.

The Islamic Bank of Britain was formed in 2004 to cater to the UK's 2 million Muslims and is able to tap into funds of Islamic finance in the Gulf and Southeast Asia. There is an internal Sharia auditor and a supervisory committee of Islamic experts.

The rise in the popularity of Islamic finance has led to an increasing demand for such legal experts – there is now a bottleneck as enough cannot be found. If this was a modest beginning in 2004, we have now reached the point in 2014 where all the major banks offer some form of Islamic banking service – not only for Muslims but also non-Muslim ethical investors such as Quakers and other religious groups.

The UK is now vying with Paris and Frankfurt for the position of leading Islamic finance centre in Western Europe. There are 23 Sharia-compliant banks, three of which have been set up since the mid-2000s. These are the Islamic Bank of Britain, the European Islamic Investment Bank and the Bank of London & The Middle East.

Evidence of London's increasing role in Islamic finance is illustrated by the fact that it is the only Western country to feature prominently – ninth with $10bn – in a global ranking of Sharia-compliant assets by country.

Islamic bonds, known as *sukuk* and issued under Sharia law, have been used to finance London's Olympic Village and the Shard building. (*Sukuk* are also discussed in Chapter 7.)

Source: Adapted from TheCityUK (2013) Islamic Finance, October.

OTHER BANKING TERMINOLOGY

There are one or two other terms that should also be explained.

Clearing Banks

The term 'clearing bank' is applied to the banks most involved in the system for clearing cheques. (We should add that this term is commonly used in the UK, but not often elsewhere!) These large domestic banks are heavily into retail banking. Banks that offer chequebook facilities and have smaller volumes will arrange for one of the larger clearing banks to handle the clearing of their cheques. Usually, each bank will clear its own cheques, that is, cheques drawn by a customer of the branch in favour of another customer of the same bank. Cheques drawn in favour of other banks are sent to a central clearing system where they can be gathered together and sent to each bank for posting to individual accounts. The customer account number, bank branch code and cheque number are already encoded on the bottom line of the cheque. Only the amount needs to be encoded for the cheques to be sorted using electronic sorting machines.

Electronic clearing is becoming increasingly important for direct debits, standing orders, salary payments, supplier payments and high-value payments made electronically by banks for corporate customers.

State or Public Banks

State or public bank refers to banks owned by the state that are not central banks but carry out some public sector activity. State-owned post offices or national savings banks are one example. Sometimes others are set up to lend to industry sectors or local authorities, or to provide finance for exports and imports. Germany has KfW, which was set up in 1948 to help finance reconstruction after the war and is now a general development bank for small and medium-sized companies. France has Crédit Local de France, which makes loans to local authorities, and Crédit Foncier, which finances house purchase and property development. Italy has Crediop, which finances public utilities and makes other industrial loans. In Spain, a major change took place that resulted in the formation of one body from various state banks:

- Banco Exterior   the finance of foreign trade
- Banco Hipotecario   subsidized loans for social housing
- Banco de Crédito Agrícola   loans for agriculture and forestry
- Banco de Crédito Local   loans for local authorities
- Banco de Crédito Industrial   loans for industry
- Caja Postal de Ahorros   post office savings banks

These were all united in 1991 as Corporación Bancaria de España, which operates under the marketing name of 'Argentaria' and has since merged with the BBVA bank.

The position regarding state banks is changing somewhat as full or partial privatization has been the trend since the early 1990s, for example Crédit Local de France and Argentaria. However, this trend has, to a certain extent, been reversed with the massive state support given to various banking systems in light of the credit crisis. Well-known banks that still remain in state ownership since their bailout as a result of the 2008 banking crisis include RBS (80% government owned in 2014), Lloyds (25% government owned), and Dexia (100% Belgium government owned). Also Northern Rock was 100% owned by the UK government but sold (after restructuring to Virgin Money in 2011), and Citigroup was 36% owned by the US government, but the bank returned to full private ownership in December 2010. AIG, the largest US general insurance firm (and ex-sponsor of Manchester United Football Club), also had to be bailed out by the US government for a cool $85bn. Since the peak of the banking crisis in September 2008 and the subsequent bailouts, the role of the government in the banking system (both explicitly and implicitly) has increased dramatically.

Banks that have a role in lending to specialist industries are also known as industrial banks.

International Banking

International banking involves a variety of activities such as deposits/loans to nationals in foreign currencies and to non-nationals in the domestic currency. It also covers cross-border operations, trade finance, foreign exchange, correspondent banking, international payments services, international finance with syndicated loans and/or euromarket instruments, dealing in precious metals, international corporate advice and corporate risk management facilities on an international basis.

Clearly, the terms we have been using are not mutually self-exclusive – they overlap. International banking with a syndicated loan, for example, is commercial wholesale banking. International banking through a Eurobond issue is investment banking and largely wholesale, but with sales at times aimed at retail investors.

Shadow Banking

One area of the financial sector that is growing rapidly is the shadow banking system. The Financial Stability Board defines shadow banking as 'lending by institutions other than banks'. It comprises a whole range of firms: investment companies, hedge funds, insurance companies, pension funds and so on – in fact, any company that 'invests' in the loan market. Estimates of the size of the shadow banking system vary, but *The Economist* in May 2014 estimated that it had assets of $71 trillion at the start of 2014, up from $26 trillion a decade earlier. Some countries are experiencing rapid growth of shadow banking, for example in China the system is estimated to have grown by more than 40% in 2012.

Shadow banking grew rapidly in the run-up to the 2007–8 banking crisis, on the back of the securitization boom where banks sold their loans to wholly owned subsidiaries (known as structured investment companies) that paid for the loans by issuing short-term securities. Buyers of the securities were happy, as they had good ratings, and they thought they were safe because the securities were backed by the loans held in the company as collateral. Most of these loans were US residential mortgage loans, but over time they became riskier (so-called sub-prime loans), and when the property market in the US collapsed, so did the value of the loans and the securities. The problem was that banks had issued billions of dollars in these securities, which were held by a wide range of investors, including the banks themselves. This led to banking sector collapse.

So post-crisis banks have been asked to be safer, have had to hold more capital and have had certain activities restricted or prohibited. This means that they cannot lend as much as they once did. So despite the problems caused by shadow banking during the 2007–8 crises, since 2011 this activity (although not through securitization, but by non-bank's lending and buying bank loans directly) has increased. Governor of the Bank of England Mark Carney announced in a speech in June 2014 that the unregulated nature of the shadow banking system was a concern and that more should be done to oversee the system (see also Chapter 5 and Box 5.2 for more details on shadow banking).

A BANK'S BALANCE SHEET

Before proceeding any further, we must look at a bank's balance sheet and the terminology used so we will be in a position to explain concepts like 'creation of credit', 'liquidity' and 'capital ratio'.

In this section and later, we use the terms 'assets' and 'liabilities'. A liability in accountancy does not have the meaning 'disadvantage' as it does in everyday English. It is money for which the entity concerned is 'liable'; for example if money is borrowed, the borrower is liable to repay it, so it is a liability.

Looking at a commercial bank, the liabilities show us where the money comes from. There are three key sources:

1   Shareholders' equity plus additions from retained profit
2   Deposits (the largest figure)
3   Borrowings (for example a bond issue)

The liabilities, therefore, represent claims against the bank.

The first category is called 'shareholders' funds' and is the main source for a bank's capital. This is the part of the liabilities that can be relied on because, being the owner's money, there is no date for paying it back. The bank has indefinite use of the money. If times are hard, even the dividend may be passed. Deposits, on the other hand, can be withdrawn, a large part without notice, and borrowings have to be repaid and interest payments met.

Assets represent how this money has been used, for example:

- Notes, coins
- Money market funds
- Securities
- Lending (the largest figure)
- Fixed assets, for example property

The assets, therefore, represent claims by the bank against others. Assets and liabilities always balance.

Banks list assets in descending order of liquidity:

- Cash
- Balances at the Central bank   *central bank reserves —*
- Money at call and short notice
- Bank and trade bills of exchange   *T Bills & Bonds —*
- Treasury bills
- Securities
- Advances to customers
- Premises and equipment

Its liabilities would be:

- Ordinary share capital
- Other share capital
- Reserves
- Retained profits
- Provisions against losses
- Bond issues
- Customers' deposits
- Other borrowing
- Trade creditors
- Tax

▼ **Figure 2.2** *Summary balance sheet*

SUMMARY BALANCE SHEET, A.N. OTHER BANK as at 31/12/14

ASSETS	LIABILITIES
(that is, how liabilities have been used)	(that is, where the money comes from)
Cash	Shareholders' funds
Money market funds	Deposits
Other securities	Borrowings
Lending	

The balance sheet is laid out with assets on the left and liabilities on the right, as shown in Figure 2.2.

The profit and loss account shows how a bank has traded during a particular period, such as 1 month, 3 months or a year, for example: 'Profit and loss account for the year ended 31 December 2014'. Note that the balance sheet shows what the bank is worth at a particular point in time, for example: 'Balance sheet as at 31 December 2014'.

Revenue is contrasted with costs, and the resulting difference is the profit or loss. After paying dividends and tax, the remaining profit is transferred to the balance sheet and added to the shareholders' funds, thus *increasing capital*. Equally, a loss will *reduce capital*.

One of the assets listed above was 'Balances at the central bank'. Most central banks insist that banks within the country maintain certain reserves with it. Usually, these are substantial sums and help the central bank in its control of monetary policy and what is called the 'money supply'. We shall examine this in more detail in Chapter 3.

Even where the reserves are very tiny, the main clearing banks have to maintain far higher working balances and *must not fall below these*. These balances are to cover things like the daily settlement for cheque clearing and the daily settlement for Treasury bill and bond purchases for themselves and clients for whom they are acting. There is also the total net payment by the bank's clients of taxes to the government. The government's balance at the central bank will rise – the individual bank's balance will fall.

THE CREATION OF CREDIT

As only a small proportion of deposits is drawn in cash, it follows that banks have considerable facilities for the creation of credit.

Imagine approaching a bank (not your own) to request flexible lending facilities up to $2,000. The bank opens an account and sends you a chequebook. You wander down the high street, writing cheques to the value of $2,000. The recipients pay the cheques into their accounts, and the amounts are credited to them 3 days later and debited to you. The bank has created $2,000 of expenditure that did not exist one week earlier. The suppliers of the goods have $2,000 in bank accounts – disposable money. Where did it come from? Not from you, because you didn't have any. It came from the bank that allowed you to overdraw to the value of $2,000 – the bank has created money. Bank lending equals spending, and excessive spending may mean unacceptable inflation and imports that the nation can't afford.

The creation of credit by banks has several implications:

1   It is a reminder that banking depends on confidence.
2   Governments and central banks will want to control it in view of the implications for inflation and imports.
3   Banks will need internal controls called 'liquidity ratios'.
4   An external control enforced by bank supervisors called the 'capital ratio' is required.

Banking Depends on Confidence

The system works because we have confidence in it and accept cheques in payment of debt. Where is the gold and silver behind this? Of course, there isn't any. Money is as much an entry on a computer disk as anything else. The economist Frederic Benham (1973), in his textbook *Economics: A General Introduction*, points out that paper money could be seen as a 'gigantic confidence trick'. It works as long as people believe in it. When people don't have confidence – they will refuse to accept banknotes and bartering will grow.

The Money Supply

Governments and central bankers will want to control credit and measure the 'money supply'. This figure is a measure of bank deposits as being the best guide to bank lending. The figure for deposits sounds like a motorway – M3 or M4, depending on the country. Another measure is M0 – notes and coin in circulation plus banks' till money and balances with the central bank. Add to this the private sector's deposits at banks, and you have the essential elements of M3 or M4. Control of inflation by controlling these monetary aggregates is part of what is meant by 'monetarism' – the economic doctrines of the American economist Milton Friedman. In the UK, the Conservative government of 1979 used them as a rather rigid instrument of government policy in the early 1980s. (Charles Goodhart, one-time economic adviser to the Bank of England, has coined 'Goodhart's law': when an economic indicator is used as an instrument of government policy, its behaviour then changes.) Later governments have interpreted the figures more flexibly. The money growth in the mid-1980s gave little warning of recessions in the US and the UK, and monetary aggregates fell somewhat out of favour. In September 2005, the Bank of England announced that, from 2006, M0 figures would no longer be published, and the US Federal Reserve dropped the publication of M3 figures in April 2006, saying, 'The role of M3 in the policy process has diminished greatly over time.' Even Milton Friedman admitted in June 2003: 'The use of the quantity of money as a target has not been a success.' However, perhaps 'the maid is not dead but sleepeth'. References to the money supply increasingly featured in the speeches of Mervyn King, governor of the Bank of England up until mid-2013, and the European Central Bank (ECB) still studies monetary aggregates. Greater attention has been paid to monetary aggregate trends in the light of the credit crisis and the era of 'easy money' that preceded the credit collapse in 2007–8 – various money aggregates were growing at annualized rates of over 20%.

Interest rates remain the main economic tool in controlling monetary conditions, being raised to curb inflation or lowered to boost economic activity. The idea is that as interest rates are raised, mortgage payments go up, and so does the cost of buying goods on credit. People therefore have less money to spend, and the price of goods has to be lowered to attract buyers. Conversely, as we have seen at the start of the new millennium, when economies slow down, they can be boosted by lowering interest rates. Mortgage payments come down, the cost of borrowing to buy goods on credit is reduced, and as people go out and spend more, this stimulates and sustains economic activity. The use of interest rates to control inflationary pressures generally worked well up until the 2007–8 crisis, although some (even Alan Greenspan, former chairman of the Federal Reserve) say that policy was too lax and promoted too much loan growth. However, since 2008, governments have aimed to inject life into recessionary economies, and interest rates have fallen to historically low levels (the UK bank rate stood at 0.5% and the US federal funds rate at 0.25%); their usefulness as a major tool of policy is limited because rates cannot fall much further.

The central bank has a number of weapons if it wishes to constrain demand and inflationary pressure. It may also not be as quick as usual to help banks' liquidity when acting as 'lender of last resort' (see Chapter 3). Monetary policy post crisis has looked to boost demand and has focused on policy guidance (reassuring markets that interest rates will stay low) over the short- to medium-term and also quantitative easing (central banks buying bank assets to boost liquidity in markets and therefore boosting banks ability to lend). See Box 2.4:

BOX 2.4

Monetary Policy and Quantitative Easing Post Crisis

The US and UK governments, have sought to rapidly inject liquidity (and capital) into collapsing banking systems in order to help preserve stability and at the same time rapidly cut interest rates to boost flagging demand.

The ECB injected over €1 trillion into eurozone banking systems between December 2011 and March 2012 in order to enhance the liquidity of, particularly, French, Italian and Spanish banks. Similarly, the Bank of England has also allowed UK banks to pledge 'doubtful' assets as collateral to borrow around £200bn of liquidity. The US Federal Reserve has pretty much done the same.

All this has the effect of exploding the balance sheets of central banks and pumping short-term cash into the system so banks can meet liquidity requirements. The approach is referred to as **'quantitative easing', or QE**.

According to *The Economist* (31 October, 2014), the US Federal Reserves balance sheet has increased five fold and the Bank of England's by a factor of 4.5.

All in all, the policy has been regarded as a success as it has avoided deflation (negative interest) and appears to have stimulated some modest growth.

Detractors say that it is storing up big inflationary problems for the future. It may also lead to a collapse in financial assets markets if massively less cheap liquidity is available to acquire such assets when QE ends (in fact the US Fed announced the ending of its QE in November 2014, although the Japanese authorities surprised markets in October 2014 by saying that they were going to start a new QE asset-buying programme).

In addition, it should be noted that governments have embraced Keynesian fiscal stimulus by injecting billions of public money into the system to boost demand in order to try and avoid a recession turning into a deflationary spiral (as partly experienced in Japan since the mid-1990s). It remains to be seen whether this will be a long-term policy success.

Liquidity Ratios

Bankers have internal controls based on liquidity ratios. They know that it would be folly to take their deposits and lend 100% as 3-year personal loans. They have internal rules on what percentage of deposits should be held as cash, what percentage at call and short notice, what percentage as short-term securities (T-bills, bills of exchange) and so on. The controls may also be *external* and laid down by the central bank, as they are in Spain, where they are called 'coefficients'. This is why banks list assets in *descending* order of liquidity, that is, the most liquid assets (cash) are first. Cash is particularly important as banks must keep a given percentage to meet cash withdrawals. In the case of the new bank account totalling $2,000, discussed above, if cash withdrawals average 5%, then the bank must have $100 cash to back these accounts.

Capital ratio is the external control imposed by bank supervisors in the interests of prudence. It is a major issue in banking, and we need to look at it in more detail.

CAPITAL RATIO

The basic concept of capital ratio has been around for hundreds of years. Bankers lend money and some people will default. Does this mean that the banks cannot repay depositors? The buffer, the money the bank can rely on, is its capital. There should therefore be a prudent relationship between capital and lending – that is the capital ratio.

All this assumes that the bank has not made things worse by an excessive exposure to a few key borrowers. In 1984, for example, it was found that Johnson Matthey Bank in the UK had lent the equivalent of 115% of its own capital to just two borrowers. This loophole was plugged in the 1987 Banking Act. If exposure to one borrower exceeds 10% of capital, the Bank of England must be informed. Before exposure can exceed 25%, Bank of England permission must be obtained. Exposure to industry sectors, for example textiles, and countries is also monitored. All central banks have 'large exposure' controls.

The older idea of relating capital to *lending* has to be extended to capital to *assets* in the modern age. However, all assets are not the same for this purpose; for example, what is the default risk with cash? Surely the answer is 'none'? Therefore we end up with the concept of 'risk-weighted assets'. A normal bank loan is weighted at 100%, that is, a loan of $500,000 counts as $500,000 for this purpose. However, cash is weighted at 0%, and a cash balance of $10m becomes $0 for risk-weighting purposes. Secured lending has a weight of 50% (see Table 2.3).

▼ Table 2.3 *Risk-weighting example*

Assets	Value $m	Risk weighting %	Risk-weighted value $m
Cash	50	0	–
T-bills	100	10	10
Mortgages	500	50	250
Loans	1,000	100	1,000
Total	1,650		1,260

The capital ratio is thus determined by applying the ratio to the figure of risk-weighted assets. If the agreed ratio were 10%, then, from the figures in Table 2.3, capital must be 10% × $1,260m = $126m.

The Basel Committee

However, every central bank had different rules. In 1974, the G10 nations (see Chapter 3), together with Luxembourg, set up the Committee on Banking Regulations and Supervisory Practices, later called the Basel Committee on Banking Supervision (known as the Basel Committee) to draw up uniform rules. It meets at Basel in Switzerland under the auspices of the Bank for International Settlements (BIS). In 1988, after several years of discussion, the committee announced agreement on uniform rules for capital ratio.

The first stumbling block was the definition of 'capital'. The committee came to a compromise – the 'best' capital is called 'tier 1' and must be at least half the necessary figure. It consists of

- shareholders' equity,
- retained profits and
- noncumulative perpetual preference shares.

'Tier 2' capital is the remainder and would include

- cumulative perpetual preference shares,
- revaluation reserves,
- undisclosed reserves and
- subordinated term debt with maturity in excess of 5 years.

For a discussion of preference shares, see Chapter 7. Subordinated debtors come after other debtors in the event of liquidation.

The minimum capital ratio itself is 8% and applied from 1 January 1993.

The risk-weighting figures were agreed, and we gave examples of some of these above. Although unsecured loans are 100%, loans to or claims on Organisation of Economic Co-operation and Development (OECD) governments, and sometimes other governments as well, are weighted at 20%. Thus, in 2007, loans to China would be given the full 100% weighting, but those to South Korea (as a member of the OECD) were weighted at only 20%.

The risk weightings are not only applied to balance sheet items but to *off-balance sheet* items that involve risk – loan guarantees, standby letters of credit, documentary letters of credit and derivative products such as options, futures, swaps and forward rate agreements (all explained in later chapters).

The banks are conscious of capital ratio rules and have tightened up the discipline regarding profit as a return on capital. If a transaction needs capital backing under the new rules, then the profit on the transaction must meet the bank's target for profit on capital employed. Some consultants call this RAROC – risk-adjusted return on capital. Although there is a capital requirement for off-balance sheet items, it is not as onerous as for on-balance sheet items and thus adds to the attraction of these transactions. For example, documentary letters of credit backed by documents giving title are weighted at 20%. A general standby letter of credit not related to a specific transaction is weighted at 100%, but a standby letter of credit which is so related is weighted at 50%. As capital has a cost, the bank will ensure that the charges to the client cover the *cost of capital* as well as any other costs.

For their results for the year ending March 1996, Japanese banks finally recognized their true position regarding bad debts and began to write these off against profit. The three long-term credit banks, the seven trust banks and 7 of the top 11 city banks all declared a loss. As a result, some of the capital ratios were close to the minimum. Despite subsequent restructuring, mergers and a brief return to profit, by 2002 the four largest banks were again reporting substantial losses (totalling $32bn) and reducing lending to maintain capital ratios. However, vigorous action to write off non-performing loans put the main Japanese banks in a much stronger position by the mid-2000s, and bad loans have continued to decline, although the ongoing poor performance of the Japanese economy and the global call for more bank capital since the credit crisis still means that the top banks are undercapitalized by international standards.

In September 1998, the Basel Committee, under its new chairman William McDonough, president of the New York Federal Reserve Bank, held the first of a series of meetings to revise the original Basel accord.

There was a general feeling that some of the rules were too crude. In March 1998, the Institute of International Finance, a Washington-based organization representing commercial and investment banks, called on the Basel Committee to change the formula. For example, lending to banks in the OECD has a ratio of only 1.6% (20% of 8%). Thus a loan to General Electric (with a 100% weighting) needed a capital ratio of 8%, but one to a South Korean bank, only 1.6%. Equally, a loan to an AAA-rated company is treated the same as a loan to a company of a much lower credit quality. In addition, where banks needed 8% capital backing for loans but internal models calculated the risk as far less, they were increasingly selling these loans to the market as securities with a lower weighting. (This is discussed later in this chapter and in Chapter 7.)

The use of credit ratings to make the risk calculation more scientific was discussed, but many European corporates do not have credit ratings. The use of statistical credit risk modelling was also discussed, but viewed with scepticism. In April 1999, a BIS committee report entitled *Credit Risk Modelling* (BIS, 1999) confirmed that regulators were not yet ready to accept them.

In June 1999, the BIS committee issued a new paper and suggested a 10-month consultation period. In spite of the absence of credit ratings in Europe, the committee came down heavily on the use of credit ratings to guide credit risk. Five 'buckets' were suggested, with sovereign governments in the AAA/AA category getting a zero weighting, a grade A 20% weighting and so on, down to 150% for grades of B– or less. Similar rules were drawn up for lending to banks and corporates. More sophisticated banks could use internal ratings as an interim measure, and supervisors could ask for more capital if they thought that banks were taking excessive risks. This has had an effect on pricing for bonds and syndicated loans. With some reservations, the new proposals were generally welcomed.

All the above relates to credit risk. There is also market risk and operational risk. Market movements in the price of financial instruments may expose the banks to losses. The EU's Capital Adequacy Directive (CAD), which effectively introduced Basel I rules into EU law, addressed this problem and applied from January 1996. In this case, however, the use of banks' internal statistical models was accepted, subject to monitoring by local central banks. These models are usually called value at risk (VaR) models. Operational risk recognizes the risk of losses through failure or weaknesses in a bank's internal processes and systems. A good example of the latter is the collapse of Barings Bank due to a failure to control the activities of one trader. A new capital adequacy accord called Basel II was agreed in June 2004 and, after various revisions, was finally agreed and introduced on 4 July 2006. It redefined credit risk and market risk but put new emphasis on operational risk – not easy to measure, as shown in Box 2.5.

BOX 2.5

Key Differences between Basel I and Basel II

The main difference between Basel I and Basel II was that the latter now not only took account of market and operational risk but also offered banks three different ways to calculate credit risk:

1 *Standardized approach:* similar to the old system, although a new rating of 150% came in for low-quality credits, and credit ratings were also to be used to inform credit risk assessments

2 *Foundation IRB (internal rating-based) approach:* where banks can use their internal models to assess credit risk, although regulators would set various parameters of these models

3 *Advanced IRB (internal rating–based) approach:* where banks can use their own models to assess the credit risk, setting their own parameters for the models, although still subject to regulatory approval

Typically, only the most sophisticated international banks – mainly the global commercial and investment banks – would adopt the advanced IRB approach. All the above was referred to as pillar 1 in Basel II.

Pillar 2 included a framework for the disclosure of other risks, such as concentration risk, liquidity risk, systemic risk and other risks; and pillar 3 introduced greater disclosure of bank risk-taking positions. In spite of much criticism from banks (particularly smaller banks that thought that under the standardized approach they would be disadvantaged), the new accord was due to be implemented from January 2007, although US banking authorities did not agree to implementation until April 2008, and this was only for 20 or so of the largest banks that planned to adopt the most sophisticated advanced approach.

Prior to implementation, some of the largest banks, like JP Morgan, noted that increasing the amount of capital to be held for high risks might tempt banks to offload these onto less regulated organizations, for example hedge funds, which they presumably did.

The main effect of Basel II was that it effectively reduced the regulatory capital that had to be held by the world's most sophisticated banks, as their models predicted that because of diversification and other risk reduction benefits, their economic capital requirements were lower than required by regulation.

In fact, it is difficult to find any bank whose capital requirements significantly increased as a result of Basel II!

Basel II cannot, however, be blamed for the credit crisis as it was implemented after the onset of the crisis, which had its origins in the collapse of the US sub-prime market in 2006–7. If bank capital regulation is to be blamed for changing the behaviour of banks to take on excessive risks, the main culprit is Basel I.

Basel II, however, has been criticized as taking a static 'engineers approach' to calculating risk, in that it failed to take account of the dynamic aspects of a bank that is constantly seeking to renew investments and refinancing. Notably, Basel II did not have a single specific measure against systemic risk.

To address this issue, new Basel III rules are planned to be introduced at the latest by 2019.

Basel III

In September 2010, global banking regulators agreed to effectively triple the size of the capital reserves that the world's banks must hold against losses (see Figure 2.3). Basel III sets a new core capital ratio ('tier 1' capital – equity and retained profits) of 4.5%, more than double the current 2% level, plus a new buffer of a further 2.5%. Banks whose capital falls within the buffer zone will face restrictions on paying dividends and discretionary bonuses, so the rule sets an effective floor of 7%. The new rules will be phased in between January 2013 and January 2019.

The accord also provides for a countercyclical buffer within a range of 0–2.5% of common equity or other fully loss-absorbing capital that will be implemented according to national circumstances. Its purpose is to achieve the broader macro-prudential goal of protecting the banking sector from periods of excess aggregate credit growth. For any given country, this buffer will only be in effect when there is excess credit growth that results in a system-wide build-up of risk. In addition, the measure of banks' risk-weighted assets has been revised to expand the range of risks covered, including counterparty credit exposure arising from credit derivatives, repos, securities lending and complex securitization activities.

Basel III also includes two new liquidity rules: a liquidity coverage ratio that requires banks to hold enough cash and other easy-to-sell assets to survive a 30 day-crisis; and a net stable funding ratio that will force banks to hold more long-term funding. Given the lack of previous experience, the adoption of the new liquidity standards is going to be preceded by a period of observation to assess their impact on funding markets.

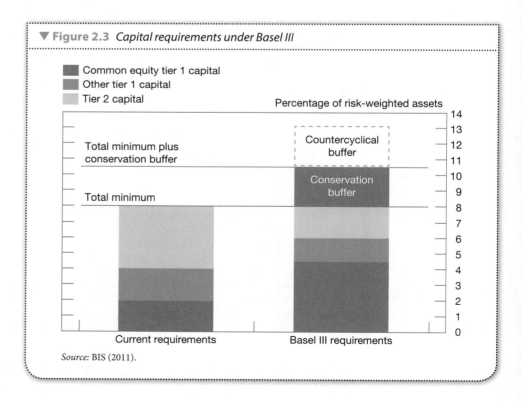

▼ **Figure 2.3** *Capital requirements under Basel III*

Source: BIS (2011).

Banks have been especially critical of the Basel III proposals, especially regarding the need to hold more equity capital. Other criticisms include the following:

- It doesn't change the risk-weighted asset (RWA) coefficients of Basel II, which are estimated on the basis of historical data, and so fails to take account of the dynamic aspects of a bank.
- There are potential problems in addressing procyclicality because of likely political opposition; for example, macro-prudential instruments might reduce returns in industries such as construction or finance. The losers from such measures may be politically powerful and able to bring considerable pressure to bear on the authorities to refrain from using them to restrain asset prices and credit expansion, and potential conflicts with the operation of monetary policy; for example, the monetary policy committee may want to lower interest rates to raise asset prices and stimulate aggregate demand and so bring inflation back up towards target, whereas a financial stability committee might want to increase capital requirements to reduce debt and leverage and contain systemic financial risk.
- It will encourage a shift of business from the regulated to the unregulated (shadow) banking sector.

European Capital Regulation

In Europe, there is a parallel regulatory framework introduced by the EU that has tended to incorporate Basel capital rules into EU law. The EU's Capital Requirement Directive (CRD) implements the revised Basel capital adequacy framework (Basel II) and applies it to all investment firms and banks. The CRD (first introduced in 2006) aims to reduce the probability of consumer loss or market disruption as a result of prudential failure. It will do so by seeking to ensure that the financial resources held by a firm are commensurate with the risks associated with the business profile and the control environment within the firm. The legislation was amended in 2008 (CRD II) and 2010 (CRD III). The European Commission has recently consulted on a CRD IV that aims to implement Basel III rules into EU legislation, covering:

- liquidity standards,
- definition of capital,
- leverage ratio,
- capital buffers and
- counterparty credit risk.

Box 2.6 highlights the main features of CRD IV.

BOX 2.6

EU's Capital Requirements Directive (CRD) IV

CRD IV is an EU legislative package covering prudential rules for banks, building societies and investment firms. The EU text was formally published in the Official Journal of the EU on 27 June 2013. The bulk of the rules contained in the legislation are applicable from 1 January 2014.

> ## EU's Capital Requirements Directive (CRD) IV (*continued*)
>
> CRD IV is made up of
>
> - the Capital Requirements Regulation (CRR), which is directly applicable to firms across the EU, and
> - the Capital Requirements Directive (CRD), which must be implemented through national law.
>
> CRD IV is intended to implement the Basel III agreement in the EU. This includes enhanced requirements for
>
> - the quality and quantity of capital,
> - a basis for new liquidity and leverage requirements,
> - new rules for counterparty risk and
> - new macroprudential standards, including a countercyclical capital buffer and capital buffers for systemically important institutions.
>
> CRD IV also makes changes to rules on corporate governance, including remuneration, and introduces standardized EU regulatory reporting. These reporting requirements will specify the information firms must report to supervisors in areas such as own funds, large exposures and financial information.
>
> *Source:* Bank of England (2014) October, http://www.bankofengland.co.uk/pra/pages/crdiv/default.aspx.

Increasing Capital Ratio

If a bank does not have enough capital to meet the new requirements, what can it do? There are essentially only two possibilities: find more capital or reduce assets.

Find more capital

Finding more capital could involve a rights issue, reducing dividends (to increase retained profit), or raising money through other forms of capital (known as 'hybrid capital instruments'). There is a well-developed market in hybrid tier 1 instruments, for example non-cumulative perpetual preference shares or perpetual variable rate notes that have features similar to equity and (up to a limit) can be included in tier 1 equity. European banks had issued $350bn of these tier 1 hybrid instruments since 1993 and raised around $55bn from them in 2008. Tier 1 capital must, of course, be 4%, and tier 2 items cannot exceed tier 1. Banks have also been active issuers of tier 2 instruments (some $700bn to date in Europe). Several German banks have issued their own type of cumulative preference share (*Genusscheine*) to count as 'hybrid' tier 2 capital. Many banks, including National Westminster, NAB, Banco Santander, RBS, Crédit Lyonnais and others, have issued perpetual variable rate notes to count as tier 2 capital. In 2004, Barclays Bank issued noncumulative perpetual preference shares to the value of €1bn to strengthen its capital. As a result of the credit crisis, many of the hybrid tier 1 and 2 instruments have been downgraded to reflect the increased risk in the banking sector, and many banks are seeking to buy back these (subordinated) debt issues.

Reduce assets

Reducing assets could involve selling off subsidiaries or selling off loans or other assets to other banks or investment firms. Post crisis many big banks have had to de-risk (reduce their risky assets so they can achieve tougher capital requirements – recall that the riskier your assets and other activities are the more capital you have to hold). As all the worlds biggest Western banks were hit by the crisis, and regulators responded by saying they have to boost their highest quality capital (tier 1 equity), there has been a massive rush for all banks to issue more equity. In a tough operating environment with low growing economies in the US and Europe, many big banks have found capital raising challenging to say the least. So, in addition, they have made a big effort to de-risk by selling assets that are viewed as risky and too capital costly. This is reflected in the fact that large banks like the two Swiss firms UBS and Credit Suisse have dramatically reduced their investment banking business, and Barclays has announced that it is moving out of some investment banking areas, as has RBS. As such, many big bank's balance sheets (and off-balance sheet positions as well) are shrinking.

One approach widely used in the past to remove assets off the balance sheet is through 'securitization'. We shall meet the word 'securitization' again in Chapter 7. In that context, it means the change in emphasis in international banking markets from 1982, by which time borrowers began to borrow on the capital markets by issuing bonds rather than by having a bank loan. The usage in our current context is similar, but here we take an existing loan off the balance sheet by converting it into securities. The best and most common example is selling off mortgage loans as mortgage bonds (pioneered in the US by Salomon Bros – now part of Citigroup). Other examples include converting car loans into notes or bonds and converting credit card receivables into bonds (frequent issues by Citigroup). Another possibility is simply to bundle bank personal loans together and sell them as bonds or shorter term notes, with the loans as the assets backing the security. The legalities are difficult, usually involving a special purpose vehicle to issue. Guarantees from insurance companies or other financial entities are involved, and the idea is for the original lender to so weaken the link to the loan that it no longer counts for capital ratio purposes. The issuer usually continues to administer the loan and will receive a fee for doing so. The securitization phenomena grew rapidly over the past decade as banks actively sought to reshuffle their balance sheets in order to release capital for more profitable activities. However, the market dried up in late 2007 because of the collapse of the US sub-prime lending market, which had primarily been financed via securitization activity – at its peak over 80% of sub-prime loans were securitized. The rise and dramatic fall of the securitization business, and how it fuelled a property boom and slump that fed the credit crisis of 2007–8 onwards is discussed in more detail in Chapter 7.

CENTRAL BANK REPORTING

All banks operating within a country make detailed reports to the central bank as part of its supervisory role, even if any action to be taken will be carried out by a separate supervisory body.

Reports will be sent at varying frequencies – monthly, quarterly, biannually, and annually – and will cover the following items:

- Maturity of assets, that is, liquidity
- Large exposures

- Foreign exchange exposure
- Capital expenditure
- Assets/liabilities for overseas residents
- Assets/liabilities in foreign currencies
- Balance sheet
- Profit and loss

Foreign banks operating in a country operate either as branches or legal entities. If only operating as a branch, no reports on capital will be made, as the capital is held by the parent company.

THE EU'S SECOND BANKING DIRECTIVE

The EU's Second Banking Directive came into effect on 1 January 1993. The original intention of the EU had been to achieve full harmonization of banking legislation throughout the EU. This has now been abandoned. Instead, under the Second Banking Directive, banks in the EU will continue to be authorized and regulated by their own national authority. This will be accepted as adequate for granting them freedom to operate throughout the EU. Thus they will acquire a European banking licence or passport which will allow them to engage in investment as well as commercial banking, because 'universal banking' has always been the tradition in Europe. In countries where this has not been so, their banks will now be free to engage in activities throughout the EU that they may still be prevented from doing in their own country. (The specific Investment Services Directive is discussed in Chapter 12.)

Third-country banks can operate within the EU if 'reciprocal treatment' is afforded in their country to EU member banks. At first, this was taken to mean that they must be allowed to engage in the same activities as third-country banks are permitted to do within the EU. This led to protest from America (where up until 1999 commercial and investment banks were separated). In response to this, reciprocity is now defined as equal 'national treatment', that is, EU banks being treated the same as local banks in third countries. But in individual cases, the EU may still insist on 'equal/comparable access'.

For some time there has been debate about whether there is need for a single European bank regulator. The rescue of Dexia Bank in September 2008 by the Belgium, French and Luxembourg governments highlighted the need for state coordination when it comes to banks with substantial cross-border banking activities. Francisco González, chairman of Spanish bank BBVA, for instance, was one of the first to call for a single European financial regulator to manage the risks of cross-border banking. This has now become a reality with the creation of a European Banking Union for banks operating in the eurozone countries, as shown in Box 2.7.

The main objective of the banking Union is to break the link between banks and sovereigns (government debt). Banks in Europe are big holders of government bonds. When banking systems have a crisis, it means that economy weakens; governments deteriorate because they have to use public money to support the banks; and the ability of government to borrow more through bond issuance weakens, as investors want to be paid much more to buy the bonds and the banks also do not have the resources to take up more government debt. So banking problems soon become government debt problems – sovereigns cannot borrow, and their creditworthiness becomes questioned by the markets – recall the euro sovereign debt crisis in 2011–12 when investors thought that Greece, Italy, Spain and Portugal might default. They all had to be supported by outside agencies including the EU

BOX 2.7

European Banking Union

In response to the financial crisis that emerged in 2008, the European Commission pursued a number of initiatives to create a safer and sounder financial sector for the single market.

These initiatives, which include stronger prudential requirements for banks, improved depositor protection and rules for managing failing banks, form a **single rulebook** for all financial actors in the 28 member states of the European Union.

The single rule book is the foundation on which the Banking Union sits.

As the financial crisis evolved and turned into the eurozone debt crisis, it became clear that for those countries which shared the euro and were even more interdependent, a deeper integration of the banking system was needed.

That's why, on the basis of the European Commission roadmap for the creation of the Banking Union, the EU institutions agreed to establish a **Single Supervisory Mechanism** (SSM) and a **Single Resolution Mechanism** (SRM) (dealing with the financing and restructuring of troubled institutions) for banks.

Banking Union applies to countries in the euro area. Non-euro-area countries can also join.

The new single supervisor is the European Central Bank, based in Frankfurt.

The SSM came into force in November 2014 and the SRM, in August 2014.

Source: EU (2014) and own updates. http://ec.europa.eu/internal_market/finances/banking-union/index_en.htm.

---

and the International Monetary Fund (IMF). The Banking Union has been put in place to reduce the likelihood of this happening again, so if a banking system does get into financial difficulties, support from the whole euro area can be provided more rapidly to resolve any individual country crisis; depositors will be protected by a much bigger guarantee scheme; resolution matters will be dealt with more systematically; and resources for bank bailouts will be backed by eurozone resources and not individual country resources.

The G20 Financial Stability Board, in addition to its European and national counterparts, has emphasized the role of systemically important financial institutions (SIFIs) that may be regarded as too important to fail. In a meeting held in Cannes, France, in April 2011, the G20 Financial Stability Board identified 28 G-SIFIs (global-SIFIs), of which 17 were European, and these are being asked to hold substantially more capital compared to regulatory norms due to their global systemic importance. It should also be noted that Basel III and CRD IV also require systemically important banks to hold more capital.

MAJOR WORLD BANKS

The UK's *The Banker* magazine publishes its annual ranking of the top 1,000 banks in July every year, highlighting the 'movers and shakers' in the banking sector over the previous year. Although 'large' banks are defined by holdings of tier 1 capital, the asset figures were also disclosed. We shall, therefore, first look at the 'top 20' of the world's biggest banks in asset terms (Table 2.4).

▼ **Table 2.4** *Top 20 world banks by assets, 2013*

Ranking		Bank	Country	Total assets		
2013	**2012**			**Amount ($mn)**	**Change (%)**	**NPL ratio (%)**
1	1	Industrial and Commercial Bank of China	China	3,100,254	11.16%	0.94%
2	3	HSBC Holdings	UK	2,671,318	−0.79%	3.22%
3	9	China Construction Bank	China	2,517,734	13.34%	0.99%
4	6	BNP Paribas	France	2,482,950	−1.32%	4.70%
5	2	Mitsubishi UFJ Financial Group	Japan	2,451,396	−1.58%	NA
6	7	JPMorgan Chase	USA	2,415,689	2.40%	3.15%
7	11	Agricultural Bank of China	China	2,386,447	13.34%	1.22%
8	5	Credit Agricole	France	2,353,553	−11.16%	3.40%
9	14	Bank of China	China	2,273,730	12.78%	0.96%
10	4	Deutsche Bank	Germany	2,222,621	−16.28%	1.76%
11	8	Barclays	UK	2,161,890	−8.03%	2.80%
12	10	Bank of America	USA	2,104,995	−4.84%	4.66%
13	15	Citigroup	USA	1,880,617	0.86%	2.39%
14	18	Société Générale	France	1,703,810	3.26%	6.00%
15	12	Royal Bank of Scotland	UK	1,693,374	−18.19%	8.61%
16	13	Mizuho Financial Group	Japan	1,669,733	−11.39%	NA
17	19	Groupe BPCE	France	1,549,683	2.36%	3.90%
18	17	Banco Santander	Spain	1,538,811	−8.13%	5.64%
19	16	Sumitomo Mitsui Financial Group	Japan	1,534,040	−2.87%	NA
20	21	Wells Fargo	USA	1,527,015	7.31%	5.19%

Source: The Banker (July 2014).

An interesting feature of Table 2.4 is the importance of Chinese banks – four out of the top ten, they have grown significantly over recent years. In contrast, the top European banks that accounted for six out of the top seven places in 2010 have all reduced their assets size (mainly to boost their capital strength). Royal Bank of Scotland was the biggest bank in the world in 2008 – its size had swelled due to the acquisition of ABN AMRO in 2007 – the largest banking takeover in history, valued at $101bn. (A consortium including

RBS, Fortis and Banco Santander acquired the Dutch bank, with the UK bank taking the bulk of its assets post merger.) The timing of the deal, just before the onset of the worst effects of the credit crisis, and the enormous amount paid were just too much. RBS had to seek state support during 2008 and the bank had to shrink its assets fast to meet capital requirements – it is now ranked 15th in the world by assets size, and remains as we noted earlier 80% owned by the UK taxpayer. In 1992, Citicorp was number 20, with no other US bank in the top 20. But in 2013, the enlarged Citigroup was number 13, although it could have disappeared from the list if the US government hadn't bailed it out in November 2008; while the merged JP Morgan and Chase Manhattan stood at number 6 and Bank of America at number 12.

Table 2.5 compares the nationality of the top 20 banks by assets in 2008 and 2013. While no major Japanese bank has failed as a consequence of the credit crisis, the presence of Japanese banks in the ranking of top global banks has declined substantially over the past 20 years or so. In 2013, the Japanese provided 3 of the world's top 20 banks. In 1992, however, they provided 11 out of the top 20 (and 8 out of the top 10). The collapse of the stock market, a serious fall in property values, a prolonged recession and high bank bad debts all caused a reduction in Japanese bank strength (the first four in the table by tier 1 capital in 1992) and some withdrawal from world markets. However, it is fair to say that the position of Japanese banks in 2013 is stronger than a decade earlier. Another noticeable feature of Table 2.5 is the increased presence of Chinese banks, a trend generally confirmed when we look at the share of global equity (tier 1) capital for banks from different regions of the world, as shown in Table 2.6. Note the increased importance of Asia-Pacific-based banks, and the relative decline in importance of Western Europeans.

The other surprise, looking at Table 2.5, is that there are only 4 US banks in the top 20. We have to realize that banking is fragmented in the US, where there are around 6,500 banks. Unlike Europe, up until quite recently branch banking across the US was unknown. The McFadden Act of 1927 limited banking activities to within a single state; some local state legislation limits it to one branch in one city within the state. The Act, however, was repealed in 1994 by the US Interstate Banking and Banking Efficiency Act, which permitted full interstate banking by 1997, unless local state laws prevent it. Many states did not wait for Congress, but changed their laws and allowed reciprocal banking facilities with other states. The passing of the Gramm-Leach-Bliley Act of 1999 created the possibility for the

▼ **Table 2.5** *Nationality of top 20 banks by assets, 2008, 2010 and 2013*

Country	Number of banks 2008	Number of banks 2010	Number of banks 2013
US	4	3	4
France	3	3	4
UK	3	4	3
Japan	3	3	3
Switzerland	1	0	0
China	2	4	4
Netherlands	1	1	0
Germany	1	1	1
Italy	1	0	0
Spain	1	1	1

Source: The Banker (July, 2009; 2011, 2014).

▼ **Table 2.6** *Global structure: Share of global tier 1 capital, 2009, 2010 and 2013*

Region	% 2009	2010	2013
Africa	1.0	1.0	0.9
Asia-Pacific	25.5	30.8	36.0
Central & Eastern Europe	2.0	2.0	2.2
Western Europe	42.5	38.1	33.8
Central & Latin America	2.8	3.0	3.2
Middle East	3.6	3.3	3.8
North America	22.6	21.7	20.1

Source: The Banker (July 2010; 2011 and 2014).

creation of financial holding companies, where banks can engage in securities underwriting, insurance sales and a broad range of investment banking and other financial services business. All major banks are part of financial holding companies, of which there were 484 at the start of 2014. Since the deregulation of branching and activity restrictions, US banks have engaged in a wave of mergers (see Appendix 1 at the end of this chapter). When we look at the top 20 global banks by tier 1 capital (Table 2.7), we see the US with five banks, as opposed to four by assets.

▼ Table 2.7 *Top 20 world banks by tier 1 capital, 2013*

Ranking				Tier-one capital	
2013	**2012**	**Bank**	**Country**	**Amount ($ million)**	**Change (%)**
1	1	Industrial and Commercial Bank of China	China	207,614	29.24%
2	5	China Construction Bank	China	173,992	26.45%
3	2	JPMorgan Chase	USA	165,663	3.54%
4	3	Bank of America	USA	161,456	3.86%
5	4	HSBC Holdings	UK	158,155	4.71%
6	6	Citigroup	USA	149,804	9.72%
7	9	Bank of China	China	149,729	23.23%
8	8	Wells Fargo	USA	140,735	11.16%
9	10	Agricultural Bank of China	China	137,410	23.24%
10	7	Mitsubishi UFJ Financial Group	Japan	117,206	−1.60%
11	11	BNP Paribas	France	99,168	−0.06%
12	15	Barclays	UK	91,960	14.79%
13	13	Credit Agricole	France	86,201	5.96%
14	14	Banco Santander	Spain	84,232	3.66%
15	12	Royal Bank of Scotland	UK	83,180	−5.65%
16	19	Goldman Sachs	USA	72,471	8.20%
17	16	Sumitomo Mitsui Financial Group	Japan	71,361	−1.62%
18	20	Deutsche Bank	Germany	69,954	5.04%
19	23	Bank of Communications	China	68,333	18.61%
20	22	Groupe BPCE	France	65,226	6.31%

Source: The Banker (2014) July.

▼ **Table 2.8** *Nationality of top 20 banks by tier 1 capital, 2008 and 2013*

Country	Number of banks 2008	Number of banks 2013
United States	6	5
United Kingdom	3	3
Japan	3	2
China	3	5
France	2	3
Netherlands	1	0
Spain	1	1
Italy	1	0
Germany	0	1

Source: Derived from *The Banker* rankings (July, 2009; 2014).

Finally, we look at the original sequence of top world banks in *The Banker*, by capital (Table 2.7). The change of bank size rankings from assets to capital came about because of the so-called Basel Agreement in 1988. *The Banker* decided that capital was the important thing for the future, and not assets.

If we compare the assets listing with the tier 1 capital rank, there is an interesting change of sequence in bank nationality, shown in Table 2.8.

There are no Swiss, Italian or Dutch banks in the top 20 ranked according to tier 1 capital. US and Chinese banks appear to be leaders in terms of capital strength. Although the spate of mergers in the run-up to the financial crisis is one reason for the strong presence of American and British banks in the listings in 2008, it is ironic that these systems (despite their perceived capital strength) suffered most in the crisis. Since then, there have been widespread calls for all banks to bolster their capital positions – this has mainly been achieved in the US and the UK by asset shrinkage (less lending and selling of other assets) plus capital issues that have improved their somewhat precarious position.

SUMMARY

- Supervision of banks may be carried out by the central bank (as in the Netherlands and in the UK) or by other supervisory bodies (as in France, Germany, Japan and the US).
- Central banks, commercial banks and investment banks are the main types of bank. There are also savings banks, cooperative banks and mortgage banks, but, with increasing deregulation, the differences are generally weakening. Finally, there are credit unions.
- Islamic banking is managing money in accordance with *sharia* (Islamic) law.
- On a bank's balance sheet, the *liabilities* are shareholders' equity, deposits and borrowings. The *assets* are cash, money market deposits, securities, loans and fixed assets like buildings.
- The shareholders' equity (including retained profits) is at the heart of the bank's *capital*.
- Bank regulators have set up a committee (the *Basel Committee*), which lays down rules that suggest the capital required not only for the credit risk in bank lending but also the market risk of the financial instruments it holds and the operational risk inherent in a bank's activities. The latest capital rules are stipulated in Basel III, which will come into force in 2019. These rules are implemented into EU law via Capital Requirements Directives (CRDs) – CRD IV implements the features of Basel III into EU law in January 2014 and has the same 2019 full bank compliance date.
- The Second European Banking Directive allows banks in the EU to open branches anywhere in the EU under licence from their *home* central bank.
- In an era where money is no longer tied to gold or silver, the ease with which a bank can advance money is called the *creation of credit*. It is limited by liquidity rules, capital ratio rules and central bank monetary policy.
- Excessive credit creation and lax monetary policy have been identified as major culprits of the recent credit crisis. Lax policy fuelled a mortgage lending boom, particularly sub-prime mortgages funded via securitization techniques, which led to a property price bubble in the US, the UK and elsewhere.

When the bubble burst during 2007 and into 2008, banks that were heavily exposed to property lending (and investments in mortgage-backed securities) suffered losses. Banks' capital strength and liquidity position came under investor and depositor scrutiny. The first bank to fail as a result of the crisis was the UK mortgage lender Northern Rock. A wave of collapses then followed, the largest being RBS and Citigroup. The US, the UK and other European governments had to engage in providing massive financial support to save their banking systems. The system experienced its largest financial collapse since the Great Depression of the 1930s, and states now play a major role in reconfiguring the world's largest market-based economies. Since the crisis, there have been massive moves to inject capital and liquidity into European and US banking systems. Pressures have mounted in the light of the eurozone crisis during 2011 and 2012, with substantial liquidity injections into the banking systems of Europe via the ECB, the US and the UK.

- The European Commission has set-out a roadmap for the creation of the European Banking Union, this establishes a **Single Supervisory Mechanism (SSM)** and a **Single Resolution Mechanism (SRM)** (dealing with the financing and restructuring of troubled institutions) for banks. It also establishes a single European Deposit Guarantee Scheme. The new regulator, will be the European Central Bank based in Frankfurt, which will oversee all the largest banks operating in the 18 eurozone countries (the 10 non-euro EU countries can opt to join the new system). The main objective of the Banking Union is to break the link between weak banks and sovereign risk.

REVISION QUESTIONS/ASSIGNMENTS

1 Analyse the role of government ownership in the banking sector of Europe and the US since the banking crisis.
2 Examine the role of liquidity in banking. How is liquidity linked to capital/solvency?
3 Discuss the main differences between Basel I, II and the proposed Basel III.
4 Outline the ways in which banks can increase their capital strength.
5 Consider the main motives for establishing a European Banking Union.

REFERENCES

Benham, F. (1973) *Economics: A General Introduction*, Pitman, London. Introductory economics text that provides some historical perspectives on economic/financial issues.

Bank for International Settlements (BIS). (1999) *Credit Risk Modelling: Current Practices and Applications*, April, Basel Committee on Banking Supervision, BIS, Basel. Technical manual providing information on early credit risk modelling approaches.

Bank for International Settlements (BIS). (2011) *81st Annual Report* BIS, Basel.

Chapman, S.D. (1984) *The Rise of Merchant Banking*, Allen & Unwin, London. Historical analysis of the evolution of merchant banking (investment banking) in the UK.

Green, E. (1989) *Banking: An Illustrated History*, Phaidon Press, Oxford. Historical perspective on the evolution of banking.

The Banker. (2009) Top 1000 world banks 2008, July, *Financial Times*, London. Highlights the 'movers and shakers' in the banking sector over the previous year.

The Banker. (2010) Top 1000 world banks 2009, July, *Financial Times*, London. Highlights the 'movers and shakers' in the banking sector over the previous year.

The Banker. (2011) Top 1000 world banks 2010, July, *Financial Times*, London. Highlights the 'movers and shakers' in the banking sector over the previous year.

The Banker. (2014) Top 1000 world banks 2013, July, *Financial Times*, London. Highlights the 'movers and shakers' in the banking sector over the previous year.

FURTHER READING

Berger, A.N., Molyneux, P., and Wilson, J.O. (2014) *The Oxford Handbook of Banking* (2nd edn), OUP, Oxford. An extensive review of key banking themes covered in over 40 chapters written by experts. Intermediate and advanced (Masters) level topics covered.

Casu, B., Girardone, C., and Molyneux, P. (2015) *Introduction to Banking* (2nd edn), FT/Prentice Hall, London. Introductory banking text with an international focus, used at all undergraduate levels.

Matthews, K., Giuliodori, M., and Mishkin, F. (2013) *Economics of Money, Banking and Financial Markets* (European edn), Pearson Education, Harlow. Standard undergraduate money and banking text used for 2nd-year undergraduate money/monetary policy courses and upwards.

▼ *Appendix 1: Top US bank mergers and acquisitions*

Deal Date	Acquiring Bank	Target (Acquired) Bank	Name of New Bank	Deal Value	Ultimate Successor (Who they are owned by today)
2007	Citizens Banking Corporation	Republic Bancorp	Citizens Republic Bancorp	$1.048 billion	FirstMerit Bank
2007	Banco Bilbao Vizcaya Argentaria USA	Compass Bancshares	BBVA Compass	$9.8 billion	BBVA Compass
2007	Bank of America	LaSalle Bank	Bank of America	$21 billion	Bank of America
2007	State Street Corporation	Investors Financial Services Corporation	State Street Corporation	$4.2 billion	State Street Corporation
2007	Bank of New York	Mellon Financial Corporation	Bank of New York Mellon	$18.3 billion	Bank of New York Mellon
2007	Wachovia	World Savings Bank	Wachovia	$25 billion	Wells Fargo
2008	TD Banknorth	Commerce Bancorp	TD Bank, N.A.	$8.5 billion	TD Bank, N.A.
2008	JPMorgan Chase	Bear Stearns	JPMorgan Chase	$1.1 billion	JPMorgan Chase & Co.
2008	Bank of America	Merrill Lynch	Bank of America	$50 billion	Bank of America
2008	Wells Fargo	Wachovia	Wells Fargo	$15.1 billion	Wells Fargo
2008	JPMorgan Chase	Washington Mutual	JPMorgan Chase	$1.9 billion	JPMorgan Chase & Co.
2008	PNC Financial Services	National City Corp.	PNC Financial Services	$5.08 billion	PNC Financial Services
2011	Capital One	ING Direct USA	Capital One	$9 billion	Capital One
2012	PNC Financial Services	RBC Bank	PNC Financial Services	$3.45 billion	PNC Financial Services

The Role of the Central Bank

HISTORY OF THE MAJOR CENTRAL BANKS

Worldwide, there are 177 central banks employing over 425 people. We shall begin by looking briefly at the historic background of nine major central banks – those of Brazil, China, France, Germany, India, Japan, Russia, the UK and the US – and also at the formation of the newest – the European Central Bank (ECB).

Brazil

Banco Central do Brasil, the Brazilian central bank, was established on 31 December 1964 and is the main monetary authority in the country. It is linked to the national Treasury, which manages (among other things) Brazil's federal public debt. Alexandre Antonio Tombini has been governor since January 2011.

China

The central bank was established in 1948 as the State Bank of the People's Republic of China. It began to function solely as a central bank in September 1983, upon approval by the state council. It is now known as the People's Bank of China. The governor is Zhou Xiaochuan, appointed in January 2003 for no specific term.

France

The Bank of France was founded by Napoleon in 1800 to restore stability, especially in banknotes, after the turbulent years of the French Revolution. It was set up as a joint stock company. Napoleon himself was a shareholder, and the top 200 shareholders elected the 'regents', the bank's principal officers.

It was brought more firmly under government control in 1808, and this process was completed in 1836 with the appointment of bank councillors by the government. A monopoly over banknote issue was given in 1848. The difficult financial years of 1929–30 allowed Banque Nationale de Crédit to go under but intervened to rescue Banque de l'Union Parisienne, which was nationalized in 1945; an Act of 1973 redefined its powers and organization.

The governor of the bank and two deputy governors are appointed by executive order of the president of the Republic for 6 years. These three head the General Council, which consists of 10 people appointed for 6 years. The bank was not originally independent of the government but was given independence in 1993, anticipating the proposed ECB. It has about 200 branches. The current governor is Christian Noyer. Many of its powers were passed to the ECB when it was set up in 1999.

Germany

The forerunner of the German Bundesbank was the Reichsbank, founded in 1876 to 'regulate the amount of money in circulation, facilitate settlements of payments and ensure that available capital is utilised'. It was a private bank, but control was in the hands of the Reich chancellor.

The terrible experience with inflation in the early 1920s led to a Banking Act of 1924, which made the Reichsbank independent of the government. Unfortunately, as Hitler acquired more power in the 1930s, he was impatient with any idea of central bank independence; this was taken away in 1937, and the bank was nationalized in 1939.

After the Second World War, the old currency, the reichsmark, was replaced by the deutschmark. A two-tier central banking system was set up. Each of the 11 federal states (Länder) had a Land Central Bank, and between them they owned a central body, the Bank Deutscher Länder. It was responsible for note creation and policy coordination. In particular, it was independent of the government.

This system was abolished by the Act of July 1957, which set up the Deutsche Bundesbank – a unified central bank. The 11 Land Banks became part of it only as regional offices. They carry out the relevant regulations in their own area.

The Central Bank Council consisted of 11 representatives from the Länder and a central directorate consisting of the president, deputy president and up to eight other people appointed by the president of the Republic and the federal government. The president is usually appointed for an 8-year term. Unification would have added five more Länder representatives to the council. It was, therefore, decided that, from 1 November 1992, the 16 Länder would have nine representatives between them. There are around 150 branch offices run by the Länder.

The Bundesbank is independent of government instructions but must support the government's policy unless it conflicts with the primary task of controlling inflation. It has clashed with various governments but usually wins. The current president is Jens Weidmann. Like France, some traditional powers passed to the ECB in 1999.

India

The Reserve Bank of India was set up in 1934 but nationalized in 1948. Its main function is to conduct monetary policy as well as to oversee supervision of the banking and non-bank financial system. The current governor, Raghuram Rajan, was appointed in September 2013.

Japan

A central bank, modelled on the Bank of England, was set up in 1882 and by 1889 had become the sole issuer of banknotes. The governor and assistant governor are appointed by the Cabinet for a 5-year term. Seven executive directors are appointed by the Ministry of Finance on the government's recommendation. These nine form the executive board.

Technically, the bank is independent of the government. This was prejudiced to some extent by the fact that the Ministry of Finance appointed so many members of the executive board. Also, the Ministry of Finance had the main responsibility for bank regulation and supervision. In April 1996, Yasuo Matsushita, the then governor, urged a review of the central bank's legal status to grant it more independence. As a result, in 1998, as part of Japan's financial market reorganization, the Ministry of Finance lost its power to order the central bank to delay interest rate rises, and banking supervision was passed to the new Financial Services Agency. The present governor is Haruhiko Kuroda.

The Zengin system for cheque clearing and electronic payments is run by the Tokyo Bankers Association.

Russia

The Central Bank of the Russian Federation (Bank of Russia) was founded on 13 July 1990 and is Russia's main monetary authority. The central bank also supervises the banking system and has been active in strengthening the system by the introduction of deposit insurance and the promotion of a Banking Sector Development Strategy (up to 2008). This strategy aimed to improve the banking sector's stability and efficiency, including:

- increasing the protection of the interests of depositors and other creditors of banks;
- enhancing the effectiveness of the banking sector's activity in accumulating household and enterprise sector funds and transforming them into loans and investments;
- making Russian credit institutions more competitive;
- preventing the use of credit institutions in dishonest commercial practices and illegal activities, especially the financing of terrorism and money laundering;
- promoting the development of the competitive environment and ensuring the transparency of credit institutions; and
- building up investor, creditor and depositor confidence in the banking sector.

These banking sector reforms were aimed at helping to implement Russia's medium-term social and economic development programmes, especially its objective to reduce the commodities bias of the Russian economy. A second stage of reforms, begun in 2009 and running up to 2015, implemented by the Russian government and Bank of Russia, will attach priority to effectively positioning the Russian banking sector on international financial markets. Elvira Nabiullina, the current chairman of the Bank of Russia, took up his post in 2013.

United Kingdom

The world's first central bank is said to be the Swedish Riksbank, which opened in 1668. However, it was the formation of the Bank of England in 1694 that more clearly showed the potential for a state bank. The bank was set up to help the government of William and Mary raise money for the wars against the French. London merchants and others raised £1.2m, and the bank was granted a royal charter. It was the only joint stock bank allowed. From about 1715 onwards, the bank was regularly raising money for the government by the sales of government bonds. By the 1826 Banking Act, joint stock banks other than the Bank of England were allowed, which led to a big increase in the numbers of banks. The Bank Charter Act of 1844 effectively gave the bank a monopoly on the issue of new banknotes. Baring Bros hit trouble in 1890 (after unwise loans in South America), and the Bank of England rescued the bank, using a fund to which it and other banks subscribed.

The powers of the bank were exercised in fact rather than law, and the bank was a private bank until it was nationalized in 1946 and banking legislation confirmed its powers in law in 1979 and 1987. In September 1984, it rescued the Johnson Matthey Bank, buying it for £1 and putting in its own managers to run it. Events during the First World War, rather than legislation, clearly established that the bank was an arm of the government and not independent. This finally changed in 1998, when the Bank of England Act set the statutory basis for the bank's new Monetary Policy Committee and the transfer of supervision to the Financial Services Authority (FSA).

The bank is run by a body quaintly called the 'Court'. It is headed by the governor, two deputy governors and 16 non-executive directors. The governor is appointed by the prime minister for a 5-year term and is usually reappointed. The current governor, appointed in 2013 is Mark Carney. Since the onset of the banking crisis and the failure and subsequent state rescue of Northern Rock, RBS and Lloyds, there has been increased discussion about the failure of bank supervision in the UK. In addition to various suggestions regarding structural reform of the banking system, it has become apparent that the tripartite regulatory structure between the Bank of England, the Treasury and the FSA did not work well during the crisis. As such, in 2011, HM Treasury set out proposed legislation in a consultation document *A New Approach to Financial Regulation: The Blueprint for Reform*, which became law in December 2012 (the revised Financial Services Markets Act 2012). The new approach is outlined in Box 3.1.

As one can see, regulatory responsibility has shifted heavily back to the Bank of England.

United States

In the US, the 1789 Constitution put management of the currency firmly in the hands of the Treasury, and the Bank of the United States was formed in 1791. As such, it predates the setting up of central banks in France and Germany, although its record is not continuous. The bank was responsible for the issue of dollar bills and control of government debt.

Due to opposition, the bank's charter was not renewed in 1811, but it was started again in 1816. Bearing in mind that the US is a federal republic, doubt about the constitutional legality behind the formation of the bank led to a withdrawal of privileges in 1836, and concessions were transferred to individual state banks. As a result, the Bank of the United States went bankrupt in 1841. An Act of 1863 distinguished between banks that were licensed and regulated by the federal government – 'national' banks – and those licensed and regulated by individual states. (In some circumstances, a bank may choose to change regulators. Thus, in November 2004, JPMorgan Chase decided not to be regulated by New York state but chose national regulation instead. Having been allowed to have branches in other states since 1994, banks find state registration clumsy.) State banks generally gave up their note issues or converted into national banks. By 1880, there were 2,000 national banks, all issuing banknotes.

It was only in 1913 that the Federal Reserve System was set up, with a single central bank controlling note issue and operating it through 12 Federal Reserve districts. The board of governors was appointed by the president, as today. Having been appointed, the board makes its own decisions on monetary policy without direction from the government, which it does through the Federal Open Market Committee. Janet Yellen is the chairman of the Federal Reserve (you maybe interested to know that she is married to the Nobel Prize–winning economist – George Akerlof – famous for his work on the 'Market for Lemons' (a 'lemon' in the US is a bad second-hand car and Akerlof highlighted how information asymmetries can lead to market mispricing). Of the key central banks we discuss here, the Federal Reserve is the one whose authority as a central body is the least clear-cut. As we noted earlier, the individual states can pass laws (and do); there is the role of the Federal Deposit Insurance Corporation (FDIC), as all deposits are insured up to $250,000; the Office of the Comptroller of the Currency supervises the national banks; and the Federal Home Loan Bank System

BOX 3.1

New Approach to UK Financial Sector Regulation

Three new bodies are as follows:

1 **The Financial Policy Committee (FPC)** acts as a single focused body to oversee financial stability of the financial system overall. It will be responsible for periodic monitoring of risks to financial stability and developing macro-prudential tools to gauge systemic risks. It is also noted that 'alongside the FPC, the Bank of England will have other financial stability functions. Most significantly, it will have clear responsibility for dealing with crisis situations, building on its responsibility for operating the special resolution regime for banks'.

▼ **Figure 3.1** *New approach to UK financial regulation*

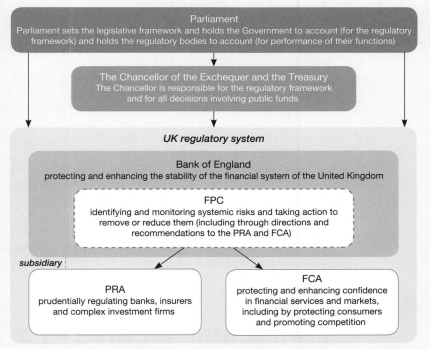

Note: FPC = Financial Policy Committee; PRA = Prudential Regulatory Authority; FCA = Financial Conduct Authority.

Source: HM Treasury (2011) *A New Approach to Financial Regulation: The Blueprint for Reform.*

2 **The Prudential Regulatory Authority (PRA)** is established as a subsidiary of the Bank of England to undertake the prudential regulation (supervision) of firms which 'manage significant balance sheet risk as a core part of their business – banks, insurers and the larger, more complex investment firms'. This used to be the job of the FSA.

3 **The Financial Conduct Authority (FCA)** is the third body established whose main brief is to monitor conduct of business for systemic firms as well as consumer protection issues.

These Authorities commenced operations in April 2013.

supervises the savings and loan associations. Finally, credit unions are regulated by the National Credit Union administrator. There has been regular discussion about simplifying bank and financial sector regulation in the US; for instance, in October 2005, a detailed report was presented to the Senate Committee on Banking suggesting a streamlining of regulation, but this received a lukewarm reception. Also, in the light of the major role played by the Federal Reserve in rescuing the US banking system from total collapse in 2008, the current structure has been substantially strengthened under the 2010 Dodd-Frank Wall Street Reform and Consumer Protection Act (see Chapter 6). In addition to its monetary authority responsibilities, the Federal Reserve also regulates all the largest domestic banks, which are typically part of financial holding companies, as well as all foreign bank subsidiaries. It has a major role under the Dodd-Frank Act of identifying SIFIs that have to hold more capital than other (non-systemic) institutions.

The European Central Bank

The European Central Bank (ECB) was created by the Maastricht Treaty of December 1991. It began operations on 1 June 1998, taking over from its predecessor, the European Monetary Institute. There is an executive board, consisting of the president (Mario Draghi), the vice president and four other members, which will carry out policy by issuing instructions to the other central banks. The policy itself is determined by the governing council, consisting of the executive board plus the governors of the 18 central banks of the member countries in the eurozone. This is usually referred to as the European System of Central Banks (ESCB). (Legally, the non-eurozone central banks are included but take no part in decisions on monetary policy.)

The prime objective of the ECB is price stability, and the Maastricht Treaty says that it is also 'to support the EU's general economic policies'. Interest rate decisions are taken by the ECB by majority vote. The national central banks still conduct the bulk of money market operations and foreign exchange interventions, but within policy set by the ECB. It is interesting to note that the president of the ECB earned $488,000 in 2012, compared with a lowly US$200,000 for the governor of the Federal Reserve. Mark Carney's package at the Bank of England is an estimated $1.3 million (the governor of the Swiss National Bank had a package worth $1.18 million).

CENTRAL BANK ACTIVITIES

We can summarize typical central bank activities as follows:

- Supervising the banking system
- Advising the government on monetary policy
- Issuing banknotes
- Acting as banker to the other banks
- Acting as banker to the government
- Raising money for the government
- Controlling the nation's currency reserves
- Acting as lender of last resort (LLR)
- Liaison with international bodies

Supervision of the Banking System

We saw in Chapter 2 that legally the central bank may not be responsible for banking supervision. There may be a separate supervisory body, like BaFin in Germany or (up until 2012 when its supervision powers were transferred to the Bank of England) the FSA in the UK. Indeed, this is more often the case than not. Even in these cases, however, the practical day-to-day supervision and collection of information from the banks will be carried out by the central bank. The amount of information to be submitted (see Chapter 2) is considerable and may is considerable and can involve significant staff resources.

Usually, the central bank will issue licences and may have to take decisions about rescues. In 1984, the Bank of England rescued the Johnson Matthey Bank and more recently, Northern Rock in 2007. There then followed the support given to Lloyds and RBS in September 2008.

During the Scandinavian banking crisis, in the autumn of 1991, the Bank of Finland had to step in and rescue the ailing Skopbank, the central bank of the savings banks. In March 1992, it was the Bank of Finland that announced a series of measures to bolster confidence in the bank sector, which was suffering due to the unprecedented recession. On the other hand, when Norway's banking sector was in trouble in 1991, it was the Bank Insurance Fund that set up a fund of state money to support the three major banks – Christiana, Norske Bank and Fokus Bank. In Sweden in 1992, the Ministry of Finance carried out rescues of Nordbanken and Första Sparbanken, and later guaranteed all obligations of the Gota Bank. When the Chicago bank Continental Illinois was in difficulty in 1984, it was the FDIC who moved in to help, not the Federal Reserve. In contrast, it was the Fed that stepped in to bail out Citigroup in 2008.

Special problems were created in the case of the infamous BCCI, which collapsed in 1991. It was active in many countries but registered in Luxembourg, which may not have had the resources to monitor it properly. This problem is potentially more serious now as, in the EU, a 'single passport' policy applies. This says that an EU bank can set up a branch in any EU country with a licence from its *home* bank and not its *host* bank, although supervision will be carried out by the *host* central bank. However, following the collapse of BCCI, the G10 Basel Committee on Banking Supervision met at the Bank for International Settlements (BIS) in Basel and formed some new international rules. In particular, these rules say that a central bank may refuse a licence if it believes that a bank is not properly supervised by its home authority.

Stung by criticism over its role in the BCCI affair, the Bank of England pointed out that in the 6 years prior to 1992, it had quietly revoked 16 banking licences and obliged 35 banks to recapitalize, change management or merge. However, in mid-1998, its supervisory powers were passed to the new FSA. But this change ultimately restricted the Bank of England from acting rapidly in the case of supporting Northern Rock, which faced serious liquidity problems prior to its collapse in the autumn of 2007. As part of the new supervisory set-up, Mervyn King argued that the central banks could not provide covert (non-reported) liquidity injections to any failing bank. Also, there were issues regarding EU law concerning preferential treatment in providing state aid to failing private sector firms on anti-competition grounds. The drawn-out support and then nationalization of Northern Rock in early 2008 was clearly not the preferred way to intervene in a crisis situation, so new legislation was passed enabling faster Bank of England support in the event of bank failures, and EU law was adapted to accommodate support for failing banks.

Monetary Policy

The decisions on monetary policy may be taken by the government if the central bank is not independent, or by the central bank itself if it is. In any case, the central bank will cooperate with the government on economic policy generally and will produce advice on monetary policy and economic matters, including all the statistics.

'Monetary policy' refers to interest rates and money supply, which we briefly discussed in Chapter 2. We noted that central banks can use various weapons to control money supply – interest rates, open market operations and changes in banks' reserves held at the central bank. The central bank's role as LLR means that it can control interest rates. The monetary authority, usually the central bank, controls the supply of money in an economy by manipulating interest rates – lower rates feed through into lower lending rates and this encourages borrowing, with the subsequent spending boosting demand and economic growth. As such, an 'expansionary (or lax) monetary policy' is often associated with falling (and low) interest rate environments that increase the amount of money (the money supply) in the economy. Alternatively, if the monetary authorities wish to choke off demand so as to reduce inflationary pressures, they increase interest rates to reduce money supply – this is known as 'contractionary monetary policy'. Often, the goals of monetary policy include maintaining relatively stable prices and low levels of unemployment, and reasonable levels of economic growth. (Remember that monetary policy differs from fiscal policy, which is concerned with government spending, taxation and borrowing.)

The main tool of monetary policy is known as open market operations. This involves the central bank buying or selling financial instruments (government bills, bonds, foreign currencies) in order to influence the quantity of money in circulation. A purchase of government bonds injects more money into the system, whereas a sale of bonds reduces the amount of the money in the system. The aim of open market operations is to influence the amount of what is known as base money in the system. Base money (or the monetary base) relates to the most liquid assets in an economy and consists of notes and coins and commercial bank reserves at the central bank. Base money is sometimes referred to as high-powered money because an increase in the monetary base by X% can have a much bigger impact on the economy as it feeds through the banking system via the credit creation process (explained in Chapter 2). To recap: if the central bank buys bonds worth $1m from a bank, this is deposited in the bank, the bank may then lend (say 90%) to a company that then saves (20%) and buys a factory with the remainder, so the builder of the factory receives $720,000 and puts this in its bank. So far, the initial $1m has created $900,000 + $720,000 = $1,620,000. The process goes on until no more money can be lent by the banking system. There is no need to go into detail regarding the features of the credit multiplier process; it is just important to realize that an increase in base money leads to a larger growth in money supply in the economy overall.

In addition to open market operations, other tools of monetary policy include these:

- *Reserve requirements at the central bank:* If the central bank increases reserve requirements, banks have to hold more low or no interest-bearing funds; this extracts money from the system and has a contractionary effect. If reserve requirements are lowered, this injects money into the system.
- *Discount window lending:* Banks and other depository institutions are allowed to borrow reserves from the central bank at a discount rate. This is the so-called 'lender-of-last-resort' facility.
- *Interest rates:* In some countries the authorities may fix interest rates of various deposit and loan products.

▼ Table 3.1 *Monetary policy, targets and objectives*

Monetary policy	Target market variable	Long-term objective
Inflation targeting	Interest rate on overnight debt	A given rate of change in the Consumer Price Index (CPI)
Price level targeting	Interest rate on overnight debt	A specific CPI number
Monetary aggregates	The growth in money supply	A given rate of change in the CPI
Exchange rate	The spot price of the currency/ or basket of currencies	The spot price of the currency/or rate on basket of currencies
Gold standard	The spot price of gold	Low inflation as measured by the gold price
Mixed policy	Usually interest rates	Usually unemployment + CPI change

Having said all this, it should be emphasized that central banks typically use open market operations to achieve a specific short-term interest rate target, although in other cases policy may be directed to targeting a specific exchange rate or the price of gold. In the US, for instance, the Federal Reserve targets a short-term interest rate known as the 'federal funds rate' (the rate at which Federal Reserve member banks lend to one another overnight). In China, however, the authorities conduct policy targeting the exchange rate between the Chinese renminbi and a basket of foreign currencies.

Table 3.1 illustrates the main types of monetary policy conducted aimed at manipulating base money in the economy in order to achieve various long-term objectives.

Box 3.2 details these six types of monetary policy.

So far, we have discussed monetary policy options under 'normal' scenarios, namely when interest rates can be increased to reduce monetary base, or reduced to boost monetary expansion. However, the latter may not be an option when interest rates reach historically low levels – the US federal funds rate has varied between 0% and 0.25% since December 2008. Similar historically low rates are being faced in the eurozone and the UK. When rates are so low, policymakers fear deflation (falling prices – negative inflation) and so undertake (extreme) measures to try and reflate, or boost, the economy.

In the US and the UK, for example, the monetary authorities have engaged in quantitative easing (QE: buying government bonds on a huge scale), credit easing (buying private sector assets – mainly off the banks) and signalling (lowering market expectations about hikes in future interest rates). All this is seen as a way of injecting money to reflate the economy. It remains to be seen whether such drastic action feeds through into prolonged and sustainable economic growth or inflationary pressures. Governments are, however, constrained on the fiscal side and don't have many policy alternatives.

Banknotes

As noted already above, as part of base money, the central bank controls the issue of banknotes and possibly, but not necessarily, coins also. Most payments these days do not

BOX 3.2

Different Approaches to Monetary Policy

1 *Inflation targeting:* Policy is conducted in a way that manipulates rates (usually) in the interbank market consistent with a desired level of inflation, usually given by a Consumer Price Index (CPI) range. Often the central bank has a target level or range of interest rates that it believes are consistent with the inflation target. The target is reviewed on a regular basis and interest rate targets adjusted accordingly. Various authorities have used the Taylor rule (devised by John B Taylor of Stanford University) that adjusts the interest rate in response to changes in the inflation rate and the output gap (the difference between actual and potential GDP). The first to use inflation targeting was New Zealand. It is currently used as the main monetary policy in many countries, including Australia, Brazil, India and the UK.

2 *Price level targeting:* This is similar to inflation targeting, although CPI growth above or below a long-term price level target is offset in following years, so a targeted price level is achieved (on average).

3 *Monetary aggregates:* In the late 1970s and early 1980s, the UK and US monetary authorities experimented with targeting the growth rate of various monetary aggregates. These are simply different definitions of money supply, with M0 (base money) being the narrowest and M1, M2 and M3 becoming increasingly broader. Definitions of the broader aggregates varied across countries but typically included base money + bank deposits + non-bank deposits and even other financial assets.

The policy (known as 'monetarism' and initially advocated by Milton Friedman) argued that the faster the growth of money in the system, the higher the rate of inflation. Think, for example, of a helicopter dropping £X on the UK in one night so that in the morning everyone had double the money to spend. In this case, the argument goes, everyone has double the spending power but the same quantity of goods and services to spend them on, as production of goods and services is limited in the short run, so what happens is that (if the rate at which money changes hands remains constant – the so-called 'velocity of circulation' of money) the prices double. The key to monetarism was that the velocity of circulation remained constant (in the short term at least).

This may seem a rather long-winded response, but to put it simply, the faster the amount of money growth in the economy, the higher the level of inflation. As such, policymakers should target money supply/monetary aggregate growth – limiting it to restrict inflationary pressures.

In the UK, Mrs Thatcher used this policy too tightly between 1979 and 1981, leading to a trebling of unemployment from 1 to 3 million over the period. From the mid-1980s onwards, the policy became discredited as policymakers could not agree on whether narrow or broad aggregates should be targeted; the link between money growth and prices became harder to empirically support; and velocity of money was viewed as not necessarily being constant. (For example, in the UK in 2012, base money exploded as the Bank of England bought government bonds to inject liquidity into markets, but prices hardly changed. This is because the velocity of circulation has collapsed – money is not changing hands – banks are hoarding and not lending.)

4 *Exchange rate target:* Monetary policy can be conducted so as to maintain an exchange rate with a foreign currency or basket of foreign currencies. The rate may be fixed or may vary within a band/range.

In a system of fixed convertibility, the central bank simply buys and sells currency to achieve the target exchange rate. If the exchange rate system is maintained by a currency board, every unit of local currency must be backed by a unit of foreign currency (correcting for the exchange rate) – known as the 'anchor currency'. This means that the local monetary base does not inflate without being backed by hard currency. It should also reduce the likelihood of a run on the local currency by those wishing to convert the local currency to the hard (anchor) currency. In the case of dollarization, foreign currency (usually the US dollar) is used as the medium of exchange exclusively or together with local currency. This type of policy is adopted if there is a lack of confidence in government policy – effectively, US monetary policy is being adopted. As noted above, China targets its domestic currency against a basket of other currencies, and Singapore also has an exchange rate target.

5 *Gold standard:* This was the main policy from the mid-19th century up until 1971. Under the gold standard, the price of the national currency is measured in units of gold bars and is kept constant by the government's promise to buy or sell gold at a fixed price in terms of the base currency.

Typically, gold standard policy can be viewed as a sort of commodity price level targeting. A minimal gold standard policy would be reflected in the monetary authority's long-term commitment to tighten policy to limit gold prices from permanently rising above parity. A full gold standard would be a commitment to sell unlimited amounts of gold at parity and maintain a reserve of gold sufficient to redeem the entire monetary base. Or to put it another way, the total amount of notes and coins plus bank reserves in an economy are backed by gold reserves. A major limitation of the gold standard policy is that economic growth is constrained by the supply of gold, so if the economy grows faster than the supply of gold, prices fall – leading to a deflationary spiral. Whether this actually does occur is open to debate, but the desire of many countries to grow faster than afforded under the gold standard eventually led to the demise of this policy.

6. *Mixed policy:* Some countries chose a mix of the above policies; for example, China targets monetary aggregates and also a basket of currencies. The ECB has also used monetary aggregate and price targeting. The UK focuses on inflation targeting, alongside secondary targets on 'output and employment', and the US also follows a mixed policy aimed at maximum employment and stable prices. India also uses a multiple target approach.

involve cash, but cheques, standing orders, direct debits, credit cards and so on. Neverthe-less, cash is important as banks' cash holdings are, as we have seen, a constraint on the creation of credit.

Generally, we can say that, if the economy grows at 2%, the central bank will be willing to issue 2% more new banknotes to oil the wheels. On the other hand, less stable central banks may print banknotes to help the government. Usually, banknotes are backed not by gold, but by securities. The cost of printing is far less than the face value, and the securities produce an income. This results in a special profit called seignorage. This special profit may go straight to the Treasury and not appear in the bank's books. The central bank will also replace used banknotes with new ones. There are local variations here. The British seem to dislike old banknotes much more than, say, the Germans. As a result, the Bundesbank replaces far fewer notes than the Bank of England.

Each year, some 75 billion banknotes are printed by 186 currency-issuing authorities in over 120 countries. Some 50 or so have state printing works, and 14 privately owned companies produce notes for the remaining 130 plus.

Banker to the Other Banks

The central bank will act as banker to the other banks in the economy, as well as hold accounts with international bodies like the International Monetary Fund (IMF) and the World Bank. It is a common habit for the central bank to insist that the other banks hold non-interest-bearing reserves with it in proportion to their deposits. Apart from helping the bank to make a profit, these serve as an instrument of control over the money supply, as we saw in Chapter 2.

For simplicity, we have talked of 'deposits'. In fact, the reserves are based on 'liabilities' in a more general sense. A bond due to be repaid by the bank is not a deposit but counts as a liability for the purposes of reserve requirements.

In any case, major banks will have to hold working balances for the day-to-day settlement for various activities. Cheque clearing will end each day with a net sum of money owed by one bank to another, or due to it. Dealings in government T-bills and bonds will be settled through the central bank accounts, and also tax payments. The total of a bank's clients' payments of tax will result in a fall in that bank's balance at the central bank and a rise in the government's balance.

The working balances that major domestic banks would need to keep at the Bundesbank, for example, are part of these reserves. The actual figures are averages of the balances held at the Bundesbank during the course of a particular month, and the calculation is based on the daily average of the various types of liabilities held. The result is that at the start of the month, the banks can hold reserves less than the required amount, provided they catch up later so that the overall average is the required figure. This leads to a lot of short-term lending and borrowing in the interbank market.

The whole system has now been reorganized for all 18 countries in the EU's Economic and Monetary Union (EMU) alternatively referred to as the eurozone. The ECB has imposed a minimum reserve requirement (similar to the Bundesbank but paying interest, which the Bundesbank did not). Banks must deposit the equivalent of 2% of deposits with their central banks. National central banks will conduct open market operations to keep interest rates within a desired range. All this is discussed in Chapter 7.

By contrast, the Bank of England abolished reserve requirements of this nature in 1979. The argument is that because there are no exchange controls, sterling can be exchanged for foreign currencies and vice versa without constraint. As London is a huge international banking centre, attempts to control the money supply by sterling non-interest-bearing reserves at the central bank would simply not be effective. The only reserve held is a cash ratio deposit as a proportion of stipulated liabilities. Cash ratio deposits are non-interest-bearing deposits lodged with the Bank of England by eligible institutions (banks and building societies) who have reported average eligible liabilities of over £500m over a calculated period. The level of each institution's cash ratio deposit is calculated twice yearly (May and November) at 0.11% of average eligible liabilities over the previous 6 months, in excess of £500m. These cash ratio deposits are not an instrument of monetary policy, but a way of 'joining the UK bank club' and helping the Bank of England to make a profit. However, the main domestic banks must still maintain working balances at the Bank of England.

Banker to the Government

Normally, a central bank acts as the government's banker. It receives revenues for taxes or other income and pays out money for the government's expenditure. Usually, it will not lend to the government but will help the government to borrow money by the sales of its bills and bonds (see next section).

One exception here is Postipankki in Finland. Perhaps because it is owned by the government, it is this bank, rather than the central bank, that handles the government's money.

As citizens pay taxes, charges are made against their bank accounts and settled through their bank's own account at the central bank. The banks' balances fall, and the government's rises. This is one reason why banks must keep working balances at the central bank. Of course, as tax rebates are made, the government's balance falls, and the banks' balances rise.

As T-bills and bonds are paid for, money is passed to the government's account. As they are redeemed, money flows back to the banks' accounts. If the central bank discounts bills of exchange to help a commercial bank's liquidity, money moves into that bank's account. As the bill is presented for payment, money is credited to the central bank. As a result, there is a constant flow of money from the banks' accounts at the central bank to the government's accounts and vice versa.

Raising Money for the Government

The government T-bill and bond markets are covered in detail in Chapter 7. While the Treasury or Ministry of Finance sometimes handles government issues, it is much more common for the central bank to control this and to settle payments through the accounts that banks and financial institutions have with it. This is one of the reasons why these banks must keep working balances at the central bank.

We have seen that in 1694 the Bank of England was formed specifically for the purpose of raising money for the government, although since 1998, responsibility has been passed to the Treasury's new Debt Management Office.

The cumulative sum of money owed by governments for all their borrowings is called the national debt. Over time, the debt grows and is not, in any real sense, ever 'paid off'. Does this matter? See Box 3.3.

BOX 3.3

National (Government) Debt – Does It Matter?

The first point is that, for any individual, how serious debt is depends on this person's income. Governments are the same.

Economists compare the national debt to the national income as a ratio to see if the situation is getting worse or better. For this purpose, the figure for gross domestic product (GDP) is used as equivalent to the national income.

In the US, due to heavy government borrowing in the 1980s, the ratio rose from 33% to over 50%, then started to fall in the late 1990s under the Clinton administration as the government was in surplus and was able to buy debt back. However, the economic slowdown of 2001–2 and the falling revenues from President Bush's tax cuts (designed to boost the economy) meant that the US was pushed back into deficit and

National (Government) Debt – Does It Matter? (*continued*)

debt increased – only to accelerate as a consequence of the credit crisis. By the start of 2014, the gross national debt/GDP ratio stood at around 108%, a staggering amount if you consider that US GDP was over $16 trillion at the end of 2013.

According to the Office of National Statistics, in the UK, the figure, which was 100% at the end of the 1960s, fell to around 37% at the start of 2000 and then gradually increased from thereon. At the end of December 2013, public sector net debt was £1,254.3 billion, or 75.7% of GDP. The national debt is increasing by approximately £107 billion per annum.

This relationship of national debt to GDP became an issue in the run-up to setting up the European economic union and single currency. The meeting at Maastricht in Holland in December 1991 set out criteria that must be met before a nation could join the single currency. One of the criteria was that the national debt/GDP ratio should not exceed 60% – a figure greatly exceeded by many eurozone countries after the recent banking crisis.

Inflation is also a key factor. As time goes by, inflation simply erodes the value of the debt. A national debt of $100bn in 1960 looks a quite different figure today.

Debt servicing costs also play a role. Interest must be paid, and this itself may limit further increases in debt. In the US in 2013, debt servicing costs approached 17% of total government revenue, and it can take more than 20% of all government tax receipts (as it also does in India).

Finally, to whom is the money owed? Often the government bonds and bills are owned by financial institutions and individuals in the domestic market. There will be foreign holders, but they will probably not account for more than, say, 20%. This is where the position of the emerging countries is so different – they largely owe the money to foreigners, and it is denominated in a foreign currency.

Is there a level of national debt that is reasonable or safe? *The Economist* (27 February–4 March 1988) had an interesting article on this subject, and this quotation provides a nice summary:

> Neither economic theory nor history gives any clue as to what is the critical level of public debt . . . The crucial factor is the willingness of investors to hold public debt. If they lose their appetite, then either interest rates must rise sharply or the government has to finance its deficit by printing more money and hence stoking up inflation.

Controlling the Nation's Currency Reserves

Each nation has reserves of gold and foreign currencies held at the central bank. If the bank intervenes in the market to buy the domestic currency, it will do so using foreign currency reserves. If it intervenes to sell the local currency, it will acquire foreign currencies.

Foreign exchange markets are examined in Chapter 11. We shall see that the transactions in major currencies are considerable. The dealing in sterling, to take one example, is so great that the Bank of England alone can't control the exchange rate by its buying and selling. It can, however, influence the rate by careful timing and the knowledge by market operators that the central bank is acting in the market. Under the newer arrangements for European cooperation, several EU central banks may act together. Equally, major countries' central banks may act together as part of the arrangements of the G7 (Group of Seven) countries (see below).

In the exchange rate mechanism (ERM) crisis of September 1992, the Bank of France is thought to have spent about 40% of its reserves defending the franc – a sum perhaps as high as Fr150bn.

Where a currency is not widely traded, the central bank will have a much better chance of controlling the rate. The central bank of Norway can control the rate for the kroner much more easily than the Bank of England can control that for the pound.

The reserves will usually include gold as well as foreign currencies, but the position of gold has changed. The central banks in the EU came to an arrangement for a controlled sale of gold in 1999. In September 2004, the arrangement was renewed, allowing the central banks to sell up to 500 metric tonnes a year. Overall, gold held in central bank reserves worldwide shrank by more than one-sixth over the 20 years from 1989 to 2009. The credit crisis, however, has reminded central bankers of gold's use as the ultimate international currency, as it is the only form of money with intrinsic value. During 2008 and at the start of 2009, global central bank gold sales slowed substantially. Having said this, however, the Bank of England has sold most of its gold.

Acting as Lender of Last Resort

As we discussed earlier, the central bank's role as an LLR not only refers to the role of the bank as a periodic rescuer of banks in trouble, but it also refers to the fact that the central bank will help other banks temporarily when they meet problems with their liquidity. From 2008 to 2014, the US, the UK and many European central banks and governments engaged in widespread liquidity schemes in order to support their banking systems (see Chapter 10). As we have just seen, tax transactions and settlements for government securities cause a continuous ebb and flow of money in and out of the accounts of the banks at the central bank. In all cases, they are obliged to keep minimum working balances, and in most cases they must also keep reserves at the central bank, although these working balances may be part of the reserves.

The central bank smoothes out the peaks and troughs by being prepared to assist other banks with short-term help. Because the banks are ultimately dependent on the central bank, the rate of interest charged governs other interest rates. How the bank carries out this role is discussed in detail in Chapter 7.

Central banks stand ready to provide liquid funds for banks that may have short-term liquidity problems. However, sometimes banks need to be rescued. It is ironic that Baring Bros, which was placed in administration in February 1995, had been in trouble some 100 years earlier and had, on that occasion, been rescued by the Bank of England and other banks. The recent liquidity and other support provided to major banks in the US, the UK and elsewhere was undertaken in order to preserve the stability of whole banking systems, and that is why the intervention undertaken has been on a much greater scale than in the case of piecemeal bank liquidity support given to troubled banks in the recent past.

The precise role of the new ECB in rescuing banks in trouble is vague in the Maastricht Treaty. As we noted in Chapter 2, the French, Belgium and Luxembourg authorities coordinated a state bailout of Dexia Bank in 2008. This raised issues about the need for a single EU regulator to deal with problems associated with institutions that had large cross-border banking business – we covered this in Chapter 2 in the context of the new European Banking Union. These issues are discussed further in Chapter 12.

Liaison with International Bodies

Central banks will liaise with other international financial bodies like the IMF and the International Bank for Reconstruction and Development (IBRD), usually called the World Bank (see Chapter 11). They also liaise with and take part in discussions at the Bank for International Settlements (BIS) in Basel. The BIS was set up in 1930. By 1929, it was evident that it was impossible for Germany to pay the massive reparations imposed on it after the First World War, and some new arrangement had to be made. A new plan called the Young Plan was devised, and part of it involved setting up the BIS to help to transfer reparation payments and other international debts (hence its name). Some 84% of the shares were held by 33 central banks, and the rest, by private shareholders. However, on 9 September 1996, the BIS announced that it was offering membership to nine other central banks, including those in areas like Southeast Asia and Latin America, and these became members in June 1997. A total of 55 central banks are now voting members of the BIS, which currently employs around 600 staff.

Today, the BIS is used by over 140 central banks and can be regarded as 'the central bankers' bank'. It handles the payments made between world banks, sponsors cooperation, handles initiatives on key topics and hosts bimonthly meetings of the world's central bankers at its headquarters near Basel's railway station. It also manages around 10% of the reserves of major world central banks.

There is far more cooperation on economic matters by the world's major powers than there was 20 years ago. Of key importance here are the periodic meetings of the seven most advanced economic nations, the G7, consisting of the US, France, Germany, the UK, Canada, Japan and Italy. These days Russia attends, making it the G8. There is also a growing pressure to admit China and India.

G7 members meet periodically to discuss world economic and financial affairs. Central bankers play a key role in preparing for these meetings and briefing the politicians. The world's top powers had realized by early 1985 that the foreign exchange markets were so big that only concerted intervention by all the major central banks could have any effect. Worried about the dollar's inexorable rise, key central bankers led by Paul Volcker, the then chairman of the US Federal Reserve, made a secret agreement. On Wednesday morning, 27 February 1985, they struck, selling dollars simultaneously. By the end of the day, the dollar had fallen from DM3.50 to DM3.30. In the process, foreign exchange markets experienced what can only be called 'pandemonium'.

Later, in September 1985, the G5 (predecessor of the G7, minus Canada and Italy) called a meeting at the Plaza Hotel in Washington. Again, the agreement was to force down the dollar, and again it worked. This first international agreement on currencies since Bretton Woods (see Chapter 11) is called the Plaza Agreement. In later years there were other meetings, for example the Louvre Accord in February 1987. Usually, these were designed to push the dollar up and were not as successful.

A wider forum for international meetings is the G10 (Group of 10 – the G7, plus Sweden, Belgium, Holland and Switzerland). The reader does not need to be a mathematical genius to see that this is 11 countries, not 10. It's all to do with Swiss neutrality: the Swiss are always there, but officially they aren't there. It's called the G10, but actually there are 11 countries participating. Sometimes, the G10 members meet with Latin American and Southeast Asian representatives on an ad hoc basis, for example to discuss the Southeast Asia crisis in 1997, forming what is usually called the G33.

There is also the G20, set up in 1999 to represent major developed and developing nations. Other forums include the so-called 'G24', which consists of eight countries each from Asia, Africa and Latin America, and is used for liaison with the IMF and the World Bank.

THE POSITION OF CENTRAL BANKS TODAY

The past 15 years or so have seen a rise in the power and influence of central bankers. Years of high inflation have led to the view that politicians can no longer be trusted with monetary policy. One by one, central banks have become independent, culminating in the formation of the ECB.

Inflation in advanced industrial countries was down to about 1.5% at the start of the millennium, its lowest rate since the 1950s, although it had risen towards the end of the 2000s up until the credit crisis. In the US in 2008, inflation fell and was close to zero, but rose to 2.9% by 2011 and has subsequently fallen to around 1.5% by mid-2014. It was below 2% in the UK by the end of 2009, although this crept up to 3.6% in 2011 but again also fell to around 1.5% by the summer of 2014. Prior to the onset of the credit crisis, many governments were concerned at the cost in growth and unemployment linked to anti-inflationary policies. Does low inflation necessarily mean low growth and high unemployment? Alan Greenspan, when chairman of the US Federal Reserve, seems to have delivered good growth with low inflation despite the 2001–2 slowdown. Rising US interest rates from 2005 to 2007, because of higher oil and other commodity prices, also did not appear to adversely affect growth and unemployment. However, the economic situation has dramatically changed since then, as the adverse effects of the credit crisis have fed through into the domestic economy – unemployment first spiralled upwards and then fell, and inflation has plummeted. So much so that there is much talk in policy circles about averting deflation in the US (and the UK). In contrast, Europe has traditionally experienced higher unemployment than the US (and the UK) because of social costs and labour market rigidities. Banking systems there were less affected by the 2007–8 credit crisis, although they have subsequently been hit hard by the eurozone sovereign debt problems. The growth and unemployment prospects here appear mixed at best – with Germany and Scandinavia offering potentially the best growth and employment prospects.

If a key role of the central bank is to combat inflation, this raises the question: How do we measure it? There is, for example, consumer inflation and industrial inflation. In particular, price indices do not usually include the prices of financial assets like shares. The collapse of these asset prices could also lead to economic and financial instability, as in Japan. In 1911, economist Irving Fisher argued that a price index should include share and property prices. Joseph Carson, an economist at Deutsche Bank, New York, has constructed just such an index with shares in at 5%. Leading indices, such as the Dow, the Footsie (Financial Times Stock Exchange – FTSE) and – most notably – the NASDAQ (National Association of Securities Dealers' Automated Quotations), surged between 1996 and 1999 at a rate not seen since the late 1980s, and people talked of the 'new economy' and 'a new paradigm'. From the highs at the end of 1999, the Dow lost around 30% and the Footsie over 40% by 2003, with falls being triggered initially by the bursting of the dot-com bubble in spring 2001, followed by the events of 11 September, and later by concerns over the validity of reported results in the wake of irregularities at Enron, WorldCom and other major corporations. Although it is not the role of central banks to maintain stock market growth – and Greenspan warned of the excessive prices of many shares before they collapsed – the knock-on economic effect of stock market instability is clearly of concern to central bank governors. Fortunately, from mid-2003 onwards, stock markets began to recover. The Dow, in fact, continued upward until 9 October 2007, when it peaked at 14,164, only to fall to below 10,000 by October 2008 – the height of the US bank bailout by US authorities. By March 2009, the Dow had fallen to 6,763 – its lowest level since 1997 (prior to the dot-com bubble), although it had recovered to hit a record high of 17,390 by the end of October 2014. In general, the Footsie followed a similar trend, peaking over 2006 and 2007, then collapsing as the credit crisis unfurled and recovering thereafter. In fact the level the FTSE 100 reached in October 2014 is similar to the peaks attained at the height of the high tech bubble in 1999 and prior to the 2007–8 banking crisis.

Accountability is another current issue. For all their independence, the Bundesbank and the Federal Reserve are basically accountable to their governments, and the Federal Open Market Committee's minutes are models of openness. There is much concern, however, at the position of the ECB. The Maastricht Treaty prohibits it from taking orders from politicians, and members of the executive are appointed for 8-year, non-renewable terms. Mario Draghi, the president, meets the European Parliament only once a year to explain policy. Outside this, however, he has stated that no minutes of meetings will be issued. It may be more difficult for the ECB, therefore, to attract public support than the Fed or the Bundesbank.

Finally, what may seem a silly question: Do we need a central bank? In 1900, only 18 countries had a central bank, compared to 160 today. Some economists still argue that private banks should issue their own banknotes in competition. This was the position before 1845 in Scotland, where notes were backed by gold, but banks competed. Adam Smith admired the system.

But surely we need the role of the LLR? Some argue that the near guarantee of a rescue encourages banks to behave imprudently – an issue called moral hazard. Given the major bank rescues that have occurred over the past couple of years, it seems that moral hazard and too-big-to-fail (TBTF) guarantees were certainly present in Western banking systems.

In his great work *Lombard Street* (1873), Walter Bagehot, that wise man, commented on moral hazard:

> If banks are bad they will certainly continue bad and will probably become worse if the government sustains and encourages them. The cardinal maxim is that any aid to a present bad bank is the surest mode of preventing the establishment of a future good bank.

Like Adam Smith, Walter Bagehot also favoured the old Scottish (free-banking, minimal regulation) system. However, he agreed that a proposal to do away with the Bank of England would be as futile as a proposal to do away with the monarchy. Now that the latter idea is no longer unthinkable in the UK, we may perhaps end up treating central banks with the same lack of reverence.

SUMMARY

- Banco Central do Brasil, the Brazilian central bank, was established in 1964; the People's Bank of China was founded in 1948; the Bank of France was founded in 1800; the Bundesbank, in 1957; the Reserve Bank of India was founded in 1934; the Bank of Japan, in 1885; the Central Bank of the Russian Federation (Bank of Russia) was established in 1990; the Bank of England, in 1694; the Federal Reserve, in 1913; and the European Central Bank, in 1998. Worldwide, there are 160 central banks.

- Central bank activities include the following:
  - *Supervising the banking system:* Here it will play a key role even if legally there is a separate supervisory body.
  - *Creating monetary policy:* This includes controlling interest rates and the money supply. The main monetary policies used focus on inflation targeting, price targeting, monetary aggregates and foreign exchange rate targeting. The most common policy is inflation targeting.
  - *Printing banknotes and minting coins:* This must be linked to growth in the economy or inflation will follow.
  - *Acting as banker to the other banks:* Domestic banks must leave sums of money with the central bank for various clearing and settlement systems. In some countries, for example the eurozone, the central bank imposes minimum reserves as part of monetary policy, although these do not apply in the UK.
  - *Acting as banker to the government:* In raising money for the government, the central bank controls the account into which the money is paid. As taxes are paid, the government balance increases, and the commercial banks' balances fall. When the government spends money, the opposite happens.
  - *Raising money for the government:* This usually involves the sale of short-term T-bills and medium- to long-term government bonds. The cumulative sum of money owed for all borrowing not yet repaid is the national debt. It is usually shown as a percentage of GDP to see whether the situation is worsening or improving. Over time, however, inflation erodes the burden of the debt. Debt burdens have increased dramatically as a consequence of the cost of financial system rescue packages resulting from the credit crisis.
  - *Controlling the nation's reserves:* From time to time, central banks will buy or sell their country's currency to influence the rate. If they buy it, they will use the nation's reserves of gold and foreign currencies to do so.
  - *Acting as LLR:* Sometimes this refers to the rescue of banks in trouble, but more generally, it is the willingness of the central bank to assist banks with liquidity problems. Usually, this means their inability to meet the necessary balance levels at the central bank (as a direct result of central bank policy). The rate of interest involved in the transaction gives the central bank control over interest rates. Although LLR actions were relatively uncommon prior to the credit crisis, they have become widespread since then, as central banks have had to inject billions into banks and economies overall to prop up failing banking systems, particularly in the UK and the US.
  - *International liaison:* This involves cooperation with bodies like the IMF, the World Bank and the BIS. It also involves supporting international meetings of the G7 and the G10. With the addition of Russia, the G7 is now the G8.

REVISION QUESTIONS/ASSIGNMENTS

1 Analyse the main functions of central banks.
2 Discuss whether it matters if a central bank is independent or not. Can a central bank ever be truly independent from political influence if the governor is always appointed by the government?
3 Examine the lender-of-last-resort function of the central bank, and explain the role of moral hazard.
4 Discuss whether monetary policy can be effective when interest rates are close to zero, making brief reference to the role of quantitative easing (QE).

REFERENCE

Bagehot, W. (1873) *Lombard Street: A Description of the Money Market*, Henry S. King, London. Classic book on the role of banks and markets in the Victorian era, much cited for Bagehot's insights into bank collapses/deposit runs and what politicians should do to limit such problems.

FURTHER READING

Congdon, T. (2009) *Central Banking in a Free Society*, Institute of Economic Affairs, London. Covers the role of central banking, with a liberal interpretation of the role. Discussion can be relatively advanced in places.

Davies, H., and Green, D. (2010) *Banking on the Future: The Fall and Rise of Central Banking*, Princeton University Press, Princeton, NJ. Intermediate text focusing on the changing role of central banks over time, with a particular focus on the US and the UK.

Matthews, K., Giuliodori, M., and Mishkin, F. (2013) *Economics of Money, Banking and Financial Markets* (European edn), Pearson Education, Harlow. Standard undergraduate money and banking text used for 2nd-year undergraduate money/monetary policy courses and upwards.

Commercial Banking

INTRODUCTION

Commercial banks are essentially banks that are in the classic banking business of accepting deposits and making loans. Banks like Barclays and Royal Bank of Scotland (RBS) are commercial banks. Other banks, like Deutsche, UBS and Citigroup, would say that they were universal banks, that is, they cover all kinds of banking, including both commercial and investment banking. In the UK, if a commercial bank carries out investment banking, it will do so through a subsidiary, for example Barclays Bank uses Barclays Capital, although in 2012, it dropped the separate name and will henceforth just be known as Barclays. In Germany and Switzerland, and to a lesser extent France, the Netherlands and Spain, they will do so within the same legal entity.

As we saw in Chapter 2, commercial banking may be retail or wholesale. Within their own country, the large commercial banks will carry out both retail and wholesale banking. Abroad, they will often focus on the wholesale markets.

We cover retail banking in this chapter. We also explain some areas of wholesale banking, mainly the question of bank lending. Other aspects of wholesale banking will be covered in later chapters – money markets in Chapter 7 and foreign exchange in Chapter 11.

RETAIL BANKING

Types of Service

Retail commercial banks offer an increasing range of services to their clients. Some relate to the handling of money – various forms of deposit accounts and loans. Others relate to services – advice, custody, purchase of stocks, shares, insurance and so on. Essentially, these are the two ways banks make their money: taking deposits – that is, borrowing money and lending it at a profitable rate of interest – and providing useful services for which they can charge. The range of products is widening as the banks react to growing competition and falling profits. Increasingly, we hear the phrase 'the financial supermarket'.

Retail banking tends to be dominated by a handful of domestic banks. According to figures from the ECB, the top five banks in the economy control 85% of banking assets in Holland and 83% in Finland. Of the largest European countries, France has the most concentrated system, with the top five banks having just fewer than 50% of banking system assets, whereas Germany has the largest number of banks (1,948) and is the least concentrated, with a five-bank asset concentration ratio of 25%. A Bank of England study found that in the UK, the top five banks accounted for 75% of individual and small firm lending.

The US used to be an exception, with a large number of banks and low concentration, although in recent years, due to a merger wave, the situation has changed. According to a recent study by the Mercatus Center at George Mason University, *The Decline of US Small Banks (2000–2013)*, the deposit share of the top five banks amounted to 40.1% in 2013, up from 19.5% in 2000. The share of the banking sector assets controlled by the five largest banks has increased from 23% in 2000 to 44% by the end of 2013. (There were 6,377 banks in the US in 2013, of which 6,279 had assets under $10 billion, and these are generally regarded as small banks). In various European countries, the mutual sector plays a major role in retail banking. In Germany and Spain, the savings banks are the main operator in retail banking business. Cooperative banks are important in Germany, France (Crédit Agricole) and the Netherlands (Rabobank). In the UK, the mutual building society sector remains an important player in the residential mortgage market.

Money Banking: Deposits

Current accounts

The principal kind of account offered by a retail bank is the current account, which is seen by the bank as a fundamental way of establishing a relationship with the customer and as a source of cheap money to sustain the various lending activities. The position regarding the charges to the client for providing the current account facility varies. In the present competitive environment, banks either make charges but offset them with interest on credit balances, or make no charges but have free use of the credit balances. French banks are not allowed in law to make charges, but many vary the amount of time to clear cheques, which can be as many as 5 days. In the UK and Spain, competition has led to the payment of interest on credit balances for the first time. The current account carries with it the obligation to provide a range of payment services – cheques, ATMs, debit cards and so on – the costs of which are quite high and consume some of the value of the low-cost deposits.

Deposit accounts

Deposit accounts are various forms of interest-bearing accounts, which usually do not allow cheques and often severely limit other withdrawal facilities. They may require a period of notice to be given before withdrawals, for example 7 days, 1 month or 3 months. The customer is paid interest on the understanding that the appropriate period of notice will be given before drawing out money. Alternatively, the money may be placed on deposit for a fixed term, similar to the above, whereupon it is repaid. Generally, the longer the customer is prepared to commit the funds, and/or the greater the amount, the greater the rate paid. The benefit for the bank is that it can rely on notice or fixed-term money much more than it can with current accounts, where the balances fluctuate.

Payments

Based on the current account, there is a range of payment products that manifest themselves in paper or electronic form. Examples of the former are cheques and giro slip payments, and a growing number of electronic payments pass from business to business and business to individuals through computer-to-computer systems. In the UK, for example, more than 80% of the workforce receive their salaries by automated transfers from their employers' systems into their current accounts. Equally, standing orders and direct debits are widely used to settle recurring payments. Mixed with electronic payments passing through the current account will be paper-based transactions. People and companies can settle indebtedness by issuing cheques, which give rise to a charge on their account and a credit on the beneficiary's account. Alternatively, a bill may be paid by completing a giro form and sending the form to the beneficiary's bank so that money can be transferred to the creditor's account, which is common in the Netherlands, Japan, Germany, Austria and Switzerland. Within the banking system, the transmission of payments between banks and the consequent financial settlement is called 'clearing', and this is discussed later.

Increasingly, payment activity is initiated by the use of plastic cards. Details of the account are embedded in a magnetic strip or a microchip, and these, when put together with value information generated at an ATM or at the point of sale (POS), give rise to a current account transaction. According to the BIS Committee on Payment and Settlement Systems (December 2013), there are over 1.5 million ATMs globally, with over 415,000 in China and an estimated 450,000 in the US. This is followed by Brazil (175,000), Russia (171,900), and South Korea (124,200). The UK has 66,100 ATMs, and they are used for over two-thirds of personal cash withdrawals. France, Germany and Italy also have large numbers of ATMs.

An alternative to the cheque for payment in a retail shop or similar outlet is the 'debit card', which is usually also the customer's ATM card. At the point of sale, a machine, sometimes integrated with the till, creates what amounts to an electronic cheque from the information on the card and the amount of the transaction. These data are passed down a telephone line so that the appropriate charge can be made to the customer's account and a credit made to the retailer's account. The customer will be called upon to identify him- or herself at the point of sale in one of two ways: by putting a signature on a paper slip for the retailer to check against a specimen on the back of the card, or by entering a personal identification number (PIN), as would be required at an ATM.

If a customer wants to make a high-value purchase, the retailer's machine will seek authorization from the customer's bank before completing the purchase. Such is the sophistication of the network connecting retailers to the world's banking systems that this takes only a few seconds. In the UK, the growing use of debit cards means that between 1991 and 2012, the volume of cheques used, which had been 3.8 billion, fell to just 848 million. In the same period, debit card purchases increased from 0.3 billion to 7.8 billion. It is interesting to note that by the end of 2012, Americans remain the biggest cheque writers, penning an average of around 58 a year, followed by the French (43 a year), Canadians (22 a year) and then the Brits (around 13 a year). Cheque usage, globally, is in decline as other card and electronic means of payment continue to replace paper-based methods.

There is a slight variation on the debit card idea in France and Germany, where they have debit cards that charge for transactions a month later. Unlike a credit card, however, this is charged to the current account, and the holder is expected to have funds to meet the charge.

When a cheque is used, the same card may serve as a 'cheque guarantee card'. A retailer will accept a cheque up to a given maximum if the card is produced so that its specimen signature can be checked against that written on the cheque. The advantage to the retailer is that the bank guarantees to pay even if the transaction is fraudulent or the cardholder has insufficient funds. These are, however, rarely used nowadays, as most retailers take electronic payment. In the US, there is no such system, and retailers are reluctant to accept cheques ('Don't you have a credit card?'). In France also, there is no such system, but retailers are happier to accept cheques, as writing a cheque when there are no funds to support it is a criminal offence.

Some interesting figures from BIS on numbers of ATMs and point-of-sale terminals are shown in Table 4.1. Note that the average American has three credit cards compared with the average person having one in the UK. Countries with high credit card usage include Canada, Hong Kong and South Korea.

Having considered all these payment systems, we should be aware that, in the UK at least, although cash transactions had dropped 14% in the 5 years up to mid-2014, cash transactions still account for 50% of the total (British Retail Consortium).

New Payments Technologies

Over recent years, a number of new technologies have emerged that make payments more accessible to a wider range of users – such as mobile phone payments – although these still rely on established currencies for transactions. A more innovative development has been the emergence of decentralized payment systems that do not rely on an established currency, but use cryptography (complex computer code) to create new digital currencies – such as Bitcoin. Most digital currencies are known as 'cryptocurrencies', as they seek consensus through means of techniques from the field of cryptography. Box 4.1 illustrates the main features of Bitcoin.

▼ **Table 4.1** *Number of ATMs, EFT-POS terminals and credit cards, end 2012*

Country	No. of ATMs per 1 million inhabitants	No. of EFT-POS terminals per 1 million inhabitants	No. of credit cards per inhabitant
Belgium	1,411	12,275	–
Brazil	890	37,506	0.84
Canada	1,703	22,881	2.26
China	308	5,270	0.25
France	897	28,094	0.41
Germany	1,008	8,789	0.04
India	94	695	0.02
Italy	839	24,963	0.47
Japan	1,075	14,628	2.52
Netherlands	451	16,153	0.35
Russia	1,200	4,853	0.16
Singapore	486	17,337	1.45
Sweden	359	22,413	1.13
Switzerland	845	21,268	0.72
UK	1,046	25,920	0.89
US	1,358	22,357	2.88

Source: BIS. (December 2013) *Statistics on Payment and Settlement Systems in Selected Countries*. Data on US ATMs estimated from data provided by the national ATM Council and on POS terminals authors' estimates.

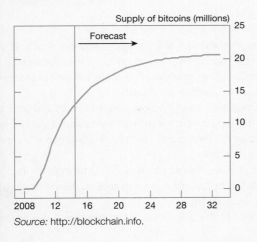

What Is Bitcoin?

BOX 4.1

Bitcoin is a digital currency scheme that uses a new decentralized payment system and a new currency. It has a publicly visible ledger which is shared across a computing network. An important feature of digital currency schemes is the process by which users agree on changes to its ledger (that is, on which transactions to accept as valid). Bitcoin users do not have to disclose who they are. They maintain a digital 'wallet' on their computers and, by use of special software, trade the currency among each other in exchange for traditional currency or goods and services.

Payments can be made at any time and between any two users worldwide. Users may acquire bitcoins as a reward for verifying earlier transactions (explained more below), by purchasing them from other users (in exchange for traditional currencies) or in exchange for goods and services.

The process of creating bitcoins is called 'mining' and employs computing power to process transactions, secure the network, and keep everyone in the system synchronized together. Users create a Bitcoin digital 'wallet' on their computer desktop or smart phone that allows them to buy, use and accept bitcoin tokens through a secure online address or a third-party service such as Multibit or Bitpay. Behind the scenes, the Bitcoin network is sharing a public ledger called the 'block chain' that keeps a record of all transactions and avoids the digital money being used more than once.

Tables 4.2 and 4.3 below illustrate the phenomenal growth of bitcoins, and the meteoric increase in price in 2013 and early 2014, with a fall thereafter.

▼ **Table 4.2** *The projected supply of bitcoins in circulation*

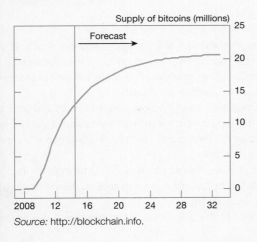

Source: http://blockchain.info.

▼ **Table 4.3** *The price of bitcoins (linear scale)*

Source: http://blockchain.info.

Advantages	Disadvantages
• Ease and speed of transactions	• Not widely accepted
• No banks involved in the process	• Used for criminal activities
• Low transaction costs	• Payments are irreversible
• No geographical and/or time limitations	• Volatile volumes
	• Digital wallets maybe lost or hit by viruses

Loans

Four types of loan are common in the retail banking sector:

- Overdraft
- Personal loan
- Mortgage
- Credit card

Overdraft

The overdraft is a popular method of borrowing in countries where it is permitted. The account holder is allowed to overdraw up to a maximum sum for a given period of time – nominally, perhaps, 6 months, but in practice renewable. Interest is charged on a daily basis (and at a variable rate) on any overdrawn balance.

From the customer's point of view, the overdraft is informal and can be arranged quickly; it is flexible in that the amount 'lent' will vary; and it can be quite economical in that when a monthly salary is paid in, the overdrawn balance will be reduced, or even eliminated, at least for a few days.

From the banks' point of view, the overdraft is also informal; the facility is reviewed at the stated time interval; and, if necessary, it is repayable on demand – a condition of which many borrowers are happily ignorant.

The overdraft is common in the UK, US and Germany, and not particularly common in France.

Personal loan

The personal loan is an agreement to borrow a specific amount over a specific period of time with a set sum repaid monthly. For example, $1,000 might be borrowed for 2 years. The rate of interest is fixed and charged on the whole amount. If the rate was 10%, then 10% p.a. on $1,000 for 2 years is $200. This results in 24 monthly repayments of $50. As some of the principal is being repaid every month, the bank is not owed $1,000 for 2 years, but, on average, a much smaller sum. The result is that the 10% rate is purely nominal, the actual rate (sometimes termed the 'annual percentage rate' – APR) will be nearly twice this.

Mortgage

Although there may be specialized mortgage lenders, commercial banks may offer mortgages too. The loan is secured on the property, and such a loan bears a much lower rate of interest than an unsecured overdraft or personal loan, as the bank is less at risk. Traditionally, in some countries, mortgage lenders would not lend more than, say, 50% or 60% of the value of the property, but this has become less common over the past few decades as competition in mortgage markets globally heated up. It became common throughout Europe for banks to offer 85–95% mortgages (and in some cases, even 110% mortgages). This increased mortgage lending was fuelled by booming property prices, the low interest rate environment and the securitization phenomena – the latter enabled banks to originate mortgage loans and then sell them on in various forms (mortgage-backed securities, collateralized debt obligations) to investors. This meant that commercial banks no longer had to rely on depositors to fund mortgage lending. As we now know, it all ended in tears with the banking sector collapses in the US, the UK and elsewhere in 2007–8. In the UK, a 20–25% deposit is now common for mortgage borrowers.

Another recent development in the UK on the mortgage product side has seen various implementations of the all-in-one account, like the Virgin One current mortgage account, which is a blend of a current account and a mortgage. The accounts are actually or virtually merged to give the customer the benefit of fluctuations in their overdraft, say, after pay day, with the lower interest rates of a mortgage.

Credit card

Another way of lending money is by a credit card account. The major international brand names are Visa, MasterCard and JCB, the Japanese branding organization, and cards are offered by banks, retailers and others. The plastic card, with coded information on a magnetic strip or microchip, is offered at the point of sale, and the purchase is charged to the credit card account. The method is exactly the same as with a debit card. A statement is sent monthly, with a given time to pay, usually 2 to 3 weeks. The consumer has the choice of paying the balance in full or paying only part and paying the rest later. It is flexible in that the cardholders can choose how much to borrow (within a prearranged limit) and how quickly to repay. Generally, the rate of interest is substantial when borrowing on a credit card account, but competitive pressures and desire for market share often cause the banks to offer keen introductory or 'balance transfer' rates. Cardholders can, of course, choose not to borrow at all, but repay in full each month, with perhaps up to 7 weeks elapsing between the purchase and the payment, at no cost to them. Most issuing banks seek to make an annual charge for the use of the card, but competitive pressures have again forced many to offer cards without fees. Recent years have seen a large increase in card issuers and types of card. Among the issuers are retailers (Tesco, Sainsbury's), bodies like AT&T, Mercedes Benz, General Electric (US) and mutual funds. In the UK, some 1,400 plus organizations – clubs (even football clubs like Queens Park Rangers have their own credit card), societies, unions and common interest groups of many kinds – have cards issued in their names. They contract the banks, or specialist organizations such as MBNA, to manage and operate the accounts, taking an introductory fee and a tiny percentage of the turnover through the accounts. Although not obvious to the cardholder, the banks also charge the retailers a percentage of 1–3% of the transaction value for providing the facilities by which the transactions are authorized, collected and cleared.

The familiar green American Express card and the Diners Club card are traditionally not credit cards and when first introduced were known as 'travel and entertainment' or charge cards. The consumer is expected to pay the balance in full every month. Nowadays, however, both American Express and Diners have expanded and they offer both the afore-mentioned as well as traditional credit cards.

In general, credit cards are now widely used. Their acceptability internationally makes them a useful way of solving foreign currency problems when travelling.

The one country where the use of credit cards is weak is Germany, where, at the end of 1995, there were only 0.6 million credit cardholders as opposed to, for example, 29 million in the UK. This was due to the opposition of the banks. However, things have changed somewhat in the UK, although not in Germany. By January 2013, there were only 3 million credit cards for a population of 82 million in Germany, whereas UK credit cards had increased to 56 million in number (according to the BIS). Some prominent stores and supermarkets in Germany still do not accept credit cards. Germans, generally, are relatively conservative spenders. By contrast, the US, with a population of 314 million, has over 904 million credit cards.

Another development using plastic cards that the banks and others are developing is electronic money, or e-money. E-money is a digital equivalent of cash, stored on an electronic device or remotely at a server. A common form of e-money is the 'electronic purse', where users store relatively small amounts of money on their payment card or other smart card, to use for making small payments. Although the development of e-money was expected to revolutionize low-value payments, it has not been a big success. One exception is the Hong Kong Octopus card system, which started as a transport payment system and has grown into a widely used e-money system. The card is a rechargeable, contactless, stored-value smart card used to transfer electronic payments in online or offline systems at stores and numerous other outlets throughout Hong Kong. (London's Oyster card is similar, but only for use on London's transport system.) Singapore has an e-money system similar to that of Hong Kong's for use on its transit system. In the Netherlands, a system known as Chipknip is widely used for low-value transactions (typically below €5). This is an electronic cash system, and all ATM cards issued by Dutch banks have smart cards that can be loaded with value via Chipknip loading stations next to ATMs.

Other Services

There are a number of other services typically offered by banks.

Securities purchases

In some countries, like Germany and Switzerland, the 'universal' bank tradition has meant that banks dominate the stock markets, and the commercial banking branches have been able to offer a full service to clients. Elsewhere, brokers have traditionally had a monopoly of stock exchange transactions, where banks would act as an agent for their customers, passing the order to the broker. Today, this might still be the case, but all over Europe deregulation has been the rule, starting with the UK's Big Bang in October 1986. As a result, banks have been allowed either to own brokerages or set up their own operations and offer their branch customers a securities service.

Securities custody

Often, bonds and shares are in 'bearer' format and not registered. The share certificate will say that 'the bearer' owns, perhaps, 2,000 shares in DaimlerChrysler. The problem is that in the event of a burglary, the burglar is now 'the bearer'. Also, since there is no register, interest payments and dividends have to be claimed, voting rights followed up and so on. The banks will, therefore, often hold the certifications for safekeeping, claim interest payments/dividends for clients, vote by proxy, notify them of annual general meetings

(AGMs), rights issues, scrip issues and other company events. Needless to say, a fee is charged for this service.

Mutual funds

Mutual funds are pools of shares run by investment managers and giving the small shareholder a spread of risk. The banks often own these, and part of the securities service might be the advice that the client would be better off in a mutual fund than owning shares directly. It would be no surprise to find that the fund recommended is one the bank owns. These are sold in France as SICAVs and FCPs, in the UK as investment trusts and unit trusts undertakings for collective investment in transferable securities, and as mutual funds in the US. The idea has spread to Spain, where *superfondos* are now being offered by the banks. Following the European single-market initiative, a range of legislation known as Undertakings for Collective Investment in Transferable Securities (UCITS) has been put in place that allows mutual funds and other collective investment schemes to operate freely throughout the EU on the basis of a single authorization from one member state (see Chapter 8). A mutual fund established in a member state country can apply for UCITS status and, if successful, can then be marketed throughout the whole of the EU. Worldwide, according to the Investment Company Institute (www.ici.org) by mid-2014 some €33 trillion are invested in all kinds of investment funds and, of these, close to one-third are managed in UCITS.

Advice

The bank manager is available for advice. This may be about investments, trust funds for children, wills and similar issues. Indeed, the manager may end up as the executor of a will and trustee of funds left for children. This position as adviser puts the bank manager in an ideal position to sell the bank's products. This has caused much anguish in the UK due to the operation of the 1986 Financial Services Act. The ruling was that either the bank manager is an agent for the bank's products or an independent investment adviser. If the former, he must inform the client of this status and is not allowed to give wide-ranging advice on a range of products; if an independent adviser, he must also make sure that the client is aware of this. If he recommends the bank's product, it must be clear, beyond reasonable doubt, that this is best for the client, or criminal prosecution may ensue. However, this was all changed in 2005 to something more complicated. There are now 'multi-tied agents' who can recommend products from a range of firms. Some independent advisers are becoming multi-tied agents, but many banks are still selling their own products only. Because of the complexities associated with providing advice, in the UK there are cooling-off periods, whereby customers have time to think and decide about products before they purchase/invest – they also have time to cancel decisions if they change their mind.

Safe deposits

Banks provide safe deposit boxes to house jewellery, other valuable items and cash. When there is a break-in and the boxes are forced open, those clients with large sums of which the tax authorities are unaware face a problem when making a claim.

Foreign exchange

Apart from the banks' wholesale foreign exchange operations, they provide a service for their customers' holiday needs. This involves supplying traveller's cheques and cash. They may also be involved in requests to transfer sums of money to accounts abroad. The rise of the credit and debit card, now widely acceptable at point of sale and in ATMs, has eroded this business, along with the advent of the euro.

Insurance

Most banks now offer insurance policies, either through an association with an insurance company or through their own subsidiary. This is discussed more fully below when we look at key current issues in retail banking.

Delivery Channels

How are the services of the bank – deposits, loans, payment products and all the other services – delivered to the customer? Traditionally, there was only one answer: the branch office. Gradually, since the early 1990s, branches have been joined by telephone banking, Internet banking and, more recently still, TV and mobile phone delivery.

Branch delivery

Branch delivery still dominates. In the UK, there were 10,600 bank branches at the start of 2012, down from 15,700 in 1990, with some of the reduction being caused by rationalization from mergers and some from branch closure programmes. Branch numbers are down in the Netherlands (down from 6,729 in 1995 to 2,515 in 2012) and have generally declined in most developed countries, but with a modest recent increase in the US (from 116,500 in 2008 to 117,007. In contrast, some emerging markets have seen big increases; for example, the number of bank branches (and agents doing branch business) in Brazil increased from just over 103,000 in 2006 to over 194,039 in 2012. China, India and Russia also experienced increases in branch numbers.

Many people now believe that the new channels are additional services rather than substitutes, with one major bank citing the fact that three out of four customers still regularly visited a branch. This all suggests that branches are here to stay, at least for the medium term. Branches are convenient for the customer, and there is still a demand for face-to-face contact, particularly when discussing more complex financial matters. Branches give the bank high visibility on the street and are a good base for attracting new customers, dealing with routine transactions and selling more complex (and profitable) products.

There has been a fairly rapid change in how the branches look to the customer. Traditionally, the customer was confined to a public space defined by the imposing barrier of the line of cashiers, behind their security screens. A customer had to go out of the way to ask to see someone who could open an account or deal with a more complicated transaction. This model of the branch is rapidly being supplanted by one in which the space has been opened up and made more welcoming. After encountering some self-service machines – ATMs, deposit machines, statement and enquiry terminals – customers see before them desks with people variously described as 'personal bankers' or 'counsellors', awaiting an opportunity to engage them in helpful conversation. The cashiers are relegated to the back of the room. The purpose of all this is to encourage customers to serve themselves for routine transactions and, as soon as they step beyond this, to expose them to sales opportunities. To make space for this more 'open' setting, something had to be displaced. This is the clerical processing of payments and correspondence, which was formerly termed 'the back office function'. These activities are still required, but they have been moved out to other units, which will, using higher-capacity technology, take on the back office work of many branches.

The use of branches is still very much a current issue. Alliance & Leicester (now part of Santander), for example, announced in mid-2004 that it intended to close one-sixth of all its branches on the grounds that more and more customers are using the telephone and the Internet. On the other hand, Abbey National (also now part of Banco Santander) and

RBS/NatWest have put greater emphasis on branches, even making them a selling point in advertisements. Barclays, after several years of flat profits in retail banking, announced in the mid-2000s through Roger Davis, its then UK retail banking chief, that it wanted customers to re-engage with their local branches, making the local manager and staff the kingpins again. There would be extensive refurbishment, more people and more branch-based technology, with the bank manager given greater autonomy. In all this, Barclays looks to more effective cross-selling of products like mortgages and insurance. Finally, when HBOS released its annual results in March 2006, it announced plans to spend £100m on 50 new branches and noted that its share of new accounts had typically doubled in areas where the bank has a branch. Although these plans to bolster UK bank branches are welcoming, it does not disguise the fact that the number of branches has systematically fallen over the past 20 years or so, and the trend is unlikely to be reversed. In fact, bank restructuring since the credit crisis is more likely to accelerate the trend – Lloyds' decision to close Cheltenham & Gloucester branches in June 2009 being a clear indication of things to come.

Although rationalization of branch networks will continue, there is no doubt that well-staffed, well-equipped, user-friendly branches still have a major role to play. The results of a survey by consultants Booz Allen Hamilton, published in March 2005, found that in Europe the most friendly branches were in Switzerland and Germany, and the least friendly in Spain and the UK. As far as product knowledge is concerned, the UK and Spain were also rated the worst. The survey covered 600 branches across Europe and found that 79% of people still prefer to buy products like basic bank deposits and savings accounts from a branch. The revolution in appearance may be more advanced overseas that in the UK. In France, Spain and the US, you can find branches run like cafés, where employees serve lattes and snacks! In Paris, BNP Paribas has a branch with chandeliers, a lounge for relaxation and a children's play area.

There were similar findings from the UK consultancy Finalta. Banks have put more emphasis on selling, but not very successfully. Another consultancy, Accenture, being in information technology (IT), thinks that better use of IT is the answer. It unveiled a demonstration of several new techniques based on IT – digital pens whose pen strokes can be transmitted to a computer, touch-sensitive video walls and video cameras to monitor how queues form. Both RBS and Lloyds claim to have used IT to analyse and optimize the design of branches and set staffing levels.

As mentioned above, the number of bank branches has barely fallen in the US; in fact, many new branches have opened following the Riegle-Neal Act of 1994, which repealed the McFadden Act and allowed banks to open in other states. Many of these new branches look more like boutiques than the old cavernous banking halls of old.

Finally, one more criticism. Chris Skinner, founder of the consultancy Shaping Tomorrow, says that branches are mostly in the wrong place – consumer traffic has moved elsewhere. His recommendation is that banks should relocate to major retail conurbations.

Telephone banking

Most banks now offer, in parallel with their branches, a service using only the telephone as a means of communication. Staff in call centres offer a service for, perhaps, 24 hours per day. In October 2005, HSBC announced that business customers had logged on to their accounts 443,000 times in the previous 12 months between 11.00 p.m. and 6.00 a.m. The busiest period was 11.00 p.m. to midnight. Customers' routine enquiries can be satisfied, and more complex services, for example bill paying, can be supported. Here, the names and bank account details for regular suppliers (gas, electricity, telephone and so on) are set up on file, and using special security passwords, a whole banking service can be initiated by the customer, using only the telephone. New accounts, loans and mortgages can be negotiated in the same way, with postal confirmation where necessary. Money can be drawn out by using plastic cards in the parent bank's ATMs. The bank has the advantage of not having the cost of a branch network and will pay a higher than normal rate of interest on credit balances.

Here are examples of such systems:

- Germany   Bank 24 (Deutsche Bank)
- UK   First Direct (HSBC)
- Spain   Open Bank (Banco Santander)
- France   Banque Direct (Paribas)

New entrants to banking, for example supermarkets and insurance companies, almost universally base their operations on a combination of telephone call centres and the Internet. Whereas telephone banking is widely used by business, it has become less important for retail customers and is increasingly being replaced by Internet services. According to UK Payments Administration, the number of people using telephone banking peaked at 16.1 million adults in 2005 and has since declined as people switch to online banking. By 2012, an estimated 14 million adults in the UK used some form of telephone banking.

Internet banking

Since the mid-1990s, there has been steady growth in the use of the Internet by individuals to access their banks. Initially, special purpose application software and diallers had to be used to provide adequate security, but now the standard Internet browsers are perfectly satisfactory for home banking purposes. Banks have been divided in their approach to Internet banking. Some have set up separately branded operations, distanced from the parent bank, whereas others have merely added the Internet as a medium for contact, along with their telephone and branch channels.

In the UK, examples of separately branded operations are Smile (started in 1999 and owned by the Co-operative Group), Cahoot (a division of Abbey National, part of Santander) and Intelligent Finance (a division of Bank of Scotland, part of Lloyds). First-e, a totally new Internet start-up established in 1999, was intended to be international, with an initial presence in the UK, Germany, Italy, France and Spain. It was, however, unsuccessful and closed down in 2001. Again, some new entrants have chosen this route, notably Egg, an Internet banking offshoot of the Prudential Assurance Company. Although heavily loss making since its founding in 1998, Egg broke into profit in the final quarter of 2001. It offers a wide range of deposit and loan accounts, credit cards, insurance and investment products as well as a 'shopping zone', where over 250 retailers have space on the Egg website to proffer their wares, which can, of course, be paid for using the Egg credit card or perhaps with an Egg personal loan. However, it cannot have been too profitable: Prudential made several unsuccessful efforts to sell Egg but announced in October 2005 that it would keep it anyway and bought the 21% of Egg that it did not own. Egg was acquired by Citibank in 2007. Internet banking has really taken off in the UK. The number of UK individuals using online banking services increased from 7.9 million in 2002 to close to 30 million by the end of 2013. Box 4.2 details recent developments in the UK.

France has an online banking facility, which has its roots in a system called Videotex, developed much earlier than the Internet. This is commonplace because the government decided to give a boost to communication links by supplying free Minitel terminals using the TV set. One early use was to make telephone directory enquiries, but other information

BOX 4.2

Britain's Bank Customers Use Internet Banking 7 Billion Times in 2013

Internet banking surges by nearly 40% in just 4 years.

Customers use these services almost 800,000 times an hour. Customers of Britain's high street banks used Internet banking nearly 7 billion times in 2013, according to industry statistics compiled by the BBA.

The figures, published in the *BBA's 2013 Abstract of Banking Statistics*, provide further evidence of the seismic change in the way millions of customers manage their finances.

In all, there were 6.9 billion customer instructions using personal computers during 2013 – up from 5 billion in 2009. This number includes:

- 316 million bill payments
- 293 million inter account transfers
- 152.6 million direct debit or standing order creations or amendments
- 1.1 billion account queries
- 10.5 million stop payment instructions – an eightfold increase on the previous year

Richard Woolhouse, the BBA's Chief Economist, said:

These figures provide more evidence of the ongoing revolution in the way millions of us spend, move and manage our money.

There are clear productivity gains for our economy from Internet banking. Many of us are spending less time queuing in branches and can avoid unnecessary fees by keeping a sharper eye on our balances. This is helping customers and providing wider economic benefits.

This data features in the first part of our annual Abstract of Banking Statistics, which is a goldmine for anyone trying to understand the industry.

The BBA has previously charted the rise of mobile banking, contactless cards and a range of other consumer friendly technology through its *Way We Bank Now* reports.

The new statistics on Internet banking featured in the first part of the BBA's 2013 Abstract of Banking Statistics are published alongside figures on household deposits, mortgages and consumer credit.

Two further parts of the abstract, one on the industry's infrastructure and another on business banking, will be published next month.

Source: British Bankers Association (2014), https://www.bba.org.uk/news/press-releases/britains-bank-customers-use-Internet-banking-7-billion-times-in-just-one-year/#.VFWoJPmzJcY.

services were soon added. There are 10 million Minitel monthly connections to the service. The banks supply software that allows balance reporting, enquiry of historical data and transfer of funds to creditors' accounts. More advanced software allows portfolio management and various financial calculations. The service has now been superseded by the Internet, and France Telecom announced the closure of the service in mid-2012.

Clearing Systems

Clearing involves the transmission, exchange and settlement for payments between banks. There are clearing systems for both paper (for example cheques) and electronic clearing. Usually, the central bank is involved, to provide interbank settlement and overall control of the process, but the extent of the involvement differs greatly from country to country.

In the US, until recently, the Federal Reserve ran 45 cheque clearing centres. In February 2003, the 12 Federal Reserve Banks announced an initiative to align their infrastructure with the declining use of cheques by reducing the number of locations at which they process cheques. Since then, they have discontinued cheque operations at many of their 45 cheque processing centres and, by 2014, had just one dedicated cheque processing site at the Federal Reserve Bank of Cleveland. There are also private clearing centres and arrangements made mutually between groups of banks. Approximately 30% of cheques are cleared internally by the banks on which they were drawn, 35% are cleared by private centres and mutual arrangements, and 35% are cleared by the Federal Reserve.

For salaries, standing orders, direct debits and supplier payments, data are encoded electronically and sent to an automated clearing house (ACH). For example, having processed salaries by computer and printed payslips for the employees, a corporate will send the data over to an ACH, there to be sorted electronically and passed to the relevant employees' banks so that their salaries can be credited. The ACHs are run by the Federal Reserve, and a few are privately operated; they processed 22 billion transactions to a value of $38 trillion in 2013. The decline in usage of cheque payments has mainly been as a result of the increase in ACH and debit card transactions since 2000.

All Federal Reserve System offices are linked for balance transfers between member banks by a system called Fedwire. The New York Clearing Houses Association runs CHIPS, an interbank funds transfer system in New York, which is used for large international, as opposed to domestic, dollar payments.

In France, there are over 100 provincial clearing houses in towns where a branch of the Bank of France is located. If presented within the same catchment area as the bank on which it is drawn, the cheque will usually clear on the second working day after presentation. Outside the catchment area, the bank will clear on the fifth working day after presentation. Six banks have their own bilateral clearing arrangements. Electronic clearing takes place through SIT (Système Interbancaire Télécompensation). It is run by the Bank of France, which operates nine centres, but policy is decided by the Bankers' Association.

In the UK, all clearing is controlled by UK Payments Administration Ltd, which took over from the disbanded Association for Payment Clearing Services on 6 July 2009. Payments Administration acts as a portal company for each of the respective sectors of UK payment services, such as Bacs, the Cheque and Credit Clearing Company and CHAPS, and a new organization known as the Payments Council sets strategy for the industry. As already noted, the three main payment systems include:

- Cheque and Credit Clearing Company Ltd, for general cheque clearing
- CHAPS Clearing Company Ltd
- Bacs Payment Schemes Ltd, accessed via a data channel known as Bacstel-IP

CHAPS is a same-day interbank clearing system for high-value electronic entries in sterling. In January 1999, CHAPS-Euro was added as a parallel system for euro-denominated payments.

BOX 4.3

The UK's New Payments Systems Regulator

A new Payment Systems Regulator was set up in the UK in April 2014 and comes into operation in April 2015. Its main objectives are threefold:

to boost competition in the payments sector
to promote innovation and finally
to make sure the payment systems are operated in the interests of users

The new regulator will be based in the Bank of England and will oversee the major payment operators, namely, those that are viewed as systemically important or because of strong market power have raised competition issues in the past. Firms to be regulated include: Visa, MasterCard, BACS Payment Schemes, CHAPS as well as various infrastructure firms.

The regulator will operate like a public utility regulator (like Ofcom in the telecoms industry), ensuring competition, innovation and minimising the likelihood of systemic failure.

Bacs is for salaries, standing orders, direct debits and direct credits, just like the ACHs in the US. It is by far the largest such operation in the world, handling over 5.7 billion items in 2013, with a total value of £4.2 trillion. Maximum payments via Bacs are for £100,000. This is same-day clearing. Over 3.5 billion transactions processed are direct debits. In April 2014, a new Payments system regulator for the UK was established, primarily to look at competition and related issues, details of which are outlined in Box 4.3.

Cross-border clearing

Cross-border clearing is a subject attracting a lot of attention. In September 1990, the European Commission published a paper on cross-border cash and electronic payments. It acknowledged that the lack of a single compatible system would be a drawback in the age of the single market. This view was also reinforced by a study published by the European Central Bank in 1999.

A group of European cooperative banks have set up a system called TIPANET (Transferts Interbancaires de Paiements Automatisés) for non-urgent transfers.

Usually the cost of the transfer is a flat fee – currently £8 from payments via the UK Co-operative Bank to elsewhere in Europe.

Giro clearing organizations in 14 countries have set up a cross-border transfer system called Eurogiro, which started in November 1992. European savings banks have set up their own network called S InterPay with links in 10 countries.

Finally, it might be possible to link national ACH systems like CHAPS (UK), SIT (France), SIS (Switzerland), EAF (Germany) and so on.

The plethora of independent and incompatible systems does not instil confidence for the future of an efficient system for cross-border payments, and there is already disappointment that within Europe's new monetary union, cross-border payments in the euro are neither easier nor cheaper. The EU passed a regulation in July 2003 requiring banks to make the same charge for cross-border payments as domestic for transactions valued up to €12,500, in spite of the higher costs. As noted below, the EU has established a single Europe-wide cross-border credit and debit transfer system for euro in 2014, and this will also be the case for non-euro EU countries by 2016. This is part of the plan to establish a Single European payments Area (SEPA). Banks set up a European Payments Council to decide how to establish SEPA, and in January 2008, more than 4,000 banks in 35 countries, representing over 95% of payment volume in Europe, took a historical first step to achieve this goal by launching the SEPA Credit Transfer Scheme for euro payments in 2008 and the SEPA Direct Debit Scheme in 2009. In 2012, the technical and business requirements were legally established for credit transfers and direct debits in euro. This regulation is also referred to as the 'SEPA end-date regulation' and defines the deadlines for the migration to the new SEPA instruments. The deadline for the euro area was 1 February 2014 and for non-euro area Member States 31 October 2016. As of these dates, the existing national euro credit transfer and direct debit schemes will be replaced. The goal is to make payments in euros and across Europe as fast, safe and efficient as national payments are today. SEPA enables customers to make low-cost cashless euro payments to anyone located anywhere in Europe by credit transfer, direct debit or debit card.

Key Retail Banking Issues

Across all the Western financial markets, commercial banks face a series of key challenges:

1   *Capital strength:* Have they got enough to back their business?
2   *Liquidity:* Can they meet predictable and unpredictable cash requirements?
3   *Risk management:* Can they manage risk properly?
4   *Executive pay:* Do they pay too much?
5   *Competition:* Can they price competitively?
6   *Cost control:* Can they be efficient?
7   *Sales of non-banking products:* What products should they offer?
8   *Use of IT:* How can IT help in reducing costs in front and back office operations?

Capital strength

Banks in many Western markets have experienced the near collapse of their systems as a result of the credit crisis. We noted in Chapter 2 and earlier in this chapter that the state has had to rescue major institutions like RBS, Lloyds and Citigroup and has also had to provide massive capital and liquidity support to the system overall. Despite unprecedented actions, many banks are still viewed as relatively undercapitalized. Major regulatory initiatives, particularly Basel III, and various national initiatives are seeking to force large complex banking groups – those viewed as SIFIs – to hold much more capital. This is because investors as well as wholesale depositors are demanding that banks look 'safer than safe' before they consider investing or placing wholesale funds. Throughout 2008, all the major US and UK banks sought to raise billions in new capital, but most of this went to cover losses incurred in loan and investment write-downs. Since 2009, the capital strength of US, UK and many European banks has become stronger, although the market clamours for more capital injections in light of the losses that many banks have made as a consequence of holding bad sovereign debt. Banks are likely to have to sell off non-core as well as their more risky activities, such as their overseas activities and maybe non-bank financial services businesses, to raise much needed capital. Contraction and risk aversion are the ongoing main strategies – and expansion has been put on hold for many large Western banks.

Liquidity

Linked to the problems caused by the crisis, some banks just did not have enough liquidity to meet deposit withdrawals. The desire to build up liquidity can be seen in Goldman Sachs' September 2008 decision to convert its legal status to a bank holding company so that it would have greater access to insured deposits and access to greater liquidity. Bank regulators have been forced to introduce rules encouraging banks to hold much more liquidity than in the past. This is enshrined in tougher new Basel III liquidity requirements, particularly for the biggest banks.

Risk management

The crisis illustrated to regulators, bank customers, senior bank managers, analysts and others that the risks being borne by many institutions were not being managed appropriately. Risks were being understated and priced incorrectly. The mispricing was compounded by assurances from credit rating agencies and monoline insurers, who also confirmed that the mispriced risks were correctly valued. One study that examined around 10 different measures of bank risk identified that in 2006, the major US and European banks were less risky than they had ever been. Bankers seemed to concur by making historically low levels of loan loss provisions and recording near record profits that year (in the UK and the US). But we know what followed – the systems collapsed. Was it all a massive confidence trick? It's difficult to say, although there is much soul-searching now. Clearly, the industry has to get its act together and measure risk more accurately. If it cannot do this, the solution is for banks to hold much more capital and liquidity. (See *The Economist* [2010] for an excellent survey of contemporary financial risk issues.)

Executive pay

Excessive salaries and bonus payments in the banking sector are said to have fuelled the lending and securitization spree that culminated in the banking sector collapses. In the UK, the Walker Review (2009) focused on corporate governance in UK banks and other financial firms. It highlighted that weak corporate governance structures were likely to have been responsible for excessive risk-taking by banks and had therefore been a cause of the crisis. Stronger oversight of the composition and role of boards is recommended, especially covering executive pay, risk management and other strategic issues. Institutional investors are also asked to play a more active role in the governance of banks and other financial institutions.

Growing competition

Banks face growing competition from other financial institutions, retailers, insurance companies and in-house corporate facilities, as illustrated in Box 4.4.

BOX 4.4

The Changing Competitive Landscape in Retail Financial Services

Growing deregulation has meant an increase in competition from other financial institutions previously precluded from offering a total banking service. This includes the S&Ls in the US, building societies in the UK, savings banks generally, post office banks in some sectors, and mutual funds that also offer savings accounts.

The Changing Competitive Landscape in Retail Financial Services (*continued*)

Competition for deposits has intensified, and we see the banks in Spain and the UK offering interest on credit balances for the first time. Also, foreign banks, such as Banco Santander in the UK, can be strong competitors. Other banks are aiming their services at customers who want 'old fashioned' branch banking with the local manager as king. The best example in the UK is the Swedish bank, Handelsbank who is opening one new branch every 8 days.

Retailers

Retailers are increasingly active. In Italy, Benetton is part of a major financial group, Euromobiliare. In Sweden, IKEA, the furniture company, offers current account facilities. In the UK, Marks & Spencer offers unsecured loans, mutual funds and life insurance.

Key supermarkets, like Tesco and Sainsbury's, have offered bank accounts. However, no chequebook facilities are offered, thus avoiding one of the key expenses of retail banking. They are being touted as the firms that may take chunks of the troubled major UK banks if the latter need to divest to raise capital.

In the US, Walmart Financial Services is now offering money transfer services, money orders, pay cheque cashing and credit cards. It handles 1 million financial transactions per week. It has also tried to obtain FDIC approval to set up a loan company to offer small loans and has applied for permission to open a bank in Utah. This latter has been strongly opposed by the banking community and so far has not been successful.

Insurance companies

Insurance companies are competing vigorously for savings with schemes that link life assurance with a savings product. These often involve the use of mutual funds to improve the return on the fund.

Although this is not new, pressure has intensified in recent years. Some are forming banks. Swedish Trygg-Hansa launched a bank in mid-October 1995 and merged with Denmark's second largest bank in 1999. The Prudential Corporation, the UK's largest life assurance and investment group, launched its own bank, which transformed itself into Egg, with loss-making interest rates in late 1998, and within 6 months had 500,000 customers and £5bn in deposits – but losses of £175m. The plan was to sell these customers lots of other financial products. As the loss-leading interest rates were brought into line with the market (although still competitive), Egg lost some of the 'hot' funds and customers, but over time it seems to have generated a self-sustaining business from a wide set of product offerings, and has finally broke into profit in the last quarter of 2001. Egg was sold to Citibank in 2007.

In-house corporate banks

In-house corporate banks are now common – Ford Motor Credit, Renault Crédit International, ICI Finance, Gemina (the Fiat financial services group), General Electric Financial Services and in Germany, bank subsidiaries of VW, Audi, BMW and DaimlerChrysler to mention a few. Although the largest effect here is usually on the banks' wholesale business, many are also active in retail finance. The General Electric subsidiary, for example, is into consumer loans and credit cards as well as leasing, property and corporate finance.

Cost control

Growing competition has made cost control even more important. Increasingly, the banks' annual reports are referring to their success (or lack of it) in cutting the cost/income ratio and increasing the return of capital on equity.

According to data from the Federal Reserve Bank of St. Louis, US banks' cost/income ratio stood at 61% in 2011, compared with 75% for French, 90% for Italian and 83% for German banks. UK banks' cost/income ratios amounted to 52% in 2009, but this shot up to 67% in 2011. China's banks have staggering low ratios – 38% for the same year. It is not surprising to find that return on equity (ROE) in the US (up until the crisis at least) averaged 15% (falling to 12% in 2006, 9.7% in 2007 and then a credit crunch collapse to 0.8% in 2008, and creeping up to just under 5% by 2011). In France, Germany and Italy, bank returns are typically below 10%. In the UK, returns for the top banks ranged between 20% and 25% from 2000 to 2007. All this changed in 2008. For example:

- Barclays posted after tax ROE of 20.5% in 2007, which fell to 14.6% in 2008 and then to 11.6% in 2010. Its performance declined with a 3% ROE in 2013.
- Lloyds Group reported an ROE of 34% in 2007, which fell to 8% in 2008 and a paltry 0.58% in 2010. The banks made a loss in 2013 with an ROE of –3.5%.
- And most spectacularly, RBS's ROE declined from 18.6% in 2007 to –43.7% in 2008 (hence the state bailout) and was still making losses in 2013, posting a ROE of –11.3%.

In retail banking, a major cost is the branch network. In recent years, we have seen rationalization and branch automation. Rationalization means dividing branches into those that only deal with corporates, full-service branches (offering the complete range of products), and local sub-branches, which are largely points for paying in cash and withdrawing it. 'Branch automation' involves withdrawing paperwork to regional centres and making more of the branch a front office for dealing with customers. Other issues relating to branches were dealt with earlier in this chapter.

Another major expense is the cost of processing paper payment transactions. Cheque usage is falling – there were just over 2 million cheques issued each day in the UK in 2013 compared with 11 million in the peak year of 1990. Nowadays, just under 2% of retail spending by value is still paid by cheque, compared with over 78% by debit or credit card. On 16 December 2009, the Payments Council announced that it had taken the decision to set a target date of 31 October 2018 to close the UK's central cheque clearing, 'effectively bringing an end to the cheque as we know it'. However, the UK Government reversed this decision in July 2011; they were somewhat annoyed that the banks had agreed to remove cheques without adequate public consultation. Nevertheless, the use of cheques is falling, so early predictions about the decline of paper-based transactions have clearly come to fruition – we mentioned earlier the shift to online banking.

One way often cited by senior bankers as a way to help cut costs has been to engage in mergers or cooperation with other banks. Appendix 2 in Chapter 2 illustrates the largest recent US bank mergers that have taken place. Outside the US, there have also been some large deals including Mitsui and Sumitomo; Mitsubishi-Tokyo and UFJ; Banco Santander and BCH; BBVA and Argentaria; Bayerische Vereinsbank and Bayerische Hypo Bank; RBS and National Westminster and then ABN AMRO; and Bank of Scotland merged with the Halifax Bank, to form HBOS, which was then acquired by Lloyds TSB Group as a consequence of the credit crisis in 2008. Prior to the forced or crisis deals, many of the earlier deals were predicated on cost savings.

A major motivation for bank mergers and acquisitions (M&A) is the desire to boost performance – increased profits and higher market valuation via share price increases. Senior executives engaged in M&A have to convince the bank owners (shareholders) that the deal will boost performance either by increasing revenues or reducing costs. It's unlikely that shareholders will sanction a deal if they believe the acquisition or merger will reduce performance. As such, CEOs make a big deal about the performance-enhancing features of any acquisitions they aim to put in place. Performance gains from mergers emanate from either cost improvements or ways in which revenues can increase – namely via market power. The latter relates to bigger banks being able to set prices above competitive levels due to market dominance in particular areas. There have been a large number of studies (by academics, analysts and consultants) that have sought to investigate the performance effects of bank mergers. Typically, these studies seek to establish whether there are cost and/or profit improvements post merger. The consensus view from studies that (mainly) examined bank M&A during the 1980s up to the mid-1990s was that cost and profit improvements resulting from bank mergers tended to be elusive, although evidence from 2000 onwards (for European bank deals at least) suggests cost improvements resulting from restructuring post merger. Other evidence also suggests that cost savings can be large – the deal between Chase Manhattan and Manny Hanny is believed to have resulted in cost savings of over $2bn.

Mergers do not, of course, necessarily go well. Wells Fargo, once a highly rated bank, bought First Interstate. Hit by service problems, many customers left, and its share price fell heavily. John Plender, writing in the *Financial Times* (12 July 2009), also identifies what he calls the 'winner's curse', citing:

> the plight of Bank of America after its takeover of Merrill Lynch. So, too, with RBS's acquisition of ABN Amro; and even more so with Lloyds TSB, where the disastrous purchase of HBOS came after years of prudent behaviour and pedestrian performance.

In addition to these mergers, we are seeing increasing cooperation. Cooperative banks are arranging for banks in other countries to offer services to their customers when abroad. A group called Unico links eight major cooperatives in the Netherlands, France, Germany, Finland, Austria, Spain, Italy and Switzerland, serving some 80 million clients. Cooperation agreements are also common in specialist areas, for instance BNP Paribas Securities Services announced a cooperation agreement with the Moroccan bank BMCI in 2009 to provide its international clients with local clearing and custody and global corporate trust services in Morocco.

Sales of non-banking products

Another way to reduce the costs of branches is to make them more productive by selling more services. Some of these are products like insurance or mutual funds, which might not have been regarded as classic banking products at one time. Other activities include the acquisition of travel agencies and estate agencies. Nowadays, bank employees are typically set sales targets for non-bank products and commission from such sales is an increasing portion of teller staff remuneration.

If banking is less profitable and costs are rising, which is certainly the case now, banks must increase their selling and marketing skills and promote a wider range of offerings than in the past. Part of the aim of branch automation is to use terminals to give access to all the information needed on the full range of a bank's services. For example, many large banks have installed terminals that provide a more holistic view of a client's relationship with the bank, highlighting the details and advantages of bank products best suited to the client and even producing the relevant application forms.

Banks now segment their customer base, typically dividing them into social sectors, each with their own needs:

- *Pre-teens:* Can we get them used to the bank's brand with piggy bank money boxes?
- *Teenagers:* This group is associated with high spending. Banks offer savings accounts, ATM cards and merchandise discounts.
- *Young marrieds:* This group has no children yet and high joint incomes, but a change to come as children arrive.
- *High net worth:* These young professionals have high incomes and are worth a special approach.
- *Over fifties:* Children have now grown up, wives are back at work, houses paid for – but retirement looms.
- *Retired people:* Often these people have high incomes from personal pension plans and savings.

This breakdown has preoccupied banks in many countries, resulting in the design of new bank accounts and mail order marketing, previously associated with consumer products. Segmentation issues are particularly sophisticated in private banking, where specialist investment advice is given to sophisticated clients.

Backing up this effort are large customer databases on computers containing not just accounting information but background details to enable the bank to sell new services, either now or later. In retail banking, 'cross-selling' has become a key feature of the industry – the main UK banks earn around 40% of their income from non-interest-based services, and French banks earn even more, around 50%.

One product of obvious relevance is insurance – life assurance, endowment policies, assurance products backing mortgages, householder policies, building policies, sickness coverage and so on. We have seen three major trends here. One has been full mergers with insurance companies; another is closer cooperation in cross-selling each other's products; and a third is banks setting up full insurance subsidiaries:

1   In the Netherlands, the ING Group merged with NMB Postbank and later bought BBL and Baring Bros; in Denmark, Tryg-Baltica merged with Unidanmark and SEB; in the UK, Halifax bought Clerical Medical; and in Belgium, Kredietbank and Cera merged with ABB Insurance.
2   Cooperation includes arrangements for cross-selling between the Swiss Bank Corporation and Zurich Insurance; Dresdner Bank and Allianz; Banco Popular and Allianz; BNP and the French insurer UAP; Banco Santander and Metropolitan Life.
3   Banks that have set up full insurance subsidiaries include Lloyds TSB, National Westminster, Deutsche, Barclays, Crédit Lyonnais, BBVA, Monte dei Paschi di Siena and Crédit Agricole. Predica, Crédit Agricole's subsidiary, has moved into France's top three insurance companies since its formation in 1987.

The scale of bank involvement in insurance is not to be underestimated. In early 2009, RBS attempted to sell its main insurance operations, including Direct Line, Churchill and Privilege for an estimated £7bn, but could not find a buyer.

Regarding the cooperative ventures, one element of doubt may be creeping in. The evidence suggests that the banks are much more successful at selling insurance products than the insurance companies are at selling banking services. These links between banks and insurance have led to much use of the French word *bancassurance* and the German word *allfinanz*. Some even suggest that bancassurance is on the decline, pointing to Citigroup selling off Travelers. However, when the economy slows and demand for traditional lending products weakens, banks traditionally seek to generate income from non-traditional areas, so the bancassurance trend is here to stay.

The growing effort to sell mutual funds, insurance, stocks, shares and other products has led to a rise in fee and commission income as opposed to interest. The desire to improve profits and control costs has also led to banks increasingly charging fees for such things as arranging loans/overdrafts, an interview with the bank manager; sending an extra copy of a statement; charging if you go overdrawn, even if you have an overdraft arrangement; and so on.

Use of IT

Modern banking is unthinkable without the use of IT. Without it, the numbers needing to be employed in banking would have made the expansion of the past 30 years quite impossible. Many of the developments discussed above have IT at their heart. Branch automation, new account databases, telephone and home banking, EFT-POS, automated electronic clearing – all are essential to the banks' new strategies, and all involve a large investment. Looking at the emerging markets in Central and Eastern Europe and the former Soviet Union, an enormous expenditure on computers and communications infrastructure is required as an essential first step in setting up modern banking systems. As John Reed, former chairman of Citicorp, has put it: 'Money is information on the move.'

One area with IT at its heart is, of course, the Internet. Early hopes (by some) for a massive migration to the Internet and a widespread shutdown of branch networks, with commensurate low costs, appear to be misplaced. The Internet has emerged as an important delivery method alongside branches and call centres as part of a multichannel strategy for most banks. This would seem to give an advantage to the larger, established banks, who have the financial resources and spread of customers to justify the expenditure in the different systems.

A Booz Allen Hamilton survey of comparative transaction costs in the US has estimated the following figures:

PC banking	13¢
Telephone	26¢
Branch	$1.08

UK building societies have produced similar estimates for the UK:

Internet	8p
Telephone	35p
Branch	70p

Could the threat be exaggerated? Internet banking may be offered by non-banks (for example computer and telecommunications companies), and progress has accelerated rapidly over recent years. Given the weak position of banks in many countries since the credit crisis, many are likely to continue to actively promote lower cost distribution channels at the expense of branches. This could mean the introduction of more or higher fees for branch-based transactions compared with those done via electronic channels. This sort of pricing has been widespread in Scandinavian banking for some time and has led to a rapid fall in branch numbers and the fastest take-up of Internet banking in Europe (and maybe the world). Other problems for commercial banks lie in the realm of wholesale banking, and that is our next topic.

WHOLESALE BANKING

Wholesale banking includes a bank's wholesale lending, which will be discussed now, and other activities, which will be covered in later chapters: money markets (Chapter 7) and foreign exchange (Chapter 17). We can begin by breaking bank lending down into uncommitted facilities and committed facilities.

Uncommitted Facilities

Here there is little formal documentation and no network of various fees to be paid to the bank for setting up the facility. The bank agrees to lend money, usually on a short-term basis, but is not committed to renew the loan. The facilities are typically on a 'revolving' basis, that is, the client can repay the loan and then redraw money. There are three types.

Overdrafts

Overdrafts are a great UK favourite with smaller firms. The client is allowed to overdraw up to a given maximum figure. Interest is charged daily on the overdrawn balance, most typically at bank base rates (not LIBOR, see below), plus a given margin. The arrangement may be for, say, 6 months. The bank is not bound to renew the agreement but may well do so. There is no formal arrangement for 'paying back' as there would be with a normal loan. In addition, the overdraft is legally repayable on demand (if necessary).

Lines of credit

Here the bank agrees to allow the client to borrow up to a maximum sum for periods such as a month, 3 months or 6 months. The rate of interest will be related to the interbank rate. The client can then repay and reborrow if required.

Bankers' acceptances

Here the bank agrees to accept bills of exchange up to a maximum figure – 'acceptance credits'. The bank accepts a bill and may also discount it, or the client may discount it with another bank. If the bill is, say, 1 month, the client is expected to repay but may do so by means of discounting another bill. If the bank discounts the bill, it may keep it on its books or sell it itself in the discount market. The best bills are bank bills or eligible bills. These bills

- are recognized as top quality by the central bank and
- must represent a genuine trade transaction and one of a type not excluded, for example property and insurance.

Eligible bills are eligible for sale to the central bank in its role of lender of last resort. As a result, they are highly liquid.

There are some bills signed by a bank *not* on the central bank list, and these are known as ineligible bank bills. There are also bills signed by the trader, known as trade bills.

However, the trader may be more creditworthy than some banks on the central bank's list. Nevertheless, the central bank still won't rediscount them.

The above three types of facility are not committed. They are also usually 'self-liquidating'. For example, a bill matures in 1 month and is repaid. The loan is often to support the working capital required for debtors and/or stocks. For example, a swimsuit manufacturer begins producing well before the season – stocks are built up and wages must be paid. As the swimsuits are sold, cash flows in and loans can be repaid.

Committed Facilities

The loan facilities here are typically for 1 year or more. The bank is committed to lend, there are formal loan agreements and a structure of fees. There are three main types and one special case – project finance.

Term loans

The term loan is typically up to 5 years but may be up to 7. The loan is amortized over the period, that is, the borrower pays back in stages, although there may be an initial 'grace' period. Sometimes the loan is payable in full at the end of the period – this is bullet repayment. The interest is floating rate, linked to the interbank rate. The money borrowed cannot be re-lent when part is repaid.

Standby credit

Here, the loan can be drawn down in stages or tranches without losing the availability of the undrawn section. Once repaid, however, the money cannot be reborrowed. It tends to be much shorter term than a term loan and may support other anticipated borrowings, for example commercial paper. The standby credit may not even be drawn if the 'normal' borrowing method is successful.

The programme will be broken down into the total maximum commitment, the used amount and the unused. Thus, a $200m programme can be drawn down in tranches, but repayments cannot be reborrowed. The banker's schedule over time might be as shown in Table 4.4.

▼ Table 4.4 *Drawing banker's commitment down in tranches*

Date		Total commitment $m	Used $m	Unused $m
1/1	Agreement	200	–	200
2/1	Borrows $75m	200	75	125
31/1	Borrows $25m	200	100	100
12/2	Repays $50m	200	100	100
1/5	Borrows $100m	200	200	–
1/7	Repays $100m	200	200	–
1/10	Repays $50m	200	200	–
1/1	Expiry	–	–	–

Note: Interest is floating rate linked to the interbank rate – LIBOR, EURIBOR or, in the US, 'prime rate'.

Revolving credit

With revolving credit, not only can the loan be drawn in tranches but, if repayments are made, the borrower can repay up to the limit, that is, the funds can be reused. Thus, the commitment is said to 'revolve' – the borrower can continue to request loans provided the committed total is not exceeded. The client gives the bank the appropriate notice and then reborrows within the terms of the agreement. If the amount were $200m, we can see the difference between this and the standby credit when we study a similar loan/repayment schedule in Table 4.5.

▼ Table 4.5 *Loan/repayment schedule*

Date		Total commitment $m	Used $m	Unused $m
1/1	Agreement	200	–	200
2/1	Borrows $75m	200	75	125
31/1	Borrows $25m	200	100	100
12/2	Repays $50m	200	50	150
1/5	Borrows $100m	200	150	50
1/7	Repays $100m	200	50	150
1/9	Borrows $75m	200	125	75
1/10	Repays $100m	200	25	175

Note: Interest is a floating rate linked to the interbank rate.

Generally, these loans are unsecured. If bankers take security, it could well be one of the following: property, accounts receivable, plant/equipment, bonds/shares, bills of lading or inventories.

If the money is raised in the London market, the loans are floating rate 'linked to LIBOR' (London Interbank Offered Rate). But what is LIBOR? To begin with, LIBOR fluctuates throughout the day. For the purposes of loan agreements, LIBOR is that stated by the reference bank(s) at 11.00 a.m. If the loan is bilateral, it may simply be the lending bank's own LIBOR at 11.00 a.m. on the quarterly or 6-monthly day on which the loan is 'rolled over' at a new rate of interest. If it is a syndicated loan, three 'reference' banks may be nominated, and LIBOR is the average of the three. It may also be quoted as the 'BBA', or, colloquially, the 'screen rate'. The British Bankers' Association lists 16 reference banks for major currencies, such as dollar, euro and sterling. Reuters omits the 4 highest and 4 lowest of the 16 quoted rates and averages the remaining 8. Reuters disseminates this on its dealing screens at 11.00 a.m. each day, hence the reference to the 'screen' rate. LIBOR, of course, may be sterling, dollar, yen or any other currency. If the currency is the euro, it is Euro LIBOR, not to be confused with EURIBOR, which is the interbank market in euros of the 18 countries of the eurozone.

A term often used in the loan documentation for standby and revolving credit is 'swingline facility'. Sometimes the borrower is due to repay investors in, say, dollars on a particular day and discovers late in the day that she cannot. Swingline is a guarantee of same-day dollars in New York to meet this emergency need. (It may not be dollars, but dollars seem to be common.) One banker has described this as 'belt and braces' and as reassuring to credit ratings organizations looking at an issuer's loan facilities.

As the bank commits to lend, whether the user draws it all or not, and as there is a formal agreement, there are fees involved.

There will be a front end, or facility, fee for setting up the arrangement. There will also be a commitment fee. For example, a bank supports a 3-year standby credit facility for $50m that is never used. The bank has committed some of its loan capacity and used up capital under capital ratio rules. As a result, commitment fees are often charged on the undrawn amount. They are typically 50% of the lending margin. The margin is the spread over LIBOR charged on the drawn amount itself, for example LIBOR + 50 basis points (bp; a basis point = 0.01%).

There are variations for commitment fees by which they may be charged on the whole facility or on the drawn amount *and* the undrawn amount (but at different rates). A recent loan to the Saudi-European Petrochemical Corporation referred to 25 bp on drawn balances and 12.5 bp on undrawn balances.

As we have seen in Chapter 3, the central bank may make all banks deposit some of their eligible liabilities with the bank, and pays them no interest. As bankers relend their deposits, they regard this as a cost of lending and will seek to recoup this.

Project finance

Project finance is simply a special case of a term loan. It is 'special' in that the projects are typically of much longer duration than the conventional term loan, and usually much more complex to structure. They are large-scale exploration or construction projects (for example the Eurotunnel, the bridge over the Bosphorus and similar projects) and require complex and time-consuming loan arrangements. In particular, a guarantee from a government or parent body may not be available (the banks' recourse is to the flow of funds from the project, called 'limited recourse financing'), in which case the banks will want to see a full set of revenue projections to ensure that debt repayments can be met. They may also wish to see firm contracts for the construction project itself and (if possible) firm contracts for the sale of the completed service.

Recent projects include a 10-year $400m facility for Neste Petroleum, a wholly owned subsidiary of a Finnish state-owned oil company; a $1.1bn facility for oil exploration for BP Norway; $600m for North Sea oil developments for Agip (UK), part of the Italian state-owned oil group; and £795m for Teesside power station. In the case of Neste, although there is no explicit guarantee, there is a tacit understanding that the parent will support the subsidiary. The Agip loan will be supported by the parent for 2 years but will revert to limited recourse thereafter.

Project finance was booming until the credit crisis reached its calamitous peak in autumn 2008, virtually disappearing until mid-2009. It is gradually re-emerging, but for smaller amounts, at a higher cost and with shorter durations than in recent years. Prior to the crisis, a typical project finance syndication loan used to last 15–20 years and pay 100 bp – or less – LIBOR. In June 2009, Qatar's Nakilat raised $949m to pay for liquefied natural gas ships. Financing deals for three other large projects – $1.7bn for Bahrain's Addur power and water project and 2 multibillion dollar deals in Abu Dhabi – were also expected to be finalized by the end of the summer. The $1.7bn raised by Addur will last for 8 years and pay 350 bp over LIBOR. Various commentators have said that international banks are unlikely to lend for more than 10 years and for less than 250 bp plus LIBOR in the current climate. A 2014 OECD report, entitled *Financing Infrastructure – International Trends*, notes that because of the tougher regulatory environment for banks, institutional investors are now playing a much bigger role in global project finance. Banks used to finance about 90% of a projects cost through debt, but this has now fallen closer to 65%.

Syndicated Facilities

Syndicated loans arise because a bank does not wish to take on the whole amount of the loan. The task of syndication is also made easier by the fact that there are many banks that will be happy to take on some of the loan exposure at a second stage – banks that may not have a close relationship with major corporates or may not have the resources to compete at the primary stage.

Syndicated loans (sometimes involving as many as 100 banks) were common in the 1970s, when we saw 'petrodollars' recycled in loans to sovereign borrowers and multinationals. This led to the LDC (less developed country) debt crisis, following Mexico's default on its debt repayments in August 1982 (see Chapter 7). The volumes of large international syndicated loans fell somewhat for several years but recovered later. Many banks found that weakened balance sheets and capital ratio constraints made further loan expansion difficult. One result was the rise in popularity after 1982 of new types of syndicated facility – NIFs and RUFs.

NIFs and RUFs

The 1980s became the era of the acronym – NIFs and RUFs, and later MOFs and many others. It was also a time of great competition, especially from Japanese banks. In 1986, the then chairman of Barclays accused the Japanese of 'dumping money', just as people had accused them of dumping goods in the 1920s and 1930s. NIF is 'note issuance facility'; RUF is 'revolving underwriting facility' (ask six bankers what the difference is, and you will get six different answers); and MOF is 'multiple option facility'.

The 1980s also saw an increasing use of tender panels of banks, bidding competitively for loan business or bankers' acceptances. For example, a corporate that frequently used bill finance would periodically approach a tender panel to accept bills. This gave us yet another acronym – the RAFT, 'revolving acceptance facility by tender'.

NIFs and RUFs were facilities by which banks agreed to support note issues by corporates to raise money. The notes were usually called Euronotes and were typically 1, 2 and 6 months. In effect, they were a sort of short-term Eurobond. On a revolving basis, the arranging bank would approach a tender panel to buy the client's notes. In the event that the notes could not be sold at or below a given lending rate, a further panel of underwriting banks stood by to lend the money. The facility was thus underwritten. It was, therefore, a mixture of commercial and investment banking techniques. Fees could be earned, and US commercial banks could join in without contravening the 1933 Glass-Steagall Act. During the period 1982–86, NIFs, RUFs and Euronotes were all the rage.

Today, the formal 1-, 3- and 6-month Euronote has disappeared, its modern equivalent being either Eurocommercial paper (ECP) or medium-term notes. (The Bank of England uses Euronotes as a generic term for short-term euro paper, whether euro certificate of deposit or ECP.)

MOFs

From 1986–87, a more flexible facility – the multiple option facility (MOF) – appeared. Instead of committing the underwriting banks to support one type of borrowing only (for example Euronotes), the banks' commitment is to a range of possibilities. The 'multiple options' might be bank loan (multicurrency), acceptances, commercial paper – domestic, ECP.

On a revolving basis, the arranging bank would approach a tender panel of banks for prices for either a bank loan or banker's acceptance to meet the client's need for, say, $10m for 3 months. At the same time, the arranging bank would contact commercial paper dealers to check rates for the same deal. The bank would then report back to the client and use the most attractive option. However, if the best option was above a given borrowing rate, a panel of underwriting banks would agree either to lend the money or sign acceptances at the agreed figure. At first this seemed to be the sort of flexible facility that the market needed, and MOFs were all the rage for several years. Later, problems emerged.

To begin with, bank supervisors saw this as a clear off-balance sheet risk and demanded capital cover. Suppose, for example, that the rate at which the underwriting panel would guarantee to lend was LIBOR + 50 bp. The supervisors argued that if the market demanded a higher figure, this might suggest that the client was less creditworthy. The underwriting panel was forced to lend to a client whose credit quality was declining. The Bank of England decided that 50% of the unused capacity must be treated as if the money had actually been lent, for capital ratio purposes. The Bundesbank took a less harsh view. Later, the rules were harmonized through the Basel agreement. The first disadvantage, therefore, was that the banks had to provide capital to back MOFs, although initially they hadn't.

The recession produced other problems. To begin with, the credit quality of many clients did indeed deteriorate, leaving the underwriting banks 'holding the baby'. Second, due to poor trading, many clients broke the loan covenants (see later). If covenants are broken, the whole agreement can be renegotiated, but *all* the banks must agree the revised terms. Sometimes, one or two banks with the smallest commitment might not agree. In a well-known incident in 1989, Laura Ashley was nearly pushed into liquidation in these circumstances.

Finally, the market became less competitive – a lenders' not a borrowers' market. In part, this was due to the departure of the Japanese. The stock market in Tokyo collapsed in January 1990, and property values fell. The Japanese drew in their horns. In 1989, they accounted for 37% of all international bank lending in foreign currencies (BIS figures). In December 2008, the figure was 5%. The departure of the Japanese, capital ratio constraints and the recession now put the banks in the driving seat. They were no longer willing to be pushed into tender panels and unattractive deals. In London, margins over LIBOR widened as a consequence. Corporates, too, saw the problems. Beating down the banks to tight margins was one thing. Expecting them to be sympathetic when the going got rough was quite another. There was much talk of 'relationship banking' – of this, more later. The OECD, in its *Financial Market Trends* for June 1992, commented on the change in the syndicated credit market and the fall in the number of syndicated facilities:

> [U]ncertainties about the creditworthiness of many potential borrowers added to the caution of financial institutions engaged in a process of profit enhancement and asset quality consolidation.

With the end of the early 1990s' recession in the West, banks were flush with cash again in 1995, and although the MOF concept had largely disappeared, margins on loans fell again. Then, the 1997–98 global crises led to margins rising yet again. For example, Powergen of the UK raised a £2.4bn 5-year loan in mid-1998 to purchase East Midlands Electricity at a rate of 50 bp over LIBOR. However, its previous syndicated loan had been at 22.5 bp over LIBOR. Equally, the bid for InterContinental Hotels by Bass was funded by a $3bn syndicated loan at a range of margins over LIBOR (depending on the loan term). The range was 22.5–27.5 bp; its previous loan had a margin of 15 bp.

To make things more flexible, banks have organized a formal secondary market in which loan commitments may be sold off to other banks. Bank loans are frequently traded in the US, but until recently Europe was well behind. This particularly applies to what is called 'distressed debt'.

The Loan Market Association was set up in London by seven banks in December 1996. It now has a corporate membership of over 473 members, comprising banks, institutional investors, law firms, rating agencies and system providers, all engaged in the international syndicated loan markets.

ICI's $8.5bn syndicated loan in 1997 was a watershed, as $1bn was traded within 6 months.

A code of conduct was issued for trading distressed debt in March 1999. This category included, for example, Disneyland Paris and Eurotunnel. The risky loan has become just another product.

Syndicated loans are usually more flexible than bond issues. The money can be drawn down as needed, and arrangements may be made more quickly. The latter can be important in takeover bid situations.

The global syndicated loan market grew dramatically before the credit crunch hit. The market stood at $4,500bn in 2007, an increase of 13% over 2006 and 32% over 2005. According to data from the BIS, global syndicated lending collapsed by over 46%, to $1,471bn in 2008. The number of deals signed also fell. Trading volumes and primary new issuance declined around two-thirds in 2008 because of the deteriorating financial climate and growing concerns over the global economy. During 2009, syndicated lending further declined in importance, with just over $1 trillion of new credits made. These were mainly used for three things: financing M&A; refinancing existing facilities; and stressed refinancing, where companies in trouble need to restructure their capital. For example, Spain's Gas Natural arranged an $18.3bn loan to take a majority stake in the utility Union Fenosa. The Italian utility Enel also arranged an $8bn loan to part-finance the acquisition of a 25% stake in Endesa, the Spanish utility. A different story emerges in 2010 with a major rebound in lending up to $1,724bn mainly because of bank and firm refinancing – an estimated 45% of new credits were attributed to firms (particularly banks) reorganizing their capital structure, replacing bond with syndicated loan borrowings. This trend has continued through 2011 and 2013.

Terminology

The facilities we mentioned earlier – term loans, standby credits and revolving credits – are usually syndicated. This leads to a variety of terms being used as illustrated in Box 4.5.

BOX 4.5

Terms Used in Syndicated Loan Facilities

1 **Arranger/lead manager:** Initially, the 'arranging bank', or lead, manager deals with the client and discusses the probable terms on which a loan can be arranged. He advises the borrower on the loan structure, maturity and covenants. The arranger coordinates the participation of other lenders. It may be, however, that a 'book-runner' is appointed, whose job is to do the 'leg work' of putting a syndicate together. Once the syndicate is together, the book-runner's role is finished. One way or another, once initial discussions with the client are concluded, an invitation is issued to co-managers to participate.

2 **Co-managers:** Along with the arranging bank, they agree to underwrite the loan so that the client is now guaranteed the funds. Each co-manager takes a share, for example $200m.

3 **Participating banks:** They now join the syndicate. A co-manager will invite perhaps four participating banks to take, say, $25m of the loan each.

4 **The agent:** The role of the bank acting as the agent bank is critically important, and a special fee is earned. The agency is an administrative role. The agent collects the loan from each participant and passes it to the borrower. Equally, the borrower payments are passed to the syndicate in agreed shares. The agent notifies the borrower of the new interest rate related to the interbank rate every 3 or 6 months as agreed. The agent is responsible for the documentation and will notify both borrower and lender of all information relevant to the loan agreement. There is no credit risk, but there is still risk. If the agent makes a mistake that loses the syndicate members money, they will be responsible for making this good.

As in the case of a bilateral loan, there will be various fees:

1 **Facility or front end fee:** For agreeing to the arrangement, there will be a front end, or facility, fee for all involved. This may be a flat fee or a percentage of the money. The arranging bank will also take an extra fee for their special role. This is called a *praecipium*.

> ## Terms Used in Syndicated Loan Facilities (*continued*)
>
> 2 ***Underwriting fees:*** These are paid to the group of underwriting banks that took on the initial commitment prior to extending the syndicate. There is a definite risk. In the case of the management buyout of Magnet Joinery, for example, a small group of lead banks led by Bankers Trust found themselves alone, as the potential syndicate members withdrew their support, sensing that the risk was unacceptable – very wisely as it happened.
>
> 3 ***Agent's fee:*** This is paid to the agent bank for the role they play, which was described earlier.
>
> 4 ***Commitment fee:*** This was mentioned before in the case of bilateral loans. It is a payment measured in basis points for the commitment to lend, which needs to be backed by capital. As we have seen, it may be based on the whole loan, the drawn section or the undrawn section (or a mixture). Usually the fee is on the undrawn section and typically 50% of the margin.
>
> 5 ***Loan margin:*** This is the actual margin over the interbank rate charged for the borrowed money, for example, LIBOR + 50 bp. It may not be a constant figure, but related to loan tranches taken by the syndicate.

In most syndications, commitment fees usually comprise around 50% of the margin, any variation is possible. For example, the German Thyssen Group arranged a $1.2bn, 7-year revolving credit facility. There was a front end fee of 8 bp, and the margin over LIBOR varies according to how much of the facility is used, for example 10 bp if less than 33% of the loan, but 20 bp if more than 66% is used.

The NIFs, RUFs and MOFs were all forms of revolving credit. In general, loans, standby credit, revolving credit and project finance are likely to involve syndicates, unless they are of a modest size.

The fierce competitive battles of the 1980s, however, led to much talk of 'relationship banking' and bilateral agreements.

Relationship banking

The inference here is that the corporate encourages a close relationship with a small number of banks and may negotiate bilaterally.

Bilateral agreements, however, can really only be used by corporates with skilled treasury departments with large resources, unless the number of banks is small. The work done by the agency bank in policing the loan should not be underestimated. A 30-bank syndicate means, for the corporate, one line of communication – the agent bank, which does the rest, whereas 30 bilateral agreements mean 30 lines of communication – one with each bank.

The Loan Agreement

If the loan is syndicated, there will be one loan agreement and one set of terms, but the amount owed to each borrower is a separate debt.

The loan agreement will typically have four sections:

1   *Introduction:* This will cover the amount of the loan and its purpose, conditions of drawdown and particulars of the participating banks.
2   *Facilities:* The loan may be drawn down in separate tranches with different terms on interest and repayment. The procedures for drawing down will be covered.
3   *Payment:* This covers the interest calculations, calculation of the interbank rate, repayment arrangements, fees, or any similar charges.
4   *Provisions:* To protect the bank, there will be covenants, events of default, procedures if basic circumstances change.

The final documentation is sent to the agent bank prior to drawing the money. The agent must ensure that the documentation embodies that which was agreed.

Covenants

These are designed to protect the bank if the 'health' of the borrower changes. If covenants are breached, the banks' commitment will cease. The loan will have to be rescheduled. The usual covenants are as follows:

- *Interest cover:* This is the relationship between profit (before tax and interest) and interest. This is to ensure that there is a comfortable margin over the loan interest. If there is not, how can the borrower repay the principal? Sometimes cash flow may be used instead of profit. After all, profit is not cash.
- *Net worth:* Suppose all assets were sold and liabilities paid – what is left? Normally, this should be the figure of share capital and reserves ± current profit/loss, minus goodwill, tax and dividends to be paid. The agreement stipulates a minimum net worth.
- *Total borrowing:* This will be limited and must cover hire purchase, finance leases and 'puttable' capital instruments (see Chapter 7).
- *Gearing:* Long-term debt to capital as defined in net worth above – a maximum ratio will be stated.
- *Current ratio:* A minimum figure will be given for the ratio of current assets to current liabilities – a measure of liquidity.

Events of default

Events of default is a list of circumstances in which the loan will be regarded as being in default, for example insolvency, change of ownership or similar circumstances. A cross-default clause is important. This means that defaults on other loans or bonds will also cause this loan to be in default.

Negative pledge

Here the client undertakes not to offer security against a loan from any other party.

Assignment

One of the syndicate banks may assign part of its loan commitment to another bank. This cannot be done without the borrower's consent, but the loan agreement usually says that 'such consent may not be unreasonably withheld'. However, there may be an initial delay in selling off any of the loan.

Subparticipation

A subparticipation simply means that part of a syndicate bank's loan allotment will be lent to them by another bank and interest payments passed on to this bank. The loan agreement with the client is not affected.

Transfer or assignment

With a transfer or assignment, the loan documentation changes, the borrower is aware of the change, and the assignee is now legally the lender for this portion. Borrowers may worry here about not having a close relationship with the assignee if they hit trouble later.

Why sell part of the loan? Capital ratio rules may make new lending difficult. A transfer would free part of the loan to be lent elsewhere, possibly more profitably. Alternatively, in order to improve capital ratio, the money may not be re-lent. If capital is no problem, the money may simply be released to take advantage of a more profitable opportunity. With a participation, we may be able to take, say, LIBOR + 22 bp from the client and pass on LIBOR + 20 bp, 'skimming' a little profit.

In the UK, subparticipation and assignment are subject to detailed regulations (Bank of England, 1989).

WHOLESALE BANKING ISSUES

The key problem for commercial banks is that corporate lending is increasingly unrewarding and becoming a shrinking market. Competition has forced loan charges down to scarcely profitable levels. The growth of international capital markets is such that bond and equity issues over the last decade or so have increased their share at the expense of bank loans. The position has been exacerbated by the arrival of the euro. A single market for corporate bonds denominated in the euro for 18 countries has hastened the substitution of bond issues for corporate loans in mainland Europe, which has so far been a market where bank loans have traditionally been a more popular source of finance than bond issues.

One consequence of this has been a move to riskier but potentially more profitable loans. There are far more loans to either non-investment-grade corporates or to hedge funds and private equity funds (see Chapter 9), which themselves are taking large risks. Indeed, a survey in October 2005 by Close Bros Corporate Finance, an independent, European corporate finance adviser, accused the banks of encouraging private equity groups to take on too much debt. Corporate debt generally is increasing. Attracted by low interest rates, corporates are borrowing to buy back equity. Another consequence of this pressure on profit from lending is to take high-quality but low-margin loans off the balance sheet and sell them as securities – a process we explain in Chapter 7.

Increased competition in wholesale banking business, especially from the capital markets, has encouraged many large commercial banks to expand via acquisition into investment banking. Early examples of such deals include Deutsche Bank and Bankers Trust; Swiss Bank Corporation and Warburg Dillon Read; and ING and Barings. These moves have not always met with success. In the UK, both Barclays and National Westminster Bank lost a great deal of money through their investment banking subsidiaries and made heavy cuts in their involvement. But Barclays narrowed its investment banking down to the debt markets with Barclays Capital. This was extremely successful. Barclays' results for 2008 showed Barclays Capital making over 40% of total bank profit, while retail earnings were pretty flat – an exception perhaps. Since 2010, however, returns from investment banking have been poor and many big banks, including Barclays, are significantly reducing these activities. Commercial banking and investment banking are different cultures, and merging them can cause severe problems. The belief seems to be that the bank should offer clients the full range of services, but do clients really care? Clients frequently use one bank for bond issues and another for corporate loans, and fail to see any particular disadvantage.

Having said this, however, over the past decade or so, banks' involvement in markets via investment banking activity has increased dramatically, partly as a reflection of the trend towards universal banking and also because technological advances have made it easier to price and trade an increasingly broad array of highly profitable, complex financial products. Banks have experienced an increasing dependence on financial markets, not only as a funding source but also for risk management (hedging) purposes and for undertaking various transactions, including the trading of syndicated loans and other credits as well as securitized issues. What has emerged is a complex web of interdependence between banks and markets. Banks have increasingly used securitization techniques to move credit off their balance sheets but also to fund a lending explosion. Since the start of the credit crunch, when interbank lending and securitized markets collapsed, investment and commercial bank failures soon followed. This has led to a massive reappraisal by bankers and policymakers of the activities of banks engaged in wholesale lending and capital markets business, discussed in Chapter 5.

SUMMARY

- *Commercial banks* are in the classic business of accepting deposits and making loans. The business is both retail (the general public, shops and small businesses) and wholesale (other banks, corporates and institutions).
- *Retail banking* covers current accounts, cheque facilities, savings accounts, credit cards and loan facilities, like overdrafts, personal loans and mortgages. Increasingly, Internet developments are leading to the spread of home banking.
- *Clearing of payments* may involve cheques or electronic payment systems. Cheques are expensive, and banks have been trying to reduce their use through Internet banking, the use of debit cards and, in some countries, e-money.
- Key issues in retail banking today relate to the need to raise capital and liquidity, executive pay, how to manage risks better, growing competition, cost control, sales of non-banking products and the use of IT. Growing links between banks and insurance companies have led to the term *bancassurance*.

- *Wholesale banking* covers bank lending to larger entities than those met in retail banking and to activities described in other chapters – money markets and foreign exchange.
- *Loans* may be uncommitted or committed. *Uncommitted facilities* include overdrafts, lines of credit and bankers' acceptances. *Committed facilities* include term loans, standby credit, revolving credit and project finance.
- *Syndicated loans* are common for large value domestic and cross-border business. There are arranging banks, co-managers, participating banks and agent banks.
- Various *fees* are involved – facility or front end fee, underwriting fees, agents fees and commitment fees. Finally, there is the loan margin.
- The *loan agreement* covers the amount of the loan, its purpose, draw down facilities, interest calculations and provisions.
- Among the provisions will be *covenants*. These are designed to protect the bank if the financial position of the borrower worsens. They include interest cover, net worth, total borrowing, gearing and current ratio.

- Other provisions cover *events of default*. There will also be a negative pledge – the client undertakes not to offer security against a loan from another party.
- A bank may assign or transfer part of the loan to another bank or it may be a less formal *subparticipation*.
- Falling profit margins on corporate loans have led many commercial banks into riskier lending. In addition, growing overlaps between wholesale banking and capital market activity through the trading of loans and related securitized products led to a boom in syndicated lending that peaked in 2007, and then collapsed with the onset of the credit crisis. Pricing has increased and maturities have shrunk. This increased overlap between banks and markets, and the wider range of services that could be offered, encouraged the largest commercial banks to become much more involved in investment banking, with disastrous consequences.

REVISION QUESTIONS/ASSIGNMENTS

1 Analyse the main payment services offered by banks, and highlight the recent trends in retail payments.
2 Discuss the key challenges faced by retail banks. Which challenges are considered the most important, and do these vary for banks in different parts of the world?
3 Examine how new technology impacts on retail banking activity. Why does Internet bank penetration vary so much in Europe?
4 What are the main differences between committed and uncommitted credit lines?

REFERENCES

Bank of England. (1989) *Notice to Institutions Authorised Under the Banking Act 1987, Loan Transfers and Securitisation*, No. BSD/1989/1. Legislation governing the syndication and securitization of loans.

Economist, The. (2010) Special Report on Financial Risk: The Gods Strike Back, 13–19 February: 1–14. Excellent review of risks faced by financial firms.

Walker Review. (2009) *A Review of Corporate Governance in UK Banks and Other Financial Industry Entities: Final Recommendations,* Walker Review Secretariat, London. UK government review examining governance issues in banking, covering the role of chairs and CEOs, exec and non-exec directors; remuneration, including bonuses; the role of risk officers and so on.

FURTHER READING

Casu, B., Girardone, C., and Molyneux, P. (2015) *Introduction to Banking* (2nd edn), FT/Prentice Hall, London. Introductory banking text with an international focus, used at all undergraduate levels.

Howells, P., and Bain, K. (2008) *The Economics of Money, Banking and Finance: A European Text* (4th edn), FT/ Prentice Hall, London. Undergraduate text covering the role of markets and institutions, with a monetary policy and European focus.

Matthews, K., and Thompson, J. (2014) *The Economics of Banking* (3rd edn), Wiley Finance, Chichester. Introductory/intermediate text on banking with an economics focus. Good on the theory of banking.

Investment Banking

INTRODUCTION

Chapter 4 highlighted the increasing overlap of commercial and investment banking and the problems both types of bank have suffered as a consequence of the credit crisis. However, we should recognize at the outset that 'commercial' and 'investment' banking do not exist in separate compartments. Some activities overlap and are carried out by both types of bank, for example accepting and discounting bills of exchange, interbank borrowing and lending, foreign exchange and some aspects of trade finance. Nevertheless, there are certain activities that would be regarded as clear 'investment' banking, for example underwriting share issues, and we shall discuss these in this chapter, as well as those activities that involve a certain amount of overlap. (The term 'merchant bank' has historically been the UK term for investment bank, but it has a far narrower meaning in the US.)

INVESTMENT BANKING

The range of activities of investment or merchant banks can be summarized as follows:

- Accepting
- Corporate finance
- Securities trading
- Investment management
- Loan arrangement
- Foreign exchange

Accepting

Although commercial banks accept bills of exchange nowadays, historically it was an investment bank activity. Chapter 2 mentioned the Medici bankers helping a Venetian firm to trade with one in London using a bill of exchange in 1463. During the Industrial Revolution in the UK, enquiries were received from firms all over the world. The role of the British (and Dutch) merchant banks in backing this trade with bills of exchange was of crucial importance. Indeed, until December 1987, the club of top UK merchant banks was called the Accepting Houses Committee.

Although bills of exchange can and are used in connection with inland business, their main use is for export/import business. An exporter sells goods for $100,000 to an importer. Their arrangement is that the goods will be paid for in 3 months, say, on 2 February 2012. The exporter makes out the bill of exchange and sends it to the importer to sign. The essence of the message is shown in Figure 5.1.

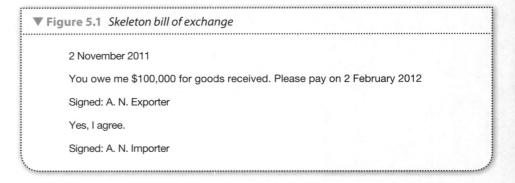

▼ Figure 5.1 *Skeleton bill of exchange*

2 November 2011

You owe me $100,000 for goods received. Please pay on 2 February 2012

Signed: A. N. Exporter

Yes, I agree.

Signed: A. N. Importer

As you can imagine, the actual document is rather more formal than this. Nevertheless, it expresses the basic idea. Notice that the *exporter* makes out the bill, that is, *draws* the bill. (There are similar documents used in international trade called 'promissory notes'. Here, the *importer* makes out the document and the exporter has less control over the wording.)

The importer now has 3 months to put the goods to work before paying. The exporter has an internationally acceptable form of debt. True, he has allowed the importer 3 months to pay (not necessary but very common), but his alternative choice might have been to send an invoice, optimistically headed by the words 'Payment terms – 30 days', with no real assurance that the money will be paid on time.

What if the exporter cannot wait 3 months, but needs the money earlier to fund cash flow? The exporter can visit the bank for a loan, armed with a heap of bills proving that cash is on the way. Alternatively, the exporter can sell the bill to a bank. The bank is being asked to put up the money now and to collect it from the importer in 3 months. As the bank is lending $100,000 for 3 months, it is not going to give the exporter all $100,000, but some lower sum reflecting risk and the cost of money – say, $97,000. The bill is sold at a discount, thus this process is called discounting the bill. Figure 5.2 shows the process in diagrammatic form.

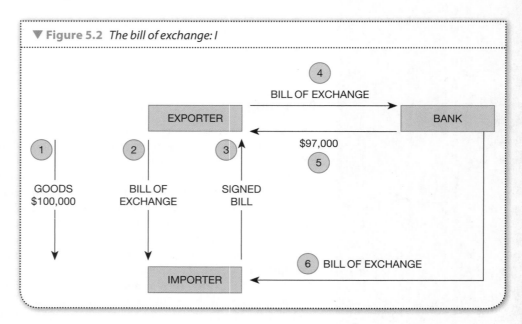

▼ Figure 5.2 *The bill of exchange: I*

The problem is that the bank may be unsure of the credit status of the trader and unwilling to discount the bill. As a result, the practice grew of asking the trader to find a merchant bank to sign the bill in its place. If, in the 19th century, the bill had been signed by Baring Bros, Rothschild or Hope & Co., the bank would have no hesitation in discounting the bill. Naturally, a fee was charged for this service, which is accepting the bill. (Whoever signs the bill, promising to pay, is accepting the bill. When people talk of 'acceptances', however, they usually refer to a bank's signature.) In effect, the bank is giving the bill its own credit status and not that of the trader; hence its importance in the Industrial Revolution. (The large number of bills in existence in 1890 whose acceptor was Baring Bros led the Bank of England to rescue it that year after unwise investments in Latin America. In 1995, however, there was no second rescue.)

We can find Josiah Wedgwood writing to an Italian customer in 1769:

My foreign correspondents name me a good house, generally in London, to accept my draft for the amount of the goods.

Or to Boulton and Watt in 1795:

We undertake no foreign orders without a guarantee being engineers not merchants (both quotes in Chapman, 1984).

Our previous diagram is now altered a little (see Figure 5.3).

Today, the whole procedure for trade finance is tied up by arrangements between the importer's bank and the exporter's bank. Usually, a documentary letter of credit is involved.

So far, we have discussed the bill in the context of an explicit trade transaction. The market in bankers' acceptances has reached a new level of sophistication today, especially in the London market. Major firms of good credit quality will ask their bank (whether investment or commercial) to accept a bill promising to pay a given sum at a future period of time. The corporate now discounts the bill in the local discount market as a way of borrowing money for trade in general rather than for an explicit transaction. Indeed, in London, firms like Harrods or Marks & Spencer will do this even though they are not selling on credit at all, but are retailers receiving cash.

Commercial banks are very involved with accepting bills, and this is one reason why the UK's Accepting Houses Committee disbanded in 1987. The committee would not

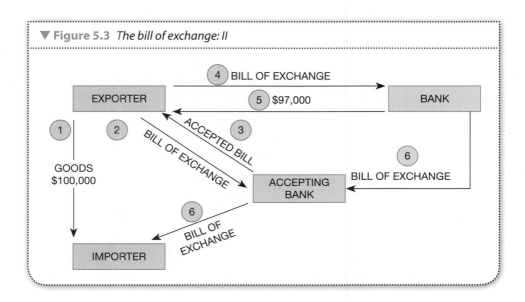

▼ Figure 5.3 The bill of exchange: II

include either commercial banks or foreign banks. This was seen to be completely out of date. In any case, accepting had ceased to be a dominant role for UK merchant banks.

Bills of exchange are used extensively in the UK, quite widely in Continental Europe generally and very little in the US. They are generally used for exports to the Middle East, East and Southeast Asia, the Indian continent, Australia and New Zealand.

Corporate Finance

Corporate finance is likely to be a department of major importance in any investment bank, managing the following:

- New issues – equities/bonds
- Rights issues
- Mergers and acquisitions
- Research

New issues

New issues of either shares or bonds involve pricing the securities, selling them to investors, underwriting and general advice regarding the regulations that must be followed. Close liaison with firms of lawyers and accountants is necessary, and their fees will be substantial, as well as those of the bankers.

Underwriting is an undertaking to buy any securities that the investors cannot be persuaded to buy. Fees will be charged (of course), and the risk will be spread among other merchant banks and investment institutions. One of the most dramatic incidents in modern times occurred when the UK government was selling off its remaining shares in BP to the public. Unfortunately, the market crash of October 1987 occurred after the price was fixed but before the offer closed. The issue was a failure, and the underwriters had to buy the shares at a substantial loss.

In the case of equities, the underwriters purchase the shares once it is clear that investors are not taking up their allocation. In the Eurobond market, on the other hand, the syndicate of underwriting banks buys the bonds from the issuer and then attempts to sell them to investors.

Rights issues

Rights issues (discussed in Chapter 8) also need to be priced and underwritten in case the market price falls below the offer price of the rights. Technically, BP was a rights issue, as some shares were already quoted but new shares were being created. The government was allowing the public to buy these shares.

The many privatizations in the newly emerging free markets of Central and Eastern Europe, the former USSR, China and India have created work for US and European investment bankers. Their advice and help are being sought for circumstances that have little precedent. The biggest names include Bank of America Merrill Lynch, Morgan Stanley, Goldman Sachs, JPMorgan Chase, Deutsche Bank and Barclays.

Mergers and acquisitions (M&A)

Firms planning a takeover will turn to investment banks for help and advice regarding price, timing, tactics and so on. Equally, the object of the takeover will turn to these bankers for help in fending off the predator. The fees involved can be substantial, and in a large takeover there may be three investment bankers or more on each side. Typically, M&A fees average between 0.125% and 0.5% of the target's value. Some fees depend on success, whereas others are linked to the premium achieved over the stock price of the company they are advising. There are also success fees and break fees for the banks on the losing side. When competition is intense, some companies will demand a limit on fees. In 2006, Indian steel-making giant Mittal's €18.6bn hostile bid for the European steel producer Arcelor generated fees of around $100m for the 14 investment banks involved. The successful €6bn bid by Linde (the German gas and engineering conglomerate) for UK's BOC generated $70m for the four banks advising Linde. M&A fee income amounted to 44% of total investment bank fee income in 2007 and since 2000 had never fallen below a third. However, M&A activity slumped in 2009, and over the year fee income from M&A business fell by around 33%, although the market returned to 2008 levels by the end of 2010. The volume of announced global M&A deals in 2013 increased to $2.9 trillion, according to Dealogic, with deals in the Americas accounting for 65% of this activity. Sectors that experienced the largest deals included the real estate, telecoms and health care. The private equity firms invested some $236.0bn in 2013, the highest amount since 2007 ($673.3bn). However, the 2013 volume was still only a third of the record high $694.0bn announced in 2006.

Many takeover bids or mergers, of course, are cross-border – notable past examples include RMC/Cemex Mexico, Allied Domecq/Pernod Banco Santander/Abbey National, UniCredito/HVB and the Mittal Steel/Arcelor deal. The biggest cross-border deal in 2013 was the $1305bn sale of Vodafone's 45% stake in Verizon Wireless to Verizon Communications, making it a wholly owned US firm. Figure 5.4 provides examples of this and other major M&A deals in 2013.

The top M&A houses in 2013 were Goldman Sachs, Morgan Stanley and JP Morgan, as can be seen in Table 5.1.

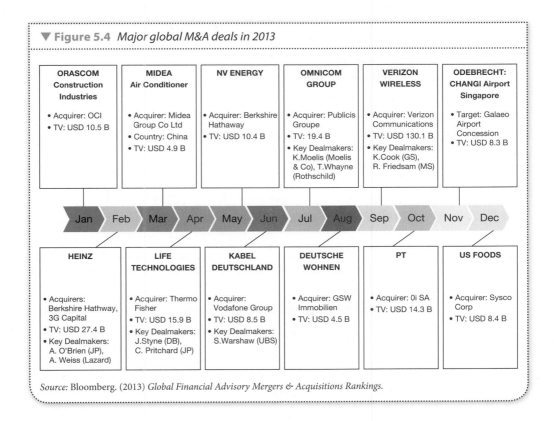

▼ **Figure 5.4** *Major global M&A deals in 2013*

ORASCOM Construction Industries
- Acquirer: OCI
- TV: USD 10.5 B

MIDEA Air Conditioner
- Acquirer: Midea Group Co Ltd
- Country: China
- TV: USD 4.9 B

NV ENERGY
- Acquirer: Berkshire Hathaway
- TV: USD 10.4 B

OMNICOM GROUP
- Acquirer: Publicis Groupe
- TV: 19.4 B
- Key Dealmakers: K.Moelis (Moelis & Co), T.Whayne (Rothschild)

VERIZON WIRELESS
- Acquirer: Verizon Communications
- TV: USD 130.1 B
- Key Dealmakers: K.Cook (GS), R. Friedsam (MS)

ODEBRECHT: CHANGI Airport Singapore
- Target: Galaeo Airport Concession
- TV: USD 8.3 B

Jan Feb Mar Apr May Jun Jul Aug Sep Oct Nov Dec

HEINZ
- Acquirers: Berkshire Hathway, 3G Capital
- TV: USD 27.4 B
- Key Dealmakers: A. O'Brien (JP), A. Weiss (Lazard)

LIFE TECHNOLOGIES
- Acquirer: Thermo Fisher
- TV: USD 15.9 B
- Key Dealmakers: J.Styne (DB), C. Pritchard (JP)

KABEL DEUTSCHLAND
- Acquirer: Vodafone Group
- TV: USD 8.5 B
- Key Dealmakers: S.Warshaw (UBS)

DEUTSCHE WOHNEN
- Acquirer: GSW Immobilien
- TV: USD 4.5 B

PT
- Acquirer: 0i SA
- TV: USD 14.3 B

US FOODS
- Acquirer: Sysco Corp
- TV: USD 8.4 B

Source: Bloomberg. (2013) *Global Financial Advisory Mergers & Acquisitions Rankings.*

▼ Table 5.1 *Top M&A advisers: Global announced deals in 2012 and 2013*

| Firm | 2013 | | | | 2012 | | Market share change |
	Rank	Market share	Volume USD m	Deal count	Rank	Market share	
Goldman Sachs & Co.	1	24.5	569,728	350	1	25.3	(0.8)
Morgan Stanley	2	21.1	491,145	291	2	21.4	(0.3)
JP Morgan	3	21.0	489,946	244	3	20.1	0.9
Bank of America Merrill Lynch	4	19.9	462,769	217	8	14.9	5.0
Barclays Capital Group	5	16.5	384,679	197	6	17.0	(0.5)
UBS AG	6	12.0	280,622	162	10	8.8	3.2
Citigroup Inc.	7	10.2	237,620	211	4	18.6	(8.4)
Deutsche Bank AG	8	9.7	226,864	156	7	16.4	(6.7)
Credit Suisse Group AG	9	8.7	203,582	211	5	17.1	(8.4)
Lazard Ltd	10	8.4	196,119	204	11	8.1	0.3
Moelis & Co	11	5.8	134,224	90	23	2.1	3.7
Guggenheim Capital LLC	12	5.7	132,825	2	-	-	5.7
PJT Capital LLC	13	5.6	130,100	1 -	-	-	5.6
BNP Paribas SA	14	5.3	122,617	101	15	4.4	0.9
Rothschild Ltd	15	4.3	100,396	184	9	9.7	(5.4)
Centreview Partners LLC	16	3.9	90,952	27	22	2.2	1.7
Evercore Partners Inc	17	3.7	85,949	110	13	5.5	(1.8)
RBC Capital Markets	18	3.3	77,600	150	14	5.1	(1.8)
Wells Fargo & Co	19	2.4	55,670	53	25	1.8	0.6
HSBC Bank PLC	20	2.1	49,385	62	17	3.3	(1.2)

Note: Includes mergers, acquisitions, divestitures, self-tenders and spinoffs. Excludes open market transactions. Total volume represents all announced transactions in US$ millions. Figures in brackets are negatives.

Source: Bloomberg. (2012, 2013) *Global Financial Advisory Mergers & Acquisitions Rankings.*

In the US, the notorious 'junk bond' era of the 1980s (Chapter 7) saw small companies raising huge sums with bonds to buy much bigger companies. (In the 1987 film *Wall Street*, the speech Gordon Gecko made to shareholders in his planned victim company was said to be based on an actual speech made by Ivan Boesky – who served a three-and-a-half-year jail sentence and paid $100m in fines in the late 1980s after being convicted for insider dealing by the SEC. He is reported to have coined the infamous phrase 'Greed is good'.) The fees earned by Drexel Burnham Lambert for bond issues and takeover bids during this era quickly made it one of the highest-earning firms on Wall Street (until its demise in 1990).

Certain jargon has come to be associated with takeover battles. If a takeover seems inevitable, the merchant bank may find a rival bidder who is preferable to the original predator. This more acceptable bidder is the white knight. For example, in April 1999, Telecom Italia, facing a hostile bid from Olivetti, turned to Deutsche Telecom as its white knight (a tactic that did not, however, succeed). Sometimes, one or two people can be found who will take a substantial minority holding and block the takeover. These are called white squires. When Lloyds Bank tried to take over Standard Chartered in 1986, the bid was blocked by holdings taken (separately) by a few entrepreneurs in Southeast Asia and Australia. As it happened, they did Lloyds a good turn, as subsequent Standard Chartered problems would have severely weakened a bank with a high reputation for profitability.

Sometimes, the white squire may become a 'Trojan horse'. When Britannia Arrow faced a hostile bid in 1985, it found a white squire in Robert Maxwell. Subsequently, he ousted the board and put in his own nominees.

Those who play computer games may be interested to hear of the Pacman defence, where the target firm turns around and tries to acquire the company that made the hostile takeover attempt. TotalFina, the Franco-Belgian group, launched a takeover bid for Elf Aquitaine, the French oil group in July 1999. Two weeks later, Elf Aquitaine made a counterbid for TotalFina.

Sometimes, the bidder may be persuaded to withdraw by the company buying back the shares at a higher price. This is called 'greenmail' (in contrast to blackmail). In 1986, Sir James Goldsmith, the Anglo-French entrepreneur, made an unpopular bid for the US tyre company, Goodyear Tire & Rubber Co. In the end, after an acrimonious fight, the firm bought Goldsmith and partners out. Goldsmith made $93m in the space of a few weeks. However, the incident damaged his reputation in the US, although he always denied the greenmail charge.

A popular defence against hostile takeover bids in the US is the so-called poison pill. This was invented by Martin Lipton, a top takeover lawyer, in 1980 and has been adopted by two-thirds of companies in S&P's 500 Index. Once one shareholder's stake rises above a given percentage (usually 20%), the poison pill device is triggered. This allows the company to give all shareholders – apart from the 20% holder – the right to buy new shares at a large discount, often 50%. This makes the bid prohibitively expensive.

In November 2004, Liberty Media raised its voting stake in News International (the main UK subsidiary of News Corp.) to 17%. The latter adopted a poison pill defence. If triggered, every shareholder except the bidder would be able to buy News International shares at half price, thus diluting the holding of the predator. A promise was made that this would be put to the shareholders for approval at the AGM in October 2005. In the event, Rupert Murdoch (chairman of News Corp.) announced that the poison pill would remain in place for a further 2 years after October 2005. The institutional shareholders were angry and threatened legal action. More recently, Yahoo put a poison pill defence in place to deter Microsoft's (unsuccessful) unsolicited $43bn bid in 2008.

Various governments have sought to introduce the use of poison pills to limit hostile takeover activity. For instance, in February 2006, the French government said that it was planning to allow French companies to use poison pills to frustrate a foreign bidder – not exactly in the spirit of the 'single market'. The South Korean authorities announced something similar in June 2009.

Up until mid-2007, M&A activity was buoyed by the continuing trend towards the globalization of industry and commerce and consolidation in specific industry sectors. However, as noted above, such activity has fallen dramatically in response to the downturn in economies caused by the credit crisis.

Research capability

Research capability is clearly essential in the corporate finance department if the bank is to be able to give advice and play a major role in raising new capital. The firm may be innovative and invent new variations on standard techniques, for example convertible capital bonds, perpetual variable rate notes, perpetual auction market preferred stock and similar instruments. Research may uncover potential victims for a takeover or give early identification of potential predators.

It is important to gain a good reputation for research. Periodically, surveys are carried out of fund managers, asking them to nominate the best houses for research. One of these is the Thomson Reuters Extel Survey, done each year in the UK, which ranks the top research teams. Individual sector analysts are also surveyed, and they and their teams often become the object of poaching by other houses.

General advice

General advice is always needed by the treasury departments of major firms. They will meet their merchant bankers regularly to discuss the outlook for exchange rates, interest rates, risk management and generally to help them to clarify their policies. Sometimes the client may be a government or quasi-government authority, for example the Saudi Arabian Monetary Agency.

Securities Trading

In corporate finance, we saw primary market activity – new issues and rights issues. Securities trading takes us into the secondary market dealing in the same equities and bonds. The trading takes place in one of the modern dealing rooms, with computer terminals and communications giving up-to-the-minute prices and contact with other dealers and investors all over the world. The dealings cover domestic bonds and equities and international bonds and equities. International bonds are discussed in Chapter 7. International equities are those of companies outside the domestic market where the investment bank is situated.

The old tradition in many countries (France, Belgium, the UK, Spain, Italy) has been to reserve domestic bonds and equities to stock exchange members, that is, they were not allowed to be owned by banks. Change began with London's Big Bang in October 1986 and spread to all the above markets. The result has been to allow banks access to these markets, breaking the previous monopolies. These banks are either pure investment banks, subsidiaries of commercial banks, or universal banks (see Chapter 2).

Alongside these traders are the experts in so-called 'derivative' products –options, futures, forward rate agreements and so on. We discuss these in later chapters, but they enable traders and their clients either to take a view on future price movements with less capital needed than if actually buying/selling the underlying instruments, or to hedge their risk. If a commercial bank has an investment bank subsidiary, the expertise in derivative products will be found in that subsidiary.

The traders in this department carry out a twofold role. They act on behalf of clients, some of whom may be in-house departments, and they take positions of their own – usually called 'proprietary trading'.

Investment Management

The investment funds these managers control may be the bank's own funds or they may be, in effect, 'looking after other people's money'. These may be

- High-net-worth individuals,
- Corporates,
- Pension funds or
- Mutual funds.

High-net-worth individuals

High-net-worth individuals may approach a commercial bank to handle all their affairs, including investments. In Chapter 2, we called this 'private banking'. They could also approach an investment bank to handle their spare funds, but a minimum sum will be stated. This type of business is also handled by stockbrokers, but with lower minimum sums than an investment bank would require.

Corporates

Corporates may either have good cash flow and wish to pay someone else to handle their investments or may build up a large 'war chest', ready for some takeover activity later, and temporarily pay an investment bank to handle this. The entity need not be a conventional corporate as such. An excellent example is the Saudi Arabian Monetary Agency.

Pension funds

Where economies have pension funds, for example the US, the UK, the Netherlands, Switzerland and Japan, they may feel that they lack the skill to manage the funds and may pay others to do so. In these economies, pension funds are usually the biggest clients of the investment management department.

Mutual funds

Mutual funds are discussed in Chapter 8. They are collective investments in money market instruments, bonds or equities. The bank may run its own fund and advertise its attractions to small investors. In addition, it will manage mutual funds for others. Independent organizations provide regular statistics on fund performance, and if the manager has performed less well than comparable funds, they may find themselves being dismissed. This has led to charges of 'short-termism' in their investment decisions. However, as a director of one major fund commented to the author: 'The long run is the sum of the short runs. If we get them right, the long run will be right too.'

Typically, fund managers will charge a small percentage fee for handling the fund and the client will meet the costs such as the broker's commission. Competition for the investment banks comes from firms of independent fund managers, who specialize totally in this business, or large pension funds that will look after the money of smaller funds as well as their own.

The role of fund managers as investment institutions who influence stock market activity will be discussed in Chapter 8.

Loan Arrangement

Where there are complex syndicated loans for special projects, we may often find that the arranger is an investment bank. The bank is using its special skills to decide on the terms of the loan and the cheapest way to find the money. It could involve using the 'swaps' market, for example, which we explain in Chapter 15. Often, several potential teams may be competing for these major infrastructure projects, for example the Channel Tunnel, the Hong Kong airport or the bridge over the Bosphorus.

Outside large, complex projects, investment bankers will help clients to raise finance for international trade. In this, there is an overlap with a major commercial bank activity. It may be a question of knowing sources of cheaper finance for exporter or importer, for example a development bank, or even acting as an agent or middleman, such as an export house or confirming house – a specialist agency that purchases and arranges the export of goods on the behalf of overseas buyers.

Foreign Exchange

The foreign exchange markets are discussed in Chapter 11. Typically, we regard this as a commercial bank activity. However, investment banks that are permitted commercial bank functions will run a foreign exchange trading desk for their clients and their own proprietary trading, and it may be an important source of profit. We make the above comment about being 'permitted commercial bank functions' because of the differing regulatory positions in various countries, which we explain towards the end of this chapter.

US and Japanese investment banks have had a modest foreign exchange section, but there are exceptions; Goldman Sachs, for example, has become a major player in foreign exchange dealing. UK merchant banks, fully licensed as banks, will often see foreign exchange dealing as a major activity and will have a 'banking' department that will also offer deposit-taking functions to clients.

Miscellaneous Activities

There is a range of miscellaneous activities that may be carried out by investment banks, possibly through separate legal subsidiaries. Commodity trading (including derivatives trading), for example, is quite common, evidenced by the links between Citigroup and Phibro and also by Goldman Sachs that have a commodity dealing arm. Other activities include insurance broking, life assurance, leasing, factoring, property development, private equity and venture capital. This latter activity covers finance for new and growing companies that are not well enough established to attract money by equities, bonds or conventional bank loans. The venture capital company puts in a mixture of equity and loans and hopes to make large capital gains later when the firm obtains a flotation on the local stock exchange.

Many of these miscellaneous activities overlap with those of commercial banks, for example leasing, factoring, venture capital and commodity dealing.

INVESTMENT BANKS AND THE CREDIT CRISIS

As illustrated earlier in Table 5.1, the world's largest investment banks come from the US – including firms such as Goldman Sachs, JP Morgan and Morgan Stanley. Their main functions, as explained above, are to help companies and governments raise funds in the capital markets by issuing new debt and equity, which they arrange on behalf of clients. They also provide corporate advisory services on M&As and other types of corporate restructuring. They trade securities on their own account and on behalf of clients and also manage investments for institutional and retail (mutual fund) clients. Box 5.1 looks at the role of investment banks in the run-up to and aftermath of the credit crisis of 2007–8.

BOX 5.1

Investment Banks and the Credit Crisis

Since 1999 and the abandonment of the Glass-Steagall Act, various US commercial banks have acquired investment banks – Citigroup now includes the investment bank Salomon Brothers and the brokerage firm Smith Barney; and the commercial bank Chase is now linked to JP Morgan. This means that banks such as Citigroup and JPMorgan Chase now offer both commercial and investment banking services.

Like the major commercial banks, the top investment banks were heavily involved in the securitization business, including both trading and investment in property-backed instruments, such as prime and sub-prime mortgage-backed securities, and also various collateralized debt obligations. Defaults on sub-prime mortgages started to accelerate in 2006 and US property prices began to fall. As this gathered pace into 2007, both commercial and investment banks had massive portfolios of securities backed by this deteriorating collateral held on and particularly off-balance sheet.

Banks could not liquidate the securities as their complex structure and uncertain collateral meant that they were near impossible to value. Banks then stopped lending to one another as they knew that all other major investment and commercial banks held a great many of these securities but they had no idea as to what losses these investments had suffered and the level of such holdings in different banks. All in all, this led to a freeze in interbank lending and a collapse of liquidity in the system; banks needed this liquidity to fund their holding of medium- and long-term securitized assets. All this culminated in collapse.

So, despite its long and successful pedigree, the US investment banking industry hit crisis times:

Bear Stearns and Lehman Brothers failed in 2008.

Merrill Lynch merged with the Bank of America.

Goldman Sachs and Morgan Stanley converted into commercial banks (via the bank holding company route) in order to diversify their funding bases.

In mid-2009, of the largest US investment banks that existed at the start of 2007, none maintained the same corporate form.

The industry has been severely impacted by the turmoil and also blamed for the excesses that led to the crisis. By mid-2009, the write-downs and credit losses incurred by the top investment banks since the third quarter of 2007 were as follows: Merrill Lynch, $55.9bn; JPMorgan Chase, $41.2bn; Morgan Stanley, $22.7bn; and Lehman, $16.2bn.

Investment Banks and the Credit Crisis (*continued*)

Investment banking slowed dramatically in 2008 into 2009, and this trend reversed in 2010, only to fall back in 2011 to 2013 – Goldman Sachs posted an ROE of barely double figures in 2013, and in 2011, it had a return of only 5.8%, the second lowest profits figure it has ever posted since it was publicly listed in 1999. The weak performance reflects weak markets and trading conditions. This contrasts with the record ROE of 41.5% it made in the boom year of 2006.

Pressure on investment banks to boost their capital (see below) has resulted in many of the universal banks stating that they will be consolidating their activities. A 2012 report by Deutsche Bank notes that 'RBS, UBS, Credit Suisse, BNP, Soc Gen, Credit Agricole and Nomura' were cutting back, along with US counterparts like Bank of America Merrill Lynch.

The consolidation trend since 2007 has led to an increase in concentration in the sector. The top five firms in 2007 accounted for 25.36% of FICC (fixed income, currency and commodities) trading, whereas this had risen to over 50% by the end of 2013. Concentration of global equities trading had also increased around 5–47% over the same period.

REGULATION

We have seen that many commercial banks have investment bank subsidiaries and that universal banks do all kinds of banking. We have also seen that many activities overlap in commercial and investment banking and that it is not always possible to draw a clear distinction. As a result, one might conclude that the distinction between the two types of banking is not really significant. However, the two terms are widely used to characterize a bank's activities and culture, and perhaps to compare or contrast it with another bank, or again, to comment on the merits and relevance or 'fit' of an acquisition. Moreover, the two types of bank were, until recently, artificially separated by law in the two biggest markets of the world – the US and Japan.

When the Wall Street Crash occurred in 1929, US authorities concluded that by engaging in stock market activities, commercial banks might be risking depositors' money. They decided to remove this risk by passing the Glass-Steagall Act of 1933 – named after the chairmen of the relevant committees of the Senate and House of Representatives. This introduced a deposit protection scheme, gave the Federal Reserve Bank greater powers of supervision, and separated commercial and investment banking. A commercial bank could take deposits but could not underwrite any securities. An investment bank could handle underwriting of securities but could not take deposits. As a result, on the one hand, we had US commercial banks (Citibank, Chase Manhattan, Chemical, JP Morgan), and on the other, investment banks (Salomon Bros, Goldman Sachs, Merrill Lynch). JP Morgan continued as a commercial bank but passed investment banking to Morgan Stanley, now a separate bank. In London, the already weak links with Morgan Grenfell were then broken.

The whole affair, however, may have been based on a misreading of the position. George Bentson, professor of finance at Emory University in Atlanta, found that allegations that securities trading weakened banks had 'almost no basis in fact'.

As the Americans (as part of the Allied Powers) occupied Japan after the Second World War, they passed the same restrictions into Article 65 of the Japanese Exchange and Securities Code. As a result, we had the commercial banks (Dai-Ichi Kangyo, Mitsubishi, Sumitomo, Sakura) and, quite separate, the securities houses (Nomura, Daiwa and Nikko).

A similar law was passed in Italy in the early 1930s, leaving Italy with just one major investment bank, Mediobanca (partly state owned). In 1988, however, the law was repealed.

From 1987 onwards, there were several abortive attempts to repeal Glass-Steagall, but although there were bitter disputes in Congress again in 1999 over a new banking bill, these were eventually resolved, and Glass-Steagall was finally repealed by the Gramm-Leach-Bliley Act of November 1999.

In Japan, in a similar way, there were various limited moves from 1993 onwards, but in June 1997, the Ministry of Finance announced plans for complete deregulation by the year 2001.

As a consequence of this deregulatory process, the largest commercial banks have transformed themselves into full-service financial firms offering a full range of investment banking services and operating as universal institutions. Nowadays, the obvious consensus is that the increasing integration of commercial and investment banking, and the increased importance of markets, has led to too much risk – in fact, a systemic collapse (and nobody seemed to see it coming). As we noted in Chapter 2, (and will discuss in more detail in Chapter 6), the world's largest universal banks are being restricted from doing a range of activities in order to reduce the likelihood of another systemic crisis recurring. In brief, the 2010 Dodd-Frank Act in the US introduced the so-called Volcker Rule that prohibits commercial banks from proprietary trading and limits investments in hedge funds/private equity fund sponsorship to 3% of capital. Similar restrictions are being placed on UK banks via the recommendations of the Vickers Commission (the Final Report was published in September 2011), which seeks to ring-fence high-risk investment banking from low-risk retail banking.

Clearly, the sector will be subject to an ongoing barrage of legislation and regulations that will be put in place to limit such risks occurring again. However, it is by no means certain what type of regulatory framework is best for the new integrated investment bank/ commercial bank model. What is certain is that in the future, banks will be strongly constrained from acting as freely as they have been in the past. They will need to hold more capital and liquidity to back securitization and other market activity. New financial innovations will come under much greater regulatory scrutiny, and they will need to be much more transparent. The industry will remain relatively unprofitable compared with the 'glory days'. Other participants involved in securities activity closely linked to banks, such as hedge funds, private equity firms and rating agencies, will also be subject to much tougher regulatory oversight.

SHADOW BANKING

An interesting recent development has been the emergence of an array of non-bank financial institutions that undertake banking style business – this diverse group of firms has become known as the 'shadow banking' industry. Its name derives from the fact that the non-banks are doing banking type business but are not subject to banking regulation. The firms include an array of investment firms – such as hedge funds, private equity companies, insurance firms, other specialist investment firms and any company that does banking business but is technically not a bank. For instance, hedge funds lend to (usually risky) businesses (they financed the Glazer Brothers purchase of Manchester United Football Club, for instance); Coca Cola has lent money in the syndicated loan market; private equity firms lend to the businesses they buy out; and investment companies buy and sell securitized bank and other assets. This sector boomed in the run-up to the 2007–8 credit crisis, fell back when the bubble burst, but is now growing again as big banks cut back on lending. Details of shadow banking (noted earlier in Chapter 2) are also shown in Box 5.2.

BOX 5.2

Shadow Banking

Many of the firms involved in the asset securitization business – hedge funds, private equity firms, structured investment companies, money market funds – all fell outside traditional banking sector regulations and therefore could operate in an unregulated environment. This is now known as the shadow banking system that grew up in parallel with the securitization business.

Investment banks, and the securities arms of commercial banks, could fund securitization activity off-balance sheet by setting up separately capitalized companies and directing business through them.

The shadow banking web created enormous complexity in linkages between a widening array of financial firms that made it near impossible for regulators to oversee, or to put it another way, the business became increasingly opaque and outside the oversight and understanding of regulators.

▼ Table 5.2 *Who does shadow banking*

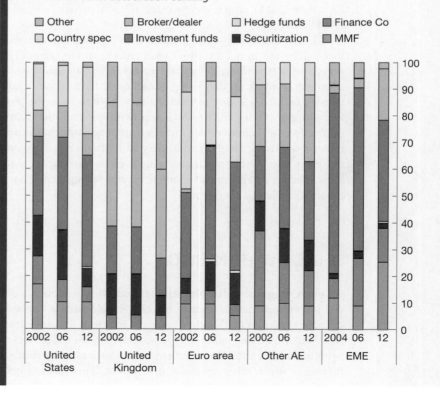

Shadow Banking (*continued*)

▼ **Table 5.3** *Size of shadow banking using alternative measures $ trillion*

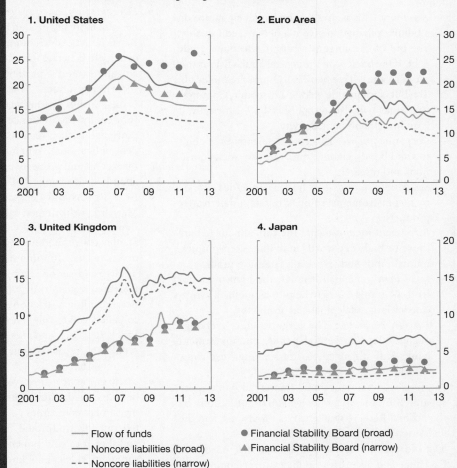

Source: IMF. (2014) Global Financial Stability Report, October, Chapter 2 Risk Taking, Liquidity and Shadow Banking Curbing Excess while Promoting Growth.

The volume of transactions in the US shadow banking system (by far the largest) grew dramatically after 2000, and by the end of 2008, it was believed to be larger than $10 trillion, although post crisis it declined substantially. By late 2009, the US shadow system had fallen to an estimated $6 trillion. The *Financial Times* reported that the 11 largest national shadow banking systems amounted to $50 trillion in 2007, declined to $47 trillion in 2008, but had increased to $51 trillion by 2011. The size of the worldwide shadow banking system is estimated to be around $60 trillion. Recent reports suggest that the UK shadow banking sector has doubled in size and nearly rivals traditional banks by 2014.

SUMMARY

- Investment banking activities can be summarized as follows:
  - *Accepting:* This is putting the bank's signature on a bill of exchange to give it a better credit quality. The bill of exchange is a promise to pay a trade debt. If the bank is on the central bank's list for this purpose, the bill is a *bank bill.* Others are *trade bills.* The bill is frequently sold at a discount. Commercial banks will also accept bills, but historically, it is an investment bank activity.
  - *Corporate finance:* This covers new issues of equities and bonds, rights issues, mergers and acquisitions and research.
  - *Securities trading:* The trading includes money market instruments, equities, bonds and derivative products.
  - *Investment management:* The funds managed are those of high-net-worth individuals, corporates, mutual funds and (especially) pension funds.
  - *Loan arrangement:* Although the bank may not lend the money, it may help to assemble a syndicate for large-scale financial products.
  - *Foreign exchange:* The large foreign exchange dealers are commercial banks, but investment banks will still need to run a foreign exchange section.
- In the US, investment and commercial banks were separated by the *Glass-Steagall Act,* but actions by the Federal Reserve weakened its provisions, and the legislation was repealed in 1999.
- The old Japanese restrictions of *Article 65* of the Exchange and Securities Code regarding commercial banking, investment banking and insurance have been swept away.
- Across Europe, banks that carry out both commercial and investment banking are called *universal banks.*
- *Deregulation* encouraged commercial banks to become more involved in investment banking activity. Banks became much more reliant on securities market activity to generate income, and this fuelled the securitization trend – particularly for mortgage-backed securities products. This, in turn, fuelled property prices, which encouraged more mortgage lending funded by the issuance of increasingly complex mortgage-backed securities (including collateralized debt obligations). When the crisis in the sub-prime market hit and property prices started to fall, the love affair between banks and securitization was over.
- Bear Stearns and Lehman Brothers failed in 2008, Merrill Lynch merged (also to avoid collapse) with Bank of America, and Goldman Sachs and Morgan Stanley converted into commercial banks in order to diversify their funding bases. The industry suffered its largest losses on record and has become subject to increased *regulatory oversight* that seeks to limit activities, including restrictions on proprietary trading (the so-called Volker rule) encompassed in the US Dodd-Frank 2010 Act, and *ring-fencing* of investment from retail banking as recommended by the UK's Vickers Commission.
- Many of the firms involved in the asset securitization business – hedge funds, private equity firms, structured investment companies and money market funds – all fell outside traditional banking sector regulations and therefore could operate in an unregulated environment. This is now known as the *shadow banking* system that grew up in parallel with the securitization business.

REVISION QUESTIONS/ASSIGNMENTS

1 Outline the main roles played by investment banks. Explain how their activities may complement traditional commercial banking.

2 Analyse the pros and cons of universal banking.

3 Discuss how the 2010 US Dodd-Frank Act and the recommendations of the UK Vickers Report will limit certain areas of investment banking activity.

4 Examine the key differences between investment and commercial banking. Explain why investment banking is considered inherently more risky.

REFERENCE

Chapman, D. (1984) *The Rise of Merchant Banking*, Allen & Unwin, London. Detailed historical perspective on the emergence of merchant/investment banks in the UK.

FURTHER READING

Coggan, P. (2015) *The Money Machine: How the City Works* (7th edn), Penguin, London. Covers the history of finance in the City of London and explains the key markets and institutions.

Fleuriet, M. (2008) *Investment Banking Explained: An Insider's Guide to the Industry*, McGraw-Hill, New York. Introductory, yet insightful text explaining key terms and strategies of investment banks.

Morrison, A.D., and Wilhelm, W.J., Jr. (2008) *Investment Banking: Institutions, Politics, and Law* (2nd edn), OUP, Oxford. Examines the theory of investment banking from a historical perspective. Focuses on the capital accumulation and allocation features of investment banking. Intermediate and academic.

Pozsar, Z., Tobias, A., Ashcraft, A., and Boesky, H. (2012) *Shadow Banking*, Federal Reserve Bank of New York Staff Reports, Report No. 458, Revised February 2012. Seminal study on the shadow banking system. Unbelievably complex; provides detailed diagrams of the shadow banking system – worth a look.

Regulation

AFTER THE CRISIS

Since the wave of government-backed bank bailouts, recapitalization plans, liquidity injections and credit guarantee schemes promulgated by the financial crisis, there have been widespread policy concerns about the business models pursued by banks and how they were regulated. Large-scale banking rescues have raised serious concerns about the social and economic costs of 'too big to fail' (TBTF) or 'too systemically important to fail'. Some small banks such as the UK's Northern Rock were rescued because it was perceived by policymakers to be of systemic importance. An important question for policymakers is whether limits should be placed on bank size, growth or concentration, to minimize the moral hazard concerns raised by banks having achieved TBTF or related status.

In addition to the actions of national governments, the European Commission has issued several communications concerning aspects of the crisis, covering

- application of state aid rules to the banking sector,
- the treatment of banks' impaired assets,
- the recapitalization of financial institutions and
- the provision of restructuring aid to banks.

Many of the regulatory or supervisory frameworks for dealing with problems in the financial system at an EU level were found to be lacking. National approaches to crisis management and depositor protection were inadequate and had adverse spillover effects. There was also a lack of cooperation and agreement over arrangements for sharing the burden of fiscal costs arising from the crisis. This has resulted in the EU introducing the European Banking Union (as discussed in Chapter 2) aimed at providing future safeguards for the eurozone banking system including decoupling both banking sector and sovereign risk. In the US, UK and elsewhere, regulators are continuing to implement tougher regulations, particularly for major banks, and this is having the impact of forcing many big banks to de-risk and shrink their balance sheets.

FREQUENCY OF CRISES AND THEIR COSTS

A key reason for regulating banks and other financial institutions is the frequency of banking crises. A survey by Laeven and Valencia (2008) indicates that, during the period 1970–2007:

- There were 124 systemic banking crises in 101 countries.
- Crises often occur regularly in the same countries, with 19 countries experiencing more than one banking crisis, for example Argentina, four; Mexico, two; and the US, two.

- Banking crises can have very large fiscal costs, for example Argentina, 75% of GDP; Chile, 36% of GDP; China, 18% of GDP; South Korea, 31% of GDP; Indonesia, 57% of GDP; and Mexico, 20% of GDP.
- Banking crises are often associated with very large output losses. For example, relative to trend output, losses reached 73% in Argentina, 92% in Chile, 37% in China, 59% in Finland and 31% in Sweden.

So we can see that banking problems are not uncommon, and their costs can be massive.

RATIONALE FOR BANK REGULATION

Economic theory suggests three purposes of regulation: limiting monopoly power, safeguarding welfare and dealing with externalities. How does this rationale apply to banking? This is shown in Box 6.1.

BOX 6.1

Rationale for Bank Regulation

Monopoly power: Regulation may be needed to prevent banks from distorting competition if they have monopoly power. In many countries, a few institutions dominate banking markets. Mergers between already large financial institutions to prevent bank failures after the 2007–8 banking crisis mean that markets are even more concentrated, for example JP Chase/Bear Stearns, Bank of America/Wells Fargo/Wachovia and Lloyds/HBOS. Many commentators argue that regulators should be tougher with large (systemic) banks, and this appears to be the direction in which the regulation of international banking is moving.

Welfare considerations: Regulating for welfare reasons mainly reflects the desire to protect people in cases where information is limited or costly to obtain. In banking, this is dealt with primarily through the provision of deposit insurance. However, the resulting moral hazard among banks and depositors means that regulators require banks to hold some minimum capital.

Externalities: The riskiness of an individual bank is the responsibility of the bank's managers, owners and debt holders, except insofar as the bank's failure impacts on the wider system via spillover externalities, that is, the fact that a bank fails is not important per se; it is that the effects can spill over to large societal costs. Externalities in banking can result from

1 informational contagion, where the failure of one bank throws doubt on the solvency of similar banks, for example Lehman's failure led to doubts about Merrill Lynch; Northern Rock's difficulties led to doubts about Bradford & Bingley.

2 the loss of access to future funding for the failed bank's customers.

3 the greater interconnectedness of banks than other firms – interbank market, derivatives markets, credit default swaps and so on.

Rationale for Bank Regulation (*continued*)

4 the forced sales of bank assets (fire sales) by troubled banks, forcing down the price of similar assets held by solvent banks.

5 credit rationing by banks to rebuild balance sheets, which adversely affects output and prices generally.

The rationale for regulation highlighted in Box 6.1 mainly relates to asymmetric information issues.

INFORMATION ASYMMETRIES IN BANKING AND FINANCE

Many problems in financial institutions and markets have the same basic source: asymmetric information. This occurs when the party to one side of an economic transaction has more information than the other party. There are two types of asymmetric information in financial institutions and markets:

1 When sellers of securities/borrowers know more than buyers/lenders about their own characteristics, it can result in adverse selection (Figure 6.1). The riskiest individuals/institutions will be the most eager to borrow, but lenders are aware of this and may not lend to low- or high-risk borrowers because they cannot distinguish between them.
2 After borrowers receive funds, they know more than the lenders about their use of the funds, which produces moral hazard. The risk arises that borrowers take actions that harm lenders, which means that lenders may not lend because they cannot monitor borrowers effectively.

▼ **Figure 6.1** *Adverse selection and moral hazard*

1 *Adverse selection:* Lenders can't distinguish good from bad credit risks, which discourages transactions from taking place.
Solutions include:
 • Government-required information disclosure
 • Private collection of information
 • Pledging of collateral to insure lenders against the borrower's default
 • Requiring borrowers to invest substantial resources of their own.
2 *Moral hazard:* Lenders can't tell whether borrowers will do what they claim they will do with the borrowed resources; borrowers may take too many risks.
Solutions include:
 • Requiring managers to report to owners
 • Requiring managers to invest substantial resources of their own
 • Covenants that restrict what borrowers can do with borrowed funds.

GOVERNMENT SAFETY NET PROBLEMS FOR REGULATORS

In almost all countries, bank regulation involves the provision of a government safety net for banks and their depositors. For the banks, the most important component of the safety net is the lender-of-last-resort (LLR) function of the central bank. Under the LLR function, the role of the central bank is to make sure that solvent banks can meet their depositors' withdrawal demands. In doing this, the central bank lends the needed funds to solvent but illiquid banks against good collateral at a penal rate of interest. The LLR function played a major role in containing the fallout from the 2007–8 financial crisis. Figure 6.2 illustrates the lending of the US Federal Reserve Bank to the banking sector in this regard. Nonetheless, the LLR function gives rise to some difficulties:

- In practice, it is difficult to distinguish an illiquid from an insolvent bank. This creates a moral hazard for bank managers (insolvent banks borrow and make risky investments).
- The existence of an LLR does not mean that it will be used. Banks may not be willing to borrow, for example preferring to meet liquidity needs through credit contraction/assets sales, or the central bank may fail to provide sufficient liquidity.
- The banks may be in need of foreign currency assets, which the central bank will only be able to lend them if it has sufficient foreign exchange reserves or if it is able to borrow them, for example from other central banks.

▼ **Figure 6.2** *Borrowing from the US Federal Reserve, 1919–2014*

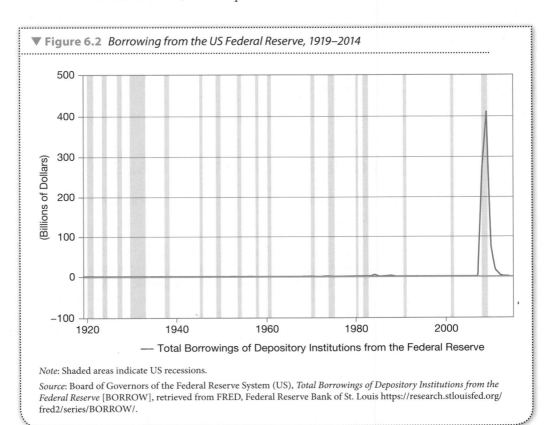

— Total Borrowings of Depository Institutions from the Federal Reserve

Note: Shaded areas indicate US recessions.

Source: Board of Governors of the Federal Reserve System (US), *Total Borrowings of Depository Institutions from the Federal Reserve* [BORROW], retrieved from FRED, Federal Reserve Bank of St. Louis https://research.stlouisfed.org/fred2/series/BORROW/.

▼ **Table 6.1** *Deposit insurance designs*

Design features of explicit deposit insurance schemes	Proportion of countries with each feature
Foreign currency deposit covered	76
Interbank deposits covered	18
Coinsurance exists	25
Payment per depositor	79
Scheme is permanently funded	84
Premiums are risk adjusted	25
Membership is compulsory	91
Source of funding	
Private	36
Joint	63
Public	1
Administration	
Official	60
Joint	27
Private	12

Source: Demirgüç-Kunt, Asli; Kane, Edward J.; Laeven, Luc. 2006. Deposit Insurance Design and Implementation : Policy Lessons from Research and Practice. World Bank, Washington, DC. © World Bank. https://openknowledge.worldbank.org/handle/10986/8376 License: CC BY 3.0 Unported.

For depositors, the most important component of the safety net is deposit insurance. This is essentially a government-backed guarantee in which depositors are paid off on their deposits, in full or in part, no matter what happens to the bank. Deposit insurance can be explicit, in the sense of a contractual obligation of the government deposit insurance agency, or implicit, in the sense that political incentives make taxpayer bailouts of insolvent banks seem inevitable. Explicit deposit insurance is increasingly popular, existing in just 20 countries in 1980, but in 87 countries by the mid-2000s. However, deposit insurance can also create problems for regulators, including these:

Moral hazard: This arises because insurance can change the behaviour of banks and depositors. Before US deposit insurance, banks had debt to equity of 4:1, now it is 13:1. In addition, others have argued that weaknesses in deposit insurance design have increased the prospect of banking crises (see Table 6.1).

Too big to fail: If government officials care more about the largest institutions, banks have an incentive to become large and then take on too much risk.

THEORIES OF BANKING CRISES

Two distinct theories seek to explain the origins of banking panics (see the survey in Allen et al., 2009):

1   The first is that they are caused by random deposit withdrawals unrelated to changes in the real economy. In this theory, economic agents have uncertain needs for consumption in an environment in which long-term investments are costly to liquidate. There are two equilibria: in one, if depositors believe that other depositors will withdraw, then all agents find it rational to redeem their claims and a panic occurs, that is, bank runs are self-fulfilling prophecies; in the other, everybody believes no panic will occur and agents withdraw their funds according to their consumption needs, that is, no panic occurs. However, this theory says nothing about which of the two equilibria will be selected and provides no account of what triggers a crisis.

2   In the second theory, crises are a natural outgrowth of the business cycle. An economic downturn reduces the value of bank assets, raising the possibility that banks are unable to meet their commitments. If depositors believe the outlook is for an economic

downturn, they will anticipate banking problems and try to withdraw deposits. So crises are not random events, but a response of depositors to bad news on the economy.

The key issue in both theories is the nature of the deposit contract – it provides an incentive for bank runs because of the first come, first served basis on which the demand for depositors' liquidity is met.

FEATURES OF SYSTEMIC RISK

To regulate banks effectively, we need to understand the causes of liquidity and solvency problems, that is, how liquidity problems can lead to solvency problems, and how relatively small shocks can cause liquidity to dry up and create financial crises. In this section, we examine risk from the perspective of the individual institution (traditional regulation) and then consider the systemic context (the focus of current efforts at regulatory reform). The bottom line is that regulation doesn't make the financial system safe just by making individual institutions safe. The thinking behind current regulatory reform is to shift regulation from a focus on individual banks to also ensuring the stability of the system as a whole. The shift reflects a better understanding about the causes of liquidity and solvency problems.

What Is 'Systemic Risk'?

Definitions of 'systemic risk' vary from author to author, but Rochet (2010) defines it succinctly as including all events capable of imperilling the stability of the banking and financial system, for example macroeconomic shocks that affect all institutions simultaneously, or situations of contagion in which the default of one bank can spread to many others. Traditionally, bank regulatory frameworks have been too focused on the health of individual institutions and not enough on the health of the financial system as a whole. This is perhaps understandable, as systemic risk in a global context did not materialize until 2007.

Solvency, Liquidity and Maturities

For it to be solvent, a bank's 'going concern' value must exceed the expected value of its liabilities. Solvency is difficult to determine in a crisis because the prices of assets become disconnected from estimates of expected cash flows and instead reflect prices that could be obtained if assets had to be sold immediately to few investors.

Solvency and liquidity issues are hard to untangle. Banks typically have an asset/liability mismatch that they fund through short-term borrowing, for example repos and commercial paper, which they rely on being able to roll over. They are able to borrow short term because they pledge collateral (the securities they own). However, they cannot borrow the entire value of the collateral – the difference between the asset price (the loan) and the collateral value (the securities they must pledge) is the haircut that has to be funded from bank capital. The major risk for banks is the inability to roll over short-term borrowing. There are two types of risk in this regard:

1   *Funding liquidity risk* arises because the size of the 'haircuts' on collateral may change or because it becomes more costly to roll over short-term borrowing, that is, short-term

interest rates rise, or because demand depositors withdraw funds. Funding liquidity risk may only be really serious in the presence of low market liquidity.

2   *Market liquidity risk* arises when the selling of assets depresses their sale price and makes it costly for banks to shrink their balance sheet.

Regulatory capital buffers traditionally reflect measures of the risk of individual institutions, not the risks of systemic failure. But funding and market liquidity risks are determined in the economy as a whole, which requires a systemic view of liquidity crisis borrowing.

Funding Liquidity and the 'Domino Effect'

Actions that strengthen individual banks do not necessarily promote systemic stability. In fact, the efforts of individual banks to remain solvent can collapse the banking system as a whole. Consider interbank relationships: a lending bank that suffers credit losses on its other (non-interbank) loans will try to reduce lending, including in the interbank market, even though the creditworthiness of the borrower bank in the market is unchanged. If the borrower bank in the interbank market cannot find alternative sources of funding, it too must reduce its exposure or sell assets, for example Northern Rock in 2007, Bear Stearns and Lehman Bros in 2008. Because of interbank linkages, there can be a 'domino effect' that spreads systemic risk through the banking system. By way of illustration, consider the depiction of interbank relationships in Figure 6.3.

Assume that Bank 1 has borrowed from Bank 2 and that Bank 2 has other assets as well as loans to Bank 1. Now, suppose that Bank 2 suffers credit losses on other loans, but the creditworthiness of Bank 1 is unchanged:

● The losses suffered by Bank 2 deplete its capital, and it is prudent for it to reduce its overall exposure (assets) so that they are sufficiently supported by capital.
● One way to do this is to reduce overall lending, including to Bank 1. But from Bank 1's perspective, the reduction in lending by Bank 2 is a withdrawal of funding.

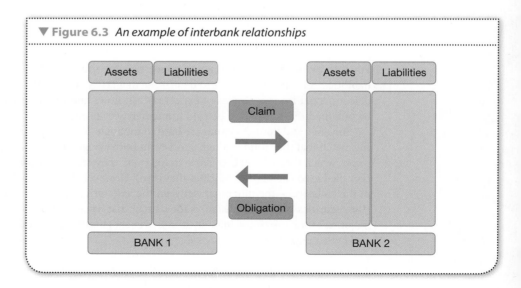

▼ Figure 6.3 *An example of interbank relationships*

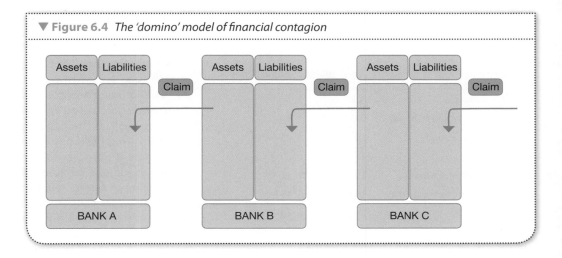

▼ **Figure 6.4** *The 'domino' model of financial contagion*

- Unless Bank 1 can find other sources, it will have to reduce its own asset holdings (curtailing lending or selling assets).
- The withdrawal of lending by Bank 2 will feel like a run from the point of view of Bank 1, if Bank 1 has no alternative funding sources; the reduction in lending by Bank 2 is severe; and Bank 1 can only sell assets at fire sale prices.

It is not difficult to imagine how this might lead to a 'domino effect' and put the entire financial system at risk. For example, consider Figure 6.4.

Here, Bank A has borrowed from Bank B, and Bank B has borrowed from Bank C and so on. If Bank A defaults, then Bank B will suffer a loss, which, if it wipes out its capital, results in Bank B defaulting. Bank C then takes a hit and so on. This is a simple domino model of contagion.

'Mark to Market' and Asset Price Effects

In market-based banking systems, balance sheets are mark to market – meaning that asset prices are changed regularly to reflect market prices. If market prices fall drastically, this may be sufficient to generate contagion and bank collapse. Changes in asset prices can lead to losses (gains) that may be large enough to transmit negative (positive) shocks to other institutions, even when they have no direct lending relation. In booms, greater demand for assets puts upward pressure on prices, with potential continuous feedback effects in which stronger balance sheets lead to greater asset demand and further increases in asset prices. In banking crises, it is the reverse that is the case – a fall in asset prices erodes equity, which banks try to rebuild by selling more assets, which reduces prices further and so on.

The 'Haircut' Spiral

Changes in the value of collateral used to support liquidity funding can also spread systemic risk. This is because a fall in the value of collateral, that is, an increase in

▼ **Table 6.2** *Haircuts on repo agreements*

Security	April 2007%	August 2008%
US treasuries	0.25	3
Investment-grade bonds	0–3	8–12
High-yield bonds	10–15	25–40
Equities	15	20
Senior leverage loans	10–12	15–20
Mezzanine leverage loans	18–25	35+
Prime MBS	2–4	10–20
ABS	3–5	50–60

Note: Mezzanine capital refers to a subordinated debt or preferred equity instrument that represents a claim on a company's assets that is senior only to that of the common shares; an MBS is a mortgage-backed security that represents a claim on the cash flows from mortgage loans through a process known as 'securitization'; and an ABS is an asset-backed security.

Source: IMF (October 2008) *Global Financial Stability Report.*

the size of the 'haircut', forces banks to reduce their leverage ratios by reducing lending or asset sales because the size of the haircut determines maximum leverage. For example, a haircut of 2% means that the borrower can only borrow $98 for $100 of securities pledged; the borrower has to provide 2% of equity so that the maximum leverage is 50. If the haircut is increased to 4%, the borrowing bank has to reduce its leverage to 25, that is, it has to sell assets and/or raise new equity. A vicious circle emerges, where higher haircuts force deleveraging and more asset sales, which increases haircuts further and forces more sales. As asset prices drop further, market liquidity essentially disappears. Table 6.2 shows the haircuts in secured lending transactions at two dates – April 2007, before the crisis, and August 2008, during the crisis (note that a repo is a sale and repurchase agreement, discussed in detail in Chapter 7). Haircuts were substantially higher during the crisis.

Systemic Risk: Spirals and the Rationale for Regulation

In the 2007–8 crisis, systemic risk spread by funding liquidity problems and adverse asset price and haircut effects. These were exacerbated by reliance on capital markets for marginal funding because of maturity mismatching and leverage and mark-to-market accounting practices. In these circumstances, it can be argued that bank regulation is justified by the externality that banks are prone to overexpose themselves to the risks of fire sale externalities and interconnectedness externalities.

THE RISE OF SYSTEMICALLY IMPORTANT FINANCIAL INSTITUTIONS (SIFIs)

The rise of systemically important financial institutions (SIFIs) is a development of crucial importance that greatly complicates financial regulation. The rise of SIFIs reflects

- the rapid rise in financial integration driven by innovation, market reforms and increased financial openness. The cross-border claims between banks at the end of September 2013 amounted to US$28 trillion.
- the fact that countries are increasingly intertwined internationally – especially among a small number of countries.
- the consolidation of national financial markets – in most countries the financial system is dominated by a small number of large institutions.
- the internationalization of institutions, with many of the largest of them operating across multiple borders (Table 6.3).

▼ **Table 6.3** *Top 20 countries with the largest system-wide bank liabilities to GDP, 2008*

Country	Ratio
Switzerland	6.293
United Kingdom	5.98
Belgium	2.916
France	2.737
Netherlands	2.469
Ireland	2.393
Denmark	2.330
Singapore	2.266
Australia	2.132
Sweden	1.982
Canada	1.799
Spain	1.749
Japan	1.657
South Africa	1.625
Greece	1.482
Italy	1.432
Israel	1.377
Germany	1.350
Hong Kong	1.301
Austria	1.251

Source: A. Demirgüç-Kunt and H. Huizinga (2010) *Are Banks Too Big to Fail or Too Big to Save?*, Table 2, p.29, © World Bank. http://elibrary.worldbank.org/doi/pdf/10.1596/1813-9450-5360. Creative Commons Attribution CC BY 3.0.

Because of the concentration of cross-border activity, changes in international bank regulations are likely to focus on France, Germany, the UK, the US, Switzerland, the Netherlands and Japan. At the end of 2009, banks from France, Germany, the UK, the US, Switzerland and the Netherlands accounted for 47% of cross-border banking assets, and the US, the UK, France, Germany, Japan and the Netherlands accounted for 50% of cross-border liabilities. European banks have reduced their cross-border exposures substantially since then.

There are particularly intense links between France and the US (some 4% of global cross-border banking assets are French banks' claims on US banks); between the UK and the US; and between Germany and France (each represents some 3% of global cross-border banking claims). Important links also arise from the claims of Swiss banks on the US (some 2.5% of global cross-border banking claims). SIFIs provide essential services by allocating capital and sharing risks across international borders, providing competitive pressures and introducing foreign technology.

Which Are the SIFIs?

The *Financial Times* identified 30 firms on a 'systemic risk' list compiled by regulators, which are listed in Table 6.4. The firms share the following characteristics:

- They are all very big and international, with non-home activities amounting to about 53% of assets.
- They are mainly European, reflecting the concentration in European banking and the central role of universal banks in Europe.
- They are extremely complex, with all 30 having at least 100 subsidiaries, many located abroad, often in offshore financial centres (OFCs).

The high degree of complexity probably intensifies the vulnerability to systemic risk. However, most countries do not want to constrain corporate structures for competitiveness reasons. Nonetheless, there are serious public policy issues at play, including the operational and financial interdependence among the financial entities and the many different regulators (national and international) involved. A more recent listing of what the IMF believes to be systemically important banks is illustrated in Table 6.5.

Why Worry about Big Institutions?

The reasons why we should be concerned about Big Banks are discussed in Box 6.2.

▼ Table 6.4 *Top 30 SIFIs*

SIFI	Total assets $bn, 2008	% of Foreign assets	% Foreign net income	Total subsidiaries	% of Foreign subsidiaries	Number of countries	Subsidiaries in OFCs	Subsidiaries in OFCs, %
Americas
JPMorgan Chase	2,175	25	68	839	49	54	61	7
Citigroup	1,936	43	74	2,631	58	89	462	18
Bank of America Merrill Lynch	1,818	17	18	2,484	38	53	236	10
Goldman Sachs	885	33	46	294	60	24	38	13
Morgan Stanley	659	30	46	1,809	58	57	323	18
Royal Bank of Canada	591	46	41	235	64	26	39	17
Averae Americas	1,344	32	49	1,382	55	51	193	14
Asia
Mitsubishi UFJ	1,921	26	28	146	58	20	8	5
Mizuho	1,509	23	30	139	45	18	16	12
Sumitomo Mitsui	1,174	17	21	144	39	14	26	18
Nomura	252	38	14	162	73	29	27	17
Average Asia	1,214	26	23	148	54	20	19	13
Europe
Royal Bank of Scotland	3,511	46	42	782	15	15	50	6
Deutsche Bank	3,066	82	75	1,992	85	61	544	27
Barclay	3,001	68	56	844	40	57	133	16
BNP Paribas	2,889	41	55	2,056	67	67	176	9
HSBC	2,527	64	70	1,765	74	73	442	25
UBS	1,888	89	47	294	97	48	31	11
ING	1,854	60	72	1,694	67	64	49	3
Société Générale	1,573	29	57	1,074	62	69	64	6
Santander	1,461	64	69	898	80	47	61	7
UniCredit	1,455	62	51	1,286	94	48	47	4
Allianz	1,310	88	78	964	85	66	41	4
Credit Suisse	1,097	85	69	267	92	39	44	16
AXA	921	75	72	1,248	85	50	82	7
Banca Intensa	885	15	12	392	62	34	87	22
BBVA	755	30	64	495	74	31	40	8
Aviva	507	64	61	454	54	26	38	8
Standard Chartered	435	71	93	298	77	49	98	33
Aegon	393	78	76	649	76	30	20	3
Zurich	309	96	84	444	98	28	31	7
Swiss Re	214	97	97	206	99	24	35	17
Average Europe	1,503	65	65	905	74	46	106	12
Grand Average	1,432	53	56	2,435	182	117	318	39

Source: Claessens et al. (2010) *A Safer World Financial System: Improving the Resolution of Systemic Institutions*, Tables 1.1 and 1.2, Geneva Report 12 ICMB and Bankscope published by Bureau van Dijk.

▼ Table 6.5 *Systemically important banks, 2012*

Bank Names		
ABN AMRO Holding N.V.	Credit Suisse Group*	National Australia Bank Limited
Allied Irish Banks PLC	Criteria Caixacorp, S.A.	National Bank of Abu Dhabi
Australia and New Zealand Banking Group	Danske Bank A/S	National Bank of Greece, S.A.
Banca Monte dei Paschi di Siena S.p.A.	DBS Group Holdings Ltd.	Natixis*
Banco Bilbao Vizcaya Argentaria S.A.*	Depfa Bank PLC	Nordea Bank AB*
Banco BPI, S.A.	Deutsche Bank AG*	OKO Bank PLC
Banco Bradesco S.A.	Dexia**	Oversea-Chinese Banking Corporation
Banco Comercial Portugues, S.A.	DNB ASA	Public Bank Berhad (The)
Banco de Chile	Emirates NBD PJSC	Raiffeisen International Bank
Banco de Oro Universal Bank	Erste Bank Der Osterreichischen Sparkassen AG	Riyad Bank
Banco do Brasil S.A.	Espirito Santo Financial Group S.A.	Royal Bank of Canada
Banco Espirito S.A.nto S.A.	First Gulf Bank PJSC	Royal Bank of Scotland Group PLC*
Banco Latinoamericano De Exportaciones, S.A.	Glitnir Banki hf	Samba Financial Group
Bancolombia S.A.	Goldman Sachs Group Inc.*	Santander Central Hispano S.A.*
Bangkok Bank Public Company Limited	Hang Seng Bank Limited	Sberbank Rosseii
Bank Austria	HSBC Holdings PLC*	Siam Commercial Bank Public Co Ltd
Bank Hapoalim B.M.	ICICI Bank Limited	Skandinaviska Enskilda Banken
Bank of America Corp.*	ING Groep N.V.*	Société Générale S.A.*
Bank of Baroda	Intesa Sanpaolo S.p.A.	Standard Chartered PLC*
Bank of China Limited*	JPMorgan Chase*	State Bank of India
Bank of East Asia Limited (The)	JSC VTB Bank	State Street Corp.*
Bank of Ireland	Jyske Bank A/S	Sumitomo Mitsui Financial Group Inc.*
Bank of New York*	Kaupthing Bank HF	Svenska Handelsbanken AB
Bank of Nova Scotia	KBC Group NV	Sydbank A.S.
Barclays PLC*	Krung Thai Bank Public Company Ltd.	Toronto Dominion Bank
Bayerische Hypo- und Vereinsbank AG	Landsbanki Islands HF	Turkiye Garanti Bankasi A.S.
BNP Paribas*	Lloyds TSB Group PLC**	Turkiye Is Bankasi A.S.
BRE Bank S.A.	Malayan Banking Berhad	UBS AG*

(continued)

▼ **Table 6.5** *(Continued)*

	Bank Names	
Cathay Financial Holding Company Ltd.	Mega Financial Holding Company	Unicredito Italiano S.p.A.*
China Construction Bank Corp	Metropolitan Bank and Trust Company	United Overseas Bank Limited
Citigroup Inc.*	Mitsubishi UFJ Financial Group*	Wells Fargo & Co.*
Commercial Bank of Qatar	Mizuho Financial Group*	Westpac Banking Corporation
Commerzbank AG**	Morgan Stanley*	
Crédit Agricole S.A.*	Moscow Municipal Bank	

Source: IMF. (2014) *Global Financial Stability Report*, April, p. 127.

Note: Systemically important banks are defined as the G-SIBs identified by the Financial Stability Board plus the three largest banks by asset size in each country if these are not G-SIBs, subject to data availability.

*G-SIBs as identified by the Financial Stability Board in 2013. When the group is not listed, the largest quoted entity is used.

**Banks previously identified by the Financial Stability Board as G-SIBs.

BOX 6.2

Why We Should Worry about Big Banks

The main reasons why we are concerned about large banks relate to the rationale for their regulation:

1 Large banks play a pivotal role in the financial system. They are a source of finance for large numbers of borrowers, and they manage the payments system.

2 There are potential systemic dangers resulting from bank runs. This is partly because of the nature of banks' deposit contracts – these are liquid deposits that finance the acquisition of illiquid assets of uncertain value; and because the interconnectedness of banks means failure of one bank can cause immediate losses to other, interconnected banks.

3 The adverse selection and moral hazard associated with the lender-of-last-resort role and other safety net arrangements are more severe for large banks.

In addition, the financial crisis made clear the following:

- The operational and financial interdependence among large financial intermediaries can create strong spillovers across markets.
- Complications in supervision, regulation and resolution could arise because of the many different regulators (national and international) involved.
- Crises impose high costs on the global real economy, such as economic recessions and larger government budgets, reflecting the direct costs of financial support, lost tax revenue, increased budget deficits and public debt. These costs tend to get more severe the bigger the institutions involved.

- It can be difficult for governments to resolve large financial institutions without putting significant public resources at risk.
- If SIFIs cannot fail, government support is inevitable, and the problem of moral hazard is exacerbated.

US REGULATORY RESPONSE TO THE CRISIS: DODD-FRANK ACT 2010

Clearly, governments and their respective regulators have moved rapidly to close the gaps and weaknesses in the system for bank regulation and supervision. The passing of the US Dodd-Frank Wall Street Reform and Consumer Protection Act in July 2010, the biggest financial reform in the US since the Great Depression, is a good reflection of this trend and is indicative of the type of measures that national governments around the world may adopt.

The Dodd-Frank Act overhauls the current system of regulation and supervision to improve disclosure, transparency and the safety and soundness of the financial system. The Act accomplished these aims:

- Established a Financial Stability Oversight Council
- Instituted new measures to deal with SIFIs
- Created a Consumer Financial Protection Bureau
- Reformed the Federal Reserve
- Improved transparency in derivatives
- Introduced new rules on executive pay and credit rating agencies

These are now discussed briefly.

The aim of the Financial Stability Oversight Council is to identify and address systemic risks posed by large, complex companies, products and activities before they threaten the stability of the economy. Council membership comprises 10 financial regulators, one independent member and five non-voting members, and it is chaired by the Treasury secretary. Its key responsibilities are to recommend tougher capital, liquidity and risk management when banks get 'too big'. By a two-thirds vote, the council can require SIFIs (banks and non-banks) to be regulated by the Federal Reserve. It is anticipated that around 35 SIFIs will be regulated by the Federal Reserve, including all banking organizations with over $50bn in assets. Also (based on a two-thirds vote), the Federal Reserve can break up complex financial intermediaries that impose a 'grave' systemic threat to the system. Finally, a broad overall goal is to monitor risk in the financial system.

The Dodd-Frank Act clearly states that 'taxpayers will not be on the hook' and the Federal Deposit Insurance Corporation (FDIC) is prohibited from losing money on SIFIs.

The so-called Volcker Rule is to be introduced, which prohibits banks from proprietary trading and limits investments in hedge funds/private equity fund sponsorship to 3% of capital. SIFIs will have to provide 'living wills' – their plans for rapid and orderly shutdown in case of bankruptcy. The Act also creates orderly liquidation mechanisms for the FDIC to unwind failing, systemically significant companies.

The new Consumer Financial Protection Bureau, housed at the Federal Reserve, has the authority to ensure that American consumers get the clear, accurate information they need to shop for mortgages, credit cards and other financial products, and to protect them from hidden fees, abusive terms and deceptive practices. It will have examiner authority over banks and credit unions with over $10bn of assets, mortgage brokers, payday lenders and others, although oversight excludes auto dealers.

Emergency lending powers of the Federal Reserve (established in 1932 under Section 13(3) of the Federal Reserve Act) give it authority to lend to non-depository institutions (investment banks, insurers) in 'unusual and exigent circumstances'. Dodd-Frank now makes this lending conditional on approval from the secretary of the Treasury. The Federal Reserve will have to disclose all its Section 13(3) lending details and will be subject to a one-time Government Accountability Office (GAO) audit of emergency lending. A new post of Federal Reserve Vice Chairman for Supervision will be created, and the GAO will also examine governance issues and how directors are appointed.

The Act forces most derivatives trading onto central clearing houses and exchange trading. Regulators and exchanges are to determine what should be exchange traded. Exchange-traded derivatives are more transparent than their over-the-counter (OTC) counterparts, and the credit risks shift to the exchange. In addition, a new Office of Credit Ratings will be set up within the Securities and Exchange Commission (SEC) to examine rating agencies, and investors will be allowed to sue agencies for 'knowing and reckless' behaviour. Shareholders are to have more say in pay and golden parachutes, and banking organizations must publish the ratio of CEO compensation to average worker compensation. There will be provisions for compensation clawback if financial performance/projections are found to be inaccurate.

Finally, other reforms encompassed in the Dodd-Frank Act are

- the abolition of the Office of Thrift Supervision – thrifts will now be regulated by the Office of the Comptroller of the Currency;
- to require the Fed to examine non-bank financial services holding companies;
- to repeal the prohibition on paying interest on business checking accounts;
- to establish a new Federal Insurance Office to oversee the insurance industry;
- to provide more financial resources to the SEC;
- to permanently increase deposit insurance to $250,000;
- to force securitizers of risky mortgages to have 'skin in the game' (a minimum of 5%);
- lenders must ensure that borrowers can repay home loans by verifying income, credit history and job status – no more 'liar loans'; and
- to place restrictions on consumer payment fees and swipe fees for debit cards – expected to cost the banking industry billions of dollars.

As can be seen, the Dodd-Frank Act radically reforms the way in which the US banking system is regulated, with greater restrictions on the type of activities banks can undertake and a continued pressure to bolster capital and liquidity strength with an end (in theory at least) to taxpayer bailouts. A main criticism of the legislation is that 'bolder 'action' should have been taken to streamline/consolidate the labyrinthine US regulatory structures.

UK REGULATORY RESPONSE TO THE CRISIS

In the UK, the Independent Commission on Banking (2011) (known as the Vickers Commission, after Sir John Vickers, who chaired review) was established to consider structural and related non-structural reforms to the UK banking sector to promote financial stability and competition. On 12 September 2011, it published its Final Report, setting out some possible reforms:

- Retail banking activity is to be ring-fenced from wholesale and investment banking.
- Different arms of the same bank should have separate legal entities with their own boards of directors.
- SIFIs and large UK retail banking operations should have a minimum 10% equity/assets ratio.
- Contingent capital and debt should be available to improve loss absorbency in the future.
- Risk management should become a self-contained, less complex business for retail banking but remain complex for wholesale/investment banking.

The cost of these reforms to the UK economy are likely to range between £1bn and £3bn per annum, which compares favourably with the estimated annual cost (of £40bn) of lost output that follows financial crises. If adopted, the proposed reforms aim to be implemented by 2019 (under successive UK governments).

EUROPEAN REGULATORY RESPONSE

In Europe, a new supervisory architecture is taking place along the lines initially highlighted in the de Larosière Report (February 2009). A key element concerns the issue of international cooperation, which is crucial given the development of cross-border banking. The European Parliament and Ecofin (Economic and Financial Affairs Council) adopted new legislation and changes to the regulatory and supervisory architecture in November 2010. New arrangements for macro- and micro-prudential supervision have been established. Specifically, a European Systemic Risk Board (ESRB) was established in December 2010 to monitor and assess systemic risks in the EU financial system. (It convenes its meeting at the European Central Bank, ECB, in Frankfurt.) If necessary, the ESRB will issue recommendations on measures required to address risks building up in the financial system.

At the micro-prudential level, a European System of Financial Supervisors (ESFS) was established in January 2011. The ESFS brings together the EU's national supervisory agencies with three new European supervisory authorities (ESAs), formed out of existing authorities, to cover

1 *Banking:* European Banking Authority (EBA), replaces the Committee of European Banking Supervisors;

2   *financial markets:* European Securities and Markets Authority (ESMA), replaces the Committee of European Securities Regulators; and

3   *insurance*: the European Insurance and Occupational Pensions Authority (EIOPA), replaces the Committee of European Insurance and Occupational Pensions Supervisors.

These authorities issue guidelines on supervisory issues and conduct peer analysis, including stress testing of EU financial institutions – the latest being in October 2011. In addition, a Joint Committee was established to ensure that effective supervision of financial conglomerates takes place.

Table 6.6 illustrates the ECB estimates of the performance of large and complex banking groups in the eurozone between 2005 and 2010, highlighting the disastrous losses made in 2008 and small pickup in ROE thereafter. Note the colossal increase in cost/income ratios in 2008 due to a collapse in income. Also witness the substantial increase in tier 1 capital and solvency ratios in 2009 and 2010. Another good example of performance scrutiny relates to the stress tests reported by the EBA, published on the 15 July 2011, which covered 90 banks operating in 21 European countries. For this exercise, the EBA allowed specific capital increase in the first four months of 2011 to be included in its calculations. This provided an incentive for banks to boost solvency prior to the tests. The main findings can be summarized as follows:

- By December 2010, 20 banks would not have achieved the benchmark 5% tier 1 capital ratio over the 2-year horizon (2010–12) of the exercise. This amounts to a capital shortfall of some €26.8bn.
- The 90 banks in question raised an additional €50bn between January and April 2011.
- Eight banks did not achieve the 5% capital threshold, amounting to a shortfall of €2.5bn.
- Sixteen banks achieved a tier 1 ratio of between 5% and 6%.

▼ Table 6.6 *Performance of large and complex banking groups in the eurozone*

Year	Return on Equity %		Impaired Loans/ Total Assets %		Cost/Income Ratio %		Tier 1 Ratio%		Solvency Ratio%	
	Median	Average	Median	Average	Median	Average	Median	Average	Median	Average
2005	10.04	11.93	0.08	0.11	60.69	58.87	7.89	8.20	11.05	11.23
2006	14.81	14.61	0.07	0.11	55.95	56.40	7.75	8.07	11.01	11.16
2007	11.97	11.65	0.05	0.10	63.00	62.95	7.40	7.72	10.60	10.72
2008	2.26	−14.65	0.27	0.31	73.36	160.96	8.59	8.58	11.70	11.37
2009	2.97	0.34	0.45	0.55	60.35	62.47	10.15	10.33	13.60	13.37
2010	7.68	6.76	0.24	0.32	60.40	62.01	11.20	11.38	14.10	14.38

Source: Adapted from ECB (June 2011) *Financial Stability Review*, Table S5, pp. S30–1.

On the basis of these findings, the EBA issued a formal recommendation to national supervisory authorities, stating that banks that have tier 1 capital below the 5% threshold should remedy the situation as soon as possible. In addition, the EBA has also recommended that national supervisory authorities request all banks whose tier 1 ratio is above but close to 5%, and with sizeable exposures to sovereigns under stress, to take specific steps to strengthen their solvency, including (where necessary) restrictions on dividends, deleveraging, issuance of fresh capital or conversion of lower-quality instruments into core tier 1 capital.

Various commentators have suggested that the stress tests performed were not tough enough, especially as the extra €50bn raised in the first quarter of 2011 was included. Other scenarios have been reported by various analysts. For instance, Goldman Sachs (2011) makes various assumptions about bank sovereign debt exposures and applying a haircut to the debt of Greece, Ireland and Portugal. This, it finds, would yield a bank capital shortfall of €25.9bn relative to the 5% core tier 1 capital benchmark. Applying a further 10% haircut to Italian and Spanish debt would see the shortfall increase to €29.8bn. On a more positive note, Barclays Capital (2011) estimated that only 4 of the top 30 banks would fail the 5% hurdle when applying mark to market also to the banking book.

A serious ongoing concern, of course, relates to how the sovereign debt crisis impacts bank funding costs. It is well known that funding costs are positively linked to sovereign risks. An increase in such risk leads to a higher spread vis-à-vis the typical risk-free asset in Europe, the German Bund, and this in turn increases the cost of servicing liabilities, especially as bonds comprise a substantial proportion of such liabilities. The aforementioned stress tests revealed that, in December 2010, the 90 banks under study had €8.2 trillion of wholesale/interbank funding, of which around 56% matures in two years. Replacing this funding is going to be a major challenge in light of the ongoing sovereign debt crisis. In fact, the ECB's *Financial Stability Report* (ECB, 2011) cautions about this growing risk. Ongoing concerns about the instability of the European banking system led to calls for a single European bank supervisor as part of a European Banking Union. The timeline of events setting up the single European bank supervisor (which will be the ECB) are noted in Box 6.3. The ultimate rationale for these moves, as we noted in Chapter 2, is to remove the 'doom loop' that exists between bank systemic risk and country sovereign risk. Or to put it simply, if big banks or a banking system fails, the state generally has to intervene to avoid economic collapse, which involves massive amounts of public money (taxpayers' money) being used to save the banks. Excessive public spending then can put the governments finances in jeopardy, as they have to raise more money by issuing government bonds to fund the rescue, and this can raise concerns about the solvency of governments/sovereigns – investors wonder whether they will be able to repay their debts. So the price of government bonds shoots up, making it more costly and problematic for public finances. This spiral (or 'doom loop') may result in major default and serious recessions for the countries involved – Greece (unfortunately) is a current example of how failed banks lead to failed government finances and subsequent serious macroeconomic consequences. The European Banking Union aims to break the banking sector/sovereign debt (country finances) link – by providing broader support across the eurozone (all euro area government will stand behind a failing individual country's banking system); supervision will be uniform; and resolution of poor-performing banks (how you restructure them or shut them in the event of a crisis) becomes similar throughout the euro area.

BOX 6.3

Key Steps toward the Single Supervisory Mechanism

4 Sept. 2014   **ECB publishes a list of significant credit institutions**

The ECB publishes the list of the 120 significant credit institutions under direct ECB supervision from November 2014, as well as the list of the less significant banks in the euro area, which remain supervised by the national competent authorities.

15 May 2014   **SSM Framework Regulation comes into force**

The SSM Framework Regulation sets out the legal structure for cooperation with national competent authorities (NCAs) within the Single Supervisory Mechanism (SSM). It governs relations between the ECB and NCAs and includes rules that apply directly to banks.

11 Feb. 2014   **Sabine Lautenschläger is appointed as Vice-Chair of the Supervisory Board**

The EU Council appointed Ms Sabine Lautenschläger as Vice-Chair of the Supervisory Board of the Single Supervisory Mechanism for a 5-year term of office starting on 12 February 2014. As required by the SSM Regulation, the Vice-Chair was chosen from among the members of the ECB's Executive Board.

16 Dec. 2013   **Danièle Nouy is appointed as Chair of the Supervisory Board**

The EU Council appointed Ms Danièle Nouy as Chair of the Supervisory Board of the Single Supervisory Mechanism for a 5-year term starting on 1 January 2014.

12 Dec. 2013   **Memorandum of Understanding between the Council of the European Union and the ECB comes into force**

The Memorandum covers practical aspects of the exercise of democratic accountability of the supervisory tasks of the ECB vis-à-vis the Council.

7 Nov. 2013   **Interinstitutional Agreement between the European Parliament and the ECB comes into force**

The Interinstitutional Agreement covers practical aspects of the exercise of democratic accountability of the supervisory tasks of the ECB vis-à-vis the European Parliament.

3 Nov. 2013   **Regulation on the Single Supervisory Mechanism comes into force**

The ECB will assume its full supervisory tasks on 4 November 2014, i.e. 12 months after the Regulation enters into force.

15 Oct. 2013   **EU Council adopts Regulation on the Single Supervisory Mechanism**

The EU Council adopts the Regulation conferring specific tasks on the ECB concerning policies relating to the prudential supervision of credit institutions. The Regulation creates a Single Supervisory Mechanism for credit institutions in the euro area and, potentially, other EU Member States, as one of the main elements of Europe's banking union.

12 Sept. 2013   **European Parliament adopts the European Commission's proposals**

European Parliament adopts the European Commission's proposals to set up a Single Supervisory Mechanism.

In parallel, Mario Draghi, President of the ECB, and Martin Schulz, President of the European Parliament, sign a declaration committing both institutions to formally conclude an Interinstitutional Agreement on the practical aspects of the exercise of democratic accountability and oversight of the tasks conferred on the ECB within the framework of the Single Supervisory Mechanism.

18 Apr. 2013 **EU Council confirms agreement with the European Parliament**

on the establishment of a Single Supervisory Mechanism for the euro area.
Bank supervision: Council confirms agreement with European Parliament.

19 Mar. 2013 **EU Council, European Commission and European Parliament reach agreement**

The EU Council, European Commission and European Parliament reach agreement on the creation of a Single Supervisory Mechanism for the euro area.

14 Dec. 2012 **European Council welcomes the agreement**

The European Council welcomes the agreement on the creation of the Single Supervisory Mechanism for the euro area and calls on EU lawmakers (EU Council, European Commission and European Parliament) to agree quickly so that the plans can be implemented as soon as possible.

13 Dec. 2012 **ECOFIN Council agrees on European banking supervision**

The ECOFIN Council (EU ministers of economics and finance) agrees unanimously on the European Commission's proposal.

5 Dec. 2012 **'Four Presidents' Report'**

The Presidents of the European Council, the European Commission, the European Central Bank and the Eurogroup present the report Towards a Genuine Economic and Monetary Union.

The report sets out a road map for the creation of a genuine Economic and Monetary Union and builds on the vision presented by Herman Van Rompuy, President of the European Council, in June 2012.

27 Nov. 2012 **European Central Bank broadly welcomes the European Commission's proposals**

12 Sept. 2012 **European Commission presents legislative proposals**

European Commission presents draft regulations and communications to set up the Single Supervisory Mechanism. These include
- assigning specific supervisory tasks to the ECB;
- aligning the role and responsibilities of the EBA with the new framework for banking supervision; and
- formulating A Roadmap towards a Banking Union.

29 June 2012 **Euro area summit statement is established**

Euro area Heads of State or Government decide to establish a Single Supervisory Mechanism for banks and assign specific supervisory tasks to the ECB. Euro area summit statement.

26 June 2012 **European Council presents Towards a Genuine Economic and Monetary Union**

The report Towards a Genuine Economic and Monetary Union by the president of the European Council, advises the establishment of a banking union and sets out a vision for the future of the Economic and Monetary Union and how it can best contribute to growth, jobs and stability.

30 May 2012 **European Commission calls for a banking union**

The European Commission promotes the move towards an integrated financial supervision to restore confidence in banks and the euro.

Source: ECB (various) Material can be obtained via the ECB's website, www.ecb.europa.eu, free of charge.

As part of the plans for a European Banking Union, the ECB assumed banking supervision tasks in November 2014 as part of its role in the Single Supervisory Mechanism (SSM). In order to prepare for this new role, the ECB conducted a comprehensive assessment of the eurozone's largest and systemically important 130 banks. The stated objectives of this exercise were to

- strengthen banks' balance sheets by repairing the problems identified through the necessary remedial actions;
- enhance transparency by improving the quality of information available on the condition of the banks; and
- build confidence by assuring all stakeholders that, on completion of the identified remedial actions, banks will be soundly capitalized.

Details of the ECB's comprehensive assessment is in Box 6.4.

BOX 6.4

ECB's Comprehensive Assessment (of Eurozone Banks)

The 130 credit institutions included in the exercise had total assets of €22.0 trillion, which accounts for 81.6% of total banking assets in the SSM. The comprehensive assessment consisted of two components:

1 The Asset Quality Review (AQR) which was a point-in-time assessment of the accuracy of the carrying value of banks' assets as of 31 December 2013 and provided a starting point for the following stress test. The AQR was undertaken by the ECB and national regulators and was based on a uniform methodology and harmonised definitions. The scale of the exercise was unprecedented; it provided a thorough health check of the banks that will be subject to direct supervision by the ECB. The exercise was based on the Capital Requirements Regulation and Directive (CRR/CRD IV) on the definition of regulatory capital as of 1 January 2014. Under the AQR, banks were required to have a minimum Common Equity Tier 1 (CET1) ratio of 8%.

2 The stress test provided a forward-looking examination of the resilience of banks' solvency to two hypothetical scenarios, also reflecting new information arising from the AQR. The stress test was undertaken by the participating banks, the ECB and national regulators, in cooperation with the European Banking Authority (EBA), which also designed the methodology along with the ECB and the European Systemic Risk Board (ESRB). Under the baseline scenario, banks were required to maintain a minimum core equity tier 1 (common equity capital) ratio of 8%; and under the adverse scenario, they were required to maintain a minimum CET1 ratio of 5.5%.

Results of the stress tests were made public on 24 October 2014, and of the 130 banks, 25 failed the stress tests, but only 12 had to raise more capital as the others had done so sufficiently during 2014.

The largest failure, with the biggest capital shortfall of €2.1 billion was the Italian bank, Monte de Paschi di Siena (the world's oldest bank, founded in 1472).

Source: ECB (2014) Aggregate Report on the Comprehensive Assessment, October, Frankfurt: ECB Material can be obtained via the ECB's website, www.ecb.europa.eu, free of charge.

Overall, the ECB exercise in evaluating the quality of eurozone banks assets and capital strength has been well regarded. It found that overall bank assets were overvalued by some €45 bn and that 25 banks had a capital shortfall of €25 bn – although, as noted in Box 6.4, 13 of these had already recapitalized during 2014 before the results (based on end of 2013 data) came out. Only 12 have to fix their balance sheets. The bank most badly hit, Monte Paschi di Siena, said it was looking to dispose assets, raise more capital and may contemplate merger as a consequence.

INTERNATIONAL ACTION

Beyond Europe and the US, there are ongoing policy discussions as to how to improve the coordination of international bank regulation, with a focus on improving the responsibilities of home and host countries in the event of large bank failures that span different jurisdictions. Opportunities for regulatory arbitrage across national boundaries are being examined, with the objective of eliminating regulatory gaps. During the crisis, meetings of the G7 and G20 were used as a forum for international discussion of various forms of policy intervention. There are obvious differences of emphasis and approach among governments, and sometimes coordinated policy action is difficult to achieve. However, a trawl through the timeline of recent post-crisis policy events does suggest a strong correlation between US, UK and (to some extent) other European policy actions, which is unlikely to be purely coincidental. As banks become more international/global, the need to coordinate international policy actions (particularly at the time of crisis) is clearly important.

The credit crisis also exposed weaknesses in the current regime for the regulation of bank capital. Under the risk-weighted capital regulation regime of Basel II, the use of backward-looking models for risk assessment created a procyclical (destabilizing) tendency for capital provisioning that appeared to amplify the economic cycle. In boom conditions, observed rates of borrower default decline. Accordingly, bank assets in all risk classes are assessed as having become less risky and require lower provisioning. In such circumstances, capital buffers can support increased bank lending, which tends to amplify the upturn in the cycle. It is now widely accepted that banks should be required to accumulate capital during booms so that reserves are available to draw upon during times of economic stress. Capital provisioning would thereby exert a countercyclical (stabilizing) effect. Past regulation may also have overemphasized capital at the expense of liquidity. In the run-up to the crisis, many banks appear to have been operating with dangerously low liquidity, that is, the ratio of liquid assets to total assets. As has become clear, severe liquidity shortages can easily trigger a full-blown capitalization crisis.

In response to these issues, and discussed in Chapter 2, the Basel Committee has set out guidelines for new capital and banking regulations (known as Basel III) that have to be fully implemented by the end of 2019. All major G20 financial centres had committed to adopt the Basel III capital framework. Basel III aims to strengthen global capital and liquidity regulations to improve the banking sector's ability to absorb shocks and reduce spillover from the financial sector to the real economy. The main features of Basel III are as follows:

- Basel III proposes new capital, leverage and liquidity standards to strengthen bank regulation, supervision and risk management. This will require banks to hold more capital and higher-quality capital than under current Basel II rules.

- A leverage ratio will be introduced as a supplementary measure to the Basel II risk-based framework. A series of measures to promote the build-up of capital buffers in good times can be drawn upon in periods of stress – reducing procyclicality and promoting countercyclical buffers.
- Risk coverage of the capital framework will be further strengthened via
  - tougher capital requirements for counterparty credit exposures arising from banks' derivatives, repo and securities financing transactions;
  - additional incentives to move OTC derivative contracts to central counterparties (clearing houses); and
  - incentives to strengthen the risk management of counterparty credit exposures.
- A global minimum liquidity standard for internationally active banks will be introduced, which includes a 30-day liquidity coverage ratio requirement underpinned by a longer term structural liquidity ratio called the 'net stable funding ratio'.

In addition to the above, the Basel Committee is also reviewing the need for additional capital, liquidity and other supervisory measures to reduce the TBTF externalities associated with SIFIs.

Effective regulation has also been constrained by a lack of transparency concerning banks' business models. Although the crisis has forced banks to provide detailed information on their exposures, the disclosure of business models, risk management and valuation practices remains limited. Likewise, the restoration of confidence in OTC markets for securitized assets and credit derivatives will require increased transparency, reduced complexity and improved oversight. In the case of credit derivatives, counterparty risk has been a serious concern, with holders of credit default swaps fearful that counterparties may default on their obligations in the event that the underlying asset defaults. Consequently, there has been a desire by policymakers to direct these transactions to clearing houses.

SUMMARY

- The financial crisis and the sovereign debt crisis present serious challenges to the preservation of financial stability of the banking system and the euro-zone itself.
- Large-scale banking rescues have raised serious concerns about the social and economic costs of *too big to fail* (TBTF) or 'too systemically important to fail'.
- An important question for policymakers is whether limits should be placed on bank size, growth or concentration, to minimize the *moral hazard* concerns raised by banks having achieved TBTF or related status.
- Between 1970 and 2007, there were 124 systemic banking crises in 101 countries.
- Banking crises can have very large fiscal costs, for example Argentina, 75% of GDP; Chile, 36% of GDP;

China, 18% of GDP; Korea, 31% of GDP; Indonesia, 57% of GDP; and Mexico, 20% of GDP.
- There are three purposes of regulation: limiting monopoly power, safeguarding welfare, and dealing with externalities.
- *Asymmetric information* causes problems of moral hazard and adverse selection. When sellers of securities/borrowers know more than buyers/lenders about their own characteristics, it can result in *adverse selection*. The riskiest individuals/institutions will be the most eager to borrow, but lenders are aware of this and may not lend to low- and high-risk borrowers because they cannot distinguish between them.
- After borrowers receive funds, they know more than the lenders about their use of the funds, which produces moral hazard. The risk arises that borrowers

take actions that harm lenders, which means that lenders may not lend because they cannot monitor borrowers effectively.

- Too big to fail is a problem if governments care more about the largest institutions, as banks have an incentive to become large and then take on too much risk.
- *Systemic risk* refers to all events capable of imperilling the stability of the banking and financial system.
- The main regulatory responses to the crisis have been the US *Dodd-Frank Act 2010*; recommendations made by the UK *Independent Commission on Banking* in September 2011; *Basel III* (to be implemented by 2019); and, in Europe, the establishment of the *ESFS, EBA and the European Banking Union*.
- The European Banking Union aims to break the banking sector/sovereign debt (country finances) link by providing broader support across the eurozone (all euro-area government will stand behind a failing individual country's banking system) and ensuring that supervision will be uniform and that the resolution of poor-performing banks (how you restructure them or shut them in the event of a crisis) will become similar throughout the euro area.
- As part of the European Banking Union, there will be a Single Supervisory Mechanism, with the ECB as the main supervisor. This SSM assumed supervisory responsibility in November 2014. Prior to this, it undertook a Comprehensive Assessment of the asset quality and capital strength of the eurozones largest and/or systemically most important 130 banks. This comprises two parts: an Asset Quality Review (AQR) which looks at asset quality, and second, stress tests on bank capital strength. Twenty-five banks failed the tests with a capital shortfall of €25 bn, although only 12 had to raise more capital. The worst affected bank was the Italian Monte De Paschi di Siena (the worlds' oldest bank, founded in 1472!)
- All seek to recapitalize the banks, boost liquidity and constrain activity.
- Recent stress tests still reveal capital shortages in the banking sector, and more pessimistic scenarios regarding sovereign debt *haircuts* suggest that many European banks in particular will have to continue to keep on raising capital into the foreseeable future.
- An overhaul of current regulatory structures will inevitably continue to take place. New rules place a greater emphasis on simple leverage and liquidity ratios, the curtailment of opaque business models and minimizing the distortions caused by TBTF and/or SIFIs. A new supervisory architecture will gradually be put in place.

REVISION QUESTIONS/ASSIGNMENTS

1 Analyse the role of information asymmetries in creating the need to regulate financial firms, making specific reference to moral hazard and adverse selection.

2 What are SIFIs? How should they be regulated?

3 Outline the major features of the US Dodd-Frank Act 2010. How is it expected to impact US bank behaviour/performance?

4 Briefly explain why the ECB undertook its Comprehensive Assessment on bank asset quality and capital strength.

REFERENCES

Allen, F., Babus, A., and Carletti, E. (2009) Financial crises: Theory and evidence, *Annual Review of Financial Economics*, 1, 97–116. Detailed analysis of financial crises from a theoretical and empirical standpoint.

Barclays Capital. (2011) *Life Goes On: The European Stress Test*, Barclays Capital Equity Research, 18 July. Brokers report on the performance of European banks and EBA stress tests.

Demirgüç-Kunt, A., Kane, E., and Laeven, L. (eds) (2008) *Deposit Insurance Around the World*, MIT Press, Cambridge, MA. Outlines the features of deposit insurance systems in developed and developing countries.

European Central Bank (ECB). (2011) *Financial Stability Review*, June, Frankfurt: ECB. Analysis of the risks faced by eurozone countries as well as the EU.

European Central Bank (ECB). (2014) *Aggregate Report on the Comprehensive Assessment*, October, ECB, Frankfurt

Goldman Sachs. (2011) *Stress Test II: Banks Not Buckling under EBA's Stress: Focus Moving to Connectivity*, Goldman Sachs Equity Research, 18 July. Brokers report on EBA bank stress tests.

International Monetary Fund (IMF). (2011) *Global Financial Stability Report*, April, IMF, Washington, DC. IMF's take on the risks faced by the global financial markets.

Independent Commission on Banking. (2011) *Independent Commission on Banking: Final Report*, Department for Business Innovation & Skills, London. Report chaired by Sir John Vickers on the causes of the crises, its impact on UK banks and proposals for reform.

Laeven, L., and Valencia, F. (2008) *Systemic Banking Crises: A New Database*, IMF Working Paper, WP/08/224, IMF, Washington, DC. A study detailing the characteristics of systemic banking crises experienced globally over the past century.

Rochet, C.-J. (2010) Systemic risk: Changing the regulatory perspective, *International Journal of Central Banking*, 6(4): 259–75. Analysis of regulatory failures during the crises and proposals for reform.

FURTHER READING

Bank for International Settlements (BIS). (2011) *The Impact of Sovereign Credit Risk on Bank Funding Conditions*, Committee on the Global Financial System, Basel, July. Technical report on how risks associated with (mainly) eurozone bonds impact on bank performance.

Fonteyne, W., Bossu, W., Cortavarria-Checkley, L., et al. (2010) Crisis Management and Resolution for a European Banking System, IMF Working Paper, WP/10/70. Detailed discussion of policy options relating to restructuring European banking post crisis.

The Money and Bond Markets

THE RATE OF INTEREST

So far, we have taken the rate of interest involved in borrowing and lending rather for granted. The time has come, however, to look at it more clearly.

The rate of interest is the price of money. We talk casually of *the* rate of interest, but of course there is no single rate. There are rates appropriate for different borrowers and rates appropriate for different time periods. A medium-sized company making machine tools will expect to pay a higher rate than a government does. A government pays a different rate for borrowing for 3 months than for 10 years.

Several factors affect the rate of interest, and we begin with the two we have just touched on – risk and maturity.

Risk

Let's take risk first. Quite simply, a lender will expect a greater reward for lending to the company making machine tools than for lending to a government. After all, the company may go into liquidation and default. We do not expect our government to default, although Mexico's government and those of other Latin American countries caused panic in international markets when they defaulted in the 1980s (more on that later). Russia's default on its Treasury bills (T-bills) in August 1998 also had widespread repercussions. The problems faced by Greece during 2011 and 2012 witnessed the severe problems that a near sovereign default may cause (see Chapter 12 for detailed discussion of the eurozone crisis).

So far as the governments of OECD countries are concerned, say, or the US government, the lowest rates of interest in their economies will apply to government transactions because they are regarded as the safest, although some have recently doubted that government debt is necessarily a safe asset in light of the eurozone debt crisis. The government rate thus becomes the benchmark for other rates. For example, an American corporate wishing to borrow for 3 months might be advised to expect to pay 'Treasuries plus 1%', that is, 1% more than the current rate for US government T-bills. It is more convenient to express it this way than as an absolute rate because rates vary in wholesale markets, even daily. For example, let's say 3-month T-bills pay 3.875%. The rate for our US company is thus 4.875%. However, tomorrow, T-bills may be 3.75%, and the corporate rate becomes 4.75%.

As a result, we find it easier to express the rate as 'Treasuries plus 1%'. Of course, the corporate may become more secure as profits increase and the balance sheet improves. Their investment bankers may express the view that they now see their appropriate rate as 'Treasuries plus 90 bp'. What does this mean? A basis point is useful for expressing small differences in rates. It is ¹/₁₀₀ of 1%. Thus, 50 bp is equal to 0.5% and 100 bp is equal to 1%. The difference between any given rate and the benchmark US government rate will be called 'the spread over Treasuries'. In the above case, the corporate has found that its spread over US government T-bill rates has fallen from 1% to 0.9%. Spreads vary according to the perceived credit risk of the borrower and are influenced by the performance of the borrower in question as well as the state of the economy. Since the start of the credit crisis, spreads on many forms of borrowing have increased – we noted in Chapter 5 that spreads on syndicated loans, for example, had increased from below 100 bp (over LIBOR) to at least 250 bp by mid-2009 due to the deteriorating economic environment.

Maturity

Maturity is another important aspect, and it doesn't always make sense in practice. Economic theory tells us that lenders will want a higher rate of interest for lending money for 5 years than for 3 months. This relationship between the rate of interest and time is called the yield curve. If rates for longer term lending are higher than for shorter term lending, we would expect the yield curve to look like that in Figure 7.1.

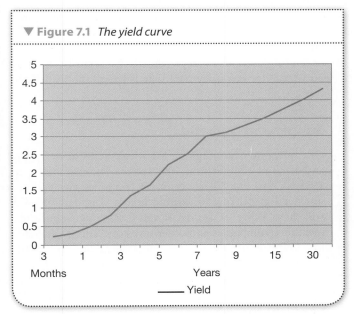

▼ **Figure 7.1** *The yield curve*

The yield curve is upward sloping, or positive. Unfortunately, although this makes complete sense, it often doesn't work that way in real life. Sometimes, short-term rates are higher than long-term ones, and we talk of a 'negative', or downward-sloping, yield curve. This may be due to government policy. They change short-term interest rates either to stimulate the economy or to slow it down. For example, from October 1989 to October 1990 in the UK, short-term rates were 15% while the government attempted to slow down a rate of inflation in excess of 10%. Investment in a 10-year government bond, however, only returned about 11%. Conversely, in mid-1992, the US government was desperately trying to 'kick-start' the economy. Short-term rates were only a little over 3%, whereas the price of a 30-year government bond was such that it yielded about 7.5%.

As interest rates fell in both the US and the UK from 2007 to 2011, the long-term yield became substantially higher than the short-term yield. By the start of March 2012, the short-term UK yield stood at just under 0.5%, whereas 25-year gilts were around 3.5% (15-year gilts yielded 2.5%). Similar trends are apparent in the US and Europe. This reflects the current recessionary features of Western economies – short-term rates have been cut in an attempt to boost depressed economies, whereas longer term rates reflect more normal economic circumstances. Financial commentators spend a lot of time looking at yield curve features, as these can change frequently and influence the pricing of many short- and long-term securities because government rates effectively are the lowest risk benchmark rate. Some, however, are rather sceptical about the use of yield curves as a forecasting tool. For instance, Milton Ezrati, an economist at Lord Abbett, fund manager, joked: 'The yield curve has predicted 12 of the last seven recessions!'

Expectations

Markets are also affected by expectations. Suppose everyone believes firmly that the general level of interest rates is due to *fall*. Lots of people will want to lend money for long periods and benefit from higher interest rates. Not many people want to borrow long term – they would rather wait until rates fall. As a result, long-term rates start to fall in relation to short-term rates. Conversely, if rates are expected to *rise*, everyone wants to lend short term, hoping to gain from higher rates later. Borrowers prefer to borrow long term and lock in to lower rates while they can. Long-term rates will now rise in order to attract funds to meet the demands of borrowers.

Liquidity

Liquidity also affects the rate of interest, that is, how quickly can the lender get the money back. This is not quite the same as maturity. There may well be one rate for 3-month money and another for 5-year money, but another consideration in the case of 5-year money is whether the lender change his/her mind and get the money back.

A savings bank will pay lower interest on a 'no notice' or 'sight' account than on a '3-months' notice' account. We have to pay (by way of a lower rate of interest) for the flexibility of being able to withdraw our money at any time.

In wholesale markets, if our lending of money is represented by a security, one way of getting the money back prior to the normal repayment date is to sell the security to someone else.

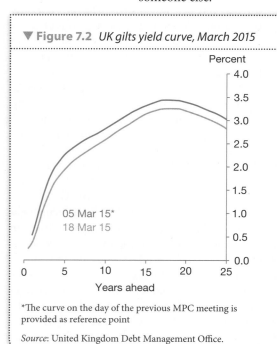

▼ **Figure 7.2** *UK gilts yield curve, March 2015*

05 Mar 15*
18 Mar 15

*The curve on the day of the previous MPC meeting is provided as reference point

Source: United Kingdom Debt Management Office.

Supply and Demand

Of course, we cannot ignore the whole question of supply and demand in different market sectors. For example, from 1988 to 1990, the UK government was in surplus and did not need to borrow by issuing bonds. The demand was still there, however, from UK and foreign pension funds, insurance companies and other investors. This contributed to a lowering of interest rates for government bonds. The supply/demand factor can perhaps be seen at its best when one looks at the yield curve for UK government bonds in March 2015 (Figure 7.2). They can also show how yields vary from year to year.

In March 2015, the yield curve for up to 5 years suggests that rates will increase to around 2.5% by 2025. Longer term bonds (20 years) yield higher returns of around 3%, irrespective of whether the borrowing is for 20 or 25 years. Remember, one can also have an inverted yield – experienced in the UK in 1996 when short-term rates were higher than longer rates. This is rather unusual and simply reflects the fact that long-term investors will settle for lower yields now if they think rates – and the economy – are going even lower in the future.

There is a higher demand for short-term paper compared to longer term issues. Long-term investors are betting that this is their last chance to lock in rates before long rates decline.

Another example of unusual market factors was in early 2006, when UK pension funds' desire for a certain income in the future led to a rush to buy the government's 50-year index-linked gilts. The *real* return (after inflation) fell at one point to only 0.5% – a clear supply-and-demand effect. In March 2009, the government failed to sell £1.75bn of 40-year bonds as investors only bid for £1.63bn of the debt. These weak demand conditions reflected concerns over the state of the public finances, because government borrowing had increased dramatically as a result of the bank bailout programme.

Inflation

Finally, whether a given rate of interest represents good value or not may depend on the rate of inflation. Economists talk of the *real* rate of interest, that is, the nominal rate of interest minus the rate of inflation.

In the UK in 1989–90, interest rates reached 15% while the government desperately tried to curb inflation, which had reached 11%. In 1992, the rate of interest had fallen to 10%, but inflation had fallen to less than 4%. Thus, although nominal rates had fallen from 15% to 10%, the *real* rate had risen from 4% to over 6%. In March 2012, with nominal rates of 0.5% and inflation at 3.6%, real rates were at a record low of −3.1%. The creation of negative real interest rates in the UK (and the US) from 2008 onwards, which is the first time negative real rates have occurred in the UK for 27 years, has been a drastic policy action aimed to stimulate demand in depressed economies – it also acts to deter savings.

Yield

Yield is arguably the most important term in the financial markets. Yield is the return to the investor expressed as an annual percentage. As the markets are all about raising capital, the yield is crucially important. Unfortunately, it's not as easy as it seems.

Suppose we have a bond issued in 1996 and maturing in 25 years – 2021. The bond pays a rate of interest of 10% once per year. What is the yield? At first, the answer seems obvious – 10%. 'If I buy the bond', you argue, 'I get 10% – where's the problem?' The problem is that your answer is only true if you paid the full price for the bond.

Par Values

Bonds have a par, or 'nominal', value. This is usually taken to be $1,000, £100, €1,000 and so on. This is the amount on which the rate of interest is based and the amount which will be repaid at maturity. You buy the 25-year 10% bond and pay the par value of $1,000. Your yield is 10%. However, as secondary market trading begins, investors may pay either more or less than $1,000 for the bond with a par value of $1,000 – this affects the yield. The price of the bond is expressed as a percentage of the par value. For example, if the price is 90, then the price for $1,000 par value is $900. In the UK, £100 is taken to be the par value. A price of 90 means that the price for £100 par value is £90.

Suppose the 25-year bond mentioned above is a UK government bond and you buy £5,000 worth at issue: After all, government bonds are the safest, aren't they? 2 years later, you need the money and decide to sell. Now, however, the level of interest rates has changed. The yield on long-dated government bonds is now 12.5%. As you try to get full price for your 10% bond, no one is interested. Why should they pay you £100 to receive £10, when they could buy a new bond for £100 and get £12.50? They might pay you £80, because your bond pays £10 once per year, and £10 for an investment of £80 is 12.5%. Therefore, as interest rates went *up*, the price of your bond went *down*. The face rate of interest is 10%, but by buying it more cheaply, the yield has increased to 12.5% because £10 is 12.5% of £80.

Let's say that you refuse to sell. 2 years later, you have lost your job and life is grim. You must sell your bonds, come what may. However, things have changed again. The yield on long-dated government bonds is now only 8%. When you attempt to sell your 10% bond, you will find no shortage of buyers willing to pay you more than par, because 10% is very attractive if current rates are 8%. As a result, as interest rates went *down*, the price of your bond went *up*. In theory, buyers might pay £125, because the income of £10 returns 8% which is the market rate, that is, £10 is 8% of £125.

Interest Yield

Just to cover more market jargon, the face rate of interest on the bond is called the 'coupon', for reasons that will be explained later. The calculation we made above when arriving at the yield was

$$\text{Coupon/Price} = \text{Yield}$$

for example £10/£80 = 12.5%
or £10/£125 = 8%

This calculation of yield is called the flat yield (the terms 'interest', 'running' and 'annual yield' are also used). It's not difficult, but not really helpful either.

Gross Redemption Yield

Let's go back to the illustration above of the effect of yields rising to 12.5%. We suggested that someone might buy your bond for £80. We argued:

1 Buy the new 12.5% bond for £100 – yield 12.5%
2 Buy the existing 10% bond for £80 – yield 12.5%.

Unfortunately, we've omitted one crucial factor – redemption. When the bond is redeemed, the government will pay £100. In case 1, there is no capital gain. In case 2, there's a capital gain of £20. As a result, the yield is more than 12.5% if we throw this factor in. Equally, if anyone paid £125, they would face a loss of £25 at redemption. The market does its calculations on the assumption that the bond is kept until redemption.

We need, therefore, an all-embracing calculation that includes the interest yield and modifies it by any gain or loss at redemption. The resultant figure is the gross redemption yield (or yield to maturity) ('Gross' means ignoring tax; as we don't know the investor's tax status, we ignore consideration of any tax that might be due on the interest or on any capital gain). The formula itself is quite complicated, as it's based on discounted cash flow. We are taking the future stream of revenue – interest and redemption – and calculating the yield that would equate this to today's bond price. Alternatively, we could feed into the formula a desired yield and calculate the price to be paid that would achieve that yield. That's why it's so important – it's how bond dealers calculate bond prices.

Suppose, however, that a bond pays 10% and the market yield is 12.5%, but redemption is not in 2021, but 2 months away. Does this make any difference? Will the bond still only sell for about £80? Surely not – here is a piece of paper that in 2 months is worth £100.

Why was the bond price so poor in our original example? It was because the bond offered 10% and the market wanted 12.5%, but if there are only 2 months' interest payments left, this hardly matters. What matters is that redemption at £100 is quite near.

The result is that the nearer we get to redemption, the nearer the secondary market price moves to £100, and the less important interest rate changes are. Thus, long-dated bonds are highly sensitive to interest rate changes (interest rates *up*, bond prices *down* and vice versa) but short-dated bonds are not.

Consider two 10% bonds. The ultimate reward for the buyer is the interest payments and the redemption value. Suppose one bond has 1 year to run, and the other, 20 years.

Case No.		Interest Payments £	+	Redemption £	=	Reward £
1	1 year to go	10	+	100	=	110
2	20 years to go	200	+	100	=	300

In case 1, most of the reward is redemption, not affected by interest rate changes. In case 2, most of the reward is interest payments. If these don't match the market yield, the effect on price will be very serious. This is shown diagrammatically in Figure 7.3.

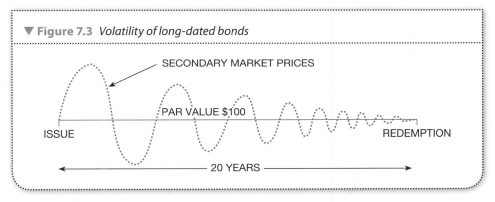

▼ **Figure 7.3** *Volatility of long-dated bonds*

SECONDARY MARKET PRICES

PAR VALUE $100

ISSUE

REDEMPTION

20 YEARS

Let's verify this against some real prices. These are prices for UK government bonds in July 2009.

Bond				Price £
Case 1	Treasury	8%	2009	100.78
	Treasury	5.75%	2009	101.67
Case 2	Treasury	8%	2021	140.31
	Treasury	5%	2025	110.86

Source: Data from United Kingdom Debt Management Office (2015) Gilt Market. Contains public sector information licensed under Open Government Licence v3.0.

Notice that in case 1 we have two bonds, one paying 8% and one 5.75%. It might be thought that the 8% would be much more expensive, when in fact the prices are almost identical – they are both near redemption (at the end of 2009). In case 2, one bond pays 8% and the other 5%, which is fully reflected in the two prices. Here, redemption is 12–15 years away.

In US bond markets, you still find the use of fractions down to $\frac{1}{32}$. Sensibly, Europe uses decimals. The smallest price movement, in one case $\frac{1}{32}$ and in the other 0.01, is called (curiously) a 'tick'. Thus, a cry of 'Treasuries are up 5 ticks' in the US would mean ⁵/₃₂. A similar cry in Germany would mean 0.05.

You will gather from the above discussion that dealers holding an inventory of long-dated bonds are at risk of interest rate changes. They may seek to hedge this risk using a futures exchange, and we explain this in Chapter 14. Equally, if you want to buy bonds as a short-term investment, it might be better to buy short-dated bonds, where the risk of market interest rate changes is less.

As an illustration of the dangers, you might like to read Michael Lewis's excellent *Liar's Poker* (1989). He tells the story of how Howie Rubin, a Merrill Lynch trader, lost $250m on long-dated bonds in 1987 in one fateful deal.

Accrued Interest

Unfortunately, there is one other factor to consider before we leave these somewhat technical questions. It is the question of the timing of the interest payments as illustrated in Box 7.1.

BOX 7.1

Timing of Interest Payments

Suppose the interest is paid twice per year on 16 January and 16 July. You buy a 10% bond in the secondary market on 16 January for £90. You have just missed the interest payment and will have to wait 6 months for the next one. Suppose that you have to sell after 3 months and that prices are unchanged. If you could only sell for £90, this would seem very unfair, as you've held the bond for 3 months and had no reward for your investment. Equally, the buyer would collect 5%, although the bond was only held for 3 months.

Naturally, it doesn't work like that. When you sell your bond, you get the accrued interest to date. If you held £100 nominal value of the 10% bond for 3 months, you would get half the biannual interest, that is, £2.50 (The calculation is simply multiplying the half-yearly interest payments per £100 – £5 in this case – by the number of days the bond is held as a proportion of the days in the half-year). The accrued interest is almost always quoted separately, although there are some exceptions in some markets, such as convertible bonds.

The price without the accrued interest is the clean price. The price you see on a computer screen or in the financial newspapers is always the clean price. If you sell, you will receive the accrued interest in addition. If you buy, you will have to pay it. One reason for accounting for the accrued interest separately is that, in many countries, any gain in this area is subject to income tax. Gains on the clean price are capital gains.

There is a complication. There must be a cutoff point, at which time everyone on the register of holders gets the interest. After this, the bond is marked XD (ex dividend). Suppose the half-year payment is on 10 June. The bonds may go XD on 3 June. However, the interest accrues from 10 December to 10 June. Any sellers selling on 3 June will get the half-year interest to 10 June, although they did not own the bond in the last 7 days. Any buyers buying the bond on 3 June will not accrue any interest until 10 June, even though they have invested their capital 7 days earlier. As a result, when bonds are sold in the XD period, the seller (who gains) *pays* the accrued interest to the buyer (who loses). This is the exception to the way accrued interest is treated.

CREDIT RATINGS

We have seen that the higher the creditworthiness of the borrower, the lower the rate of interest. Some markets (for example the US) want the credit rating of the borrower officially assessed so as to guide them as to the risk and the appropriate rate of interest. There are several companies in the credit rating business but the three most important are Standard & Poor's (McGraw-Hill), Moody's Investors Service (Dun & Bradstreet) and Fitch Ratings. The credit ratings business began in 1909 when John Moody issued his first-ever ratings of company debt – 200 American railway companies.

These organizations look at bond issues and commercial paper issues (to be covered later) and rate them according to the risk. To quote Standard & Poor's (S&P), the ratings are based, in varying degrees, on the following considerations:

1   Likelihood of default – capacity and willingness of the obligor as to the timely payment of interest and repayment of principal in accordance with the terms of the obligation
2   Nature and provisions of the obligation
3   Protection afforded to, and relative position of, the obligation in the event of bankruptcy, reorganization or other arrangement under the laws of bankruptcy and other laws affecting creditors' rights.

A bond that is the best risk is rated AAA by S&P and Aaa by Moody's. The full list for S&P is: AAA, AA, A, BBB, BB, B, CCC, CC, C and D. A bond rated 'D' is either in default or expected to default. As a further refinement, the grade may be modified by plus (+) or minus (–), for example, AA+ or AA. A bond may be issued as AAA but be reduced later to A if the position of the issuer deteriorates. This will increase the borrowing costs of the issuer. Suppose the appropriate rate for an AAA bond is 10%; the rate for an A bond might be 10.75%.

Below the BBB rank there is a sort of invisible line. Bonds rated BBB and above are investment grade – top quality if you like. Many investment funds will only invest if the grade is BBB or higher. Below BBB, to quote S&P again:

> Debt rated 'BB', 'B', 'CCC', 'CC' and 'C' is regarded as having predominantly speculative characteristics with respect to capacity to pay interest and repay principal. 'BB' indicates the least degree of speculation and 'C' the highest degree of speculation. While such debt will likely have some quality and protective characteristics, these are outweighed by large uncertainties or major risk exposures to adverse conditions.

Junk bonds are simply bonds that are not investment grade. This is quite a long story, and we'll tackle it later.

Moody's have a similar system but use slightly different lettering.

The view of risk for a 3-month loan may be quite different from that for a 5-year loan. As a result, both organizations use a simpler system for the shorter term commercial paper. For S&P, this is: A1, A2, A3, B, C and D.

Default could range from simply missing a payment to bankruptcy. Up to the end of 2008, 0.6% of S&P's AAA and 0.5% of Moody's corporate bonds had defaulted. For bonds rated CCC (Caa in the case of Moody's), the default rate was 69%. The fall from grace during the 2000s of top companies, like Enron, WorldCom, Marconi, Parmalat and various banks has led to more defaults from highly rated bonds. Both Moody's and S&P

experienced an increase in default on high-yield debt during 2009 and 2010 due to the worsening economic environment.

Clearly, non-investment grade will have to pay more than investment grade to compensate for the risk. The interest rate spread over investment-grade debt was 300 bp in 1997 but went much higher as we moved into the Russian-inspired crisis in 1998. Since the credit crunch of 2007, spreads over investment grade have exceeded 500 bp – and there has been reasonable activity in the market as companies have sought to raise funds via this market to refinance bank loans. For instance, MGM Mirage (the US casino operator) issued a 5-year $827m senior note paying 11.125% in mid-May 2009.

As an example of the way organizations can lose ratings, we have only to look at the banks. In 1990, there were eight banks (not owned by the state) whose bonds were rated AAA by both organizations – Rabobank, Deutsche, Morgan Guaranty, Barclays, Swiss Bank Corporation, Union Bank of Switzerland, Credit Suisse and Industrial Bank of Japan. Due to commercial bad debts following the recession, by mid-1992, the proud band of eight had shrunk to four – Rabobank, Deutsche, Morgan Guaranty and Union Bank of Switzerland – and then, by January 1997, to one – Rabobank. By March 2012, Rabobank was rated AAA by Moody's and AA by S&P – *Global Finance* ranked it the World's Safest Bank in the same month (although by 2014 its rating had fallen to AA–). In industry and commerce, previously blue-chip companies have also been downgraded, with Corus and Cable & Wireless acquiring junk status in 2002. Finally, in 2005, the downgrades of Ford and General Motors led to shock waves, especially in the derivatives markets; however, in 2012, Ford and General Motors' S&P ratings stood at BB+, a significant improvement compared to the CCC+ of mid-2009.

S&P and Moody's do not always move together. In 1992, for example, Moody's downgraded the Swiss Bank Corporation from AAA, whereas S&P did not follow suit until early 1995.

Credit ratings are used extensively in the domestic US market and the euromarkets (to be explained later). It has not generally been a habit in Europe, but the default of Polly Peck's commercial paper issue in the UK in 1990 led to an increasing use of ratings in this market. Corporate credit ratings are now widely used in Europe. Ratings are not only applied to corporate issues but also to government issues ('sovereign issues'). In December 2008, Moody's downgraded Icelandic debt to 'Baa1' and in July 2009, it also reduced Irish debt to 'Aa1' (following similar moves by S&P and Fitch). In January 2012, S&P downgraded France and Austria (two of the eurozone's six AAA sovereign borrowers), as well as seven other countries not in the top tier, including Spain and Italy, which prompted the French Finance Minister François Baroin to call for a downgrade of the UK on the grounds that the UK economy was in just as bad a shape, if not worse, than France's. All these recent moves simply reflect the troubles faced by the eurozone economies resulting from the banking collapses that had wrecked their systems.

Since the onset of the recent credit crisis, rating agencies have been accused of being too lenient in rating securitization transactions, that is, giving low-risk assessments to complex products, making them more marketable to investors. There are also allegations about major conflicts of interest arising from the fact that advising and rating such assets became a major source of rating agency income, and this may have corrupted their incentives for accurately rating the issuers involved in such structures. As such, there have been various plans announced to increase the regulation of credit rating agencies – in the US these are aimed at restricting agencies from providing consulting services to any firm they rated and would require them to disclose rating fees, although their main business model would not be affected. The eventual outcome of how rating agencies are to be regulated are outlined in detail in the Dodd-Frank Act 2010. Similar action has been taken in Europe, where the new regulatory body – the European Securities and Markets Authority (ESMA) – now oversees the activities of the rating agencies. We will discuss more of these issues in Chapter 10 on the credit crisis.

DOMESTIC MONEY MARKETS

We have previously mentioned that some markets are domestic, that is, transactions are in the local currency and under the control of the local central bank, and some are regarded as international, for example a bond denominated in Japanese yen issued in London through a syndicate of international banks.

There are also money markets, which are short term, that is, borrowing/lending money for 1 year or less, and bond markets, which are markets handling medium- to long-term borrowing/lending. In this chapter, we deal with domestic markets first, covering the various instruments and practices of the money markets, and follow this with bonds. Then we will look at the international markets, both short and long term.

When we look at domestic money markets, we find that there is no single market-place here, like a stock exchange floor. All over the Western financial markets, there are large numbers of people who spend their day buying and selling money in one form and another. Huge sums of money are borrowed or lent, sometimes simply 'overnight'.

Transactions involving the general public and small businesses, like shops, are called the 'retail market'. Transactions between the big players are typically called the 'wholesale market'. The players are central banks, other banks, financial institutions, corporates and specialists, like money brokers and hedge funds. Most of this chapter will be concerned with the wholesale markets.

Call Money

There is a market in money that is borrowed/lent for a very short period of time and is not represented by a marketable instrument or security. Bankers talk of call money and the 'call money market'. Money is lent by one bank to another and may be 'called back' at any time. There is also money lent overnight by one bank to another. 'Overnight' usually means 12.00 p.m. one day to 12.00 p.m. the next day. Sometimes the money may be lent with a right to have the money back with, say, 3 or 7 days' notice. The result, on a bank's balance sheet, becomes 'money at call and short notice'. In most markets, the overnight rate is averaged and used for a variety of purposes. The rate for the 17 eurozone countries is EONIA (Euro Overnight Index Average). For example, Crédit Immobilier de France, the French public entity, issued a 2-year bond where the interest rate is reset every night to EONIA. In London, the equivalent rate (confusingly) is EURONIA, the overnight indexed rate for dealings in the euro in London as opposed to the 18 eurozone countries. The rate for overnight dealings in London in sterling is SONIA (Sterling Overnight Index Average). There is also RONIA (Repurchase Overnight Index Average) for secured sterling overnight cash transactions.

The Interbank Market

Apart from the very short-term money mentioned above, there is generally a strong interbank market, in which banks lend money to one another for periods ranging from several weeks to 1 year. We say that there is 'generally a strong interbank market', but there can be times where demand for liquidity outstrips supply and can lead to near gridlock. This happened in early September 2007 in the UK, when interbank lending rates hit a 20-year high as banks stopped lending to one another due to concerns about credit quality resulting from the onset of the credit crisis. The authorities eventually had to inject liquidity into the system to get things working. A similar 'dry-up' of liquidity in eurozone and other interbank markets occurred from September 2011 to March 2012, leading to the ECB having to inject around €1 trillion into the market via its long-term refinancing operations (LTRO 1 and LTRO 2), which took place in December 2011 and February 2012 (see Chapter 12).

In our discussions on commercial banking, we concentrated on the idea of banks taking money from deposits and lending it to other people. The banks also top up their funds by borrowing from other banks that have spare liquidity. As this is the marginal cost to the banks for raising new money, their wholesale lending rates are based on the interbank lending rate.

The terms 'bid rate' and 'offer rate' are usually met in securities markets. The bid rate is the dealer's buying rate, and the offer rate is the dealer's selling rate. Obviously, the offer is higher than the bid, as the dealers will buy cheaper than they sell. The difference is called the spread.

Curiously, when it comes to wholesale money, the deposit rate offered by a bank is called the 'bid rate', and the lending rate is called the 'offer rate'. Thus, the interbank rates in London are called LIBOR (London Interbank Offered Rate) and LIBID (London Interbank Bid Rate). We find TIBOR in Tokyo, and EURIBOR for the 18 countries of the EMU. One exception is the US, where the interbank rate is called the 'federal funds rate'.

We have already seen that interest rates vary with time, and so the interbank rates will probably be different for 1 month, 3 months, 6 months and 1 year. The most common maturity used in the market is 3 months. If someone asks, 'What's the £ LIBOR rate today?', she will be referring to 3-month LIBOR. Of course, the interbank market in London deals in dollars, yen, Swiss francs and other currencies and so, although LIBOR refers to London, it doesn't necessarily mean sterling. Again, these wholesale rates vary all the time, and each bank's rate could be different. If we say £ LIBOR is 5.0625%, we mean the average of major banks in the market. Rates quoted for 3-month money in currencies in London in December 2011 are shown in Table 7.1.

As London is a huge international market, the rate we hear of most commonly is LIBOR. We have seen that as LIBOR is the marginal cost of new money, the lending rate in wholesale markets may be quoted as 'LIBOR + ¼', 'LIBOR + 35 bp', 'LIBOR + 0.5%'. Equally, floating rate notes issued in London will have the rate reset periodically (typically every 3 or 6 months) as LIBOR plus a given margin. If the rate for a loan or floating rate note is reset every 3 months, but LIBOR is different at different times of the day, then we need to define this precisely. It is usually quoted as the average of the LIBOR rates given by nominated banks at 11.00 a.m. on the relevant day.

In early July 2012, Barclays was fined £290m after it was found that some of its derivatives traders had attempted to rig this key rate. Evidence stretching back to 2005 suggested that both LIBOR and EURIBOR had been fixed. By the end of July 2012, there were ongoing investigations into other banks surrounding a full-blown LIBOR and other rate fixing scandal. Details of the scandal and the new LIBOR rate – ICE LIBOR – are shown in Box 7.2.

▼ **Table 7.1** *Three-month LIBOR, 4 August 2014 (%)*

$	0.23710
€	0.17286
£	0.56050
¥	0.13000

Source: ICE Benchmark Administration Limited.

BOX 7.2

London Interbank Offered Rate (LIBOR) Scandal

The LIBOR scandal refers to the fraudulent activity related to fixing of the major global interbank rate.

LIBOR is calculated as an average interest rate submitted by major banks in London who decide on a daily fix.

Problems arose in 2012 when it was revealed that some banks were artificially increasing or decreasing their submitted rates to manipulate the LIBOR setting and to profit from trades related to these prices. Some of the rate fixing also sought to give the impression that some banks were more creditworthy than they actually were.

LIBOR rates underpin pricing in the $350 trillion global derivatives market as well as in other wholesale banking markets. It was administered by the British Bankers Association, but responsibility was transferred to the Intercontinental Exchange (ICE) which had acquired NYSE Euronext in December 2012.

In January 2014, ICE Administration took up responsibility for setting the new price benchmark now known as ICE LIBOR.

Problems regarding the setting of LIBOR came to a head in June 2012 when Barclays made major financial settlements relating to manipulation of the rate. This also revealed collusion and fraudulent activities of other member banks related to rate submission.

A report on 27 July 2012 in the *Financial Times* suggested that manipulation had been commonplace since the early 1990s, and other reports in Europe and the US also highlighted various rate-rigging activity. As LIBOR is used to price derivatives, and the biggest market is in the US, the price fixing effectively meant that US derivatives markets had been manipulated, and this is a criminal offence (as indeed it is in many other jurisdictions). In addition, the rate rigging was alleged to have cost investors billions of dollars due to adverse mispricing.

Since these revelations, major banks (among others) have had to pay massive fines/settlements regarding these rigging activities: Barclays ($500m), UBS ($1.7bn); Rabobank ($1.1bn); RBS ($300m); Lloyds ($370m); Deutsche ($260m); JP Morgan ($120m); Citibank ($120m); and so on.

Due to the aforementioned rigging allegations, the UK Government set up a review (Wheatley Review) that recommended a new administrator for LIBOR setting. The new administrator, as noted above, is ICE, and the new rate is known as ICE LIBOR.

ICE LIBOR (formerly known as BBA LIBOR) is a benchmark rate produced for five currencies with seven maturities quoted for each – ranging from overnight to 12 months, producing 35 rates each business day.

ICE LIBOR provides an indication of the average rate at which a LIBOR contributor bank can obtain unsecured funding in the London interbank market for a given period, in a given currency. Individual ICE LIBOR rates are the end product of a calculation based upon submissions from LIBOR contributor banks.

ICE Benchmark Administration (IBA) maintains a reference panel of between 11 and 18 contributor banks for each currency calculated. IBA currently fixes in the following five currencies: CHF (Swiss franc); EUR (euro); GBP (pound sterling); JPY (Japanese yen) and USD (US Dollar).

Following on from the LIBOR scandal it was revealed in June 2013 that major banks had also been involved in rigging foreign exchange rates – a market with total daily turnover exceeding $5.3 trillion. A handful of major banks were fined over $4bn in November 2014 for manipulating benchmark foreign exchange rates (see Table 7.2 for the details).

With the arrival of EMU, we now have the interbank market of the 18 countries in the eurozone and its reference rate, EURIBOR; and we have the interbank market in London in the euro and its reference rate, Euro LIBOR. As LIBOR has always been a major reference rate for bond issues, derivatives, and other transactions, the question arose – which one would win? The answer was EURIBOR. Even London's derivatives exchange LIFFE (now part of NYSE Euronext) admitted defeat in February 1999 and changed its contracts to EURIBOR.

Money Market Securities

The markets we have described above – the call money market and the general interbank market – deal with wholesale borrowing and lending among banks and financial institutions. The transactions are not represented by any security that can be traded. We will now deal with money market transactions that do result in trading in securities.

Typical instruments are T-bills, local authority/public utility bills, certificates of deposit, commercial paper and bills of exchange.

Treasury bills (T-bills)

Governments find that their income from taxes does not come in at a steady rate, nor is their expenditure at a steady rate. Apart from raising money with medium- to long-term government bills, it's convenient and useful to be able to borrow for shorter periods and balance their cash flow. The chosen instrument is the Treasury bill (T-bill) (the UK and the US), *bon du Trésor* (France), *Schatzwechsel* (Germany, Austria), GKOs in Russia or similar terms.

The bills may or may not be offered to the same organizations who buy government bonds. In the US, T-bills for 3 or 6 months or 1 year are sold by weekly auction to the same primary dealers who buy federal notes and bonds. In the UK, the 3- and 6-month T-bills are sold every Friday by auction to banks. In France, anyone who has an account with the central bank can buy 3- or 6-month or 1-year T-bills. They are sold weekly, and money market dealers are usually called *opérateurs principaux du marché*. In Germany, the Bundesbank sells 6-month bills called *Bubills* every quarter.

The payment of interest on an instrument that only lasts 3 months is not necessarily convenient. Most typically, money market instruments are sold *at a discount*. For example, suppose we are talking about a 1-year US T-bill, value $100, sold by auction. A dealer may bid $94. If accepted, the dealer pays $94 and 1 year later receives $100 from the government. The dealer discounted the $100 by 6% but now earns $6 for investing $94, which is 6.38%. Thus, the market refers to the discount rate and the resulting yield.

We have mentioned the term 'sale by auction' (or tender). There are two kinds. In one, everyone pays the price he ('bid price auction'). In the other, everyone pays the same price (often called a 'uniform price auction', where the price is known as the 'strike price'). Anyone bidding at or above the strike price will receive an allocation, but not necessarily all he bids for. Both types of auction are used in financial markets. For example, the Bank of England sells weekly T-bills by tender to the highest bidders – the bid price technique. Government bonds are also sold on a bid price basis unless they are index-linked stock, and then the striking price is used.

Just to confuse matters, a German publication we have seen says that the money market instruments are sold by auction on a bid price basis, which it calls 'US style', calling a striking price auction a 'Dutch auction'. A French publication says that money market instruments are sold on a bid price basis, which it calls a 'Dutch auction'. Although the Germans are probably right, let's avoid all mention of Dutch auctions and simply say that if everyone pays the price she bids, it is a 'bid price' auction, and if everyone pays the same price, it is a 'strike price' auction. Both methods are used. On balance, the bid price method seems to be the most common, although Federal Reserve auctions are now using the strike price.

Local authority/public utility bills

These may be offered by municipalities, geographic departments, federal states, or public bodies like railways, electricity, gas and so on. There is a strong market in public sector bills as well as bonds in France and Germany. There are issues by SNCF or EDF, or by the railways and post offices in Germany (Bundesbahn and Bundespost), as well as by the individual federal states. The market in the UK for local authority/municipal bills is weak, but it is large in the US. By 2011, the US municipal bond market alone comprised over 1.5 million issues sold by 50,000 municipal issuers with a wide range of credit ratings, and traded and underwritten by around 2,000 securities dealers. The US municipal bond market amounted to $3.7 trillion by the fourth quarter of 2013, the same level as in 2011. This market alone represents many times the number of issues listed on all US stock exchanges.

Certificates of deposit

Certificates of deposit (CDs) are receipts issued by banks when soliciting wholesale deposits. The lenders may be other banks, corporates or investment institutions. The advantage to the *borrower* is that the money is lent for a specific period of time, for example 3 months. The advantage to the *lender* is that if they need the money back earlier, the certificate can be sold to someone else quite easily. There is a strong CD market in the US and the European economies, with the exception of Germany.

There is usually an active and efficient CD market. As a result, yield rates will be a little less than those for 'sight' deposits, as we must pay for the advantage of liquidity.

Commercial paper

So far, we have looked at short-term borrowing by governments, municipalities, public sector bodies and banks. There remains the question of corporates. Commercial companies can borrow in the wholesale markets and offer a security called commercial paper (CP). It's just another promise to pay back. Central banks have to agree, as this is a deposit-taking activity and must be controlled. There will be rules by which companies can or cannot borrow using CP. For example, in the UK, companies must have a balance sheet capital of £25m and be publicly quoted on a stock exchange, although not necessarily in the UK. The minimum denomination is £100,000.

Commercial paper is an older market in the US, where it is a huge market with outstanding money at the start of 2014 amounting to just over $1,000bn. It has hit Europe in the past 15 years. Germany was the last major market to allow CP issues, in January 1991. Before that, it was not practical due to a securities tax and the need for prior notification to the Treasury. Outside Europe, China started a CP market in late 2005. Let's have a look at some figures on CP markets (from the BIS) in Table 7.2, which focuses on international CP issues, namely issuers raising funds outside their home country or currency. The US Fed reports that in March 2014 the US CP market stood at $1.027 trillion (a big decline

▼ **Table 7.2** *International commercial paper issuance, March 2014 (amounts outstanding)*

Market	$ billion
TOTAL	513.7
By currency	
US dollar	194.7
Euro	178.4
Yen	1.5
Pound sterling	107.1
Swiss franc	3.5
Canadian dollar	3.4
Other currencies	20.3
By issuer	
Financial institutions	445.5
Governments	35.3
International organizations	19.0
Corporate issuers	13.9

Source: BIS https://www.bis.org/statistics/secstats.htm.

on the $1.7 trillion reported in mid-2008 before the onset of the credit crisis). Nevertheless, the US still has by far the largest CP market, with banks being the main borrowers. The decline is because banks used CP issuance in a big way to finance their securitization activity up to the crisis, but this business has now disappeared. In addition, the credit-worthiness of banks has also collapsed, making it difficult (if not impossible) for them to issue large amounts of CP.

CP issues are, of course, just another way of borrowing money and may provide an alternative to borrowing from the bank. In early 1990, the Bank of Spain was struggling to control the credit explosion and limiting banks' ability to lend. The result was a huge increase in CP (*pagares de empresa*) issues, as companies borrowed by selling CP – in some cases to the same banks who couldn't lend them money.

International debt securities for Q4 2013. Note that 'other' international money market instruments amounted to $356.3 billion compared with the $513.7 billion of commercial paper.

Deregulation applies here as in other markets. The French now allow non-French entities to issue domestic CP, and Germany did so from August 1992. At the end of 1995, outstanding CP in Germany from foreign issuers was higher than that from domestic issuers.

How do the CP issuers find the lenders? They set up a programme (perhaps a 5-year programme) and announce a bank or banks as dealers. If the programme is $500m, then the issuer does not intend to raise $500m now, which would be the case if it were a bond issue, but will borrow money from time to time and repay it from time to time, up to the maximum figure. If they wish to borrow $50m for 2 months, they would notify the bank dealer(s), who ring round typical lenders (other corporates, banks and investment institutions) and tie up the deal, all for a small commission. The banks do not *guarantee* to find lenders but if lenders are scarce; they may buy the CP themselves as a matter of goodwill. The effect of borrowing from lenders directly, instead of borrowing from the bank, means that the rate may be less than the interbank rate.

Bills of exchange

Another way in which a corporate might raise money short term is by selling on a short-term trade debt (we met this in Chapter 5). The seller draws up a bill promising to pay for the goods supplied in, say, 3 months and asks the buyer to sign it. This is the bill of exchange. The seller of the goods can now sell this at a discount to the banks or general money market operators. We have seen that a bank's promise to pay may be better than a trader's, and there is always a distinction between bills with the trader's signature (trade bills) and those with a bank's signature (bank or eligible bills). Bills may change hands several times in their short life. There are usually restrictions on the type of transaction that can be represented by a bill, and so not all corporates can use bills of exchange. They are not especially popular in the US but are widely used in Europe, especially in the UK. In France, the bill is called a *lettre de change*, and in Germany, *Wechsel*.

We have now met several ways in which a corporate might raise money short term – bank overdraft, a general uncommitted bank line of credit, a revolving credit programme, a CP issue or using bill of exchange finance.

CENTRAL BANK ROLE

A key role is played in domestic money markets by central banks. They have a function as lender of the last resort, which we met in Chapter 3. They are prepared to help the other banks (especially commercial banks) with their liquidity problems. As mentioned earlier, UK and US authorities have been very active since the autumn of 2007, injecting liquidity into their troubled banking systems, as has the ECB via its LTRO 1 and 2 in December 2011 and February 2012, respectively.

Why would banks meet liquidity problems? In the first place, the key commercial banks must maintain working balances at the central bank. Where central banks insist on special reserves being left (Chapter 3), there will be times when the reserves look comfortable and times when they don't. The reserves are usually based on average balances over a month. Until the end of the month, the banks are not sure what the figure will be. Those banks in surplus will lend to other banks; those in deficit will borrow from other banks. At times, all the banks may have problems. This happens when heavy tax payments are being made. The government's bank balance is going up; the banks' balances at the central bank are going down. The central bank will relend the money to keep everything on an even basis and to avoid wide fluctuations in money market rates. The rate set for the central bank's help gives it control over interest rates. When interest rates change, it is because the central bank changes the rate for its help to other banks.

There are usually two ways in which a central bank will help: direct assistance at special rates such as the 'discount rate' or 'Lombard rate'; or by what is called 'open market operations'.

What are these rates? The discount rate is the rate at which the bank will discount eligible bills of exchange (that is, top-quality bills) for other banks. The maturity of the bills must not exceed 3 months. As this rate is below other rates, there is a quota for each bank, or life would be too easy. If we could discount a bill at 9.5% and then refinance ourselves at 8.75% at the central bank, we would soon make a lot of money.

The Lombard rate is an emergency lending rate against top-quality securities (eligible bills, bills of exchange or government/federal bonds). Usually, as it is higher than money market rates, no limit to the quantity need be set. At times, however, limits have had to be set for temporary periods because the Lombard rate was lower than money market rates.

Open market operations means that the central bank may be prepared to buy bills of exchange, T-bills or similar securities to help the banks' liquidity or to sell bills to help drain excess liquidity.

A popular method nowadays is the 'sale and repurchase agreement', commonly called the repo. The central bank will buy nominated securities from the other banks for a stated period, for example 7 days, 14 days, 28 days. At the end of the period, the banks must be ready to buy them back at a rate that includes the rate of interest on the money. The banks sell the securities to the central bank but must repurchase later. This is a common method all over Europe. In the UK, the more common method used to be that the Bank of England would simply buy eligible securities outright. Later, repos became much more common.

These operations exist not only to help commercial banks with their liquidity but can also be used to influence money supply and market conditions. The central banks may keep the banks short of liquidity to keep credit scarce and stiffen interest rates. For example, when a repo falls due, there will normally be another repo to keep the banks funded, but the second repo may be for a smaller sum than the first.

- With the arrival of EMU in Europe, the previously separate systems of the 18 countries have been unified into one system. Policy is laid down by the ECB but is operated on a decentralized basis by the member central banks. Its rates up until 2014 are shown in Box 7.3.

BOX 7.3

Key ECB Interest Rates

There are three main rates:

1 **Deposit Facility** – the rate that banks make use of to place deposits overnight with the Eurosystem. You can see that since June 2014 this rate is negative – so banks actually have to pay to deposit overnight. This is to discourage banks from doing this hoping to prevent more lending.

2 **Fixed Rate** – the rate on the main refinancing operations of the system that provides the bulk of liquidity to the banking system. The main refinancing operations are weekly tenders for funds with a 2-week maturity. There are also monthly tenders with a 3-month maturity. These tenders are essentially repos.

3 **Marginal Lending Rate** – the rate charged for overnight credit to banks from the Eurosystem.

YEAR	Date	Deposit Facility	Fixed Rate	Marginal Lending Rate
2014	10 Sept.	−0.20	0.05	0.30
	11 June	−0.10	0.15	0.40
2013	13 Nov.	0.00	0.25	0.75
	8 May	0.00	0.50	1.00
2012	11 July	0.00	0.75	1.50
2011	14 Dec.	0.25	1.00	1.75
	9 Nov.	0.50	1.25	2.00
	13 July	0.75	1.50	2.25
	13 Apr.	0.50	1.25	2.00
2009	13 May	0.25	1.00	1.75
	8 Apr.	0.25	1.25	2.25
	11 Mar.	0.50	1.50	2.50
	21 Jan.	1.00	2.00	3.00
2008	10 Dec.	2.00	2.50	3.00
	12 Nov.	2.75	3.25	3.75

YEAR	Date	Deposit Facility	Fixed Rate	Marginal Lending Rate
	15 Oct. (5)	3.25	3.75	4.25
	9 Oct. (4)	3.25	-	4.25
	8 Oct.	2.75	-	4.75
	9 July	3.25	-	5.25
2007	13 June	3.00	-	5.00
	14 Mar.	2.75	-	

Source: ECB (2014) and authors' own commentary.

By way of contrast, the Bank of England used to operate on a daily basis using a mixture of repos and outright purchase of securities. (For those with long memories and who seem to recall that the bank did all of its refinancing operations through specialists called 'discount houses', this method has now been abandoned.) However, in May 2006, the whole system changed. From a small group of a dozen banks having to balance their books with the bank every evening, in the future some 40 or so banks and building societies – accounting for nearly all of the UK banking system's sterling balance sheet – will instead maintain a target balance with the bank on average over the month between Monetary Policy Committee (MPC) meetings. To encourage this averaging, for the first time the Bank of England will pay interest, at the MPC's rate, on those bankers' balances.

At the start of the new system, these reserves were more than £20bn. In addition, banks and building societies will be eligible to use standing facilities to place deposits with the bank or borrow from it against high-quality collateral – without limit, but at a penalty rate of interest, which will place a corridor around the market rate. These measures should help to stabilize short-term interest rates, give the banking system more flexibility in managing liquidity and make sterling money markets more user-friendly for non-specialists.

The new system draws on the best elements from elsewhere, such as the US and the eurozone, which tend to operate on a monthly basis rather than daily. The aim is to make the overnight rate more stable – it has tended to be more volatile than in other main currencies.

The decisions are made by the MPC, consisting of the governor, two deputy governors, two bank executives and four outsiders.

In the US, the Federal Reserve operates by influencing the overnight interbank federal funds rate and also the deposit rate for bank assistance. The rates are announced by the Federal Open Market Committee, consisting of the seven-member board of governors and twelve members from the regional Federal Reserve Banks.

DOMESTIC BOND MARKETS

The term 'bond' applies to instruments that are medium to longer term. The term 'note' is also used in some markets. The US, for example, has 2-, 5- and 10-year Treasury notes and a 30-year Treasury bond. In the UK, the same 5-year instrument would be called a bond.

Language is a problem here, in that there is no consistency. The French, for example, call instruments up to 5 years (but prior to 1992, up to 7 years) *bons du Trésor* and from 7 years *obligations assimilables du Trésor* (OATs). The Spanish have *bonos del estado* (Bonos) up to 5 years; after that they are *obligaciones del estado*. On the other hand, the 10-year issue in Italy is *buoni del Tesoro*.

Let's look at some general characteristics of bonds. As we saw in Chapter 1, they are simply receipts, or promises to pay back money lent. We are not talking here of short-term money, however, but medium- to long-term borrowings – in excess of 1 year and possibly for 30 years or more.

The general features of bonds are as follows:

- The name of the bond
- The nominal or par value in the currency of denomination
- The redemption value – usually the nominal value, but there are other possibilities, index linking, for example
- The rate of interest, expressed as a percentage of nominal value, which is called the 'coupon' and in which the frequency of payment is stated
- The redemption date

The rate of interest is called the 'coupon' because 'bearer' bonds have no register of holders. The bond states that the issuer owes the 'bearer', whoever that may be. The bond therefore has attachments called coupons, so the bearer may detach these as required and claim the interest. Even where bonds are registered and the interest can be posted to the holder's home, the market still refers to the 'coupon' or coupon rate.

The coupon could be variable in cases where the rate of interest is changed periodically in line with market rates. As the word 'bond' implies a fixed rate of interest, instruments like this are usually called floating rate notes (FRNs). If issued in London, the coupon may be defined as 'LIBOR + 45 bp' and reviewed 6 monthly.

Some stocks have no redemption date and are called 'undated' or 'perpetual'. If the holder needs the capital, he must sell the bond to someone else in the secondary market.

Typically, bonds are classified by remaining maturity. The scale may well be as follows:

- *Shorts*: life of up to 5 years
- *Mediums:* life of 5–15 years
- *Longs:* life of 15 years or over

Notice that this is the *remaining* maturity. A 20-year bond is a 'long' at first, but 10 years later it's a 'medium', and 6 years later it's a 'short'.

At original issue, bonds may be sold as an open offer for sale or sold directly to a smaller number of professional investors and called a private placing.

In an offer for sale, a syndicate of banks with one bank as lead manager will buy the bonds en bloc from the issuer and resell them to investors. In this way, they underwrite the issue, because if the investors don't buy, the banks will be forced to keep them. Needless to say, they charge fees for this risk.

If the lead bank buys all the bonds and sells them to the syndicate, it's usually called the 'bought deal'. The syndicate members may themselves then sell the bonds at varying prices. More commonly these days, the lead manager and syndicate buy the bonds simultaneously and agree to sell at the same price for a period – the 'fixed price reoffering'.

This is common in the US and in the so-called 'euromarkets'. Less frequently (apart from government bonds), there may not be a syndicate, but the bonds are sold by competitive auction.

There are several types of bond according to the issuer:

- Government bonds
- Local authority/public utility bonds
- Mortgage and other asset-backed bonds
- Corporate bonds
- Foreign bonds
- Junk bonds

Corporate bonds may also be debentures, or convertibles, and there is a hybrid type of instrument, the preference share or participation stock.

Government Bonds (Sovereigns)

Almost always, government bonds seem to dominate the bond markets. Most modern governments are running a budget deficit, and this leads to large-scale issues of bonds. Sometimes the secondary market is run on stock exchanges (France, Germany, the UK) and sometimes outside stock exchanges (the US).

As regards the types of bonds and method of issue, there are many variations:

- The bonds may be issued by the central bank (the US, Germany, France), by the Ministry of Finance (Netherlands, Japan) or by general Debt Management Offices (the UK, Ireland, Sweden, Portugal, New Zealand).
- They may be sold on a regular day per month.
- The issue may be to specialist dealers (the US, the UK, France, Germany, Italy) or to a syndicate of banks in agreed proportions (Switzerland).
- Bonds may be 'bearer' status or registered. For example, in the UK, government bonds are registered, and the registrar's department handles 5 million interest payments per year and 1 million changes of ownership. In Germany, the most important government bonds for the wholesale markets are bearer bonds. There are no certificates, and buying/selling is entered on the computerized Bundesschuldbuch.
- Some markets pay interest twice per year (the US, the UK, Italy, Japan), whereas others only pay once per year (France, Germany, Netherlands, Spain, Belgium).
- US government bonds are priced in fractions (down to $\frac{1}{32}$). Elsewhere, bonds are priced in decimals.

Let's look at some examples.

In the US, 2-year Treasury notes are sold every month, and 5- and 10-year Treasury notes are sold every quarter. They are sold by auction, on regular dates, to some 40 primary dealers. The issue of 30-year bonds was stopped in November 2001 but resumed in 2006 after requests from the Bond Market Association. In general, markets have been keen to lock in relatively low interest rates. Since 2008, it has been regularly rumoured that the US may issue a 50-year (and even 100-year) bond to ease the governments financing obligations, but this has not yet occurred. Canada issued a 50-year bond in April 2014.

In France, government bonds are called OATS and are sold on a regular monthly auction basis (on the first Thursday in each month). They are sold to primary dealers who have an obligation to support the auction. They must take up 3% of annual bond issuance and trade 3% of secondary market turnover. The primary dealers are called *spécialistes en valeurs du Trésor*. However, at each auction, the offerings are usually of existing bonds rather than offering new ones each time. A point to note is that there are 2- and 5-year issues called T-bills rather than bonds. These are known as BTANs (*bons du Trésor à intérêt annuel*), and they are sold on the third Thursday in each month (short-term T-bills are BTFs – *bons du Trésor à taux fixe*).

In line with the trend towards longer dated bonds, the French Treasury issued a 50-year bond in February 2005.

In Germany, there were 2- and 4-year medium-term notes –*Bundesschatzanweisungen*, but these maturities were lowered in mid-1996 to 2 years and referred to as 'Schätze'. There are also 5-year government bonds – *Bundesobligationen*, and 10–30-year bonds – *Bundesanleihen*. The 10-year issues are the popular ones (rather than those of longer duration), and most are fixed rate, although there is the occasional floating rate bond. There are bond issues from the federal states (Länder), the railways and the post office. There are also issues from the German Unity Fund (Fonds Deutsche Einheit). All are issued for them by the Bundesbank. The dealers in German bonds are known as the Federal Loan Bidding Group, and there are about 70 dealers. *Bundesobligationen* are issued in series. A series is offered continuously for 4–6 weeks 'on tap'. They are aimed at retail buyers, as are the Treasury financing notes (*Finanzierungschätze*). At the end of the period, the unsold bonds are offered for sale by auction. The main retail bond for savers, however, is the *Bundesschatzbriefe*. These are sold continuously by all banks and financial institutions and are for 6 or 7 years. The bonds can be sold back at par at any time, but the longer the holder keeps them, the greater the rate of interest.

All French and German bonds are now issued in the new currency, the euro, and all outstanding bonds have also been converted to the euro.

In Japan, government bonds are sold by auction by the Ministry of Finance. Some 40% are sold to a bank syndicate in agreed proportions and 60% are sold by the auction method. 2, 4-, 5-, 6- and 10-year bonds are sold monthly, and 20-year bonds are sold quarterly. Interest payments are biannual. Government, municipal and public sector bonds are 60% of issuance and dominate the market. In May 2009, the Ministry of Finance made the fifth issue of 40-year bonds, raising $2.1bn – this is the longest maturity in the Japanese fixed-income market.

In the UK, government bonds are called gilts or 'gilt-edged', meaning a very secure investment (the term came into widespread use in the 1930s). The bonds are issued on regular dates and sold to 13 specialist dealers called 'gilt-edged market makers'. Bonds not taken up at an auction are bought by the Debt Management Office and sold whenever the dealers want them as tap stock. Maturities range typically from 5 to 25 years, but 50-year bonds have now been issued. There was particular interest in the issue in September 2005 of the world's first index-linked 50-year bond. It was not sold as usual by an auction, but to a syndicate of investment banks; this allowed the issue to be increased if there was high demand. It was, in fact, increased from £1bn to £1.25bn. There was a large demand from pension funds and insurance companies, anxious to match long-dated liabilities with assets.

Gilts are divided into three main classes: dated, undated and index linked. New undated gilts are no longer issued, but there are six still in existence, although in October 2014, the UK government announced that it was to repay some of these bonds off. The Treasury said it would pay off £218m from a 4% consolidated loan next February, as part of a redemption of bonds stretching as far back as the 18th century. They also relate to the South Sea

Bubble crisis of 1720, the Napoleonic and Crimean wars and the Irish potato famine. In fact, almost £2bn of First World War debt remains, and the government said it was looking into the practicalities of repaying it in full. The bonds being paid off are '4% consols' that were issued in 1927 by Winston Churchill, then chancellor, to refinance national war bonds originating from the First World War. The government's Debt Management Office (DMO) estimates that the nation has paid £1.26bn in interest on these bonds since 1927.

The aforementioned bonds have no redemption date. In bond markets, bonds with no redemption date are called undated, perpetual or irredeemable. There is speculation that the UK government is considering issuing 100-year gilts and possibly undated bonds to meet both the long-term financing needs of the state as well as to fill demand for longer dated instruments by institutional investors. There is very little trading of undated gilts by the wholesale markets.

Index-linked gilts pay a rate of interest and a redemption value based on the change in the Retail Price Index (RPI) in the same period. In July 2009, the UK issued £5bn worth of 33-year index-linked bonds, and the Treasury offered the 0.625% bonds, due to yield 0.886% in 2042, or seven basis points lower than comparable securities maturing in 2037. The UK index-linked sector accounts for around a quarter of all outstanding government bonds, further long-dated index-linked bonds, maturing in 2062 and 2068, were issued in October 2011 and September 2013, respectively. Other governments that offer index-linked bonds are Australia, Canada, Iceland, Israel, New Zealand, Sweden and, more recently, the US, France, Japan (10-year inflation-linked bonds were introduced in 2004) and Germany. China issued an index-linked bond in 1998. In May 1996, the US Treasury announced that it would issue index-linked Treasury notes and bonds for the first time, and began in January 1997. In the US, they are known as Treasury inflation-protected securities (TIPS), and the principal is adjusted to the Consumer Price Index (CPI). Of the $6.7 trillion of US government bonds issued between October 2008 and June 2009, around $44bn were TIPS, so it's a relatively small part of the market. The French government issued its first inflation-linked bond in September 1998, and many others have followed.

In 1973, the French government issued Giscard bonds linked to the change in the price of gold between then and 1988. As the price of gold rose, this caused great embarrassment. A fictitious example of a Giscard bond was used by Tom Wolfe in *The Bonfire of the Vanities* (1987) to highlight the 'wheeling and dealing' of Wall Street investment bankers, although some say the fictitious transactions were based on an actual Salomon Brothers deal.

Given prospects for greater inflation, there has been renewed interest in issuing index-linked bonds. For example, the Australian Office of Financial Management announced in August 2009 that it was to offer its sixth issue of index-linked bonds, as the massive fiscal stimulus resulting from the credit crisis was expected to stimulate price increases. The Japanese and Thailand authorities have also recently stated that they are considering similar issues. This followed on from the long-dated issue made by the UK authorities in July 2009 and explained above.

Why do governments issue index-linked bonds? There are three. reasons:

1   Risk-averse investors, such as pension funds and retired people, like the idea.
2   Monetary policy is more credible – the government has an incentive to keep inflation low.
3   The yield helps the government and others to estimate market views on further inflation. The difference between the yield on index-linked stock and ordinary stock should equal the expected inflation rate.

The idea is not totally new. In 1780, the state of Massachusetts issued a bond where payment of interest and principal was linked to a commodity basket of corn, beef, wool and leather.

Spanish government bonds are called *bonos del estado*, with maturities of 3 and 5 years, but the 10-year maturity is called *obligaciones del estado*. The central bank sells these on a regular date each month.

Italian government bonds are called BTP (*buoni del Tesoro poliennali*) if fixed rate. These are 2–10 years in maturity. However, there are floating rate bonds of similar maturity called CCT (*certificati credito del Tesoro*). Both are sold by the central bank to 20 primary dealers on fixed dates every month. There are also 6-year bonds that buyers can sell back after 3 years called CTO (*certificati del Tesoro con opzione*).

There seems to be a trend towards governments issuing longer dated bonds than in the past. In early 1999, Japan and Greece issued their first 30-year bonds, and Switzerland issued a 50-year bond (the first for Switzerland since 1909). In the whole eurozone area from the mid-2000s onwards, there were substantially more issues of bonds with maturities of 15 years or more than in previous years.

As explained earlier in this chapter, some auctions of government stock are bid price and some strike price. A bid price auction might seem to be the obvious answer. The argument for the strike price, however, is that it avoids the problem of the 'winner's curse', that is, where some bidders may pay a higher price and end up with bonds they can't sell. The belief is that strike prices may encourage more bidders to participate. Either way, the evidence does not seem to be very strong. The US used to use bid price but now uses strike price; the UK, which used to use strike price, now uses bid price (except for index linked). (An example of the result of a bid price auction is given in the Appendix 1 to this chapter.)

Most government bond markets allow dealing to begin a few days before the auction – the 'when-issued', or 'grey', market. Institutions can buy from primary dealers at an agreed price, which reduces the dealers' risk.

Local Authority/Public Sector Bonds

We have already mentioned issues in Germany by the railways, post offices, federal states and the German Unity Fund. Public sector issues are also common in France. There are the utilities like SNCF, EDF and Gaz de France. There are also public sector bodies like Crédit Foncier (housing credits) and Crédit Local de France (local authority financing). Bonds may, of course, be issued by cities, like New York, or regions, like the Basque Country.

Local authority and public sector issues are rare in the UK, although some long-dated bonds issued in the 1970s are still traded. Municipal bonds are a big market in the US. According to the Securities Industry and Financial Markets Association, issuance of municipal bonds amounted to $330bn in 2013, with $3,671bn outstanding (although the market has hardly grown since 2008, when total outstandings stood at just over $3.5 trillion).

Mortgage and Asset-backed Bonds

In some markets, there is a big market in mortgage bonds. In the US, for example, it has been the custom for many years to bundle up mortgages and use them as the backing security for mortgage bonds. The mortgages may be guaranteed by bodies with names like Ginnie Mae, Fannie Mae and Sallie Mae (naturally, they stand for something much more formal, for example Government National Mortgage Association – GNMA and hence Ginnie Mae). The US mortgage bond market is huge – over $2bn bonds were issued in

2007, although this fell to $1.3bn in 2008 as the credit crunch hit. The market has grown rapidly from $3.6 trillion in 2000 to $8.7 trillion in 2013; it is the second largest part of the domestic bond market, after Treasuries ($11.9 trillion) and bigger than the corporate debt market ($7.5 trillion). The mortgage-backed bond market has been driven by booming house prices, a benign monetary policy and the increasingly inventive ways that banks have structured securitized issues – it was also a major cause of the credit crisis.

In Germany, the 35 members of the Association of German Pfandbrief Banks account for 97% of mortgage bond (*Pfandbrief*) issues. Outstanding mortgage bond issues stood at €390.6bn in 2011. Banks also issue mortgage bonds in various other countries like Denmark, Finland, France and Spain. These are not, however, the same as US mortgage bonds. The latter involve taking the original mortgages off the balance sheet, placing them in a separate special purpose vehicle (SPV) and issuing bonds financed by the stream of principal and interest payments of the mortgages (see Figure 7.4). The German *Pfandbriefe* are simply a way for the banks to raise money to fund their mortgage loans, although they are, of course, a very secure investment.

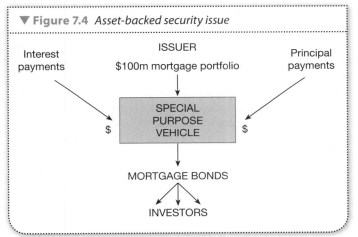

▼ **Figure 7.4** *Asset-backed security issue*

The technique involved in the US case is called securitization of assets, and we refer to asset-backed securities (ABS). You may also see reference to collateralized mortgage obligations (CMOs) or commercial mortgage-backed securities (CMBS). Although we have so far only mentioned the US, the technique has been widely used in the UK and, to a lesser extent, in Europe and Japan. The massive growth in securitization activity and its key role in fuelling the property boom and eventual collapse of the US, UK and other banking systems are outlined in Chapter 10.

Again, we have so far only referred to mortgages, but securitization can and has been used to take any stream of income payments (or income and principal payments) and use them to fund an ABS issue (why banks and others do this will be explained shortly). The market is growing in ingenuity, as will be seen from the following list of income streams that fund ABS issues:

- Auto loans — VW, GM, Porsche, BMW and others
- Record royalties — David Bowie, Rod Stewart, James Brown
- Telephone calls — Telemex, Mexico
- Future export revenues — Brazilian Iron Ore
- Football season tickets — Real Madrid, Lazio, Fiorentina
- Property rentals — British Land and others
- Rolling stock leases — Nomura in the UK
- Credit card receivables — Citibank, MBNA
- Bank corporate loans — National Westminster, Hypovereinsbank
- Non-performing loans — Banca di Roma
- Tax arrears — Portugal
- Life insurance premiums — Swiss Re

Let's look at some examples. The National Westminster Bank issue aroused tremendous interest. It was first used in November 1996 and again in 1997 under the acronym ROSE (repeat offering securitized entity) funding. The first issue was to the value of $5bn and represented as much as one-third of NatWest's corporate loan book, being loans to some 300 large corporates in the UK, Continental Europe and the US. They were issued as 11 classes of notes – various levels of seniority offering a range of risk/return ratios. The bank guarantees anonymity and continues to administer the original loans.

The securitization of intellectual property rights was initiated by the issuance of (David) Bowie bonds in 1997. The bonds were bought for US$55m by the Prudential Insurance Company and paid an interest rate of 7.9%, with collateral from the royalties from the 25 albums (280 plus songs) that Bowie had recorded prior to 1990 – on which he held copyright and recording rights. The average life of the bonds was 10 years. Unfortunately, the bonds did not do well and were downgraded a number of times, reaching just above junk status in May 2003 – mainly due to flagging royalties on Bowie's music. However, there has been a recent increase in interest in securitizing similar rights from royalty flows from established performers since Apple's iTunes came online.

To be feasible, all we need is a pool of homogeneous assets like mortgages, trade receivables, motor car loans and so on. The funds are pooled in the same SPV, which has a 'firewall' between it and the original issuer. The payments are sometimes (but not always) guaranteed against default, and usually the bonds attract a high credit rating. What, then, are the attractions of this technique for the issuer?

So far as banks are concerned, it is the ability to lighten the balance sheet and make better use of capital. Basel Committee capital ratio rules make it expensive to keep low profit items on the balance sheet. The money can, when released, be used for more profitable investments. For NatWest, this was a major motive in the ROSE case. Low-yielding loans were removed from its books without jeopardizing client relationships.

The example in the list above of 'tax arrears' refers to an issue by Portugal in April 2004, when bonds worth €1.7bn ($2.0bn) were sold, backed by tax and social security arrears. Portugal had a budget deficit of over 6%, easily exceeding the eurozone limit of 3%. The bond was an attempt to accelerate cash flow. Unfortunately, by August 2005, receipts were only 56% of the forecast figure, and the bond was downgraded by Moody's and Fitch. As a result, further issues planned by Greece and Belgium were withdrawn.

Also in the list above is the securitization of anticipated life insurance premiums by Swiss Re. These insurance bonds are likely to become more popular in the future. The Swiss Re issue in January 2005 followed issues by National Provident Institution, Barclays Life and Friends Provident.

Commercial mortgage-backed securities (CMBS) are a specific example of ABS or CMO. Being based on commercial property, they are at risk if property values fall. For example, hurricane Katrina materially affected some US CMBS bonds. More recently, the 40% fall in commercial property values in the UK since mid-2008 has seriously impacted the CMBS of UK banks. The UK accounted for just under 50% of all outstanding European CMBS at the start of 2009 (some €148bn); this compares with the larger US CMBS market of €471bn for the same period.

'Covered bonds' is another term one may meet in the field of ABS. In an ABS transaction, the bond is issued by an SPV and is removed from the balance sheet of the issuer. With covered bonds, the assets remain on the balance sheet of the issuer, and investors have recourse to the company in the event of bankruptcy. As the risk to the investor is reduced, the cost to the issuer is lower. The FSA, the UK regulator, has ruled that 20% of bank or building society assets may be covered by these bonds before additional capital is required. We have seen issues from a wide range of European banks and other institutions, including Barclays (its first covered bond issue was for two £1bn FRNs in July 2008),

HSBC France (an €8bn issue in September 2008), Eurohypo AG, BNP and Portugal's Caixa Geral de Depósitos. Germany (and Denmark) are large markets, as *Pfandbriefe* are covered bonds with no SPV. Again, Basel II has made these products more attractive to the issuer. According to the ECB, the covered bond market has developed into the most important privately issued bond segment in Europe's capital markets, with over €1.8 trillion outstanding at the end of 2011. Danish and German issuers account for 50% of the market, with other major issuers being France, Spain and the UK.

Structured bonds or structured finance are also terms applied to ABS issues, which appear in a different form. The assets that might form part of a normal ABS issue are pooled and transferred to an SPV as before. Instead of mortgages or auto loans backing the security issue, there is a range of ABS backing the issue. However –and this is the crucial difference – the asset pools are tranched according to credit risk – some low risk, some high risk. Investors are sold securities backed by different tranches, some low risk and others right through to high risk. This is a more sophisticated way of handling the transfer of credit risk to the investor. One of the most common (and complex) structured finance instruments is the collateralized debt obligation (CDO), where 'senior' CDOs were backed by highly rated mortgage-backed security (MBS) and other ABS while mezzanine tranches pooled together a higher proportion of 'junior', poorer quality tranches. In contrast to an MBS, where the underlying pool of assets was actual mortgages, in the case of CDOs, the assets were the securities that received mortgage payments as well as other ABS. CDOs, therefore, can be viewed as resecuritized securities. Once the pool of ABS and MBS were pooled, these could then be tranched, and CDO securities could be issued via SPVs with varying risk/return and maturity profiles. CDOs have been constructed with a variety of assets and have earned different titles, including:

- Corporate bonds – collateralized bond obligations (CBOs)
- Corporate/leveraged loans – collateralized loan obligations (CLOs)
- ABS – mezzanine CDO
- Tranches of other CDOs – CDO squared

Credit rating agencies rated the tranches of CDOs and similar securities, and issuers used credit enhancement techniques to lower the credit risk associated with the various tranches to make them more attractive to investors. Global CDO issuance amounted to $430bn in 2007, but this had collapsed to a meagre $14.2bn by the start of 2012.

The creation of CDOs – or the further securitization of already securitized assets (ABS and MBS) – made these instruments increasingly complex. A significant proportion of them were backed by sub-prime mortgages, and when this market collapsed, banks that held billions of these 'investments' were left with near valueless assets and massive losses. According to the *Securitisation Data Report*, in the third quarter of 2011, the value of all outstanding securitized assets (ABS, CDOs, MBS) amounted to €6582.4bn in the US and €2031.7bn (of which around 11% each were for ABS and CDOs) in Europe. ABS and CDO markets are dwarfed by the size of the residential mortgage-backed securities (RMBS) markets. The US RMBS market stood at €4.6 trillion, and the European market at €1.2 trillion, with the UK accounting for around one-third.

Corporate Bonds

There are, of course, bonds issued by corporates, and there is a strong market in the US. In Europe, as a generalization, the corporate bond market is weaker, being overshadowed by the government and public sector bond market. In Germany, there is a tradition of reliance on bank finance as opposed to either bonds or equities. Very large European corporates may, in any case, find it easier to issue the bond in London as a Eurobond rather than as a domestic bond (see later in this chapter).

Corporate bonds can, however, be quite long-dated. In the UK, MEPC, a property company, issued a 44-year bond in 1988 that will redeem in 2032, and British Land did a 40-year issue in September 1995. Property companies look far ahead to long-term leases and commitments. Apart from these, we have seen a 50-year bond issued by Tesco in February 2007 that raised £500m, and even 100-year bonds issued by bodies like Walt Disney, Coca-Cola and IBM, although sometimes the issuer has an option to redeem the bond after 30 years. These bonds are so long-dated, they are almost equity, but the interest is tax deductible. IBM's 100-year bond only cost it 10 basis points more than its 30-year bond. Who among investors looks so far ahead? The answer is pension funds and life assurance companies who have to meet long-term liabilities. Table 7.3 illustrates key features of the US corporate bond market in 2013, illustrating major issues by Verizon, KfW, Barclays and Sprint. Over the year, there were 9,026 issues with a total value of $1.59 trillion, average issue size being $176mn.

There are a number of variations on the bond theme, which we now discuss.

Debentures

Debentures are corporate bonds that are backed by security, for example land and buildings. If the issuer goes into liquidation, these assets must be sold to pay the bondholders.

▼ **Table 7.3** *US corporate bond market in 2013*

US corporate bond issuance in 2013 reached a record $1.6 trillion as fixed-income markets were boosted by proactive monetary policies (quantitative easing, QE) around the world. Record low interest rates were a major contributing factor. QE in the US boosted asset prices and reduced yields, encouraging investors to seek out higher yields. This boosted the high-yield debt market which also witnessed record issuance of $370bn. Most of the US high-yield issuance was used for refinancing as the average coupon declined to 6.78% in 2013 compared with 7.4% in 2012 and 8.05% in 2011. Top US bond issues are listed below.

Month	Issuer	Amount ($ million)	Month	Issuer	Amount ($ million)
January	KfW	4,000	July	KfW	5,000
February	KfW	5,000	August	Credit Suisse	2,500
March	JPMorgan	4,250	September	Verizon Communications	1,500
April	Apple	5,500	October	KfW	4,000
May	BR Petrobas	3,500	November	Barclays	2,000
June	EMC Corp	2,500	December	Sprint	2,500

The financial sector was the biggest issuer, accounting for 40% of the value of new bond issues, followed by telecommunications (13%) and consumer goods (12%)

Source: Adapted from Bloomberg. (2014) Global Fixed Income League Tables.

Because they are more secure, however, the rate of interest is less. Some investment funds will only invest in corporate bonds that are debentures. Again, language is a problem. The definition given is the UK usage of the term. In the US and Canada, 'debenture' may be used to describe any bond. Just bear in mind that corporate bonds may be unsecured (the majority) or secured on specific assets. Although securing a bond gives a corporate cheaper finance, it's also inconvenient to tie up assets in this way. Lengthy and tedious legal procedures must be gone through before these assets can be disposed of and replaced by others. MEPC and British Land have both unsecured bonds and debentures on the market. The unsecured bonds pay 1.1% more than the debentures in the case of MEPC and 70 basis points in the case of British Land.

Convertibles

A convertible is a bond that can be converted later, either into another type of bond (for example convertible gilts) or into equity. The difference between the implied conversion price of the equity and the market price is called the 'premium'. For example, the bond may confer the right, after 3 years, to convert $100 of bonds into 50 shares. The conversion price is $2 per share; if the market price is $1.60 at the time, the initial premium is 25%. If the conversion price remains above the market price, the bond will redeem in the normal way.

The attraction to the *investor* is the mix of risk and return – the steady income we associate with a bond with the possible capital gain we associate with a share. For the *issuer*, the finance is cheaper, as the interest rate will be less due to its attractiveness. If investors wish to convert, where do the shares come from? The issuer creates *new* shares. Suppose the bond is $500m. The issuer hopes that instead of having to find $500m to redeem the bond, it will issue $500m of new shares instead. True, the equity will be diluted, but probably not by a large margin. In Europe (but not as clearly in the US), shareholders typically must give approval for the issue of convertibles because, generally, any new shares issued for cash must be offered to the existing shareholders.

Sometimes convertibles hit unforeseen problems. The general fall in the Japanese stock market since 1990 meant that the market price of many shares was below the conversion price. With Japan seen as somewhat risky, refinancing these convertibles was expensive. Moody's studied the default rates of convertible bonds between 1970 and 2000 and found that out of 280 failed issues, the amounts investors managed to recover were significantly lower than those for nonconvertible bonds, and investors eventually received $29 on average compared with $43 per $100 par for defaulting straight bonds. They also found that loss rates (the proportion of convertible bonds defaulting), at over 1%, were higher than for standard bonds, reflecting the subordinated nature of convertibles compared to straights.

Exchangeable bonds

Sometimes the right to convert is into another company's shares, which the issuing company owns, known as an 'exchangeable bond'. For example, Deutsche Bank issued €1.5bn in early 1999 to help fund its takeover of Bankers Trust. The bonds, however, were exchangeable into Allianz shares, which Deutsche owned. This was a way of Deutsche reducing its holding in Allianz without directly selling the shares and moving the price against it. The premium was 30%. Deutsche had previously done a convertible with the right to convert into shares of Daimler-Benz (as it then was), which the bank also owned. (Over the past decade or so, German banks have gradually reduced their shareholdings in large domestic corporates.) Société Générale issued a convertible bond in 2005 in which the conversion is into the shares of the Italian oil company, ENI. More recently, in July 2009, KfW (the German Länder bank) successfully placed €750m in bonds exchangeable into ordinary registered shares of Deutsche Post, and these are due in 2014.

Warrants

An alternative to a convertible bond is to issue a bond in which the right to buy shares later at a certain price is contained in a separate warrant. This is more flexible than the convertible in that the warrant can be used later to buy shares more cheaply while still keeping the bond. The warrants are often detached from the bonds and sold separately.

Sometimes, an entity that is not the company may issue warrants on the company's shares, for example Citigroup offered warrants on Eurotunnel shares. This is often called the 'covered warrants market' because Citigroup must cover the risk by owning the shares. If Eurotunnel issued a bond with warrants, it has the right to issue new shares if need be. Naturally, Citigroup does not have that right and must obtain the shares conventionally. Warrants may be (and frequently are) offered on a 'basket' of different shares. These covered warrants (very popular these days) are really part of the traded options market and are priced accordingly (see Chapter 12).

Preference shares

Preference shares usually pay dividends as a fixed percentage rate. If there is any shortage of money, their dividends must be paid out before other dividends. In the event of liquidation, preference shareholders have priority over ordinary shareholders. They normally have no voting rights. If the dividend cannot be paid, it is legally owed to them. Hence they are cumulative (normally). In Continental Europe, these are typically called 'participation certificates' or, in Germany and Switzerland, *Genusscheine* or *Participationsscheine*.

The Americans use the term 'preferred stock', and the French have several variations on this theme:

- *Certificats d'investissement*
- *Titres participatifs* – public sector only and the dividend may be partly fixed and partly linked to profit
- *Actions à dividende prioritaire* – where the dividend is the ordinary dividend plus a given percentage

The general features of all the above are that they are non-voting, preference in the event of liquidation and cumulative. They are hybrid instruments with some characteristics of a bond and some of an equity. Banks have done many issues to raise capital to count as tier 1 capital (RBS in September 2004 and HSBC in October 2005) or tier 2. To count as tier 1, they must be undated and noncumulative. In June 2008, Westpac, the Australian bank, announced that it was raising around $600m of tier 1 capital through an issue of 5-year convertible preference shares that would yield between 2.3% and 2.8% above the 90-day bill rate. This followed on from a $600m issue by Macquarie Bank in May the same year, which were convertible or cashable in 2013. As conversion at some point is mandatory, the issue counts as tier 1 capital.

Hybrid Bonds

Although preference shares were referred to above as a hybrid instrument, there are bonds called hybrid bonds, which aim more specifically at having characteristics of bonds and equity. They are perpetual and deeply subordinated and may defer coupon payments (noncumulative). Rating agencies tend to view them as quasi-equity, and capital can thus be raised without putting credit ratings at risk. Early in 2005, Moody's clarified the terms on which they could be treated as 70% equity. They are more expensive to the issuer but are treated as debt for accounting purposes and thus are tax deductible. As a result of Moody's decision, the market took off in the second half of 2005, with issues from Thomson, the Scandinavian energy groups DONG Energy and Vattenfall, and the German corporations Bayer and Südzucker. The Bayer issue, for example, paid 175 basis points more than the equivalent Bund (the German government bond). One final point: if the issuer falls below investment grade, the bonds must be called at par.

As hybrid bonds seem to offer cheaper financing than alternative (equity or ordinary) bonds and can be treated as part of bank capital, they have become popular with bank issuers. More than $800bn of these types of hybrid bond have been issued globally, according to Dealogic, reaching a peak of $175bn in 2007, with most of the issuance from banks. Their importance in supporting bank balance sheets during the crisis is shown in the $137bn of deals undertaken in 2008. A recent controversy with regard to hybrid bonds is the case of Deutsche Bank, which announced in December 2008 that it was not going to redeem a €1bn hybrid in January 2009. These bonds are typically repaid at the first opportunity after an initial period when redemptions are not allowed. If an issuer does not redeem them then, it must pay a higher penalty coupon rate. The German bank decided it was more cost-effective to pay the penalty rate than to replace the funding in expensive market conditions (in fact, coupon and capital payments on hybrid instruments, such as perpetual bonds, upper tier 2 bonds and preference shares, can be postponed or even cancelled when the bank makes losses or is inadequately capitalized). Typically, when banks decide not to redeem bonds at the earliest opportunity, the market value of the instruments falls. However, this event did not seem to deter Indian banks from making major hybrid issues in 2009. State Bank of India and ICICI Bank, the country's largest banks, raised more than Rs12bn each (around $240m per issue) via hybrids, and the government has also been using these instruments to infuse capital in certain state-run banks. The flexible nature and acceptability of hybrids as capital, coupled with a relatively small premium prevalent in Indian markets, has made these instruments popular with Indian banks that are increasing their capital. In the post-crisis period, many European and UK banks have been buying back the previously issued hybrid instruments in order to boost their capital positions.

Foreign Bonds

Foreign bonds are domestic issues by non-residents – bulldogs in the UK, yankees in the US, matador bonds in Spain, samurai bonds in Tokyo and kangaroo bonds in Australia. In November 2005, the International Finance Corporation, the private sector finance arm of the World Bank, issued the first foreigner renminbi bond in Hong Kong – a panda bond. China's central bank announced in mid-2009 that it will allow more foreign companies to issue renminbi-denominated bonds on the mainland. Daimler was the first corporate to issue a panda bond in March 2014, a 1-year issue for $81.5mn.

Notice that the bonds are domestic bonds in the local currency, it's only the *issuer* who is foreign. They should not be confused with international bonds (also called Eurobonds), which are bonds issued outside their natural market.

Non-US firms seeking dollar funding, for example, have a choice. The bonds may be issued in London as Eurobonds or in the US as yankee bonds. The investment community is different in both markets. Although the ultimate investors in the US might have a slightly parochial attitude to European firms, the investment institutions themselves have sophisticated credit assessment teams. In the absence of formal credit ratings, they will make up their own minds. The Eurobond market might be guided by credit ratings (or their absence) rather more slavishly. Nevertheless, market conditions change from time to time; sometimes it's easier to raise dollars in New York, sometimes in London.

Foreign bonds may be subject to a different tax regime or other restrictions. For example, yankees can only be sold to qualified institutional buyers in the first 2 years.

Junk Bonds (High-yield Debt)

Junk bonds were a phenomenon that occurred in the US domestic markets in the 1970s and 1980s. Earlier in this chapter, we noted that bonds rated below BBB grade were essentially speculative. As a result, they offered a much higher rate of interest. Box 7.4 details the evolution of the market.

BOX 7.4

Evolution of the Junk Bond Market

Michael Milken, a researcher at Drexel Burnham Lambert, did a study of the behaviour of such bonds in the early 1970s. He proved that an investment in these bonds would return a better yield than investment-grade bonds, even deducting the loss due to greater defaults. He was not the first to discover this – other academic studies had come to the same conclusion – but he was the first to do anything about it.

At first, his firm dealt in underpriced bonds in this category in the secondary markets. Drexel then began to look at the potential for new issues. At that time, the bonds of 90% of US corporates would, if issued, not be investment grade. Drexel (and Michael Milken) began to do primary issues too, arguing that the judgement of the rating agencies was too harsh.

Then the bonds were used to raise large sums of money for takeover bids. The market began to refer to them as 'junk bonds', but Drexel called them 'high-yield bonds', a more respectable title.

Junk bonds slowly became notorious because huge sums of money were raised with these bonds by entrepreneurs who bought companies much bigger than they were – the 'leveraged' takeover – for example Nelson Peltz/National Can; Ronald Perelman/Revlon; Carl Icahn/TWA

Each year at Beverly Hills, Drexel would hold a High Yield Bond Conference at which the wheeler-dealers and potential investors would sit at the feet of the 'junk bond king' Michael Milken and be entertained in lavish style. The rather less formal name for the conference was the Predators' Ball (The whole amazing story is told in Bruch's 1988 *The Predators' Ball*).

Later, the US SEC decided that Drexel and Michael Milken had broken the law in various ways during the course of their activities. In addition, banks and other investors realized that they had gone too far, especially with the arrival of the recession. The bubble eventually burst. Drexel Burnham Lambert collapsed in early 1990, and Michael Milken was jailed for 10 years for infringing various laws, although the sentence was reduced later.

Opinion is still divided between those who believe that Milken revitalized corporate America and those who think that his sentence wasn't nearly long enough.

For a long time the junk bond issuance in the US was muted, and non-existent in London's Eurobond market. In April 1997, however, Doughty Hanson, a UK venture capital company, issued a non-investment-grade 10-year bond for DM157m to finance the takeover of a Swiss firm. Other issues followed. Foreseeing monetary union, interest rates in many European countries were falling, and investors were anxious to find higher yields, albeit at higher risk. The Southeast Asian crisis in 1997 and the Russian default in 1998 dealt the market a severe blow, as investors' liking for risk cooled dramatically. However, memories are short, and with the general recovery of the markets in the mid-2000s, investors were once more seeking higher interest payments for higher risk. The European High Yield Association reports that the value of high-yield bond issuance ranged from €30bn to €40bn between 2005 and 2007, but in 2008, there were no issues due to the adverse market conditions brought about by the credit crisis. The average size of European issues in 2006–7 was around €300m. The market has grown substantially since the collapse in 2008, and during 2013, European high-yield debt issuance amounted to €202bn, including a €1.25bn issue by the car maker Fiat in March 2013 and a $1bn issue by Commerzbank in September. US high-yield bond issuance peaked in 2006 at $147bn and fell slightly to $136bn in 2007, before collapsing to $44.5bn in 2008, although it has revived dramatically since then, with 2013 witnessing $324bn of issuance.

Islamic Bonds

In Chapter 2, we mentioned Islamic banking techniques that conform with Islamic (sharia) law. There are also Islamic bonds issued on a similar principle and known as *sukuks*. For example, to fund its proposed takeover of P&O Ports, DP World, from Dubai, issued the biggest *sukuk* to date – $3.5bn (£2.1bn) with a duration of 2 years. To conform with Islamic law, no interest payments will be made. The bond was to be repaid in 2 years with conversion rights for part of the value into DP World shares. Islamic bonds were among the fastest growing instruments in the world before the credit crisis hit in August 2007, and total issuance stood at $80bn at the start of 2009 – a dramatic increase since 2000 when the market consisted of just a handful of deals. Like other investment markets, Islamic bond issuance has stalled as a result of the credit crisis and there have even been defaults. In June 2009, there was a default on a $650m Islamic bond issued in 2007 by an offshore arm of the troubled Saudi Group owned by billionaire Maan Al-Sanea. Major problems also emerged in November 2009 when Dubai World, the government-backed Dubai property conglomerate, revealed that it faced difficulties in making partial repayments on an outstanding $3.2bn *sukuk* issued by one of its subsidiaries (Nakheel) and due on 14 December. A last-minute $10bn loan from the government of Abu Dhabi to the Dubai Financial Support Fund averted default. Despite these difficulties, however, *sukuk* business continues to grow, with issuance reaching $115bn in 2013.

In June 2014, Britain became the first western country to issue a *sukuk* after it sold a £200 million Islamic bond to investors. Orders totalled about £2.3 billion. Allocations were made to sovereign wealth funds, central banks and domestic and international financial institutions.

INTERNATIONAL MARKETS

Background: Eurocurrencies

Some markets are called international markets or, misleadingly, euromarkets. We are talking here of dealing outside the natural market of the transaction. For example, December 1996 saw the second biggest privatization of all time – Deutsche Telekom (the

Japanese NTT being the biggest). Shares were offered in tranches to Germany, the UK, the rest of Europe, the Americas and Asia.

In late 1991, Kuwait raised a huge dollar loan, $5.5bn, from a syndicate of banks in London to repair the damage caused during the Gulf War. It's an 'international loan'.

Bonds are frequently raised in London by syndicates of banks of all nationalities and in dollars, yen, euros and other major currencies. We call them 'Eurobonds' or, more correctly, 'international bonds'. For example, SNCF (the French national railway company) may decide to issue a bond in London, and in dollars, instead of in Paris, in French francs.

How did all this begin? Its origins lie in the period after the Second World War. Russia and so-called 'Iron Curtain' countries that held dollars were worried that the US authorities might seize them for political reasons. The Russians owned a bank in France, Banque Commerciale pour l'Europe du Nord, and concentrated their holdings there. This bank lent dollars to other non-US banks in Europe. Some say that the term 'Eurodollars' was used because the telex code of the bank was 'Eurobank'. Others believe that it was a natural name for dollar dealings outside the US.

In the postwar years, there were plenty of dollars in the hands of non-Americans. American spending in Europe through the Marshall Plan was one source. The year 1957 saw the Treaty of Rome and the arrival in Europe of American multinational firms – earning dollars and spending them. A European firm might earn, say, $20m for sales to US firms. The dollars were credited to its account with, perhaps, Banque Nationale de Paris. These were now Eurodollars and could be lent to other entities in Europe. They were dollars outside the control of the US authorities. For years, for example, there was a strict control on interest rates called 'Regulation Q', which put an upper level on interest rates offered to depositors. If our mythical European firm chose not to convert the dollars into francs but to lend them to BNP Paribas on deposit, BNP Paribas's interest rate was not constrained by Regulation Q – hence an increase in dealings in dollars held by non-US residents.

(The *Oxford English Dictionary* in 1972 suggested that the first recorded reference to the phrase 'Eurodollar' was in the financial review of *The Times*, 24 October 1960.)

In July 1963, President Kennedy decided to tax yankee bonds – dollar bonds issued in the US by non-residents. The perception was that perhaps these bonds could be issued in Europe, finding investors among those non-US residents who held dollar balances. In 1963, SG Warburgs managed a bond issue in London worth $15m for the Italian motorway authority Autostrade, generally believed to be the first Eurobond – a dollar bond issued in Europe and not the US. London, with its non-protectionist policies and long traditions, became the natural market for this new business. To quote Al Alletzhauser in his interesting history *The House of Nomura* (1990):

> Almost overnight the world's financial centre shifted to London. The big four Japanese stockbrokers wasted no time in setting up offices there. If they could not sell Japanese stock to the Americans, they would sell them to the Europeans. Over the years, it proved to be one of the most profitable moves Japan's brokers ever made abroad.

In 1950, there were 140 foreign banks in London; by 1973, the number had risen to 340, and the number increased to over 500 by the mid-1980s. It was a vital shot in the arm for the London financial market, which had suffered from the postwar decline of the UK as a major economic power. However, by 2012, the number had dropped to 241, mainly due to merger and acquisitions.

We said earlier that the term 'euro-' is misleading. For example, dealings might take place in Tokyo, relending dollars held by Asian organizations. The terms 'euromarkets' and 'Eurobonds' are well established, however, although 'international markets' is a more correct term for dealings in a currency outside its natural domestic market (and thus outside the *control* of its domestic market). There is now a further confusion between a Eurobond and a bond denominated in the euro. 'Eurocurrencies' is a wider term, reminding us that the currency might not be dollars, but yen, euros, Swiss francs and so on.

For reasons we shall see below, eurocurrency dealings grew enormously from an estimated $1bn in 1959 to an estimated $14 trillion in 2012 (Thompson Financial and BIS figures). The irony is that although these markets grew as a result of restrictions in the US, they did not disappear when the restrictions were later abolished.

The Syndicated Loan Market

In 1973–74, the Organization of the Petroleum Exporting Countries (OPEC) oil price increases led to a large increase in dollars held by non-US residents. The price of oil went from $3 per barrel in October 1973 to $10.5 per barrel by January 1974. This led to a huge rise in dollar balances held by OPEC countries and a huge reduction in the dollar balances of many sovereign states. The services of international banks were required to recycle these dollars from those with surpluses to those in deficit, many of whom were underdeveloped countries – largely in Africa and South America.

The original use of Eurodollars was for the short-term interbank market. Then we saw syndicates of banks getting together to lend the dollar balances as part of, say, a 7-year loan to Mexico. As the source was dependent on what might be short-term balances, the loans were all at floating rate so that rates could be adjusted according to the new LIBOR rates in London. The banks might argue (as we look back on this period) that they were encouraged to lend by the world's financial and political authorities, worried about a bottleneck in the world's financial system.

To share the risk, banks spread each loan across a syndicate of banks, perhaps with as many as 100 banks in a syndicate. Notices of these loans would appear in the London *Financial Times* and other relevant publications – 'as a matter of record only'. What was the notice for then? It was an advertisement for the banks concerned – a tombstone notice, in the jargon of the trade (some say because in the 19th century financial notices were placed next to those for births and deaths).

Whether the banks were encouraged to lend or not, they did so and on a large scale – plenty of dollars, plenty of borrowers and nice rates of interest. To be fair, they must have looked at some borrowers, for example Mexico or Nigeria, and thought: 'How can we go wrong, when they have this precious commodity, oil?'

The biggest lender was Citibank, whose chairman, Walter Wriston, encouraged the others with the words: 'Sovereign borrowers do not go bust.' He meant that governments come and go, but countries would always survive, and they had assets that could, if necessary, be seized.

The International Debt Crisis

Walter Wriston couldn't have been more wrong. For a time, indeed, 'all went merry as a marriage bell' as the poet Byron says in his poem 'The Eve of Waterloo'. However, the next line is: 'But hush! hark! a deep sound strikes like a rising knell!' The deep sound in this case was the voice of the Mexican finance minister telling an audience of bankers in New York, on 20 August 1982, that repayment of principal on bank loans was to be deferred for 3 months. Brazil, Argentina and others quickly followed suit.

Falling oil prices, falling commodity prices generally and a large rise in dollar interest rates (remember, the loans are floating rate) had done the damage. Mexico followed its announcement by imposing total exchange controls and nationalizing all the banks.

To understand the banks' reaction to this, we must realize that the three largest South American debtor nations owed commercial banks $150bn, and that Mexican debt alone accounted for 44% of the capital of the nine largest US banks. The very survival of some of the world's largest banks was in question, and that meant that the whole international financial system was in jeopardy.

The banks met in fear and panic at the IMF and the World Bank's annual meeting in Toronto in September 1982. A wit described the meeting as 'rearranging the deckchairs on the Titanic'. The key figures – Jacques de Larosière, IMF managing director, Paul Volcker, chairman of the Federal Reserve Board, Gordon Richardson, governor of the Bank of England, and Fritz Leutwiler, chairman of BIS – mapped out a strategy. The essence was to buy time – to ask the debtors to implement economic policies to reduce the deficits that had led to the initial problems and to ask the banks to give the new policies time to work. The loans were to be rescheduled and repayments of interest deferred.

In a sense, it was a cat-and-mouse game. J.M. Keynes once said: 'If you owe the bank £1,000, you may be in trouble; if it's £1 million, maybe the bank's in trouble.' The banks were as much at risk as the debtors. Cut them off from new supplies of money, and they can no longer buy Western goods. Drive them into the ground with austere economic programmes and you may provoke a coup d'état and a communist government. America didn't want a communist government in Mexico, on its doorstep.

Things were not easy. In 1985, the IMF suspended loans to Brazil and Argentina as economic targets were missed. Peru announced a limit on debt repayments. In December, the oil price halved from $30 per barrel to $15 – Mexico's situation worsened. Everyone called it the 'LDC (less developed countries) debt crisis', and 1987 was the crisis year, as Brazil suspended interest payments and spent all year arguing with the banks.

Up to 1987, banks had had bad debt reserves of only about 5%. John Reed, Walter Wriston's successor at Citibank, decided in May 1987 to grasp the nettle and increased the bad debt charge against profit to $3bn (30%), plunging them into loss. Other banks followed suit. Of the UK's big four banks, Midland and Lloyds, the two smallest, had the largest exposures, and in 1987 declared their first losses of the century. This was followed by their second losses of the century in 1989, as all the banks added to these bad debt reserves, which now ranged in total from 40% at Citibank to 100% in the case of JP Morgan's medium- to long-term LDC debt.

The LDC debt crisis was sad news for the ordinary citizens of these countries. It would be nice to think that the money (about $300bn in total) had been spent strengthening the infrastructure of the countries, but a great deal was wasted on grandiose, prestige projects. Even worse, much had found its way into bank accounts abroad. Meanwhile, at home, the poorer citizens suffered the consequences.

Several attempts to solve the LDC problem were tried:

- Banks sold LDC debt at a large discount to other banks, simply spreading the risk.
- In debt for equity swaps, some LDC debt was exchanged (at a discount) for equity in the country concerned. For example, the American Express Bank swapped $100m of its Mexican debt at a discount for equity in Mexican hotels. In a bizarre incident,

some Brazilian debt was used to buy a Brazilian centre forward for PSV Eindhoven, the Dutch football team. Other Brazilian debt was purchased at a discount and invested to protect the rainforests.

- In 1985, James Baker, US Treasury secretary, unveiled the Baker Plan – economic reform to promote growth in LDC countries, combined with increased lending by commercial banks.
- In 1989, Nicholas Brady, the new US Treasury secretary, launched the Brady Plan. Building on experience gained with the Baker Plan, this envisaged encouraging the creditor banks to allow debt reduction. For example, LDC debt would be exchanged at a heavy discount for 30-year LDC government bonds backed by 30-year zero-coupon US Treasury bonds, thus guaranteeing eventual repayment of the principal. Alternatively, banks prepared to lend new money would be rewarded by no write-downs on the existing debt.

The first case was Mexico in 1989–90. Of the creditor banks, 90% swapped $42bn of debts for bonds on terms implying a discount of 35%. Some 10% of the banks lent new money. Later, Brady Plan-type deals were struck with the Philippines, Uruguay, Venezuela, Costa Rica, Peru, Brazil and Argentina. These bonds, which are still traded in secondary markets, are known as Brady bonds. With the recovery of the Latin American economies generally, many governments are buying back their Brady bonds. At its peak, the IMF estimated the total was $156bn (£93.6bn). When the buy-backs are finished, JP Morgan estimates that there will be only $10bn (£6bn) outstanding.

Later, Latin America reappeared in the world's financial markets and new capital inflows increased rapidly. Unfortunately, history repeated itself. Excessive bank lending led to further crises in 1997/98.

Whatever the eventual outcome, the LDC crisis was a disaster for the banks concerned. S&P and Moody's didn't like what they saw and reduced credit ratings. Not only did this mean that the cost of new money for the banks went up, but often their best customers had a better credit rating than they did. In 1982, banks like Chase, Bank America and Manufacturers Hanover were all of AAA status. By 1990, they were hanging on to single A if they were lucky. Manny Hanny was BBB – almost a junk bond. Yet in June 1986, Marks & Spencer, the well-known UK retailer, issued a $150m Eurobond rated AAA by both the main organizations. Why should M&S borrow from Lloyds or Midland Bank in 1986? Its credit rating was better than either.

Capital, too, was hit by bad debt reserves and the changed situation. Due to capital ratio constraints, banks found it difficult to expand their lending but still needed to earn money. In Chapter 4, we saw how new techniques were tried – the NIFs, RUFs and RAFTs, followed by the MOF. Unfortunately, however, many corporates could avoid the banks by borrowing from other lenders, using the securities market. For example, top-quality borrowers could raise money by selling commercial paper to lenders, with the bank role limited to taking a commission. The classic role of the bank is that of intermediary. It takes money from depositors and lends it to borrowers. Cutting out the bank, borrowers meeting lenders directly is often called disintermediation. Another term is 'securitization', that is, borrowers borrow by selling a security to lenders rather than borrowing from the bank. The biggest illustration of this process of either disintermediation or securitization was the rise in the issue of Eurobonds from 1982 onwards.

In any event, banks that had suffered big losses in the debt crisis started applying more sophisticated risk pricing to syndicated lending – relying in part on techniques initially developed in the corporate bond market. They also started to make wider use of covenants that acted as triggers that linked pricing explicitly to corporate events such as changes in ratings and debt servicing. In addition, banks began to use guarantees and various risk transfer techniques such as synthetic securitization, which enabled them to buy protection against credit risk while keeping the loans on the balance sheet. The BIS notes that the development of these new risk management techniques enabled a wider circle of financial institutions to lend on the market, including those whose credit limits and lending strategies would not have allowed them to participate beforehand. Partly, lenders saw syndicated loans as a loss leader for selling more lucrative investment banking and other services. More importantly, in addition to borrowers from emerging markets, corporations in industrialized countries also developed an appetite for syndicated loans. They saw them as a useful, flexible source of funds that could be arranged quickly and relied upon to complement other sources of external financing. Box 7.5 outlines the main benefits from loan syndication.

BOX 7.5

Advantages of Loan Syndication

The main advantages of this form of borrowing are listed here:

- Arranging a syndicated loan is less costly, in terms of setup fees, compared with a bond issuance.
- Borrowers can achieve lower spreads than they might have to pay to individual banks if they intended to borrow through a series of bilateral bank borrowing.
- Syndication can also provide a more flexible funding structure, which guarantees the availability of funds in the currency of their choice.
- It widens a company's circle of lenders through syndicates that include foreign banks.
- A syndicate provides the borrower with a stable source of funds, which is of particular value in the event that other capital markets (like the bond market) are subject to disruption.
- Syndication allows borrowers to raise larger sums than they would be able to obtain through either the bond or equity markets under a time constraint.
- The facilities can be arranged quickly and discreetly, which may be of value for certain transactions such as takeovers.
- Commitments to lend can be cancelled relatively easily compared to borrowing via securities markets, where such actions could have an adverse impact on investor confidence.

By 2003, signings of new loans totalled $1.6 trillion in 2003, and this increased to over $2.3 trillion by 2008, and grew further to around $4.5 trillion by 2013. Borrowers from emerging markets and industrialized countries alike tap the market. In fact, syndicated loans have also been increasingly traded, and as a consequence, according to a 2009 ECB study, have become much more like corporate bonds and are a clear substitute. Typically, access to the syndicated loans market is restricted to only the largest firms, as the smallest loans on average exceed $50m, with the most common maturity being 5 years. Spreads over LIBOR for the pricing of such loans used to hover around the 100 basis point level for good credits, but since the credit crisis these have moved out to 250 basis points plus, reflecting tougher credit conditions. One of the largest European syndications in 2013 was by the Linde Group, who arranged a $3.3bn facility to refinance existing debt.

The Eurobond Market

From 1982, there was a fall in the size of the international syndicated loan market and a rise in the issue of Eurobonds. Banks that could not expand their lending due to capital ratio constraints could make some money by underwriting bond issues. Borrowers found that the holders of eurocurrencies, which provided a short-term deposit market, could now be persuaded to buy bonds denominated in the same currencies, and create a longer term market. As before, London became the major market for these bond issues.

Typical terms for Eurobonds were in the range of 3–25 years (the longest so far – 50 years – was issued by British Gas in 1994). A syndicate of banks with a lead manager underwrote the issue, sold the bonds to investors and ran secondary markets.

Settlement between the professionals (in the secondary market) is 3 working days, that is, buy the bond on Monday, pay on Thursday; buy the bond on Tuesday, pay on Friday; and so on. There are two settlement and clearing organizations – Cedel and Euroclear. The first is owned by Deutsche Börse, and the second by banks; the first is in Luxembourg, and the second in Brussels. They ensure that bonds are transferred to the ownership of the buyer and that money is taken from the buyer's account to pay for them. Using another technique, which always seems curious to an outsider, they can arrange to lend bonds to sellers who have sold bonds they don't actually own. The sellers can use these bonds to settle the deal and buy them later in the market in order to return them to the lender. This is stock lending and is very common in bond markets everywhere. Lenders earn a small fee for their trouble, and it makes life easier for sellers.

There is an International Primary Markets Association and an International Securities Markets Association to coordinate issues in the secondary market.

The techniques for selling these bonds are investment banking techniques, as opposed to the commercial banking techniques used for syndicated loans. The rise in Eurobond market activities after 1982 led to a big increase internationally in investment banking at the expense of commercial banking.

The borrowers in this market are governments, quasi-governments (for example the EU), international financial organizations (for example the World Bank), banks and large corporates. The lenders are retail investors, that is, well-off private individuals, banks and investment institutions.

The interest on the bond is paid gross, and therefore the onus is on the retail investor to declare this to the local tax authority. On the other hand, the bonds are bearer bonds, that is, no one knows who owns them. As a result, there is a strong incentive for the retail buyer to indulge in tax evasion and enhance the yield on the bond by not paying any tax. The cliché in the market for the retail buyer is the 'Belgian dentist'. The idea is that she crosses the border into Luxembourg (where the paying bank often is), presents the coupons and pays the money into a local bank account (Luxembourg banks have a great tradition of secrecy, like the Swiss). The EU is determined to put an end to this and has implemented a Savings Directive that came into force on 1 July 2005. The aim is to reduce tax evasion by people living in one EU country who earn savings income in another. Some countries have agreed to exchange information, and others (Austria, Belgium, the Channel Islands, Monaco, Switzerland) to impose a withholding tax of 15%, which increased to 35% by 2011. In Luxembourg, clients themselves can decide whether they exchange information or pay the withholding tax. The Directive applies to bank deposits, corporate and government bonds and some investment funds, but not to dividends or pension income.

In Luxembourg, however, certain types of SICAV funds (mutual funds) are exempt as they are not widely offered to individual investors, but to institutional investors or private clients. As a result, by October 2005, there was a huge flow of money into Luxembourg funds launched by Swiss banks. Were people moving money to escape the Directive's net? (Probably.)

For professional investors, who will not indulge in tax evasion, there is still a cash flow advantage because the interest is paid gross. By the time they come to year end and auditors agree the tax figures with the authorities, it may be 18 months before the tax is actually paid.

▼ **Table 7.4** *A selection of Eurobond issuers*

Issuer	Currency
Abbey National (now Santander Group)	Swiss franc
Vietnam	US dollars
Shell International Finance	US dollars
Nestlé	Australian dollars
Province of Quebec	New Zealand dollars
KfW	Icelandic krona
KfW	Mexican peso
EIB	Turkish lira
GE Capital	pounds sterling
BBVA	pounds sterling
Air Products	euro
Fortis Bank	euro
Eurohypo	Swiss franc
Leaseplan Finance NV	Slovenian tolar

As a result of the tax situation, Eurobonds may offer a yield that seems less than general market rates.

An early variation on the theme was the FRN. This pays a variable, rather than a fixed, rate of interest. This appeals to financial institutions, which *lend* at floating rate and therefore find it easier to *borrow* at floating rate. If rates fall, their income falls, but so do their costs. Assets and liabilities are nicely matched.

Let's look at some Eurobond issues to get the flavour of the market, both for types of issue and types of currency (Table 7.4).

You may wonder why some of these issuers want a particular currency and why, for example, a financial institution like the UK's Abbey National was borrowing at a fixed rate. The curious answer is that perhaps they don't want the currency at all, nor does Abbey National want a fixed rate commitment. It's all to do with the world of swaps, which we discuss fully in Chapter 15. The investment bankers advise you in which currency in the prevailing market conditions it will be easier to raise the money. They then swap it for the currency you really want. They advise you whether a fixed rate bond or FRN will be best received by the market, and then swap the interest rate obligation with you.

Let's take the Abbey National case. First we have the currency swap:

Abbey National   Swap bank
Swiss franc ——————————▶
◀—————————— £

At the same time, they arrange to swap back at maturity so that Abbey National can redeem the bond.

Then we have an interest rate swap for the interest element:

Abbey National   Swap bank
Floating £ rate ——————————▶
◀—————— 4.875% Swiss franc

The swap bank passes Abbey National a stream of money in Swiss francs to pay the interest. Abbey National passes them a stream of money in sterling at the floating rate. The obligations of Abbey National to the bondholders are unaltered.

Notice that in the above case, we have not only swapped a fixed commitment for a floating one, but the floating rate is in sterling and the fixed rate is in Swiss francs, that is, we have arrived at the CIRCUS (combined interest rate and currency swap). The result is that issuers raise money where it is easiest and cheapest to do so, and then the investment banks swap it into the arrangement they really want. In November 2005, Wind, the Italian telecoms company, raised $50m in 10-year bonds and swapped the proceeds into euros, saving 40 basis points over borrowing in euros in the first place.

Our main discussion on swaps is in Chapter 15, but it's impossible not to mention them here, as it is estimated that 70% of Eurobond issues are swapped one way or another. The market is very innovative and ingenious. It was noted at an early stage that some professional investors were stripping off all the coupons separately, leaving behind a bond paying no interest. Perhaps they wanted a capital gain rather than income from a tax point of view. As a result, the market invented the zero-coupon bond in the primary market. If the bond pays no interest, why buy it? The answer is that the investor buys it at a substantial discount. Suppose market yields for 5-year bonds are 10%. Investors could buy a 10% bond at par. Alternatively, they could buy a zero-coupon bond for $62.09 for each $100 nominal. They invest $62.09 and in 5 years receive $100 – also a yield of 10%. For example, British Gas offered a 30-year zero-coupon bond in dollars. The bonds were sold at $8.77 for each $100 nominal value.

From a tax point of view, it may suit the investor to receive capital gain and not income. In Japan and Italy, for example, the increase in the bond price is taxed as a capital gain, not as income (but this is not the case in the UK). In addition, if the bond is in a foreign currency, the exchange rate risk is limited to the principal, not the coupons. These bonds are even more sensitive to interest rate changes than a normal bond. This might suit a speculator who was convinced that interest rates would fall. Remember – interest rates *down*, bond prices *up*.

Take a conventional 10-year bond paying 10%. The market yield falls to 9%, and the price goes up to $106.4 (a rise of 6.4%). Suppose an investor had bought a 10-year zero-coupon bond instead. A price of $38.55 per $100 nominal would give a yield of 10%. However, when yields fall to 9%, the price goes up to $42.24 (a rise of 9.6%). This is due to the gearing effect. In taking a position on a 10-year bond for $38.55 instead of $100, the investor has increased her exposure to the market. This is another aspect of gearing / leverage, which we met in Chapter 1.

Of course, if bond yields go up and not down, then the loss on the zero-coupon bond is even greater. (The unfortunate Merrill Lynch dealer mentioned earlier was not only holding zero-coupon bonds but had made them zero-coupon by selling the coupons separately.)

In early 1992, the perception was that yields in European bond markets (especially in Spain, Portugal and Italy) would slowly fall to those on deutschmark bonds. As a result, there were several zero-coupon issues to take advantage of later price increases as interest rates fell.

Coupon Stripping

We mentioned earlier that it is not uncommon for innovative investment banks to take an ordinary bond and remove the coupons, making it a zero-coupon bond. This is called 'coupon stripping' or 'bond stripping' and is very common with US Treasury issues (see Figure 7.5).

▼ **Figure 7.5** *Coupon stripping*

	Normal bond	Stripped bond coupons					Principal	Total
		1	2	3	4	5		
Payment now	100	9.09	8.26	7.51	6.83	6.21	62.1	100
Receipt:								
Year 1	10	10						10
Year 2	10		10					10
Year 3	10			10				10
Year 4	10				10			10
Year 5	10					10		10
Year 5	100						100	100
TOTAL	150	10	10	10	10	10	100	150

For example, take a $100m 5-year 10% bond and assume that the market yield is 10%, the bond selling for $100. The interest payments are stripped to form five zero-coupon bonds of $10m each, maturing one per year in years 1–5. The principal of $100m is itself now a zero-coupon bond. Someone needing $10m in 3 years can buy the 3-year zero-coupon bond for $7.51m in 3 years. This enables investment institutions to match future assets and liabilities more closely.

The first US government bond was stripped in 1982. Strips began in Canada in 1987, in France in 1991, in the UK and Germany in 1997 and in Italy and Spain in 1998. Almost all markets have stripped bonds now.

Other Variations

There are many variations on the theme in the Eurobond market – far too many to cover them all here. Let's just look at a few to get some idea of the possibilities.

Callable/puttable bonds

If *callable*, the issuer can redeem the bond at a stated earlier date if he chooses to. The investor is compensated for this disadvantage by a higher coupon. If *puttable*, the investor can sell the bond back at a stated earlier date. The investor has an advantage now and pays for it by receiving a lower coupon. The UK government's huge $4bn FRN issued in 1986 was both callable and puttable.

Convertibles

Corporate bonds that can be converted into equity are common, as in domestic markets. However, conversion could be from fixed into floating or floating into fixed.

Warrants

Again, as an alternative to a convertible, separate warrants entitling the investor to buy equity later may be attached. When the Nikkei Index in Japan rose strongly up to 1990,

Japanese convertibles and bonds with warrants were so popular, they accounted for 20% of the market. When the bubble burst as the Nikkei fell, Eurobond issues in 1990 fell as a result.

Dual currency

Dual currency bonds pay interest in one currency but redeem in another.

Rising/falling coupon

A 10-year bond might be 3% for the first 5 years and 10% for the last five (or some other variation).

The above two variations were combined in one with an issue by Banca Nazionale del Lavoro. The issue was in yen, with 60% of the redemption in yen and 40% in dollars at a fixed rate of ¥163. In addition, the coupon was 4.7% for the first 5 years and 7.5% thereafter.

Collars

In mid-1992, several banks, led by Kidder Peabody, issued FRNs with both a lower and upper limit to the interest paid, called 'collars'. This idea had been used in 1985 and called 'mini-max'. The revival was due to the unprecedentedly low US interest rates in mid-1992. A floor giving a lower limit was attractive, even if there was a maximum upper level to the interest paid.

Reverse FRNs

As the interest rates go *up*, the interest on the FRN goes *down* and vice versa. In December 1997, the World Bank issued a complex 12-year reverse floater in lira. For the first 4 years, rates were fixed on a falling scale, 12% down to 7%. For the next 7 years, the rate was calculated by a formula: 15.5% − 2 × LIBOR. Thus, as LIBOR went up, rate fell. This expressed the view that Italian rates would fall due to the arrival of the euro. As a further variation of the FRN theme, Aegon, the Dutch insurance company, did a 12-year issue in 1992, which was an FRN for the first 2 years and fixed at 8.25% for the remaining 10.

Global bonds

Pioneered by the World Bank in 1989, global bonds are designed to be sold in the Eurobond market and the US at the same time, thus increasing liquidity for the bond. The two markets have different conventions – Eurobonds are bearer, pay interest gross and annually; US bonds are registered and pay interest net semi-annually. However, the Eurobond issues are registered with the SEC in the US and can be sold to all classes of US investors. Eurobonds cannot be sold into the US initially unless registered under SEC rule 144a, when they can only be sold to qualified institutional investors anyway. In September 2005, Brazil issued a 10-year global bond denominated in its own currency, the real. More recently, in September 2013, IFC, a member of the World Bank Group, issued a $3.5 billion, 5-year global bond as part of its programme of raising funds for private sector development lending.

Dragon bonds

A dragon bond is similar to a Eurobond but is listed in Asia (typically Singapore or Hong Kong), aimed at investors in the region and launched in the East Asian time zone. The first issue was made by the Asian Development Bank at the end of 1991. With the growing importance of China, dragon bond issues have become very frequent.

The market is very competitive, and each investment bank is seeking ways to score over its rivals with some new innovation. The cliché here is the rocket scientist – the highly numerate trader who invents more and more complex instruments.

Medium-term Notes

Medium-term notes (MTNs) became popular in 1991–92 and have remained popular since. They are very flexible programmes. Within the same programme and legal documentation, the issuer can issue bonds in various quantities, maturities and currencies, and either fixed or floating. MTNs were designed in part to meet investor-driven transactions. In other words, an investor might request, say, $10m more of a previously issued bond, and the issuer will release more to meet this demand. The issuer can thus issue a new bond, more of an existing bond, or create a bond to a specification suggested by the investor. The structure is particularly useful for issuing small tranches of notes/bonds. Indeed, one investment banker has suggested that issues down to as little as $500,000 are now practical.

For borrowers, the MTN allows them to bypass the costly and time-consuming documentation associated with issuing a stand-alone bond. The market can then be tapped at very short notice, compared with a delay of several days for a stand-alone offering. Borrowers can thus react quickly to a given opportunity.

Among those who launched programmes are IBM International, Abbey National, the European Bank for Reconstruction and Development, GMAC Europe (the finance arm of General Motors), Monte dei Paschi di Siena, Finnish Export Credit and GE Capital, the market's most frequent issuer.

Sometimes the programmes are underwritten, like bond issues; sometimes not.

The Money Markets

We have been looking at syndicated loans and Eurobonds. Short-term transactions in eurocurrencies, which are not simply deposits/loans, but are represented by securities, result in eurocertificates of deposit (ECDs) and Eurocommercial paper (ECP). The generic term for these short-term transactions is usually Euronotes. The committed loan facilities, which we mentioned in Chapter 4, like NIFs/RUFs and MOFs, have largely died.

The strong interbank market in London in the eurocurrencies gives rise to references to Eurodollar LIBOR, Euroyen LIBOR and similar expressions for other currencies.

Repos

Earlier in this chapter, we mentioned that a central bank may use a 'repo' to help out other banks in its role as lender of last resort. A repo is a sale and repurchase agreement. Party A may sell stock to B and receive a collateral payment. At a later point in time (which may be fixed or variable), Party A must buy the stock back and return the collateral plus interest to Party B (Figure 7.6).

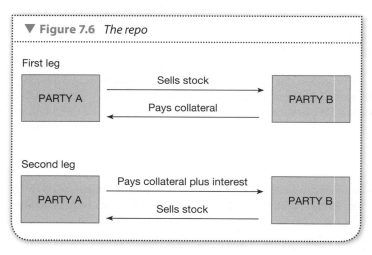

▼ Figure 7.6 *The repo*

First leg

PARTY A — Sells stock → PARTY B

PARTY A ← Pays collateral — PARTY B

Second leg

PARTY A — Pays collateral plus interest → PARTY B

PARTY A ← Sells stock — PARTY B

The repo technique is used very widely outside its use by central banks. Any dealer may find that she has a short position in stock, that is, she has sold stock, but not yet purchased it. As an alternative to buying the stock, the dealer can get hold of the stock on a temporary basis, using the repo technique. The stock is used to settle the deal and purchased later for its return in the second leg of the repo. Why bother? Maybe the dealer found some difficulty in buying the stock at an attractive price. Perhaps the dealer believed that stock would be cheaper in a few days' time. Sometimes, the dealer has actually bought and sold stock, but the buy side of the deal fails settlement, and it is the settlement department that uses the repo to fulfil the bank's obligation to deliver. This, of course, gives the market more flexibility and encourages liquidity. For this reason, the technique is often referred to as 'stock borrowing and lending' (the classic repo is not quite the same as stock borrowing and lending).

Often the repo is used for the opposite reason, that is, not to get hold of the stock, but to get hold of the collateral. A dealer must fund his position. If the bonds that have been purchased are not needed at once, they can be sold via the repo to obtain the cash to fund the purchase. As the borrowing is secured, it will be at a cheaper rate than unsecured borrowing. The repo here is simply a technique for borrowing money.

The repo thus suits everyone. The bond dealer can use it either to run a short position or to borrow money at the best rates. An institution that chooses to lend stock earns a small percentage to enhance yield on the portfolio, and the deal is secure, as collateral has been received.

Repos are widely used in the US Treasury markets; the Bank of England allowed repos in UK gilts in 1996; and the market began properly in Japan in April 1996 after new regulations solved problems with the previous rather weak repo technique (collateral surrender could not be enforced).

Participants and Top Traders

As we have seen, these are large wholesale markets and the transactions involve the following:

- Governments
- Municipalities
- Public sector bodies
- International financial institutions
- Commercial banks
- Investment banks
- Investment institutions:
  - Pension funds
  - Insurance companies
  - Mutual funds
  - Hedge funds
- Large corporates

There are also brokers who act as intermediaries, displaying anonymously on computer the best prices in the market and putting principals in touch with one another for a small commission (as little as two bp). The top underwriters for international bonds are shown in Table 7.5.

▼ **Table 7.5** *Top underwriters in international debt, 2013*

1/1/13 – 12/31/13 FIRM	RANK	MKT SHARE	2013 VOLUME USD (Min)	DISCL FEES (%)*	DEAL COUNT	2012 RANK	MKT SHARE	MKT SHARE CHG (%)
JP Morgan	1	7.2	261,087	0.35	1312	1	7.3	(0.1)
Deutsche Bank AG	2	7.2	260,828	0.28	1251	3	6.6	0.6
Barclays	3	6.8	246,756	0.28	1027	2	6.7	0.1
HSBC BANK PLC	4	5.7	207,961	0.25	1178	5	5.3	0.4
Citi	5	5.6	205,369	0.35	1039	4	5.6	–
Goldman Sachs & Co	6	5.3	193,909	0.30	739	8	4.3	1.0
BNP Paribas Group	7	4.9	179,450	0.22	800	6	4.5	0.4
Bank of America Merrill Lynch	8	4.4	161,050	0.44	906	7	4.3	0.1
Morgan Stanley	9	4.2	151,620	0.34	696	10	3.5	0.7
Credit Suisse	10	3.3	121,056	0.32	647	11	3.4	(0.1)
RBS	11	2.8	102,901	0.45	626	13	3.0	(0.2)
UniCredit	12	2.8	102,150	0.20	444	12	3.0	(0.2)
Société Générale	13	2.6	95,121	0.21	458	15	2.1	0.5
Credit Agricole CIB	14	2.3	85,474	0.23	427	14	2.5	(0.2)
RBC Capital Markets	15	2.0	72,934	0.27	379	17	1.6	0.4
UBS	16	1.7	62,098	0.47	477	9	3.7	(0.2)
Nomura Holdings Inc	17	1.4	52,496	0.13	428	21	1.1	0.3
Natixis	18	1.4	51,545	0.25	285	16	1.6	(0.2)
Intesa Sanpaolo SpA	19	1.2	43,240	0.58	146	22	1.1	0.1
Commerzbank AG	20	1.1	40,088	0.18	290	20	1.1	–
TOTAL		100%	3,640,980	0.31	11,674	3,821,720	100%	

Note: Includes all eligible international bonds – bonds that can be sold outside their domestic market. *Weighted average disclosed fees – only issues that have fee information available are used in calculating this value.

Source: Bloomberg. (2014) *Global Fixed Income League Tables*.

The euromarkets are the most important financial development of the past 30 years. They have created a vast pool of international money seeking investment in the best place it can, with no especial loyalty to any particular market.

It seems appropriate to close this chapter with a quotation from Walter Wriston, Citicorp's chairman from 1970 to 1984 (quoted in Hamilton, 1986):

The information standard has replaced the gold standard as the basis of world finance. In place of systems, like the gold standard, based on government established rules, communications now enable and ensure that money moves anywhere around the globe in answer to the latest information or disinformation. Governments can no longer get away with debasing the coinage or controlling the flow of capital. There now exists a new order, a global marketplace for ideas, money, goods and services that knows no national boundaries.

SUMMARY

- The rate of interest is the price of money. It varies with risk, maturity and liquidity. There is, finally, supply and demand.
- Bonds have a *par*, or nominal, value. They may sell at below or above par value, and the resulting return to the investor is *yield*. If we ignore the profit or loss at redemption, it is *interest yield*. If we do not, it is *gross redemption yield*. As interest rates go up, bond prices go down and vice versa. This volatility is most marked for long-dated bonds. If the bond is sold before going ex dividend, the buyer pays *accrued interest*.
- *Credit ratings* (such as AAA or BB) are assigned to bonds to guide investors as to the risk and hence the necessary yield.
- Money markets cover transactions whose maturity is 1 year or less. They include:
  - *Money at call and short notice:* Liquid funds lent for very short periods.
  - *Interbank market:* The rate at which one bank will lend money to another is the offer rate for money, hence London Interbank Offered Rate (LIBOR) or Tokyo Interbank Offered Rate (TIBOR).
  - *T-bills, local authority and public sector bills:* These represent the short-term borrowing of these entities, say, 3, 6 and 12 months.
  - *Certificates of deposit:* Short-term borrowings by banks.
  - *Commercial paper:* Short-term borrowing of corporates, very big in the US.
  - *Bills of exchange:* Discussed in Chapter 5.
- *Central banks* control short-term interest rates using key rates such as Lombard rate, discount rate, repo rate and similar terms.
- *Bonds* are transactions in excess of 1 year. The face rate of interest is called the *coupon* and they may be short-, medium- or long-dated. They may be sold through an offer for sale or a private placing.
- Government and public sector bonds are usually the most important. Frequently, they are sold at monthly auctions on set dates to specialist dealers.
- Mortgage and other asset-backed bonds use the flows of interest and capital to back bond issues – these are *asset-backed securities* (ABS). Other terms used are

- *collateralized mortgage obligations* (CMOs), *commercial mortgage-backed securities* (CMBS), *covered bonds* and *structured bonds*. The growth in structured products and other securitized instruments has been stratospheric since 2000; it peaked in 2006–7, and then activity collapsed. The growth of these instruments has been widely cited as the main cause of the property price boom and bust and the credit crisis that followed.
- *Debentures* (in the UK) are corporate bonds secured on assets.
- *Convertibles* are bonds that may be converted to another bond or equity. The right to buy equity later at a set price may be contained in an attached *warrant*.
- *Preference shares* usually pay the dividend as a fixed rate of interest. They are preferred to other shareholders for dividends and in the event of liquidation, and are non-voting.
- *Hybrid bonds* have the characteristics of both bonds and equity, being perpetual, deeply subordinated and noncumulative. They are growing fast in popularity.
- *Foreign bonds* are those issued in the domestic market by non-residents.
- *Junk bonds* are bonds below investment grade, offering high yields.
- *Islamic bonds* are issued to conform with Islamic law and do not pay interest in the conventional way. They are known as *sukuks*.
- *International* or *euromarkets* refer to primary market activity (loans, bonds or money market instruments) outside the domestic market of that currency, for example a dollar loan raised in London or a dollar bond issued in Singapore. London is the major centre for these activities.
- *Coupon stripping* refers to detaching the coupons from a bond and selling the principal and the coupons all separately. They are all now *zero-coupon bonds*.
- *Medium-term notes* are flexible programmes for issuing paper in any currency, any maturity, any quantity, and fixed or floating.
- *Repos* stands for sale and repurchase agreements. These are used either to borrow bonds for short positions or finance long positions.

REVISION QUESTIONS/ASSIGNMENTS

1 Analyse the main types of bonds and their different features. Highlight the main differences between corporate and government bonds.
2 Discuss the main differences between bonds and floating rate notes. When would a company issue floating rate notes?
3 Examine the role of the euromarkets, and discuss the main debt instruments linked to these markets.
4 Outline the role of credit rating industries in bond markets. When would rating agencies upgrade a bond issue?

REFERENCES

Alletzhauser, A. (1990) *The House of Nomura: The Rise to Supremacy of the World's Most Powerful Company: The Inside Story of the Legendary Japanese Dynasty*, Bloomsbury, London. Detailed historical account of the evolution of one of Japan's leading investment banks.

Bruch, C. (1988) *The Predators' Ball: The Inside Story of Drexel Burnham and the Rise of the Junk Bond*, Simon & Schuster, New York. Racy account of the rise and fall of Michael Milken and his firm Drexel, which pretty much created the junk bond/high-yield debt market.

Hamilton, A. (1986) *The Financial Revolution: The Big Bang Worldwide*, Penguin, Harmondsworth. Discusses change in global financial services and its impact on firms and economies.

Lewis, M. (1989) *Liar's Poker: Two Cities, True Greed*, Hodder & Stoughton, London. A tale of lies, corruption, greed and loathing on Wall Street; if you liked the film *Wall Street* (Gordon Gekko: 'Lunch is for wimps'), this is for you.

FURTHER READING

Fabozzi, F. (2010) *Bond Markets, Analysis and Strategies* (7th edn), Pearson Education, Harlow. Advanced, but useful, text on bond markets.

Matthews, K., Giuliodori, M., and Mishkin, F. (2013) *Economics of Money, Banking and Financial Markets*, European edition, Pearson Education, Harlow. Stand-ard undergraduate money and banking text. Used for 2nd-year undergraduate money/monetary policy courses and upwards.

Walsh, C.E. (2010) *Monetary Theory and Policy* (3rd rev. edn), MIT Press, Cambridge, MA. An overview of recent theoretical and policy-related developments in monetary economics.

▼ *Appendix 1:* *Announcement of result of a UK bid price auction for government bonds*

United Kingdom
Debt
Management
Office

46/05

DMO-TAS041/404

Eastcheap Court
11 Philpot Lane
London EC3M 8UD

Tel. 020 7862 6500
Fax. 020 7862 6509

27 September 2005

PRESS NOTICE

RESULT OF THE SALE BY AUCTION OF £2,750 MILLION OF 4 3/4% TREASURY STOCK 2020

The United Kingdom Debt Management Office ("DMO") announces that the auction of £2,750 million of 4 3/4% Treasury Stock 2020 has been allotted in full.

(Note: all prices in this notice are quoted in pounds and pence)

1   All bids which have been accepted at the lowest accepted price have been allotted approximately 78.0% of the amount bid for.

Competitive bids made at prices above the lowest accepted price have been allotted in full.
Competitive bids made at prices below the lowest accepted price have been rejected.

2   The range of bids accepted was as follows:

	Price	Yield
Highest Accepted	£104.61	4.32%
Non-competitive allotment price	£104.59	4.32%
(i.e. the rounded average accepted price)		
Lowest Accepted	£104.57	4.32%
Tail in basis points		0*

3   The total amounts allotted and bids received were as follows:

Amount allotted to competitive bids	£2,471.300 million
Amount allotted to non-competitive bids	
Gilt-edged market makers	£275.200 million
Others	£3.500 million
Total	£2,750.000 million
Total bids received	£5,194.674 million
Times covered	1.89 times

4   Cheques may be presented for payment. Refund cheques, where appropriate, will be sent as soon as possible by post. Stock allotted to members of CREST will be credited to their accounts by member-to-member deliveries on the relevant settlement date if they so requested.

*Tail is calculated as the yield at the lowest accepted price less the yield at the average accepted price (using unrounded yields). This figure is then multiplied by 100 to convert it into basis points.

Note: A non-competitive bid is one in which no bid price is entered, and it is allocated at the rounded average price of the auction.

Equity Markets

HISTORY OF ASSOCIATIONS FOR TRADING

The early associations for trading were sole owners, mutual associations or partnerships. The first modern shareholding enterprise is generally recognized as the proposal by Sebastian Cabot, the British explorer, to set up an enterprise to find a northeast trade route to China and the Orient.

The origins of modern-day stock exchanges are generally ascribed to 13th-century commodity traders in Bruges, Belgium, who met in the house of a man named Van der Burse, and in 1309 the institution became known as the 'Bruges Bourse'. At the same time, Italian merchants in Genoa, Florence and Verona traded government securities.

In 1553, 250 merchants put up £25 each to equip three ships for the voyage, sharing the cost and thus any eventual profit. Two ships foundered but one reached the Russian port of Archangel, and the crew were taken to the court of Ivan the Terrible. Trade was started between England and Russia, and the company's short name was the Muscovy Company. As the shares were held jointly, they were 'joint stock companies'. The famous East India Company was formed in 1600 and was dominant in trading up to about 1850. Of these early trading companies, several are still in existence, the most famous being the Hudson's Bay Company (1670). With the importance of the Dutch Empire, we also see the formation of the Dutch East India Company in 1602 and the Dutch West India Company in 1621.

Trading began in the shares of these companies. Amsterdam opened a stock exchange in 1611. The Austrian Bourse opened in Vienna in 1771, largely to trade government bonds to finance war. By the end of the 19th century, it had 2,500 equities listed and was one of Europe's most important financial centres.

In London, brokers and jobbers (as they were called) met in coffee houses:

> Mr Affery went about to other counting-houses and to wharves and docks, and to the Custom House and to Garraway's Coffee House and the Jerusalem Coffee House. (Dickens, *Little Dorrit*, Chapter 24)

To regulate the market, New Jonathan's Coffee House was converted into the 'Stock Exchange' in 1773. Curiously, there seems to be some doubt about the formal start of securities trading in New York. A newspaper called *The Diary* indicated in an issue of March 1792 that dealers in stock met each noon at 22 Wall Street (so called because the early Dutch traders who founded New York built a wall to keep livestock in and Indians out). Most trading was in government bonds and bank shares. Inspired by the success of an organization set up by brokers in Philadelphia, a New York Stock Exchange and Board was set up in 1817. In 1850, the US actually had 250 stock exchanges. However, by 1900, New York was totally dominant due to the introduction of the telegraph and ticker tape.

In France, we can trace an early shareholding company, the Société des Moulins du Bazacle in Toulouse, with 96 lots or shares that could be bought and sold. This became the local electricity company in the 19th century and was quoted on the Toulouse Stock Exchange until 1946. This was an earlier example than the Muscovy Company but more of an isolated instance. A form of stock exchange, a 'bourse', appeared in Lyons in 1540, with dealers called, in a decree of 1639, *agents de change*. A bourse was established in Paris in 1724 but does not seem to have been particularly active. With the revolution, *agents de change* were abolished in 1791, and the exchange closed in 1793. Under Napoleon, the bourse was officially opened again in 1801, with the *agents de change* given a monopoly of trading, but not allowed the privilege of limited liability.

THE ROLE OF A STOCK EXCHANGE

We should perhaps begin by considering the role of a stock exchange. It provides the regulation of company listings, a price formation mechanism, the supervision of trading, authorization of members, settlement of transactions and publication of trade data and prices.

However, sometimes listing rules are made by government-sponsored bodies, like the Securities and Exchange Commission (SEC) in the US and the China Securities Regulatory Commission in China. Separate settlement and custody bodies may be taking over this role, as in the UK, where Euroclear carries out the settlement from the London Stock Exchange (LSE). Some people are questioning the future role of a stock exchange, as rules that forced securities to be traded on exchanges (so-called 'concentration trading' rules) become eroded and computerized matching systems outside exchanges capture business (like Posit Match, INET and NYSE Arca in New York, and Turquoise, acquired by the LSE in December 2009, and Chi-X in Europe), or trades are handled by broker/dealers like Instinet. With the arrival of the Internet, the growth of online trading and the development of a wide range of competing electronic communication networks (ECNs) forcing down transaction costs, maybe Microsoft could be the exchange of the future?

One recent major development has been the emergence of 'dark pools' which are system that allows stock market traders to transact large blocks of shares anonymously, with prices posted publicly only after deals are done (see Box 8.4). They were initially developed by large banks – like Goldman Sachs, Barclays, UBS – so institutional and other large investors could make big transactions that were not adversely effected by technology driven high-frequency traders (HFTs). The HFTs made famous in Michael Lewis's 'Flash Boys' use advanced technology (such as placing their servers very close to exchanges), so they can 'get ahead' or 'trade ahead' of conventional transactions. Put simply, the HFTs can buy or sell large amounts of stock in the microseconds before a regular investor does, which means that the investor either has to pay more to buy or accept less to sell. Public stock exchanges are supposed to provide a level playing field for all investors by providing equal access to pricing information. When they get an order, the price of the stock is adjusted and everyone with a data feed sees it. So, if a lot of people want to sell a stock, the price goes down, and if a lot of people want to buy, it goes up. But dark pools are the exact opposite of this as they report data only after a trade has occurred. This denies investors critical information. The aim is to provide big traders with confidentiality in their transactions that are only revealed after a certain amount of time. The worry is that so many transactions have been routed through dark pools, it may distort pricing on public exchanges, which disadvantages retail investors. The US Securities and Exchange Commission announced (another) investigation into the operations of dark pools in early November 2014, and it looks like they will be subject to increasing regulatory oversight.

STOCKS AND SHARES

We refer to 'stocks and shares' as though there is a clear difference. Strictly speaking, shares are equities in companies, paying (typically) a variable dividend. Stocks are instruments where the payment is by way of interest, such as bonds and similar instruments. Unfortunately, although the term 'shares' is only used to refer to shares in companies, 'stocks' is a much more vague term. In the US, shares are 'common stock' and the shareholders are the stockholders. In the UK, the term 'stocks' is frequently used to mean either shares or bonds, and we shall follow this practice.

Generally, however, exchanges always split turnover between the fixed interest element and equities. Although most transactions in number are usually equities, the bond values are high because of the importance of professional investors with high-value deals. In the UK, for instance, the average domestic equity deal is about £70,000, and the average government bond deal about £5m. In general, bonds are about 56% of turnover in London; 68% in Spain, the European exchange with the most bond trading; and 35% in Germany. However, in New York, almost all turnover is in equities, as few bonds are traded on the exchange.

Figures for the world's largest exchanges are shown in Table 8.1. NASDAQ stands for National Association of Securities Dealers' Automated Quotations, and OMX is the Swedish company that has a dominant position on Scandinavian exchanges. OMX bid for the London Stock Exchange in 2001 but failed in its attempts to acquire its much larger competitor. NASDAQ agreed to acquire OMX in 2007 for $3.7bn, but a contested battle for OMX ensued with Borse Dubai. In a complex deal, NASDAQ eventually merged with OMX in February 2008; thus we have NASDAQ OMX. In November 2013, the NYSE merged with the *Intercontinental Exchange* (ICE), a US holding company. Previously, it was part of NYSE Euronext, which was formed by the NYSE's 2007 merger with the fully electronic stock exchange *Euronext*. NYSE and Euronext now operate as divisions of ICE.

Looking at Table 8.1, one can see that there is no simple answer to the question: Which are the world's biggest stock exchanges? What does 'biggest' mean? It could be market value, total value of trading, total turnover (total value of trading/number of outstanding shares), equity turnover or just the number of companies listed.

The market value is the number of shares in existence multiplied by the share price, also called capitalization (but beware – it's nothing to do with capital on the balance sheet). Share prices go up and down, and the capitalization is only that at the moment when the calculation is done. That's part of the problem. Had one taken Tokyo at the end of 1989, before its market crashed, Tokyo would have appeared as the world's biggest exchange.

Of the London equity value of shares traded amounted to $822bn, the claimed foreign equity content is around 25%, one of the highest in the world, similar to the foreign turnover of NYSE (9%) and the NASDAQ OMX (1%).

▼ **Table 8.1** *International stock market comparisons, equity turnover, market capitalization and number of companies listed, January 2014*

Exchange	Value of share trading $bn	Domestic market capitalization $bn	Number of companies listed	
			Domestic/Foreign	
NASDAQ OMX	1,059	5,998	2,343	306
NYSE (US)	1,302	17,006	1,855	521
London	822	4,429	1,643	832
Tokyo	543	4,421	3,407	11
Germany	147	1,852	638	79
Euronext (Europe)	176	3,443	933	127
Shanghai	225	2,414	957	na
Shenzhen	362	1,510	1,575	na
Spain	96	1,068	3,221	32
TMX Group (Canada)	116	2,034	3,794	79
Hong Kong	134	2,958	1,566	91

Source: The World Federation of Exchanges, *Annual Statistics* (2014), www.world-exchanges.org and the London Stock Exchange.

Taking capitalization in January 2014, our sequence is:

1 NYSE (US)
2 NASDAQ OMX
3 London
4 Tokyo
5 Euronext
6 Hong Kong.

Taking the total value of trading, the next question is whether we take equities only or total turnover including bonds. If we do the latter, it may not seem fair for exchanges where bonds are traded outside the exchange. If we take equity turnover only, however, our top six become:

1 NYSE
2 NASDAQ OMX
3 London
4 Tokyo
5 Shenzhen
6 Shanghai.

From the above, you will see that the question, 'Which are the world's biggest stock exchanges?', elicits a somewhat complicated response. The very statistics are themselves controversial. Some exchanges insist that trades handled by local brokers are recorded locally for regulatory reasons even if the trade is actually passed to a foreign exchange. For this reason, London's claim for its foreign equity share has been attacked by many as an exaggeration. In January 2014, there were over 45,000 companies listed on global exchanges that had a total market capitalization of just over $63 trillion (compared with global GDP that amounted to $78 trillion).

EFFICIENT MARKETS

The behaviour of financial markets and the potential returns generated from such investments have long been of interest to academics and market participants. Probably the most common (and some say important) area of study has been tests of the efficiency of financial markets. This massive body of empirical work was stimulated by Eugene Fama's efficient market hypothesis (EMH) developed in the early 1960s.

The EMH asserts that financial markets are 'informationally efficient', or to put it another way, investors cannot consistently generate returns in excess of the average market returns on a risk-adjusted basis given the information available at the time the investment is made.

There are three main versions of the EMH, weak, semi-strong and strong:

1 *Weak-form EMH* asserts that prices on any traded asset (equity, bonds, commodities, property and so on) already reflect all past publicly available information. In this case, the future prices of these assets cannot be predicted by analysing prices from the past.
2 *Semi-strong-form EMH* claims that prices reflect all publicly available information plus any new public information. In semi-strong-form efficiency, asset prices vary according to publicly available new information very rapidly, so no excess returns can be earned by trading on that information.
3 *Strong-form EMH* argues that prices instantly reflect all public and private information – even 'insider' information. In strong-form efficiency, no one can earn excess returns. It should be noted that if there are various legal and other barriers to private information becoming public, as with insider trading laws, strong-form efficiency is impossible (apart from the case where the laws are ignored).

There has been an extensive literature that has sought to test the various forms of the EMH on a variety of asset markets. Typically, empirical evidence is mixed at best. One area where the EMH does not appear to hold is the case regarding assets/shares with a low price/earnings ratio (and similarly, low price to cash flow or book value) as these tend to outperform other similar assets. This has led to new theories on financial markets espoused by behavioural finance/economics.

During the 1990s, there was increased interest in alternative explanations of financial asset returns based on behavioural/psychological factors. More formally, it is argued that cognitive biases (variations in individual judgement that occur in particular situations, giving rise to perceptual distortions and inaccurate and/or illogical interpretations) lead to investors making 'irrational' decisions. These 'irrational' decisions may be driven by factors such as overconfidence, overreaction to events, information bias, and various other predictable human errors in reasoning and information processing. (Leading behavioural economists, including Daniel Kahneman, Amos Tversky and Richard Thaler, investigate such issues, complemented by Robert Schiller, among others, in the finance field.)

Behavioural finance, for instance, would argue that cognitive biases lead investors to purchase overpriced growth stocks (firms that exhibit signs of above-average growth, even if the stock price appears expensive in terms of P/E or price to book ratios) rather than value stocks (where stocks appear underpriced). Irrational behaviour leads investors, therefore, to avoid value stocks and buy growth stocks at expensive prices. This allows those who acquire value stocks to outperform.

Since the 2007–8 global financial crisis, there has been much discussion about the irrationality of markets and scepticism surrounding EMH. Even Paul Volcker, the former Federal Reserve governor, has stated that it is 'clear that among the causes of the recent financial crisis was an unjustified faith in rational expectations [and] market efficiencies'. However, as noted by Ray Ball from Chicago University, it was claimed that:

> belief in the notion of market efficiency was responsible for an asset bubble, for investment practitioners miscalculating risks, and for regulators worldwide falling asleep at the switch. These claims are without merit. Despite the evidence of widespread anomalies and the advent of behavioural finance, we continue to follow practices that assume efficient pricing.

INDICES

Share indices are usually based on market capitalization. If the index is of, say, the top 50 companies, then 'top' means biggest by market capitalization. Sometimes, the index is described as 'weighted'. This simply means that a 1% change in the price of the largest company in the index will have more impact than a 1% change in the price of the smallest. Because the share price is always changing, it follows that the top shares are not always the same. There is provision for removing some shares and adding others, say, every quarter. There are rules on this designed to prevent firms moving in and out as they go from 99 to 101 in the index and back.

In the modern age, the desire to use an index for the purposes of options and futures transactions (see Chapters 13 and 14), as well as the evolution of an industry geared to passive investments (like exchange-traded funds) and benchmarked performance, has led to the creation of a wide range of new indices, which are recalculated every minute of the day.

Indices are some form of weighted average. In 1884, for example, Charles Dow (publisher of the *Wall Street Journal*) began publishing share averages, beginning with an average of 11 railway stocks. The modern Dow Jones Industrial Average began in 1896 with 12 shares and was increased to the present 30 in 1928. The Dow simply averages the share prices and (but for stock splits) would divide the total of all 30 prices by 30. It is a price-weighted index, so the change in the value of a share contributes to the change in the overall index, with a weight equal to the ratio of the share price and the sum of all the other share prices. If, however, a stock split causes a price to fall from $100 to $50, this must be taken into account. The method used is called 'constant divisor'. The Dow used to be calculated hourly but is now done every minute.

In London, the Financial Times Ordinary Share Index began in 1935. Its average is even more complicated. The 30 share prices are multiplied together, and a thirtieth root of the answer taken.

Modern indices are based on taking the number of shares and multiplying by the price. This gives proper weight to the companies worth the largest capitalization. In 1957, for example, Standard & Poor's introduced the S&P 500. In 1983, the Chicago Board Options Exchange began trading options on its 100-share index, changing its name to the S&P 100 in July of that year. Both these indices are based on market capitalization.

Also based on market capitalization was the New York Stock Exchange Index, introduced in 1966, now known as the NYSE Composite and consisting of over 2,000 stocks. The American Stock Exchange (AMEX) introduced its American Stock Exchange Index in 1973, later known as the AMEX Composite. It is another capitalization index, based on around 800 stocks. (Note that AMEX was acquired by NYSE Euronext in 2008 and was renamed the NYSE Amex Equities in January 2009.) One interesting and unusual feature is the inclusion of dividends as additions to the index. Thus, the index measures a *total* return (as does the German DAX – see later). Other important US indices are the S&P 100 and S&P 500.

In Japan, the main index is the Nikkei Dow 225, an index of 225 shares. It is, however, based on average prices, not capitalization. As a result, a Nikkei 300 was introduced in 1984. There is another index based on capitalization, the Tokyo Stock Exchange Price Index (TOPIX), an index of all shares listed in the first section of the Tokyo Stock Exchange. Other indices include TOPIX Core 30 (the 30 most liquid and highest market capitalization stocks), TOPIX 100, TOPIX 500 and TOPIX Small (stocks outside the TOPIX 500 stocks and non-eligible stocks).

In London, the need for a more satisfactory measure than the 30 ordinary share index led to the Financial Times Stock Exchange 100 Index in January 1984. This is known as the FTSE 100 Index and thus known locally as the 'Footsie'. It is also based on capitalization, but only using the 'free float' shares, that is, those freely available for sale and not held by founders or similar entities (this adjustment was made in June 2001). It is calculated every 15 seconds from 8.30 a.m. to 4.30 p.m. (with a pre-index level calculated from 8.00 a.m.). The index began at the level of 1,000. It represents 81% of the capitalization of the whole market. The FTSE 100 is the top 100, regardless of sector.

In October 1992, it was decided to broaden the indices, and two new ones were added. The FTSE 250 is the 250 shares after the FTSE 100, and the FTSE Supersectors 350 is the addition of the FTSE 100 and 250. It is calculated every minute and includes figures for market sectors. An older, larger index is the Financial Times Actuaries Indices, started in 1962 and widened to include over 800 stocks in December 1992. Now referred to as the FTSE All-Share Index, it accounts for 98–99% of the market's capitalization.

In France, the CAC 40 was started in 1987. It takes its name from the Paris Bourse's early automation system Cotation Assistée en Continu (Continuous Assisted Quotation). It is based on capitalization and is calculated every 30 seconds. It is 60% of the capitalization of the whole bourse, but the top seven stocks account for 43% of the CAC 40. One interesting point is that the CAC 40 is chosen to represent *all* major market sectors. (Other French indices are the CAC Next 20 and CAC Mid 100.) The older index in Paris is the SBF 240, which is based on opening prices and only calculated once per day. In September 1993, this was replaced by the SBF 250 index, which is calculated every minute and integrates dividends as well. At the same time, a new index – the SBF 120 – was introduced. This is based on the 40 shares in the CAC 40 and 80 others. It is calculated every minute. In May 1995, an additional index of middle capitalization stocks – the CAC Mid 100 – was launched.

The older German indices are the FAZ 100 (from the business newspaper *Frankfurter Allgemeine Zeitung*) and the Commerzbank index of 60 shares on the Dusseldorf exchange. They were both started in the 1950s and are calculated once per day. The most important index is the DAX (Deutscher Aktienindex), consisting of 30 shares introduced in

December 1987. This is calculated continuously (every second since 2006) but includes dividends and thus calculates a total return. This makes it especially attractive for some 'swap' transactions of a kind we discuss in Chapter 15. It represents over 80% of stock market capitalization and covers all the country's exchanges. The next 70 shares provide the Mid-Cap DAX (MDAX). There is also an L-DAX (Late DAX) that calculates the index for a few hours after electronic trading has ceased.

We mentioned above that some indices will attempt to apportion sectors (for example CAC 40), and some will take all sectors if their market capitalization warrants it (for example FTSE 100). In June 2011, the financial sector constituted 22.1% of the index, followed by the oil and gas sector (17.05%), basic materials (13.25%), consumer goods (11.76%) and consumer services (9.59%). In the US, the pattern for the S&P 500 includes IT (20.21%), financials (14.31%) and energy (11.95%). The Paris CAC 40 is more varied, including retailers, contractors, civil engineering, media companies and fashion and beauty (LVMH, L'Oreal). Of the DAX 30 shares, 18 are manufacturers with some large financial organizations like the banks and Allianz.

Other prominent indices are listed here:

- Amsterdam   AEX
- Brazil   Bovespa

               IBrX

               IBrX50
- Brussels   BEL 20
- China   SSE Composite (Shanghai)

               SSE Component (Shenzhen)

               Hang Seng (Hong Kong)
- India   BSE SENSEX 30 (Bombay/Mumbai Exchange)
- Madrid   IBEX 35

               MADX
- Milan   S&P MIB

               MIBTel
- Russia   RTSI
- Switzerland SMI

With the growth of international equities in investor portfolios and the ongoing pressure to benchmark performance, we also have the use of international indices. There are world indices, such as the Morgan Stanley Capital International (MSCI) World Index, run by Citigroup and Russell, and the Financial Times/Standard & Poor's Actuaries World Indices. There is also the S&P Global 100, 700 and 1200; the FTSE All-World Index (covering 2,700 stocks); the FTSE Global Equity Index (covering 8,000 stocks in 48 countries); the FTSE Global Small Cap Index; and various others.

For Europe, there is the FTSE Euro 100 Index, representing the 100 largest capitalized firms in the eurozone. There is also the FTSE Eurotop 100 Index, representing the 100 most highly capitalized blue-chip companies in Europe (in and out of the eurozone). In addition, there is also the FTSEurofirst 80 Index – the 60 largest companies ranked by market capitalization in the FTSE Eurozone Index and 20 additional companies selected for their size and sector representation. In competition, there is the S&P Europe 350 (an equity index drawn from 17 major European markets accounting for around 70% of the region's market capitalization) as well as the S&P Euro Plus (eurozone companies plus those from Denmark, Norway, Sweden and Switzerland) and the S&P Euro Index (companies from the eurozone). There is also a family of Dow Jones Stoxx indices (see stoxx.com) that track various European markets.

As the previous list of S&P indices suggests, one problem for Europe is, what exactly is meant by 'Europe'? There is the Europe of the 18 countries in the eurozone, which excludes an important market in the UK; the EU of 28 countries, which excludes an important market in Switzerland; and some wider geographical definitions. All this leads to a proliferation of European indices.

The indices mentioned above may actually be traded as exchange-traded funds (ETFs). These are listed securities that mimic the behaviour of stock market indices or other benchmarks, for example the Dow Jones, the S&P 500, the FTSE 100 or any other popular index. ETFs can be bought and sold on a continuous basis and are traded between investors on a stock exchange. They are popular in the US, but interest elsewhere is growing. In January 2014, according to the World Federation of Exchanges *Annual Statistics* (www .world-exchanges.org), there were 6,289 ETFs globally, with an annual turnover of about $634bn of assets. By the start of 2014, 50% of all the worlds ETFs were traded on NYSE. Using these funds, investors can 'buy' the performance of a market/sector/area (known as 'buying beta') at a low price. Only when investors buy 'alpha' (performance in excess of the market) should they pay asset managers more. The market for these so-called 'tracker products' has continued to grow substantially relative to managed funds since 2009.

THE LISTING PROCESS: GOING PUBLIC

Handling issues of shares of new companies coming to the market is very much the essence of a stock exchange. We should, perhaps, begin by asking: Why do companies go public? There are a variety of reasons.

In the first place, the company may be seeking new capital for an expansion plan. This may be a more attractive way of getting the money than, say, bank loans or trying to attract more private shareholders. If a company feels that it is not yet ready to go public, but is looking for more capital, it may seek as a new shareholder a bank that specializes in this – usually referred to as a venture capital company. In later years, if the company needs more capital, it can go back to the shareholders with a rights issue (which we discuss shortly).

Second, going public produces a price for the shares and a market. Without this, if one of the original private shareholders wishes to sell out and retire, there may be a problem. What price do we put on the shares? Who can afford to buy them? In addition, giving staff the right to buy shares through one of a variety of share purchase schemes provides a valuable incentive. It is also cheap for the company. To sell shares to the staff, the company usually creates new shares. The number is so small that any dilution of the share price is not noticeable.

Finally, in a takeover situation, the company can now offer new shares in its own company instead of cash to the victim company's shareholders. This can be useful and is also common. If the victim shareholders would prefer cash, institutions can be found to buy the shares, usually referred to as a vendor placing.

In general, there are two systems – the public offer for sale and the placing, or private placement.

In the case of a public offer for sale (known as an initial public offering, IPO, in the US), the offer receives wide publicity, and investors are invited to submit applications for the shares. If oversubscribed, some form of rationing or allocation must take place. Usually, a comprehensive prospectus giving details of the firm's history and accounts must be produced. The issue is brought to market by a bank or stockbroker, who will advise on the pricing of the issue and attempt to persuade the market of its merits and arrange under-writing. This means that insofar as the investing public does not buy the shares, the group of underwriters undertakes to purchase them. For this they receive a fee, perhaps 1.5–2% of the value underwritten. The risk is spread widely, and investment institutions will often participate, hoping to keep the fee and sleep well at night. In 1987, Black Monday occurred in the middle of the UK government's privatization of further shares in British Petroleum. The underwriters had to purchase the shares at the offer price and incur a considerable loss. Sometimes, if the market is seen to be weak, a planned issue is withdrawn.

In the placing, the broker concerned contacts investment clients with the details of the offer and sells the shares without any public offering. The number of shareholders for a given sum raised is usually set at a minimum by local stock exchange rules.

From an administrative point of view, the placing is much easier and cheaper and also saves underwriting fees. Other things being equal, firms may prefer a placing. However, there are usually local stock exchange rules on this subject. For example, in the UK, if the sum of money raised was more than £3m, a placing was not allowed. In 1986, this limit was raised to £15m, and in 1991 more complex rules were introduced. These envisaged the possibility of a new issue that was part placing and part offer for sale, a 100% placing being ruled out if the amount raised exceeded £50m. In 1992, there were several new issues that were 50% offer for sale and 50% placing. However, from 1 January 1996, these rules were abolished, and there is now no limitation on the amount that can be raised by a placing.

Sometimes, we hear of an unquoted company taking over a shell company. This is a company with few assets, profits in decline or non-existent and a low share price. The takeover company usually imposes its own name. It's a way of gaining a listing without going through all the procedures of an official new issue.

Another possibility is for a company to be admitted to the list of shares that are being traded on an exchange by an introduction. This is typically a firm quoted on a foreign stock exchange that seeks an admission to the list of firms traded on a domestic exchange. Normally, no new money is being raised at this time. This became common in the 1980s as part of the 'international equity' idea, discussed earlier in this chapter. The Japanese firm Toshiba, for example, is listed on nine European stock exchanges. Daiwa began to trade on seven European stock exchanges simultaneously in April 1990. Volkswagen was listed on all four Spanish stock exchanges in June 1990, and Volkswagen and Bayer Chemicals became the first foreign companies to be listed on the Milan Stock Exchange in the same year. Daimler-Benz became the first German company to list on the NYSE in 1993, and the National Bank of Greece listed on the NYSE in mid-1999. However, the 2002 Sarbanes-Oxley legislation is now something of a deterrent to listing in the US. Indeed, some US companies are considering having their IPO in London instead.

Foreign shares listed in the US would have a disadvantage if quoted and dealt in their own currency. There are also higher costs for investors in buying foreign shares and worries (in some cases) about receiving share certificates. As a result, many foreign companies' shares trade in the US as American depository receipts (ADRs). The receipt for one or more of a foreign company's shares is held by a trustee (often

Morgan Guaranty Trust Co.), and the receipt is traded rather than the shares themselves. For example, a BP ADR is worth 12 ordinary shares. The US investor avoids the inconvenience of collecting dividends and converting them to dollars. The sponsor bank takes care of this. The first ADR was issued in 1927 for the British American Tobacco Company. In 1999, the amount of capital raised via ADRs rose to a record $22bn, as 33 companies and governments sought funding in US capital markets. Since then, the number of ADR-listed programmes has risen more than three times from 176 to 700+. Typically, it is the largest companies that have ADR listings, including banks such as Barclays, Lloyds, HSBC and Mizuho Financial. A more general theme is global depository receipt (GDR), which refers to using the same technique as ADRs for listing shares on exchanges outside the US. The first of these was issued in 1990, and they have proved useful for emerging markets. For example, by 2014, there were 315 companies from 48 different countries that had their GDRs traded in London. Among these were Sistema (Russia's largest float up to that point), Investcom (Lebanon) and Kumho Tires (South Korea). (Over £40 bn has been raised in the London market through GDRs since 2001.) Issuance of GDRs has continued to increase since then due to booming emerging markets, although they did fall back as a result of the credit crisis. A recent GDR announced in 2013 involved the Qatari Doha Bank, raising over $1bn via a combination of a rights issue and GDRs.

There is also now the European depository receipt (EDR) launched by the Paris Bourse and Citibank in 1998. The EDR accesses the euromarkets, but not the US market. It settles and trades through the euromarket clearing systems, Euroclear and Clearstream, and may be listed on a European stock exchange, normally London or Luxembourg. EDRs and GDRs are generally denominated in US dollars but may be denominated in any currency.

RIGHTS ISSUES

Later, a firm may decide to offer existing shareholders the right to buy some new shares in proportion to the shares they already hold. This is why they are typically called 'rights issues'. Across most of Europe, the law requires that existing shareholders have pre-emptive rights to any new shares issued for cash. New shares may not necessarily be issued for cash – they may be issued in order to fund a takeover bid by offering them to the shareholders of the company to be taken over.

In the US, shareholders' rights to new shares are not so firmly established. The whole question of these pre-emptive rights is controversial. Periodically, articles appear arguing that firms should be able to issue a block of new shares by auction without offering them first to the existing shareholders.

Although pre-emptive rights are common across Europe, one exception is Germany. In March 1998, Mannesmann, the industrial conglomerate, issued new shares to the value of DM3bn without offering them to existing shareholders. In March 1999, Deutsche Bank was raising money to fund its takeover of Bankers Trust. It raised DM4bn by means of a rights issue to existing shareholders but also sold a further DM2bn of new shares worldwide on a non-rights basis.

Of course, shareholders may be approached to waive their rights. When Midland Bank sold 14.9% of its shares by way of new shares to the Hong Kong and Shanghai Bank in 1987, it approached the existing shareholders for their permission.

The new shares will be offered at a discount to the existing shares, for example an offer of one new share at $90 may be made for every three existing shares whose market price is $110. The discount is more apparent than real. The firm is regarded as having diluted the value of the issue by this offer of extra shares at a discount. An averaging or pro-rating now takes place as follows:

	$
3 existing shares	at $110 = 330
1 new share	at $90 = 90
Therefore, each block of 4 shares	= 420
So 1 new share	= 105

When the shares are declared ex rights (XR), the price will be $105 if the market price remains at $110. 'XR' means that anyone buying the shares does not enjoy the rights to the new shares. It now seems that the shareholder will not gain from taking up the rights in any explicit sense but will lose if they do not. They may have 100 shares at $110 per share and soon will have 100 shares at $105 per share.

They may not have the money to buy the new shares. Some shareholders sell some of their existing shares to buy new ones, or the rights may be sold to someone else for a quoted premium. In the above case, the premium would be $15. The purchaser of the rights will pay the shareholder $15 and later pay the company $90, paying $105. The shareholder has shares at present for which each set of three are valued at $330 and will soon be valued at $315; however, they sold the rights for $15.

The market price does not obligingly remain stable while the shareholders make up their minds. The premium for buying the rights thus goes up and down. What is particularly serious is if the rights price ends up above the market price. Suppose the market price in this case falls to $80. How many people will wish to buy shares at $90 if the existing shares can be purchased for $80? This reminds us that a rights issue must be underwritten just like a new issue.

In 1991, in the UK, British Aerospace announced a rights issue at £3.80 at a time when the market price was £5.00. The announcement of poor profit prospects, however, saw the market price plunge to £3.60 as the market lost faith in British Aerospace. The underwriters took up 95% of the offering.

Rights issues are examined carefully by the market. The new money needs to be used wisely if profit per share and dividend per share are not to suffer. Sometimes, the rights issue is seen as positive and well received, sometimes as negative, a sign of a firm in trouble, and the share price suffers.

Banks had major rights issues during 2008–9 as they sought to boost their capital strength in light of their troubled on- and off-balance sheet positions. Lloyds Group, for instance, successfully raised £13.5bn in a rights issue in December 2009 instead of having to tap the UK government's asset protection scheme (APS). This followed on from major rights issues by all the major UK banks in 2008. The problem by mid-2009, however, was that so many banks had made rights issues that very large issues were unlikely to meet investors' approval as they would significantly push down valuations, although the success of the Lloyds issue at the end of the year appeared to buck this trend. Another interesting event is the case of Arsenal Football Club, whose board agreed not to go for a rights issue before the start of the 2009–10 season as it believed that it had enough resources to cover its £320m debt. Red and White Holdings, the second largest shareholder and the investment vehicle owned by Russian businessman Alisher Usmanov and his business partner Farhad Moshiri disagreed with this decision but said that it would see how things worked out before reconsidering a rights issue to pay down debt.

SCRIP ISSUES, SPLITS AND SCRIP DIVIDENDS

Sometimes firms offer shareholders free shares in proportion to the shares they own. For example, they may be offered one free share for every share owned. This is the scrip issue (or bonus issue). Alternatively, the shares are split. For example, every share, 'par' or 'nominal' value $1, is replaced by two shares, 'par' or 'nominal' value 50¢.

In each case, the market value of the share will fall to half of the previous figure. The idea is that markets recognize a broad range of trading prices for shares. With growing profits and dividends over the years, the share price increases. Sometimes, the market feels that the new price is inconvenient and deters small shareholders from buying. The theory is that shareholders are happier with 100 shares at $50 than 10 shares at $500. If this doesn't seem logical, it is because it is, in fact, quite illogical – it's pure investor psychology. For example, the UK market likes share prices in a range of, say, £1–10. Above this level, companies frequently do scrips or splits to bring the price down to a 'better' trading price, one thought to lead to a more widespread holding and more liquidity. Thus, in the autumn of 1998, the Logica share price was £20. It did a 4-for-1 scrip issue to bring the price down to £4.

In the US, the same idea prevails, but at much higher share price levels. In Continental Europe, too, shares typically trade at far higher prices than in the UK. When Paribas was privatized, for example, 3.8 million investors applied for shares and received just four each – but the price was about FFr450 each. Switzerland is a place where, traditionally, the shares of banks, pharmaceutical companies and Nestlé have traded at a price equivalent to several thousand dollars. However, the law, which required a minimum legal value of SFr100 per share, was altered to lower this to SFr10 per share. In May 1992, Nestlé took advantage of this to replace each share, legal value SFr100, by 10, with legal value of SFr10 each. The effect was to lower the price of each share from SFr9,600 to SFr960. Other large Swiss companies have followed suit.

In the US, they become uncomfortable when share prices exceed $100. Fast-growing shares end up doing many splits. In January 1999, Intel announced its 12th split when the share price hit $137. In the US, buying in multiples of 100 attracts cheaper commission – the split makes this easier. In the same week, IBM and Microsoft also did splits.

We have seen from the above that shares typically have a 'par', or legal, value, which may not bear any relationship to the market price – IBM at $1.1.25 for example, or AT&T at $1. There is no minimum for the legal value either in the US or the UK. In Germany, however, there was a minimum legal value of DM50, but this was lowered to DM5, which may have been part of a move to a lower average price. A low par, or legal, value enables the company to issue more shares when it is first formed and gives it greater flexibility later.

The scrip issue does not change the par value but gives, say, one additional share free. This doubles the par value on the balance sheet, and the money is taken from reserves. A split does not alter the *total* par value owned, as, say, one share at $75 is replaced by three at $25 – the total par value on the balance sheet is unchanged, but the par value of each share is. Thus Barclays' 4-for-1 split in 2002 reduced the par value of each share from £1 to 25p.

Finally, let's note that a reverse split, or consolidation, is possible. Here, say five existing shares are replaced by one new one whose par value is five times as high. This is for situations where the share price is so low that it suggests a firm in serious trouble. Again, it's simply psychology. For example, in June 1992, the British advertising group Saatchi & Saatchi carried out a 1-for-10 consolidation when the share price touched a low of 15p each.

A common practice in many markets is to offer a choice of cash dividends or more shares – the scrip dividend. From the firm's point of view, it saves cash, as it's easier to create new shares than pay dividends. From the investor's point of view, if dividends are not needed as income, it's a way of gaining new shares without paying share tax or brokers' commission.

INTERNATIONAL EQUITY

In the 1980s and 1990s, it became common for multinational companies to seek a listing on several foreign stock exchanges. This may have been to attract a wider investor market or because the local exchange was too small for the ambitions of the company (for example Stockholm and Electrolux). The result has been a large expansion in primary market issues and secondary market trading in non-domestic equities.

For example, although German accounting rules are not as tight as those in the US, Daimler-Benz listed in New York and accepted the implications for greater transparency. AXA, the French insurance group, became the first French financial services company to secure a US stock exchange listing in mid-1996. There are still problems, however, as SEC rules require approval for rights issues. Ericsson had to wait 3 months, during which its share price fell 56%. New legislation following the scandals of Enron and others have also brought in new restrictions. Senator Paul Sarbanes and Michael Oxley, chairman of the House of Representatives Financial Services Committee, brought in the Sarbanes-Oxley (SOX) legislation. This makes managers fully responsible for maintaining 'adequate internal control structures and procedures for financial reporting'. It also lays down new rules for audit and accounting and has established a Public Company Oversight Accounting Board. New criminal penalties await transgressors.

SOX is controversial, not least because of the huge cost of compliance (a bonanza for accountancy firms for the same reason). As a result, some firms, for example the Rank Group, have withdrawn their listing in the US. However, this is not as easy as it sounds. The firm must prove that they have less than 300 US shareholders – difficult when so many shares are held in nominee accounts. There are 519 foreign firms with listings on the NYSE, and over 300 on NASDAQ. BP calculated that the cost of confirming to SOX is about £67m. Has it worked? Again, doubts have been expressed in some quarters, but perhaps a better prevention may be the jail sentences handed out to various fraudsters – Bernie Ebbers (WorldCom), 25 years; John Rigas (Adelphi), 15 years; and Dennis Kozlowski (Tyco), 8–25 years. Having said all this, however, it should be noted that SOX has encouraged the listing of Chinese, Indian and other companies in the US, as it demonstrates the desire of firms from emerging markets to provide investors with greater shareholder rights than in their home market – so the argument can work both ways.

Large new equities are now offered on an international basis, and there have been many involving national telephone companies. The second biggest privatization of all time was Deutsche Telekom, offered to markets all over the world at the end of 1996. The offering was split as follows:

- Germany   462 million shares
- Americas   98 million shares
- UK   57 million shares
- Rest of Europe 38 million shares
- Rest of world   34 million shares

A further slice was offered in June 1999, again on a worldwide basis, leading Deutsche Telekom to claim that it has more shareholders outside its domestic market than any other company. One key factor here is that US mutual funds and pension funds have gradually become less parochial and are investing more abroad.

TRADING IN THE MEDIUM AND LONG RUN: WHO OWNS SHARES?

Small Investors versus Institutions

The pattern of share ownership varies in different world markets. In the US, there is still a strong tradition of equity ownership by private investors who own slightly under 35%. In Germany, the figure is 14% and in France 20%. The UK, after a rise because of the many privatizations, is now down to 11.5%. In general, the trend is for institutional investors such as pension funds, insurance companies and also mutual funds to be the biggest owners of shares, and the importance of individual investors is declining.

Private share ownership is usually contrasted with that of the 'institutions', by which we mean pension funds, insurance funds and mutual funds. In some markets, private pension funds look after the pensions of individuals, whether collected by their firms or contributed individually. Life assurance companies collect premiums for years in order to provide a payout at death. General insurance companies also invest premiums paid in advance but face greater uncertainty with regard to payouts. Storms, hurricanes or oil disasters lead to unexpectedly large payouts. Mutual funds are explained below.

Sometimes people compare market capitalization as a percentage of GDP. Figures for leading centres in 2012 (reported by the World Bank's *World Development Indicators 2014*) are presented here:

- UK   122.7%
- US   114.9%
- Japan   62.0%
- France   69.8%
- Germany 43.4%
- Brazil   54.7%
- China   44.9%
- India   68.0%
- Russia   43.4%

Pension Funds: Funding versus Unfunding

How active the equity market is usually depends on the activity of the institutions, especially the pension funds. The precise effect may depend on the asset allocation policy of the pension fund as between equities and bonds.

This brings us to a fundamental question as to how pensions are funded. Box 8.1 illustrates the issues.

BOX 8.1

How Are Pensions Funded?

The first point is whether pensions are largely provided by private funds or the state. The second is whether there is a fund or whether the pensions are paid out of current taxation and contributions. The World Bank classifies pension provision into three tiers:

Tier 1 pensions provide security against destitution in old age and are mandatory and normally government owned; in the UK, it is the state pension that everyone is eligible for at retirement age, whether they be a pauper or a billionaire.

Tier 2 pensions are geared to smooth the distribution of consumption spending over a lifetime; they are usually privately managed, although they can be publicly managed. They also tend to be linked to the first tier, as is the case in the US and the UK, where contributions to private pensions receive advantageous tax treatment because the government wants to encourage individuals to save for retirement.

Tier 3 pensions provide insurance to those with exceptional longevity; they are entirely privately funded, voluntary and intended to increase individual choice.

Where the money contributed by private individuals is invested in funds to provide pensions, the biggest markets are the US, Japan, the UK, Canada, Australia, the Netherlands and Switzerland.

There are two types of pension scheme:

Defined benefit schemes relate to pension benefits being linked to final salaries – you know roughly what your pension will be years before you retire, as it's linked to the number of years of contributions and a calculation relating to final salaries. **Defined contribution** schemes are like any other long-term investment – pension payments are linked to the performance of the pension fund over its lifetime. Many individuals who had defined contribution schemes have seen their pension assets fall by 40% since the start of 2007 due to market collapses, meaning their pensions will be much reduced, especially for those just about to retire.

Because defined benefit schemes have become much more costly to finance (because people are living longer), many companies are closing their defined benefit pensions to new members and just allowing defined contribution schemes. In Britain, Tesco, British Airways and a number of other leading companies have decided not to offer guaranteed salary-related pensions to employees, as the cost of doing so becomes prohibitive, and recent accounting rules require this cost to be disclosed as a contingent liability. This is exacerbating the general concerns over pension provision.

Table 8.2 illustrates the features of various pension markets for 2014.

▼ **Table 8.2** *Global pension assets, 2014*

Country	Pension fund assets$ billion	Pension fund assets% GDP	Pension type %	
			Defined benefit	Defined contribution
Australia	1,675	113	15	85
Brazil	268	12	na	na
Canada	1,526	85	96	4
France	171	6	na	na
Germany	520	14	na	na
Hong Kong	120	41	na	na
Ireland	132	54	na	na
Japan	2,862	60	97	3
Malaysia	205	61	na	na
Mexico	190	15	na	na
Netherlands	1,457	166	95	5
South Africa	234	69	na	na
Switzerland	823	121	na	na
UK	3,309	116	71	29
US	22,117	127	42	58
TOTAL	36,119	84	53	47

Source: Towers Watson, 2015 *Global Pension Assets Study*, http:/.www.towerswatson.com.

It is also important to note the distinction between funded and unfunded pension schemes. Many state pension schemes, like National Insurance in the UK and the social security system in the US, pay pensions out of current tax revenues – not a pot of money that has been put aside and accumulated to pay pensioners in the future – they are known as 'pay-as-you-go' systems. A funded scheme is when funds are put aside and invested to meet future pension obligations.

In France, Germany and Italy, pension provision is largely by the state. In France, for instance, although the state also handles most pension payments through the Caisse de Retraite, they are not funded but paid for out of current taxation. Private pension provision is largely confined to schemes for wealthy individuals and only accounted for 6% of GDP in 2013. Sweden has a fully funded state pension scheme.

Over the past decade or so, there has been growing concern in policy circles that a pensions crisis is upon us, and the state, as well as many defined benefit schemes, will just not be able to meet its pension obligations. This is likely to be exacerbated by demographic factors, as all across Europe (and Japan), populations are ageing. With six or seven employees funding each pensioner, the older systems may have been satisfactory; however, the future is likely to see two or three workers for every pensioner. Figure 8.1 shows the incidence of ageing populations.

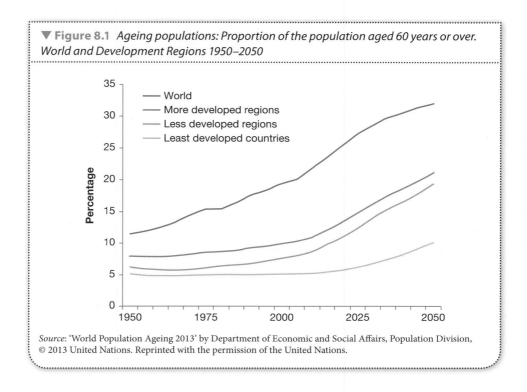

▼ **Figure 8.1** *Ageing populations: Proportion of the population aged 60 years or over. World and Development Regions 1950–2050*

Source: 'World Population Ageing 2013' by Department of Economic and Social Affairs, Population Division, © 2013 United Nations. Reprinted with the permission of the United Nations.

The World Bank estimates that by the year 2030, the number of people over 60 will triple to 1.4 billion. The Federal Trust for Education and Research, a British think tank, published a report entitled *The Pensions Time Bomb in Europe* (Taverne, 1995). It calculated a dependency ratio, that is, the ratio of people aged 65 plus to the 15–64 age group. Over the 12 countries of the EU (prior to 1995), this ratio is expected to increase from 21% in 1990 to 43% in 2040, and to 48% in Italy and the Netherlands (see Table 8.3). The Netherlands, at least, has funded pensions; Italy does not. In Germany, by 2030, pension contributions could be 30% of gross income, with one worker for every pensioner. China is in an even worse position. The 'one-child' policy means that the flow of young people to replace those retiring will not be enough. By 2040, today's young workers will be retired, and there could be 100 million people aged over 80 (the second largest population figure outside India). At present, funded or unfunded pensions are not remotely big enough to cope with this.

Countries are slow to make progress on this issue. How can we persuade people to pay tax now to fund today's pensioners and put aside extra money for their own retirement at the same time? The French have increased the number of years private sector personnel must work for a full pension, from 37.5 to 40. An attempt to do the same for the public sector met with strikes and was withdrawn. This is in spite of the fact that, by 2040, France is expected to have 70 people over 60 for every 100 people aged between 20 and 59, double the current level. In November 2011, the UK government announced

▼ **Table 8.3** *Age dependence ratio, persons over 65 as a percentage of persons aged 15–64*

Country	1990	2040
Belgium	21.9	41.5
Denmark	22.2	43.4
France	21.9	39.2
Germany	23.7	47.1
Greece	20.5	41.7
Ireland	18.4	27.2
Italy	20.4	48.4
Luxembourg	20.4	41.2
Netherlands	17.4	48.5
Portugal	16.4	38.9
Spain	17.0	41.7
UK	23.5	39.1
All EU	21.4	42.8

Source: Taverne (1995).

that the state pension age will increase to 67, and this will take place between 2026 and 2028. The Germans passed a law in 1992 making it less worthwhile to retire before 65.

In Japan, pension funds are big but past protectionist rules have curtailed competition, and performance has been poor. However, deregulation from April 1996 opened the markets to foreign investment advisers on a wide scale. Table 8.2 above shows that Japan has the world's third largest pool of pension assets – 97% being for defined benefit schemes.

The coming of the European single market should have resulted in abolition of many restrictions on pension fund investment. For example, Italian funds cannot hold more than 20% in private company equities; Portuguese and Danish funds cannot invest in other countries' securities; German funds cannot hold more than 5% in foreign bonds; and in Belgium, 15% of the fund must be held in domestic government bonds.

Work was done on a European Commission Pensions Directive, which sought to abolish these restrictions or at least modify them. After fierce argument, however, it was withdrawn in 1995. Eventually, a revised Pension Fund Directive came into force in 2003 and was implemented into member state law in 2005. Various restrictions were removed, but the Directive did not tackle the thorny issue of tax treatment of pensions. Attempts to change taxation require a unanimous vote.

Pensions still remain a national industry, with virtually no pan-European activity. It remains one of the least integrated financial sectors in Europe.

Equity Investment

The effect of pension fund activity depends, of course, on the attitude to asset allocation. The key choice is between equities and bonds, with a further subdivision between domestic and international. Boots, the British retailer, announced in autumn 2001 that it would in future be investing exclusively in bonds and switched funds out of equities. Property is a popular investment in some markets, and clearly there will also be liquid funds on deposit and invested in money market instruments like certificates of deposit.

Table 8.4 shows pension asset allocations for the main markets. With pension funds usually the major operators in stock exchanges, their importance for the equity and bond markets can readily be seen. In previous editions, we commented on the then 'cult of equity', but this seems to have reversed a little. Comparing 1998 with 2013, the US's percentage in equities is down from 62 to 57, Japan's from 67 to 40 and the Netherlands from 46 to 35. The UK always had a relatively high percentage (now 50%) in equities, partly due to its poor performance on inflation. The general belief is that equities will give better protection than bonds, that is, firms will put their prices up and make more money in nominal, if not real, terms. However, the equity market's prolonged decline in 2001–2, together with lower inflation and the problems of some pension funds, has led to a change in attitude. In the UK, legislation has been passed forcing pension funds to be more cautious in matching future liabilities with assets. The UK's 71% in equities in 2000 was down to 67% in 2004 and fell to 50% by 2013. Bond totals of 21% in 2000 were up to 33% by 2013.

Many have noted that the general move to bonds, although bringing more certainty, may, ironically, lead to poorer performance over the long term. They believe that, in the

▼ **Table 8.4** *Pension fund asset allocation 2014*

Country	Pension fund assets $bn	Asset allocation %			
		Equities	Bonds	Other	Cash
Australia	1,675	51	15	26	8
Canada	1,526	41	35	22	2
Japan	2,862	33	57	7	3
Netherlands	1,457	30	55	14	1
Switzerland	823	29	36	28	7
UK	3,309	44	37	15	3
US	22,117	44	25	29	2
TOTAL	33,769	39	37	20	4

Source: Towers Watson, 2015 *Global Pension Assets Study*, www.towerswatson.com.

end, equities will recover, driven by technology, productivity and world trade. However, given the crisis in global capital markets, those funds that are overweight in bonds will have performed much better than pensions dominated by equities.

Share Buy-backs

An interesting issue is that of companies buying back their own shares. This is common in the UK and the US. See Box 8.2.

BOX 8.2

Share Buy-backs

The idea of share buy-backs is to cancel the shares so that profit and dividend per remaining share are then enhanced.

In 2002, GlaxoSmithKline bought back the first of two instalments of £42bn of its shares. In France, however, it is common to buy shares back as a defensive move, either to support price or prevent a takeover. Under a new law passed in 1998, the AGM has powers to authorize a buy-back of up to 10% in the next 18 months. Once bought, the shares may be cancelled (subject to EGM approval) or allocated to employees.

Critics point out that if a company is unable to employ surplus capital profitably, it is a sad reflection on the business vision of the company's management and does not augur well for the company's prospects. Consequently, a share buy-back may actually result in a fall in the share price (this happened in the case of GlaxoSmithKline and also Reuters).

Share buy-backs were illegal in Germany until a new law in March 1998 permitted companies to buy back up to 10% of their shares in an 18-month period. The BHF-Bank took advantage of this to buy back 3.4% of its shares.

In Japan, share repurchases have not typically been as common and have traditionally been frowned upon as a way of manipulating share prices. However, since the slump in markets heralded by the credit crisis, Japanese companies have been active in buy-backs. During 2008, there were buy-backs at 587 listed companies, up 33% on 2007 and nearly reaching record levels. Canon spent ¥50bn ($544m) and bought back more than 1% of its outstanding equity in November, and the largest single buy-back was by Mitsubishi UFJ Financial Group, which acquired ¥239bn (around $2.5bn) of stock from its own subsidiaries in July. These figures suggested that Japanese managers were heeding investors who criticize them for keeping cash rather than giving it back to shareholders. Alternatively, some managers may simply feel that their share price is too low.

We said above that the idea of the company buying back its own shares is to cancel them to enhance profit and dividend per remaining share. The company, however, may not necessarily be obliged to cancel the shares, depending on local legislation. In the UK, for example, cancellation was mandatory until a law in 2003 allowed a company to continue to hold the shares as Treasury stock. Why would a company do this? Treasury stock allows the shares to be reissued later, either for a rights issue or even as part of a takeover bid. BP holds 7% of its own shares and UBS 10%. Typically, 10% is a maximum limit.

Mutual Funds

If a small investor has, say, $3,000 to spend on equities, there are two choices. The money can be spent on just 1 or 2 companies' shares or spread widely over 10 companies' shares. In the first case, the risk is great if one company performs badly. In the second case, with $300 spent on each share, the dealing costs are discouragingly high. The answer may be to put the money into mutual funds. These are collective investments, run by fund managers. They may be investments in money market instruments, equities or bonds. Indeed, nowadays, there are funds whose investments are in financial futures (see Chapter 14).

In the case of equities, the fund will invest in a wide range of equities; the $3,000 is thus spread over a range of shares, but without excessive risk. The fund is run by skilled managers, and fees must be paid. There are two kinds of funds:

1 *The open-ended fund* (unit trusts in the UK) raises, say, $50m and spends it on a wide range of shares. Simplifying, the fund is divided into 50 million units at $1 each. Later, investors can buy units from the managers or sell them back to the managers. If investors with $5m to spend *buy* units, the managers buy more shares, and the fund is now $55m. If investors with holdings worth $10m now *sell* the units back to the managers, shares will have to be sold to raise the money, and the fund is now only $45m. Hence, the term 'open-ended fund'. As the shares grow in value, so do the units, and this is how investors make their money. In practice, there are fees to pay and also the basic costs. Units thus have a bid/offer price like an ordinary share.

2   *The closed-ended fund* (investment trusts in the UK) is a shareholding company, much like any other. It raises $50m and, instead of being in engineering or groceries, invests the money in a portfolio of equities. If, later, investors with $5m to spend want to join in, they buy the shares of the fund on the open market *from someone else who sells them*, that is, the fund doesn't get the money but remains at $50m – hence, 'closed-ended fund'. The idea is that if, in 3 years, the shares double in value, so should the market share of the fund itself. The investors can now sell and take their profit this way. The extent to which the share price may not double, but remain at a discount to the asset value per share, attracts a lot of attention from analysts and needs to be studied by potential investors. This is because the share price of the closed-ended fund will reflect supply and demand as well as the underlying asset value.

These mutual funds are well established in the US, the UK, the Netherlands, France, Germany, Italy and Spain. In France, they are very popular, partly due to tax concessions. The open-ended fund is the SICAV (*société d'investissement à capital variable*) and the closed-ended fund, the FCP (*fonds communs de placement*). As well as equity funds, SICAVs and FCPs are popular for money market instruments.

As one might expect, the concentration in the UK is on equity investments and in Germany, bonds. Mutual funds were allowed in Italy in 1983, but equity funds lost popularity after the October 1987 crash. Today, some 50%+ of the money is invested in T-bills.

The US is a huge market for mutual fund investment. By the end of 1999, $6.85 trillion was invested in 7,791 mutual funds, and 45% of US households were fund holders. This had increased to $15.2 trillion in 7,707 funds by the start of 2014. It is interesting to note that in 1999, 59% of mutual funds were equity; 23.6%, money market; 11%, bond funds; and the remaining 5.6% were hybrids (combining a variety of equity, bond and other securities). By the first quarter of 2014, equity funds accounted for 54% of US mutual funds (in net asset terms), followed by bond funds (22.4%) and money market funds (17%). The remainder are made up by municipal and hybrid bond funds. The size of the US mutual fund sector hit $12 trillion in 2007 (it reached this level again at the start of 2012), but the effects of the credit crisis via falling markets substantially reduced the value of equity funds, which declined from $6.5 trillion to $3.7 trillion by the end of 2008. There was also a flow into safer money market funds over the period, although equity funds picked up thereafter, reaching $8.3 trillion in early 2014. Low money market rates led to a decline in the attractiveness of these funds. Leading mutual fund companies in the US include Pimco, Vanguard Group, American Funds Investment Company of America, and Fidelity. Table 8.5 provides a snapshot of the global mutual funds industry and illustrates the importance of Luxembourg, Ireland and France in Europe.

UCITS (undertakings for collective investment in transferable securities) is a term that has arrived due to an EC Directive in October 1989. The Directive sets minimum standards for open-ended funds (not closed-ended). For example, no more than 10% of the investment can be in one security. Investment in commodities, property and money market instruments is excluded. The UCITS managers can take a fund that has domestic authorization and offer it anywhere within the EU. It must be recognized by regulators in the country where the fund is to be marketed. However, although the marketing regulations are those which are in use locally, investor compensation is from the home country of the fund.

▼ **Table 8.5** *Worldwide total net assets of mutual funds, $m†*

COUNTRY	2010	2011	2012	2013	2014 Q3
World	**24,709,854**	**23,795,808**	**26,835,850**	**30,030,312**	**31,315,091**
Americas	**13,597,527**	**13,529,258**	**15,138,443**	**17,156,410**	**17,818,766**
Argentina	5,179	6,808	9,185	11,179	15,695
Brazil	980,448	1,008,928	1,070,998	1,018,641	1,064,407
Canada	636,947	753,606	856,504	940,580	996,638
Chile	38,243	33,425	37,900	39,291	41,132
Costa Rica	1,470	1,266	1,484	1,933	2,390
Mexico	98,094	92,743	112,201	120,518	133,036
Trinidad & Tobago	5,812	5,989	6,505	6,586	7,107
United States	11,831,334	11,626,493	13,043,666	15,017,682	15,558,361
Europe	**7,903,389**	**7,220,298**	**8,230,059**	**9,374,830**	**9,715,781**
Austria	94,670	81,038	89,125	90,633	84,910
Belgium	96,288	81,505	81,651	91,528	91,719
Bulgaria	302	291	324	504	511
Croatia					2,236
Czech Republic	5,508	4,445	5,001	5,131	5,363
Denmark	89,800	84,891	103,506	118,702	121,257
Finland	71,210	62,193	73,985	88,462	87,938
France	1,617,176	1,382,068	1,473,085	1,531,500	1,456,443
Germany	333,713	293,011	327,640	382,976	368,575
Greece	8,627	5,213	6,011	6,742	6,278
Hungary	11,532	7,193	8,570	12,158	11,945
Ireland	1,014,104	1,061,051	1,276,601	1,439,867	1,551,999
Italy	234,313	180,754	181,720	215,553	238,907
Liechtenstein	35,387	32,606	31,951	36,235	32,821
Luxembourg	2,512,874	2,277,465	2,641,964	3,030,665	3,224,702
Malta		2,132	3,033	3,160	3,433
Netherlands	85,924	69,156	76,145	85,304	77,987
Norway	84,505	79,999	98,723	109,325	129,248
Poland	25,595	18,463	25,883	27,858	26,944
Portugal	11,004	7,321	7,509	9,625	9,074
Romania	1,713	2,388	2,613	4,000	4,819
Russia	3,917	3,072			
Slovakia	4,349	3,191	2,951	3,292	4,010
Slovenia	2,663	2,279	2,370	2,506	2,612

COUNTRY	2010	2011	2012	2013	2014 Q3
Spain	216,915	195,220	191,284	248,234	275,519
Sweden	205,449	179,707	205,733	252,878	271,342
Switzerland	261,893	273,061	310,686	397,080	407,921
Turkey	19,545	14,048	16,478	14,078	14,678
United Kingdom	854,413	816,537	985,517	1,166,834	1,202,594
Asia and Pacific	**3,067,323**	**2,921,276**	**3,322,198**	**3,356,204**	**3,636,276**
Australia	1,455,850	1,440,128	1,667,128	1,624,081	1,681,893
China	364,985	339,037	437,449	460,332	611,761
India	111,421	87,519	114,489	107,895	123,556
Japan	785,504	745,383	738,488	774,126	794,495
Korea, Rep. of	266,495	226,716	267,582	285,173	314,166
New Zealand	19,562	23,709	31,145	34,185	40,034
Pakistan	2,290	2,984	3,159	3,464	3,791
Philippines	2,184	2,363	3,566	4,662	4,942
Taiwan	59,032	53,437	59,192	62,286	61,637
Africa	**141,615**	**124,976**	**145,150**	**142,868**	**144,268**
South Africa	141,615	124,976	145,150	142,868	144,268

Note: Components may not sum to total because of rounding.

Source: National mutual fund associations; European Fund and Asset Management Association (EFAMA) provides data for all European countries except Russia.

† Funds of funds are not included, except for France, Germany, Italy, and Luxembourg. Home-domiciled funds, except for Hong Kong, New Zealand and Trinidad & Tobago, which include home- and foreign-domiciled funds.

Source: Investment Company Institute, www.ici.org and International Investment Funds Association.

Amendments to the UCITS Directive were ratified in February 2002 and were adopted in February 2007. The new UCITS III allows greater flexibility, including some use of derivatives.

As indicated in Table 8.5, Luxembourg and Ireland have become popular (low-tax) centres for UCITS to be sold across Europe. This is because the dividends can be paid gross. A UK UCITS, for example, will deduct tax on dividends at source. Although foreigners can reclaim tax, French and German investors, for example, will be reluctant to fill in the forms of the UK's HM Revenue & Customs.

Active versus Passive Management

It is beyond the scope of an introductory book of this nature to explain the various theories that exist on asset allocation and pricing of securities. One issue, however, should be mentioned, and that is the question of active versus passive management of the funds, as shown in Box 8.3.

BOX 8.3

Active versus Passive Fund Management

Active management can be summarized as 'picking winners', that is, active selection of specific securities with frequent reorganization of the portfolio. This is typically driven by good picking and timing of investments. (Firms can use sophisticated computer models known as 'program trading' to do this, but it is more common for stock index arbitrage and dynamic portfolio insurance strategies.)

Passive management, on the other hand, makes an investment in all the stocks in a well-known index, such as the S&P 100, and leaves the fund to perform as the S&P 100. The argument for this is that statistics show that less than 50% of funds beat the index anyway and that 'index tracking' (as it is called) incurs fewer dealing costs. The subject is, naturally, controversial. It appears that in the US, some 50% of pension funds are indexed, and perhaps 15–20% in the UK.

The first tracker fund was launched by Wells Fargo in 1973, but the idea did not catch on until the mid-1980s. Some 50% or so of US public sector pension funds are based on tracking. CAPS, the UK pension performance measurement company, pointed out that although the UK's FTSE 100 rose some 14% in 1998, the median performance of active funds was only 10.4% – the biggest difference in 10 years. Only 21% of the active funds beat the FTSE 100.

The UK's National Association of Pension Funds estimates that 39% of private UK pension funds and 49% of public funds use tracking for at least part of their portfolio. On the question of costs, active funds usually charge fees of some 50 basis points, as opposed to 5–10 basis points for tracker funds.

As one might expect, the idea of active versus passive is not completely black and white. Many so-called 'passive' funds also use quantitative models to add a little to their performance and are not purely tracking.

The activity of tracker funds is now distorting some of the indices, following the mergers of large companies – Vodafone/AirTouch, BP/Amoco, Astra/Zeneca.

When a company drops out of the index, the tracker funds immediately sell it; when one joins the index, they immediately buy it. When Aegon, the Dutch insurance group, joined the MSCI Pan-Euro Index in early 1999, its price jumped 10% in one day; when Shell left the S&P 500 in June 2002, the opposite happened.

As noted earlier, there has been substantial growth in tracker funds over the past decade or so as investors have chosen to invest in those funds that charge a lower fee and emulate market movements. One development in the UK has been the arrival of Vanguard. The *Financial Times* reported that the low-cost US fund provider is offering a FTSE All-Share Index tracking fund and charging an annual fee of 0.15% – up to 10 times cheaper than other tracker products on the market (and lower than the 1%+ charged for actively managed funds). It is also offering US, European, Japanese and emerging market trackers, with annual charges ranging from 0.25 to 0.55% a year, plus three bond trackers charging between 0.15 and 0.25%.

Custodians

One term we should mention in this context is that of the custodian. Acting for pension funds, mutual funds and the like, the custodian actually looks after the securities, carries out settlement, handles stock lending (if the fund rules permit) and notifies the fund of corporate actions such as rights issues, dividend notification, AGMs and so on. They will also collect and remit dividends and reclaim withholding taxes. These days this is big business and dominated by large global custodians like Bank of New York Mellon, JPMorgan Chase, State Street, Deutsche Bank, Citigroup, BNP Paribas, HSBC and Northern Trust. To do this worldwide, they either have their own offices or use subcustodians.

TRADING IN THE SHORT RUN: DEALING SYSTEMS

Systems in stock exchanges for buying and selling stock usually follow one of three patterns: order-driven systems, quote-driven systems, or a mixture of the two.

Order-driven Systems

Most systems in Continental Europe are order driven, that is, an intermediary matches buy and sell orders at a given price. As the name suggests, the systems are driven by orders. Orders contain information essential for the transaction: the price, the quantity and the instruction of what to do in case the order does not find its match or 'twin'. Shares will not be bought or sold unless there is a counterparty with the equivalent deal on the other side. The systems in France, Germany, Belgium, Italy, Spain and Switzerland are of this type.

The older type of system saw activity on a physical floor, with the broker for a given share surrounded by others calling out buy and sell orders. The broker then matched the orders and declared an official price, which might last until the next session. Today, computer systems are usually used, at least for the major shares. A popular system in Europe is the one taken from the Toronto Stock Exchange, called CATS (computer-assisted trading system). Sometimes, it is given a different name locally, such as CAC in Paris. The French have rewritten the system as NSC (Nouveau Système de Cotation) or SuperCAC and sold it back to Toronto. It is also used in São Paulo, Brussels, Lisbon and Warsaw.

Let's take Paris as our example. Orders may be keyed into the system directly, fed to member firms or fed to the CAC system from member firms. Orders may be 'limit orders', where they are entered with a price limit, for example a buyer is prepared to buy 500 shares up to a limit of €154 or a seller will sell 400 shares, but at a price no lower than €151. Otherwise, they are known as 'market orders' filled at the 'market price'. (Note that some stock exchanges forbid the introduction of limit orders to specific categories of trades, for example those on market quote-driven systems.) From 9.00 a.m. to 10.00 a.m., these orders are fed into the system. At 10.00 a.m., the market opens. The computer then calculates the opening price at which the largest number of bids and offers can be matched (see Table 8.6).

In this example, the market reaches equilibrium at €153, with 1,700 shares at the offer rate (that is, 200 +

▼ **Table 8.6** *Opening prices*

Stock XYZ			
Buyers		**Sellers**	
Quantity	**Price limits**	**Price limits**	**Quantity**
500	Market price €	Market price €	400
200	156	150	250
250	155	151	400
500	154	152	500
750	153	153	600
1,000	152	154	1,250
3,000	151	155	1,700

250 + 500 + 750 – all these are prepared to pay at least €153) and 1,750 shares at the bid rate (that is, 250 + 400 + 500 + 600 – all these are prepared to accept €153). All the orders at the market price are now filled insofar as it is possible. Unfilled orders at the market price are carried forward, with €153 as the limit price. From 10.00 a.m. to 5.00 p.m., trading takes place on a continuous basis and the arrival of a new order will trigger a match if matching orders exist on the centralized book. An in-depth display of data on a given security is shown at the same time.

The London Stock Exchange's SETS (Stock Exchange Electronic Trading Service) is used for trading FTSE 100, FTSE 250 and the FTSE Small Cap Index constituents as well as other liquid securities. The exchange also operates a modified version of SETS known as SETSqx (Stock Exchange Electronic Trading Service – quotes and crosses) for trading securities less liquid than those traded on SETS. They are order matching systems like the French NSC. Orders can be placed at a limit price or simply 'at best'. Further options allow the user to decide if a part-match is acceptable and whether any unmatched order is to remain on the order book.

The information shown on a screen once continuous order input takes place is shown in Figure 8.2. On the left, we can see that the best 'buy' price for GlaxoSmithKline is £17.46, and the best 'sell' is £17.47. Total buy orders are 6,661, and total sell orders are 62,482. Stock exchange members, however, can still do deals outside SETS, reporting them through the system. This is why some prices reported are AT (automatic trading), and some are not.

Figure 8.2 *SETS screen*

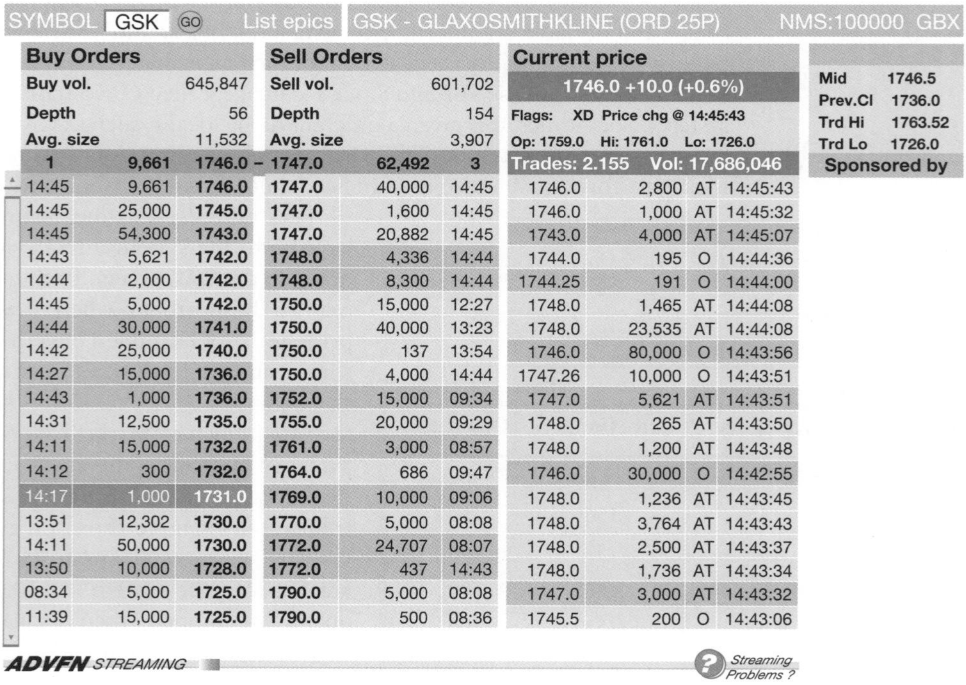
SYMBOL GSK GO List epics GSK - GLAXOSMITHKLINE (ORD 25P) NMS:100000 GBX

Buy Orders			Sell Orders			Current price			
Buy vol.		645,847	Sell vol.		601,702	1746.0 +10.0 (+0.6%)			
Depth		56	Depth		154	Flags: XD Price chg @ 14:45:43			
Avg. size		11,532	Avg. size		3,907	Op: 1759.0 Hi: 1761.0 Lo: 1726.0			
1	9,661	1746.0 –	1747.0	62,492	3	Trades: 2.155 Vol: 17,686,046			
14:45	9,661	1746.0	1747.0	40,000	14:45	1746.0	2,800	AT	14:45:43
14:45	25,000	1745.0	1747.0	1,600	14:45	1746.0	1,000	AT	14:45:32
14:45	54,300	1743.0	1747.0	20,882	14:45	1743.0	4,000	AT	14:45:07
14:43	5,621	1742.0	1748.0	4,336	14:44	1744.0	195	O	14:44:36
14:44	2,000	1742.0	1748.0	8,300	14:44	1744.25	191	O	14:44:00
14:45	5,000	1742.0	1750.0	15,000	12:27	1748.0	1,465	AT	14:44:08
14:44	30,000	1741.0	1750.0	40,000	13:23	1748.0	23,535	AT	14:44:08
14:42	25,000	1740.0	1750.0	137	13:54	1746.0	80,000	O	14:43:56
14:27	15,000	1736.0	1750.0	4,000	14:44	1747.26	10,000	O	14:43:51
14:43	1,000	1736.0	1752.0	15,000	09:34	1747.0	5,621	AT	14:43:51
14:31	12,500	1735.0	1755.0	20,000	09:29	1748.0	265	AT	14:43:50
14:11	15,000	1732.0	1761.0	3,000	08:57	1748.0	1,200	AT	14:43:48
14:12	300	1732.0	1764.0	686	09:47	1746.0	30,000	O	14:42:55
14:17	1,000	1731.0	1769.0	10,000	09:06	1748.0	1,236	AT	14:43:45
13:51	12,302	1730.0	1770.0	5,000	08:08	1748.0	3,764	AT	14:43:43
14:11	50,000	1730.0	1772.0	24,707	08:07	1748.0	2,500	AT	14:43:37
13:50	10,000	1728.0	1772.0	437	14:43	1748.0	1,736	AT	14:43:34
08:34	5,000	1725.0	1790.0	5,000	08:08	1747.0	3,000	AT	14:43:32
11:39	15,000	1725.0	1790.0	500	08:36	1745.5	200	O	14:43:06

Mid	1746.5
Prev.Cl	1736.0
Trd Hi	1763.52
Trd Lo	1726.0
Sponsored by	

ADVFN STREAMING
Streaming Problems ?

Source: advfn.com.

Very large orders present a problem. They may wait quite a long time until they can be matched, and their very presence will tend either to raise or lower the price. Block trades between institutions can be matched by brokers if there is a matching price, but stamp duty (among other things) prevents a market maker in Paris (*teneur du marché*) either buying a large block (not knowing to whom they will sell the stocks) or selling a large block they will now have to buy. The liquidity in trading for large orders attracts business to London from Paris, Frankfurt, Milan, Brussels and Madrid.

In Germany, on the official market, there are official price fixers (*Amtliche Kursmakler*), and on the second market, there are independent brokers (*Freimakler*). The whole system is dominated by the banks handling their own and client orders. As a result of conflicts of interest, there have been three rival computer systems – the banks with IBIS, the *Kursmakler* with MATIS and the *Freimakler* with MIDAS. However, IBIS eventually became the sole system for top shares and was itself replaced by Xetra in December 1997. The Irish and Vienna exchanges also use Xetra.

In Japan, there are seven stock exchanges – Tokyo (which merged with the Osaka exchange in 2013) and six others. The Tokyo exchange trades the shares of 2,292 companies and accounts for 90% of Japan's trading. Investors place their orders with stock exchange members. Specialists – *saitori* – match orders through an open outcry system. The details are circulated on computer screens.

Quote-driven Systems

In quote-driven systems, there is someone called a market maker, who continuously quotes bid and offer prices at which they will buy or sell shares. The difference is the spread, that is, their profit margin. As a result, they will buy shares at the bid price, not knowing to whom these shares will be sold. They also agree from time to time to sell short, that is, to sell stock that they don't actually own but will now have to go out and buy. This clearly involves risk and needs capital.

The systems, therefore, tend to be driven by the quotations. The prices, especially first thing in the morning, do not necessarily reflect the prices at which deals have taken place, as the market makers can change the quotations whenever they wish. Usually, these prices are firm for a given quantity of shares and may be shown thus:

Share XYZ	Bid	Offer	Bid quantity	Offer quantity
100 102	50	50		

Seen on a computer screen in the UK, this would indicate that the market maker will buy shares at, say, £1.00 or sell them at £1.02 for any quantity up to 50,000 shares. For higher quantities, brokers will then negotiate on behalf of clients.

The main quotation-driven systems are the US NASDAQ and London's SEAQ (Stock Exchange Automated Quotations), which was heavily modelled on NASDAQ. Although the top shares in London are traded on the SETS, SEAQ is the London Stock Exchange's service for fixed interest market and alternative investment market securities that are not traded on either SETS or SETSqx. Where there are such systems, there are now two types of trader – the broker and the market maker.

The broker approaches market makers on behalf of clients and buys shares from them for the clients or sells the clients' shares to them. Brokers make a living by charging a commission and do not take risk. In London, a broker may match buy or sell orders from a client provided the price is better than that available from a market maker. This is a slight complication and leads to the term 'broker dealer'. Generally, however, the role of the broker is that of an agent, especially for smaller clients.

▼ **Figure 8.3** *SEAQ screen*

| Screen | Quote changes | | | | | | | | | |

| SYMBOL IMG GO | List epics | IMG - IMAGINTN. TECH (ORD 10P) | | NMS:75000 GBX |

SEAQ Market Maker Quotes						Current price				Mid 39.5
Spread		5.0	Market Makers		8	39.5 -3.0 (-7.1%)				Prev.Cl 42.5
Spread %		11.9%	Total Trades		11	Flags:	Price chg @ 11:03:07			Trd Hi 44.0
Buy Quotes			Sell Quotes			Op: 42.5	Hi: 42.5		Lo: 39.5	Trd Lo 37.25
4	300,000	37.0 –	42.0	300,000	4	Trades: 11	Vol: 119,601			Sponsored by
07:53	75k NMRA	37.0	42.0	WINS	75k 09.28	37.25	2,400	O	11:03:07	
09:28	75k WINS	37.0	42.0	MLSB	75k 10.29	37.6	1,000	O	11:02:00	
10:29	75k MLSB	37.0	42.0	UBSW	75k 10.30	39.0	655	O	10:17:10	
10:30	75k UBSW	37.0	42.0	CSFB	75k 10.31	39.25	500	O	09:38:48	
09:19	75k KLWT	36.0	43.0	KLWT	75k 09.19	40.0	62,500	O	09:31:50	
10:30	75k NITE	36.0	43.0	NITE	75k 10.30	39.3	546	O	09:29:00	
10:30	75k AITK	36.0	44.0	AITK	75k 10.30	41.5	35,000	O	09:14:42	
10:31	75k CSFB	35.0	47.0	NMRA	75k 07.53	41.6	4,000	O	09:07:00	
						41.25	6,000	O	08:59:50	
						44.0	1,000	O	08:36:51	
						44.0	6,000	O	08:01:00	

Source: advfn.com.

Large clients, like investment institutions, don't have to use a broker, but may approach a market maker directly. If they do use a broker, it will be on a quid pro quo basis, that is, in return for the business, the broker will make available equity research reports free of charge. As a result, providing top-quality equity research is essential to attract business.

The market is very competitive, and there may be 15–20 market makers competing in a particular share, with the prices freely available to all. This ability to take risk is useful for large deals, as the market maker will buy and sell and keep liquidity going. Very large deals hit problems with order-driven systems. On the other hand, market makers are reluctant to handle small company shares in which there is little trading. The spreads are very wide, and this further discourages trading.

The NASDAQ and SEAQ systems are very similar. Let's examine the SEAQ type of display for a high-tech stock like Imagine Technologies, as in Figure 8.3.

Normal market size (NMS) is the minimum quantity of shares for which a firm quotation is given. (Smaller market makers can register as 'reduced size market makers' and post half this figure.) We can see that for Imagine Technologies, there are eight market makers competing for the business. The main display shows the market makers' initials, the bid/offer price and the bid/offer quantity. For example, on the left towards the bottom, we see that CSFB are quoting a price of 35p bid and 40p offered for quantities of 300,000 shares bid and offered.

We don't even need to search for the best prices, as the panel halfway down shows us the best bid and offer, 37–42. These are called the touch prices. The spread (5p) at the touch is usually measured and a record kept as an indication of the market's efficiency. Above these figures are shown the cumulative volume of shares traded so far and the latest price and trading history. All prices must be entered within 3 minutes of the conclusion of the deal.

Note that the trading itself is not automated. If the broker wishes to deal, the arrangement is concluded on the telephone. Only the SETS is automated.

Hybrid Systems

There has been a trend over the past decade or so for hybrid systems to emerge with both order-driven and quote-driven features. Hybrid systems have been in place for a while in the NYSE, where an order-driven automated system coexists with a physical deal market. We have also witnessed quote-driven systems move to hybrids, as in the case of London's SETS and the US's NASDAQ. The main European exchanges have moved from order-driven systems to hybrids, for instance Milan's STAR and SeDex.

In New York, each share is allocated to a specialist. The specialist acts as a broker, executing orders for other brokers on a commission basis. However, they may act for their own account (like a market maker) by buying from the public when there are no other buyers and selling to the public when there are no other sellers, all at or near the price of the last transaction. In other words, they match buyers and sellers when there are plenty of them but will keep the market going by buying on their own account when there is a shortage. There are about 60 specialists on the NYSE and the system dates from before the First World War.

In a given stock, a specialist may have buyers at $45.25 and sellers at $45.50 – these are the best prices, that is, highest bid and lowest offer. A broker approaches and is quoted '$45.25/$45.50'. The broker's client wants to buy 100 shares. He tries '$45.375' in case anyone in the crowd surrounding the specialist wishes to match this. If this fails, he raises the bid to $45.50, and the specialist calls out 'sold' and gives the broker the name of the first order on his book at that price.

At the start of the day, the specialist is faced with many orders – some at the closing market price, some at limit prices. His duty is to set a price as near as possible to the close (to maintain an orderly market) and yet also to match as many orders as possible. Sometimes the system works well in a crisis, sometimes not. On Monday, 26 September 1955, following President Eisenhower's heart attack the previous day, there was frenzied trading. Specialists, holding stocks worth $50m, bought almost another $50m to help stabilize the market. However, on Black Monday, 19 October 1987, the specialists were overwhelmed, and for hours there was no trading in two key stocks, IBM and General Motors. In London, the market makers kept going, but there were frequent accusations of not answering the telephone.

There is an important automatic electronic order execution service in New York, DOT (Designated Order Turnaround), which was introduced in 1976 to transmit to the trading posts orders of up to a given maximum size and to send back confirmation of completed orders. In 1984, this was replaced by SuperDOT, able to handle bigger volumes. This itself was integrated with OARS (Opening Automated Report Service), which collected and stored the opening orders each day. The system pairs buy and sell orders, and specialists can quickly see imbalances and determine the day's opening prices.

An order matching system called Direct Plus has been introduced. This matches orders directly and accounts for some 10% of all trades in New York.

In Amsterdam, the market is split between retail and wholesale. Retail orders go via the *hoekman*, who may match orders or take a position like a market maker. Wholesale orders go through an order matching system called AIDA. Banks and brokers can also advertise their desire to buy and sell via a system called ASSET.

Although the London SETS is essentially order matching, in practice it is more of a hybrid system. Users are not obliged to enter orders via the system. For years, London's culture has been one of market making. As a result, many institutions still telephone stock exchange members and ask if they want to buy or sell and take the risk. Sometimes, the dealer will accept a large order at a protected price but attempt to better it by feeding it through the system in smaller batches or offering it to other institutions. These very large orders are called 'worked principal orders' and publication details are delayed. Because currently less than half the orders are going via order matching for automatic execution, we can describe the SETS system as a kind of hybrid with characteristics of both order-driven and quotation-driven systems. A new system, SETSqx, specifically incorporates market maker quotes into the system.

A rival system to SETSqx is PLUS, operated by PLUS Markets, owners of the OFEX market, described later in this chapter. The system operates for 220 quoted (Plus-quoted) and another 400 listed (Plus-listed) companies, typically with capitalization less than £50m.

All the above systems may be suspended at moments of crisis (such as the 9/11 attacks in New York), when trading becomes frantic. In London this is called a fast market. When the bombs went off in London on 7 July 2005, the LSE declared a fast market for a period.

Interdealer Brokers

In some markets (for example London), transactions between market dealers are facilitated by interdealer brokers (IDBs). Their function is like brokers in money markets or foreign exchange. They publish (on computer screens) large potential deals at bid and offer prices, but anonymously. Another dealer may see the quotation and decide to make a trade. The transaction is carried out by the broker, and the two counterparties never learn of each other's identity. The dealer who identifies a trade and indicates a willingness to conclude it pays the commission and is called (curiously) the 'aggressor'. Anonymous order matching systems have not impacted the market as much as many people thought. Interdealer broking exists for equities, bonds, foreign exchange and derivatives. The world's biggest is ICAP, active in the wholesale markets in interest rates, credit, commodities, foreign exchange, emerging markets, equities and equity derivatives. In October 2014, it had an average daily transaction volume of just under $800bn. Other top firms include GFI Group, Tullett Prebon, Tradition Financial Services and BGC Partners. Combined, these five firms have 90% of the interdealer market.

Stock Borrowing and Lending

Dealers may sell shares or bonds they don't have, going 'short'. An alternative to buying the stock prior to settlement is to borrow it from institutions who will lend stock for a commission and pass over money (or other securities) as collateral. Typically, the stock is paid for and the money returned when the dealer actually buys the stock and returns it. This facility greatly assists the liquidity of the market.

On the other hand, dealers have to fund their long positions. One way to fund them is to lend stock not needed and take the money to help fund other positions. Thus, stock lending may be done by institutions merely to enhance income, or may be done by dealers as a means of financing their position. To complicate matters, although everyone calls it stock lending; in fact, the stock is *sold*, albeit on a temporary basis. In other words, the whole arrangement is the sale and repurchase agreement, or repo, which we met in Chapter 7. There it was a means of banks funding their liquidity by selling stock (temporarily) to the central bank.

This market is particularly large for bonds, although there is some lending of equities.

The language, as usual, is used loosely. Generally 'stock lending' is used where dealers want to cover short positions and is driven by borrower demand. 'Repo' is used where the transaction is to meet funding needs. The legal agreements for stock lending and repos are, however, different.

As we will see in Chapter 9, hedge funds use stock borrowing extensively to cover their short positions.

Bought Deals/Block Trades

Another interesting type of transaction is bought deals or block trades, which recently have led to the development of dark pool trading as shown in Box 8.4.

BOX 8.4

Block Trades and Dark Pool Trading

Occasionally, very large share deals, called 'bought deals' or 'block trades', are executed. The investment bank involved buys the shares using its own capital and hopes to sell them to investors at a profit. It can be very lucrative but also involves great risk.

It is usually a competitive process. In December 1995, for example, NM Rothschild held an auction for the sale of the UK government's remaining stake in BP. SBC Warburg won the business by offering £5.08 per share and later sold the shares for £5.13, making about £5m. The sales total was £500m.

In March 1999, Veba, the German energy group, sold its 10.2% stake in Cable & Wireless – the biggest block trade in the European stock markets. Some 246 million shares were placed by ABN AMRO at £7.35, raising £1.8bn, a discount of 11.5% to the latest stock price. ABN AMRO was believed to have paid £7.24 for the stake, leaving a profit of £26m, about 1.5%. In February 2004, UBS sold a block of 21.2 million shares in AstraZeneca on behalf of Investor, the Swedish investment company. The block was sold for £550m in 30 minutes at a discount to the market price of 1.51%.

It doesn't always go well, of course. In May 2005, *The Banker* magazine reported losses on two block trades of €35m for Citigroup and €40m for Goldman Sachs.

Over recent years, there has been rapid development of 'dark pool' trading systems that allow the trading of large blocks of shares to be carried out away from the public, or order book of an exchange or other type of publicly available share trading platform.

Prices are not revealed until after trades are completed. These have grown rapidly in the US and Europe, and are emerging elsewhere – Singapore announced the introduction of such a Chi-X system in early 2009. For instance, in July 2009, the *Financial Times* said that SmartPool, a European dark pool share trading facility (launched by NYSE Euronext at the start of the year), had signed up 14 banks and independent brokers to trade on its platform.

SmartPool is one of 45 dark pools operated in Europe by either exchanges, platforms such as Chi-X – commonly referred to as 'multilateral trading facilities' – and independent operators such as Liquidnet. The largest dark pools include Crossfinder (Credit Suisse), Barclays LX (Barclays), UBS Securities LLC, Instinct X (Merrill Lynch), MS Trajectory Cross (Morgan Stanley), Super X (Deutsche Bank) and Sigma X (Goldman Sachs).

Block Trades and Dark Pool Trading (*continued*)

In June 2014, the State of New York filed a lawsuit against Barclays, saying that it had misrepresented to clients the level of high-frequency (automated) trading that used its dark pool.

Source: Financial Industry Regulatory Authority (FINRA) (2015)

THE TRADING PROCESS: CLEARING AND SETTLEMENT

Clearing relates to all activities that take place in between making a commitment to undertake a transaction until it is paid for (settled). Most security transactions nowadays have compulsory clearing systems run by a clearing house that acts as a counterparty to reduce settlement risk (the risk that the transaction will not be paid for). Clearing houses were once more typical in derivatives markets, but they are now widespread in all exchanges. Since the credit crisis, there have been major moves to push over-the-counter (OTC) derivatives contracts onto exchanges with clearing house facilities so as to reduce risk.

Settlement is the basic question of paying money and receiving stock or receiving money and delivering the stock. If the stock can be delivered with money being credited to pay for it, this is called 'delivery versus payment' and is the ideal. It is a recommendation of a 2003 Group of Thirty report on settlement.

Sometimes settlement systems are rolling settlements, for example, rolling 5 working day settlement. This means that a deal on Tuesday must be settled on the next Tuesday, a deal on Wednesday must be settled on the next Wednesday and so on. This is called 'T+5', that is, 'trade date +5'. The Group of Thirty report recommends rolling settlement systems and 'T+3' if possible. The US is T+3; Germany, T+2; and France, T+3 under its RELIT system (*règlement livraison de titres*).

The alternative is the system of an account period. For example, Paris has its *règlement mensuel*, which can still be used to settle if requested. The 'month' is the 5 last working days of the month plus the next month up to 5 working days from the end. All deals within this month are settled on the last trading day of the month. There is, however, also a cash market (*marché au comptant*). This is used for less actively traded stocks, all the second markets, OTC markets and all bonds.

In New York, the Depository Trust Corporation (DTC) holds large blocks of stocks registered in its name for safe custody. Between the New York Stock Exchange (NYSE) and the DTC is the National Securities Clearing Corporation, which acts as a clearing function for the exchange and passes the transfers to the DTC. Net money due to or from a broker is settled daily by a single payment.

The UK had a fortnightly account system. Settlement day was a week on Monday, following the end of the 2-weekly account ending on the Friday. All member firms' deals were then settled as one net figure. Its successor abolished the use of share certificates, but only for professionals, and implemented T+2 rolling settlement. Private investors are still able to use share certificates if they wish. UK security trades are normally settled in Euroclear UK and Ireland, the UK's central security depository. Where paper certificates no longer exist and transfer of ownership is on a computer register only, this is called 'dematerialization'. The French RELIT system is of this type.

Italy dropped its monthly settlement system and moved to T+5 rolling settlement in February 1996.

In general, the trend is towards new rolling settlement systems and dematerialization.

SECOND MARKETS

It is quite common to have a 'second market' for shares that do not fulfil all the requirements for a full official listing. The UK has the alternative investment market (AIM), and Germany used to have a Neuer Markt, but this and other segments disappeared and became part of the official market in November 2007. Similarly, second-tier markets in Paris and the Netherlands have been phased out under Euronext ownership.

There may be an active OTC market. Paris has its 'Hors Cote', the US has the huge NASDAQ market, and the UK had a market called PLUS Markets although this failed to make money and was sold to the interdealer broker ICAP in 2012 and renamed ICAP Securities and Derivatives Exchange (ISDX). It has around 120 companies listed (including Arsenal football club) and has a quote-driven system.

Usually, the key requirements that the second-tier (or even third-tier) market firm may not fulfil are the number of years' trading record and the percentage of shares in outside hands. The general European rule, under the 'Mutual Recognition of Listing Particulars', is that 3 years' trading is needed for a full listing and for recognition of a firm already listed on another EU exchange.

In London, for the official list, 25% of shares must be in outside hands. By October 2014, there were 1,096 firms listed on the AIM with a market capitalization of £72bn, and they are now handled by SETSqx.

A consortium of US and European banks formed a new pan-European market called EASDAQ, modelled on the US NASDAQ market. The aim was to attract high-growth companies. Here, 20% of the shares must be in outside hands. It began in late 1996, but by mid-1999, had only 43 companies listed with a total capitalization of €21bn. In 2001, it was taken over by NASDAQ.

ANALYSTS' RATIOS

When a firm makes an offer for sale (or IPO) of its shares, how does it decide what price to ask for the shares? A simple answer seems to be 'divide the value of the company by the number of the shares'. The problem is that the value of the company is the share price.

Sometimes people suggest 'asset values' as a possible guide. However, on 1 October 1987, companies' share prices were a great deal higher than at 31 October 1987, after the market crash, and yet the assets were the same. In any case, some firms are quite valuable but have few assets. 'People' companies like computer software houses or stockbrokers are like this.

The fact is that price is simply what the market will pay. We must, therefore, look at what the market does pay for similar companies. Their share prices will all be different, which doesn't immediately help. There are two rewards for buying a share – dividends and an increase in the share price. Both of these depend on profits, so what we need to do is see how the price per share of comparable companies compares with the profit per share. We might find an overall relationship of, say, 10; that is, if the profit is $4 per share, the share price is typically $40. If our profit per share is $3, this suggests a price of $30. Let's make it $28 and persuade everyone that it's a bargain. This relationship of share price to profit is the price/earnings ratio (P/E ratio) – the most famous ratio of them all. We've seen one of its key uses, to help us initially set a price. Each time new profits are announced, a new P/E ratio is calculated, and the share may seem cheap or dear now compared to its peers in the market sector.

Sometimes analysts look at the P/E ratio for the whole stock market and compare this with historic values to see if the market is overpriced or not. Analysts gauge the performance of IPOs and also offer periodic announcements of forecasts and opinions on 'fair' securities prices. The truth is that they sometimes advise to buy, often advise to hold and rarely advise to sell (especially if they hold the shares in their own balance sheets).

Sometimes it is not easy to find the market sector. When the composer Andrew Lloyd Webber went public as the Really Useful Group, it was difficult to find anything comparable. In that case, what took place was the 'offer for sale by tender'. Investors put in their various bids, and the share allocation was decided accordingly. In that case, it was a 'strike price' tender, that is, everyone paid the same price.

As dividends are part of the reward for holding shares, the market looks at dividend income as a percentage of the share price. To avoid complications, the dividend is grossed up if it is normally paid net, for example:

$$\text{Gross dividend/Share price} = \$2.5/\$50 = 5\%$$

This ratio is the gross dividend yield or, simply, the yield. It will be compared with the yield on other shares and with the yield on bonds in particular. Analysts talk of the yield ratio – the ratio between the yield on government bonds and the yields on shares. As shares may have capital gains, the yield is usually less than that on medium maturity bonds, although this has not always been the case. Typical P/E ratios and yields for key exchanges in December 2008 are shown in Table 8.7.

Looking at the dividend paid, we may want to see how comfortable the firm was when paying the dividend out of profit. Was all the profit used? How much profit is retained for growth? We compare the profit per share with the *net* dividend per share, for example:

$$\text{Profit per share/Net dividend} = \$5/\$2 = 2.5$$

▼ Table 8.7 *P/E ratios and yields, 1 August 2014*

Exchange	Index	Yield	P/E
US	S&P 500	1.93	18.8
Germany	DAX 30	2.2	16
UK	FTSE 100	2.7	14.2
France	CAC 40	1.8	24.8
Japan	TOPIX	1.8	14.4

Source: Yahoo Finance and various market indices.

This ratio is the cover. If the profit is small but the firm feels it must maintain the dividend, the net dividend paid may exceed the profit per share. We say the dividend is *uncovered*. Clearly, it is being financed out of the reserves (that is, previous years' profits), and the firm's capital is being weakened.

At a time of recession, there is fierce argument about the extent to which firms should try to maintain dividends even if they are not justified by profits. Pension funds or insurance companies who need income to meet commitments are concerned when dividends are cut or not paid. Trustees of some investment funds will not allow investment in any firm that has passed a dividend in a given previous time period.

Finally, analysts look at earnings per share and use this as a record of the firm's performance. Problems arise when accounting conventions may allow (legitimate) massaging of the profit figure. Should extraordinary items for unprecedented events, for example acquisition costs, be charged against profit for this purpose? More recently, analysts have focused on a new measure – earnings before interest, tax, depreciation and amortization (EBITDA), which gives a useful guide to cash flow.

For the EU, trying to impose common national standards is a veritable minefield. However, the International Accounting Standards Board (IASB), a new standard for public companies, came into force on 1 January 2005. The aim of the IASB is to develop a single set of 'high quality, understandable and international financial reporting standards for general purpose financial statements'. The EU has adopted many of its recommendations, affecting some 7,000 companies, and involving such things as the treatment of R&D, goodwill, stock options and accounting for off-balance sheet vehicles. The idea is to make interfirm comparisons easier. In 2009, the EU published proposals regarding whether banks and insurers should value a financial investment as a long-term holding or as a trading position. If a bank's investment produces predictable cash flow like a government bond, it can be valued in accounts using an accounting mechanism that smoothes out market fluctuations. If the investment's cash flow is unpredictable, like some derivatives for instance, it should be valued at current market levels. These proposals could see more investments reported at current market values, a move that may improve the transparency of accounts but increase volatility in earnings. The EU appeared keen to implement these new rules, although the US wanted to water down the proposal, as it believed it would lead to too much volatility in earnings. This latter view is based on the argument that 'fair value' accounting, where various financial contracts were valued at market prices, led to a collapse in bank assets and in part contributed to the credit crisis. Accounting rules known as IFRS 13 on Fair Value Measurement were adopted by the International Accounting Standards Board in mid-2011, and this provides a guide as to how to perform fair value measurement under International Financial Reporting Standards. These came into effect in January 2013 and are enshrined into EU legislation; in fact in October 2014, the EC published a report investigating the extent of compliance with these fair value rules.

US STOCK MARKET: THE NEW PARADIGM AND THE BURSTING OF THE DOT-COM AND SECURITIZATION BUBBLE

The performance of the US economy up to and beyond the millennium seemed to have broken all normal economic rules. The stock market also experienced a period of unprecedented expansion.

For 3 years, US GDP grew at 4% per annum with no sign of inflationary pressures. Consumer price inflation at the end of 1998 was 1.7%, the lowest for 20 years, and unemployment, at 4.2%, the lowest for 30 years. At this point (according to normal rules), labour shortages should have appeared, and competition for labour would have forced wages and inflation up. Instead of declining productivity as poorer quality labour is employed, productivity in 1997–8 doubled.

People referred to this as the 'new paradigm' – an era in which the old rules no longer applied. They pointed to declining commodity prices, cheaper imports due to the strong dollar, high productivity due to technology and the intensification of global competition, making companies reluctant to increase prices for fear of losing market share.

The Dow Jones responded in kind, rising two and a half times in the period 1996–98, and continuing to rise in 1999 – the only small blip coming with the Russian crisis in August 1998. The number of US households in mutual funds rose from 10 million to 40 million. At one point, Alan Greenspan, then chairman of the Federal Reserve, issued warnings about 'irrational exuberance', but seemed to content himself with pointing out that share prices implied confidence in a strong growth in corporate profits.

Would the old rules reassert themselves in the end? Those who wanted to spoil the party pointed out that the stock market rose threefold between 1925 and 1929 and everyone talked of 'a new era'. The market then fell 89% from its peak to a low point in 1932 (the Great Depression).

With the bursting of the dot-com bubble in 2001 and accounting scandals in 2002, the markets fell around 40%, and the Dow, having peaked at over 12,000, fell to 7,528 in October 2002. The FTSE 100 peaked at 6,930 in December 1999, fell to a low of 4,122 in September 2001, recovered somewhat in 2002, but the Iraq War uncertainty led to a new low of 3,281 in March 2003. After that, the market recovered steadily, moving to 6,716 by July 2007, had a reversal in August and increased again to 6,661 by October 2007. Then the credit crunch happened, and the FTSE generally declined, hitting a low of 3,530 in late February 2009. However, since then, central banks in the US and UK have been boosting market liquidity via their quantitative easing and near zero market interest rates. This has rallied their equity markets; the Dow hit over 17,000 and the FTSE over 6,800 in September 2014.

EU RULES

Investment Services Directive

At the end of June 1992, EU finance ministers reached agreement on the final shape of the Investment Services Directive (ISD). This extends the 'single passport' idea seen in the Second Banking Directive. Stockbrokers in one country have the right to deal in the shares of any other EU country, without having to set up a local office or a local stockbroker. The ISD took effect on 1 January 1996. From this date, firms have been able to operate in any EU member state provided they are regulated in one of them. This operation is subject to local rules on the conduct of business.

In addition, all exchanges and futures and options markets can trade throughout the EU. The effect of all this is to increase competition between the EU's stock exchanges and derivatives exchanges. Thus, from 1 January 1996, NatWest Markets began trading on the Swedish Stock Exchange, but from its office in London, and there was no longer any need to pay a local Swedish broker. Equally, the German DTB, the derivatives exchange, opened an access point in London for local members to do business directly with Frankfurt.

Markets in Financial Instruments Directive

The Markets in Financial Instruments Directive (MiFID) came into effect on 1 November 2007, replacing the ISD. As noted above, the aim of the ISD was to establish provisions governing the organization and conduct of business requirements that should apply to firms engaged in investment activities. It also aimed to harmonize certain conditions governing the operation of regulated securities markets. MiFID has the same basic purpose as the ISD, but it makes major changes to the way in which investment firms are regulated. Thus, the MiFID:

- widens the range of investment services and activities that firms can undertake on an EU-wide basis;
- sets out more detailed requirements governing the organization and conduct of business of investment firms, and how regulated markets operate;
- includes new pre- and post-trade transparency requirements for equity markets, the creation of a new regime for 'systematic internalizers' of retail order flow in liquid equities, and more extensive transaction reporting requirements;
- improves the 'passport' for investment firms by drawing a clearer line between the respective responsibilities of home and host states; and
- requires investment firms that fall within its scope to comply with the new Capital Requirements Directive (CRD).

In general, the MiFID covers most, if not all, firms that were subject to the ISD, plus others that were not. It now covers investment banks, portfolio managers, stockbrokers and broker dealers, corporate finance firms, many futures and options firms, and some commodities firms. One of the main criticisms of MiFID is that it requires extensive changes to computer systems and compliance. Banks and investment groups are groaning under the weight of a raft of regulations – Basel II, Sarbanes-Oxley and MiFID. They are likely to continue to groan as a new wave of regulations are bound to be implemented to tighten up banking sector oversight (see Chapter 6). The crucial innovation of MiFID as far as stock exchanges are concerned is the abolition of the principle of concentration of trading in a stock exchange, thus allowing competition from alternative trading venues. The most relevant two are (from the original MiFID definition):

1 *mutualized trading facilities (MTFs)*, multilateral systems, operated by an investment firm or market operator, which bring together multiple third-party buying and selling interests in financial instruments in accordance with non-discretionary rules; and
2 *systematic internalizers*, investment firms that, on an organized, frequent and systematic basis, deal on their own account by executing client orders outside a regulated market or an MTF.

In October 2011, plans were set out to update the above EU legislation – MiFID II aims to further strengthen the single market and ensure its resilience. The MiFID II proposals comprise revisions to the original Directive and seek to advance:

- *conduct of business* rules by
  - developing clearly defined powers for national regulators to intervene to protect consumers from inappropriate products or services;
  - raising at the EU level the issue of the adverse effects of payments between product providers and intermediaries;
  - strengthening the best execution framework; and
  - setting clear standards for firms' dealings with eligible counterparties.
- best execution in markets by
  - providing a level playing field;
  - adapting for developments in technology and market infrastructures;
  - providing for the necessary transparency to investors and regulators across a wider range of instruments and markets; and
  - allowing stronger supervision of commodity derivative markets.

MiFID II is not expected to be in place until late 2016/early 2017.

Capital Requirements Directive

Alongside the MiFID is the Capital Requirements Directive (CRD) that introduces the capital requirements set-out in Basel III into EU law. CRD was introduced in mid-2013 and sets out the new capital and related standards for global banks under Basel III. This includes requirements for banks to hold more capital and liquidity. Basel III has to be in place by 2019 so the deadline for full implantation of the CRD is the same. Note that banks that are viewed as systemically important have to hold more capital and liquidity than non-systemic institutions. Also, banks have limits/restrictions placed on some of their more risky activities, such as proprietary trading and involvement with hedge funds and other investment firms. (Note that the CRD replaces the old Capital Adequacy Directive).

Mergers and Acquisitions

The EU agreed a Merger Regulation in 1989. This defined circumstances in which a merger would have a 'European dimension' and come under the rules of the EU, and when a merger would be decided by national bodies. In one case in particular, in 1991, the European Commission vetoed the takeover of de Havilland, the Canadian aircraft maker, by Aérospatiale of France and Alenia of Italy (to the fury of all concerned). On the other hand, objections to the Nestlé takeover of Perrier had little effect, and Nestlé and BSN of France now control 75% of the French mineral water market. In the UK, Airtours abandoned its bid for First Choice in June 1999, following objections from the regulatory authorities in Brussels.

The EU has abandoned the idea of a detailed takeover bid directive in favour of one that outlines principles with which local legislation must comply, for example equal treatment of all shareholders. However, the problem was stalled for 13 years, despite a clear need for general principles to be adopted. In France, BNP made a bid for Société Générale and Paribas. The last two could (and did) deal in BNP shares, but BNP could not deal in theirs. Gucci, facing a hostile bid from LVMH, sold 40% of new shares to an ally, François Pinault. This was only possible due to lax takeover rules in Amsterdam, where Gucci is listed. One current compromise floats the idea of 'joint jurisdiction', where a company is listed in one country, but registered in another (like Gucci).

In 2002, a new takeover code was agreed by EU lawmakers. It curbs companies' use of poison pill takeover defences (see Chapter 5) and requires bidders and targets to treat all shareholders equally. Also, predators will be required to make a formal bid once their stake reaches a certain threshold. EU member states should have implemented the rules by now, but, as usual, some have not. However, in early 2006, various countries, especially France, were finding loopholes in the code to allow them to permit poison pills to frustrate foreign takeover bids.

By July 2005, the European Commission was still investigating possible barriers to M&As in the financial sector – legal, tax, economic, attitudes and the need for a supervisor's approval. There was much anger at actions by the Bank of Italy to frustrate a takeover of Banca Nazionale del Lavoro by Spain's BBVA Bank and also a takeover of Banca Antonveneta by the Dutch ABN AMRO. Even the Italian authorities criticized Bank of Italy actions in the latter case, and the takeover went through.

EU competition law now covers 4 key areas: cartels (price and output fixing agreements by major banks), market dominance (major banks charging uncompetitive prices), mergers and state aid. There has been interest post crisis as to how bank bailout impacted competition in the banking sector. Some evidence suggests that concentration and market power aided stability – banks earn monopoly profits and so can retain more profits to boost capital and be safer – while others find that competition aids stability – prices are lower so less default on loans. It remains an empirical question. See Schaeck and Cihák (2013) for a good review of this literature.

CHALLENGES TO TRADITIONAL STOCK EXCHANGES

As we have mentioned, stock exchanges do not necessarily have a monopoly of trading. As noted above in the case of MiFID, rival order matching systems are common, and these have been assisted by the rapid growth of electronic networks. Traditional brokers face competition from brokers like Charles Schwab who offer cheaper Internet trading.

In the UK, Tradepoint opened up in 1995 in competition with the LSE. Initially, it was a failure and ran up losses of £30m. However, in a rescue package in May 1999, new partners took a 55% stake and revitalized it by putting their own trades through it. These new partners included Instinet, Morgan Stanley, Dean Witter, JP Morgan and Warburg Dillon Read. In addition, Tradepoint became the first foreign exchange to receive clearance to operate in the US from the SEC. In 2001, it was bought by the SWX Swiss Exchange (formerly the Zurich Stock Exchange) and renamed Virt-X as a cross-border trading system for blue chips. In 2008 it changed its name to SWX Europe, but closed in 2009 with all its business being transferred to Six Swiss Exchange (Switzerland's main exchange).

In the US, electronic communications networks (ECNs) act as mini-exchanges. They include Posit Match, INET, NYSE Arca, Turquoise and Chi-X to name just a few. Even worse for the traditional exchanges, the SEC and other regulators have been considering recognizing ECNs as official exchanges for some time, but this has not yet happened, and they are still regarded as alternative trading systems.

By March 2014, the LSE Group was the main trading venue in Europe, accounting for 23% of turnover. Alternative trading venues – BATS Chi-X and Turquoise – account for 25% of equity market turnover. Euronext and Deutsche Boerse account for 12.3% and 9.8% of turnover, respectively. Dark pool trading – large trades done through proprietary systems aimed at 'hiding' big trades – is also significant. These are estimated to account for about 10–15% of European equity market turnover.

One reaction of stock exchanges has been to offer more flexibility with evening sessions. After hours trading has taken place on the NASDAQ, NYSE and other major exchanges via brokers/ECNs for some time.

In order to have greater flexibility for raising capital many exchanges have demutualized, as illustrated in Box 8.5,

Other moves to cut costs include mergers with derivatives exchanges and mergers with other stock exchanges.

Key stock exchanges and derivatives exchanges have merged in the following markets: Germany, France, the Netherlands, Sweden, Austria, Switzerland and Hong Kong. In the US, NASDAQ merged with the AMEX and acquired the Instinet electronic exchange, and the NYSE merged with Archipelago in 2006 to offer both floor and electronic trading.

In Scandinavia, Sweden and Denmark announced a common system, Norex, and expect to include Norway and Finland. The new Stockholm system, SAX-2000, will be used, and trading, regulations, clearing and settlement will all be unified.

The big talking point in Europe, however, was a planned pan-European exchange spurred on by EMU. The first move was the announcement in mid-1998 that the London and Frankfurt exchanges planned to merge. Paris was understandably upset and began to talk of a rival merger with other European exchanges. Nevertheless, a meeting took place in December 1998, attended by the exchanges from London, Frankfurt, Paris, Brussels, Madrid, Milan, Zurich and Amsterdam. At a further meeting in May 1999, the six other exchanges signed a memorandum of understanding with London and Frankfurt.

BOX 8.5

Demutualization of Stock Exchanges

Stock exchanges originated as mutual organizations, owned by member brokers. There has been a trend for stock exchanges to demutualize, where the members sell their shares in IPOs. When this happens, the mutual becomes a company with shares listed on an exchange.

Proponents of demutualization argue that the main advantages are that it provides the business with more capital, greater accountability to its owners, improved governance and (overall) a better competitive position. It also, of course, makes it more vulnerable to takeover.

The LSE went public in June 2000, and NASDAQ did so in early 2003. The Chicago Mercantile Exchange was the first major US market to float when it went public in December 2002, with a market capitalization of about $1bn. Finally, the NYSE went public in 2006.

Examples of other demutualized stock exchanges include Australian Securities Exchange (1998), Euronext (merged with NYSE), Bursa Malaysia (2004), Bolsas y Mercados Españoles, São Paulo Stock Exchange (2007) and, most recently, the Nigerian and Pakistan Stock Exchanges in 2011 and 2012, respectively.

The long-term objectives included a single electronic trading platform, common trading regulations, and common access and trading hours. London and Frankfurt had already announced common trading hours and one or two minor trading details. All German company trades are now handled in Frankfurt, and UK company trades in London.

There were, however, severe problems to be overcome. Which trading system to use – London or Frankfurt? Which settlement system? (CREST, London's system, formed an alliance with the Deutsche Börse Clearing in May 1999.) Which indices will be used? How will ownership of the exchange be structured? Will the latter be based on turnover or capitalization? Germany's share based on capitalization, for example, would be about 15%, but 20% based on turnover. So severe are these problems that in September 1999, the partners announced an alliance rather than a new unified exchange, giving access to all exchanges on one screen, with anonymous trading and a central counterparty. In 2001, plans for a merger between Frankfurt and London were abandoned, and in 2002, the LSE announced that it was purchasing a 76% stake in OM, the Swedish exchange (previously an unsuccessful bidder for the LSE).

While they deliberated, the competition did not stand still. Euronext was created in September 2000 as an amalgamation of stock exchanges in Amsterdam, Brussels and Paris, with the goal of becoming a fully integrated, cross-border, European market for equities, bonds, derivatives and commodities. One major step towards this goal was the acquisition of LIFFE, London's derivatives exchange, in January 2002. Later Lisbon joined as well. Switzerland's SOFFEX and Germany's Deutsche Terminbörse formed Eurex to offer derivatives trading.

In 2005 and early 2006, the market was swept by offers or proposed offers for the LSE by Deutsche Börse, Euronext, the Australian Macquarie and NASDAQ. The UK competition authorities were worried about the threat to competition if an exchange also controlled settlement. What the EU (and many users) wants is pan-European clearing and settlements.

At the time, nothing came of any of these moves, but in May 2006, NASDAQ started to build up a holding in LSE shares, which eventually became 25%. However, after a hard-fought battle, on 20 August 2007, NASDAQ announced that it was abandoning its plans to take over the LSE and sold its stake to Borse Dubai. In October, the LSE announced that it was to acquire Borsa Italiana.

At much the same time, the NYSE offered a 'merger of equals' to Euronext (the union of the exchanges in Amsterdam, Brussels, Paris and Portugal as well as LIFFE). In early June 2006, Euronext announced that its board was recommending the offer to shareholders. The newly created exchange was called NYSE Euronext and brought together six cash equities exchanges in 7 countries and 8 derivatives exchanges. NYSE was acquired by Intercontinental Exchange (ICE) in November 2013, so now Euronext and NYSE operate as divisions of ICE.

SUMMARY

- Strictly speaking, *stocks* are fixed interest securities, and shares are equities.
- *Share indices* are usually based on market capitalization and calculated every minute.
- In most economies, the major shareholders are investment institutions (pension funds, insurance companies and mutual funds) rather than private shareholders. The world's ageing populations will lead to a growth in funded pensions.
- Mixed pools of shares are popular investments. They may be *closed-ended* (for example UK investment trusts) or *open-ended* (for example US mutual funds).
- *Order-driven dealing systems* are those where orders of buyers and sellers are matched. *Quote-driven systems* are those where market makers quote firm bid and offer prices. Hybrid systems, like New York, involve elements of both types.
- Dealers with *long* positions can lend stock to gain collateral to fund their position and those with *short* positions can borrow stock (offering collateral) to match their sales. This is *stock borrowing and lending*. Very large deals are *bought deals* or *block trades*.
- Sometimes firms buy their own shares back in order to cancel them and enhance dividends and earnings per share.
- Settlement systems are usually *rolling settlement*, although settlement of all deals in a given trading period still exists (for example France).
- With new issues, shares may be a *public offer for sale* (or *initial public offering*). The alternative is the *private placing*, although sometimes a mixture of both is used.
- An offer of more shares to existing shareholders is a *rights issue*.

- A *scrip issue* offers shareholders free shares, and a *split* divides the par value of the existing shares. The objective in both cases is to lower the price to improve liquidity. A *consolidation* replaces a number of existing shares by one new one to enhance the price. A *scrip dividend* is an offer of shares instead of cash dividends (optional).
- As well as the normal market for shares, there may be a secondary market for newer companies that do not meet the requirements for a full listing. There may also be dealing outside the exchange – *over the counter* (OTC).
- When a firm goes public, we look at the relationship between the price of similar shares and the profit per share to guide us as to the correct offer price of the new share. This is the *price/earnings ratio* (P/E). We also look at the likely dividend as a percentage of the share price to calculate the *gross dividend yield*.
- To check if the latter is achieved by giving away all the profit, we compare the profit per share to the net dividend to calculate the *cover ratio*. Finally, analysts look at the *earnings per share*.
- The Markets in Financial Instruments Directive (MiFID) came into effect on 1 November 2007, and replaced the existing Investment Services Directive (ISD), introducing new rules for a wider range of EU investments firms, covering transparency of trades and increasing reporting requirements. It is being updated by MiFID II, which should come into force by late 2016 or early 2017. Investment firms also have to adhere to the EU Capital Adequacy Directive.
- In the US, the NYSE acquired Archipelago, the electronic exchange, and then Euronext, creating *NYSE*

Euronext, which covered trading in New York and various European capital and derivatives markets. NYSE was acquired by Intercontinental Exchange (ICE) in November 2013, so now NYSE and Euronext operate as divisions of ICE. NASDAQ has merged with the AMEX and acquired Instinet, the electronic exchange.

- Over recent years, there has been rapid development of *dark pool* trading systems that allow the trading of large blocks of shares to be carried out away from the

public, or order book of an exchange or other type of publicly available share trading platform. In Europe, there are 45 dark pools operated by exchanges, smaller platforms such as Chi-X (commonly referred to as 'multilateral trading facilities') and independent operators such as US-based Liquidnet.

- In general, the future for traditional exchanges is under threat from Internet trading and the growth of *electronic communications networks* (ECNs).

REVISION QUESTIONS/ASSIGNMENTS

1. Outline the major market indices, and briefly explain how they are constructed. Discuss the reasons why their coverage and construction vary.
2. What is the difference between exchange-traded and OTC transactions? If the latter are cheaper, why don't small investors trade OTC?

3. Why does stock borrowing and lending occur? In your answer, provide a general explanation of short selling.
4. Analyse the main features of an order-driven system.

REFERENCES

Schaeck, K., and Cihák, M. (2013) Competition, efficiency and stability in banking, *Financial Management*, 43, 215–241.

Taverne, D. (1995) *The Pensions Time Bomb in Europe*, Federal Trust for Education and Research, London. Looks at issues surrounding the liberalization of pensions provision in Europe.

FURTHER READING

Burrough, B., and Helyar, J. (1990) *Barbarians at the Gate: The Fall of RJR Nabisco*, Harper & Row, New York. Racy, bestselling tale about greed and glory in the leveraged buyout of one of the world's biggest companies.

Cuthbertson, K., and Nitzshe, D. (2008) *Investments*, John Wiley & Sons, Chichester. Intermediate text covering a spectrum of investment areas.

Elton, E., Gruber, M., Brown, S., and Goetzmann, W. (2010) *Modern Portfolio Theory and Investment Analysis* (8th edn), Wiley, New York. Advanced text on portfolio theory and investment analysis written by leading researchers in the field.

Lewis, M. (2014) *Flash Boys: Cracking the Money Code*, Allen Lane, London. How computerised trading may

be used to rig the markets and how one group set out to expose it.

Malkiel, B.G. (2003) *A Random Walk Down Wall Street: The Time-tested Strategy for Successful Investing*, WW Norton, New York. Bestselling book offering practical investment advice.

Mobius, M. (2007) *Equities: An Introduction to the Core Concepts*, John Wiley & Sons, New York. Detailed introduction to equity markets and analysis.

Parameswaran, S. (2011) *Fundamentals of Financial Instruments: An Introduction to Stocks, Bonds, Foreign Exchange, and Derivatives*, Wiley Finance, New York. Student-friendly guide to financial instruments and investment.

Hedge Funds and Private Equity

INTRODUCTION

The hedge fund industry has come a long way since the dramatic collapse of Long-Term Capital Management (LTCM) in August 1998 (discussed later in the chapter). Private equity only came into the picture with specific deals, like the takeover of RJR Nabisco by Kohlberg Kravis Roberts (KKR) in the late 1980s for $25bn, a story captured by Burrough and Helyar (1990) in their book *Barbarians at the Gate: The Fall of RJR Nabisco*. Nowadays, we can't open the financial press without seeing reference to both hedge funds and private equity companies and their large-scale activities, often apportioning blame to these firms for helping to fuel the excesses that led to the credit crunch and now profiting from 'bottom feeding' off wrecked banks and other companies.

Because hedge funds are largely unregulated and private equity companies are somewhat secretive about their activities, the size of their interventions in the market depends on estimates. According to TheCityUK (2013), a non-profit organization promoting the UK financial services sector, the number of hedge funds increased from 4,000 with $324bn of assets in 1999 to a peak of 10,700 with $2,150bn in 2007 and then declined to 10,100 hedge funds and $2.054bn by the start of 2013, after the Madoff scandal (discussed later in the chapter) and the credit crisis. There are also funds of (hedge) funds, and these experienced a similar collapse. Another excellent source of hedge fund market news is Hedge Fund Intelligence, publishers of *Eurohedge*, which came up with similar figures. Note that the fall in fund assets size since the crisis is partly due to trading losses and partly due to investors pulling out money from these funds.

The private equity market has followed a slightly different trend to the hedge fund sector. The latter was boosted in the early 2000s, despite the fall in markets after the dot-com bubble burst, as many funds managed to generate positive returns in 2001–2 when equity markets slumped. This encouraged investors to the hedge fund sector even in the declining markets of the early 2000s. In contrast, the private equity business pretty much follows stock market trends. A report from TheCityUK (2012) shows that global private equity investment amounted to $176.6bn in 2000, and this fell to $82.2bn by 2002 and then rocketed on the back of rising markets to $317.6bn by 2007. The size of the market was then hit by the credit crisis, and investments fell to $246bn. The largest markets are in the US, the UK, France, China, India and Japan. Table 9.1 provides a regional breakdown of the percentage share of private equity activity.

▼ **Table 9.1** *Regional breakdown of private equity activity, 2001 and 2011, % share*

Regional breakdown of private equity activity

% share	North America	Europe	Rest of world
INVESTMENTS			
2001	54	30	16
2011	50	33	17
NEW FUNDS RAISED			
2001	70	23	7
2011	57	23	20

Source: TheCityUK (2012).

The growth in the hedge fund and private equity sectors led the major consulting firm McKinsey to refer to them as the new financial power brokers in global markets – along with oil-rich countries and Asian central banks.

Given the importance of these activities, it is time for an initial look at what these organizations do. A more detailed look will come later.

Hedge Funds

A hedge fund is an actively managed investment fund that seeks an attractive absolute return, that is, a return whether markets go up or down. This contrasts with investors in an index tracker, for example, who will only gain if the index goes up. To achieve this absolute return, hedge funds use a wide variety of investment strategies, many of them quite complicated. They are not designed for the retail investor, but either high-net-worth individuals or investment institutions. Unlike mutual funds, they are typically limited partnerships. The funds themselves may be small, $100m to $1bn, but a hedge fund company may run many funds, each differentiated by its particular strategy. These companies think of themselves as small and nimble. Because their interest is an absolute return, they are not interested in relative returns, unlike conventional fund managers. The latter will claim victory if a given index grows by 7%, but they have achieved 9% – this is definitely not the world of hedge funds. Although we shall discuss detailed strategies later, one common way of achieving this is short selling, that is, selling securities the fund does not own. This is achieved by borrowing the securities. Hedge funds will also borrow a lot of the capital, hence frequent references to a word we met earlier – 'leverage'. If the security falls in price, the hedge fund can now buy it and close the deal at a profit. Although this is a common hedge fund technique, it is not unique to hedge funds – the proprietary trading desks of investment banks have done this for years. A list of the largest funds appears in Table 9.2, and the returns generated by global hedge funds are shown in Table 9.3.

What are the origins of hedge funds? Generally, one refers here to Alfred Winslow Jones in the US, who formed a partnership, AW Jones & Co., in 1949. The company took both long and short positions in the shares of similar companies in the same sector, thus hedging the portfolio. If its preferred firm did well, it made money. If its shares fell due to a fall in the sector, the shares sold short made money. This is the origin of the word 'hedge' in hedge funds, which puzzles people because they are well aware that hedge funds take speculative positions. Jones raised $100,000 from friends and borrowed more money to leverage the position, producing extra profit. His aim was to charge a management fee of 2% and offer a 20% share of profits. However, as the years went by, he would not be the only one doing this. *Fortune* magazine stumbled on this in 1966, and a score of imitations started up. Even the prudent Warren Buffett started a hedge fund in the 1950s and produced a 24% annualized return. He used the profits to buy Berkshire Hathaway in 1966 and dissolved the hedge fund in 1969. George Soros

▼ **Table 9.2** *World's largest hedge funds, 2012*

Largest hedge funds, 2012, assets under management	Location	$bn
Bridgewater Associates	Westport CT, US	76.1
JP Morgan Asset Man.	New York NY, US	53.6
Man Group	London, UK	36.5
Brevan Howard Asset Man.	London, UK	34.2
Och-Ziff Capital Man. Group	London, UK	30
BlackRock Advisors	New York NY, US	28.8
BlueCrest Capital Management	New York NY, US	28.8
Baupost Group	London, UK	28.6
AQR Capital Management	Boston MA, US	25.2
Paulson & Co	Greenwich CT, US	23.2
Angelo, Gordon & Co.	New York NY, US	22.6
Renaissance Technologies Corp.	New York NY, US	22.1
DE Shaw & Co.	East Setauket NY, US	20
Ellion Management Corp.	New York NY, US	19.5

Source: TheCityUK (2013).

▼ **Table 9.3** *Global hedge fund returns 2002–12*

%, Return	
2002	−2.8
2003	23.5
2004	10
2005	6.7
2006	13.5
2007	9.3
2008	−21.3
2009	18.2
2010	9.7
2011	−4.6
2012	6.1

Source: TheCityUK (2013).

is another well-known name. He left a Wall Street brokerage in 1974 to go independent and form his Quantum fund.

Box 9.1 illustrates the trends in the size of the hedge fund industry and highlights the role of prime brokers.

Private Equity

Private equity is a mixture of venture capital for early stage companies and management buyouts – a public company is taken private for a few years and then either sold to a private buyer or floated on the stock exchange again. The European Private Equity and Venture Capital Association estimated that in 2004, venture capital (early stage financing) accounted for 28% of the investments; and buyouts, 72%; since then, the focus on buyouts increased up until 2007, when, according to TheCityUK, they amounted to 89% of total global private equity investments. Therefore, buyout deals, usually heavily leveraged, were the mainstay of the industry. However, buyouts' share of the value of private equity investments fell dramatically in 2008, to 41% of total investments, as liquidity in the markets disappeared and it became more difficult for private equity firms to obtain bank loans to finance deals. Figures for 2011 suggested that buyouts accounted for 97% of total private equity investments in the UK and 78% globally. Table 9.4 illustrates the top firms ranked by amount of capital raised between 2006 and 2011.

BOX 9.1

Hedge Funds and Prime Brokers

The hedge fund industry has experienced its ups and downs over the last decade or so. The numbers increased from 6,420 in 2002 up to 10,070 in 2007 and then fell back after the crisis to re-emerge with 10,100 by the end of 2012. Assets under management now amount to just over $2 trillion.

To undertake their sophisticated and sometimes complex investment activities, the hedge funds need access to major banks that can provide finance as well as undertake transactions on their behalf. These are known as 'prime brokers' – and as you can see below – they are among the world's largest banks.

Prime brokers offer brokerage and other professional services, including financing, clearing and settlement of trades, custodial services, risk management and even operational support facilities, to hedge funds and other large institutional customers. The bulk of prime brokers' income derives from cash lending to support leverage and stock lending to enable short selling.

	Number of hedge funds	$bn assets
2002	6,420	600
2003	6,800	850
2004	8,100	1,050
2005	8,800	1,350
2006	9,500	1,750
2007	10,070	2,150
2008	9,600	1,500
2009	9,400	1,700
2010	9,550	1,955
2011	9,860	1,936
2012	10,100	2,054

Top prime brokers servicing hedge funds, 2012	% of hedge funds serviced	
Goldman Sachs	US	19
JP Morgan	US	13

Morgan Stanley Prime Brokerage	US	13
Credit Suisse Prime Fund Services	Switz.	9
UBS Prime Services	Switz.	8
Deutsche Bank Global Prime Finance	Germ.	7
Citi Prime Finance	US	5
Bank of America Merrill Lynch	US	4
Barclays	US	4
Newedge Prime Brokerage Group	France	3

Top prime brokers by proportion of hedge fund launches in 2012 serviced		
Goldman Sachs	US	17
Credit Suisse Prime Fund Services	US	15
JP Morgan	Switz.	13
Morgan Stanley Prime Brokerage	US	12
Deutsche Bank Global Prime Finance	US/Germ.	5

Source: TheCityUK (2013).

Buyouts occur for many reasons. Perhaps a company is in difficulties and wishes to sell a subsidiary. Alternatively, it may have made a major acquisition but does not want to hold on to some of the non-core assets. Sometimes, the original owners of the business may want to retire or sell their stake. Private equity firms like to have the existing management team on board, as they know the business well, and may offer them a 20% stake to keep them committed and give them an incentive to improve the business. The nature of the private equity is such that the timescale is much longer than the normal hedge fund deal – probably a return is sought in 3 to 5 years. This affects the investors in private equity firms, as liquidity is thus constrained. Although we normally talk of a 'management buyout', there is sometimes a management *buy in*. For example, when Legal & General Ventures bought nine hospitals from BUPA, a UK private health care provider, they brought in new managers to run them. Usually, private equity deals involve large sums of money, and it is rare to see deals of less than $100m, but common to see deals in excess of $1bn. To summarize, private equity firms seek to make good returns by buying public companies or neglected subsidiaries at good prices and turning them into more attractive businesses.

▼ Table 9.4 *Largest private equity firms total funds raised, 2006–11*

Largest private equity firms

Funds raised in 5 years between 2006 and 2011	Location	$bn
TPG Capital	Fort Worth, Texas	50.6
Goldman Sachs Principal Investment Area	New York	47.2
The Carlyle Group	Washington, DC	40.5
Kohlberg Kravis Roberts	New York	40.2
The Blackstone Group	New York	36.4
Apollo Global Management	New York	33.8
Bain Capital	Boston	29.4
First Reserve Corporation	London	25.1
Hellman & Friedman	Greenwich, Connecticut	19.1
Apax Partners	San Francisco	17.2

Source: TheCityUK (2012).

Usually, debt forms a large part of the purchase price, at least twice the capital put in by the private equity firm.

Like hedge funds, private equity activity is not particularly new. We saw this in the UK from Slater Walker in the 1970s and Hanson in the 1980s. As we noted above, in both cases a downturn in the markets brought this to an abrupt halt. As markets began to recover from the recession of 2000–2, we began to see a strong resurgence of both hedge fund and private equity activity that surged up until 2007 and then collapsed, but began picking up as we moved into 2012–13. We will talk more about recent trends in the private equity sector later in this chapter.

HEDGE FUNDS

Hedge funds must not be confused with ordinary fund managers. Apart from the objective of absolute, not relative, return, they have a freedom most funds don't enjoy. Mutual funds (unit trusts) have limitations on borrowing, short selling and the use of derivatives. Investment trusts may borrow but have the other two limitations. Pension funds, too, usually have limits, although, curiously, they are now making investments in hedge funds, as we shall see later. Another problem for mutual funds and investment trusts is that they must provide daily liquidity for their investors – this would be a big handicap for hedge funds that operate on a monthly or quarterly cycle and sometimes less often. Finally, hedge fund managers have a major personal investment in the firm that the ordinary fund manager does not. Hedge funds have a small base of much more sophisticated investors.

We cannot understand hedge funds without looking at their strategies. As a simplification, we can say that they carry out the typical operations of the proprietary trading of an investment bank but often use a much greater range and with less restraint on volatility of earnings. So far, hedge funds have been free of the regulation and control under which investment banks operate, although there have been calls to toughen up regulations. For instance, Silvio Berlusconi, then Italian prime minister, told a news conference at the conclusion of a G8 meeting in 2008 that fighting hedge fund speculation in commodities (particularly oil) markets should be a priority. In mid-2009, the International Organization of Securities Commissions (IOSCO) called for funds to register and accept scrutiny of their positions and working practices. Regulators, it argued, should also share more information to help monitor funds' cross-border activities. The EU has also made recommendations that hedge funds should hold minimum capital requirements like banks – a proposal that has not gone down well with the industry. In April 2009, the European Commission published its proposal for an Alternative Investment Fund Managers Directive (AIFMD) to establish EU-level regulation. This was altered in October 2010 to include a European passport scheme to make it easier for hedge fund firms, once registered to do business in one EU country, to move to other countries. The AIFMD entered into force in July 2013.

There has also been debate in the US as to whether the sector should be more heavily regulated. A June 2009 announcement by Tim Geithner, the US Treasury secretary, that hedge funds would not be overseen by the Federal Reserve (which regulates major US and foreign banks) also came in for serious public criticism. The Dodd-Frank Act introduced various registration requirements for hedge fund advisers, but this will have little impact on the industry. In the UK, hedge fund managers need to register at the Financial Services Authority (FSA). Despite all these moves, the industry is still almost immune from bank-like regulation.

Leverage and Short Selling

Before looking at the strategies in detail, we shall remind ourselves of two tools that are important here.

We will meet leverage in Chapter 13 – the ability to carry out a deal with only a small amount of the investor's capital. One way is to put forward a premium or margin. Another is to borrow all or most of the money. The effect in both cases is the same – a given percentage change in the price of the security produces a bigger percentage profit or loss for the investor. This is known as 'leverage' and explained in Box 9.2.

BOX 9.2

Attractions and Risks Associated with Leverage

Suppose an investor buys $100,000 shares in IBM, using $20,000 of her own capital and borrowing $80,000. After 3 months, the IBM share price goes up 20%, and the shares are now worth $120,000. The investor sells the shares and pays back to the lender the original $80,000 plus, let's say, $2,000 interest. Deducting this from $120,000, we have a profit of $38,000, a 90% profit on the original $20,000.

Note that the share price only went up 20% but has given the investor 90% – this is the essential attraction of leverage.

Attractions and Risks Associated with Leverage (*continued*)

The problem is risk. Suppose the IBM price falls 20%, and the shares are only worth $80,000. If the shares are sold now and the lender paid back $82,000, the investor has lost all the capital of $20,000 and an extra $2,000. This is a loss of 110%, although the share price only fell 20%.

Leverage may bring huge percentage profits but risks high percentage losses and even the whole of the original capital. Nevertheless, in view of its attraction, leverage is used frequently in hedge fund transactions and also private equity, hence the term 'leveraged buyout'. (In the above examples, dealing costs have been ignored in the interest of simplicity.)

Short selling is a way of making money out of a price fall. The first step is to sell a security we don't own, let's say the $100,000 of IBM shares. Because we will be expected to deliver them in the required timescale, the next step is to borrow the stock from one of the many lenders and use this borrowing to deliver the shares (sometimes the stock is not even borrowed – this is known as 'naked short selling'). The lender requires collateral to the value of the shares and a little more (see repos and stock borrowing and lending in Chapters 7 and 8). This could be cash or securities. The cash could be borrowed if necessary, but this will only be for a short period as we will receive the payment for the shares of $100,000. If we have left securities as collateral, the money can now earn interest. Let us say that later the shares fall 20%, to $80,000. We can now buy the shares with the money received from the sale and repay the stock to the lender, who will return the collateral. Forgetting the interest and dealers' costs, we bought shares for $80,000 we had sold for $100,000 – a gross profit of $20,000. It will be evident that if the price of the shares goes up, the short seller faces a losing position. For hedge funds that are seeking absolute returns, short selling is an essential weapon and often used to provide the 'hedge' part of the transaction. Short selling may have to follow rules of the exchanges that limit it, for example the NYSE, or it may be banned – as it was at the height of market turmoil in September 2008, when various banks failed. During this month, the US, the UK, France, Germany and Australia banned the short selling of bank and other financial firms' shares (for around 3 months or so), as there was concern that hedge fund shorting could drive down bank share prices and lead to further bank failure. *The Telegraph* reported that the FSA had banned short selling due to fears in the City that the battering of shares in HBOS – which agreed a quick takeover by Lloyds TSB – would spread to other large banks. On 23 September 2008, the FSA banned new short positions in 32 companies with either banking or insurance operations, and forced investors to disclose existing short holdings worth more than 0.25% in a company by 3.30 p.m. on 22 September. The positions revealed are shown in Table 9.5.

▼ **Table 9.5** *Most shorted banks on 22 September 2008*

Bank	Shorter	Amount %
Anglo Irish Bank	Lansdowne Partners	1.63
	Calypso Capital Management	0.4877
Lloyds TSB	Paulson & Co	1.76
Barclays	Lansdowne Partners	0.51
	Paulson & Co	1.18
Bradford & Bingley	Steadfast	0.9047
	Samlyn Capital	0.41
Alliance & Leicester	Blue Ridge Capital	0.95
HBOS	Paulson & Co	0.95
Royal Bank of Scotland	Paulson & Co	0.87

Source: Telegraph (23 September 2008).

John Paulson, the New York-based hedge fund manager that made an estimated £1.9bn from the global credit crisis by shorting companies involved in US sub-prime mortgages, announced to the London Stock Exchange that it had short positions equivalent to 1.76% of Lloyds TSB and 0.87% of RBS. In HBOS, Paulson was short 0.95% and in Barclays, 1.18%. *The Telegraph* (23 September 2008) reported that in defending its position, the firm said:

> Paulson & Co empathises with financial firms as to the difficult positions in which many find themselves ... Our primary objective is to preserve capital for our investors and to show positive returns in all market environments. We do this by going long stocks we think will rise in value and going short stocks we think will fall in value – in each case based on extensive research on the company and its fundamentals, rather than short-term market movements.

Strategies

There are many hedge fund strategies, and Hedge Fund Research, a research organization, tracks the results of 39 strategies. We will concentrate on five main headings, within which there may be subheadings for more specific strategies:

- Equity hedge funds
- Global asset managers
- Relative value arbitrage
- Event-driven investing
- Short sellers

Equity hedge funds

Equity hedge funds are equity managers that will sell short and use leverage. They will analyse individual companies and individual shares. Some may specialize in geographic sectors, others in either large or small capitalized companies. We may find that some managers are 'long' biased, with perhaps 50% of long positions, whereas others are 'short' biased with the opposite. Some will be looking for good long-term growth, others at shares that look cheap in view of their potential. A manager may take the view that a sector is now overvalued, for example technology stocks prior to the bursting of the dot-com bubble. Timing is, however, crucial, and many hedge funds got out too early – the sector kept rising. Some managers will take a shareholding in a company whose shares have underperformed with a view to taking aggressive action, ousting managers or forcing other changes. This happened to Time Warner late in 2005 as three hedge funds led by Carl Icahn started to 'rock the boat'. More recently, during 2009, Harbinger Capital Partners and Firebrand Partners amassed a combined 5% stake in the *New York Times* in order to shake up its board and try go redirect the performance of the company.

Equity long/short strategies typically account for the leading share of strategies. According to Eurekahedge, data provider and research house, the figure was about 30% in 2012, significantly down from their 41% share in 2007.

Global asset managers

Although equity hedge managers focus on specific stocks, global asset managers take a broader view. They look at stocks, bonds, currencies and physical commodities from a global point of view. If they believe that the UK is a better prospect than, say, Italy, they will be long of UK and short of Italy – probably using stock indices and not individual stocks. They may be referred to as 'macro-investors' because they look at broad themes, as opposed to 'micro-investors', who look at individual stocks. As with conventional managers and analysts, there are those who use technical analysis. The technical analysts or *systemic* managers identify trends using basic techniques or complex algorithms and primarily focus on past price trends to identify future price movements. Others use what is known as 'fundamental analysis', which includes macroeconomic, industry and company analysis to determine future security price movements and related investment strategies.

Relative value arbitrage

Relative value arbitrage concentrates on the relative value of individual shares, bonds, currencies and so on. Managers will put in place extensive hedges. They concentrate on the difference in performance of two given securities in a homogeneous universe. For example, if they believe that, say, BP will do better than another firm in the oil sector, the manager goes long on BP and short on the other firm. So long as the relative gain of BP over the other firm gets bigger, it will gain whatever happens to the price. This also applies to bonds in the same way. For example, many investment funds are not allowed to hold non-investment-grade bonds. When a bond falls below investment grade, this forced selling may cause an exaggerated fall in price. Hedge funds buy the bonds cheaply but go short on bonds of similar issuers in case the whole market falls – another example of the 'hedge' in hedge funds.

A common strategy within the relative value arbitrage is to take positions with convertibles. As we saw in Chapter 7, a convertible bond gives the holder the right, but not the obligation, to convert into the underlying equity. It is, therefore, a special form of options, which we meet in Chapter 13. In view of the attraction of a possible conversion later, the interest paid is less than the normal rate for that organization. Suppose the right to convert is at a price of $9 per share, and the market price is $7. If the share price goes up to $8, the convertible has a better chance of future profit, and the price will go up. On the other hand, if the share price goes down to $6, the possible conversion looks less likely, and the price of the convertible will go down. The hedge fund manager will buy the convertibles if there is a belief that in the end a profitable conversion is possible. However, as a hedge against the share price falling (and the convertible falling), the manager will short the shares. If the share price keeps changing, as is likely, the amount of hedge needs to be changed. The relationship is complex. To try and keep this simple, suppose the conversion price is $9, and the share price is $2. The share price changes to $2.30. The likelihood of profitable conversion has hardly altered; it is still remote and therefore the convertible price will not change. The amount of shares shorted to form a hedge need not be altered. Suppose, however, the share price is $11 and changes to $11.30; the profit has increased by 30¢, and other things being equal, the convertible will increase by 30¢, and so the amount of the hedge needs to increase. Thus, the amount of shares shorted to provide a hedge needs continually to be altered as the share price changes – technically known as 'dynamic delta hedging'.

Other factors to be taken into account are the interest earned on the convertible and interest on money received from the short sale. There are, of course, risks other than that of the share price falling. If market interest rates rise, the convertible will fall in price. If the credit status of the company itself falls, so will the convertible price, in view of the greater risk of default.

Nevertheless, hedge funds have become huge buyers of convertibles on first issue – good news for the company. They also then short the shares, which is bad news for the company.

Event-driven investing

Event-driven investing looks at special situations and seeks to exploit them. One strategy relates to takeover bids. The victim's price usually does not rise to the offer price due to uncertainties: Will the offer be withdrawn? Will there be a referral to the competition authorities? Often, in an all-share offer, the bidder's price goes down due to the costs of takeover and delay in producing profits. The hedge fund will buy the victim's shares and short the bidder. The worst-case scenario is if the deal is referred or does indeed collapse. In the UK, in the autumn of 2005, HMV (owning one bookshop chain) made a bid for Ottakar's, another one. Everyone expected the deal to go through, but to general surprise, due to fierce lobbying by authors, the deal was referred to the competition authorities. A more spectacular case occurred in the US in October 2000 when General Electric bid for Honeywell. Honeywell's share price moved up from $35 to $52 – the US authorities approved the deal. Then came the bombshell – European regulators blocked the deal (to the fury of the Americans), and the Honeywell price fell back again.

Periodically, there are changes in indices like the FTSE 100, which are based on capitalization, as the capitalization of underlying shares changes. Index trackers must sell the shares of any firms that fall out of the index and buy those of new entrants, but they cannot do this until the news is confirmed. Hedge funds will move in earlier and go long on the shares expected to join and short those expected to leave. Of course, once again, there is risk, as a late share price may mean that a 'leaver' stays or a 'joiner' fails to join. Another point that applies to many of these strategies is that once all the hedge funds start to do it, there is very little profit left.

A major activity under event-driven investing is 'distressed debt'. This relates to shares and bonds in companies that go into bankruptcy. An analysis of the real value may lead to profit in buying these shares/bonds, especially if there is a capital reorganization. For example, when Delphi, the US spare parts supplier, filed for bankruptcy, Appaloosa Management, a hedge fund, bought a 9.3% stake. A capital reorganization may take a long time. Rather than wait for the outcome, trade and bank creditors may sell their debt to a hedge fund. Hedge funds may buy the high-yield bonds, which, in the end, may be exchanged for a combination of debt and equity in the reorganized company. Mutual funds and pension funds may need the money and will be prepared to sell defaulted bonds. Again, there is risk – interest rates generally may go up, or a change in the economy may worsen the defaulter's position.

Short sellers

Short sellers are specialist funds that are looking exclusively for overvalued assets – whether bonds, shares, currencies or commodities. As illustrated in Table 8.3, hedge funds have been major short sellers of banks over the 2008 crisis period, but even if the main focus of the hedge fund is shorting (like Paulson), they may still engage in long strategies – Paulson acquired major stakes in Bank of America (becoming its fourth largest shareholder), Goldman Sachs and Gold Fields (South Africa) in the summer of 2009. It appears that Paulson went long on these banks and gold. In practice, few hedge funds focus solely on short selling.

In all the above strategies, extensive use will be made of derivatives (covered in Chapters 13, 14 and 15). Some funds will even concentrate on this exclusively. Among other things, they offer a form of leverage in that positions can be taken on premiums and margins without having to invest the full capital. As credit risk is one of the hedge fund's problems: they are frequent users of credit derivatives, described in Chapter 15. Indeed, Fitch, the ratings organization, estimates that hedge funds account for 35% of the trading volumes in credit derivatives.

Range and Activities of Hedge Funds

The range of hedge funds is considerable – from large organizations like the Man Group, which operates a large range of funds, to small niche operators that concentrate on one strategy. For example, Clarksons, one of the world's biggest ship brokers, has launched a hedge fund investing solely in shipping securities and derivatives, especially freight derivatives. The Man Group, on the other hand, lists over 100 funds in the appropriate page in the *Financial Times*.

Here are some examples of hedge fund activity:

- In May 2005, DaimlerChrysler said that 15% of its shares were owned by hedge funds.
- Two UK-based hedge funds, Toscafund and Lansdowne Partners, bought aggressively into Commerzbank, about whose future there were endless rumours.
- In August 2005, Saint-Gobain, the French group, first bid for British Plaster Board at £7.32 a share – hedge funds bought 15% of the shares, sensing a later much higher bid, and they were right.
- In the autumn of 2005, Dubai-based DP World made a bid for P&O, the UK's port and ferry operator, at £4.43 a share. Although there were murmurs of interest from Singapore's state-owned PSA, the market was a little surprised to see it launch a firm bid on 10 January 2006 at £4.70 a share. Among the buyers of P&O was the hedge fund DE Shaw, which bought 450,000 shares at £4.59, anticipating a bid battle from two state-owned institutions with plenty of cash. At close of business on 11 January, the price was already over £4.90.

Research by Goldman Sachs at the end of 2005 suggested that as much as 20% of the huge oil price increase that year was as a result of hedge fund buying, which continued up until early 2008. In fact, the boom in commodities prices from 2005 through to 2008 is partly explained by hedge fund investment. The record spike in sugar prices in August 2009 has not only been attributed to poor harvests in the main producer countries – Brazil and India (India is also the largest consumer of sugar) – but also to hedge fund speculation. Of course, when the expectation is of security or commodity values spiralling upwards, then hedge funds go long, and when they expect a tumble, they go short. Where there is more uncertainty, that is, greater volatility in prices, they will mix long and short strategies.

All the hedges we have discussed depend on one thing – liquidity, that is, they can get out when they want to. If they want to sell, there will be buyers. If they want to buy, there will be sellers. The classic case of LTCM illustrates the pitfalls. In 1998, LTCM was long on Russian government bonds, denominated in dollars. If dollar interest rates went up, the chance of default would be greater, but other dollar bonds would fall in value. Thus, shorting US Treasury bonds seemed a logical hedge. Unfortunately for LTCM, in August 1998, the Russian government defaulted. There began a panic-stricken rush to buy Treasury bonds. As LTCM had gone short on the bonds, to unwind was to buy them – but everyone else was buying too. No one wanted to sell, and LTCM was caught in a vice. In addition to the losses on the Russian bonds came the losses on the Treasury bonds. To make matters worse, LTCM was leveraged to a huge degree; it had borrowed $125bn on a capital of $2.3bn, wildly excessive by any standards. The Federal Reserve board saw a threat to market stability and persuaded the major Wall Street firms that were involved to act together. The creditors seized the whole LTCM portfolio and organized a gradual unwinding of positions. Those who were not involved may have derived some pleasure from the irony that on the LTCM board were two academics who had been awarded Nobel Prizes for their contribution to risk theory.

When General Motors was dramatically downgraded to non-investment status in the spring of 2005, many hedge funds bought the bonds and sold the stock in a classic move. However, the stock suddenly rose as Kirk Kerkorian, an existing shareholder, moved to buy more – sending the share price up and spoiling the hedge.

The Deutsche Börse made a bid for the London Stock Exchange (LSE) in early 2005. Many shareholders thought that this was a bad move, and one of them, the London-based Children's Investment Fund (a hedge fund), was active in forcing the resignation of both the chairman and chief executive of Deutsche Börse. This caused great disgust in Germany, which announced, in January 2006, a proposed change in the law to tighten the disclosure level for holdings in shares, down from the current level of 5% to 3%.

Energis was the UK's third biggest fixed line telecoms operator. It was taken over by a consortium of banks in 2002 after it became insolvent following heavy losses. In August 2005, a bid came from Cable & Wireless. A group of hedge funds controlling a large part of Energis's junior debt tried to block the deal, holding out for a higher price. The group of nine hedge funds claiming to control 25% of junior debt was coordinated by Close Brothers. For the deal to go through, 75% acceptance was needed. In the end, the group was unable to block the deal, and in due course Cable & Wireless took over Energis.

In another case, hedge funds achieved success and unexpected praise. US hedge funds, holders of shares in Medidep, a French retirement home operator, arranged a takeover by a similar operator, Suren, at a price 15% higher than that obtaining over the previous 6 months. Colette Neuville of Adam, the country's leading small shareholders' group, said that, for once, the hedge funds should be praised.

Some market watchers say that hedge funds probably account for one-third of the turnover of the NYSE and the LSE and perhaps 30–40% of all foreign exchange trading. As a result, they provide huge business for the brokerage sections of investment banks, known as 'prime brokers', as noted in Box 9.1. According to Eurekahedge, the largest prime brokers in 2012 were Goldman Sachs (19% market share), JP Morgan (13%), Morgan Stanley (13%), Credit Suisse (9%) and UBS (8%).

There are, of course, more commissions to be earned than from a conventional fund manager due to hedge funds going long and short and using derivatives. The leverage also means that their lending will create further fees from the bank. In an article in the *Sunday Telegraph* on 4 December 2005, the head of one of Europe's largest conventional fund management operations said that he had become a second-class citizen in the City. He instanced two funds, each starting with $1bn invested. One is a conventional fund, the other a hedge fund. He showed that the hedge fund will create 16 commission opportunities compared with 2 from the conventional fund. In addition, there will be fees and interest on the loan. He estimated that 30–40% of large investment banks' income comes from hedge funds, compared with almost nothing 10 years before. Although the latter may be somewhat of an overestimate, there is no doubt that fee structures at hedge funds are typically much higher than those for conventional fund managers. A hedge fund manager typically receives both a management fee and a performance fee (also known as an 'incentive fee') from the fund. The management fee is usually around 2% of the fund's net asset value but can vary between 1% and 5%, and performance fees, though usually around 20% of profits, can go as high as 40–50%. In the booming days of hedge fund growth before 2008, some star performers were charging what the *Wall Street Journal* referred to as 'outrageous fees', given the high demand from investors. For instance, SAC Capital Partners has charged a 35–50% performance fee in the past, and the Medallion Fund has charged up to 50%. A fund that charges a 2% management fee and a 50% performance fee is known as a '2 and 50'. Also, the performance fee may have a hurdle rate that has to be achieved before this is paid. Some charge redemption fees – a charge for withdrawing funds, although funds can be locked in for a set period, making it almost impossible for investor withdrawals. Although fees can be onerous, they have fallen after 2008 and 2009 in an attempt to stem investment withdrawals from the industry – especially in the light of credibility concerns since the collapse of the fraudulent Madoff fund in the latter part of 2008.

Investors

Who are the investors in hedge funds? Originally, they were confined to high-net-worth individuals, but today the various institutions are big investors – insurance companies, pension funds, banks, endowments and foundations.

In an attempt to reduce the entry price, Rydex Investments, a US mutual fund, launched a fund in September 2005 to give investors access to hedge fund–like strategies for a minimum investment of $2,500. The problem is that fees are higher than for mutual funds, and hedge funds cannot offer the liquidity that private investors expect. More realistically, individuals need assets of $1–5m to consider investing directly in hedge funds. However, there is one possible exit for retail investors who do not have the liquidity they would like – a forum for secondary trading has started on the Internet. Hedgebay is the largest secondary market trading firm.

Another way for small investors to spread risk is to buy into a 'fund of funds'. As the name implies, this is a hedge fund that invests in a wide variety of funds to spread the risk. Unfortunately, there are now two lots of fees to be paid.

Regarding the prominence of institutional investors, there are various estimates. Tremont Capital, a US research firm, estimates that institutions account for well over 50% of new inflows into hedge funds. Greenwich Associates, another research organization, found that 32% of all European institutions invested in these funds in 2004, and a later study indicated that this had increased to over 45% by 2007. Kinetic, an investment management consultancy, surveyed 70 hedge funds that confirmed that the profile of investors is moving heavily towards institutional investors. David Butler, founding member of Kinetic, commented, 'The era of high net worth investors is fading as institutions become the main investors.' In fact by 2012, TheCityUK estimates that individuals only provided 20% of capital to hedge funds; 25% each was from companies and fund of hedge funds, with 23% from pension funds and the remainder from endowments and foundations.

A slightly curious development in 2006 was the decision by some hedge funds to list themselves on the stock market. One of their characteristics had been the ability to operate with as little scrutiny as possible. Nevertheless, Close Brothers raised £145m ($240m) through an alternative investment market flotation of Close AllBlue in May 2006. Goldman Sachs Dynamic Opportunities Limited is a Guernsey-registered closed-ended fund of hedge funds, which is listed and traded on the main market of the LSE, and there are various others.

One big attraction for investors is liquidity. We mentioned above that hedge funds cannot offer the liquidity that private investors expect. For shares, however, there is always a quoted price, and investors can get in or out easily.

Returns

How profitable are hedge funds? The increase in the number of funds and the rush of investors up until 2007 would suggest high returns. Certainly, most funds aim to produce returns of 20% plus, but how many do? Frankly, the evidence is mixed and even contradictory – there are over 10,000 funds, so some make sparkling returns, whereas others do not. In addition, there are a number of indices that track the sector with different coverage, such as the Greenwich Alternative Investments (GAI) Global Hedge Fund Indices, Eurekahedge, Credit Suisse/Tremont Hedge Fund Index and a family of Dow Jones hedge fund indices to name just a few. All can arrive at different return estimates. For example, after a disastrous year in 2008, hedge funds seem to have had mixed performance since then. A report in *The Economist* (20 August 2011) highlights this by noting:

> With bold promises of strong returns in good times and bad, hedge funds have seduced many an investor. But as often happens when a courtship develops into something more serious, blind love has been followed by a bitter let-down. Hedge funds first disappointed investors en masse in 2008, when the average fund fell by 19%. Since then they have struggled to beat the market . . . This year performance has continued to be lacklustre. The hedge-fund industry needs to produce outsize returns for the rest of 2011 if it is to restore its reputation.

According to the GAI Global Hedge Fund Index, in the 5 years up to 2008, the global industry made annualized returns of 4.2% (1.7% over the previous 3 years), and though this looks poor, it compares favourably with the S&P 500, which lost 2.2% annually between 2003 and 2008, and lost nearly 9% in the 3 years up to 2008. So hedge funds at least performed better than equities, although bonds posted returns of around 4–5% over the same period – so given the risk, these were no doubt the best risk-adjusted returns.

Hedge fund returns over the past few years have been massively adversely affected by the impact of the credit crisis. The GAI Global Hedge Fund Index fell by 15.7% in 2008 (the S&P 500 fell 38%), making it the worst return for the hedge fund sector on record. Nearly 75% of hedge funds and 85% of fund of hedge funds made losses in 2008 – most occurring in September and November. This was because of a number of factors:

- a number of major bank failures in Europe and the US – banks that provided prime broker facilities to hedge funds,
- a decline in equity markets,
- bans on short selling,
- increased liquidation of positions due to margin calls and
- an acceleration of redemptions.

As we said earlier, the sector rebounded in 2009 from the doldrums of 2008, and performance is up. Often the performance of the sector is presented according to different strategies undertaken. A report in the *Financial Times* (19 August 2009) identified the best performing hedge fund strategies for 2009:

The industry is also seeing a 'back to the future' trend, say big investors now looking to allocate, as traditional strategies such as arbitrage and equity long-short make a come-back. Convertible arbitrage – which bets on price inefficiencies in convertible debt – continues to be the best-performing hedge fund strategy this year, up on average 5.4% in July, according to Credit Suisse/Tremont, and more than 30.7% on the year to date. GLG's convertible arbitrage fund is up more than 20% this year. Emerging market and fixed-income arbitrage strategies – which bet on relative changes in value between bonds – have also done well. 'The crisis has thinned the players in the markets – both funds and banks – considerably,' said one London-based credit hedge fund manager. 'The result is that there are fewer crowded trades and almost any arb strategy can now outperform.' The worst-performing strategy so far this year, however, has been that most commonly asso-ciated with the industry in the public imagination: dedicated short selling. The strategy had a dreadful July as equities rallied, with the average dedicated short bias fund losing 8.32%, according to HFN. Dedicated short funds, which make up only a tiny proportion of industry, are languishing on the back of the powerful rally in global equities.

As we noted earlier in Box 9.1 the sector made big losses in 2008, figures from Hennessee Hedge Funds show that in that year, funds on average lost 21.3% of their value, but returns were up in 2009 at 18.2% and have been mixed since then – 9.7% in 2010, –4.6% in 2011 and 6.1% in 2012.

Regulation

Generally, hedge funds have been described as 'unregulated funds'. However, this is now changing. The US SEC ruled that from February 2006 any fund with holdings in excess of $25m must post results through them for all to see. In the UK, the FSA, having spent more than 12 months analysing the sector, set up a hedge fund supervisory scheme in the mid-2000s and identified 25 hedge funds (later extended to 35) which it said it would watch carefully. Also, IOSCO announced that it was carrying out its own review, eventually culminating in recommendations for greater regulatory oversight (as noted earlier). We have already mentioned that since the dramatic increases in oil and other commodity prices from 2005 to 2008, various bodies – including the G8 – have called for greater regulation of the industry. This is because hedge funds have been blamed for pushing up oil, commodity and other securities prices to excessive levels (gaining from long positions) and then speculating on dramatic falls (gaining from shorting).

Historically, hedge fund managers in the US have not been subject to regular SEC oversight like their investment banking counterparts. To be exempt from direct regulation in the US, a hedge fund must be open to a limited number of 'accredited' investors only. Accredited investors are wealthy individuals with investments typically in excess of $1m who are therefore viewed as professional investors who do not need regulatory protec-tion. Various rule changes were introduced by the SEC in February 2006 that required hedge fund advisers to register their activities with the regulatory authorities, but this was overturned by the US federal court in the same year.

Since 2007 and the onset of the crisis, there have been growing calls for regulation of the industry. Although hedge funds did not play a major role in the emergence of the credit crisis (only around 5% of their assets were in mortgage-backed securities), it has been argued by various market commentators that they created excessive volatility in 2008 by short selling banks and other securities and also due to massive deleveraging and redemp-tions. To make matters worse, the industry was hit by the largest ever financial fraud – the collapse of Bernard Madoff's $50bn (£33bn) fund. International Financial Services London (IFSL, 2009) neatly summarizes the scandal:

> The Madoff investment scandal occurred after the discovery that the asset management business of former NASDAQ chairman Bernard Madoff was actually a giant 'Ponzi' scheme. (A Ponzi scheme, named after the fraudster Charles Ponzi, who ran such an activity in the 1920s, simply involves promising high returns from an investment and paying these from current or new investors rather than any actual profit from investment. Such schemes work so long as the scheme can attract a decent number of new investors and so long as nobody finds out what is happening.) Alerted by his sons, federal authorities arrested Madoff on 11 December 2008. On 12 March 2009, Madoff pled guilty to 11 felonies and admitted to operating the largest investor fraud ever committed by an individual. According to a federal criminal complaint, client statements showing $65 billion in stock holdings were fictitious, and there is no indication that any stocks had been purchased since the mid-1990s. Although Madoff did not operate as a hedge fund, he operated through various funds of hedge funds. This has inflicted great reputational damage and reduced investor confidence in the hedge fund industry, particularly funds of funds which are the source of around 40% of hedge fund assets.

The Madoff scandal and the associated lack of regulation, plus concerns about the industry's contribution to the economic slowdown post credit crisis, have led to increasing pressures to regulate the industry. Various regulatory initiatives aimed at curbing hedge fund excesses include those below:

- In the US the Dodd-Frank Act of 2010 introduces regulations that stipulate that hedge funds with more than US$150 million in assets are to be registered with the SEC, and they have to disclose detailed information about their trading strategies and funds under management. Those with under $100 million have to register with state supervisors. Offshore hedge funds (doing business into the US) with more than US$25 million of assets also are overseen by the SEC. Part of the Dodd-Frank legislation known as the 'Volcker Rule' limits bank business with hedge funds and prohibits proprietary trading.
- In Europe, the 2010 EU's Directive on Alternative Investment Fund Managers (AIFMD) requires hedge funds to be registered with their home regulatory authorities. It provides for a single passport, and also has new capital and leverage requirements. Rules on hedge funds are country specific and vary from one jurisdiction to another, but they all have requirements on licensing, leverage, short-selling and report requirements.
- In the UK, which accounts for over 80% of hedge fund activity in Europe, fund managers and advisers are required to obtain authorization from the Financial Conduct Authority (FCA). There are also rules restricting the sales and marketing of hedge funds to retail UK investors, and on the use of derivatives and short-selling. Approximately one-half of the world's hedge funds are registered in offshore financial centres to benefit from low tax. Unlike onshore operations, the number of investors are usually not restricted. Onshore funds typically establish complementary offshore funds to attract additional capital without exceeding limits on the number of investors. The bulk of offshore funds are registered in the Cayman Islands (45%) and Delaware (20%) followed by the British Virgin Islands (10%), Ireland (8%) and Bermuda (6%). They are subject to less oversight than in onshore jurisdictions.

There have also been unprecedented proposals for regulatory coordination at the international level. Three major European and US hedge fund groups – the Alternative Investment Management Association, the President's Working Group on Financial Markets and the Managed Funds Association – have all announced that they will continue to develop best practice standards for the industry, covering issues such as disclosure rules and risk management. IOSCO has also announced proposals for increased regulations of the hedge fund industry. It remains to be seen how this new regulatory oversight of the industry will pan out, although there is no doubt that hedge funds are subject to tougher rules nowadays.

PRIVATE EQUITY

As we have seen, private equity is not in the same business as hedge funds, although activity can overlap and both have incurred the same criticism over the amount of leverage involved.

To recap: private equity firms make good returns by buying public companies or neglected subsidiaries at good prices and turning them into more attractive businesses. They will gear up with debt that a public company would not want to risk – private equity purchases will normally be turned into non-quoted companies. Although debt may be high, one advantage is that interest payments are tax deductible. It is, however, essential to have good, reliable cash flows. Private equity firms get involved in the business, bringing in their own expertise and giving existing managers big incentives to improve the business. They seek to cut costs, squeeze suppliers and sell unwanted assets. In addition, they may sell and lease back property. As we shall see later, there are certainly many cases where they have made considerable improvements. In rarer cases, they may buy a stake in a private company that simply looks undervalued and wait until it goes public later (see the example of QinetiQ below). As private companies, they escape some obligations of public companies – scrutiny of share price, rules on appointments to the board and, of course, financial disclosure. They look to fees of 1–2% and take 20% of profits as 'carried interest'.

The private equity companies take their profit in a variety of ways. One is to refloat the company. Another possibility is to sell the company to someone else in the same business. Another popular way of getting an early return is refinancing. Once some improvements are clear, the private equity company goes back to the banks and borrows more money, paying itself a substantial dividend from the proceeds. This was particularly common in 2005, and S&P reported in October 2005 that private equity firms had taken out more capital in Europe in the 9 months up to September than they had put in – a figure of €11.4bn compared with €5bn in the whole of 2004. Sometimes, the results of refinancing are spectacular. In December 2003, a group of private equity firms – Texas Pacific, CVC and Merrill Lynch Global Private Equity – bought Debenhams, the UK department store, for £1.7bn, of which £600m was their own capital. In two refinancing in 2004 and 2005, they reconstructed the balance sheet with new borrowings and paid themselves back £1.3bn – twice their original capital – in about 18 months. They refloated Debenhams in May 2006, although the share price fell by 24% in the following year.

In fact, 2005 and 2006 witnessed some of the largest private equity deals, as illustrated in Table 9.6. The earliest megadeal was Nabisco, purchased in 1989 by KKR.

Sometimes debt has to be sold as 'distressed debt' to hedge funds. There are two US funds specializing in this – Apollo Management and Cerberus.

One other development in 2005 was that trade buyers seemed to be less willing to be pushed aside when opportunities presented themselves. For example, when it became

▼ **Table 9.6** *Largest private equity transactions*

	Announcement Year	**Deal** value ($ bn)	**Inflation adjusted** value ($ bn)
RJR Nabisco	1989	31.1	50.6
Energy Future Holdings	2007	44.4	47.2
Equity Office Properties	2007	38.9	40.5
Hospital Corp. of America	2006	32.7	40.2
First Data	2007	29	36.4
Harrah's Entertainment	2006	27.4	33.8
Alltel	2007	27	29.4
Clear Channel	2006	25.7	25.1
Hilton Hotels	2007	26	19.1
Alliance Boots	2007	24.8	17.2

Source: TheCityUK (2012).

clear that Amana, the Spanish telecoms operator, was for sale, France Telecom battled two strong private equity consortiums and won.

The whole private equity industry has become widespread and influential. In the UK, well-known firms that are or have been owned by private equity groups include Alliance Boots, Iceland, Debenhams, the AA, Saga, Odeon and UCI Cinemas, Kiwi-Fit, New Look, United Biscuits, Jimmy Coho, Weetabix and National Car Parks. The British Venture Capital Association (BVCA) calculates that British private equity firms invested over £12.2bn in 2012 (down from £20bn in 2010), including investments made in 1,009 companies. Due to the state of the UK economy, early stage investments amounted to a lowly 6% of all investments, with over 45% dedicated to management buyouts (MBOs).

Investors

Who are the investors who are putting money into private equity? These include institutions like insurance companies, pension funds desperate for higher yield, subsidiaries of investment banks and, in the US, endowments like Yale. For private investors, the inability to withdraw money quickly is a major disadvantage, together with the minimum funds involved. The best way for them is through private equity investment trusts, a private equity fund of funds and venture capital trusts.

Investment levels in private equity firms can vary substantially year on year and pretty much reflect the performance of equity markets. According to the BVCA, in 2004, the sector raised only $3.3bn (the lowest for a decade), but the following year managed to obtain investments of £27.3bn, peaking at £34.3bn in 2006. Investments fell to £29.3bn in 2007 and then £23.1bn in 2008. In 2011 the sector raised a more modest £4.5bn (31% from UK investors and 29% from the US), but in 2012 when the industry raised £6bn funds from US investors dried up – only 9% from the US, with 73% of funds coming from the UK.

Box 9.3 provides examples of various private equity deals, failures as well as successes.

BOX 9.3

Private Equity Deals – Successes and Failures

Successes

Debenhams was mentioned earlier as an example of refinancing. The turnaround, however, is impressive. The buyout took place in December 2003. Before this, Debenhams had a profit of £153.6m on a turnover of £1.7bn. For the year to September 2005, the profit was £212.3m on a turnover of £2.0bn.

- Also in 2005, SunGard Data Systems was purchased by seven private equity groups for $11.3bn. In terms of finance, some of the money was found by an asset-based bond (see Chapter 7), the assets being future rentals.
- In November 2005, five private equity groups, including KKR, announced a bid for TDC, Denmark's leading telecommunications group. The bid was worth $12bn, Europe's largest ever. The offer was recommended by TDC's board, but the bid hit a snag in early January 2006 when ATP, a Danish pension fund holding 5.5% of TDC shares, the biggest shareholder, said that it would not accept the offer. The offer was conditional on receiving a 90% acceptance rate. Somehow, TDC succeeded in lowering the acceptance rate to 85% and got 88.2% acceptance in the end.
- In 2006, Bain Capital, KKR and Merrill Lynch linked up with Thomas Frist, co-founder of HCA, and paid a record $33bn for HCA, the American hospital chain (passing the $31.3bn buyout of RJR Nabisco, although not in real terms).
- CVC Capital Partners bought Kwik-Fit from Ford for £300m and later sold it for £800m. It also bought Halfords from Boots and doubled the value in 3 years.
- Energy proved to be a fruitful area for private equity firms when the market boomed in 2005. Some had picked up energy firms when prices were low. Triana Energy Holdings, an affiliate of Merrill Lynch, bought Columbia Natural Resources for $330m in 2003 and sold it late in 2005 for a figure in excess of $2.2bn. A group including KKR, Texas Pacific and Blackstone bought Texas Genco in 2004 for $900m and sold it late in 2005 to NGR for $5.8bn.
- The UK government found itself in an embarrassing situation in early 2006. QinetiQ, the Ministry of Defence's advanced research laboratory, was partially privatized in 2003. The US Carlyle Group took the opportunity to invest £42.4m and acquired 31.1% of shares. The government decided on a full flotation late in 2005, and in early 2006, it looked as though it would be valued at £1.1bn, making Carlyle's stake worth £340m, eight times as much as it had paid and forgetting a payment to it of £28.5m in 2004. In June 2006, it actually floated at £1.3bn – not easy for a Labour government to accept.
- Private equity firms operate right across the globe. This is even hitting China, in spite of the general resistance to foreign ownership. Carlyle Group took over Xugong Group, the construction machinery maker, taking an 85% holding from the state owner. China, however, says that it wants to encourage its own private enterprise and venture capital funds.

Failures

Naturally, it is not all sweetness and light. There are also the deals that did not do well:

- Cinven bought Dunlop Slazenger in 2001 and in the end lost all the £70m equity it had put in.

- Carlyle Group owned Edocha, a German vehicle component maker, and carried out a recapitalization to enable it to withdraw €80m of its €185m equity stake. Unfortunately, Edocha then experienced a serious downturn.
- In 2005, there was a well-publicized strike at Gate Gourmet, supplier of catering to BA and others, doing great damage to BA in particular. It had been bought by Texas Pacific Group and earlier in the year had stopped payments on its SFr760m debt. A squeeze by Texas Pacific followed and resulted in industrial unrest and much opprobrium for the owners.
- Among private equity-owned firms that collapsed are Gateway Supermarkets, Le Meridien Hotels, Allsports, Furnitureland, Unwins (wines/spirits retailer) and MVC (music retailer).
- In many cases, the burden of debt has proved to be the problem.

We noted earlier that buyouts' share of the value of private equity fell in 2008 as it became more difficult to obtain finance. According to IFSL, the largest buyouts in 2008 included the $3.5bn acquisition of the Weather Channel by NBC Universal, Bain Capital and Blackstone, and Carlyle's $2.5bn takeover of consulting firm Booz Allen Hamilton. Blackstone was the most active private equity firm in 2014, sealing nearly 40 deals, including taking a stake in the luxury goods firm Versace. Many recent deals, however, are relatively small compared with some of the megadeals in the years preceding the credit crisis, as already shown in Table 9.5 above.

Leverage

The question of heavy borrowings has been mentioned several times. Is leverage a threat, is it really excessive? Debt is usually measured as a multiple of earnings (strictly, earnings before interest, tax, depreciation and amortization, EBITDA – a figure aimed at showing the cash flow of the company). A consortium bought Rexel, a subsidiary of Pinault-Printemps-Redoute, for €3.7bn – debt was seven times EBITDA. This was 2004, when S&P found that over 60% of deals were based on debt multiples in excess of 5. Close Brothers Corporate Finance estimated in October 2005 that multiples averaged 5.6 compared with 4.2 in 2002. Blackstone and Lion Capital bought Cadbury Schweppes' European beverage arm for €1.85bn in late 2005 on a multiple of 7.

Despite concerns the sector boomed, typically increasing leverage from 2005 to 2007. Then the deleveraging trend began. Market commentators say that debt multiples have collapsed and there was even talk about regulations imposing maximum leverage ratios in Europe.

In Chapter 15, we explain the world of credit derivatives where those faced with debtors buy insurance against default and pay a premium measured in basis points. Naturally, the higher the risk, the higher the premium. As soon as a bid for VNU, the Dutch media group, was launched and terms were known, the credit derivative premiums for VNU widened considerably. The same thing happened once the bid for TDC was launched.

Finally, a spirited defence of the current levels of leverage was launched by George Roberts, founder of the well-known KKR, in January 2006. He dismissed the idea that private equity groups were recklessly applying too much debt to the businesses they were buying: 'We are not being reckless with our investments.' Though one has to respect the opinion of such a successful market practitioner, one also recalls the words of Mandy Rice-Davies: 'Well, he would, wouldn't he.'

Hedge Funds and Private Equity Coming Closer

There is now growing evidence of firms with a foot in both camps. Many private equity funds have set up hedge funds, especially in the US, for example Blackstone, which include activities that focus on the areas of distressed debt, long/short equity and multistrategy business.

This does raise questions of conflicts of interest and insider trading. The advantage of the alliance is that both groups can share information about market trends and attract investors looking at either vehicle. The disadvantage is the scope for insider trading. The private equity groups acquire intimate knowledge of the firms in which they have invested. Most of these will not be public companies, but what of those that are or are near to being floated? If hedge funds trade shares based on information passed on to them by their associates, they would be in breach of US regulations.

Sometimes the titans clash. In 2000, a powerful consortium of hedge funds challenged private equity groups KKR and Hellman & Friedman when both made a bid for Texas Genco. Many will argue that hedge funds do not have the experience in running a company to do this – another argument for an alliance. The word on everybody's lips these days is 'convergence'. The *Financial Times* (June 2007) has highlighted what it called the 'symbiotic' relationship between the two industries, noting that:

> Hedge fund investors are adding fuel to the buy-out fire as enthusiastic buyers of high-yield debt – helping to keep it cheap and plentiful. So far this year, hedge funds and similar investors have bought more than 20% of leveraged loans.

Profits on Private Equity

Everyone knows that there are deals which are spectacularly profitable, and we have seen some – but what about average profitability, taking losses into account? George Roberts of KKR says that his firm continues to anticipate beating the S&P index by 5–7%, but of course this is one of the biggest and most successful firms.

An academic study from the University of Chicago Graduate School of Business and the Sloan School of Management at MIT did a survey of 700 private equity funds and found that returns, net of fees, from 1980 to 2001 were a little less than those on the S&P 500 Index. The academics even warn of suspected underreporting by the worst performing funds. The reporting was based on completed transactions, where cash was paid to investors from liquidated funds, and not valuations of unsold investments. The study also concludes that funds raised in boom years (like 2005) tend to perform poorly. It is clear that returns between different funds vary considerably. It is also true that we tend to hear of the successes and not the failures.

Is private equity somehow a superior form of ownership? Has it, as John Lovering (a key private equity player) claims, 'added freedom to Britain's commercial scene because

▼ **Table 9.7** *UK private equity returns, 3-, 5- and 10-year average*

10 years (% p.a)	
Private equity	15.7
Pension assets	7.8
FTSE All-share	8.8
5 years (% p.a)	
Private equity	11.1
Pension assets	10.1
FTSE All-share	14.3
3 years (% p.a)	
Private equity	10
Pension assets	7.6
FTSE All-share	9.4
2013	
Private equity	19.2
Pension assets	11.0
FTSE All-share	20.8

Source: British Venture Capital and Private Equity Association (BVCA) (2014) Performance Measurement Survey.

it has introduced a parallel universe to traditionally owned and managed firms'?

Surely, overall, only a small number of firms can be relatively inefficient and subject to a dramatic turnaround. Is public ownership such a disadvantage, when the quarterly reports, dividends and transparency also provide a discipline? Can one believe that private equity companies understand debt better than public companies? The claim is that they can borrow much more than a public company and that public companies are thus at a disadvantage – but what does theory say here? The Modigliani and Miller research in 1958 on the cost of capital concluded that a company's enterprise value is not increased by borrowing other than by way of a minor tax advantage.

The disadvantages for private equity are the lack of liquidity for its investors, the need to pay a premium to obtain control and the fact that sometimes there are no obvious industrial synergies. As we have seen, most research concludes that returns overall are no better than the S&P 500 in spite of the risks. The best, of course, do very well and employ talented people, but the average may not be impressive. Table 9.7 illustrates the returns of the UK private equity industry in and up to 2013.

SUMMARY

- A *hedge fund* is an actively managed investment that seeks an attractive *absolute* return, that is, a return whether the market goes up or down. To achieve this, a wide variety of strategies are used, especially *short selling* of securities – the selling of borrowed assets in the hope of buying them back at a lower price.
- *Private equity* is a mixture of venture capital for early stage companies and management buyouts. The company that is bought out may be refloated on the stock market later to achieve a profit or sold to a trade buyer.
- Both activities seek to enhance profits by heavy borrowing, known as *leverage*.
- Hedge funds use a wide variety of strategies, many of them very complicated. They are similar to those used by the proprietary trading desks of investment bankers, but with much greater freedom for risk and leverage because the funds are not regulated in the way that investment bankers are. As a result, it is claimed that they often account for 30–40% of trading of bonds, equities, foreign exchange and credit derivatives.
- Around 9% of hedge funds closed in 2008 as a consequence of the economic slowdown and particularly the collapse of banks and their prime brokerage arms in late autumn. The industry's reputation has also suffered from the collapse of the fraudulent Bernard Madoff investment firm that operated as a Ponzi scheme and embezzled $50bn from clients. The performance of the sector has improved modestly since then.

- The US Dodd-Frank Act of 2010 introduced more regulations for the hedge fund industry. Funds with more than US$150 million in assets are to be registered with the SEC, and they have to disclose detailed information about their trading strategies and funds under management. Those with under $100 million have to register with state supervisors; and offshore funds with more than US$25 million and if doing business with US clients also have to register. Part of the Dodd-Frank legislation, known as the 'Volcker Rule,' limits bank business with hedge funds and prohibits proprietary trading.
- In Europe, the 2010 EU's Directive on Alternative Investment Fund Managers (AIFMD) requires hedge funds to be registered with their home regulatory authorities. It provides for a single passport, and also has new capital and leverage requirements. Rules on hedge funds are country specific and vary from one jurisdiction to another but they all have requirements on licensing, leverage, short selling and report requirements.
- UK hedge funds have to obtain a license and are subject to regulation by the Financial Conduct Authority.

- Investors in hedge funds were originally high-net-worth individuals, but now the various institutions are big investors – fund of funds, pension funds, banks, endowments and foundations.
- The investment institutions are also heavy investors in private equity companies. They have a disadvantage for private investors due to the inability to withdraw money quickly, as these companies will be prepared to wait 3–5 years for a return. There are, nevertheless, private equity investment trusts, private equity funds of funds and venture capital trusts. Private equity companies are so called because they are usually private companies as this gives them greater freedom of action.
- The high leverage used by private equity groups has drawn attention – up to as much as seven times profit before tax, interest, depreciation and amortization.
- Both hedge funds and private equity groups have attracted investment in view of the large profits apparently being achieved, with returns of the order of 20% p.a. being claimed. However, no academic studies have been able to verify high *average* profits over the whole range of activity. Although there are, without doubt, spectacular successes, there are also many wind-ups and failures.

REVISION QUESTIONS/ASSIGNMENTS

1 Analyse the main characteristics of hedge funds, and explain their role in modern financial markets.
2 Examine the key differences between hedge funds and private equity firms. Why are they becoming increasingly similar?

3 Outline the role of leverage for both hedge funds and private equity firms.
4 Discuss the recent regulatory initiatives aimed at regulating the hedge fund sector.

REFERENCES

Burrough, B., and Helyar, J. (1990) *Barbarians at the Gate: The Fall of RJR Nabisco*, Harper & Row, New York. Racy tale about the leveraged buyout of RJR Nabisco – the biggest private equity deal ever.

IFSL (International Financial Services London). (2009) *Hedge Funds*, IFSL, London. Review of the global hedge fund industry. IFSL changed its name to TheCityUK in 2010.

TheCityUK. (2012) *Private Equity*, TheCityUK, London. Well-illustrated contemporary insight into the private equity sector.

TheCityUK. (2013) *Hedge Funds*, TheCityUK, London. Well-illustrated contemporary insight into the global hedge fund sector.

FURTHER READING

Coggan, P. (2008) *Guide to Hedge Funds: What They Are, What They Do, Their Risks, Their Advantages*, Profile Books/The Economist, London. Practical guide to the risk and return features of hedge fund investment.

Lo, A.W. (2010) *Hedge Funds: An Analytic Perspective (Advances in Financial Engineering)*, Princeton University Press, Princeton, NJ. Detailed guide to the hedge fund sector. Useful for those thinking of investing in hedge funds or funds of funds.

Zask, E. (2013) *All About Hedge Funds* (2nd edn), McGraw-Hill, New York.

Financial Crisis

Financial Crisis

INTRODUCTION

The global financial crisis has had a massive impact on banks and financial markets as well as the way in which they are regulated. From 2007 to mid-2009, global financial markets and systems experienced the worst financial crisis since the Depression era of the late 1920s. Major banks in the US, the UK and Europe collapsed and were bailed out by state aid. AIG, the largest US insurer, suffered a similar fate. The investment banking world was decimated by the collapse of Lehman Brothers and Bear Stearns, and all the major US bulge-bracket firms – Merrill Lynch, Morgan Stanley, Goldman Sachs – were either acquired by commercial banks or converted into bank holding companies. Both Royal Bank of Scotland (owners of NatWest) and Citigroup, pillars of the UK and US financial systems, respectively, are now under state ownership. Since the deterioration of the US property market in 2007 and the failure of sub-prime lending, much of which was securitized, markets of many types of financial assets collapsed. The response to the crisis by US and European governments and central banks was significant and unprecedented. Measures enacted range from initiatives dealing with impaired bank assets, the recapitalizing and/or financial restructuring of troubled banks, and actions designed to inject liquidity into the banking system. Governments have also poured billions into their respective economies, and interest rates have been cut to record low levels. The objective is to provide both a fiscal and monetary stimulus to stave off recession.

The crisis had a massive adverse impact on global banking systems. The International Monetary Fund's *Global Financial Stability Report* (IMF, 2009) reported an estimate of $2.7 trillion for write-downs of US-originated assets by banks and other financial sector institutions between 2007 and 2010. Estimated write-downs for all mature market-originated assets for the same period are in the region of $4 trillion. The same report contains estimates of the implications of these write-downs for bank recapitalization. To restore bank capital/assets ratios to the average 4% level before the crisis, the required capital injections were $275bn for banks in the US, $325bn for the euro area, $125bn for the UK, and $100bn for other mature European countries. To restore capital/assets ratios to the average level of 6% that existed in the mid-1990s, the required injections are $500bn, $725bn, $250bn and $225bn, respectively. Faced with such enormous losses, many banks have retrenched, selling off non-core businesses and looking to boost their own capital strength (with or without the help of government). This has become increasingly apparent as a result of the eurozone crisis (see Chapter 12).

This chapter looks at the causes and key events of the crisis and highlights the role of the securitization business and sub-prime lending activity and how it helped to trigger the crisis. We then look at the impact of the crisis in the US, the UK, Europe and elsewhere, and end with the lessons learned and policy response. Many of the major developments that have impacted global banking systems since mid-2007 have been triggered by events in the US, so a significant portion of the chapter outlines these events.

WHAT WENT WRONG

The *79th Annual Report* of the Bank for International Settlements (BIS, 2009) provides an encyclopaedic coverage of the causes, impact and consequences of the financial crisis and is an excellent analysis of what went wrong. The BIS identifies key macroeconomic and microeconomic factors that led up to the crisis.

Macroeconomic Factors

Several macroeconomic factors led up to the crisis:

- *Global financial imbalances:* This refers to large and persistent current account deficits and surpluses that came from capital flows from capital-poor emerging market countries (Asia and the oil-rich Gulf) to capital-rich industrial economies (particularly the US). Typically, high saving rates in the emerging world and the low level in the US were associated with these flows. The BIS notes that from 1999 to mid-2007, the cumulative US current account deficit was $4.6 trillion, and the external debt was around $13.4 trillion (some four times larger than it had been in 1998). There are a number of reasons why these imbalances occurred, ranging from the desire of emerging market investors wishing to hold their assets in more stable currencies as well as changes brought about by new trade flows. Whatever the reason, the surplus countries of the emerging world – China and the Gulf in particular – were paying for the indebtedness of the West.
- *Long period of low real interest rates:* Concerns over deflation led policymakers in the West to run an accommodating monetary policy that resulted in low rates of interest. In the US, for instance, from 2001 to 2005, the federal funds rate was consistently below 1%, and the real rate was negative for most of the period. In the eurozone, real rates were around 1% over the same period and even lower in Japan. Low interest rates in the US have a bigger effect than low rates elsewhere because most international contracts are denominated in US dollars and also many fixed or quasi-fixed exchange rate systems use the dollar as a reference currency. A low interest rate environment had the following effects:
  - It fuelled a credit boom in many industrialized countries, and annual credit growth ranged between 7% and 10% in the US and the UK between 2003 and mid-2007. Much of this was in the form of residential mortgage lending, which helped to fuel property prices.
  - Low rates increase the present discounted value of revenue streams from earning assets, so this pushed up asset prices (recall the inverse relationship between bond prices and interest rates). The BIS reports that real property prices in the US and UK increased by more than 30% between 2003 and mid-2007. Global equity markets rose by 90% over the same period.
  - A low-interest-rate environment encourages banks and other unregulated institutions (the so-called 'shadow banking' system described in Chapter 5) to

take on more risk so they can meet the relatively higher nominal returns they have committed to in various long-term contracts. For instance, asset managers may promise high nominal returns from, say, investing in mutual funds or other investments, and these returns can be difficult to achieve if they stick to their usual portfolio mixes, so they shift to higher return (and higher risk) investment areas to meet client demand. Low interest rates therefore lead to greater risk taking.

These factors – the credit boom that fuelled the housing market, consumer spending and the desire to obtain greater returns – 'helped distort the macroeconomic structure of a number of countries' (BIS, 2009), most notably the US and the UK.

Microeconomic Factors

From the onset of the credit crisis in mid-2007, a range of microeconomic causes of the ensuing financial crisis became apparent:

- *Households* were generally unaware that the banks and investment firms through which they were conducting business were taking on extensive risks and that their solvency was threatened.
- *Managers* of such firms were being incentivized to take on greater risks to generate higher returns for shareholders who were not fully aware of the risks they were engaging in.
- *Rating agencies* were rating what turned out to be high-risk firms and investments as low risk, driven by the desire to grab larger market shares of rating business revenues.
- *Insurance firms* were insuring the credit risk of a variety of financial instruments, mainly securitized products, which they believed had low probabilities of loss, but which turned out to default.
- *Investment and commercial banks* became increasingly sophisticated in creating innovative products that were well-nigh impossible to price accurately, given the limited risk measurement approaches.

The misaligned incentives encompassing the above are neatly summarized by the BIS as follows:

- *Consumers failed to watch out for themselves:* Complexity was mistaken for sophistication, and consumers believed that their investments and deposits were safe: 'The system that consumers so readily assumed was sophisticated and safe was, in fact, recklessly complex and opaque' (BIS, 2009). If financial experts, regulators and experienced bankers are looking after our money, surely it must be safe? This, of course, turned out to be not the case.
- *Managers of financial firms increased returns by boosting leverage:* Increased pressure on managers to generate higher returns for their shareholders encouraged them to take on more risk. The major gauge of firm performance is return on equity (ROE), which is the net income generated for shareholders. ROE simply equals the return on assets (ROA) multiplied by the ratio of assets to equity. If you hold less equity (more debt or leverage), then ROE increases. As the BIS (2009) notes: 'This private incentive to increase leverage created not only fragile institutions but also an unstable financial system.'

- *Manager compensation schemes further encouraged risk-taking:* Senior managers at banks and other financial firms were incentivized to take on greater short-run risks, irrespective of whether the longer term implications of such strategies would lead to disaster, because this boosted returns and therefore wage packets that were linked to ROE and/or stock price performance. Asset managers were rewarded for beating various benchmarks, and to exceed these hurdles, they were also incentivized to take on more risk, even though they probably knew that the assets were bubble-like and likely to collapse. So long as benchmark or hurdle performance levels were exceeded over a short period, they earned their significant bonuses: 'In the end, the overall difficulty in distinguishing luck from skill in the performance of asset managers, combined with compensation based at least in part on the volume of business, encouraged managers and traders to accumulate huge amounts of risk' (BIS, 2009).

- *Skewed incentives of the rating agencies:* The rapid growth in new securitized financial instruments created a massive demand for credit rating agency services. Securities backed by mortgages and other debt instruments proliferated (see the later section on securitization). However, for these securities to be attractive, investors needed to know the risks associated with the mortgages or other debt backing these instruments. In particular, as traditional low-risk (AAA) bonds paid low returns, there was a strong desire from investors for higher return, low-risk investments. Complex and opaque structures developed in the securitized market, to which the rating agencies assigned high-grade (low-risk) ratings. Rating agencies were happy because they earned substantial revenues from the booming rating business, banks were happy because they could sell rated instruments to investors, and investors were happy because they could acquire what appeared to be low-risk investments that generated higher returns than similar risk bonds. It all seemed too good to be true, and of course it was.

- *Limitations of risk measurement, management and regulation:* As already noted, a whole range of financial market participants were incentivized to take on more risks to obtain greater returns, and a major route through which this was undertaken was via the securitization business. Banks made loans to households (including risky households – sub-prime lending), packaged them up as securities in increasingly complex forms, created new legal structures off balance sheet to do this, had them rated, issued other instruments (such as short-term commercial paper) to fund this activity, had the securities rated and then sold them on to investors and also held a portion themselves. They also bought other banks' securitized issues. This complex web of interactions meant that the risk features of all these dimensions needed to be measured and managed accurately and effectively. However, there were problems. Many of the securitized products were new and backed by assets (such as sub-prime mortgages) that had only experienced a short (booming) life span. The risk measurement models, run by 'rocket scientists', only had data on the good times to predict losses and default outcomes. This led to an exaggeration of the low risk associated with securitized assets. Risk managers, whose job it was to look at the broader risk implications of such activity, typically found it almost impossible to accurately gauge the risks and, given that such positions are generally not regarded as 'revenue generating', had limited say in altering things even if they identified problems: 'Why change things if we are making great returns and bonuses?' Finally, regulators, being one step behind the market, were further removed from the process and appeared to have only limited insight as to the risks being taken. In any event, the various legal structures that banks had created off balance sheet in order to engage in the securitization business shielded much of this activity from the gaze of the regulators.

It's a long and, in retrospect, rather sorry story, summed up in the title of Gillian Tett's (2009) excellent book on the crisis: *Fool's Gold: How Unrestrained Greed Corrupted a Dream, Shattered Global Markets and Unleashed a Catastrophe.*

STAGES OF THE CRISIS

Because losses appeared in the US sub-prime residential mortgage market in June 2007, the financial crisis unfurled. The BIS identifies five main stages of the crisis:

- *Stage 1:* Losses in the US sub-prime market starting in the summer of 2007 – June 2007 up to mid-March 2008
- *Stage 2:* Events leading up to the Lehman Brothers bankruptcy – mid-March to mid-September 2008
- *Stage 3:* Global loss of confidence – 15 September to late October 2008
- *Stage 4:* Investors focus on the global economic downturn – late October 2008 to mid-March 2009
- *Stage 5:* Signs of stabilization – from mid-March 2009

Characteristics of these stages are illustrated in Table 10.1, and a timeline of key credit crunch events is shown in Table 10.2. We will cover many of the events illustrated in the timeline later in this chapter.

SECURITIZATION AND HOW IT FUELLED THE CRISIS

Start of Securitization

One area that has been widely referred to as a major cause of the crisis has been the massive growth in securitization business undertaken by banks and the shadow banking system. This activity has had a major impact on the funding of residential property markets and also on the flexibility with which banks can manage their loan books. The collapse of sub-prime mortgage lending in the US and related securitized products is seen by many as the start of the credit crisis.

The origin of the US securitization business starts from the failure of the savings and loans associations (S&Ls) (similar in many respects to UK building societies) in the mid-1980s. Traditionally, the S&Ls took retail savings deposits and used these to finance long-term mortgages. In the mid-1980s, the S&L sector faced collapse because as market interest rates increased, the S&Ls had to pay higher deposit rates to maintain funding, but because of various restrictions, they could not change the rates on mortgages to cover the increased cost of funding. S&Ls therefore undertook higher risk commercial property lending to try to generate higher returns, but this resulted in substantial losses. Also, at that time, the US had restrictions on interstate banking, so many S&Ls had concentrated

▼ **Table 10.1** *Stages of the crisis*

Stages of the crisis	Markets and institutions	Industrial economies		Emerging market economies (EMEs)	
		Macroeconomic conditions	Policy responses	Macroeconomics conditions	Policy responses
1. Pre-March 2008: prelude to the crisis	Sub-prime mortgage defaults create widespread financial stress. Uncertainty about size and distribution of losses. Crisis starts when interbank markets are disrupted in August 2007; waves of increasing intensity until March 2008.	Growth weakens.	Central bank (CB) rate cuts. Liquidity operations targeted at money markets.	Robust growth with inflation rising. Many inflation targeters above their targets.	Rate increases in response to high inflation.
2. Mid-March to mid-September 2008: towards the Lehman bankruptcy	Takeover of Bear Stearns in March slows decline, but bank losses and write-downs accumulate as downturn weighs on asset prices. More countries affected. Liquidity crisis reveals underlying solvency crisis, increasing pressure on financial institutions.	G3 economies contract even as oil prices fall steeply after August.	Initially further rate cuts. Liquidity facilities grow. GSEs put into conservatorship in early September.	GDP growth slows after June but remains positive. Exports weaken in central Europe.	Further rate increases due to high inflation.
3. 15 September 2008 to late October 2008: global loss of confidence	Demise of Lehman Brothers on 15 September 2008 triggers a bigger run on key funding markets. More financial institutions fail or are rescued. Loss of confidence affects markets and countries globally. Reprieve only after unprecedented and broad-based policy intervention.	As confidence falls and financing conditions tighten, forecasts are revised down sharply.	Sharp rate cuts, CB swap lines expanded, rapid CB balance sheet growth. Large-scale bank rescues, deposit and debt guarantees.	Confidence slumps. Financing conditions tighten. Steep currency depreciations.	Rate cuts, more flexible provisions of central bank liquidity. Deposit and debt guarantees. Capital injections.
4. Late October 2008 to mid-March 2009: global downturn	Markets remain volatile, with increasingly dire economic data releases, weak earnings reports and uncertainties over ongoing government intervention. Downturn means that credit losses keep mounting.	Spending drops, leading to declines in goods trade and GDP. Inflation falls, with the price level declining in some countries.	Rates cut to near zero, liquidity provision to non-banks. Outright purchases of public debt. Big fiscal stimulus packages.	GDP growth declines sharply in Q4 2008 as exports slump. Capital inflows reverse.	Further rate cuts, lower reserve requirements. FX intervention, CB swap lines. Large fiscal stimulus packages in some EMEs.
5. Since mid-March 2009: downturn deepens but loses speed	Asset prices recover somewhat after more policy action. But signs of market dysfunction remain, as official efforts have failed to fully restore confidence in the global financial system. Continued credit losses.	Consumption and production continue to decline, with possible signs of bottoming-out.	Further rate cuts in some countries. Accounting rules for banks eased.	Equity markets recover, and exchange rates stabilise.	Increased external official financing to support EMEs.

Source: BIS (2009) *79th Annual Report*, Table 1.1, p. 15, www.bis.org/publ/arpdf/ar2009e.pdf.

▼ **Table 10.2** *Timeline of key events*

2007

9 Aug.	Problems in mortgage and credit markets spill over into interbank money markets when issuers of asset-backed commercial paper encounter problems rolling over outstanding volumes, and large investment funds freeze redemptions, citing an inability to value their holdings.
12 Dec.	Central banks from five major currency areas announce coordinated measures designed to address pressures in short-term funding markets, including the establishment of US dollar swap lines.

2008

16 Mar.	JPMorgan Chase agrees to purchase Bear Stearns in a transaction facilitated by the US authorities.
4 June	Moody's and Standard & Poor's take negative rating actions on monoline insurers MBIA and Ambac, reigniting fears about valuation losses on securities insured by these companies.
13 July	The US authorities announce plans for backstop measures supporting two US mortgage finance agencies (Fannie Mae and Freddie Mac), including purchases of agency stock.
15 July	The US Securities and Exchange Commission (SEC) issues an order restricting 'naked short selling'.
7 Sept.	Fannie Mae and Freddie Mac are taken into government conservatorship.
15 Sept.	Lehman Brothers Holdings Inc. files for Chapter 11 bankruptcy protection.
16 Sept.	Reserve Primary, a large US money market fund, 'breaks the buck', triggering large volumes of fund redemptions; the US government steps in to support insurance company AIG (and is forced to repeatedly increase and restructure that rescue package over the following months).
18 Sept.	Coordinated central bank measures address the squeeze in US dollar funding with $160 billion in new or expanded swap lines; the UK authorities prohibit short selling of financial shares.
19 Sept.	The US Treasury announces a temporary guarantee of money market funds; the SEC announces a ban on short sales in financial shares; early details emerge of a $700 billion US Treasury proposal to remove troubled assets from bank balance sheets (the Troubled Asset Relief Program, TARP).
25 Sept.	The authorities take control of Washington Mutual, the largest US S&L institution, with some $300 billion in assets.
29 Sept.	UK mortgage lender Bradford & Bingley is nationalized; banking and insurance company Fortis receives a capital injection from three European governments; German commercial property lender Hypo Real Estate secures a government-facilitated credit line; troubled US bank Wachovia is taken over; the proposed TARP is rejected by the US House of Representatives.
30 Sept.	Financial group Dexia receives a government capital injection; the Irish government announces a guarantee safeguarding all deposits, covered bonds and senior and subordinated debt of six Irish banks; other governments take similar initiatives over the following weeks.
3 Oct.	The US Congress approves the revised TARP plan.
8 Oct.	Major central banks undertake a coordinated round of policy rate cuts; the UK authorities announce a comprehensive support package, including capital injections for UK-incorporated banks.
13 Oct.	Major central banks jointly announce the provision of unlimited amounts of US dollar funds to ease tensions in money markets; euro area governments pledge system-wide bank recapitalizations; reports say that the US Treasury plans to invest $125 billion to buy stakes in nine major banks.
28 Oct.	Hungary secures a $25 billion support package from the IMF and other multilateral institutions aimed at stemming growing capital outflows and easing related currency pressures.
29 Oct.	To counter the protracted global squeeze in US dollar funding, the US Federal Reserve agrees swap lines with the monetary authorities in Brazil, Korea, Mexico and Singapore.

▼ **Table 10.2** *Timeline of key events (continued)*

15 Nov.	The G20 countries pledge joint efforts to enhance cooperation, restore global growth and reform the world's financial systems.
25 Nov.	The US Federal Reserve creates a $200 billion facility to extend loans against securitizations backed by consumer and small business loans; in addition, it allots up to $500 billion for purchases of bonds and mortgage-backed securities issued by US housing agencies.

2009

16 Jan.	The Irish authorities seize control of Anglo Irish Bank; replicating an approach taken in the case of Citigroup in November, the US authorities agree to support Bank of America through a preferred equity stake and guarantees for a pool of troubled assets.
19 Jan.	As part of a broad-based financial rescue package, the UK authorities increase their existing stake in Royal Bank of Scotland. Similar measures by other national authorities follow over the next few days.
10 Feb.	The US authorities present plans for new comprehensive measures in support of the financial sector, including a Public-Private Investment Program (PPIP) of up to $1 trillion to purchase troubled assets.
10 Feb.	G7 Finance Ministers and central bank Governors reaffirm their commitment to use the full range of policy tools to support growth and employment and strengthen the financial sector.
5 Mar.	The Bank of England launches a programme, worth about $100 billion, aimed at outright purchases of private sector assets and government bonds over a 3-month period.
18 Mar.	The US Federal Reserve announces plans for purchases of up to $300 billion of longer term Treasury securities over a period of 6 months and increases the maximum amounts for planned purchases of US agency-related securities.
23 Mar.	The US Treasury provides details on the PPIP proposed in February.
2 Apr.	The communiqué issued at the G20 summit pledges joint efforts by governments to restore confidence and growth, including measures to strengthen the financial system.
6 Apr.	The US Federal Open Market Committee authorizes new temporary reciprocal foreign currency liquidity swap lines with the Bank of England, ECB, Bank of Japan and Swiss National Bank.
24 Apr.	The US Federal Reserve releases details on the stress tests conducted to assess the financial soundness of the 19 largest US financial institutions, declaring that most banks currently have capital levels well in excess of the amount required for them to remain well capitalized.
7 May	The ECB's Governing Council decides in principle that the Eurosystem will purchase euro-denominated covered bonds; the US authorities publish the results of their stress tests and identify 10 banks with an overall capital shortfall of $75 billion, to be covered chiefly through additions to common equity.

Source: BIS (2009) *79th Annual Report*, pp. 18–19, www.bis.org/publ/arpdf/ar2009e.pdf.

lending that focused on particular geographical areas, that is, mortgage loan portfolios were not very geographically diversified, and states such as Texas and California suffered high default rates during the 1980s.

The crisis situation faced by the S&L sector led the US authorities to set up the Resolution Trust Corporation, which took assets off the S&Ls' books and sold them on to investors and other banks. This process was not costless – US taxpayers faced losses of around $150bn resulting from this process – but it did manage to avoid a system-wide collapse of the whole banking system.

The process outlined above, whereby S&Ls moved loans off the balance sheet and sold them on to investors, was the first major securitization. The process was viewed as a solution to the problem faced by the S&L sector, and it freed mortgage lenders from liquidity constraints imposed by their balance sheets. Put another way, banks no longer had to rely on deposits to make loans; they could make loans and then sell them on to investors in the form of securities that finance the lending activity. These two different approaches to funding credit have been referred to as follows:

1 *Originate and hold model:* where lenders find borrowers, originate loans and then hold these on the balance sheet until maturity – the traditional approach
2 *Originate-to-distribute model:* where lenders find borrowers, originate loans but then sell the loans (repackaged as securities) on to investors – the securitization approach

Before securitization, banks could only make a limited number of loans based on the size of their balance sheets; however, the new form of financing allowed lenders to sell off their loans to other banks or investors, and the funds raised could be used to make more loans.

Role of the US Government-sponsored Enterprises

A major push to the US securitization trend was led by the development of mortgage-backed securities (MBS) promoted by government-sponsored enterprises (GSEs), notably Fannie Mae (Federal National Mortgage Association) and Freddie Mac (Federal Home Loan Mortgage Corporation).

The GSEs had been established some years earlier to promote home ownership in the US. Mortgages that fit certain rules (known as 'conforming mortgages') can be sold by banks and other originators to Fannie Mae and Freddie Mac. The GSEs then package geographically dispersed mortgage loans together and sell MBS in the financial markets. This is the first stage of the securitization process, where investors acquire financial assets, MBS, whose returns reflect the returns on the underlying mortgage pool held by the GSEs. Investors have to bear some risks, mainly interest rate risk. Importantly, however, the risks of default in the mortgages were retained by the GSEs. They guaranteed buyers of the securitized mortgages against the loss of default and prepayment losses (losses associated with early repayment). So, in theory at least, investors can acquire low-risk investment securities, because they are backed by good collateral/security – namely a pool of diversified mortgages. Also, because the GSEs had implicit government backing – they were viewed as being guaranteed by the federal authorities even though no formal guarantee existed and could issue their own finance (by issuing bonds) at the finest rates (only one or two basis points above government Treasury yields – investors believed GSE bonds to be nearly as safe as the US state). This meant that the GSEs could raise cheap finance to also purchase the MBS that they were creating.

Over recent years, the securitization activities of the GSEs have been highly profitable, and their business has boomed, until they faced various regulatory restrictions pushed by Alan Greenspan, then Federal Reserve chairman, and others. The GSEs were key participants in the mortgage market, accounting for much of the expansion of prime mortgage lending in the early 2000s. They also bought sub-prime (higher risk) loans, and expanded that portfolio after 2003, in part because the US Congress encouraged (some say pushed) them to provide more loans to low-income borrowers to justify the capital advantage they had because of the implicit federal guarantee.

The increase in sub-prime mortgage defaults in the summer of 2007 resulted in the GSEs suffering major write-downs, pushing them into losses – Fannie Mae and Freddie Mac had nearly $15bn of write-downs at the end of 2007, according to their regulator, the Office of Federal Housing Enterprise Oversight. However, despite these problems, by the end of 2007, they remained by far the largest buyer of mortgages originated, and some 75% of new mortgages written in the fourth quarter of 2007 were placed with Fannie Mae and Freddie Mac. Growing concerns about the value of the massive portfolio of MBS held by the main GSEs (estimated at $5 trillion) led to a collapse of their share prices in July 2008, and the federal authorities had to step in and bail them out in September 2008.

It is also important to note that although the discussion of securitization focuses on the role of the GSEs, other financial institutions also issued MBS. As the GSEs' original remit was to promote home ownership to US citizens, they only dealt with conforming mortgages up to a certain size and those that had (in theory at least) moderate credit risk features. As such, other institutions tended to be involved in securitizing larger 'jumbo' mortgages or those in the higher risk sub-prime market. This leads us on to the emergence of the sub-prime market.

Sub-prime Lending

The growth of the US sub-prime mortgage business (and related securitizations) deserves special mention. Sub-prime refers to loans to higher risk borrowers – those who are not prime borrowers. Mortgage lending to sub-prime lenders grew rapidly from around $200bn in mid-2003 to more than $500bn by mid-2004, peaking at around $600bn in 2005–6. At this time, sub-prime mortgages accounted for about 20% of all new US residential mortgages.

The attraction of sub-prime mortgage lending for banks was that it offered higher interest rates than prime mortgages – typically 2% more than fixed rate prime lending. In the low-interest-rate environment, this was attractive, and banks used securitization techniques to finance this lending. The use of sub-prime loans in the underlying collateral allowed MBS and collateralized debt obligation (CDO) packagers to enhance their profit margins while offering competitive returns on their securitizations.

Sub-prime loans therefore proved extremely attractive both as candidates for securitization and as investments. In addition, securitization became a major profit source for financial intermediaries and came to be viewed as an indispensable source of yield enhancement for many asset managers. By 2006, around 81% of sub-prime mortgages had been securitized. When sub-prime mortgage borrowers began to default due (mainly) to a decline in property prices, the securitization business of such loans collapsed and fuelled the credit crisis.

Modern Securitization Business

We have explained the origins of the securitization process in the US and the importance of the GSEs in the process. However, GSEs did not originate mortgages; they purchased these from banks that acted as originators, packaged them together and sold them on to other investors (or invested in the MBS themselves). In general, securitization relates to the pooling of credit-risky assets, traditionally residential mortgage loans (but nowadays other types of credit such as car loans, credit card receivables or any credit generating some form of predictable cash flow), and their subsequent sale to a special purpose vehicle (SPV), which then issues securities to finance the purchase of the assets. The securities issued by the SPV are usually fixed-income instruments – known as MBS if backed by mortgages, or asset-backed securities (ABS) if backed by a variety of different types of loans – which are then sold to investors where the principal and interest depend on the cash flows produced by the pool of underlying financial assets. Figure 10.1 shows this process.

Box 10.1 highlights the main features of the process and draws on the exposition presented by Berger et al. (2012).

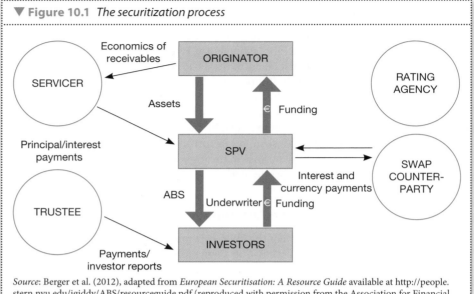

▼ **Figure 10.1** *The securitization process*

Source: Berger et al. (2012), adapted from *European Securitisation: A Resource Guide* available at http://people. stern.nyu.edu/igiddy/ABS/resourceguide.pdf (reproduced with permission from the Association for Financial Markets in Europe).

BOX 10.1

Stages of the Securitization Process

The main stages of the securitization process are as follows:

- *Stage 1:* The originator makes the mortgage (or other types of) loans.
- *Stage 2:* The SPV buys the mortgages (or other loans) from the originator in what is known as a 'true sale'. (Note that many large banks created their own SPVs for this purpose.) The 'true sale' aims to guarantee the separation or 'remoteness' of the cash flows from the underlying assets (mortgages or other loans that have been acquired) from the solvency of the originator. More simply, if the bank that made the loans becomes insolvent, then the SPV remains (in theory) legally separate, and the loans that have been purchased are protected. The SPV usually has no other function apart from holding the purchased underlying assets and issuing securities backed by the pool of assets (mortgages or other loans) being held. This structure reduces the likelihood of the SPV being placed into bankruptcy.
- *Stage 3:* The cash received from investors who buy the (credit rated) securities issued by the SPV is then passed back on to the originator via the SPV.
- *Stage 4:* The SPV also appoints a servicer to collect interest and principal payments on the underlying loans.
- *Stage 5:* Two other key parties to the transaction are, first, the swap counter-party (normally any interest rate risk or currency risk associated with the pool of underlying assets is hedged (or reduced) using a variety of swap transactions). The second party is the trustee who performs the function of ensuring that money is transferred from the servicer to the SPV and that investors are paid in accordance with the promised priority (investors in the ABS or MBS are paid at

different times, different rates and in accordance with varying rules, depending on how the securities being backed by the assets are 'sliced and diced' – different tranches of assets back different securities from low risk to high risk, as explained below).

All this seems rather complicated (and it can be), but one must remember that a critical feature is that if the originator (bank making the loans) goes bust, there is no recourse to the collateral (underlying assets) held by the SPV, and the servicer continues to ensure that payments on the underlying assets continue to be made and that investors who have bought the securities from the SPV still receive interest and principal payments.

So (in theory), investors do not have to worry about the risks the bank is taking in its lending activity, all they have to worry about is the credit quality of the underlying assets held in the SPV – and because the regulators in the US and elsewhere classified such SPVs as 'bankruptcy remote', they were viewed as legal structures that held low-risk pools of diversified mortgages (or loans) and, as such, were seen to be corporate structures containing high-quality, low-risk collateral.

Another important feature, illustrated in stage 3 of the process, is that most securities issued by SPVs were rated by credit rating agencies – S&P, Moody's and Fitch.

Credit rating agencies evaluate the credit risk of financial instruments issued by companies (as well as governments and other public bodies).

The higher the credit (default) risk associated with a security, the lower the rating, and investors will demand higher returns to hold such instruments.

S & P's credit rating scale rates the lowest risk and therefore highest quality investments as AAA. The credit rating ranges from the aforementioned excellent rating down to poor – AAA, AA, A, BBB, BB, B, CCC, CC, C, D. Anything lower than a BBB rating is regarded as high risk, referred to as 'speculative grade' or a junk bond.

So as to assure investors that the ABS or MBS are of a high quality, the SPVs required the credit rating agencies to rate these securities to reflect the credit risks of the pool of assets backing these securities. Although the credit quality of individual loans in the underlying pool of assets may be low, the credit quality (and therefore the credit rating) of the overall portfolio held in the SPV can be increased by pooling the portfolio of credit-risky assets so as to gain various diversification benefits.

Risks of the portfolio can further be improved by various credit enhancement techniques such as third-party guarantees (insurance cover to protect the value of assets), overcollateralization (holding a larger pool of assets than securities issued) and by something known as 'excess spread' (originators, namely banks, inject cash into the SPV that will bear certain early losses). All these practices, getting the ABS or MBS rated and the various credit enhancement techniques, were put in place to increase the attractiveness of the securities issued to investors.

Another important feature relates to the 'tranching' of the liabilities of the SPV so that different types of securities with varying risk and maturity features can be offered to meet varying investor demands. In its simplest form, securities issued by the SPV can be broken down into three main 'tranches', and these have different risk/return features: the senior tranche (least risky with the highest credit ratings, typically AAA and AA), the mezzanine tranche (usually rated BBB and below), and the unrated equity tranche.

In reality, the number of tranches is normally much more than three, and senior tranches can be broken down into further tranchettes (sub-tranches) that usually have the same credit rating, but different maturity dates. An important feature of the tranching process is that though all tranches are backed by the same pool of assets, if some of these go bad (default), there is a 'cascade' of payments, with the highest risk tranche – the equity tranche – the first to suffer losses. If losses are so great that they exceed the value of the equity tranche, the mezzanine tranche suffers losses and then the senior tranche. All income paid out from the pool of underlying assets first goes to the senior tranche (investors); then the mezzanine; and then, if funds are left over, to the equity tranche.

Because of the high-risk nature of the equity tranche, traditionally the originators (banks) would hold part of this on their balance sheet – again to enhance the credit risk of the underlying pool of assets. It also maintains the incentive for originators to continue to monitor the credit quality of borrowers. However, in recent years, the equity tranche securities have increasingly been sold on to speculative investors such as hedge funds. As such, originators (banks) have had less incentive to monitor the credit quality of borrowers after the loans have been made because all the risks have been passed onto investors (via the SPV) in the form of securitized assets (MBS and ABS).

Typically, the pools of loans held by SPVs, as in the case of the US GSEs, comprised a large number of relatively small mortgage loans. More recently, the structures include a much broader array of credits including car loans, student loans, credit card payments, and other assets. Although credit enhancement techniques have been used to reduce the default risks of the underlying assets, this still does not make these assets immune from major shocks – such as major macroeconomic risks like a collapse of the property market or economy.

From early to mid-2007, a wave of defaults accumulated in the US sub-prime mortgage market, and property prices began to fall. As we noted earlier, 80% or so of sub-prime mortgages had been securitized, packaged with higher quality mortgages, credit enhanced and placed in SPVs that issued various tranches of securities backed by the aforementioned collateral. As the value of the collateral declined, investors realized that their investments were rapidly evaporating. Also, the complexity of the structures meant that it became well-nigh impossible to value the securities, as it was also virtually impossible to accurately value the underlying collateral. Securities that had been rated as low risk and investment grade by the rating agencies became speculative and even unsaleable. This prompted the meltdown in the sub-prime (and other) mortgage-backed securities markets. Banks stopped lending to each other because they did not know each other's exposure to securitized assets held on and off their books. The interbank market dried up, and central banks had to inject short-term funding into the markets by the end of 2007. The situation was made more complex by a new wave of securitization that had occurred, as explained below.

Securitizing the Securitizations: Recent Developments

The creation of securities known as CDOs (collateralized debt obligations) formed a new wave in the securitization process. CDO issuers purchased different tranches of MBS and pooled them together with other ABS (backed by car loans, student loans, credit card payments and other assets). They were tranched in a similar fashion as noted above: 'senior' CDOs were backed by highly rated MBS and other ABS, whereas 'mezzanine' tranches pooled together a higher proportion of junior tranches. In contrast to an MBS, where the underlying pool of assets was actual mortgages, in the case of CDOs, the assets were the securities that received mortgage payments. CDOs, therefore, can be viewed as resecuritized securities. Once the pool of ABS and MBS were pooled, these could then be tranched, and CDO securities could be issued via SPVs with varying risk/return and maturity profiles. CDOs have been constructed with a variety of assets and have earned different titles, including these:

- Corporate bonds – collateralized bond obligations (CBOs)
- Corporate/leveraged loans – collateralized loan obligations (CLOs)
- BBB ABS – mezzanine CDO
- Tranches of other CDOs – CDO squared

Rating agencies were actively engaged in rating the tranches of CDOs and similar securities, and issuers used credit enhancement techniques to lower the credit risk associated with the various tranches to make them more attractive to investors. The size of US CDO issuance amounted to $300bn in 2007. The creation of CDOs – or the further securitization of already securitized assets (ABS and MBS) – made it even more difficult to evaluate the risk and prices of these instruments when the sub-prime market collapsed. During 2007, many high-grade CDOs suffered losses, reflecting the mirage associated with the high credit rating of these instruments.

Another important securitized product is asset-backed commercial paper (ABCP). ABCP is (to a certain extent) similar to traditional ABS, as it uses a variety of ABS funded by the issue of commercial paper. Typically, ABCP uses short-term debt (with maturities starting from 1 day to several months) to finance a pool of credit assets, such as trade receivables, corporate loans, mortgage loans, CDO tranches or other credit assets obtained from the market, including US sub-prime mortgages. The underlying assets have relatively long maturities compared with the funding liabilities, and as such, ABCP structures have large maturity mismatches (or less formally, specific types of SPVs set up by banks, known as structured investment vehicles (SIVs), issue short-term ABCP to finance the assets in the pool and must continue to roll over the issues). Typically, the originator will provide liquidity support (enhancement and other guarantees) to meet investors' fears about the liquidity mismatch. Many banks (particularly in the US) used this type of structure to hold large pools of medium-term loans in SPVs financed by the issue of short-term paper. They could raise short-term finance at attractive terms to hold higher yielding assets in their SPVs that were not subject to onerous capital requirements, which would have been the case if they had been held on balance sheet. With the onset of the credit crunch, liquidity in the ABCP market collapsed, forcing banks to honour the liquidity guarantees they had made to their SPVs and forcing many banks to take these back onto their balance sheets – bearing massive losses as a consequence. Given that the size of the ABCP market was estimated at $1.4 trillion in 2007, the collapse of this activity had serious implications for bank performance, which we are still experiencing.

The Role of Rating Agencies and Monoline Insurers

Banks' increasing involvement in markets via the securitization process could not have taken place without the role of two important players – credit rating agencies and monoline insurers. Box 10.2 outlines the role of rating agencies in the securitization process.

Many securitization structures also benefited from credit enhancement techniques that reduced the perceived risks of the underlying assets backing the ABS, MBS and/or CDO

BOX 10.2

Role of Credit Rating Agencies (CRAs) in the Securitization Process

Rating agencies were key in boosting the attractiveness of many securitized assets by assigning a rating to the different tranches of securities issued via SPVs (or SIVs). However, the lack of transparency of various securitized assets – particularly CDOs and ABCP – meant that investors became reliant on the ratings as a guide to the risk/return features of these ABS.

The main agencies used complex models to assess the probability of default of the securitized assets and also advised issuers on how to structure the securitized assets (CDOs and the like) so as to minimize funding costs.

Put simply, unlike in the corporate bond and other debt markets (syndicated lending) where issues are passively rated, the agencies actively engaged in advising on the creation of increasingly complex structures from which they earned substantial consulting fees.

Issuers could shop around to get more attractive ratings.

All this resulted in a boom in profits for the credit rating firms – Moody's profits increased threefold between 2002 and 2006 to $750m – mainly as a result of fees from advising on securitization structures.

As we noted earlier, rating agencies have been accused of being too lenient in rating various tranches in securitization transactions (particularly the senior tranches). In addition (and as inferred above), various commentators have made allegations about conflicts of interest arising from the fact that advising and rating securitized assets became a major source of rating agency income, and this may have corrupted their incentives for accurately rating the issuers involved in such structures.

issues. One of the main providers of such enhancement is the so-called monoline insurance companies, major operators being MBIA and Ambac. They emerged in the US in the 1970s, offering insurance to back municipal bonds. The insurance companies had strong balance sheets and sold default insurance to issuers of municipal bonds – the municipalities purchased this insurance to obtain higher credit ratings (typically AAA) on the bonds they were issuing and could therefore borrow at lower cost. Monoline insurers earned fees for their services.

Over time, monoline insurers expanded their activities into the securitization of MBS and then other ABS and CDOs. At the start of 2008, it was estimated that seven (AAA-rated) monoline insurance companies insured around $100bn in CDOs linked to sub-prime MBS.

Monoline insurers can provide credit enhancements via two main channels, traditional credit insurance and through the use of instruments known as credit default swaps (CDS). A CDS is similar to credit insurance, but there are major regulatory differences between the two. A CDS transaction (like credit insurance) involves a 'protection buyer', for example a CDO bond issuer trying to raise ratings and reduce default risk, and a 'protection seller', a counterparty who receives a fixed-income stream in return for assuming the default risk. CDS are not, however, overseen by any regulatory authority, and therefore there is no guarantee that in the case of default, the seller will have sufficient funds to make full payment.

In general, the purchase of credit protection (either via insurance or CDS) reduces the credit risk of mortgage-backed securities, allowing them to obtain AAA ratings. In addition, the credit insurance was provided at relatively low expense because it was believed that the risks were low. All went well until various asset-backed securities went bust following the start of the sub-prime crisis. When, for instance, a CDO issued by the Swiss bank Credit Suisse defaulted during 2006, virtually all its $341m was wiped out. However, Credit Suisse had bought credit insurance protection from MBIA for its senior tranches (but not mezzanine). Although the mezzanine bondholders lost everything, most AAA holders were reimbursed, as MBIA had to pay $177m to cover the losses. During 2007, the monoline industry made massive losses in the light of the collapse of the sub-prime market and securitized issue business in general. The two top firms posted combined losses of around $4.5bn, and their own AAA ratings were removed. Ambac's rating was reduced to speculative grade by S&P in July 2009, to CC from triple BBB, after it warned that it would report a $2.4bn loss.

As well as monoline insurers, hedge funds and other major insurance companies were active in the credit protection business. The stellar example is probably AIG, which reported that it sold a staggering $446bn in credit insurance, mainly in the form of CDS. By the end of 2008, losses on its CDS book amounted to $30bn and prompted a rescue by the federal authorities in September 2008. Commenting on the AIG collapse in March 2009, Mark McKissick of Denver Investment Advisors stated: 'People took risks, which the market never fully reflected in prices, and then looked the other way . . . The whole CDS market was part of the bubble.'

The Impact of Securitization and Its Future

The growth in securitization activity has increased the linkages between banks and markets. It has also created a complex web of interlinkages between banks and the shadow banking system – hedge funds, investment companies, money market funds, SPVs and so on, firms that do banking-linked business but are not subject to traditional or as tough regulation. From a positive perspective, the securitization trend offers the potential for banks to manage their balance sheets more effectively and to move risks to those most willing to bear it. This can result in a more efficient use of capital resources and a better allocation of risks in the system overall. It also enabled banks and other financial intermediaries to generate extra revenue and therefore helped boost financial performance. Although securitization, well managed and appropriately overseen, can offer such benefits, we know since the advent of the sub-prime crisis that there is a serious negative downside to such activity.

The written testimony of US Treasury Secretary Timothy F. Geithner, before the House Financial Services Committee on 23 July 2009, summarizes what went wrong and notes areas for further regulations:

> Loan originators failed to require sufficient documentation of income and ability to pay. Securitizers failed to set high standards for the loans they were willing to buy, encouraging underwriting standards to sag. Investors were overly reliant on credit rating agencies, whose procedures proved no match for the complexity of the instruments they were rating. In each case, lack of transparency prevented market participants from understanding the full nature of the risks they were taking. In response, the President's plan requires securitization sponsors to retain 5 percent of the credit risk of securitized exposures; it requires transparency of loan level data and standardization of data formats to better enable investor due diligence and market discipline; and, with respect to credit

rating agencies, it ends the practice of allowing them to provide consulting services to the same companies they rate, requires these agencies to differentiate between structure and other products, and requires disclosure of any 'ratings shopping' by issuers.

Box 10.3 highlights the regulations imposed on credit rating agencies (CRAs) since the crisis, in response to the criticism outlined by Timothy Geithner above.

BOX 10.3

Regulation of Credit Rating Agencies (CRAs) in Europe and the US

Europe

In June 2013, new EU rules came into force, aiming to improve the way in which credit rating agencies (CRAs) operate in the following ways:

1. Reduce financial market overreliance on credit ratings.

In line with our G20 commitments, the new EU rules will reduce reliance on external ratings, requiring financial institutions to strengthen their own credit risk assessment and not to rely solely and mechanistically on external credit ratings. European Supervisory Authorities should also avoid references to external credit ratings and will be required to review their rules and guidelines and where appropriate, remove credit ratings where they have the potential to create mechanistic effects. The regulatory package also contains a Directive introducing the principle to reduce reliance on external ratings in sectoral legislation for collective investment funds (UCITS), alternative investment fund managers (AIFMD) and institutions for retirement provision.

2. Improve quality of ratings of sovereign debt of EU Member States.

To avoid market disruption, rating agencies will set up a calendar indicating when they will rate Member States. Such ratings will be limited to three per year for unsolicited sovereign ratings. Derogations remain possible in exceptional circumstances and subject to appropriate explanations. The ratings will only be published on Fridays after close of business and at least 1 hour before the opening of trading venues in the EU. Furthermore, investors and Member States will be informed of the underlying facts and assumptions on each rating which will facilitate a better understanding of credit ratings of Member States.

3. Credit rating agencies will be more accountable for their actions.

The new rules will make rating agencies more accountable for their actions, as ratings are not just simple opinions. Therefore, the new rules ensure that a rating agency can be held liable in case it infringes intentionally or with gross negligence the CRA Regulation, thereby causing damage to an investor or an issuer.

4. Reduce conflicts of interests due to the issuer pays remuneration model.

The Regulation will improve the independence of credit rating agencies and help eliminate conflicts of interest by introducing mandatory rotation for certain complex structured financial instruments (re-securitizations). There are also limitations as regards the shareholding of rating agencies. To mitigate the risk of conflicts of interest, the new rules will require CRAs to disclose publicly if a shareholder with 5% or more of the capital or voting rights of the concerned CRA holds 5% or more of a rated entity, and would prohibit a CRA from rating when a shareholder of a CRA with 10% or more of the capital or voting rights also holds 10% or more of a rated entity.

To ensure the diversity and independence of credit ratings, the Regulation prohibits ownership of 5% or more of the capital or the voting rights in more than one CRA, unless the agencies concerned belong to the same group (cross-shareholding).

5. Publication of ratings on a European Rating Platform

All available ratings will be published on a European Rating Platform, available as from June 2015. This will improve the comparability and visibility of ratings of financial instruments rated by rating agencies registered and authorized in the EU. This should also help investors to make their own credit risk assessment and contribute to more diversity in the rating industry.

As part of the package, the Commission will also review the situation in the rating market and report to the European Parliament and the Council on the appropriateness of the development of a special European system for creditworthiness assessments of sovereign debt. By 31 December 2016, the Commission should submit a report to the European Parliament and to the Council on the appropriateness and feasibility of supporting a European credit rating agency dedicated to assessing the creditworthiness of Member States' sovereign debt and/or a European credit rating foundation for all other credit ratings.

United States

The Dodd-Frank Wall Street Reform and Consumer Protection Act of 2010 introduced a number of requirements on credit rating agencies (CRAs); in particular, it set up a new Office of Credit Ratings, based in the Securities and Exchange Commission (SEC) which opened in 2012, whose aim it is to provide greater regulatory oversight of the sector. Other recent rules on rating agencies cover:

- Annual reports on internal controls
- Conflicts of interest with respect to sales and marketing practices
- Fines and penalties
- Disclosure of performance statistics
- Application and disclosure of credit rating methodologies
- Form disclosure of data and assumptions underlying credit ratings
- Disclosure about third party due diligence
- Analyst training and testing
- Consistent application of rating symbols and definitions
- Specific and additional disclosure for ratings related to ABS products

In August 2014, the SEC adopted new rules on internal controls over the ratings process, transparency of ratings performance, steps to be followed when adopting or revising credit ratings procedures and methodologies, and a requirement for third parties retained for the purpose of conducting due diligence related to asset-backed securities to provide a certification containing specified information justifying the rating of ABS. It also adopted standards for rating analysts, rules regarding ratings symbols.

Source: SEC (2014) Press Release, http://www.sec.gov/News/PressRelease/Detail/PressRelease/1370542776658.

EC (2013) Press Release http://europa.eu/rapid/press-release_IP-13-555_en.htm?locale=en.

Since the collapse of the sub-prime lending market, the securitization business has collapsed, and banks that were heavily engaged in this activity (both issuing and investing in CDOs and other ABS on their own account) have experienced major losses, if not failure. At the end of 2008, Bloomberg reported that bank losses stemming from the meltdown in the US sub-prime market amounted to $744.6bn – Wachovia had the biggest loss of $96.5bn, followed by Citigroup with $67.2bn and Merrill Lynch with $55.9 bn.

The major losses faced by banks involved in securitization activity have been a key feature of the global financial sector collapse. Subsequently, both US and European regulators have announced plans to limit securitization activity.

CREDIT CRISIS IN THE US

The US banking system has been traumatized since the onset of the credit crisis, which started with the demise of the sub-prime mortgage lending market and the loss of value of the loans and securities underpinning this business. The issuance of sub-prime and other mortgage loan–backed products (otherwise known as 'structured credit products') grew from around $150bn in 2000 to around $1.2 trillion by 2007. As we have already explained, everything rested on the belief that (despite the complexity of the products) they were backed by good collateral (mainly property values) and as there had been a boom in property prices over the period, even high-risk mortgage lending seemed relatively immune. So far, so good. Up until mid-2007, the demand for these structured credit products boomed. Investors were attracted because they appeared to offer higher returns than equivalently rated alternative investments. Banks were attracted to the business, as it allowed them to reduce the amount of capital they had to hold for regulatory purposes, and rather than holding onto the credit risk, they could sell these risks on to investors. The whole process was generally viewed as beneficial, as it allowed greater risk to be shared across a broader spectrum of investors.

At the top of the US credit cycle in 2006, around 20% of US mortgage originations were sub-prime, and 75% of these were securitized, of which 80% were funded by AAA-rated paper. When foreclosures and defaults on US sub-prime mortgages accelerated from late 2006 onwards, the value of the securities backed by such assets rapidly declined, particularly because the complex nature of their structures and lack of transparency of the bank's off-balance sheet vehicles made it almost impossible to value such assets. Holders of investments backed by sub-prime mortgages did not know what they were worth, and banks stopped lending to each other because they also did not know the extent of losses held by other banks in their off-balance sheet (structured credit) vehicles. When property prices crashed in the US, causing prime and sub-prime borrowers to increasingly default, this put further downward pressure on the value of securitized mortgage products and bank loan books. This resulted in a liquidity gridlock in interbank markets and the subsequent 'credit crunch'. Key events in the US credit crisis are shown in Table 10.3.

The US response to the crisis has been unprecedented in recent banking history. Although some of the government actions noted in Table 10.3 appear complex, it is important to remember that the actions are designed to do three main things. The Term Auction Facility (TAF) was designed to pump liquidity back into banks to free up interbank lending. The Troubled Asset Relief Program (TARP) and the later Term Asset-backed Securities Loan Facility aimed to remove bad or doubtful assets from bank balance sheets (or off-balance sheet) so as to strengthen their financial position – indirectly helping them

▼ **Table 10.3** *US credit crisis: Key events*

Dec. 2007	The Federal Reserve introduced the Term Auction Facility (TAF). This was a temporary programme managed by the Federal Reserve aimed to 'address elevated pressures in short-term funding markets'. Under the TAF, the authorities auction collateralized loans with terms of 28 and 84 days to depository institutions that are 'in generally sound financial condition' and 'are expected to remain so over the terms of TAF loans'. Eligible collateral included a variety of financial assets. The programme aimed to help banks raise short-term funds due to gridlock in interbank markets. (The initial programme envisaged $20bn of loans under the TAF, but this ballooned – $1.6 trillion in loans to banks were made for various types of collateral under the TAF by November 2008).
Mar. 2008	Bear Stearns became the largest casualty of the 'credit crunch' to that date when the failing investment bank was purchased by JPMorgan Chase for a nominal amount ($2 per share, or $236m) following the provisions of earlier liquidity support (a revised offer of $10 per share was made on 24 March, enabling JPMorgan Chase to acquire 39.5% of Bear Stearns). In addition, the Federal Reserve extended the safety net arrangement to ensure that JPMorgan Chase would not suffer significant losses on loans extended to Bear Stearns.
June 2008	The FDIC took over IndyMac Bank, a large alt-A mortgage lender (alt-A mortgages are considered riskier than 'prime' and less risky than 'sub-prime', and often do not require income verification of the borrower) that suffered large losses on these mortgages. The bank had $32bn in assets, making it the second largest bank failure in US history. The estimated cost of the failure at the time of this writing is $8.9bn. The takeover followed a slow run, or 'walk', on the bank of $1.3bn in deposits withdrawn between 27 June and 10 July. This followed a public warning about the bank from Senator Charles Schumer. At the same time, Fannie Mae and Freddie Mac, who hold or guarantee over $5 trillion in US mortgages (about half of the total), were having their own problems of a 'walk' on their outstanding stock and shares, both of which declined by more than 80% in value from a year earlier.
July 2008	Treasury Secretary Henry Paulson announced a plan to ensure that Fannie Mae and Freddie Mac would continue to support the housing market. This consisted of a proposal that the Treasury would temporarily increase its credit lines to the organizations, that they could borrow from the Federal Reserve under certain circumstances, and that the Treasury would get temporary authority to buy their shares should that be necessary.
Sept. 2008	Freddie Mac and Fannie Mae were placed into conservatorship of the Federal Housing Finance Agency.
Sept. 2008	Lehman Brothers collapsed, and Merrill Lynch was sold to the Bank of America. The two remaining large investment banks, Goldman Sachs and Morgan Stanley, converted into commercial banks. AIG, the world's largest insurance company, was rescued by the Federal Reserve courtesy of an $85bn emergency loan, and in exchange, the federal government acquired a 79.9% equity stake. Washington Mutual was acquired by the US Office of Thrift Supervision and the bulk of its untroubled assets sold to JPMorgan Chase.
Oct. 2008	The Fed announced that it was to expand the collateral it would lend against to include commercial paper, to help address ongoing liquidity concerns.
Nov. 2008	Citigroup failed and was rescued by the US government. In a complex deal, the US government announced it was purchasing $27bn of preferred stock in Citigroup and warrants on 4.5% of its common stock. The preferred stock carried an 8% dividend. This acquisition followed an earlier purchase of $25bn of the same preferred stock using Troubled Asset Relief Program (TARP) Funds. The TARP was a plan under which the US Treasury would acquire up to $700bn worth of MBS. After various revisions, the plan was introduced on 20 September 2008 by US Treasury Secretary Henry Paulson. Under the agreement, Citigroup and regulators would support up to $306bn of mainly residential and commercial property loans and certain other assets, which would remain on the bank's balance sheet. Citigroup would bear losses on the first $29bn.
Nov. 2008	The Federal Reserve announced the $200bn Term Asset-backed Securities Loan Facility – a programme supported by the issuance of ABS collateralized by loans related to autos, credit cards, education, and small businesses. In the same month, the Federal Reserve also announced a $600bn programme to purchase MBS of government-sponsored enterprises (such as Freddie Mac and Fannie Mae) in a move aimed at reducing mortgage rates.

▼ **Table 10.3** *US credit crisis: Key events (continued)*

Feb. 2009	The US authorities present plans for new comprehensive measures in support of the financial sector, including a Public-Private Investment Program (PPIP) of up to $1 trillion to purchase troubled assets.
Mar. 2009	The US Federal Reserve announces plans for purchases of up to $300bn of longer term Treasury securities over a period of 6 months and increases the maximum amounts for planned purchases of US agency-related securities. The US Treasury provides details on the PPIP proposed in February.
Apr. 2009	The US Federal Open Market Committee authorizes new temporary reciprocal foreign currency liquidity swap lines with the Bank of England, ECB, Bank of Japan and Swiss National Bank. The US Federal Reserve releases details on the stress tests conducted to assess the financial soundness of the 19 largest US financial institutions, declaring that most banks currently have capital levels well in excess of the amount required for them to remain well capitalized.

Sources: Adapted from Berger et al. (2014); BIS (2009), p. 19.

to boost their soundness (capital strength) and also hopefully provide greater confidence in the system so as to encourage lending. By July 2009, the US Treasury had announced that out of the $700bn earmarked for TARP, banks held $178bn, and the major insurer AIG (alone) had been given $69.8bn. (In fact, the US auto industry had also dipped into TARP for the princely sum of $85bn.)

Direct injections of capital, such as in the Citigroup and AIG cases, effectively nationalized these institutions – so that they could continue to operate. One can see that these momentous government actions were needed to restore the lifeblood of banks – liquidity and capital. Without sufficient liquidity, banks cannot meet their short-term obligations, and without the appropriate level of capital, they become insolvent (or bankrupt). All these actions by the US government (and similar drastic action in the UK and throughout Europe) sought to inject liquidity and capital into the systems to stave off imminent collapse.

The passing of the US Dodd-Frank Wall Street Reform and Consumer Protection Act in July 2010, the biggest financial reform in the US since the Great Depression, is a good reflection of the international trend in re-regulation since the crisis (which was discussed in detail in Chapter 6). To recall, the Act overhauls the current system of regulation and supervision to improve disclosure, transparency and the safety and soundness of the financial system. The Act accomplished the following aims:

- Established a Financial Stability Oversight Council
- Instituted new measures to deal with SIFIs
- Created a Consumer Financial Protection Bureau
- Reformed the Federal Reserve
- Improved transparency in derivatives
- Introduced new rules on executive pay and credit rating agencies

The aim of the Financial Stability Oversight Council is to identify and address systemic risks posed by large, complex companies, products and activities before they threaten the stability of the economy. Council membership comprises 10 financial regulators, one independent member and five non-voting members, and it is chaired by the Treasury secretary. Its key responsibilities are to recommend tougher capital, liquidity and risk management when banks get 'too big'. By a two-thirds vote, the council can require SIFIS (banks and non-banks) to be regulated by the Federal Reserve. It is anticipated that around 35 SIFIs will be regulated by the Federal Reserve, including all banking organizations with over $50bn in assets. Also (based on a two-thirds vote), the Federal Reserve can break up complex financial intermediaries that impose 'grave' systemic threat to the system. Finally, a broad overall goal is to monitor risk in the financial system.

The Dodd-Frank Act clearly states that 'taxpayers will not be on the hook', and the FDIC is prohibited from losing money on SIFIs. The so-called Volcker Rule was introduced that prohibits banks from proprietary trading and limits investments in hedge funds/private equity fund sponsorship to 3% of capital. SIFIs will have to provide 'living wills' – their plans for rapid and orderly shutdown in case of bankruptcy. The Act also creates orderly liquidation mechanisms for the FDIC to unwind failing systemically significant companies.

The new Consumer Financial Protection Bureau, housed at the Federal Reserve, has the authority to ensure that American consumers get the clear, accurate information they need to shop for mortgages, credit cards and other financial products, and to protect them from hidden fees, abusive terms and deceptive practices. It will have examiner authority over banks and credit unions with over $10bn of assets, mortgage brokers, payday lenders and others, although oversight excludes auto dealers.

Emergency lending powers of the Federal Reserve (established in 1932 under Section 13(3) of the Federal Reserve Act) give it authority to lend to non-depository institutions (investment banks, insurers) in 'unusual and exigent circumstances'. Dodd-Frank now makes this lending conditional on approval from the secretary of the Treasury. The Federal Reserve will have to disclose all its 13(3) lending details and will be subject to a one-time Government Accountability Office (GAO) audit of emergency lending. A new post of the Federal Reserve, Vice Chairman for Supervision, will be created and the GAO will also examine governance issues and how directors are appointed.

The Act forces most derivatives trading onto central clearing houses and exchange trading. Regulators and exchanges are to determine what should be exchange traded. Exchange-traded derivatives are more transparent than their OTC counterparts, and the credit risks shift to the exchange. In addition, a new Office of Credit Ratings was set up within the SEC (in 2012) to examine rating agencies, and investors will be allowed to sue agencies for 'knowing and reckless' behaviour. Shareholders are to have more say in pay and golden parachutes, and banking organizations must publish the ratio of CEO compensation to average worker compensation. There will be provisions for compensation clawback if financial performance/projections are found to be inaccurate.

Finally, other reforms encompassed in Dodd-Frank are

- the abolition of the Office of Thrift Supervision – thrifts will now be regulated by the Office of the Comptroller of the Currency;
- to require the Fed to examine non-bank financial services holding companies;
- to repeal the prohibition on paying interest on business checking accounts;
- to establish a new Federal Insurance Office to oversee the insurance industry;
- to provide more financial resources to the SEC;
- to permanently increase deposit insurance to $250,000;
- to force securitizers of risky mortgages to have 'skin in the game' (a minimum of 5%);
- to establish that lenders must ensure that borrowers can repay home loans by verifying income, credit history and job status – no more 'liar loans'; and
- to place restrictions on consumer payment fees and swipe fees for debit cards – expected to cost the banking industry billions of dollars.

As can be seen, the Act is likely to radically reform the way in which the US banking system is regulated, with greater restrictions on the type of activities banks can undertake and a continued pressure to bolster capital and liquidity strength with an end (in theory at least) to taxpayer bailouts. A main criticism of the legislation is that 'bolder action' should have been taken to streamline/consolidate the labyrinthine US regulatory structures. By mid-2014, according to *USA Today*, only 40–50% of Dodd-Frank had been incorporated into US law.

CREDIT CRISIS IN EUROPE

United Kingdom

The retail bank Northern Rock was the first major UK casualty of the financial crisis. On 13 September 2007, Northern Rock announced that it had received emergency financial support from the Bank of England. Following a run on Northern Rock's high-street branches, on 17 September, the UK government announced a full guarantee of the bank's retail deposits. On 1 October, the UK authorities strengthened the deposit guarantee scheme by eliminating a provision whereby deposits between £2,000 and £35,000 were only 90% guaranteed. On 17 February 2008, having finally exhausted attempts to find a private sector buyer, the nationalization of Northern Rock was announced. On 21 February, new provisions were announced for faster intervention in cases of imminent bank failure, in recognition that the authorities' powers to intervene had been inadequate in September 2007. The underlying causes of the Northern Rock failure included overaggressive growth in mortgage lending, overdependence on short-term wholesale funding, and regulatory failure.

In April 2008, the Bank of England announced a 'special liquidity scheme', to allow banks to temporarily swap high-quality mortgage-backed and other securities for Treasury bills. Swaps for up to 3 years, to the value of £50bn, would be available. Although the monetary authorities attempted to inject liquidity into the banking system, several major write-downs of non-performing assets were announced. In April, Royal Bank of Scotland (RBS) announced plans for a £12bn rights issue. In July, Barclays announced that only 18% of the shares in a £4.5bn rights issue had been taken up, and HBOS similarly announced that only 8% of a £4bn rights issue had been taken up.

On 17 September 2008, Lloyds TSB announced that it was to acquire HBOS for £12bn, creating the Lloyds Banking Group, with a market share of around one-third in the UK savings and mortgage markets. The UK competition authorities deemed that the aim of preventing the collapse of HBOS overrode any competition policy concerns. On 29 September, after several months of uncertainty and a sharply declining share price, the UK government announced its acquisition of the mortgage-lending arm of Bradford & Bingley. The still-viable depositor base and branch network were sold to the Spanish Santander Group. On 6 October, the UK government lifted the ceiling on the deposit guarantee scheme from £35,000 to £50,000, and on 8 October, a blanket guarantee was announced for UK retail deposits in Icesave, the Internet banking arm of the failed Icelandic bank Landsbanki.

In October 2008, the UK government announced the creation of a £50bn fund for the recapitalization of ailing banks. The mechanics would involve government purchase of preference shares. At the same time, the special liquidity scheme was extended, making available on demand T-bills to the value of at least £200bn, to be swapped for illiquid, high-quality securitized assets. Treasury guarantees would be provided on commercial terms for up to £250bn of wholesale funding. On 13 October, capital injections were announced for RBS (£20bn), and Lloyds (£17bn), increasing the public ownership stakes in these banks to around 60% and 40%, respectively. In return, commitments were made to lend at competitive rates to homeowners and small businesses, reschedule mortgage payments for homeowners facing difficulties, and exercise restraint over executive compensation.

Loan guarantees of up to £20bn to small and medium-sized firms were announced in January 2009, along with further measures to restore confidence, including

- an extension of the credit guarantee scheme;
- a new facility for asset-backed securities to be used as collateral for banks seeking funds to support mortgage lending;
- extended provisions for banks to swap illiquid assets for T-bills (replacing the special liquidity scheme);
- a new Bank of England facility for purchasing up to £50bn of high-quality assets; and
- a new capital and asset protection scheme for selected eligible bank assets.

In February 2009, a permanent 'special resolution regime' was established, to strengthen provisions for intervention in the case of banks facing financial difficulties. Details of recourse to the capital and asset protection scheme by RBS and Lloyds were unveiled soon afterwards. RBS would participate in respect of £325bn of assets, in exchange for a fee of £6.5bn. The Treasury also agreed to acquire a £13bn equity stake, with an option for a further £6bn. Exercise of this option would leave 95% of RBS in public ownership. Lloyds announced subsequently that it had agreed to participate in respect of £260bn of assets, increasing its public ownership stake from 43% to 65%.

By the summer of 2009, RBS was 70% owned by the state and 43% by Lloyds Group (by the end of March 2014, they were 80% and 25%, respectively). HSBC and Barclays had not dipped into the government pot for financial support and appeared to have fared better in weathering the financial storm. It is not surprising to find out that these two UK banks have many more international activities than their two aforementioned competitors. Typically, UK banks that had significant activities outside the UK have fared better than those with business concentrated in the UK. Standard Chartered stands out as a star performer – only 5% of its revenues originate in the UK.

As a response to the aftermath of the crises, the UK government set up an Independent Banking Commission (known as the Vickers Commission after its chairman, Sir John Vickers) to consider structural and related non-structural reforms to the UK banking sector to promote financial stability and competition (see Chapter 6). On 12 September 2011, the Vickers Commission published its Final Report, setting out some possible reforms:

- Retail banking activity is to be ring-fenced from wholesale and investment banking.
- Different arms of the same bank should have separate legal entities with their own boards of directors.
- SIFIs and large UK retail banking operations should have a minimum 10% equity/ assets ratio.
- Contingent capital and debt should be available to improve loss absorbency in the future.
- Risk management should become a self-contained, less complex business for retail banking, but remain complex for wholesale/investment banking.

The cost of these reforms to the UK economy is likely to range between £1bn and £3bn per annum, which compares favourably with the estimated annual cost (of £40bn) of lost output that follows financial crises. If adopted, the aim is to implement the proposed reforms by 2019.

Switzerland

By international standards, the Swiss banking sector is large. In 2007, the ratio of total banking sector assets to GDP was 9.2 for Switzerland (although this had fallen to around 4.5 by 2013). The corresponding ratios for France, Germany, Italy and the UK were 3.1, 2.9, 1.6 and 3.6, respectively. Swiss banking is dominated by UBS and Credit Suisse, both of which provide services in investment banking, private banking and asset management. The large relative size of the banking sector reflects Switzerland's importance as an offshore banking centre and capital of the global private banking market. UBS and Credit Suisse are less dominant in their domestic market, with a combined market share of around one-third. The rest of the Swiss banking sector comprises the semi-governmental cantonal banks, the Raiffeisen Group consisting of a large network of local cooperative banks, and a number of regional banks specializing in lending and deposit business.

Offshore assets held by Swiss private banks were valued at $2 trillion in 2008. A reputation for competence and discretion has been essential in attracting business from overseas clients. As part of the fallout from the credit crisis, however, the culture of secrecy that pervades offshore banking centres, including Switzerland, has become increasingly subject to critical scrutiny. Concerns have been raised in the US and elsewhere that the balance struck between client privacy and matters of public interest leans too heavily towards the former, and that offshore banking centres offer safe havens for some clients with dubious motives, such as tax evasion, avoidance of divorce settlements, or criminal activities.

Having invested heavily in US mortgage-backed securities during the run-up to the credit crisis, an area in which it had previously lagged, UBS has experienced heavy losses subsequently. Following a series of smaller write-down announcements, in April 2008, UBS announced a further write-down of SFr19bn on its mortgage investments. A SFr15bn capital injection, underwritten by a syndicate of banks, was accompanied by the departure of UBS's chairman. In October 2008, the Swiss government injected SFr6bn into UBS through a convertible bond issue, giving the government an eventual ownership stake of up to 9.3%. At the same time, SFr60bn of troubled UBS assets were transferred into a new fund, managed and 90% funded by the Swiss National Bank, with UBS providing the remaining 10% funding. By the end of 2008, UBS had posted almost SFr50bn in write-downs and losses, more than any other European bank. Credit Suisse's sub-prime exposure was less extreme than that of UBS. However, in October 2008, Credit Suisse was obliged to raise SFr10bn through the sale of assets including Treasury shares and convertible bonds, representing about 12% of the bank assets when the bonds convert to shares.

UBS has suffered considerable reputational damage but has also drawn some praise for taking steps towards recovery faster and more decisively than many other European banks. UBS started to recapitalize relatively early, while some private finance was still available. The transfer of assets into what is effectively a publicly funded bad bank was a decisive step towards cleaning and shrinking UBS's balance sheet. Steps towards internal reorganization include the installation of new leadership, staff cuts, and the separation of the investment banking, private banking and asset management functions into separate divisions. In the future, UBS is committed to focusing primarily on its core asset management specialism.

However, in February 2009, the bank became engulfed in fresh controversy when the US government demanded disclosure of the names of all 52,000 American UBS clients, alleging conspiracy to defraud the US Inland Revenue Service and federal government of tax revenue. UBS's chief executive stepped down from his post 1 week later.

Since 2009–10, Swiss banks have been reducing their exposures to investment banking and continuing to focus more on private banking and wealth management. By the end of 2013, two of the four biggest private banks in the world – UBS with $2 trillion assets under management (Aum) and Credit Suisse with $888bn Aum – were Swiss banks (the other two in the top four are Bank of America, $1.95 trillion; and Morgan Stanley, $1.5 trillion).

Iceland

The collapse of Iceland's banking system in autumn 2008 has been adjudged the largest of all time by the IMF. Following financial deregulation in 2001, Iceland's three major banks, Landsbanki, Kaupthing and Glitnir, developed a business model that circumvented the constraints on growth implied by the small size of the Icelandic economy, by attracting funding from international capital markets. Between 2006 and 2008, Landsbanki and Kaupthing both set up online banking operations offering high-interest Internet accounts to depositors in the UK and the Netherlands via Landsbanki's Icesave brand, and through subsidiaries trading under the Kaupthing Edge brand in nine European countries.

Prior to the banking crisis, Iceland's current account deficit was clearly unsustainable, having reached 25% of GDP in 2006, and 15% in 2007. Between January and September 2008, consumer price inflation was running at around 14%, and domestic interest rates reached 15.5%. Despite a 35% decline in value against the euro during the first 9 months of 2009, the krona was still significantly overvalued, bolstered by short-term capital inflows attracted by the high domestic interest rate. When liquidity in the interbank markets dried up in mid-September 2008 following the liquidation of Lehman Brothers in the US, the Central Bank of Iceland had inadequate reserves to be able to guarantee the banks' debts as lender of last resort. The European Central Bank, the US Federal Reserve, the Bank of England and the three Nordic central banks collectively declined to provide sufficient assistance to avert the imminent crisis.

On 29 September 2008, it was announced that the Icelandic government was to acquire a 75% stake in Glitnir. This part-nationalization was not completed, however, and a few days later Glitnir was placed into receivership. Reports in the *Financial Times* over the weekend of 4–5 October 2008 appear to have triggered a run on savings in Icesave by UK and Dutch online depositors, and Landsbanki was placed into receivership on 7 October. Because Icesave was a branch (not a subsidiary) of Landsbanki, its UK depositors were not protected under UK deposit insurance; however, on 8 October, the UK government froze Landsbanki's UK assets, and announced it would compensate UK retail depositors in full. A number of UK local authorities and other governmental organizations, which had deposited spare funds with Icelandic banks, would not be guaranteed reimbursement. (The full extent of their losses amounted to around £5bn, of which over half had been recovered by the start of 2012.) Meanwhile, on 8 October, the UK's Financial Services Authority placed Kaupthing's UK subsidiary into administration and sold its Internet bank Kaupthing Edge to the Dutch group ING Direct. In Iceland, Kaupthing followed into receivership on 9 October, and over the next few days Kaupthing's other subsidiaries were either wound up or taken into public ownership by the respective national authorities.

With the krona continuing to fall precipitously against the euro, the Icelandic government applied for IMF assistance in late October 2008. In November, the IMF agreed to provide a $2.1bn standby programme over 2 years, supplemented by assistance in the form of loans and currency swaps from the governments of the Nordic countries, Russia, Poland, the UK, the Netherlands and Germany, which brought the headline value of the full package to over $10bn. The terms of the IMF package impose obligations on the Icelandic government in the areas of currency stabilization and inflationary control, bank restructuring and fiscal retrenchment. Icelandic GDP fell by over 10% in 2009, and several years of austerity appear inevitable. The new Icelandic government, elected in April 2009, was committed to applying for full EU membership and adoption of the euro. This was viewed as offering future protection against the exposure that destroyed the Icelandic banking system in 2008, and may alleviate the banks' difficulties in raising short-term foreign funds to cover their foreign debts, although enthusiasm has waned by 2013–14.

Germany

Unlike many European countries, Germany ran a current account surplus during the 2000s and avoided a housing market bubble of the kind experienced in the US, the UK, Spain and Ireland. During the financial crisis, however, German banks have encountered difficulties similar to those experienced elsewhere.

IKB Deutsche Industriebank was one of the first casualties of the credit crisis. In August 2007, Rhineland Funding, the IKB's SIV, called on a €12bn line of credit underwritten by IKB and several other banks. One of these, Deutsche Bank, exercised an option to cancel the commitment. IKB was bailed out by the public development bank KfW (Kreditanstalt für Wiederaufbau). In August 2007, Sachsen LB, a small Landesbank with a large subprime exposure, entered into negotiations that led to its eventual acquisition by the largest Landesbank LBBW (Landesbank Baden-Württemberg), with the first €12bn of losses guaranteed by the Saxony state government. In January 2008, WestLB, a former Landesbank that had converted to a commercial bank in 2002, secured €5bn of loan guarantees from the North Rhine Westphalia state government and a consortium of local banks. Hypo Real Estate, a holding company comprising a number of specialist property finance banks, including the troubled Depfa Bank (a German bank headquartered in Dublin which specialized in financing infrastructure projects), was the most prominent German casualty of the liquidity crisis of autumn 2008. In October, an initial €50bn rescue package was agreed, comprising a €20bn credit line from the Bundesbank and €30bn of support from other German banks. By April 2009, with total government support for Hypo Real Estate having exceeded €100bn, a transfer into public ownership appeared imminent.

In October 2008, the Bundestag issued a policy declaration providing an informal guarantee for all non-banks' bank deposits, and established the Financial Market Stabilization Fund (SoFFin). SoFFin was authorized to provide loan guarantees of up to €400bn for new debt and liabilities incurred up to the end of 2009. There were provisions for the recapitalization of banks up to a normal limit of €10bn per institution. To qualify for capital injections, commitments would be required to curb executive pay and suspend dividends. SoFFin was also authorized to temporarily acquire risk exposures held by banks or their SIVs prior to 13 October 2008 of up to €5bn per institution. And SoFFin was authorized to raise finance of up to €100bn to support these interventions. Commerzbank, Germany's second largest bank, received €18.2bn of support from SoFFin between November 2008 and January 2009, required partly to cover losses emanating from the acquisition by Commerzbank of Dresdner Bank in August 2008.

Spain

Two distinctive features of the Bank of Spain's regulatory approach in the run-up to the crisis have attracted particular scrutiny. The first concerns the dynamic provisioning regime introduced in 2000, requiring banks to harmonize loan loss provisioning with the lending cycle and achieve an accurate accounting recognition of ex ante credit risk. Under dynamic provisioning, the loan loss provision is created at the inception of the loan, reducing the cyclical impact of provisioning, and correcting biases and volatility that would otherwise affect the bank's profit and loss account. The second aspect is the requirement that assets channelled through SIVs are subject to the same capital requirements as on-balance sheet assets. The opportunity for regulatory arbitrage through the creation of SIVs having been blocked, most Spanish banks abstained from creating these off-balance sheet vehicles.

During 2007 and 2008, BBVA and Banco Santander, the two largest Spanish banks, wrote off smaller proportions of their loans portfolios than many of their European competitors. However, a sharp downturn in the Spanish economy in 2008, coinciding with the collapse of the property market, seemed certain to increase non-performing loan ratios and erode capital buffers. Having both made major forays into Latin American markets during the 2000s, BBVA and Santander were susceptible to recessions in several countries in this region in 2008 and 2009. The Spanish government bailout in March 2009 of Caja Castilla La Mancha, a small mutually owned savings bank, raised concerns that the fallout from the property market collapse could yet impact severely on the banking sector. Mortgage lending to households appears to be of lesser concern than lending to builders and property developers, to which Spain's savings banks are heavily exposed. There has been wholesale restructuring of the Spanish savings banks sector up to 2014.

Belgium, the Netherlands and Luxembourg

Bank bailouts in the Benelux countries provide an interesting insight into the resolution of failing cross-border banks, as shown in Box 10.4.

BOX 10.4

Cross-Border Bank Bailouts – Experience from BENELUX countries

Prior to the credit crisis, Fortis Holdings was a large financial services conglomerate based in Belgium, the Netherlands and Luxembourg.

In late September 2008, Fortis's share price plummeted amid rumours of difficulties in raising liquid funds through the interbank markets. On 28 September, it was announced that the three BENELUX governments would acquire stakes in Fortis of €4.7bn, €4bn and €2.5bn, respectively.

On 3 October, however, in the face of Belgian accusations that the Dutch had reneged on their earlier commitment, the Dutch government announced the full €16.8bn acquisition of the Dutch banking and insurance subsidiaries of Fortis. The Dutch government would also acquire the Fortis share of ABN AMRO's retail business.

On 5 October, the press reported that the French bank BNP Paribas would acquire Fortis Bank, with the Belgian and Luxembourg governments reduced to minority shareholder status in exchange for shares in BNP Paribas.

Cross-Border Bank Bailouts – Experience from BENELUX countries (*continued*)

Subsequently, the break-up of Fortis was subject to protracted litigation by disaffected shareholders. The sale of a 75% stake in Fortis Bank to BNP Paribas was eventually approved in April 2009.

The governments of Belgium, Luxembourg and France contributed to a joint €6.4bn recapitalization plan for the Dexia Group, announced on 30 September 2008. Dexia's difficulties appear to have originated in a large loan it had granted to the German-Irish Depfa Bank.

The Belgian government also provided guarantees for new borrowing by Dexia and a capital injection of €1.5bn for the insurance company Ethias.

In the Netherlands, a €20bn bank recapitalization fund was established, and on 13 October, the Dutch deposit guarantee scheme was extended to cover individual deposits of up to €100,000 in Icesave.

On 19 October, ING Group accepted a €10bn Dutch government recapitalization plan in exchange for securities and government participation in operational and investment decisions. Smaller capital injections were provided to Aegon (€3bn) and SNS Reaal (€750m). The Dutch government has provided guarantees for €200bn of new bank debt, and a €50bn fund has been earmarked for the purchase of high-quality bank assets, either temporarily or permanently.

Other European Countries

Ireland

Rapid economic growth in Ireland during the period prior to 2006 coincided with a housing and commercial property market boom, with much of the bank lending for property development financed in the interbank markets. After the property bubble burst in 2007 and interbank lending dried up in 2008, it was clear that the Irish banks' liquidity and solvency would be severely tested. On 20 September 2008, coverage under the Irish deposit guarantee scheme was raised from 90% to 100% of each individual's deposit, subject to a limit that was increased from €20,000 to €100,000. On 29 September, the government announced a 2-year guarantee of all deposits and some categories of senior debt, for certain banks. This scheme took effect from 24 October 2008 for the three major domestic banks, Bank of Ireland, Allied Irish Banks (AIB), and Anglo Irish Bank; three other domestic banks; and one foreign-owned bank. On 15 January 2009, the nationalization was announced of the third largest bank, Anglo Irish Bank, amid allegations of inappropriate or fraudulent accounting practices involving the concealment of loans from shareholders. On 11 February, the government announced a €7bn recapitalization package for Bank of Ireland and AIB. In return for capital injections of €3.5bn each, the government received preference shares and an option to purchase 25% of the ordinary shares of each bank. In 2009, the Irish government set up an asset management company, National Asset Management Agency (known as a bad bank), to acquire non-performing bank assets and to invest €2bn in building projects.

France

In France, the banking sector entered the financial crisis in a relatively healthy condition, following several years of sustained growth and strong profitability. Subsequently, however,

Société Générale has been hit by exposure to sub-prime lending losses and an alleged fraud on the part of one of its traders that became public knowledge in early 2008. Both Crédit Agricole and Caisse d'Epargne have sustained substantial losses. In October 2008, the French government announced that it was setting aside €40bn for bank recapitalization and the purchase of assets. A fund to provide guarantees covering bank lending totalling €320bn was also established. Between October 2008 and March 2009, two tranches of €10.5bn were allocated to the six largest French banks in the form of subordinated debt, subject to obligations for the banks to sustain growth in lending. Public funds of €1bn were contributed to the bailout of the Belgian Dexia Bank. French banks suffered increasing difficulties through 2011 and 2012, as they were larger holders of eurozone debt, which continued to be downgraded.

Italy

Having largely abstained from securitization and the creation of SIVs during the run-up to the credit crisis, Italy's banks faced a lower sub-prime exposure than those in some other countries. One exception, however, is Unicredit, which has experienced losses following its acquisition of the German bank HypoVereinsbank in 2005. No bank recapitalization fund has been publicly announced in Italy, although individual consideration will be given to cases requiring support. In October 2008, the government established a €40bn swap facility for the conversion of bank debt into T-bills. Five-year guarantees are available for all new bank bonds. In February 2009, a new measure was implemented for the government purchase of bank bonds. Italian banking sector performance improved throughout 2009–10, only to be severely adversely affected by the eurozone crisis. In fact, levels of profitability in the industry have been relatively low; the big banks have relatively high cost ratios due to big branch networks, and some are still overburdened with poor-quality assets. This view of some banks in Italy was confirmed in October 2014 when the ECB released the results of its bank stress tests, highlighting that of the 25 major EU banks that failed the test, 9 were based in Italy; the largest failures were Banca Monte Paschi di Siena and Banca Carige. The former had a €2 bn capital shortfall that it will have to fill by issuing more equity via a rights issue (which could be challenging), or more likely it will seek a merger partner.

Denmark

In October 2008, Denmark introduced a 2-year blanket guarantee scheme for bank liabilities. In January 2009, an Dkr100bn capital injection fund was established to provide hybrid capital in the form of loans of infinite maturity, subordinate to primary debt, convertible to equity if demanded by the regulator, or redeemable after 3 years.

Norway

In October 2008, Norway allocated Nkr350bn for a new swap facility, allowing the conversion of bank loans to government debt. In January 2009, Nkr50bn was allocated for bank recapitalization, with terms to be negotiated on an individual basis.

Sweden

Carnegie Investment Bank, temporarily nationalized on 10 November 2008, was the first bank in Sweden to be bailed out during the present crisis. However, concerns have been raised over the size of the exposures of several Swedish banks, including Swedbank and SEB, in Eastern Europe, especially in the Baltic states. In February 2009, the Swedish government announced the allocation of Skr50bn for bank recapitalization.

Austria

In October 2008, Austria announced the allocation of €100bn in response to the crisis: €15bn for bank recapitalization; €10bn for increased limits for deposit guarantees; and €75bn for guarantees on interbank lending. Austrian banks carry significant exposures in a number of countries in Central, Eastern and Southeastern Europe.

Greece

Greece has set up a €28bn fund for support of the banking system: €5bn for bank recapitalization in the form of purchase of preference shares; €15bn for guarantees of new bank debt; and €8bn for the issue of government debt deposited with Greek banks, enabling them to access liquid funds from the ECB. The problems faced by Greek banks eventually spilled over into the eurozone crisis, which had serious repercussions for the Greek economy and financial system throughout 2011 and into 2012 (see Chapter 12).

Portugal

In October 2008, Portugal announced a €20bn package to guarantee new bank lending. The availability of public funds for bank recapitalization was announced in November, alongside plans to nationalize the troubled Banco Portugues de Negocios. The economy faced ongoing difficulties due to sovereign debt concerns.

CREDIT CRISIS IN JAPAN

Japanese financial firms have been operating in a slow-growing, near deflationary environment since the onset of an earlier financial crisis in 1998. The banks have restructured their activities and reduced their levels of bad loans, although over the past decade they have posted low profitability by international standards and still remain undercapitalized. While struggling along, the financial system has been hit by the fallout from the credit crisis. Unlike the US, however, Japan does not have a sub-prime mortgage market, and securitization of mortgages (or other loans) is not common and property prices have followed a different trend from those in the US and the UK for nearly two decades. The Japanese property bubble burst in the early 1990s, and after that, prices in the major cities fell continuously until 2004, although they did increase by around 25% between 2004 and 2008. By 2008, residential property prices in Japan still were not at the level they had been in 2000. So the country did not face a property bubble funded by securitization and lending excesses as in the US and the UK.

Also, Japanese banks did not hold significant amounts of sub-prime and other securitized securities that collapsed in value at the start of the crisis. For instance, the largest three banking groups (Mizuho, Mitsui Sumitomo and Tokyo-Mitsubishi UFJ) are estimated to have had less than 1% of their balance sheet invested in sub-prime MBS and ABS or CDOs by the end of March 2008. No Japanese bank has failed as a consequence of the credit crisis, although the downturn in the global economy and the adverse impact on the already weakened Japanese economy will continue to put pressure on the system.

Japanese banks were not large buyers of sub-prime-related products, but they have still suffered in the financial fallout from the crisis. Bank margins are particularly low and credit to the corporate sector (with even thinner spreads than to retail customers) forms the bulk of their business. When loan growth stalls, so does bank profitability. The stock market also fell 40% between April 2008 and April 2009, creating losses that have further reduced banks' capital. A major consequence is that all the main Japanese banks have sought to raise more capital – some $34bn – through the issue of new equity and preferred stock between January 2008 and April 2009. The Bank of Japan has offered to buy a modest $10bn worth of shares and has intimated that it may buy banks' subordinated debt – this is a pitiful amount compared to the amounts injected into UK and US banks post crisis. However, it indicates that Japanese banks at least fared relatively well during the credit crisis compared with their US and UK counterparts. Other figures from the IMF's *Global Financial Stability Report* (2009) note that losses by banks over 2007 to the end of 2009 in the US amounted to an estimated $2.7 trillion, $1.193 trillion in Europe and a much more modest $149bn in Japan.

The major ongoing concern for the system is the state of the domestic economy, which poses the greatest threat to the performance of financial firms. As a consequence, the authorities have announced a series of fiscal stimulus and quantitive easing actions in order to stave off deflationary pressures. What is startling about the Japanese banking system is that, like its economy, it has hardly grown since 2000 – as a consequence of the major banking collapse the country experienced in 1998–9. Worries remain in the US, UK and Europe that they may follow along the same path as Japan – an era of near zero interest rates, deflationary pressures and a (very) slow growing economy.

CREDIT CRISIS IN CHINA AND INDIA

Unlike its Western counterparts, China did not suffer too badly; instead, some banks, like the Bank of China, posted only modest losses on holdings of securitized assets. However, it suffered from secondary effects, namely the collapse in exports. During 2007, annual export growth exceeded 25%, and exports made up 36% of the country's GDP. By November 2008, exports actually declined by 2.2% and have continued to fall during 2009. Various estimates suggest that this dramatic decline has resulted in knocking 3–5% off previous GDP growth forecasts.

The government responded quickly to this reversal of fortunes by announcing, in November 2008, a major fiscal stimulus package amounting to a staggering $580bn – some 14% of GDP. This has helped to keep the economy on track, with GDP growth exceeding 8% for 2009. Although the country can afford the stimulus package – government debt amounts to only 20% of GDP – there are concerns that such stimulus packages lead to credit booms fuelling capital and property market.

During the first 6 months of 2009, bank credits grew by Rmb7,300bn – way above the official annual target for the full year. Credit growth rocketed, and this has fuelled excess liquidity in the system, boosting property and stock market activity. This excess liquidity has led to the resurgence of asset bubbles and caused various financial commentators to talk about a significant readjustment and growing inflationary pressures. The lending boom has also had the effect of stalling various banking sector reforms that aimed to introduce more competition in domestic retail markets and provide greater oversight of the system. Just when Chinese banks were getting to grips with their substantial bad loan portfolios, it seems that they may be creating a new set of problems for the future. The central bank has tightened credit controls, reserve requirements and pushed interest rates up a few times to try and dampen market excesses, although by 2014, property prices in the main urban centres were still increasing substantially.

India has been hit harder than China in the wake of the credit crisis. The domestic stock market fell 50% during 2008, and the country's second largest bank, ICICI Bank, suffered a major collapse in its share price following rumours of overexposure to toxic assets. Foreign institutional investors withdrew nearly $10bn of investments during 2008, compared with an inflow of $17.4bn in 2007. Also, the rupee fell to a 6-year low in October 2008, despite massive intervention by the Reserve Bank of India. This has resulted in money market liquidity shortfalls and spikes in wholesale money market rates.

The government enacted various policies to stabilize the situation, including a reduction in the cash reserve ratio in October 2008, which was expected to inject some $4bn into the banking system. As in China, the indirect effects of the credit crisis – particularly stalling exports – have pushed GDP growth downward. Official figures put growth at over 8% for 2009, although this has fallen to between 4.5% and 5% in 2012 and 2013. The government has continued with its policy of not selling more than 49% stakes in its state banks, which account for some 67% of banking sector assets. This has aided stability in the system, although loan losses in these institutions remain high by Western standards. Nevertheless, a major ongoing issue for the government is its lack of fiscal resources to deal with a banking sector meltdown. This was clearly illustrated in the summer of 2009 when Moody's placed all the major listed Indian banks on credit watch due to concerns about the level of potential government support in the event of a crisis.

WHAT HAVE WE LEARNED FROM THE CRISIS?

The first thing we have learned from the crisis is that such events can be costly! Box 10.5 illustrates this case.

BOX 10.5

Cost of Banking Crisis

The first table below shows different measures of crisis costs relating to 147 banking crises that have occurred from 1970 to 2011. One can see that, on average, systemic banking crises cost about 30% in lost output and 20% of financial sector assets. They last longer in advanced economies (5 years) compared with emerging economies (3 years) and developing economies (2 years)

Banking Crises Outcomes, 1970–2011

Country	Output loss	Increase in debt	Monetary expansion	Fiscal costs	Fiscal costs	Duration	Peak liquidity	Liquidity support	Peak NPLs
					Medians				
		In percent of GDP			In percent of financial system assets	In years	In percent of deposits and foreign liabilities		In percent of total loans
All	23.0	12.1	1.7	6.8	12.7	2.0	20.1	9.6	25.0
Advanced	32.9	21.4	8.3	3.8	2.1	3.0	11.5	5.7	4.0
Emerging	26.0	9.1	1.3	10.0	21.4	2.0	22.3	11.1	30.0
Developing	1.6	10.9	1.2	10.0	18.3	1.0	22.6	12.3	37.5

Source: Leaven, L. and Valencia, F. (2013) Systemic banking crises, database, *IMF Economic Review*, 61(2): 221–70 (IMF: Washington, DC).

An illustration of the financial costs of the bank bailouts in Europe are shown in the table below. State aid measures amounting to 45.8% of EU GDP were taken between 2008 and October 2014.

Parliamentary approved amounts of state aid in the period 2008 to 1 October 2014.

Years	Recapitalization €billion	Guarantees €billion	Asset relief interventions €billion	Liquidity measures other than guarantees €billion	Total capitalization and asset relief €billion	Total capitalization and asset relief % GDP	Total guarantees and liquidity measures €billion	Total guarantees and liquidity measures % GDP
2008	269.87	3,097.34	4.8	85.48	274.67	2.2	3,182.82	25.3
2009	110.04	87.63	338.50	5.49	448.54	3.8	93.12	0.8
2010	184.01	54.81	77.98	66.75	261.99	2.1	121.56	1.0
2011	37.40	179.70	6.30	50.23	43.77	0.3	229.93	1.8
2012	150.81	266.82	157.48	37.46	308.29	2.4	304.28	2.4
2013	29.56	37.86	14.73	23.55	44.29	0.3	61.42	0.5
2014	39.37	168.42	69.53	110.94	108.71	0.8	279.35	2.1
TOTAL	821.06	3,892.58	669.32	379.9	1,490.26	11.9	4,272.48	33.9

Source: Adapted from http://ec.europa.eu/competition/state_aid/scoreboard/financial_economic_crisis_aid_en.html

Bank Recapitalizations and Cleansing of Bank Balance Sheets

During the credit crisis, national governments and central banks adopted several alternative approaches to dealing with troubled assets on bank balance sheets and banks in need of recapitalization. As discussed earlier, in October 2008, the US government earmarked $700bn of public funding for the purchase of troubled assets, through the Troubled Assets Relief Program (TARP). A fundamental difficulty soon emerged, however, in valuing illiquid troubled assets for purchase. With mark-to-market asset prices often having fallen below balance sheet valuations, many banks were reluctant to sell. TARP was quickly adapted into a vehicle for public funded bank recapitalizations, including Bank of America and Citigroup. In March 2009, a revised variant of TARP was launched, involving joint private–public purchase of troubled assets, but it appears similar difficulties still arise in striking a fair price at which to trade.

The UK has favoured retaining troubled assets within banks and providing credit insurance guarantees for a fee. Since the Northern Rock disaster, UK authorities have responded vigorously to subsequent episodes of bank distress; however, concerns have been raised that the UK approach risks repeating the experience of Japan during the 1990s, when troubled assets were retained on balance sheets and the banks deleveraged gradually by implementing restrictive lending policies. The Japanese economy entered a long-lasting deflationary spiral and may have suffered more in terms of lost output over the past 20 years than any other financial crisis victim. The Japanese experience was in marked contrast to that of Sweden, which dealt with a banking crisis in the early 1990s by transferring troubled assets into a separate 'bad bank' and restoring the troubled bank that originated the transferred assets to 'good bank' status with a cleaned-up balance sheet. As noted above, in the present crisis, the 'good bank/bad bank' model has been adopted by Switzerland in respect of UBS, and the Irish authorities are following a similar route, despite mounting public criticism.

Willem Buiter, former member of the Bank of England's Monetary Policy Committee, has argued that public recapitalization, as practised in the US, the UK and elsewhere, constitutes a surrender on the part of the authorities to lobbying for government bailouts by unsecured creditors and that the risks of systemic failure are overstated (Buiter, 2009). For example, pension funds are not highly leveraged and can adjust to write-downs of their assets simply by reducing their liabilities. Orderly restructuring of an insurance company following insolvency need not entail the collapse of the entire financial system, as was suggested and feared at the time of the US bailout of AIG.

Capital and Liquidity Regulation

Current arrangements for capital provisioning have been subject to intense scrutiny during the crisis. Under the risk-weighted capital regulation regime of Basel II, the use of backward-looking models for risk assessment creates a destabilizing tendency for capital provisioning to amplify the economic cycle. In good times, observed rates of borrower default decline, and bank assets in all risk classes are assessed as being in need of lower provisioning. Existing capital buffers can support increased lending, with a tendency to amplify the cycle. Conversely, during a downturn, risk is perceived to have increased, and banks need either to recapitalize, liquidate existing assets or reduce new lending in order to achieve sufficient provisioning.

Banks with a higher proportion of short-term debt (rather than long-term debt or equity) and banks with a higher proportion of illiquid assets (which might have to be disposed of rapidly in a fire sale) probably should be subject to higher capital requirements. Further, the introduction of a simple leverage ratio (ratio of capital to assets), alongside risk-based capital regulation, should simplify supervision and make regulatory arbitrage more difficult, as suggested by the Group of Thirty in 2009.

To avoid requiring banks to hold excessive capital during normal or boom conditions, while providing an automatic mechanism that allows banks to recapitalize during periods of stress, various commentators have suggested creating a long-term debt instrument that converts to equity under conditions that might be either bank specific (contingent on the bank's performance or capitalization) or general (contingent on the regulator's judgement that a systemic failure might be imminent) or both. Another proposal is that banks should be required or given the option to purchase capital insurance against systemic failure. Investors such as sovereign wealth funds or pension funds would deposit the full sum insured with the insurer in exchange for receiving the premium paid by the bank and the return of the sum insured at the end of the period if no catastrophic event had occurred. Others suggest using market indicators, such as credit default swap (CDS) spreads, to trigger the recapitalization mechanism. These schemes raise complex issues over how precisely contracts should be specified and how the banks might be able to 'game the system', that is, to manipulate the rules that are supposed to protect the system for an alternative desired outcome. However, both are motivated by the core principle that the cost of the systemic risk should be borne by the banks ex ante, and not by the taxpayer ex post.

The drying up of wholesale funding and the interbank markets during 2007 and 2008 suggests that past regulation may have overemphasized capital at the expense of liquidity. By itself, capital regulation is insufficient to guarantee the viability of any financial institution. A liquidity crisis can rapidly develop into a full-blown capitalization crisis due to fire sale risk, arising from the need for institutions selling large positions in illiquid assets (perhaps in order to reduce leverage in compliance with capital adequacy requirements) to offer price concessions in order to attract buyers, with knock-on effects for the balance sheets of other institutions obliged to mark their assets to the fire sale price. Therefore, new liquidity requirements, separate from capital adequacy standards, should focus on the ratios of liquid assets to total assets, and liquid liabilities to long-term liabilities. Liquidity standards for individual institutions should also take account of their systemic linkages.

Ed Kane (2009) notes that although the seizing up of liquidity in the wholesale and interbank markets in autumn 2008 was the proximate cause of the ensuing crisis, the underlying cause was the recognition in these markets of the severity of the failures in the sub-prime lending and securitized assets markets. Accordingly, the realignment of incentives and the correction of other forms of market failure in mortgage and securitized markets are necessary conditions for the repair of the system. Obliging the originators of securitized assets to retain a portion of the risk should provide the necessary incentives for the appropriate monitoring of lending standards, rather than a dereliction of this prime banking responsibility – this is, in fact, a proposal adopted by the US government, which has suggested that banks must hold 5% of the credits they securitize on their own books. Stronger emphasis on the quality of the underlying assets, simplification of some of the more complex securitized products and tighter constraints (through capital and liquidity requirements) on investors are measures expected to feature prominently in the eventual recovery of markets for securitized assets.

Scope of Regulation, and Separation of Bank Functions

Clearly, major gaps and weaknesses in the system for the regulation and supervision of financial institutions should be addressed. There is wide support for the principle that all systemically important financial institutions (SIFIs) should be subject to capital regulation, regardless of legal status. SIFIs other than banks that should be subject to regulatory oversight include some large insurance companies, hedge funds, private equity funds and clearing houses. SIVs should not be permitted to escape capital and liquidity regulation and disclosure requirements that apply to their parent companies.

More radical and controversial, a case has been made for the reintroduction of the separation of narrow banking from investment banking, originally introduced in the US by the Glass-Steagall Act of 1933 and repealed in 1999. A heavily regulated commercial banking sector would provide basic deposit and lending services under central bank lender-of-last-resort protection, whereas a more lightly regulated investment banking sector would undertake risky investment business without government protection. Another lesson of the crisis is that the banking system has hitherto been underwritten by a large but only partially recognized public subsidy, which enabled some large banks to exploit their status as 'too big to fail' (TBTF) in order to recklessly expand their balance sheets. A return to Glass-Steagall, it is argued, would prevent universal banks from sheltering their risky investment activities under the implicit public subsidy umbrella of TBTF. However, ring-fencing narrow banking would present formidable technical and practical challenges, and strong support for this proposal has so far failed to coalesce.

Systemic Risk

One of the key lessons of the financial crisis is that past financial regulation has overemphasized measures to preserve the soundness of individual institutions and underemphasized the interconnectedness of financial institutions and the implications for systemic stability. Principal sources of systemic instability include counterparty risk, the risk of default on the part of counterparties to over-the-counter (OTC) transactions and fire sale risk. Central banks should be specifically mandated to oversee systemic stability in addition to their existing responsibilities for price stability and (in the case of the US Federal Reserve) maximizing employment. Forms of oversight should include the gathering and analysis of information on asset positions and risk exposures in a standardized format that permits comparisons between institutions; the publication of data, subject to time-lags, that strike an appropriate balance between disclosure and transparency objectives and legitimate concerns over the protection of financial innovation and proprietary business models; and the preparation of an annual report on systemic stability and risk.

Credit Rating Agencies

We have already discussed the misaligned incentives of rating agencies in securitization activity. By using backward-looking models to evaluate risk, and by underestimating systemic correlations and probabilities associated with extreme events, the agencies succumbed to the fallacy that the absence of a crisis in the recent past implies a reduced or negligible probability of a crisis in the near future.

A wide range of remedies has been floated, from the creation of a free market in ratings data (in the US, rating agencies have to obtain licences) to the nationalization of the agencies. The complete separation of advisory services from the award of ratings would address conflicts of interest, although it might be difficult to prevent issuers from using multiple ratings applications as a means of accessing advice. Transparency might be improved by replacing the letter grading system with numerical estimates of exposures and default probabilities, and the time periods to which these data apply. However, models capable of generating refined numerical estimates for complex structured products are not well developed. One proposal that has gained some traction is for the creation of an intermediary between the issuer and the agency in the form of a centralized clearing platform administered by the regulator, which would charge the issuer a flat fee dependent on the security's attributes and complexity. The platform would then commission an agency to supply the rating. This system would address the conflict-of-interest problem because the regulator rather than the issuer selects the agency, but it would also impose a heavy burden on the regulator in monitoring the agencies' performance.

Credit Derivative Markets

The restoration of confidence in OTC credit derivative markets will require increased transparency and improved oversight. During the crisis, counterparty risk has been a serious concern, with CDS investors fearful that counterparties may default on their obligations in the event that the underlying asset defaults. Concern over counterparty risk is compounded by a lack of transparency. Following the collapse of Lehman Brothers, $400bn of CDS was presented for settlement, but after offsetting bilateral trades were netted out, the figure was reduced to $6bn. Shortcomings in the supporting infrastructure for OTC derivatives markets include trade confirmation delays, lack of transparency on transaction reporting and pricing, contract closeout procedures, valuation practices and collateral disputes, and direct and indirect counterparty credit issues.

The advantages of a centralized clearing system for credit derivative markets that are sufficiently large to have implications for systemic stability are widely recognized. The Group of Thirty (2009) reports that the leading credit derivative market participants are working on the creation of such a system. The major gain from developing a centralized clearing system accrues through the elimination of counterparty risk. However, the development of a formal exchange, requiring standardized contracts, might not be desirable in view of the complex and thinly traded nature of some credit derivative instruments. There are moves to push a lot of OTC derivatives contracts, particularly interest rate swaps as well as credit derivatives, onto organized exchanges so as to reduce risk. The new regulatory requirements in both the US and Europe are complex but are expected to be implemented by 2016–18.

Cross-border Supervision and Regulation

The growth of cross-border banking within the EU (and elsewhere) raises complex issues for supervision. Strains are placed on a supervisory framework organized on national lines, with considerable variation between countries in supervisory and regulatory practice. During the crisis, the market valuation of cross-border banking groups has declined by more than that of single-country banks, with inadequate regulatory oversight cited as a contributory factor.

The cross-border bank's legal structure determines the division of responsibilities among national supervisory authorities: branches are subject to home country supervision, whereas subsidiaries are under the jurisdiction of the host country supervisor. This violates the principle that regulatory treatment should be neutral with respect to the internal organizational structure of the bank. Home country supervision creates difficulties in the case of a bank failure, with systemically damaging implications for a host country. The Icelandic banking collapse illustrates the danger of a mismatch between the size of a cross-border bank and the size of a home country's resources, creating a so-called 'too large to save' dilemma. The UK and Dutch governments provided guarantees for their own citizens' deposits in Icesave, even though they were not responsible for the supervision of Landsbanki.

As the Fortis bailout demonstrates, crisis management requiring cooperation between national supervisors has sometimes proven inefficient and ineffective. Disputes between countries can delay action in situations where speed is essential, and equal treatment for creditors and debtors in different countries can be hard to achieve. Supervisory fragmentation may even constitute a threat to the integrity of a European single market in financial services, with the break-up of Fortis illustrating an alarming tendency for reversion towards banking within national borders in the event of a crisis. Strings attached to publicly funded bank bailouts, in the form of commitments to prioritize domestic lending, also push in the direction of fragmentation.

Most commentators accept that the coordination of mechanisms for bank regulation and supervision within the EU should be improved. The de Larosière Report (2009) on the reform of EU and global supervision and regulation recommended the creation of a new coordinated supervisory structure. Under these proposals, bank supervision would remain decentralized at the national level, but supervisory and regulatory practices would be harmonized. For example, standardized deposit guarantee provisions should be adopted, and consistent principles and tools should be deployed in crisis management. For each cross-border banking group, a college of national supervisors would be established, with provisions for binding arbitration at EU level. Three functional EU-level authorities would be responsible for coordinating the regulation of banking, insurance and securities. Finally, a European Systemic Risk Council would oversee the entire system and monitor systemic risk at the macro level. This has all now happened as part of the EU's plan to create a European Banking Union, the ECB became responsible in November 2014 for supervising the eurozone's largest banks, and a single-deposit insurance and resolution scheme is being put in place. The aim, ultimately, is to try and decouple (or break) the link between banking sector risk and sovereign risk. It remains to be seen whether this will be a success.

Burden-sharing between countries in the event of a cross-border bank failure, however, remains a thorny issue. Charles Goodhart and Dirk Schoenmaker (2009) have argued that ex-post negotiations on sharing the costs of a cross-border bailout will result in an underprovision of capital, as participants outside the home country have an incentive to understate involvement in order to minimize their costs. Two ex ante burden-sharing mechanisms are suggested. The first, a general mechanism, is financed collectively by the participating countries, based on their GDP. The second is a specific mechanism, funded by participants, based on the geographical spread of their banks' business. The latter might be more effective because each country's benefits in terms of financial stability are more closely aligned to their contributions to the scheme.

SUMMARY

- The *credit crisis* ran from June 2007 through to early 2009. The main causes of the crisis were macroeconomic and microeconomic.
- *Macroeconomic causes* included the build-up of global financial imbalances and low real interest rates. The latter fuelled a credit boom, especially in mortgage lending.
- *Microeconomic causes* were that consumers failed to understand the risks they were taking, managers of financial firms sought higher returns via increased leverage, compensation schemes were geared to encourage financial professionals to take on more risk, skewed incentives of credit rating agencies, and the substantial limitations in risk measurement, management and regulatory oversight.
- The BIS identified five stages of the crisis: *Stage 1* (June 2007 up to mid-March 2008) – losses in US sub-prime market starting in the summer of 2007; *Stage 2* (mid-March to mid-September 2008) – events leading up to

the Lehman Brothers bankruptcy; *Stage 3* (15 September to late October 2008) – global loss of confidence; *Stage 4* (late October 2008 to mid-March 2009) – investors focus on the global economic downturn; and *Stage 5* (from mid-March 2009) – signs of stabilization.
- The rapid growth in *securitization* was a major cause of the crisis. This activity has not only had a major impact on the funding of residential property markets but also on the flexibility with which banks can manage their loan books. The collapse of sub-prime mortgage lending in the US and related securitized products is seen by many as the start of the credit crisis.
- Securitization involves the process where banks find borrowers, originate loans but then sell the loans (repackaged as securities) on to investors. This is known as the *originate-to-distribute* model in contrast to the traditional *originate-and-hold* approach.
- Securitization relates to the pooling of credit-risky assets, traditionally residential mortgage loans (but

nowadays other types of credits such as car loans, credit card receivables or any credit generating some form of predictable cash flow), and their subsequent sale to an SPV, which then issues securities to finance the purchase of the assets.

- The securities issued by the SPV are usually fixed-income instruments – known as MBS if backed by mortgages or ABS if backed by a variety of different types of loans – which are then sold to investors where the principal and interest depend on the cash flows produced by the pool of underlying financial assets.

- The first major securitization activity in the US was by the S&Ls that moved mortgage loans off their balance sheet and sold them on to investors. The *government-sponsored enterprises* (GSEs), such as Fannie Mae and Freddie Mac, were major operators in the US mortgage securitization business, and they held an estimated $5 trillion in mortgage-backed securities by mid-2008 (federal authorities had to step in and bail them out in September 2008).

- *Sub-prime* refers to loans to higher risk borrowers – those that are not prime borrowers. Mortgage lending to sub-prime lenders grew rapidly from around $200bn in mid-2003 to more than $500bn by mid-2004, peaking at around $600bn in 2005–6. At this time, they accounted for about 20% of all new US residential mortgages. Around 80% of sub-prime mortgages were securitized.

- The attraction of sub-prime mortgage lending for banks was that it offered higher interest rates than prime mortgages – typically 2% more. The use of sub-prime loans in the underlying collateral allowed MBS and CDO packagers to enhance their profit margins while offering competitive returns on their securitizations.

- Most securities issued by SPVs were rated by credit rating agencies – S&P, Moody's and Fitch – to make them more attractive to investors. Although the credit quality of individual loans in the underlying pool of assets may be low, the credit quality (and therefore the credit rating) of the overall portfolio held in the SPV can be increased by pooling the portfolio of credit-risky assets so as to gain various diversification benefits.

- In addition, the risks of the portfolio could further be improved by *various credit enhancement techniques* such as *third-party guarantees* (insurance from *monoline insurers* to protect the value of assets), *overcollateralization* (holding a larger pool of assets

than securities issued) and by something known as *excess spread* (originators, namely banks, inject cash into the SPV that will bear certain early losses). All the aforementioned practices, getting the ABS or MBS rated and the various credit enhancement techniques, were put in place to increase the attractiveness of the securities issued to investors.

- From early to mid-2007, a wave of defaults accumulated in the US sub-prime mortgage market, and property prices began to fall. As the value of the collateral declined, investors realized that their investments were rapidly evaporating. Also, the complexity of the structures meant that it became well-nigh impossible to value the securities as it was also virtually impossible to accurately value the underlying collateral. Securities that had been rated as low risk and investment grade by the rating agencies became speculative and even unsaleable. This prompted the meltdown in the sub-prime (and other) mortgage-backed securities markets. Banks stopped lending to each other, as they did not know the exposure of each other to securitized assets held on and off their books. The interbank market dried up, and central banks had to inject short-term funding into the markets by the end of 2007. The situation was made more complex by a new wave of securitization including CDOs and asset-backed commercial paper (ABCP).

- At the end of 2008, Bloomberg reported that bank losses stemming from the meltdown in the US sub-prime market amounted to $744.6bn – Wachovia had the biggest loss of $96.5bn, followed by Citigroup with $67.2bn and Merrill Lynch with $55.9bn.

- The credit crisis spread rapidly, having a particularly disastrous impact on the financial systems of the UK, Ireland and Iceland. No major European system was immune from its effects as banks failed or had to be supported via capital and liquidity injections. Japanese banks appeared less affected by the crisis than most, although they have had a poorly performing domestic economy to worry about for over a decade. Governments and various international organizations have *introduced major reforms to the financial system*, such as the Dodd-Frank Act in the US, covering the cleansing of bank balance sheets, increased capital and liquidity requirements, increased oversight and regulation of securitization business, hedge funds (as discussed in Chapter 9) and credit rating agencies.

REVISION QUESTIONS/ASSIGNMENTS

1 Analyse the main causes of the 2008 global financial crisis. How much was lending to the property sector to blame for the crisis?

2 Discuss the role played by rating agencies in the securitization business. What are the potential conflicts of interest for rating agencies in this business area?

3 Analyse the US regulatory response to the crisis. How will the 2010 Dodd-Frank Act impact on future bank behaviour?

4 Examine the role of too big to fail (TBTF) in banking.

REFERENCES

Berger, A., Molyneux, P., and Wilson, J.O. (eds) (2012) *The Oxford Handbook of Banking* (1st edition), OUP, Oxford. Covers contemporary issues in banking and finance, with over 40 chapters by leading scholars.

Berger, A., Molyneux, P., and Wilson, J.O. (2014) Overview of banking, in Berger, A., Molyneux, P., and Wilson, J.O. (eds) *The Oxford Handbook of Banking* (2nd edn), OUP, Oxford. Review of developments in banking.

BIS (Bank for International Settlements). (2009) *79th Annual Report* (1 April 2008 to 31 March 2009), BIS, Basel. Good on the credit crisis.

Buiter, W. (2009) Regulating the new financial sector, www.voxeu.org/index.php?q=node/3232. Some insights into causes and cures of the crises. Advanced in places.

De Larosière, J. (2009) *The High-level Group on Financial Supervision in the EU Report*, The De Larosière Group, European Commission, Brussels. Outlines new supervisory framework for European financial system regulation post crisis.

Goodhart, C., and Schoenmaker, D. (2009) Fiscal burden sharing in cross-border banking crises, *International Journal of Central Banking*, 5: 141–65. Empirical analysis of which governments should bear the costs asso-ciated with bank failure for large cross-border banks, highlighting how different arrangements change the fiscal burden for various countries.

Group of Thirty. (2009) *Financial Reform: A Framework for Financial Stability*, Group of Thirty, Washington, DC. Proposals for reform of the global financial system, partially shaping post-crisis legislation in the US, the UK and Europe.

IMF (International Monetary Fund). (2009) *Global Financial Stability Report: Responding to the Financial Crisis and Measuring Systemic Risks*, IMF, Washington, DC. Advanced level discussion of reform of the financial system.

Kane, E.J. (2009) Incentive roots of the securitization crisis and its early mismanagement, *Yale Journal of Regulation*, 26: 504–16. Academic analysis of the adverse impact of securitization activity.

Tett, G. (2009) *Fool's Gold: How Unrestrained Greed Corrupted a Dream, Shattered Global Markets and Unleashed a Catastrophe*, Little, Brown, New York. Intriguing and witty analysis of those who made and broke the financial system by top FT journalist.

FURTHER READING

Acharya, V. (2009) Some steps in the right direction: a critical assessment of the de Larosière Report, www.voxeu.org/index.php?q=node/3185. Critique of post-crisis reform suggestions.

Bailey, M., Elmendorf, D., and Litan, R. (2008) *The Great Credit Squeeze: How it Happened, How to Prevent Another*, Brooking Institution, Washington, DC. Suggestions for reforms aimed at minimizing the likelihood of another credit crisis.

Brunnermeier, M.K. (2009) Deciphering the liquidity and credit crunch 2007–8, *Journal of Economic Perspectives*, 23(1): 77–100. Detailed review of the credit crisis, advanced in places.

Calomiris, C.W. (2009) The sub-prime turmoil: What's old, what's new, and what's next, *Journal of Structured Finance*, 15(1): 6–52. Interesting insights in the new and not so new factors that resulted in the crisis.

Caprio, G., Demirgüç-Kunt, A., and Kane, E.J. (2008) The 2007 meltdown in structured securitization: Searching for lessons, not scapegoats, *World Bank Policy Research Working Paper*, WPS4756. Pros and cons of securitization.

Caprio, G., and Honohan, P. (2014) Banking crises, in Berger, A., Molyneux, P., and Wilson, J.O. (eds) *The Oxford Handbook of Banking* (2nd edn), OUP, Oxford. Excellent review of the banking crises by two distinguished scholars.

Goddard, J.P., Molyneux, P., and Wilson, J.O. (2009a) The financial crisis in Europe: Evolution, policy responses and lessons for the future, *Journal of Financial Regulation and Compliance*, 17(4): 362–80. Review of the impact of the crisis in Europe.

Goddard, J.P., Molyneux, P., and Wilson, J.O. (2009b) Crisis in UK banking: Lessons for public policy, *Public Money and Management*, 29(5): 277–84. Review of the impact of the crisis in the UK.

Herring, R., and Carmassi, J. (2014) The corporate structure of international financial conglomerates: complexity and implications for safety and soundness, in Berger, A., Molyneux, P., and Wilson, J.O. (eds) *The Oxford Handbook of Banking* (2nd edn), OUP, Oxford. Review detailing the increased complexity of financial firms.

Lewis, M. (2010) *The Big Short: Inside the Doomsday Machine*, Allen Lane, London. The author (of *Liar's Poker* fame) approaches the problem of the banking collapse by talking to those clever enough to bet against the system and asking why they did it. Very clear, very revealing and even frightening, particularly the role of the rating agencies.

Litan, R.. and Bailey, M. (2009) *Fixing Finance: A Road Map for Reform*, Brooking Institution, Washington, DC. Proposals for reform of the financial system.

Milne, A. (2009) *The Fall of the House of Credit*, CUP, Cambridge. Racy insights into the credit collapse.

Philippon, T. (2009) An overview of proposals to fix the financial system, www.voxeu.org/index.php?q=node/3076. More discussion on potential reform options for the financial system post crisis.

Foreign Exchange

11

....

INTRODUCTION

The Market

Foreign exchange dealing rooms at times of peak activity resemble bedlam. Shirtsleeved dealers look at computer screens, talk into several phones at once and yell to colleagues. They talk in the space of minutes to key centres – London, New York, Paris, Zurich, Frankfurt. The phrases are terse and mysterious – 'What's cable?', '50/60', 'Mine!', 'Yours!', 'Cable 70/80 – give five, take three', 'tomnext'. A broker may quote, 'Cable 70/80 – give five, take three'. Cable is sterling/dollar and the broker has a client who will buy £3m at, say, $1.7370 and sell £5m at $1.7380.

The foreign exchange market is international, open 24 hours a day, adjusts prices constantly and deals in huge sums. 'Five' always means 5m, whether dollars, yen or sterling, and yards is a billion. Central bankers have now fallen into a pattern of doing a full survey of the size of the market every 3 years. The year 1986 showed a total world market that traded over $300bn every *day*. According to the BIS *Triennial Central Bank Survey of Foreign Exchange and Derivatives Market Activity* (2013), daily turnover had reached $5.3 trillion by April 2013 – a huge increase even from 2004, when daily turnover stood at $1.9 trillion.

London accounts for 41% of global foreign exchange turnover, compared with 35% in 2007, followed by New York (19%), Tokyo (6%), Singapore (6%), Hong Kong (4%), Switzerland (3%) and Australia (3%).

Buyers and Sellers

Who is buying and selling all this foreign exchange? One's first thought is of importers and exporters. BIS calculates the daily value of imports and exports. The latter are around 3% of the value of daily foreign exchange dealing. What drives the market these days is huge capital transactions. Looking at buyers/sellers of foreign currencies, we see the following:

- Importers/exporters
- Tourists
- Government spending, for example for troops abroad
- Speculators
- Banks and institutions

We've mentioned importers/exporters and the role of tourism and government spending is easy to understand and not crucial.

As exchange controls have been abandoned by major centres, pension fund managers, investment fund managers and insurance companies can invest in foreign equities and bonds. They then need the foreign currencies to pay for them.

Investors with spare funds will move money around freely. For instance, during the 1980s investors were convinced that Spain, Italy and the UK offered high interest rates together with low exchange rate risk due to the EU's exchange rate mechanism (ERM), so they put their funds into these currencies. The head of research at Mitsubishi Bank in London, for example, estimated that free funds of some £40–50bn flowed into the UK during 1985–92, attracted by high interest rates. As the ERM all but collapsed in the dramatic days of September 1992, the funds flowed out of the high-yielding currencies as exchange rate risk became a reality once more. Among these investors could be corporate treasurers at multinationals trying to protect their overall position. Those with heavy dollar earnings might worry if the dollar weakened and move spare funds into euros. We saw huge currency outflows again in 1997 as East Asian countries, like South Korea, hit trouble.

One recent popular strategy by foreign exchange investors has been to borrow currency in low-interest environments and invest these in currencies where there are high (or higher) interest rates. This is known as the 'carry' trade – see Box 11.1. Throughout the 2000s, Japan experienced very low interest rates (a consequence of monetary policy actions such as quantitative easing that were used to try to boost the economy post the late 1990s banking crisis). During this period a common investment strategy was to borrow Japanese yen and invest in Australian dollars.

The 2013 BIS *Triennial Central Bank Survey* notes that the increase in foreign exchange trading over the last few years has been driven by financial institutions – and small banks in particular. Smaller banks (not participating in the 2013 survey as reporting dealers) accounted for 24% of turnover. Institutional investors (pension funds and insurance

BOX 11.1

The 'Carry' Trade

One popular trading strategy for making money in the foreign exchange market is known as the 'carry trade'.

In the first-half of 2014, investors have put on carry trades using less volatile major-market currencies and investing in emerging-market currencies as they search for investments offering higher yields amid generally low interest rates globally.

Carry trades involve investors borrowing in a currency from a country where interest rates are low, such as dollars and euros in 2014. They then exchange it for currency in a country where rates are higher, such as India, Indonesia, the Philippines or Turkey. By 'carrying' the higher-yielding currency, they can collect the difference in interest rates.

Such trades can be profitable. According to data revealed by the Wall Street Journal on 30 June 2014, from February to late June, a Deutsche Bank index that tracks trades between lower-yielding, developed-market currencies and higher-yielding, developing-market currencies shows them generating returns over the 3-month LIBOR of 7.7%. Timing, of course, is the essence – as the same index shows that such trades lost 3.4% in 2013.

Carry trades are particularly popular when there is lower volatility in exchange rates, as this makes the interest differential more certain.

companies) accounted for 11%, and hedge funds and proprietary trading firms for another 11%. Trading with non-financial companies fell between 2010 and 2013, reducing their share of global turnover to only 9%. As one would expect, the US dollar remained the dominant vehicle currency; it was on one side of 87% of all trades in April 2013, and the euro was the second most traded currency (although its share had fallen to 33% in April 2013, from 39% in April 2010. According to the BIS, 'turnover of the Japanese yen increased significantly between the 2010 and 2013 surveys. So too did that of several emerging market currencies, and the Mexican peso and Chinese renminbi entered the list of the top 10 most traded currencies'.

Bank Profits

Foreign exchange profits are important for the major banks. The US Office of the Comptroller of the Currency at one time calculated that foreign exchange dealing accounts for half of the profits made by the big commercial banks.

The risks have grown, too. Big corporate customers have become more sophisticated, some with their own dealing rooms; new capital ratio rules have increased the cost of foreign exchange exposures; counterparty risk has become a major worry; and dollar volatility in recent years has become more unpredictable. As a result, the business is increasingly concentrated in a handful of major banks. Top traders according to *Euromoney* magazine are shown in Table 11.1. The market share of each of the top five banks rose in 2013, with Citi recording a rise in market share of 1.14 percentage points. In total, the market share of the top five banks was 60.62%, compared to 57.36% last year. It is the first time the combined market share of the top five banks has exceeded 60% since 2009.

▼ Table 11.1 *Top 5 traders by % share of foreign exchange market, 2013*

Rank	Bank	% share
1	Citi	16.04
2	Deutsche	15.67
3	Barclays	10.91
4	UBS	10.88
5	HSBC	7.12

Source: Euromoney (2014).

Similar to the scandal that emerged in the fixing for LIBOR rates (see Box 7.2), the foreign exchange market was embroiled in a similar scandal with UK, US and European regulators investigating whether there had been manipulation of key foreign exchange rate 'fixes' by some of the leading traders. Typically, a variety of foreign exchange rates are set by the major traders every day, and on this basis, the $5.3 trillion daily turnover of foreign exchange rates are priced. There were allegations that traders at some of the main banks manipulated the rates set so they could profit from such trades. In November 2014, the UK Financial Conduct Authority (FCA) and the US Commodity Futures Trading Commission (CFTC) and Office of the Comptroller of the Currency (OCC) fined some major banks a staggering $4.3bn – with the total fines paid by JP Morgan and Citibank amounting to over $1 billion each.

WHAT DETERMINES EXCHANGE RATES?

Among economists, the most popular theory for explaining exchange rates is that of purchasing power parity (PPP). At its simplest, if a given basket of goods is priced at £10 in the UK and $20 in the US, this suggests the exchange rate should be £1 = $2. If the exchange rate is actually £1 = $1, the Americans can buy a basket of goods in the UK at half the price it costs them at home, and dollar imports will rise heavily, causing the dollar to weaken. As time goes by, one factor causing US goods to become either more or less expensive than British goods is inflation. If UK inflation is higher than the US, they may sell less goods to the US, but if the sterling/dollar exchange rate moves in the dollar's favour, the cost to the Americans is the same.

At least, that's the theory. Like most economic theories, it raises serious problems in practice. To begin with, what should go in the basket of goods, as nations' purchasing habits are different? Again, many of the prices in the basket will be for goods and services not traded internationally. It also assumes that the price is not distorted by tax differences (value-added tax [VAT] or sales tax) and that there are no artificial barriers to trade, such as tariffs.

The Economist has some fun periodically with its McDonald's Big Mac™ PPP: it compares the price of a hamburger in key world capitals and arrives at an exchange rate, which it compares with the real one. It started as a bit of fun but has inspired several serious studies, for example *Burgernomics: A Big Mac™ Guide to Purchasing Power Parity* (Pakko and Pollard, 2003).

If inflation in one country is consistently higher than in another, then the expectation is that the exchange rate will deteriorate in the country with the higher inflation. How do we persuade foreigners to hold this currency? Answer: by offering them higher interest rates than they can get at home. The higher interest rates compensate for the anticipated higher inflation rate. Thus, interest rates enter the equation along with inflation and balance of payments figures.

The relationship between inflation and the exchange rate was nicely shown by Samuel Brittan of the *Financial Times* (9 October 1992) (using original figures from Datastream). Brittan plotted the declining purchasing power of the pound against the declining deutschmark/sterling exchange rate from 1964 to 1992. The correlation was striking. Underlying this is the fact that beginning with £1 in 1950, we needed £17 to buy the same goods in 1992. Beginning with DM1 in 1950, we only needed DM3.5 in 1992 to buy the same goods. The German consciousness of the risks of inflation reflects the horrifying experiences following the First World War. In 1918, a loaf was 63 pfennigs and in November 1923, DM200bn.

The balance of payments is the difference between what a country buys and what it sells. It buys and sells physical goods and services as well as financial items called 'invisibles'. A French investment bank holds US government bonds and earns interest on these bonds. A German firm pays Lloyd's of London premiums for insurance. The balance between all the above items is the current account. Then there is the holding of assets – foreign securities, factories, land and so on – called the 'capital account'. The balance of payments is said to always balance because any deficit on the current account will be offset by a surplus on the capital account. Unfortunately, the figures don't always balance, and so we have 'balancing items' to account for errors and transactions that cannot be traced. Sometimes, the balancing items are huge, reducing confidence in the figures. If a country has a consistent deficit on the current account, the inference is that the country is not competitive, and the expectation is that the exchange rate will weaken in the future.

Because trade sales/purchases only account for a small amount of foreign exchange daily dealing as opposed to capital movements, attention has switched away from PPP to the question of investments. Investors are looking for high real interest rates, that is, the return after taking account of inflation and currency risk. The theory is that investors will shift assets from one country to another according to the relative prices of international assets, expectations of inflation, expectations of exchange rate stability or volatility and actual exchange rates. This is the 'portfolio balance model'.

In a way, this is more attractive than PPP if we look at the sheer volatility of exchange rates. In January 1991, for example, the dollar had weakened dramatically – it was virtually $2 = £1. Within weeks, however, the dollar strengthened to $1.70 = £1. Had the price of a basket of goods changed in this period? Surely not.

The problem with all these theories is when artificial systems, like the ERM, interfere with market forces. For example, in October 1990, the UK joined the ERM with a target rate of DM2.95 = £1. Although UK inflation rates fell over the next 2 years and German rates increased, the UK had, on average, higher inflation in the period and lower productivity in manufacturing. In the middle of a severe recession, the UK was running an extraordinary deficit on its current account, suggesting structural problems and severe difficulties to come as the economy came out of recession. In addition, UK interest rates were barely higher than Germany's in September 1992. Although inflation, then, on a like-for-like basis, was much the same as Germany's, investors' *expectations* were different. They were far more confident that Germany would get inflation lower than they were that the UK would stop it rising further. They also had greater confidence in the Bundesbank holding interest rates high (unpopular politically, but the Bundesbank is independent) than in the Bank of England (not independent at that time) keeping interest rates high in the middle of a severe recession.

In spite of this, sterling moved over the 23 months within its ±6% band compared to the deutschmark. However, sentiment that the pound was overvalued and would have to devalue grew stronger. Financial institutions and corporates holding pounds sold them. Speculators joined in. Finally, the leak that the Bundesbank thought that sterling should seek a new parity was all that was needed for the dam to burst. On 17 September 1992, the UK government withdrew sterling from the ERM and saw the rate fall in 2 weeks from a level of about DM2.80 to DM2.50, causing the experts to produce their favourite quotation: 'You can't buck the market.' The Italian lira had a similar experience. This was followed by further turbulence in July 1993, when currencies like the French franc were attacked, leading to a fundamental change in ERM rules.

Finally, what we can't ignore in looking at exchange rate determinants is the sheer psychology of the markets – the 'herd' instinct, for example, which causes dealers to act in concert and for the market to frequently 'overshoot' when new data are released. Paul de Grauwe and Danny Decupere of the Catholic University of Leuven in Belgium produced a study entitled *Psychological Barriers in the Foreign Exchange Market* (1992), which found, for instance, that traders tended to avoid certain exchange rates, especially those ending in round numbers.

Perhaps because of psychology, there are forecasters of movements called 'chartists' who plot historic price data and look for patterns and trends such as 'heads and shoulders', 'double bottoms/tops', 'broadening top' and so on. This is also called 'technical analysis'. They talk of upper (resistance) levels and lower (support) levels. If a level is broken, the chartists believe that the break will be decisive. Those who look at the underlying economic factors – interest rates, inflation, productivity, balance of payments – are the 'fundamentalists'. The same two approaches are used in equity and bond markets. The chartists and fundamentalists often clash in battle, like the Guelphs and the Ghibellines in medieval Italy, or Catholics and Protestants. In fact, all banks use a blend of both techniques.

BRETTON WOODS

In the postwar period up to the early 1970s, currencies did not fluctuate as they do today, but operated on a fixed basis. The system was set up at a conference in Bretton Woods (New Hampshire, US) in 1944. World finance ministers and major economists, like J.M. Keynes, attended the conference from 44 countries. It was called to discuss the international financial arrangements that would apply after the Second World War. In particular, it set up

- a system of exchange rate stability,
- the International Monetary Fund and
- the World Bank.

Exchange Rate Stability

Exchange rate stability was achieved by members adopting an external, or 'par value', for their currency, expressed in terms of either gold or the US dollar. America had no choice but to adopt a par value for the dollar expressed in gold; the dollar was convertible to gold on demand at $35 per oz, but all other members pegged to the dollar. This Bretton Woods system was therefore termed the 'gold exchange standard', with the dollar being linked directly to gold and other currencies indirectly linked to gold via the dollar. Having adopted a par value, the central banks of member countries had to routinely intervene in the foreign exchange markets to keep their exchange rate against the dollar within 1% either side of the par value: selling their currency (and buying the dollar) when it threatened to rise above 1%; doing the opposite when it fell 1% below the par value. The central banks' efforts to keep their currency at the agreed rate could be supported by the International Monetary Fund (IMF) – hence its relevance to these arrangements.

International Monetary Fund

The decision to set up the IMF was taken at the Bretton Woods Conference in 1944, but it did not come into operation until 1946. Its headquarters are in Washington, DC. The prime object in setting up the IMF was to prevent any return to the restrictive international trade environment and erratic exchange rate fluctuations of the interwar period. The IMF's main task was to preside over a system of fixed exchange rates. Ancillary to this, it provided borrowing facilities for its members, which also allowed trade deficit nations to embark on more gradual corrective policies that would be less disruptive for trading partners.

When a member country had a balance of payments deficit, it borrowed from the IMF to finance it, as well as to obtain supplies of foreign currency with which to buy up its weak currency in the foreign exchange markets, in order to prevent it falling more than 1% below its par value. Thus, in this way, the borrowing facilities' function was ancillary to the stable exchange rate goal. When members exhausted their borrowing entitlement, they had perforce to adopt a new, and lower, par value. Devaluation (and revaluation) was possible but had to be carried out in discussion with the IMF, the latter having to be satisfied that a state of 'fundamental disequilibrium' in the member country's balance of payments did exist. Thus, although exchange rates were fixed under the Bretton Woods system, they were not immutably fixed.

For example, the UK, having sold every foreign asset to pay for the war, was in a weak position. After the war, it adopted (possibly foolishly) an exchange rate of $4 = £1. In 1949, however, it devalued to $2.80 = £1. Devaluation is always difficult. Governments cannot announce devaluations in advance, as everyone will immediately sell their currency. As a result, they always deny any intention to devalue in the strongest terms. Then, they suddenly devalue. The result is that protestations about a determination not to devalue may, in the end, simply be disbelieved. When enough people disbelieve it, devaluation is inevitable due to the massive selling of the currency. The chaos in the ERM in September 1992 illustrates these forces at work.

Member countries had to pay a subscription to the IMF, originally related to their prewar value of trade. This subscription had originally (but no longer) to be one-quarter in gold, with the remainder in the member's own currency. In this way, the IMF acquired a vast pool of gold and members' currencies, giving it the resources to lend. Borrowing entitlements were basically 125% of subscription, although the needs of small subscription countries, as well as the oil price rises of the 1970s, called for additional categories of borrowing facilities to be brought into being. IMF loans are conditional upon the borrowing country agreeing to adopt certain corrective economic policies, generally of an unpopular, restrictive nature.

In the late 1960s, there had been concern that international liquidity (the means of payment for international trade) would not keep pace with the volume growth in trade, thus exerting a deflationary pressure. A new function for the IMF was therefore brought into being, that of creating man-made international liquidity in the form of special drawing rights (SDRs). These were credits created in the books of the IMF and allocated to members to pay for their balance of payments deficits (surplus countries accumulating SDRs). SDRs were first issued in 1971, but with the fear now being one of inflation rather than deflation, further subsequent issues of SDRs have been limited. The value of an SDR is calculated daily, based on an average of the exchange rates of the world's major currencies. As Switzerland did not join the IMF formally until 1992, Swiss francs were not used.

The World Bank

The main operating company is the International Bank for Reconstruction and Development (IBRD, more commonly known as the World Bank). It began operations in 1945 and was initially concerned with the 'reconstruction' of war-devastated Europe. Nowadays, it is primarily concerned with helping less developed countries (LDCs) to develop their economies. It makes loans for up to 20 years at rates of interest slightly below the commercial level, with repayment being guaranteed by the government of the borrowing country. The majority of these loans are for specific projects in the areas of agriculture, energy and transport. Recently, more generalized 'programme' and 'structural adjustment' loans have also been extended to aid less developed economies. The World Bank obtains its funds from members (the same 100 or so countries that are members of the IMF) as well as by the issuance of international bonds. It is a major borrower in the Eurobond market. Along with the IMF, two other institutions come under the umbrella title of the World Bank:

1   The International Finance Corporation (IFC) was set up in 1956 as a multilateral investment bank to provide risk capital (without government guarantee) to private sector enterprises in LDCs, as well as being a catalyst in encouraging loans from other sources. In the latter respect, the IFC is also concerned to stimulate multinational corporations' direct investment in LDCs, this being further encouraged by the Multilateral Investment Guarantee Agency to provide insurance against non-commercial risks.

2 The International Development Association (IDA) (created in 1960) is the soft loan arm of the World Bank. It gives interest-free loans for up to 50 years to the poorest of the developing countries. The IDA's resources come from donations from the rich members of the World Bank, with the US usually contributing not less than 25% of funds.

FLOATING RATES

By August 1972, there were huge pressures on the dollar, partly due to the cost of the Vietnam War. In August, the US authorities abandoned any guaranteed convertibility of the dollar into gold. An international meeting took place in Washington and attempted to hold the fixed exchange rate system together, but the effort failed. The European Common Market was concerned that freely floating rates would upset the operation of the Common Agricultural Policy and set up an arrangement known as the 'snake', designed to keep currencies within a band of ±2.25%. The oil price rises of the 1970s put the arrangements under pressure, and membership gradually dwindled.

The arrival of floating rates meant that central banks didn't have to intervene to the same extent and didn't need the IMF to help with intervention. However, nations still needed to finance their balance of payments deficits. The fact that these were often LDCs with large international debts and seeking World Bank assistance has led some observers to comment on a confusion between the roles of the IMF and the World Bank and, indeed, to a certain amount of rivalry.

In this period of floating exchange rates, the dollar has proved to be a volatile currency. Foreign trade as a proportion of GDP is much less for the US than for many countries, and it seems to be able to live with wild fluctuations that would cause havoc elsewhere. It has implications for world trade that may cause international central banks to wish to intervene, and we shall examine this later in the chapter.

Sterling has not exactly been a stable currency either. Table 11.2 provides a sample of dollar/sterling rates over the years 1972–2014, and Figure 11.1 provides a graphical description of the trends. The Table shows that since 1999, the pound generally increased in strength against the US dollar, peaking in mid-2008 at £1 = $1.96 but falling to $1.66 by March 2014 – a fall of about 15%.

Our previous comments about the effect on an exchange rate of one country's higher inflation and lower productivity are dramatically illustrated by looking at the list of sterling/deutschmark exchange rates, shown in Table 11.3, up until EMU in 1999 and its equivalent rate since.

Over the last couple of years, various price-setting arrangements in financial markets have been under scrutiny since the discovery of price fixing in the London interbank market – the so-called LIBOR scandal. Box 11.2 highlights that price rigging also occurred in the foreign exchange markets and illustrates the major fines recently imposed on major banks for this wrongdoing.

▼ **Table 11.2** *Sterling/dollar exchange rates, 1972–2014*

	Year	Sterling/dollar rate
	1972	2.50 (year of floating)
	1977	1.75
	1980	2.32
Jan.	1985	1.03
Late	1985	1.40
Jan.	1991	1.98
Mar.	1991	1.70
Aug.	1992	1.98
June	1993	1.55
June	1999	1.60
June	2002	1.52
Nov.	2005	1.72
June	2008	1.96
Mar.	2009	1.41
Mar.	2010	1.51
Mar.	2011	1.62
Feb.	2012	1.58
Mar.	2013	1.58
Mar.	2014	1.66

Source: Federal Reserve Bank of St Louis, stlouisfed.org.

▼ **Figure 11.1** *US dollar/UK pound rates,1971–2014*

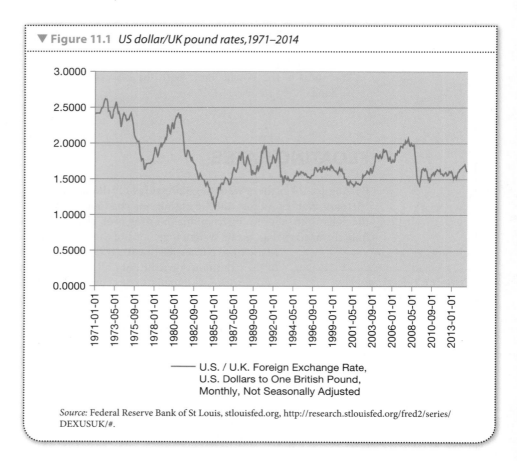

—— U.S. / U.K. Foreign Exchange Rate,
U.S. Dollars to One British Pound,
Monthly, Not Seasonally Adjusted

Source: Federal Reserve Bank of St Louis, stlouisfed.org, http://research.stlouisfed.org/fred2/series/
DEXUSUK/#.

▼ **Table 11.3** *Sterling/deutschmark exchange rates, 1960–2002*

Month	Year	Sterling/deutschmark rate	
	1960	11.71	
	1980	4.23	
Feb.	1987	2.85	
July	1989	2.76	
Oct.	1990	2.95	(ERM target)
Sept.	1992	2.51	(Sterling leaves ERM)
Apr.	1996	2.27	
Dec.	1998	2.80	
Sept.	2002	3.13	(Equivalent – introduction of the euro)

Source: Federal Reserve Bank of St Louis, stlouisfed.org.

BOX 11.2

Fines Imposed on Major Banks for Foreign Exchange Rate Rigging

Regulators fined six major banks a total of $4.3 billion for failing to stop traders from trying to manipulate the foreign exchange market, following a yearlong global investigation.

HSBC Holdings Plc, Royal Bank of Scotland Group Plc, JPMorgan Chase & Co, Citigroup Inc, UBS AG and Bank of America Corp all faced penalties resulting from the inquiry, which has put the largely unregulated $5-trillion-a-day market on a tighter leash, accelerated the push to automate trading and ensnared the Bank of England.

Authorities accused dealers of sharing confidential information about client orders and coordinating trades to boost their own profits. The foreign exchange benchmark they allegedly manipulated is used by asset managers and corporate treasurers to value their holdings.

Dealers used code names to identify clients without naming them and swapped information in online chatrooms, with pseudonyms such as 'the players', 'the 3 musketeers' and '1 team, 1 dream'. Those who were not involved were belittled, and traders used obscene language to congratulate themselves on quick profits made from their scams, authorities said.

Wednesday's fines bring total penalties for benchmark manipulation to more than $10 billion over 2 years. Britain's Financial Conduct Authority levied the biggest penalty in the history of the City of London, $1.77 billion, against five of the lenders.

'Today's record fines mark the gravity of the failings we found, and firms need to take responsibility for putting it right,' FCA Chief Executive Officer Martin Wheatley said.

He said bank managers needed to keep a closer eye on their traders rather than leaving it to compliance departments, which make sure employees follow the rules.

The investigation already has triggered major changes to the market. Banks have suspended or fired more than 30 traders, clamped down on chatrooms and boosted their use of automated trading. World leaders are expected to sign off on regulatory changes to benchmarks this weekend at the G20 summit in Brisbane, Australia.

In the United States, which has typically been more aggressive on enforcement than other jurisdictions, the Department of Justice, Federal Reserve and New York's financial regulator are still probing banks over foreign exchange trading.

Exasperation

Regulators said the misconduct at the banks ran from 2008 until October 2013, more than a year after US and British authorities started punishing banks for rigging the London interbank offered rate (LIBOR), an interest rate benchmark.

The foreign exchange probe has wrapped up faster than that investigation did, and Wednesday's fines reflected cooperation from the banks. Britain's FCA said the five banks in its action received a 30% discount on the fines for settling early.

The US Commodity Futures Trading Commission ordered the same five banks to pay an extra $1.48 billion. Swiss regulator FINMA also ordered UBS, the country's biggest bank, to pay 134 million francs ($139 million) and cap dealers' bonuses over misconduct in foreign exchange and precious metals trading.

The US Office of the Comptroller of the Currency fined the US lenders a total of $950 million. It was the only authority to penalize Bank of America.

Fines Imposed on Major Banks for Foreign Exchange Rate Rigging (*continued*)

More penalties are likely to follow. Barclays Plc, which was not included in Wednesday's settlement, said it had pulled out of talks with the FCA and the CFTC to try to seek 'a more general co-ordinated settlement' with other regulators that are investigating its activities.

The FCA said its enforcement activities were focused on those five plus Barclays, signalling it would not fine Deutsche Bank AG.

The CFTC declined to comment on whether it was looking at other banks.

Britain's Serious Fraud Office is conducting a criminal investigation, and disgruntled customers can still pursue civil litigation.

RBS, which is 80% owned by the British government, received client complaints about foreign exchange trading as far back as 2010. The bank said it regretted not responding more quickly.

The other banks were similarly apologetic.

Bank of England

The currency inquiry struck at the heart of the British establishment and the City of London, the global hub for foreign exchange dealing.

The Bank of England said on Wednesday that its chief foreign exchange dealer, Martin Mallet, had not alerted his bosses that traders were sharing information.

The British central bank, whose governor, Mark Carney, is leading global regulatory efforts to reform financial benchmarks, has dismissed Mallet but said he had not done anything illegal or improper.

It also said it had scrapped regular meetings with London-based chief currency dealers, a sign the BOE wants to put a distance between it and the banks after the scandal.

Source: Reuters, 12 November 2014, http://uk.reuters.com/article/2014/11/12/us-banks-forex-settlement-cftc-idUSKCN0IW0E520141112.

EUROPEAN ECONOMIC AND MONETARY UNION

Moves to European Economic and Monetary Union (EMU) led to changes that had an important impact on foreign exchange markets – the introduction of the ERM in 1979 and the adoption of a single currency, the euro, for 11 countries in January 1999. These moves are so significant that they have a chapter of their own (Chapter 12).

Between 1996 and 2002, the pound increased in value against many other currencies, including the deutschmark, as shown in Table 11.3. For instance, in 1996, you could buy DM2.27 with £1, whereas by 2001, you could buy DM3.09. This strengthening of the pound had adverse consequences for UK exporters as it made their goods substantially more expensive. Even companies like Toyota and Honda, which had set up businesses in the UK to export, had to reduce their car prices so they were competitive in Europe. However, this situation soon changed with the introduction of the euro, as this increased rapidly in value against the pound from 2002 to 2008. A similar trend has occurred in euro/dollar rates. Figure 11.2 illustrates the euro to US dollar rate in recent years and shows the strengthening of the former over a similar period.

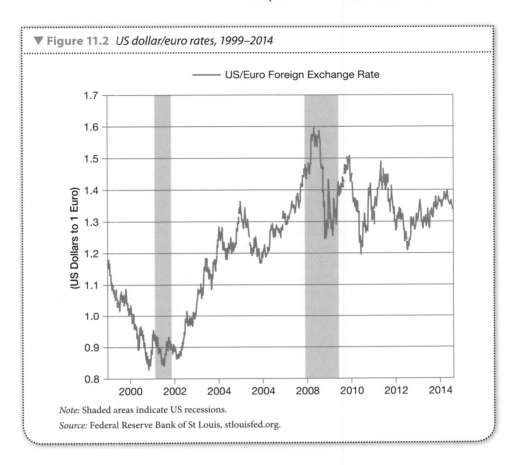

▼ Figure 11.2 *US dollar/euro rates, 1999–2014*

Note: Shaded areas indicate US recessions.

Source: Federal Reserve Bank of St Louis, stlouisfed.org.

FOREIGN EXCHANGE RISK FOR CORPORATES

Types of Risk

Companies that compete in an international marketplace are vulnerable to changes in foreign exchange rates. This vulnerability stems from three types of risk: transaction risk, translation risk and economic risk.

1   *Transaction risk:* This is the most obvious and common risk. A Swiss importer needs to pay for dollar imports in 6 months that are ordered today. If the Swiss franc weakens against the dollar, the imports will cost more. A Swiss exporter has sold goods to someone in the US to be paid for in dollars. By the time the goods are shipped and paid for, say, in 9 months, the Swiss franc may have strengthened against the dollar, making the dollar earnings worth less money. Most corporates will decide to reduce this risk by the technique called 'hedging'. This chapter concentrates on this type of risk.

2   *Translation risk:* Suppose a French firm has overseas subsidiaries reporting profits in Swiss francs, and it also owns land and property in Switzerland. If the Swiss franc weakens against the euro, the profits are worth less in euros when included in the annual report. The value of the land and property may be unchanged, but translated

into euros, the assets seem to have lost value. Should these exposures be hedged? This is a subject of huge controversy. Not hedging may distort asset values and earnings per share. On the other hand, hedging means spending real money to protect account-ancy figures. In any case, sophisticated investors will take the exposure into account. Knowing that our French firm has a heavy exposure to Switzerland, they will adjust their view of the firm's prospects. If, however, the risk has already been hedged away, their view will be incorrect. It may be complicated by the fact that the French firm makes extensive purchases in Swiss francs, thus giving a natural offset of risk.

We can sum this up with the totally opposite views of two firms in not dissimilar businesses. SmithKline Beecham, the former UK-listed pharmaceuticals group, made 90% of its profits outside the UK. In the *Financial Times* (27 November 1991), its treasurer argued in favour of producing less volatile earnings by hedging: 'Stable and predictable earnings are more valuable to investors'. On the other hand, ICI, the UK chemicals and pharmaceutical group, made 55% of its earnings overseas but did not hedge. In the *Financial Times* (1991), its treasurer argued: 'Translation exposures do not have any immediate cash flow consequences, yet any hedging activity will involve cash expenditure.'

3 *Economic risk:* This is by no means as obvious as the other two. Suppose a Dutch firm is selling goods into the US, and its main competitor is a British firm. If sterling weakens against the dollar, the Dutch firm has lost competitive advantage. The UK left the ERM in September 1992. Sterling fell 15% against the deutschmark in a matter of weeks, but the Dutch guilder did not. Obviously, this is serious for the Dutch firm, but it may not be easy to hedge such a risk. It does need to be considered as part of marketing and competitive strategy.

Transaction Risk: Forward Rates

Box 11.3 provides an example of how a company manages transaction risks.

BOX 11.3

Managing Transaction Risk with Forward Rates

Let's take a German computer software company that imports computers from the US, paid for in dollars. It resells them with its added-value services – software, installation and so on. A contract has just been signed with a German customer and two computers ordered from the US in order to fulfil the contract. In its own accounts, the German firm would use euros. The rate for the euro/dollar could fluctuate. The computers cost $100,000, and the exchange rate is $1 = €1.10. The cost is therefore €110,000.

By the time the computers arrive and the German firm is due to pay for them, say, in 3 months' time, the dollar may have strengthened and the exchange rate changed to $1 = €1.25. The cost in euros is now €125,000. If the German firm costed the computers at €110,000 when making the sale, then €15,000 has just been lost from its profit. How can it prevent this happening?

This is, of course, the standard problem facing all importers and exporters.

Importers pay later but don't know what the exchange rate will be.

Exporters earn foreign currencies at a later date but, equally, don't know how rates will move.

One simple solution for the importer is to buy the dollars today at $1 = €1.10. The dollars are not needed for 3 months, so the $100,000 is put on deposit to earn interest. In 3 months' time, they are taken out of deposit and used to pay for the machine.

In principle, there's nothing wrong with this solution, apart from the assumption that the importer has the €110,000 now to do this, as opposed to having to find it in 3 months when, perhaps, his own customer has paid.

However, there is another solution that is so common that this is probably the one that would be used. The importer buys the dollars from the bank 3 months forward – the forward contract.

The bank is requested to provide $100,000 in 3 months in exchange for euros. Today's rate (called spot) is €1.10. The bank may quote, say, €1.1055 for the 3-month deal. The importer now has certainty. The rate could depreciate later to €1.25 but the purchase of dollars will be made at €1.1055. It's a little bit worse than the spot rate, but it has bought peace of mind.

The question is, how did the bank decide that €1.1055 was the correct rate? Does the bank have analysts studying key exchange rate trends and making a forecast? Does it have, in a discreet corner of the dealing room, a gypsy and crystal ball?

The bank is, of course, now at risk instead of the importer. If it does nothing, then in 3 months it faces buying dollars at, say, a rate of €1.25 and only getting €1.1055 from its customer. Earlier, we suggested that the firm could buy the dollars today and put them on deposit. The bank can do the same. It can buy the dollars today at €1.10 and simply lend them in the interbank market for 3 months until its client needs them. The question is – what is the cost to the bank?

The consequence of the bank's action is that money which had been in euros and earning interest (or borrowed – the argument is much the same) is now in dollars and earning interest.

But suppose dollar rates for 3 months' money are 3% p.a., and euro rates are 5% p.a.? The bank has lost 2% p.a. (that is, 0.5% in 3 months) by being in dollars. It is what economists call the 'opportunity cost'. It has lost the opportunity to earn interest on euros, and the cost is 0.5%. This will be charged to the client as a worsening of the spot rate from €1.10 to €1.1055.

Forward rates arise **from the difference in interest rates in the two currencies concerned**.

We can try this argument from another angle. A rich American, with $1m on deposit in the US, earning 3%, sees that euro interest rates are 5% and moves into euros for 1 year to earn an easy extra 2%. The snag is that if euros depreciate by, say, 5% against the dollar, then the original $1m will later only be worth $950,000, and this loss has wiped out the interest rate gain. To prevent this, the American arranges to sell the euros (and buy back the dollars) 1 year *forward*. If the charge for this is any less than 2%, then our American has a locked-in profit and no risk. This will apply to dozens of other Americans with spare funds. The result is that billions of dollars will flow into euros until the laws of supply and demand put up the cost of the forward rate by 2%, making the whole exercise no longer worthwhile. The activity of trying to make a risk-free profit by exploiting price discrepancies is known as 'arbitrage', but of course supply and demand eliminate the possibility very quickly, if, indeed, it arises in the first place.

As dollar interest rates are less than euro interest rates, we say the dollar is at a *premium* (and the euro at a *discount*). Notice, however, the effect of this on an *exporter* in Germany. This firm will, say, earn $100,000 in 3 months and ask the bank to quote a forward rate for buying the dollars from them and providing euros instead. What steps can the bank now take to avoid risk? As it's a little more complicated than our previous example, let's lay out the steps the bank can take:

Today:

1   Borrow $100,000 for 3 months.
2   Buy €110,000 with the dollars at today's rate of €1.10.
3   Put the €110,000 on deposit for 3 months.

3 months later:

1   The €110,000 comes off deposit and is sold to the bank's client for dollars.
2   The client gives the bank the $100,000 earned from exports/
3   The dollar loan is repaid with the $100,000.

The effect of this is that the bank has paid 3% p.a. interest on the dollars and earned 5% p.a. interest on the euros for 3 months (that is, gained 0.5%). The bank has now made money from the interest rate difference, and the forward rate is *more favourable* than the spot rate. (In all these examples, the question of bid/offer spreads has been ignored in the interests of simplicity.)

Where the dollar is at a *premium* to the euro, this means that

- for the *importer*, the forward rate is *less* favourable, and
- for the *exporter*, the forward rate is *more* favourable.

The importer may not be quite sure when it will pay for the dollars and so asks for a forward purchase of dollars, for example 'between 1 and 28 February'. This is a forward-dated option contract, not to be confused with 'options' as such. (In today's market, there is nothing like this difference between US and euro rates, as you may be aware. For the purposes of illustration, however, it is easier to pick figures that can easily be understood.)

Transaction Risk: Options

Let's go back to the case of our German importer. The $100,000 needed for imports is bought forward at a rate of €1.1055. However, in 3 months, the rate is actually €1.05 and has improved from the euro point of view. The $100,000 could be bought spot for only €105,000. However, it can't be bought spot, as the importer has already committed to buy forward at €1.1055. This illustrates a most important point about forward purchases:

The forward purchase protects against a deterioration in the rate, but the forward buyer cannot now gain should the rate improve.

The importer will probably not worry about this, being happy to have protected the profit in the computer deal. Others may not take this view and argue as follows:

Today's spot rate is €1.10. I want protection if the rate worsens in 3 months to €1.25 – I still want to buy dollars at €1.10. On the other hand, if the rate improves to €1.05, I want to forget the above protection and buy spot at €1.05.

In other words, there are those who wish to have their cake and eat it. The markets, being advanced and ingenious, provide a means by which this can be done, called 'options'. Options can become quite complicated when considered in detail. Happily, the principle is easy. The importer does not commit to buy the dollars forward at €1.10, but pays for an option to do so. If, later, the rate has worsened, the importer takes up the option at €1.10. If, however, the rate has improved to, say, €1.05, the importer abandons what was only an option and buys dollars spot at the better rate.

This is clearly more flexible and advantageous than buying forward and naturally costs more (or who would buy forward?). The cost is called the 'premium' and is usually paid in advance. We can, therefore, say of options:

The option purchase protects against a deterioration in the rate, but the option buyer can still benefit from an improvement in the rate. There is a cost – the premium.

Where would the importer (or exporter) go to buy this option? There are two possibilities:

1   Deal through a traded options exchange.
2   Deal through a bank – called OTC ('over the counter').

There are few currency options contracts available in Europe on trading exchanges. This is largely due to the strength of the OTC market there. The biggest currency option deals are handled in the US at either the Chicago Mercantile Exchange (CME) or the Philadelphia Stock Exchange (PHLX, the oldest stock exchange in the US, founded in 1790, and now owned by NASDAQ). In Europe, the main market is the International Securities Exchange.

The characteristics of an exchange are that there are standard contract sizes and standard expiry months. If we take our German importer, he could go to either the CME or PHLX for dollar/euro options and would find the terms shown in Table 11.4.

The first problem for the importer is that €110,000 needs to be covered, and the contract size is €125,000 (or 2 × €62,500). The next problem may be that the expiry in 3 months is 18 February, and neither exchange handles this expiry date.

▼ Table 11.4 *Dollar/euro options terms*

US exchange	Contract size dollar/euros	Options contract months.
CME	125,000	Jan/Mar/Apr/Jun/Jul/Sept/Oct/Dec and spot month
PHLX	62,500	Mar/Jun/Sept/Dec plus 2 near months

The advantage of the standard contract is that, being standard, there is plenty of competition for the business. In particular, the contracts can be sold back later, called 'trading the option'.

Finally, the exchange protects contracts from default by the use of a body called a 'clearing house', and we shall explain this further in Chapter 13.

Going to the bank, the terms can be tailored to the needs of the option buyer, for example €110,000, expiring 18 February. The bank may also offer a number of variations on the deal (see below). However, the options cannot normally be traded and, if the bank crashes into liquidation, the contract is not guaranteed. In currencies, the OTC market with the banks is huge. Perhaps this is because the bank may be helping the importer/ exporter with general finance for trade anyway, and it seems natural to ask it to handle the options business. In addition, banks may construct attractive variations on the options theme, some of which have proved very popular. Here are three examples.

Break forward

Break forward was devised in the mid-1980s by Warren Edwardes while he was at Midland Bank. Here the client is offered a forward rate (at a rate not quite as good as the normal forward), but at a predetermined rate, the contract can be unwound, leaving the client to benefit from a future favourable rate.

For example, a British firm needs to import dollar goods and buy dollars in 3 months. The forward rate is £1 = $1.89. The firm wants downside protection but feels that it is just as likely that sterling will improve. The bank offers a 'floor' rate of $1.88 and a 'break' rate of $1.91. The effect is that, up to a rate of $1.91, the client will buy dollars at $1.88. Above $1.91, the client is freed from this obligation and can buy dollars at the spot rate less 3¢ (that is, the difference between the 'floor' and the 'break' rate which the bank is cleverly using to buy an option). Thus:

- If the future spot rate is $1.80, client buys at $1.88.
- If the future spot rate is $1.91, client buys at $1.88.
- If the future spot rate is $1.98, client buys at $1.95.

The firm gets almost complete downside protection but can, to a large extent, benefit from a forward rate. This leads naturally to participating forward.

Participating forward

Again, a 'floor' rate is agreed as is a participation level in future favourable rates. Let us say that the normal forward rate is $1.89, the 'floor' is $1.86 and the agreed participation in improvement above $1.86 is 80%. If the spot rate later is worse than $1.86, the client buys dollars at $1.86. If the rate is, say, $1.96, the client rate is based on 80% of this improvement. The spot rate is 10 points better than $1.86, so the client can have a rate 8 points better, that is, $1.94. Thus:

- If the future spot rate is $1.80, client buys at $1.86.
- If the future spot rate is $1.91, client buys at $1.90.
- If the future spot rate is $1.96, client buys at $1.94.

Again, the client has substantial downside protection but can also, to a large extent, benefit from an improvement in the rate. The client can discuss the desired participation level with the bank – the higher the level, the lower the floor rate.

Cylinder, or collar

The cylinder, or collar, technique is identical to the 'collar' technique used in interest rate futures. Again, a UK importer needs to buy dollars in 3 months. Let us say that today's spot rate is $1.90. The importer can come to an arrangement with the bank that the future dollars will be bought within a range of, say, $1.85–1.95. (As a result, the technique is also called 'range forward'.) Thus:

- If the future spot rate is worse than $1.85, client buys at $1.85.

- If the future spot rate is better than $1.95, client buys at $1.95.
- If the future spot rate is between $1.85 and $1.95, client buys at that rate.

The client now gets some downside protection and also some upside gain. Depending on the rates chosen, the cost may be small or even none at all.

How does the bank achieve the above end objectives for the client? The answer lies in very ingenious use of option techniques. The whole question of option trading is covered in detail in Chapter 13.

FOREIGN EXCHANGE DEALING

Quotations

The foreign exchange dealer is surrounded by computer terminals giving exchange rates quoted by banks all over the world. The main information providers are Reuters and Electronic Broking Services (EBS), which is owned by ICAP, the world largest interdealer broker. The rates quoted are 'indicative' only. For a firm rate, the dealer must telephone and ask for a quotation for a given currency pair. The dealer merely asks for a quote and does not say if this is a sale or purchase.

The market has its own curious jargon for exchange rates, for example:

- Cable – dollar/sterling
- Swissy – dollar/Swiss franc
- Stocky – dollar/Swedish kroner (from Stockholm)
- Copey – dollar/Danish kroner (from Copenhagen)

In London, even Cockney rhyming slang is used. The Japanese yen rate is the 'Bill and Ben'.

As elsewhere in financial markets, rates are given as 'bid and offer', that is, buying/selling. For example, asked for a 'Swissy' quote, the reply might be SFr1.4250/SFr1.4260 or more likely '50/60' as the dealers are following rates every second of the day. If in any doubt, the enquirer will ask, 'What's the big figure?' and the reply is, '1.42'. This means that the fellow dealer will *buy* dollars at SFr1.4250 or *sell* dollars at SFr1.4260. The 10 bp in the rate is the profit margin, or 'spread'.

We can see this by following it through slowly. Suppose the dealer begins with SFr1.4250 and buys $1. Now the dealer owns $1 (this would be said as 'is *long* of dollars'). On a second enquiry, the dealer sells the dollar at the selling rate of SFr1.4260. Now the dealer, having started out with SFr1.4250, has ended with SFr1.4260 after buying and selling dollars.

If this all seems terribly obvious, we apologize. The problem is that foreign exchange can be confusing for the newcomer. For example, two currencies are involved, not one (as when buying bonds or equities in the domestic currency). Thus, if the dealer buys dollars at SFr1.4250, that is also the rate at which he *sells* Swiss francs. If the dealer sells dollars at SFr1.4260, that is also the rate at which he *buys* Swiss francs. So bid/offer is buy/sell for dollars. For Swiss francs, it is best viewed as sell/buy.

It gets more confusing if we consider sterling. Here the convention is to quote a rate of *dollars for the pound sterling*, for example, the rate is given as $1.70. Everywhere else, we give a rate for each currency against the dollar. Asked to quote for 'cable' (sterling/dollar), the dealer quotes '60/70' or, in full, $1.7360/$1.7370. This time, the buy/sell rate is in terms of *sterling*, that is, the dealer buys sterling at $1.7360 and sells it at $1.7370. In dollars, it's the sell/buy rate.

The result of this way of quoting sterling can be seen when we consider an importer who wishes to buy dollars. One importer is in Switzerland and the other in the UK. The quotes are (mid-point rates):

> dollar/Swiss franc – SFr1.50
> dollar/sterling – $1.73

Later, the rates change to SFr1.55 and $1.78, respectively. For the Swiss, the increase gives a *worse* rate, as they must give up SFr1.55 to buy $1, instead of SFr1.50. For the UK importer, the increase has given a *better* rate. For each £1, they obtain $1.78 instead of $1.73. (Notice that, for an exporter, the results would be exactly the opposite.)

Foreign exchange rates can be confusing for the newcomer unless these basic points are borne in mind from the outset:

> The market is oriented to the dollar. Dealers' quotes are normally given as an amount of the currency to the dollar, and the bid/offer is buy/sell from a dollar point of view. Sterling is the exception, typically quoted as an amount of dollars for the pound sterling. From the dollar point of view, the bid/offer is now sell/buy.

Cross-rates

When a Swiss firm contacts its bank to buy Canadian dollars, the bank will buy US dollars with the Swiss francs and then buy Canadian dollars with the US dollars. The market is wedded to the dollar and finds organization easier and simpler if dealers go in and out of the dollar, even if some 'double counting' is involved. To attempt to deal directly between any pair of currencies would be too complex. The April 2013 BIS survey found that around 87% of deals involved the dollar. The dollar is the world's reserve currency – by the end of 2013, 60% of the world's foreign exchange reserves were in dollars, with 25% in euros, 5% in yen and sterling and the remainder in other currencies. A reserve currency needs a home economy with a large share of global trade and finance. It must also be a currency in which people have confidence.

An exchange rate between two currencies, neither of them the dollar, is a cross-rate. If a dealer goes directly from Swiss francs to sterling, it would be called a direct cross-rate deal, or *cross*. Due to the anticipated arrival of the euro, crosses between European countries became more popular. With the replacement of 11 currencies by the euro in 1999 (and the increase in euro members to 18 by the start of 2015), the figure has fallen.

Foreign Exchange Swaps

When we discussed the problem of our German importer earlier, we suggested that the bank, requested to *sell* dollars to its client in 3 months, might buy the dollars today and put them on deposit. For a client wanting the bank to *buy* dollars in 3 months, the procedure was more complex but involved borrowing dollars for 3 months, buying euros and putting them on deposit. Although both techniques are quite feasible, they tie up balance sheet assets and liabilities. They impact on the banks' credit limits, involve counterparty risk and use up capital under capital ratio rules.

As a result, the problem is usually solved by the 'foreign exchange swap'. Before going any further, these swaps have nothing to do with the swaps market for interest rate and currency swaps. The use of the same term can cause confusion. Many foreign exchange dealers simple call them 'forward' deals because that's how they handle forward requirements. Box 11.4 details features of a foreign exchange swap.

BOX 11.4

Foreign Exchange Swaps

The foreign exchange swap is *one* transaction that combines *two* deals, one spot and one forward. In the first deal, a bank buys a currency spot and, in the second, simultaneously sells it forward for delivery at a later date. The bank will therefore return to the original position at the future date. For example, bank A may have £10m and enter into a swap with bank B for dollars:

1 Bank A sells £10m *spot* for, say, $20m to bank B

2 Bank A sells the $20m *forward* for £10m in 3 months.

At the moment, then, bank A has $20m. In 3 months, bank A will exchange the $20m for £10m, returning to the original position. Thus, the foreign exchange swap is a combined spot and forward deal.

When a bank commits to sell a customer a currency at a future date, there may be others wanting to buy the currency for the same date. However, though some deals will offset in this fashion, in most cases dealers won't be so fortunate. If they have sold $2m for delivery on 20 March, they may find that they are due to buy $2m for pounds on 30 March – leaving an exposure 'gap'. Alternatively, they are due to buy dollars for pounds on 20 March, but only $1m, leaving the dealer 'short' of $1m for 20 March delivery.

One way of handling the problem is to buy $2m today and put it on deposit until 20 March. This may mean having to borrow the pounds to do it. This involves finding suitable lenders and borrowers, and ties up lines of credit with other banks.

Instead, it will be easier to buy $2m spot. The dollars, however, are not required until 20 March, so the dealer now enters the swap:

1 The dealer sells the $2m spot for pounds, returning back to a pound position

2 At the same time, the dealer sells the pounds forward for $2m to be delivered on 20 March.

The counterparty to the swap that had pounds originally is now sitting on dollars until 20 March. If dollar interest rates are lower than the pound, the swap rate will reflect the difference in interest rates.

Thus, if UK interest rates were 6% higher than the US, then a 6-month forward deal would involve a premium of 3% (ignoring yield curve variations). If spot were, say, $1.80, then the 6-month forward premium would be about 5.40¢. The spot rate might thus be quoted as $1.8000/$1.8010 with a forward margin or spread of, say, 5.40¢/5.30¢ (or quoted as basis points, 540/530). As the dollar is at a premium, these rates will be *subtracted* from the spot rates (if at a discount, the rates would be added to the spot rates).

Foreign Exchange Swaps (*continued*)

Thus, an *importer* wanting to buy dollars for pounds in 6 months will be quoted as follows:

Spot $ 1.8000
Premium 540 –
Forward rate $1.7460

An *exporter* wanting to sell dollars for pounds in 6 months will be quoted as follows:

Spot $ 1.8010
Premium 530 –
Forward rate $ 1.7480

The *importer* has a *worse* rate than spot, as it only gets $1.7460 for £1 rather than $1.80, and the *exporter* has a *better* rate than spot as it only gives up $1.7480 to obtain £1 rather than $1.8010.

Thus the swap handles the request from a customer for a forward deal. It would also handle a situation where the dealer was 'long' in spot dollars (and thus at risk) but 'short' of the same quantity for delivery in 3 months. The dealer sells the dollars spot for pounds (and is no longer 'long' of spot dollars) and sells the pounds back for the dollars in 3 months.

Those who have quick minds will see that, while the dealer is no longer at risk to changes in currency rates, it may be at risk to changes in interest rates. The cost of the swap is based on an interest rate difference between dollar/sterling of 6% p.a. But what if this changes to 4% p.a. or 7%?

There is, indeed, a potential problem here, but the solutions are outside the scope of an introductory book of this nature. Suffice it to say that there is a risk – market risk – which could result in losses if not hedged, and which will be taken into account by the risk management policies and practices of the bank as well as by regulators in setting capital ratios.

Often swap deals are very short term. Many are for delivery spot (2 days) but will be reversed the following day, called 'spotnext'. Others are for delivery the next day and reversed the following day, called 'tomnext'. It all adds to the horrible jargon of the markets.

The foreign exchange swap is different from the forward transaction we met earlier in the chapter. The BIS 2013 survey analysed the market over spot, forward and swaps. Average daily dealings were as follows:

Spot – $2,046bn
Forwards – $680bn
Swaps – $2,228bn
Currency swaps – $54bn
Options and other products – $337bn
Total – $5,345bn

Brokers

In these markets, extensive use is made of brokers. A dealer who is long on dollars and anxious to sell may not wish to reveal its position to others. The desire to sell, say, $50m for sterling at a given rate can be passed to a broker who will disseminate this information anonymously, using computer screens or voice boxes. Another dealer, who finds this rate acceptable, may close the deal via the broker. The broker takes no risk. The clients settle directly, and the broker takes a small commission.

An innovative Reuters system, Dealing 2000/2, was released in mid-1992. This enabled the computer system itself to match spot foreign exchange deals automatically and anonymously, and was followed by even more powerful systems – the most recent being the Reuters spot matching system. The main competitor to Reuters is the Electronic Broking Services (EBS), created in 1990 by a partnership of the world's largest foreign exchange market-making banks to challenge Reuters' threatened monopoly in interbank spot foreign exchange, and now owned by ICAP. When the Bank of Japan surprised markets by saying it was going to engage in more quantitative easing in late October 2014, transactions on the EBS spot dealing system hit a record high, with daily volumes at the start of November exceeding $220bn. The decision whether to use EBS or Reuters primarily depends on the currency being traded. EBS is the main trading venue for €/$, $/¥, €/¥, $/CHF and €/CHF, and Reuters is the main trading venue for all other interbank currency pairs. EBS accounts for the majority of the spot interbank market.

In July 1999, Bloomberg, the US company, announced that it would join with Tullett & Tokyo Liberty (now known as Tullett Prebon), the London-based voice broker, to launch an electronic broking system, known as FXall, for the forward market. This electronic trading platform for foreign exchange began operating in 2000. It is integrated with large foreign exchange banks and by 2012 dealt with over 1,000 worldwide institutions. It offers spot and forward transaction services and dealt with around $90bn daily transactions in 2013.

Settlement

Getting paid is, naturally, crucially important. Doing the deal on the telephone is called 'front office'. Getting paid, reconciling accounts and so on is 'back office'.

In some systems, the dealer writes the details of the deal on a slip of paper. These are later encoded into the computerized back office system. In other cases, the dealer enters the deal into the computer system used for front office, which prints a deal slip and holds the data electronically for transfer to the back office system.

A domestic bank thinks of its account with a foreign bank in the foreign currency as its nostro account. For example, BNP Paribas thinks of its dollar account with Citibank in New York as its 'nostro', or *our* account with you. Equally, it regards Citibank's account with itself, BNP Paribas, in euros as the 'vostro', or 'loro', account, that is, '*your* account with us'. This all goes back to those clever Italian bankers years ago.

The department dealing with settlement and reconciliation is thus the 'nostro department'. Agreeing our calculation of the value of the foreign currency account with the foreign bank's statement for the same account is 'nostro reconciliation', an important but tedious chore for which computer systems are used to speed up the process.

Banks today are most concerned about counterparty risk (even before the collapse of BCCI in 1991). For example, all spot deals are settled in 2 working days. What if we settle the foreign currency deal but the counterparty doesn't? The bankers call this 'Herstatt risk', following the spectacular failure, on 26 June 1974, of the German bank Herstatt to settle the dollar side of its transactions (6 hours behind), although the deutschmarks had been paid to it. This risk has led to the use of a technique called 'netting'. The Group of Thirty, a Washington-based think tank, headed by Paul Volker, a past chairman of the

Fed, produced an important report on settlement. Among other things, it recommended netting arrangements to reduce risk.

The first system of bilateral netting in London was provided by FXnet, a trading platform involving 16 banks and IT companies. It will serve to illustrate the principle. Netting no longer requires the exchange of two payments for each pair of currencies dealt with. The two parties make or receive one net payment for each currency deal for each settlement date. For example, suppose counterparty A and counterparty B enter into the four transactions for the same settlement date, as shown in Figure 11.3. In the conventional way, each counterparty would process eight transactions, paying away four and receiving four.

In the FXnet system, running accounts were maintained for each currency and settlement date, and at settlement, each counterparty would process three *net* deals, one for each currency. The running accounts would appear as shown in Figure 11.4.

Settlement of the net amounts occurs as each settlement date is reached. Using conventional settlement methods, if we take the dollar account, A will pay B $40m, and B will pay A $20m. Taking the pound account, A will pay B £10m, and B will pay A £5m. Suppose A defaults and does not settle? B will lose $40m and £10m. Under the netting, B would lose $20m and £5m. In other words, a key reason for net settlement is to reduce substantially the underlying risk of foreign exchange dealing.

If bilateral netting has advantages, then multilateral netting has even more. A multilateral netting system called ECHO began operations in London in 1995, as did a similar system called Multinet in the US. Then, in March 1996, came the announcement that 20 major banks, 'the group of 20', were setting up a global clearing system to handle foreign exchange settlement, which would operate in real time. This was an instantaneous settlement system in which payment by one bank is immediately offset by payment by another, eliminating the Herstatt risk. With this announcement, ECHO and Multinet merged, and later merged with the new system, called CLS Services (now CLS Bank).

▼ **Figure 11.3** *Netting by counterparties*

1

A	B
$10m ⟶	
	⟵ £5m

2

A	B
	⟵ $20m
£10m ⟶	

3

A	B
$20m ⟶	
	⟵ 30m

4

A	B
$10m ⟶	
	⟵ 15m

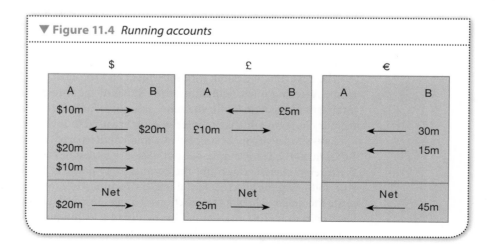

▼ **Figure 11.4** *Running accounts*

This became operational in September 2002, having completed trials in July 2002. Since then, an increasing number of trades have been settled through CLS Bank. Owned by a group of the world's largest financial institutions, it runs a daily system for netting payments between its members that dramatically reduces settlement risk. Currencies accounting for about 95% of daily trading can be settled through CLS, and all large banks use the system. CLS settled a record $2 trillion daily in August 2013 (record daily settlements in value terms was on 19 March 2008, when 1,113,464 payment instructions were settled to a value of $10.3 trillion).

An interesting feature of the credit crisis has been to show how resilient foreign exchange settlement systems are. Only one transaction by a German bank suffered from Herstatt risk – resulting from the collapse of Lehman Bros on 15 September 2008. On this day, KfW Banking Group allowed a €300m payment for a currency swap to go out to Lehman Brothers, and it never received the dollars it was owed in return. According to the *Financial Times* (21 August 2009), if the transaction had been undertaken via CLS, then KfW would have got its money back:

> CLS processes trades in real time for settlement for most of the main banks today, handling about 50% of global FX [foreign exchange] trading volumes. The system matches both sides of a trade – it does not stand as a central counterparty – and then nets each member bank's total obligation. If KfW had settled its Lehman trade through CLS, it would have got its €300m back, because if CLS can't reconcile both sides of a deal, the funds are returned.

ARBITRAGE

Arbitrage is a term first used in the foreign exchange markets. In the days when communications were not as good as today, one might find a disparity in rates quoted for the same pair of currencies. Perhaps the offer price for dollar/sterling in Paris is less than the bid price for dollar/sterling in London or any similar disparity in rates quoted by various banks. A currency could be bought in Paris and resold in London for an easy profit.

In general, arbitrage is taking advantage of any pricing anomaly. More and more sophisticated arbitrage opportunities than ever before are being spotted due to the use of computers, often linked to constant feeds of live prices and using 'expert systems' techniques. At the same time, the paradox is that a dealer has to be quicker than ever to take advantage of an arbitrage opportunity, because everyone else is using computers too.

For example, a dealer may spot that another dealer's forward rate does *not* eliminate the difference in interest rates. As a result, perhaps the low-interest-rate currency is borrowed, sold for the high-interest-rate currency and this put on deposit for, say, 6 months. At the same time, to avoid currency risk, the low-interest-rate currency is bought back forward in 6 months' time so that the original loan can be repaid. The forward rate cost, however, is less than the interest rate difference, leaving a risk-free profit. This is called 'covered interest rate arbitrage'.

Arbitrage can be found in any market these days, not just foreign exchange. As it is essentially risk free, it's good business if you can find it. All the banks employ arbitrage specialists who look for these opportunities, especially in the derivative products marketplace. The argument in its favour is that it keeps pricing efficient. In spite of this, arbitrage between equities and futures markets (stock index arbitrage) rouses great suspicions and is a subject of considerable controversy.

One of the earliest records of telegraphic links was that between the Rothschilds of London and the Behrens of Hamburg in 1843 to exchange prices of securities, currencies and bills of exchange – rich arbitrage opportunities for those quick off the mark.

CENTRAL BANK SURVEYS

At the start of this chapter, we explained that global central banks carried out a simultaneous survey of their markets in 1986, 1989, 1992, 1995, 1998, 2001, 2004, 2007, 2010 and 2013. The BIS, in Basel, collects all the figures and eliminates double counting (a deal done in London with a New York bank will be reported in both centres). Recent results in the major centres can be seen in Table 11.5.

The first point to note is the huge size of the figures. London trades $2,726bn worth of business each and every day. The total figure in 1986 was just in excess of $300bn daily, but by 2013 the figure was $3.98 trillion.

Second, note that the geographical breakdown in Table 11.5 is calculated on the so-called net-net basis, which takes account of domestic and cross-border interdealer double counting. Here the daily turnover is estimated at $5,345bn.

Trading in the individual currencies of the euro member countries against the dollar accounted for 37% of total volume in 1998; dollar/euro trading now accounts for 24.1%. The Appendix 1 to this chapter gives the breakdown of trading by currency pair. Note that the dollar is the main traded currency, featuring in 87% of deals, followed by the euro (33.4%), yen (23.4%) and then sterling (11.8%). (Note the percentages sum to 200% because all transactions involve two different currencies.)

One problem for central banks, intervening from time to time to support their currencies, is that the forces that can be marshalled against them are much bigger. If we look at the ERM crisis as it unfolded in August–September 1992, we see the Bank of England sitting

▼ Table 11.5 *Central bank foreign exchange surveys: Daily foreign exchange dealing*

Centre	2004		2007		2010		2013	
	Amount $bn	Share %	Amount $bn	Share %	Amount $bn	Share %	Amount $bn	Share %
UK	753	31.3	1,359	34.1	1,854	36.7	2,726	40.9
US	461	19.2	664	16.6	904	17.9	1,263	18.9
Switzerland	79	3.3	242	6.1	263	5.2	216	3.2
Japan	199	8.3	238	6.0	312	6.2	374	5.6
Singapore	125	5.2	231	5.8	266	5.3	383	5.7
Hong Kong	102	4.2	175	4.4	238	4.2	274	4.1
Australia	81	3.4	170	4.3	192	3.8	182	2.7

Source: BIS (2010, 2013) *Triennial Central Bank Survey.*

on reserves of gold and foreign currencies of about $44bn. The trading in deals involving sterling, including cross-rate, amounted to some $79bn every single day. Even with the assistance of the Bundesbank, the resistance was simply swept away.

What we saw at one time was concerted action by major central banks, usually agreed at G5 (France, Germany, Japan, the UK and the US) and later G7 (G5 plus Canada and Italy) meetings. It all began at the start of 1985. The rise of the dollar was making US exports uncompetitive, and the pound/dollar rate was nearing parity. After a series of secret telephone calls, the world's major central banks hit the dollar simultaneously on Wednesday morning, 27 February 1985. There was near pandemonium on the foreign exchange markets, and within an hour the dollar had fallen 6% against the deutschmark, from DM3.50 to DM3.30.

Intervention came again in September 1985. Ministers from the G5 countries met at the Plaza Hotel, New York on 22 September. A statement was issued that the dollar was overvalued, and although this was only words, it did the trick. The following day, Monday, 23 September, the dollar fell 3.5% without the central banks spending anything. The dollar/deutschmark rate was then DM2.70. Later, the central banks did intervene to reinforce their wishes, and by November, the dollar/deutschmark was DM2.50. This has become known as the Plaza Agreement and was, perhaps, the first international agreement on currencies since Bretton Woods.

If the Plaza Agreement seemed to mark a new milestone, this has not really proved to be the case. Ministers from the G7 countries met again at the Louvre in Paris in February 1987, and this time declared the dollar undervalued and also announced a resolve to hold major world interest rates within narrow bands. This became known as the 'Louvre Accord'. However, this and several later attempts to boost the dollar were not nearly as successful as the earlier attempts to halt its runaway success. Nevertheless, the US and Japan moved to support the yen in June 1998 and for a time moved the rate from ¥143 to the dollar to ¥136.8; by 2002, it was trading in the ¥120–125 range. Generally, these concerted central bank moves have become less common over the past decade, although individual central bank intervention is more common. For example, the *Financial Times* (19 June 2009) reported the following:

> Speculation that the Bank for International Settlements was intervening on behalf of the Swiss National Bank [SNB] to stem the rise of the Swiss franc sent the currency tumbling yesterday. Traders said they saw bids from the BIS to buy the euro and sell the Swiss franc in the currency market. As the news spread across the world's trading floors, the euro rose from SFr1.50 to above SFr1.51 against the Swiss franc in a matter of minutes. Markets have been on the alert for any intervention from the SNB after the central bank stunned currency markets by selling the Swiss franc against the euro and the dollar in March in an attempt to stop the currency's strength hampering the domestic economy. Neither the SNB nor the BIS confirmed any action.

Although the Swiss authorities intervened in the foreign exchange markets between 2009 and 2011 to influence the value of the Swiss franc, it is typically the case that since the mid-1990s, monetary authorities in most large developed countries have backed away from foreign-exchange intervention. According to the Cleveland Federal Reserve Bank, 'Switzerland's recent experience goes a long way to illustrate why: foreign-exchange intervention did not afford the Swiss National Bank with a means of systematically affecting the franc independent of Swiss monetary policy, and it left the Bank exposed to foreign-exchange losses. To affect exchange rates central banks must change their monetary policies. Any monetary authority contemplating intervention should consider the recent Swiss experience'.

WHY LONDON?

The figures shown above reveal London not only as the biggest foreign exchange market in the world, but also by a considerable margin, as it accounts for 40.9% of world foreign exchange dealings. In view of the decline of the UK as an economic power and the weakness of the pound as a major currency, one may well ask why it is the major foreign exchange market. There are, perhaps, four factors:

1   *Time zone:* London is well placed here. It can talk to Tokyo for an hour in the morning, the Middle East at about 11.30 a.m., New York/Chicago at 1.30 p.m. and Los Angeles/San Francisco at 4.30 p.m. New York and Tokyo are in non-overlapping time zones.
2   *Tradition:* London has a historical and traditional role as a major financial centre. Around 1,400 foreign financial firms (according to TheCityUK) trade in London including around 200 banks (the Association of Foreign Banks has 198 members in 2014) and it also has the professional services infrastructure needed – accountants, lawyers, speciality printers and so on.
3   *Euromarkets:* The euromarkets have large implications for foreign exchange. London's traditional role and its lack of protectionism led to the euromarket business (the issue of non-sterling denominated bonds, equity and other instruments including syndicated credits) emanating from London and the large number of foreign banks.
4   *English language:* English is the major language in international finance. The use of English as a first or second language is actually growing. This certainly helps London to score over Paris or Frankfurt. Indeed, the French insistence (at the highest official level) on the use of French militates against their desire to promote Paris further as an international centre.

SUMMARY

The foreign exchange market is huge, trading $5,345bn ($5.3 trillion) a day in 2013, with London the biggest market.

The demand for foreign exchange arises from trade, tourism, government spending, international security trading and speculation.

Interbank business in London accounts for over two-thirds of the market by value and the top five banks dominate.

One economic theory for explaining exchange rates is *purchasing power parity* (PPP). Pricing the same basket of goods in two countries should result in the exchange rate. If a country consistently has higher inflation than another, its currency will tend to weaken compared with that of the country with lower inflation. The high inflation country will have to offer higher interest rates to persuade non-nationals to hold its currency. The theory that investors will shift assets according to factors like these is the *portfolio balance model*.

The postwar period of fixed exchange rates was agreed at a meeting at *Bretton Woods* in 1944. This also set up the IMF and the World Bank.

Foreign exchange risk for corporates has three elements – *transaction risk*, *translation risk* and *economic risk*.

Spot rates are today's exchange rates with settlement in two days. *Forward rates* are fixed rates for a transaction at a later date. They are determined by the difference in interest rates in the two currencies concerned. Worldwide, 42% of deals by the volume of turnover are FX swaps, 38% spot and 13% forwards.

The forward rate, being fixed, protects against the currency moving to the buyer's/seller's disadvantage, but they cannot benefit if it moves in their favour. This can be achieved by *currency options*. Options can be dealt on an exchange or over the counter (OTC).

Foreign exchange quotations are shown as a *bid/offer rate*. The dollar lies at the heart of foreign exchange dealing, as most transactions involve moving in and out of the dollar. Sterling and currencies that were linked to sterling quote so many dollars to the domestic currency. Other currencies quote a quantity of that currency to the dollar. A rate between two currencies, neither of them the dollar, is called a *cross-rate*.

The purchase of a currency spot accompanied by its simultaneous sale forward is the *foreign exchange swap*.

Brokers are active and link buyers and sellers on an anonymous basis. Electronic broking systems like Reuters and EBS's spot matching systems are widely used.

A bank's foreign currency holdings with banks abroad are its *nostro* accounts. The foreign banks' balances with it in the domestic currency are *vostro* accounts.

Multilateral netting is now used to reduce settlement risk and the main system is CLS, which settled $2 trillion daily transactions in August 2013. Record daily settlements in value terms was on 19 March 2008 when 1,113,464 payment instructions were settled to a value of $10.3 trillion.

Arbitrage is taking advantage of an anomaly in rates to make risk-free profit.

Central banks carry out a foreign exchange survey every 3 years (2013 was the last occasion), with the results coordinated by the BIS.

REVISION QUESTIONS/ASSIGNMENTS

1 Briefly explain the main theories relating to exchange rate determination.

2 Can PPP be used to forecast future exchange rates? What are the limitations of PPP?

3 Examine the main features of spot and forward rates. Why are forward products used more widely than spot contracts?

4 Why has London become the main foreign exchange market?

REFERENCES

BIS (Bank for International Settlements). (2013) *Triennial Central Bank Survey of Foreign Exchange and Derivatives Market Activity*, BIS, Basel. Definitive 3-yearly survey of the global foreign exchange market.

BIS (Bank for International Settlements). (2010) *Triennial Central Bank Survey of Foreign Exchange and Derivatives Market Activity*, BIS, Basel. Definitive 3-yearly survey of the global foreign exchange market.

Euromoney FX Survey 2014, May, http://www.euromoney.com/Article/3338848/Euromoney-FX-survey-2014-results-revealed.html.

De Grauwe, P., and Decupere, D. (1992) *Psychological Barriers in the Foreign Exchange Market*, discussion paper no. 621, January, CEPR, London. Technical paper analysing behavioural features of the foreign exchange market.

Pakko, M.R., and Pollard, P.S. (2003) *Burgernomics: A Big Mac™ Guide to Purchasing Power Parity*, Federal Reserve Bank of St Louis, St Louis. Classic explanation and analysis of the Big Mac index.

FURTHER READING

Chen, J. (2009) *Essentials of Foreign Exchange Trading*, John Wiley & Sons, New York. Detailed and insightful text of foreign exchange trading.

Copeland, L. (2014) *Exchange Rates and International Finance* (6th edn), FT/Prentice Hall, London. Intermediate text on foreign exchange, with detailed analysis of the theory and practice of foreign exchange market volatility.

Pilbeam, K. (2013) *International Finance* (4th edn), Palgrave Macmillan, Basingstoke. Covers the theory and practice of international finance in a clear, thoughtful manner, discussing exchange rate determination, international organizations and balance of payments issues.

Sarno, L., and Taylor M.P. (2003) *The Economics of Exchange Rates*, CUP, Cambridge. Advanced text covering theory and econometrics of exchange rate markets.

▼ *Appendix 1:* *Foreign exchange turnover by currency pairs, daily averages in April 2004, 2007, 2010 and 2013, in billions of USD*

Currency pair	2004 Amount	2004 Share %	2007 Amount	2007 Share %	2010 Amount	2010 Share %	2013 Amount	2013 Share %
US$/€	501	28	840	27	1,101	28	1,289	24
US$/Yen	296	17	397	13	568	14	978	18
US$/£	245	14	361	12	360	9	472	9
US$/AUS$	90	5	175	6	249	6	364	7
US$/SwFr	78	4	143	5	168	4	184	3
US$/CAN$	71	4	115	4	182	5	200	4
US$/Other	292	16	572	19	445	11	1,168	22
€/Yen	51	3	70	2	111	3	147	3
€/£	43	2	64	2	109	3	102	2
€/SwFr	26	1	54	2	72	2	71	1
€/Other	39	2	112	4	102	3	182	3
Other currency pairs	39	2	122	4	514	12	195	4
All currency pairs	1,773	100	3,081	100	3,981	100	5,345	100

Source: BIS (2013) *Triennial Central Bank Survey.*

Europe and the Eurozone

INTRODUCTION

The world is increasingly becoming one vast global market – general deregulation, the collapse of artificial barriers to trade, modern electronic communications – all have contributed to this state of affairs.

A supreme example of globalization is surely Europe's Economic and Monetary Union (EMU) and the creation of the eurozone. Eighteen sovereign states, with an estimated total population of 333 million, have accepted a single currency and central bank. The term 'cross-border' has become less significant as the EMU area moves (with limitations) to become simply one market. In many ways, it is the most dramatic political and economic development of our time; hence this separate chapter, looking at this phenomenon in more detail.

We shall begin by examining the history of the European Union (EU), which comprises 28 member countries with an estimated population of 507 million, and then look at its institutions. We shall then discuss the objectives of EMU. Why create it in the first place? What advantages should it bring? What are the problems? During this, we consider the effect of EMU (actual and anticipated) on banking and securities markets in their various aspects, and in particular we discuss the new European Banking Union.

Major countries in Europe not yet members of the eurozone include the UK, as well as Denmark and Sweden. The 2008 financial crisis initially increased interest in Denmark and Poland joining the EU, although with the onset of the eurozone crisis, this enthusiasm has been somewhat dampened. The ability of Ireland's crippled banking and economic system to withstand collapse has, however, been put down to EMU membership. This was another reason why Iceland stated that it wished to join the EU, a precondition for eventually adopting the euro, although again, like Portugal and Denmark, enthusiasm has waned.

Finally, we look at the general arguments for and against the UK joining the EMU, outline EU legislation that impacts the financial sector and discuss recent European banking sector trends, including the recent eurozone crisis and the establishment of a European Banking Union.

HISTORY OF THE EUROPEAN UNION

Early History

Most of us believe that the impetus for European Union came in the years after 1945. Although this is generally true, the concept has a long history. Several people have thought of the idea of drawing Europe together by military conquest, from the Romans through Charlemagne to Napoleon. The general idea then was to maintain peace and provide defence against enemies.

A landmark event was the establishment in 1923 of a 'Pan-European Union' by an Austrian aristocrat named Richard Coudenhove-Kalergi. He argued for a European federation and, importantly, attracted several young politicians as members who later were able to wield considerable influence. Among these were Konrad Adenauer, Georges Pompidou and Carlos Sforza. One key objective (as today) was to compete better in the world's economic markets. Interestingly, the UK was never regarded as a potential participant. No practical results were achieved, although the idea had general support.

1945

After 1945, things changed. Europe was devastated by the Second World War (1939–45). There was a widespread feeling that the nation state had no future. There was an awareness of Europe's weakened state economically, the dominance of the US and fear of Russia and communism.

In 1948, the Organisation for European Economic Co-operation (OEEC) was formed to oversee the distribution of US aid in Europe. It had a Council of Ministers, with each state having one voice, and decisions required a unanimous vote. After the widespread currency devaluations of 1949, the OEEC set up a European Payments Union in 1950 to act as a sort of central bank for intra-European trade and payments.

The OEEC was not a foundation stone: it had no political implications and limited economic power. It was still, however, a major exercise in Europeans working together. In 1960, it became the wider Organisation for Economic Co-operation and Development (OECD), the original 18 members growing to 30 today, including the US, Canada and Japan. Many more countries are being invited to join, including China and Russia.

The Council of Europe

In 1947, an International Committee of the Movements for European Unity was formed and held a Congress of Europe in the Hague in May 1948. Several hundred delegates attended from 16 states. Delegates wanted a European assembly and a European court. A European movement was formed to carry on the debate and put pressure on politicians.

After the UK's unique position in the war, many looked to it for leadership here, but did not get it. The Attlee government was preoccupied with its own problems in implementing a socialist economy. The idea of a European assembly was, however, supported by many pro-Europe politicians, notably Paul-Henri Spaak of Belgium and Robert Schuman, France's foreign minister.

In May 1949, representatives of the states agreed to set up a Council of Europe in Strasbourg to achieve

> a greater unity between its members for the purpose of safeguarding and realizing the ideals and principles which are their common heritage and facilitating their economic and social progress.

The Council of Europe met in August 1949, with a Committee of Ministers, meeting twice a year, and a Consultative Assembly. Paul-Henri Spaak was the first president. No positive move towards European integration took place, and the Committee of Ministers and the Assembly were often at loggerheads. Nevertheless, the Council did useful work on human rights and founded the European Court of Justice in 1959. It also worked on coordinating policies on transport, civil aviation and agriculture. Again, Europeans were trying to work together.

The European Coal and Steel Community (1952–2002)

In May 1950, Robert Schuman, the French foreign minister, produced the Schuman Plan, proposing a pooling of coal and steel resources. They were to be pooled and administered by a new supranational authority in conjunction with the various states involved. Tariff barriers would be eliminated gradually.

It is most important, however, to see the political motivation here. There was recognition that stability and security in Western Europe rested on France and Germany coming together. Indeed, the initial proposal was for a Franco-German coal and steel pool with others invited to join (the Council of Europe had made a similar recommendation earlier). It was also seen as the first step to political integration.

A specific plan was drafted by Jean Monnet, head of the French Planning Commission. The Treaty of Paris, setting up the European Coal and Steel Community (ECSC), was signed in April 1951, and ratification by local parliaments took a further year. Members were France and West Germany, along with Italy, the Netherlands, Belgium and Luxembourg – the Common Market's original 'six'. Although the Attlee government in the UK lost the 1951 election, the new government under Churchill (a supposed European) was no more enthusiastic about the ECSC than the previous government, to the disappointment of many dedicated Europeans.

People committed to a form of common future for Europe were now in positions of power – Schuman and Monnet in France, Adenauer in Germany, de Gasperi in Italy, Spaak in Belgium and Beck in Luxembourg.

It is common for people in the UK to talk of a 'hidden agenda' behind EMU, namely some form of political federation. Certainly, some UK pro-Europeans have played this aspect down, but the agenda has always been in the open. The founders of the ECSC wanted to foster economic expansion, growth in employment and a rising standard of living, it is true. They were, however, clear about their political motives – a check on Germany to reduce the risk of war, and ultimately a form of political federation. Schuman's declaration said openly: 'Europe must be organised on a federal basis' and also that this was 'a first step in the federation of Europe'.

This is not to say that the mass of people were in favour of this move, but, as today, they were led towards it by political leaders dedicated to the idea.

Jean Monnet was the first president of the ECSC. There was a Common Assembly of 78 members, a Council of Ministers and a new High Authority, whose supranational powers had caused a long debate before the various parliaments ratified the treaty. The first meeting of the High Authority was in 1952.

'All Roads Lead to Rome'

The ECSC was not a total success but did much useful work on trade discrimination and restrictive practices. Although nothing political was achieved, it had started a process of European decision making on matters of vital interest.

However, whatever aspirations some politicians may have had, Europe was not yet ready to make any dramatic move towards political union. A treaty was actually signed in May 1952 for a European Defence Community, but defeated in the French Assembly in August 1954 – France was alarmed at any idea of rearming Germany.

The ECSC move led to discussions within the OEEC and the Council of Europe on cooperation in other sectors such as transport, agriculture, health, postal services and communications. Gradually, however, the 'six' felt that a number of separate organizations was not the way forward, but rather a single body to oversee integration of the economies was needed.

The idea of some form of common market had gathered strength by the mid-1950s, and the foreign ministers of the six met at Messina in Italy in the middle of 1955 to launch 'a fresh advance towards the building of Europe'. They agreed to set up a committee under Paul-Henri Spaak to report back on concrete proposals. The Spaak report was discussed at the ECSC Common Assembly in March 1956 and approved by the foreign ministers of the six in May. The Spaak Committee then drafted two treaties – one for a European Economic Community (EEC) and one for a European Atomic Energy Authority. The six made it clear that other countries, especially the UK, could join. In March 1957, the two treaties were signed in Rome. The atomic energy initiative became known as 'Euratom' and was largely a failure. The same could not be said of the EEC (commonly known as the Common Market).

The European Economic Community (1958–93)

The start of what is regarded as modern Europe began in December 1957, with the ratification of the Treaty of Rome by the six states, and the first meeting of the Common Assembly (later the European Parliament) took place in Strasbourg in March 1958. The first elected president was Robert Schuman. Support had come from France, who saw in it export potential for its agriculture, and Germany, who saw the export potential for its industrial goods.

The treaty emphasized that the problems of one member state would be the problems of all. The treaty was to remain in force for an unlimited period and could not be revoked. The main objectives were expressed in economic terms – setting up a common market, ending price fixing, dumping and unfair subsidies, and ensuring free competition. Behind it all lay the political motives. The treaty's preamble spoke of 'the foundations of an even closer union among Europe's peoples'. Walter Hallstein, the first president of the European Commission (originally the High Authority), said: 'We are not integrating economies, we are integrating policies.' In 1964, Paul-Henri Spaak reminded the Council of Europe:

> Those who drew up the Rome Treaty . . . did not think of it as essentially economic; they thought of it as a stage on the way to political union.

So much for the 'hidden agenda'.

Membership of the EEC meant a commitment to the free movement of capital and labour, a common investment policy and coordination of social welfare policies. Three funds were set up, a European Social Fund, a European Investment Bank and a European Development Fund. The general institutions of the EEC/EU are discussed in the next major section.

Progress continued over the next 10–11 years in moving to a common market. A customs union was declared operational in 1968, with a single external customs duty and the abolition of all internal tariffs. That year also saw the commencement of the Common Agricultural Policy. The 1960s generally saw the greatest tensions over the future direction of the EEC. These concerned the extension of the EEC to other members and the question of the powers of the European Commission.

Wider Membership

Ireland, Denmark and the UK formally applied for membership of the EEC in 1961, followed by negotiations with Norway. However, the 1960s also saw a French government headed by Charles de Gaulle, who vetoed the UK's application in 1963 and again in 1967. What particularly incensed France's partners was that de Gaulle's 1963 veto was announced at a press conference and without prior consultation with the other governments.

A summit at the Hague in 1969 agreed on the principles for enlargement, and discussions reopened with Ireland, Denmark, the UK and Norway. Treaties were signed in 1972, but a referendum in Norway rejected the idea, leaving the other three to join in 1973. (Norway is still not a member.) The '6' were now 9 at last. Greece joined in 1981, and Spain and Portugal in 1986. The 9 were now 12. Sweden, Austria and Finland joined in January 1995 giving us 15, and then 10 countries joined in June 2004, with two more members in 2007, giving us the 28 EU members we have today, with a total population of some 507 million. Here is a brief recap of EU members and when they joined:

- 1952 – Belgium, France, Germany, Italy, Luxembourg, Netherlands
- 1973 – Denmark, Ireland, UK
- 1981 – Greece
- 1986 – Portugal, Spain
- 1995 – Austria, Finland, Sweden
- 2004 – Cyprus, Czech Republic, Estonia, Hungary, Latvia, Lithuania, Malta, Poland, Slovakia, Slovenia
- 2007 – Bulgaria, Romania
- 2013 – Croatia

As mentioned earlier, Iceland stated that it wished to join the EU in the light of the severe difficulties faced as a result of the collapse of its banking system and economy during 2008, although given the eurozone crisis over 2011–12, it appears to have backtracked on this view.

The de Gaulle Stalemate

Apart from arguments with de Gaulle (president of France) about accession of other members, a more serious dispute took place with France in the mid-1960s about the whole question of EEC powers as opposed to those of the members. Margaret Thatcher (later to become the UK's prime minister) was not the first to question the powers of the Commission. They were also questioned by an equally dominant personality – de Gaulle.

In 1965, the European Commission, under Walter Hallstein, proposed that the EEC should have its own independent source of revenue and budget (instead of direct contributions from national treasuries). It was also proposed that the European Parliament should have more powers, especially over control of the budget. The third proposal concerned the setting up of a more formal agricultural policy. De Gaulle wanted the agricultural policy, but not the first two. He was against them because they would increase the supranational characteristics of the EEC.

The EEC then faced its biggest crisis so far. De Gaulle attacked the powers of the Commission as taking away the powers of national governments. A federal Europe did not appeal to him any more than it did to Margaret Thatcher. To make things worse, the Treaty of Rome had envisaged a switch to majority voting for most cases after January

1966. De Gaulle was totally opposed to this. The French simply boycotted the Council of Ministers for 7 months. However, this also meant no progress on the agricultural policy, which France wanted. A compromise had to be found.

In Luxembourg, in January 1966, the six agreed that a state could continue to exercise a veto if it felt that its own vital interests were at stake. As a result, majority voting was de jure but not necessarily de facto. The Commission, in turn, agreed that it would consult more closely with the Council of Ministers and inform governments at all stages of any new initiatives.

The Hague Conference of 1969 was much more positive. It agreed proposals for the financing of the Common Agricultural Policy – itself finally agreed in 1968 – and also the budgetary powers of the European Parliament. The latter had been discussing plans for direct elections, and these began in 1979. The Hague Conference also agreed on the principle of monetary union, to be reached by 1980. We discuss this more fully in the history of EMU in a later section.

The European Council

Periodically, heads of government had met to discuss issues affecting the EEC. The meetings of heads of state were institutionalized in 1974 by calling it the 'European Council'. This was a body that could resolve disputes, set new objectives and decide on future progress. It was outside the Treaty of Rome and therefore not subject to, for example, the European Court.

The whole question of the future for a more political union for the EEC was on the agenda in the late 1970s and early 1980s. This included the vexed question of majority voting. The European Council meeting of June 1983 ended with a rather extraordinary 'Solemn Declaration on European Union'. The Council saw itself as responsible for a general political impetus to the construction of Europe. There was fine rhetoric, but not much action.

However, the European Council meeting in Milan in June 1984 decided to set up an intergovernmental conference to discuss the future for the EEC and the question of majority voting. Their proposals, put to the European Council in December 1984, became the Single European Act.

The Single European Act

As shown in Box 12.1, the Single European Act established a date for introducing a single market throughout all EU member states.

BOX 12.1

Single European Act

The Single European Act (SEA), signed in 1986, set the target of a genuinely single internal market by the end of 1992.

It aimed to sweep away all the obstacles that still remained to achieving a genuine single competitive market. In addition, it referred to new forms of decision making and legislative processes within the EEC, extending its scope to cover foreign policy and some matters of defence.

Single European Act (*continued*)

The economic aim of a single market, however, involved questions like tax, law, accountancy, national standards and social welfare as well as the question of frontiers themselves. In other words, we were back to politics.

On the question of the veto, it was agreed that this applied to the introduction of new members and the general principles of new policies. The actual implementation of the policies in detail would be subject to qualified majority voting, in practice 54 out of 76 votes then available at the Council. This was a significant change, and one accepted by Margaret Thatcher, the arch-anti-European.

The reforms for the European Parliament did not go as far as many people would have liked. Where the Council of Ministers had decided on a proposal by qualified majority, the Parliament could amend or reject the proposal. The Council of Ministers could then only override this by *unanimous* vote – a significant change, not totally appreciated at the time.

Finally, the SEA asserted that member states should formulate a European foreign policy and should work more closely together on defence issues.

After some delay, the SEA was finally ratified by all parliaments and came into force in July 1987.

European Free Trade Area

As an alternative to full membership of the EEC, the UK had raised the question of forming a free trade area within the Community, during the late 1950s. When this failed, the UK joined with Austria, Denmark, Norway, Portugal, Sweden and Switzerland in forming the European Free Trade Area (EFTA). Its aim was to work for the reduction and eventual elimination of tariffs on most industrial goods between the members. Special provisions were made for fisheries and agriculture. EFTA was launched in May 1960. It was not nearly as ambitious as the EEC, being simply, as the name implied, a free trade area.

With the projected arrival of the single market, post-1992, many EFTA members were worried about its future. Austria, in particular, had decided to join the EEC anyway. As a result, they opened discussions with the EEC (now simply called the European Community – EC) about a European Economic Area (EEA). The two sides reached agreement in October 1991. Essentially, the EEA was a large free trade area with no internal tariffs, but no common external tariffs. The EFTA states, for example, did not necessarily have to accept the Common Agricultural Policy (by then, Denmark, Portugal and the UK were members of the EC anyway, but Iceland had also joined EFTA). The EEA came into force in 1993, but in rather unreal circumstances. Switzerland rejected the idea in a referendum in December 1992, and all the states except Iceland had either applied for full membership of the EC or were very near to doing so.

The Maastricht, Amsterdam and Nice Treaties

The most important decisions taken at Maastricht in December 1991 concerned monetary union, and for that reason they are covered under that heading later in this chapter. However, once again, many people failed to notice that the treaty was in two parts – economic and monetary union and *political* union. We shall cover the latter aspects now.

The political section of the Maastricht Treaty decided on the following points:

- An intergovernmental foreign and security policy
- A concept of 'European citizenship'
- A central role for the principle of 'subsidiary'
- A new 'social chapter' (the UK opted out)
- An increase in the powers of the European Parliament – co-decision authority with the Council of Ministers on certain subjects
- An intergovernmental framework for justice and home affairs

There is nothing too dramatic here, and the European Community became the European Union (EU) on 1 November 1993, when the Maastricht Treaty (Treaty on the European Union) became effective.

Some of the perceived shortcomings of the Maastricht Treaty were redeemed by the Amsterdam Treaty, signed in 1997. Unlike Maastricht, the Amsterdam Treaty was solely concerned with political issues. The key points were as follows:

- Safeguarding human rights, with penalties for states in breach
- Providing for the establishment of 'an area of freedom, security and justice in the EU'
- Gradually bringing asylum, visas, immigration and external border control under common rules
- Allowing the UK and Ireland to opt out of the above two provisions
- Allowing the European Parliament co-decision policy within the Council over a wider range of issues than Maastricht
- Giving the Commission president greater powers in selecting commissioners
- Making the promotion of high employment an EU goal
- Providing for a 'high representative' to put a name and face to EU foreign policy

The Amsterdam Treaty came into effect in March 1999.

The Nice Treaty of December 2000 again did not involve EMU as such but was held largely to resolve issues caused by the prospective admission (at that stage thought to be from 2004 onwards) of 12 new members – Bulgaria, Cyprus, Czech Republic, Estonia, Hungary, Latvia, Lithuania, Malta, Poland, Romania, Slovakia and Slovenia. The key points were as follows:

- Expansion of qualified majority voting while retaining vetoes in key areas
- Reallocation of votes to a total of 342, allowing for the new members
- A Charter of Human Rights
- A European Rapid Reaction Force
- An increase in European Parliament members to 738 when all new members had joined
- Changes in the composition of the European Commission

However, all these splendid ideas suffered a setback when Ireland rejected the Nice Treaty in a referendum in June 2001. In spite of this, it was decided in December 2001 that 10 of the 12 new applicants could still be ready for membership in 2004, Romania and Bulgaria being the exceptions. The latter two countries joined in 2007. Ireland voted again on 19 October 2002, and this time passed the Nice Treaty by 63% to 37%. The key question asked had been altered to reassure the Irish on neutrality in view of the Rapid Reaction Force. Once again, the reaction of the EU when faced with a setback was to move the goalposts.

Admission of the 10 new members in 2004 was formally confirmed at the Copenhagen summit in mid-December 2002. Much of the meeting was taken up by the subject of Turkey, which was pressing hard for an early date to discuss its admission. Some countries (the UK and Italy) were sympathetic, but others were not (France and Germany). In the end, October 2005 was set as the date to begin consideration of Turkey's entry, although despite ongoing debate, full EU membership is not expected before 2020 at the earliest.

Before we look at more recent developments in the EU, we shall look at the institutions of the EU and then the development of EMU itself. Finally, we shall bring ourselves up to date with the key current issues.

THE INSTITUTIONS OF THE EUROPEAN UNION

The European Council

In a sense, the European Council is not really an institution of the EU, as it does not appear in the Treaty of Rome. From the early days, frequent 'summit' meetings of heads of government were called to resolve key issues of principle. At a summit in Paris in September 1974, it was decided to regularize these meetings under the name 'European Council' (not to be confused with the Council of Europe). It consists of the heads of government with the president of the Commission entitled to attend. A decision to meet three times a year was amended to twice a year in 1985; the presidency of the meeting to rotate over the various countries of the EU every 6 months.

The Council of Ministers

The Council of Ministers is the main political body of the EU, representing the elected governments of the 28 countries. It makes the main strategic decisions, leaving the Commission to draw up the necessary Directives. On some issues, each country has a veto.

The European Commission

The European Commission is, in effect, the civil service of the EU. The commissioners are the permanent officials. The president of the Commission (currently Jean-Claude Juncker) is picked by the Council of Ministers. The president, in turn, decides on the 28 individual commissioners, with the usual horse trading to ensure that each country gets it fair share. The choice of commissioners needs to be approved by the Parliament. The Commission prepares recommendations on broad macroeconomic guidelines and monitors member states' performance.

The European Parliament

The European Parliament is an elected body. Until recently, its powers were limited, leading to complaints about the undemocratic nature of the EU generally. However, its powers have been strengthened by both the Maastricht Treaty (1993) and the Amsterdam Treaty

(1999). Although a formal vote of censure failed, its criticisms of the commissioners for a mixture of incompetence and fraud led to the resignation of all of them, including Jacques Santer, the president, in March 1999. This dramatic move was seen as a 'sea change' so far as the Parliament is concerned (not quite as dramatic as was then thought, as the incompetence and fraud don't seem to have diminished).

The powers of the Parliament are summarized as follows:

- The Maastricht Treaty gave the Parliament co-decision with the Council of Ministers in 15 areas. The Amsterdam Treaty increased this to 38 areas. The exceptions are tax, agriculture and EMU itself. In the 38 areas, the Parliament can amend drafts of the Commission, can reject them by majority vote, or work with the Council on a compromise.
- It has the power to amend the draft budget prepared by the Commission and also to approve (or not) the Commission's handling of the budget.
- It has the right to approve or veto the appointment of the Commission's president and the commissioners themselves. It can also pass a motion of censure on the commissioners.
- It has the right to ratify any foreign treaties.

Ecofin

Ecofin replaces the former EU Monetary Committee and is more formally known as the Economic and Financial Affairs Council. It is the prime forum for macroeconomic policy, monitoring of member states budgets, the euro (legal, practical and international aspects), financial markets and capital movements, and is responsible for broad economic guidelines. It decides mainly by qualified majority, in consultation with the European Parliament, with the exception of fiscal matters, which are decided unanimously. In agreement with Parliament, Ecofin also adopts the €145bn budget every year (around 1% of the EU's gross national income). A subgroup, known as the Eurogroup, represents members of EMU, and any decisions relating to euro countries is decided by EMU members only.

The European Central Bank (ECB)

Although the setting up of the European Central Bank (ECB) is clearly part of the move to economic and monetary union, we discuss it here, together with the other key institutions of the EU generally. On paper at least, the European System of Central Banks includes the non-members of EMU, as we shall see.

There are technically no less than three terms here. There is the European Central Bank (ECB, which has its headquarters in Frankfurt), which with the 28 national central banks (NCBs) form what is called the 'European System of Central Banks' (ESCB). Note that this includes countries that are not part of EMU/eurozone. They do not, however, take part in the decision making regarding the single monetary policy for the eurozone and the implementation of such decisions. To avoid confusion, the governing council of the ECB has introduced a fourth term – the Eurosystem – for the ECB and the 19 NCBs that constitute euro members. Unfortunately, it has, perhaps, created further confusion, as even the technical press do not seem to be aware of this distinction.

There are two decision-making bodies in the ECB:

1 *The Governing Council:* The supreme decision-making body of the ECB and the 19 NCBs, that is, the Eurosystem. The council adopts guidelines and makes decisions

to ensure performance of the tasks entrusted to the Eurosystem. It formulates the monetary policy of the eurozone – monetary objectives, interest rates and reserves.

2   *The Executive Board:* This consists of the president, vice president and four other members. They are appointed by the governments of the 19 member states on a recommendation from the European Council, after consultation with the Parliament and the governing council. The main responsibilities of the board are to prepare the meetings of the governing council, to implement monetary policy in the eurozone that the council has laid down and generally to be responsible for the ECB.

The president and vice president serve for a minimum of 5 years, and the other four members serve for 8 years, non-renewable. To prevent all eight from terminating at once, in the first instance, there was a staggered system. The first six appointments in July 1998 were as follows:

1   President – Wim Duisenberg – Netherlands
2   Vice president – Christian Moyer – France
3   Otmar Issing – Germany
4   Tomasso Padoa Schioppa – Italy
5   Eugenio Domingo Solas – Spain
6   Sirrka Hamalainen – Finland

The members in October 2014 were as follows:

1   President – Mario Draghi – Italy
2   Vice president – Vitor Constâncio – Portugal
3   Sabine Lautenschläger – Germany
4   Benoît Cœuré – France
5   Yves Mersch – Luxembourg
6   Peter Praet – Belgium

The basic tasks to be carried out by the Eurosystem in the eurozone are listed here:

● To define and implement monetary policy
● To conduct foreign exchange operations
● To manage the official foreign reserves
● To promote the smooth operation of member systems

The Maastricht Treaty stipulates that the ECB's main goal is 'price stability'. It also directs the ECB 'to support the general economic policies of the Community' but 'without prejudice to the objective of price stability'. The bank itself decides what price stability means.

ECB monetary policy is based on a maximum inflation figure of 2% and a mixture of economic indicators, including money supply. Inflation is based on the Harmonized Index of Consumer Prices (HICP). It uses a narrower range of goods and services than most national indices and (for the technically minded) is based on a geometric mean rather than an arithmetic mean, to reduce the impact of sharp movements in a small number of prices. (In the case of the UK, the HICP usually produces a figure about 1% less than the local RPI, although the HICP has now been adopted as well as the RPI.) Figure 12.1 illustrates the success of the ECB at controlling inflation up to 2007, when there was a spike up to 4% over

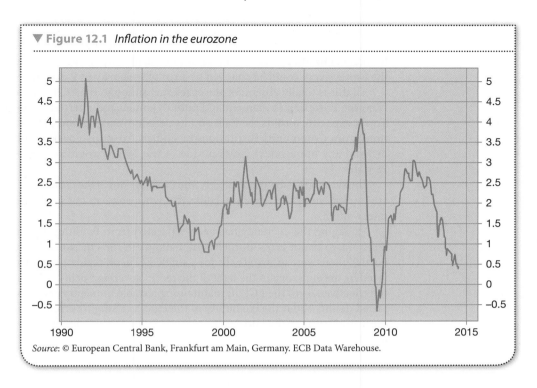

▼ Figure 12.1 *Inflation in the eurozone*

Source: © European Central Bank, Frankfurt am Main, Germany. ECB Data Warehouse.

2008, a big fall to 0.5% in 2009, a rise through to 2013 and a fall thereafter – amounting to 0.5% by the end of 2014.

All banks in member countries will deposit reserves with their central bank equivalent to 2% of their eligible liabilities. By October 2014, gold was some 55% of the total (€597bn) international reserves held at the ECB. Each central bank surrenders a percentage of its gold and foreign currency reserves to be held at the ECB. This percentage is based on a formula taking account of relative GDP and population. There has been a trend in recent years for the world's central banks to sell off gold, and even the ECB announced in August 2009 that it was to commence a 5-year programme of yearly sales not exceeding 400 tonnes 'and total sales over this period will not exceed 2,000 tonnes'.

The total system is a decentralized one, as discussed in Chapter 6. The ECB sets three interest rates – a fixed rate tender, or repo, rate; a marginal lending rate; and a rate at which deposits with central banks are paid. (Initially, on the 1 January 1999, these rates were 4.5%, 3% and 2%, respectively, and on 10 November 2014, they were 0.05 %, 0.3% and – 0.20% (yes, this deposit rate is a minus – banks have to pay interest to have funds deposited at the ECB – the negative rate was set to deter banks from doing this and to try to encourage them to lend).) The fixed rate tenders are carried out by the 19 central banks, which will also carry out any foreign exchange transactions called for by the ECB.

The monetary system is similar to that of the Bundesbank, showing the influence of Germany on the final decisions and the need to gain agreement from the German public to the diminution of the power of the mighty Bundesbank. As Jacques Delors once said, 'Not all Germans believe in God, but they all believe in the Bundesbank.'

Nevertheless, various aspects of the Eurosystem have attracted criticism. To begin with, this is the most independent and unaccountable central bank the world has ever seen. In the US, the Federal Reserve chairman has to appear before Congress every 3 months and knows that politicians could, if they wished, change the law. Equally, the Federal Open Market Committee publishes minutes of its deliberations. In Germany, the law regarding the Bundesbank could be changed by a simple majority in Parliament.

All this is totally absent for the eurozone, although the ECB must submit to questions from the European Parliament and publish annual and quarterly reports. The Maastricht Treaty explicitly forbids the ECB and its decision-making bodies to 'seek or take instructions from Community institutions or bodies, from any government of a member state or from any other body'. Any revision of the Treaty would require unanimity from all 28 states.

The system is also decentralized. The ECB lays down the crucial interest rates, but repos are carried out by the 19 central banks that will also carry out any forex (foreign exchange) intervention.

Managing the currency has been separated from banking supervision. However, in light of two major cross-border bank bailouts in the eurozone during 2008 (Dexia and Fortis), there were growing calls for a single EU bank regulator. Also, the major problems faced by the eurozone in the light of the recent sovereign debt crisis raised concerns about the effectiveness of the ECB in maintaining a stable monetary and banking system. It also raised doubts about the credibility of the euro as a single currency. This ultimately led to the introduction of the European Banking Union. We will discuss these momentous issues at the end of the chapter.

STEPS TO EMU AND THE CREATION OF THE EURO

The Werner Report

As early as 1962, the European Commission had started discussing proposals for a single currency as a way of binding the original six countries together. Little progress was made, however, until 1969, when Willy Brandt revived these original plans. The theme was taken up in the Werner Report of 1970, which proposed a move to a single currency by 1980. The report was approved by European heads of state in 1971, but the collapse of the Bretton Woods system in 1971–72 stopped developments in their tracks. The 'snake' was set up in 1972 to align European currencies to the deutschmark, with an allowed fluctuation of ± 2.25%. The snake did not work well, especially with the oil price explosion at the end of 1973. The UK joined in May 1972 and left 6 months later. France and Italy joined, but left twice. The next move was the European Monetary System (EMS).

European Monetary System

The European Monetary System (EMS) was set up in March 1979 and had three elements:

1   The Exchange Rate Mechanism (ERM)
2   The European Currency Unit (ECU)
3   The European Monetary Cooperation Fund

The ERM was the successor to the snake. This time, two bands of fluctuations were allowed – the narrow band of ± 2.25 % and the wide band of ± 6%. Target rates for each currency against the others were established (the 'parity grid'), and periodic realignments were allowed for. If rates moved near to their limit, the central bank concerned was expected to defend the currency by buying it and perhaps also raising interest rates. Currencies could be borrowed from other central banks to enable it to do this. By 1992, of the 12 countries of the EU, Greece was not a member; the UK, Spain and Portugal were members at the wide band; and the other eight were members at the narrow band.

The ECU was calculated from a weighted basket of all European currencies (not just those in the ERM). It produced a common unit of accountancy and was used for all EU statistics, some currency dealings, some cross-border public sector invoicing within Europe, and as a denomination for some T-bills and bonds (government and corporate). Clearly, the idea was that this laid the basis for a genuine future currency. If all countries in the ERM could move in time to the narrow band on a stable basis, this would make the transition to a single currency easier.

The European Monetary Cooperation Fund was actually set up following the Werner Report, but was effectively dormant until the EMS. Each country in the EU deposited 20% of its gold and foreign currency reserves and received ECUs in exchange. The funds were held at the BIS in Basel. This was the *official* ECU as opposed to the *private* ECU, as used for T-bills and bonds. This central fund was only to be used for transactions between EMS central banks and named monetary institutions. Central banks obliged to intervene in the markets because of ERM rules could draw on an unlimited credit within the system. Apart from this, it had little practical use during the life of the system.

Changes to the ERM

In September 1992, the growing belief that a realignment was due and that sterling and the lira were overvalued led to great turbulence. The UK and Italy left the ERM, and devaluations of the peseta, escudo and punt followed. Further turbulence returned in July 1993, with attacks on the French franc and other currencies. In early August, a decision was taken to widen the bands to ± 15% (except for the deutschmark/guilder, which remained at ± 2.25%). These were black days for the ideal of monetary union.

The Delors Plan

The ultimate aim for Europe was the Economic and Monetary Union (EMU). In 1989, central banks drew up a blueprint chaired by Jacques Delors, president of the European Commission, and thus called the Delors Plan. This set up three stages towards EMU:

1 All members in the ERM, no exchange controls, achievement of a single market in financial services
2 Setting up the European System of Central Banks (ESCB)
3 Locked exchange rates, monetary policy controlled by the ESCB and, eventually, a single currency.

The Maastricht Treaty

This blueprint was broadly endorsed by the Madrid EC summit in mid-1989, and mid-1990 was set as the starting date for stage 1. The matter was further discussed at the inter-governmental conference, which began in December 1990, and prepared for a treaty to be drawn up at Maastricht in December 1991. The Maastricht summit laid down a timetable for EMU as follows:

- By the end of 1996, a decision would be made on possible EMU in 1997, if a minimum of seven nations could meet the convergence conditions (described below).
- By 1999, there would be EMU in any case if two nations were able to meet the convergence conditions.
- A European Central Bank would be set up 6 months prior to EMU, but a body called the European Monetary Institute (EMI), to be set up in 1994, was to coordinate policies prior to setting up the central bank.
- Special protocols allowed the UK to opt out of a final move to a single currency and for Denmark to hold a referendum in June 1992.
- The convergence conditions were
  - _ inflation rate within 1.5% of the best three nations;
  - _ long-term interest rates within 2% of the average of the lowest three nations;
  - _ currency within the 2.25 % ERM band, and no devaluation in the previous 2 years; and
  - _ budget deficit to GDP ratio not to exceed 3% and national debt not to exceed 60% of GDP.

The Danish referendum in June 1992 rejected the Maastricht Treaty by a narrow majority. Nevertheless, the other states decided to continue with the process of having the treaty accepted by their parliaments. A French referendum in September 1992 narrowly voted in favour, and the German parliament passed it in December, although this was challenged by the German Constitutional Court. Finally, after concessions, Denmark accepted the Maastricht Treaty in a new referendum in May 1993.

The EMI started operations in January 1994, located in Frankfurt. Sweden, Finland and Austria joined the EU on 1 January 1995, and Austria joined the ERM. Later, Finland joined the ERM; Italy rejoined in November 1996; and Greece joined in early 1998.

The EMI laid down firmer plans for monetary union in November 1995:

- 1 January 1999 – start of monetary union, with locked exchange rates
- 1 January 2002 – introduction of new notes and coins
- 1 July 2002 – the new currency to be legal tender

The December meeting in Madrid decided to call the new currency the 'euro' (not the 'ecu'). The rates, to be locked on 1 January 1999, were decided at a meeting in May 1998, which also decided which countries would join the monetary union.

EMU

The countries joining EMU should have met the Maastricht conditions described above. Embarrassingly, Belgium and Italy, key candidates, had a national debt/GDP ratio well in excess of 100%. The budget deficit/GDP ratio of 3% was based on 1997 figures. Many countries used what could only be called 'creative accounting' to come in below the 3% level. Such was the strong political will to have EMU, however, that these problems were ignored, and the system began as planned in January 1999, with 11 members – Austria, Belgium, Finland, France, Germany, Ireland, Italy, Luxembourg, Netherlands, Portugal and Spain. This left Greece, Sweden, the UK and Denmark outside. Greece joined EMU in 2001. Membership was

▼ **Table 12.1** *Euro rates against eurozone currencies*

Country	Currency	€	Country	Currency	€
Austria	Sch	13.7603	Italy	L	1,936.27
Belgium/Lux	BFr/LFr	40.3399	Luxembourg	LFr	40.3399
Cyprus	C£	0.585274	Malta	Lm	0.429300
Estonia	EEK	15.6466	Netherlands	Fl	2.20371
Finland	FM	5.94573	Portugal	Es	200.482
France	FFr	6.55957	Slovakia	Sk	30.1260
Germany	DM	1.95583	Slovenia	SIT	239.640
Greece	GRD	340.750	Spain	Pta	166.386
Ireland	I£	0.787564	Latvia	Lats	0.702804
			Lithuania	Litas	3.4528

Source: http://ec.europa.eu/economy_finance/euro/adoption/conversion/index_en.htm

expanded to the current 19 countries when Slovenia (joined on 31 December 2006), Cyprus (1 January 2008), Malta (1 January 2008), Slovakia (1 January 2009), Estonia (1 January 2011), Latvia (1 January 2014) and Lithuania (on 1st January 2015) introduced the euro.

The permanently fixed rates for the euro against eurozone currencies are shown in Table 12.1.

As the rates for, say, the French franc and the euro, and also the Italian lira and the euro, are fixed, it follows that one multiplication gives us a fixed franc/lira rate and so on.

No notes and coins were issued until January 2002, but the euro was used for domestic bonds and Eurobonds as well as interbank transactions. It was also used for cheques or credit cards or any transaction where notes and coins are not used. Control of interest rates and monetary policy was in the hands of the new ECB.

The Maastricht Treaty laid down a target budget deficit/GDP ratio of 3%, but said nothing about variations once EMU had started. This is covered by the Stability and Growth Pact. The position of the ERM, now that EMU has started, is ERM II. We discuss both these subjects now.

The Stability and Growth Pact

Further changes to the EU were discussed at Amsterdam in June 1997, leading to the Amsterdam Treaty, which became law in May 1999. While at Amsterdam, heads of government discussed the question of control over excessive budget deficits once EMU had started. They agreed on a common code of fiscal conduct to uphold discipline in the management of government finances. Budgets are normally to be kept close to either a balance or small surplus. This should ensure that even in recession, the maximum deficit/GDP ratio can be kept to 3%. Sound government finances are regarded as an indispensable requisite for macroeconomic stability. This common code is known as the Stability and Growth Pact.

Technically, all countries in the EU are part of this pact, not just the 19 of the EMU. All countries submit their forward budgetary plans to the Ecofin. This should enable early warning to be given of any slippage. Deficits in excess of 3% are only permitted in exceptional circumstances, such as a fall in GDP in excess of 2%. See Box 12.2.

BOX 12.2

Stability and Growth Pact – Some Problems?

The issue of sanctions for those who break the rules caused much argument, with the Germans wanting much tougher action than most other countries. It was decided that Ecofin would formulate recommendations for correction, and measures would have to be taken within 4 months. The decision would be taken by qualified majority, and Ecofin could impose sanctions – a non-interest-bearing deposit that might be converted later into a fine if effective action was not taken.

In April 1999, the ECB issued a sharp warning that many governments risked breaking the budget limits agreed and that safety margins were not sufficient. Following this warning, we saw the pact in action in May 1999. Italy, whose forecast deficit was 2.0%, asked permission to raise this to 2.4%. Weak growth and high unemployment had led to this position. GDP was due to grow 1.5% in 1999. Ecofin agreed to Italy's request, and many saw this as an ominous sign for the future. The euro then fell sharply on the forex markets.

Worse was to follow. Ironically, Germany, which had been so keen on tough action, found itself facing a formal warning for breaking the pact in February 2000. With the usual EU compromise, Germany said it would 'endeavour' to balance its budget by 2004. Otmar Issing, chief economist of the ECB, said, 'If all other European states want the same treatment in future, the early warning system is useless.'

Then, in June 2002, Ecofin finance ministers criticized France for not balancing the budget. However, François Mer, French finance minister, refused to say that the country would be in balance by 2004, although it had promised to do so at the Barcelona summit in March. Pressed again at the Seville summit in June 2002, France agreed (reluctantly) to bring its budget 'close to balance' by 2004. Then, later, in June 2002, Portugal admitted that its budget deficit as a percentage of GDP would probably be 3.9%, well above the limit of 3%.

Despite all these moves, the original stability pact was effectively wrecked by late 2003, by which time France and Germany had engineered the suspension of the original rules in order to avoid heavy fines for running persistent deficits.

In March 2005, a new, more flexible pact emerged. Under the new rules, countries could still be fined for persistently breaching the pact's 3% of GDP ceiling, but a number of 'get-out' clauses meant that such an eventuality was highly unlikely. The main feature of the new pact was an emphasis on its 'preventive arm' – the idea that countries should be forced into running a balanced budget during economic upturns, cutting deficits by at least 0.5% a year.

In theory at least, the new pact aimed to discourage procyclical spending, and the focus on balanced budgets should help meet the costs associated with the eurozone's ageing population.

Since the new pact, there has been ongoing debate about fiscal credibility in the eurozone, especially since the credit crisis, as French and other countries' public spending and deficits have soared.

In June 2009, the *Financial Times* noted that 'Angela Merkel, the German chancellor, has been a vocal critic of deficit spending in Europe and repeatedly urged governments to develop "exit strategies" and return to fiscal discipline quickly' in order to preserve the threatened pact.

The pact (and the credibility of EMU) has also been tested to its limits with major public sector deficits and other problems faced by Greece in early 2010. EMU member countries have provided massive financial resources to bail out the Greek economy and preserve the eurozone. The continued inability of various governments to achieve the limits set by the pact ultimately resulted in the eurozone crisis.

ERM II

On 1 September 1998, the Governing Council and Executive Board of the Eurosystem of central banks agreed on a text for the successor to the ERM. The Maastricht Treaty had a condition that countries joining EMU had to have had a 2-year period in the ERM at the narrow band. This led to the creation of what is called 'ERM II'. Countries wishing to join EMU have to agree to maintain their currencies within a band of an agreed rate against the euro. The 19 central banks will intervene, if necessary, to support a currency, and loans are available to the participating countries from the ECB. These loans can only be drawn after first drawing on the country's own reserves. The loans are repayable in 3 months and subject to a ceiling on cumulative borrowings.

Next Members?

Of the 10 new members that joined the EU in 2004, 4 have joined the single currency (Cyprus, Malta, Slovakia and Slovenia). All the others, plus the two most recent EU members, Bulgaria and Romania, have aspirations to join as well. Estonia adopted the euro in 2011, and Latvia in 2014. The Czech Republic seemed to be the one of the non-EMU recent members holding out hope for early membership as its economy met all the entry requirements, although this has not happened. Hungary and Poland had plans to introduce the single currency in 2012; Romania, in 2014; and Bulgaria in 2015, but none of these has been achieved. In fact, it remains to be seen if any join the euro, given political worries following on from the eurozone crisis in 2011–12.

In terms of new members to the EU, probably the most talked about EU enlargement candidate is Turkey, and in mid-2009, the Turkish prime minister again stated the country's desire to push ahead with membership. France and Germany, however, are not enthusiastic and have talked about providing some interim membership, referred to as a 'privileged partnership', which the Turkish authorities are not keen on. A major stumbling block in EU negotiations relates to the tensions between Greece and Turkey over Cyprus and especially the treatment of Turkish Cyprus. Other official enlargement countries (in 2014) included Albania, Iceland, Macedonia, Montenegro and Serbia. In addition, Moldova, Ukraine and Georgia have all expressed European aspirations.To join the EU itself, countries must meet all the rules and obligations of membership. The document recording these runs to 80,000 pages – banking laws, competition policy, state aid, veterinary inspection standards and so on. They also need efficiency in public administration to enforce the rules.

EMU Statistics

Some interesting statistics are shown in Table 12.2. We can see that the EU now exceeds the US, and is much bigger than Japan, in terms of population and GDP (in PPP terms). The EU economy is larger than the US in PPP terms, with a GDP of €13.5 trillion compared to €13 trillion, respectively. According to IMF figures for 2013, the EU now accounts for 23% of global GDP compared with around 22% for the US. Within the eurozone itself, the market is dominated by Germany, France and Italy, who together account for 66% of the total GDP – Germany alone accounts for 29%. In contrast, China's nominal GDP stood at over $9.5 trillion in 2013, making it the second largest single country economy after the US (nominal GDP of $16.8 trillion).

One can also see in Table 12.2 that the EU (and eurozone) has a larger public sector (central expenditure) than the US or Japan, although deficits (public spending minus public income) are larger in the latter.

Finally, Table 12.2 also reveals that despite its larger size, the EU still has smaller capital markets compared to the US. This is because many European countries have had bank-based systems where commercial banks have been the main providers of finance to the corporate sector and capital markets (traditionally at least) have played a lesser role. This contrasts with the US market-based system, where capital markets are more important. Stock market capitalization to nominal GDP stood at 114% in the US compared to 45–55% for the EU and eurozone.

Payment Systems

The official interbank payments system for the euro is TARGET (Trans-European Automated Real-time Gross Settlement Express Transfer). After some controversy, access to TARGET is open to national central banks and participants in real-time gross settlement (RTGS) systems in non-eurozone member states. These non-eurozone central banks must

▼ **Table 12.2** *Key characteristics of the eurozone and EU, 2013*

Characteristics	Unit	Eurozone	EU	US	Japan
Population	million	335.4	508.1	316.5	127.5
GDP (PPP)	€ trillion	9.6	13.5	13.0	3.5
GDP per capita (PPP)	€ thousands	28.6	26.6	41.2	27.4
Labour force participation rate	%	72.2	72.0	72.8	74.9
Government expenditure	% of GDP	49.7	49.0	34.5	40.5
Deficit (−)	% of GDP	−3.0	−3.3	−6.4	−8.7
Debt securities outstanding	€ trillion	16.4	22.2	25.5	10.6
Stock market capitalization	€ trillion	5.6	8.7	20.2	3.3

Source: © European Central Bank, Frankfurt am Main, Germany (July 2014) *Statistics Pocket Book*.

deposit a sum of money with the Eurosystem by 8.00 a.m. each day (for example €3bn for the Bank of England). This is to ensure the availability of intraday liquidity.

This system was superseded by TARGET2 in November 2007, which unifies the technical infrastructure of the 28 central (note-issuing) banks of the EU. Sweden and the UK have elected not to participate in TARGET2 (the UK terminated its connection on 16 May 2008), so banks in these two countries have had to use alternative means to make large cross-border euro payments. In 2013, TARGET2 processed a daily average of 369,099 payments, representing a daily average value of €1.9 trillion. The average value of a TARGET2 transaction was €5.3m. The system accounts for around 91% of the total value of payments (and 59% in volume terms) of euro large-value payments.

In addition to TARGET2, there are euro clearing systems available through the Euro System of the EBA Clearing Company (EURO 1), the French Paris Net Settlement (PNS), the Finnish Pankkien On-line Pikasiirrot ja Sekit-järjestelmä (POPS), and CLS, the continuous linked settlement system for foreign exchange transactions. (There have also been individual national systems for the clearing of high-value, euro-based payments, for example CHAPS-Euro in the UK, but this was closed in May 2008, after 9 years of activity, due to a decline in volumes.)

EMU: The Benefits

Having looked at the history and all the facts and figures, we are still left with the basic question: Why? What are the objectives of EMU? What advantages should accrue? The benefits are illustrated in Box 12.3.

BOX 12.3

Benefits of EMU and the Euro

One key argument is that the use of a single currency (the euro, €) in 19 countries with a population of around 335 million will lead to more transparency of prices and make it much more difficult to sell goods at a higher price in the Netherlands than, say, Italy.

The argument goes that as a major barrier to cross-border trading has been eliminated, this will make it easier for firms to compete in various member states and it will also be simpler for consumers to compare prices denominated in the same currency.

Also, producers will have larger markets to target and therefore may benefit from various scale and other efficiency gains. All this should, in theory at least, put a downward pressure on prices.

Many studies have drawn attention to the disparity in motor car prices. Pre-tax differentials can exceed 20%, and the European Commission even produces a 6-monthly car price report.

A report in July 2011 notes that pre-tax price differences for new cars between member states continued to fall in 2010, with the average standard deviation ('indicator') going down from 8.5% to 8.2%. The fact that the British Pound appreciated by 10.3% against the Euro in 2010 led to relatively lower prices in the eurozone compared to the UK, which used to be the least expensive country for new cars in the EU. This exchange rate adjustment contributed significantly to the overall price convergence.

Benefits of EMU and the Euro (*continued*)

Within the eurozone, the indicator remained stable at 6.5%, as in the previous year. Greece became the cheapest country for new cars within the eurozone in terms of pre-tax prices (average list prices were, in 2010, 5.6% below the eurozone average), followed by Slovenia (4.8% below the eurozone average) and Malta (4.6% below the eurozone average). In 2009, Malta was the least expensive country in the eurozone, followed by Greece. Germany and Luxembourg remain the most expensive countries in the EU (with pre-tax list prices of 7.7% and 7.0% respectively above the eurozone average), followed by Austria and France (with pre-tax prices of 4.8% and 4.3% respectively above the eurozone average).

Car price variation is lower in the eurozone than outside, perhaps giving credence to price convergence.

Also, a large number of EU and other studies have sought to investigate price convergence of retail and wholesale financial services. Again, the assumption is that the single currency boosts competition and this should lead to lower and convergent pricing.

> *Typically, these studies find convergence in wholesale financial services, but little convergence in many retail products – like credit card prices, mortgage rates, personal insurance and so on. Retail banking and financial services typically remain the preserve of domestic firms where foreigners (until recently at least) have not made major inroads.*

Some retail products like private pensions and mortgages also may benefit from special tax treatment that varies from country to country. Simply put, there are more obstacles to creating a single market in retail financial services than in wholesale activity, where business is typically more international.

In general, the single currency is predicated on the view that greater price competition will lead to lower prices and more trade. With no worries about currency movements, it will be easier for producers to move production to cheaper areas. There may be pressure in high-cost countries for lower taxation and more flexible labour markets.

All the above are part of a wider argument that a single currency will make the eurozone more of a genuine single market.

A more obvious example of the benefit of the introduction of a single currency is the saving to importers and exporters of buying/selling foreign currency. As we noted earlier, there are spreads to be paid on spot and forward deals and perhaps premiums if options are chosen. Not only is useful money now saved, but it is easier to look at the eurozone as a single area. In particular, it streamlines European Treasury operations. Cash can be managed on a pan-European basis, saving currency and interest rate spreads and leading to greater efficiency.

Another area of cost saving for corporates is a reduction in the cost of capital. We know that Europe has relied far more on bank finance than the US, which uses capital markets much more. Prior to the introduction of the euro, fund managers and investors all over Europe were constrained by forex risk (and sometimes regulations) when it came to cross-border purchases of securities. These constraints have now gone. If the eurozone produces more of a single market in bonds and equities, then raising finance should be cheaper, to the benefit of the companies concerned.

Of course, there is still a basic question: What is Europe? There is the Europe of the 19, the Europe of the 28, and then Europe including Switzerland. This is a country with two of the world's biggest pharmaceutical companies (Novartis and Roche), two huge banks (Credit Suisse and UBS), two of the world's biggest insurers (Swiss Re and Zurich Financial Services) and the world's biggest food company (Nestlé), yet it isn't in the EU.

Interestingly, as well as bonds and equities, the syndicated loan market has also expanded in the eurozone. We have seen major acquisitions funded in the first place by a syndicated loan (for speed and confidentiality). Later, these are often replaced by a bond issue.

Although it is unlikely that a true single market can be created while tax differences, consumer protection laws and other obstacles to full integration remain in place, there is no doubt that the creation of the single currency has removed one major barrier to doing business in the EU.

The Counterarguments

Having looked at the benefits of EMU, we must also acknowledge that naturally there are those whose views are different. Perhaps the most common counterargument relates to the 'one size fits all' implication of the ECB, with its single interest rate and exchange rate. The fact that countries are at different phases in the economic cycle means that some may need high interest rates while others need lower ones. We had a perfect example of this as EMU started. Italy and Germany were growing GDP at 1.5% while Spain and Portugal were growing at 3% and Ireland at a massive 7%. Irish interest rates prior to EMU were 6% and then fell to 2.5 % on entry, with a later rise to 3%. Inflation took off and soon reached 7%, with little the Irish government could do about it.

One response to this would be to change fiscal policy. However, this is limited by the Stability and Growth Pact. If a country is in recession, but interest rates are going up in EMU because others are in a boom, it would normally stimulate its economy by lowering its taxes and raising government spending, but it no longer has the right to do this except within defined limits. Those in recession when interest rates are high may find that unemployment rises to socially unacceptable levels. One result of all this is that the Stability and Growth Pact has come under immense strain at various periods since the introduction of the euro. The recent eurozone crisis and near Greek debt default is a key example of the strains that can become apparent.

Another argument is that the promised convergence within EMU is not happening and is unlikely to happen. There are differing rates of inflation, unemployment and growth. If one state is in recession and one experiencing strong growth, one response is for labour to move from one to the other. Economists claim that a monetary union needs high labour mobility. After all, the US is a monetary union. Texas may be suffering where New England is prospering. This is where the eurozone faces severe problems. The US has high labour mobility, whereas the eurozone has poor mobility.

Another problem with 'one size fits all' is that different states react differently to changes in interest rates and exchange rates. In Ireland, for example, 80% of people own their homes, and variable rate mortgages are the most common. An interest rate increase has much more effect on consumers than in, say, Germany, where households usually rent their property.

To the above can be added what some people see as the weaknesses of the ECB and the Eurosystem – its lack of accountability or any kind of control, the separation of managing the currency from supervision, and the possible struggle between the executive board and the ECB governors who could outvote the former.

One of the key benefits claimed for EMU is the transparency of prices, which will lead to growing competition, higher efficiency and lower prices. Critics, however, point to the effect of varying VAT rates and, in particular, transport costs. Goods made in Spain that have higher transport costs will certainly not sell for the same price in Finland as they do in, say, Spain and Portugal.

The eurozone (and the EU overall) is now a substantial market competing with the US. However, major weaknesses remain. One is high labour costs due to the social security costs borne by employers. A Morgan Stanley Dean Witter study estimates social costs at 28% of hourly compensation in the US, and 45% in Germany. It estimates the hourly compensation in manufacturing in the eurozone at 12% higher than the US. Another study shows Europe well behind the US in the use of IT, with Western Europe spending 2.26% of GDP on IT as opposed to 4.08% in the US, and white-collar workers in the US having 103 personal computers (PCs) per 100 workers, as opposed to 52 in Western Europe.

Labour laws are more inflexible in Europe than the US. In the latter, it is much easier to restructure and lay workers off. One's first humane reaction may be to see this as a bad thing, until it is realized that the alternative may be for all employees to lose their jobs as the firm is put out of business by global competition. It is much harder to sack people in the eurozone than in the US, yet the eurozone has unemployment at 11.5% of the labour force, and the US at 5.9% (in late 2014). In addition, as we saw from Table 12.2, government expenditure in the eurozone is 49.7% of GDP and only 34.5% in the US. High government expenditure means high taxes and potential crisis – as we will explain later.

Many of the counterarguments generally relate to the fact that countries follow different business cycles. Business cycle convergence is widely regarded as a necessary condition for the implementation of a monetary policy that is appropriate for all single currency member countries. Furthermore, when trade barriers are eliminated, advances in technology and knowledge are more easily transferred across borders; consequently, demand shocks have similar effects in each country. Paul Krugman, winner of the 2008 Nobel Prize for Economics, has argued that the tendency for increased specialization within a single market might induce less closely synchronized business cycles.

Of course, synchronicity of business cycles may cause co-movements in bank risks and performance, given that European banks face common exposures to specific industries, countries and even projects (via interbank lending and linkages). These linkages became apparent after the 2007–8 credit crisis. Even in the retail banking segment (where integration is less complete), EU banks are more likely to face common shocks. Ultimately, as we now know, such common shocks and interbank linkages can reduce financial stability if the distress or failure of banks in one country is transferred across borders. Many have argued that this increases the importance of intercountry regulatory and supervisory cooperation.

The UK Position

The major EU economy absent from EMU is, of course, the UK. We shall look briefly at the arguments made prior to the recent eurozone crisis to get a flavour of the arguments for and against joining EMU. Given the eurozone crisis, the arguments for joining the single currency, of course, look weaker than ever. See Box 12.4.

Officially, prior to the eurozone crisis, the government's policy on EMU is that the UK will join 'when the time is right'. The decision as to whether the time is right or not will be taken after a periodic examination of five tests:

1   Convergence of business cycles with those of the EMU countries over a sustained period

BOX 12.4

Should the UK Join the Eurozone/EMU?

The general arguments *for* the UK joining the eurozone can be summarized as shown below:

- Stability of the exchange rate.
- Lower foreign investment in the UK if outside. In recent years, 40% of foreign direct investment in Europe has come to the UK.
- The UK will progressively have far less influence on monetary and economic policy in Europe if outside. Frankfurt will gain, and the City of London will lose. The ECB is already in Frankfurt, and EURIBOR is used as the reference rate, not Euro LIBOR.
- There will be savings on forex transactions.
- The UK is too small an economy to stay outside – it would gradually lose business and influence.
- As a matter of philosophy, the UK should join in this exciting historic venture and take its full place in Europe.
- The fear of federalism and political integration is exaggerated because in practice it will never happen.

The arguments *against* joining are as follows:

- Stability of the exchange rate will only apply in the eurozone. The UK will still have instability against the dollar, the yen and the Swiss franc.
- Decisions on foreign investment are not only influenced by currency risk – the UK has low labour costs, flexible labour laws and lower taxes than most of the eurozone.
- The UK's GDP would only be 16% of the GDP of the eurozone if it joined; thus the extent of its probable influence would be modest.
- Most currency transactions in London are not sterling anyway. London has 40.9% of world forex trading and Frankfurt only 1.7%. London trades over two-thirds of the international bond market and has a far bigger OTC derivatives market (more than 44% of world activity) than the rest of the eurozone. London has a pool of skilled labour, lower social taxes, the infrastructure of accountants and lawyers and the use of English as a language.
- The UK is small, but big enough to survive outside – look at Switzerland. 'One size fits all' would be a major problem with a business cycle out of line with France and Germany and the highest ratio of outstanding variable rate mortgage debt to GDP in Europe.
- EMU and the euro area needs political integration to work properly.

2 The flexibility of the economy's adjustment to economic shocks
3 Investment – would EMU and the adoption of the euro create better conditions for inward investment into the UK?
4 Impact on financial services
5 Promotion of higher growth, stability and a lasting increase in employment.

This fifth test is largely a summary and conclusion of the previous four.

The typical British attitude (rightly or wrongly) is summarized in the following quotation:

> We see nothing but good and hope in a richer, freer, more contented European commonality. But we have our own dream and our own task. We are with Europe, but not of it. We are linked, but not compromised. We are interested and associated, but not absorbed.

This was written by Winston Churchill in an American periodical in 1930. In spite of the huge decline in British influence and power since then, it's probably still a fair summary of the attitude of many people in the UK today, even more so in the light of the recent problems faced by the eurozone.

EUROZONE SOVEREIGN DEBT CRISIS

The European/eurozone sovereign debt crisis relates to the financial crisis faced by various countries concerning their inability to finance their spending due to their excessive levels of previous borrowings. The crisis emerged during 2009 as a consequence of the increased debt levels (partly because of banking system bailouts in 2007–8) and also because of the downgrading of various government debt by the rating agencies, which made new borrowing and the financing of existing debt more expensive. Countries in the eurozone have been most affected, namely Greece, Ireland and Portugal, and there has been a wave of rescue packages coordinated by the European Commission, the ECB and the IMF, aimed at stemming the crisis. Although, to a certain extent, the causes and impact of the crisis vary from country to country, the overall impact has led to a crisis of confidence in the eurozone, with increased discussion as to whether the euro can remain as a single currency or whether countries most hit by the crisis – like Greece – should be forced to leave the euro, resulting in a break-up of the single currency. Figure 12.2 illustrates the situation of indebtedness of various major eurozone and other countries relative to the size of their economies by the end of first quarter 2015.

▼ Figure 12.2 *Gross government debt as a % of GDP*

	2008	2009	2010	2011	2012	2013	2014	2015
Australia	13.9	19.4	23.6	27.0	32.1	33.1	35.2	35.9
Austria	68.7	74.3	78.8	80.6	86.0	83.4	90.0	89.5
Belgium	92.6	101.0	100.9	104.1	106.4	106.7	106.8	105.4
Canada	74.7	87.4	89.5	93.6	96.1	93.6	94.2	93.6
Czech Republic	34.4	40.8	45.2	48.2	55.7	57.1	58.8	60.9
Denmark	41.4	49.3	53.1	59.9	59.3	55.2	56.5	59.3
Estonia	8.5	12.6	12.4	9.6	13.3	13.1	13.0	12.7

▼ **Figure 12.2** *Gross government debt as a % of GDP (continued)*

	2008	2009	2010	2011	2012	2013	2014	2015
Finland	40.3	51.8	57.9	58.2	64.0	66.4	69.3	70.1
France	79.3	91.4	95.7	99.3	109.3	112.6	115.1	116.1
Germany	69.9	77.5	86.2	85.8	88.5	85.9	83.9	79.8
Greece	122.5	138.3	157.3	179.9	167.5	186.0	188.7	188.2
Hungary	77.2	86.4	87.7	86.8	90.0	89.4	90.3	90.1
Iceland	76.4	94.5	100.1	106.8	103.7	97.9	96.0	91.3
Ireland	50.1	71.1	88.5	103.9	127.8	134.6	133.1	132.0
Israel (1)	72.9	75.3	71.5	69.7	68.2	67.8	67.6	67.0
Italy	118.9	132.4	131.1	124.0	142.2	145.5	147.2	147.4
Japan	171.1	188.7	193.3	209.5	216.5	224.6	229.6	232.5
Korea	28.3	31.0	31.8	33.3	34.8	36.5	37.9	39.0
Luxembourg	19.3	19.2	26.2	26.3	30.2	30.3	31.6	33.5
Netherlands	64.8	67.6	71.9	76.1	82.7	86.2	87.5	87.7
New Zealand	28.7	34.0	37.8	41.3	42.4	40.6	39.3	38.1
Norway	55.2	49.0	49.3	33.9	34.7	35.6	36.7	39.6
Poland	55.5	57.6	62.2	63.0	62.3	63.8	56.8	58.4
Portugal	80.8	94.0	104.0	118.4	134.6	139.4	141.3	142.2
Slovak Republic	32.2	40.4	45.9	48.3	56.9	59.3	59.1	60.1
Slovenia	28.9	43.3	47.6	51.2	61.6	80.5	85.9	89.7
Spain	48.0	63.3	68.4	78.8	92.6	104.0	108.5	111.5
Sweden	48.3	50.2	47.3	47.6	46.7	47.1	48.5	48.3
Switzerland	48.3	47.5	46.2	46.3	46.5	46.2	45.9	45.3
United Kingdom	57.3	72.1	81.7	97.1	101.6	99.3	101.7	103.1
United States	72.6	85.8	94.6	98.8	102.1	104.3	106.2	106.5
Euro area (15 countries)	78.0	88.8	93.9	95.9	104.4	106.7	107.7	106.9
OECD-Total	79.9	91.2	97.5	102.1	107.1	109.5	111.1	111.2

Figures in green are eurozone countries

1. Information on data for Israel: http://oe.cd/israel-disclaimer.

Source: OECD Economic Outlook No. 95 (database), 2014.

Although the origins of the crisis are varied and complex, a number of factors have been identified as major causes of the eurozone crisis, as shown in Box 12.5.

Experiences vary from country to country, with Greece and Ireland being the worst affected. Ireland's problems, for instance, mainly emanated from the government's bailout of the banks that had lent excessively to property developers. In Greece, the problems emanated mainly from generous pensions and other welfare benefits that could not be

BOX 12.5

Causes of the Eurozone Crisis

The main causes of the crisis include the following:

- *Lax monetary policy and easy credit conditions* in the run-up to the banking crisis, fuelled a borrowing boom in both the private and government sectors
- *International trade and capital imbalances*, particularly the massive surpluses being generated in emerging markets, which heralded an era of cheap financing, helping to fuel a boom in global capital markets
- *Property market bubble collapses in 2008*, which put massive pressure on global financial systems and resulted in a sudden downgrading of economic growth, making it more difficult for debtors (both private and public) to repay
- *Profligate government spending in the pre-crisis era*, which led to an explosion of the welfare state (particularly in Greece) as well as excess borrowings needed by government to bail out their troubled banks

The impact of the eurozone crisis was reflected in a big, big spike upwards, particularly in Greek, Irish and Portuguese governments borrowing costs compared to the (safer) Dutch and German economies.

---

sustained. As we all know, various crises have been headline news since 2009; the global financial crisis has been followed by the euro sovereign debt crisis, and by mid-2015 the Greek crisis. Over the last few years a series of momentous events have occurred in order to 'save' particularly troubled countries, to limit contagion in the eurozone and ultimately to save the single currency itself. The key events that unfurled during the sovereign debt crisis are highlighted in Table 12.3.

The ongoing sovereign debt crisis has been a major factor destabilizing financial markets and the eurozone overall, despite the fact that the main countries affected, Greece, Ireland and Portugal, only account for about 5% of eurozone GDP. However, possible contagion effects via the sovereign debt markets and bank holdings of debt instruments have made it imperative that the authorities stem contagion, and despite all the problems highlighted above, the euro has remained surprisingly stable – presumably because markets assume that eurozone governments will do what it takes to support their systems.

One area of major concern has been talk of another banking crisis linked to the debt problem. This is because many eurozone banks hold large quantities of eurozone sovereign debt – Italian and Spanish banks, for instance, are the largest holders of their country's government bonds. Some large French and German banks were also big holders of Greek government debt. If the value of this debt falls, then these 'safe' assets become less safe, and these are held for capital purposes. A weakening of eurozone bank capital positions has meant that banks have found it difficult to borrow via private bond issuance, and they have also started to stop lending to each other, resulting in liquidity concerns in interbank markets. These issues came to a head on 21 December 2011 when the ECB announced its long-term refinancing operation (LTRO 1), where it lent €489bn to 523 banks for 3 years at a rate of just 1%. It was reported that €325bn was tapped by banks in Greece, Ireland, Italy and Spain – mainly so they could pay off their €200bn of maturing debts in the first quarter of 2012 and

▼ **Table 12.3** *Timeline of events associated with eurozone debt crises, 2010–12*

Feb. 1992	Maastricht Treaty signed by 12 members of the European Community: establishes European Union (EU), commits members to 'irrevocable' monetary union. Convergence criteria include rules for public deficit < 3% GDP, debt < 60% GDP.
Sept. 1992	ERM (European Exchange Rate Mechanism) crisis forces devaluations of Italian and UK currencies and later, Irish and Spanish currencies. When crisis threatens more counties in 1993, ERM is weakened by considerably widening bands in which exchange rates fluctuate.
June 1997	Stability and Growth Pact (SGP), proposed by Germany, imposes financial penalties on countries that violate 3% deficit rule.
Jan. 1999	Euro becomes currency in Austria, Belgium, Finland, France, Germany, Ireland, Italy, Luxembourg, Netherlands, Portugal, Spain. ERM II replaces ERM.
Jan. 2001	Greece enters eurozone.
Nov. 2003	Germany and France announce that they have violated SGP deficit rule.
Mar. 2005	EU finance ministers relax SGP deficit rule.
Jan. 2007– Jan. 2009	Slovenia, Cyprus, Malta and Slovakia enter eurozone.
Oct. 2009	New Greek government of PM George Papandreou announces deficits have been much higher than reported.
Jan. 2010	EU report condemns 'severe irregularities' in Greek government's accounting, announces public deficit in 2009 was 12.7% GDP.
Apr. 2010	EU revises Greece's 2009 public deficit up to 13.6% GDP and Ireland's 2009 public deficit up to 14.3% GDP.
May 2010	EU and International Monetary Fund (IMF) provide €110 bn. rescue package for Greece.
May 2010	EU establishes European Financial Stability Facility (EFSF) with initial capital guarantees of €440 bn. European Central Bank (ECB) launches Securities Market Program (SMP) to buy Greek, Irish, Portuguese bonds over the next 9 months.
Nov. 2010	EU and IMF provide €85 bn rescue package for Ireland.
Jan. 2011	Estonia enters eurozone.
May 2011	EU and IMF provide €78 bn rescue package for Portugal.
July 2011	EU Summit starts to plan second rescue package for Greece, plans to force EU banks to accept 'voluntary' 50% haircut on Greek bonds.
Aug. 2011	ECB resumes SMP, buying Irish, Italian, Portuguese and Spanish bonds.
Nov. 2011	Greek PM George Papandreou resigns, replaced by Lucas Papademos. Italian PM Silvio Berlusconi resigns, replaced by Mario Monti. Papademos and Monti are 'technocrats' – not politicians.
Dec. 2011	ECB cuts repo rate (interest rate on repurchase agreements – loans to banks collateralized by bonds) to 1% per year and eases collateral rules.
Dec. 2011 – Mar. 2012	EU leaders negotiate treaty that includes new rules to control deficits, signed by all EU members except the UK and Czech Republic in March. Treaty requires ratification by at least 12 countries by 2013. Only countries that ratify treaty will be eligible for rescue packages.
Mar. 2012	EU and IMF finalize second Greek rescue package of €130 bn. Enough bond holders agree to 53.5% face-value haircut with restructuring that lengthens maturities and reduces interest payments (for a total haircut of 75%) to allow the Greek government to invoke CACs (collective action clauses) that force settlements on all bond holders. These CACs are controversial because they were introduced retroactively by Greek government.

Source: Kehoe, T.J., Arellano, C., and J.C. Conesa. (2012) Chronic Sovereign Debt Crises in the Eurozone, 2010–12, Federal Reserve Bank of Minneapolis Economic Policy Papers, May 29, https://www.minneapolisfed.org/research/economic-policy-papers/chronic-sovereign-debt-crises-in-the-eurozone-20102012.

continue 'normal' activities. A second round of cheap financing, LTRO 2, took place on 29 February 2012, where another €529.5bn of such loans was taken up by some 800 plus banks.

Solving the Sovereign Debt Crisis

The policies needed to bring an end to the eurozone's sovereign debt crisis have been fairly clear for some time, especially to observers of debt crises in emerging markets and developing economies. These policies are a combination of

- sovereign debt write-offs,
- bank recapitalizations,
- ECB support for the banks and sovereign debt markets,
- medium-term commitments to fiscal discipline and
- cuts in labour and other business costs to restore competitiveness and growth (euphemistically called 'structural reform').

Unfortunately for private creditors, these policies have important linkages that mean that, in some cases, the sovereign debt write-offs have to be very large indeed. Eurozone leaders began to understand that these were the policies that needed to be implemented. Debt write-offs are needed for some countries because the sovereign has all but lost access to capital markets and because just cutting spending and raising taxes is proving to be self-defeating – it is worsening economic conditions and fiscal deficits. The only solution was for fiscal adjustment to include a large write-off of sovereign debt. Fortunately, this process began with the debt exchange by the Greek government in February 2012 that implied a 'haircut' of up to 53.5% of the principal bond value and a net present value reduction of 75–80% when reduced coupon payments on the new bonds are taken into account. Although the haircut seemed large, it was accepted because the majority of bondholders knew that it was the best deal they were likely to get. Moreover, if creditors had also looked at the debt sustainability exercise underlying the exchange offer that was prepared by the staff of the IMF and leaked to the *Financial Times*, they would have known that the odds were against even a debt reduction of this magnitude being sufficient to restore debt sustainability for Greece. In other words, more write-offs of Greek debt were likely down the road, so best take what you can get now.

Although the Greek debt write-off was the first of several sovereign write-offs, eurozone leaders have demonstrated that elements of hubris remain by declaring Greece to be a unique case, not to be repeated elsewhere in the eurozone. But these are the same people who told us in 2009 that Greece had no need to go to the IMF because fellow governments would help out with a generous loan of about €20bn and, when that didn't work, declared in 2010 that Greece had been 'saved' by a €110bn aid package and, when that didn't work out, told us that a new €750bn package would do the trick. Well, that didn't either.

Of course, although sovereign debt write-offs are a necessary part of the solution to the crisis, they have adverse consequences that have to be dealt with. Because European banks hold so much debt of European governments, the debt write-offs will weaken many banks and probably bankrupt some. To avoid a contraction of money and credit and an associated economic meltdown, European governments will have to provide public funds to assist with private bank recapitalization. But doing this will raise countries' sovereign public debt/GDP ratios, which means that only very large debt write-offs will bring the debt burden down to a sustainable level where growth-enhancing policies will have some chance of working. Debt write-offs that don't go far enough will place too big a burden on fiscal adjustment through public spending cuts and tax increases. That will mean lasting austerity and deep economic recession, which is likely to generate social protest and disorderly debt defaults, such as happened in Ecuador in 1999 and Argentina in 2002. Thus, the choice is large-scale, managed public debt write-offs now, or disorderly defaults and debt write-offs in the not too distant future. That European leaders finally accepted that this was inevitable for Greece was encouraging; that they believe it can be limited to Greece suggests that their capacity for self-delusion has not been exhausted.

The good news on bank recapitalization front is that eurozone leaders have finally endorsed the view that recapitalization is necessary. Unfortunately, the steps considered were not ambitious enough: the amount of recapitalization under consideration was too small, and the insistence that banks first have to try to raise their capital themselves forced them to contract their lending, given the environment of reduced bank profitability and a poor appetite for bank stocks. To avoid a 'credit crunch', some argued that banks needed to be given immediate access to the resources of an enlarged European Financial Stability Facility (EFSF). Up until recently (and the set-up of the new European Banking Union) such access was considered as a last resort option. Moreover, as the EFSF has been called upon to backstop sovereign debt markets to avoid contagion, it presently lacks the resources to support the scale of recapitalization that is likely to be needed. Maybe eurozone leaders are worried about an adverse reaction from the general public to more bank bailouts. If so, they should clarify that, though banks will need to be bailed out, bailouts will be done in a way that minimizes moral hazard and maximizes taxpayer protection – and that means wiping out shareholders and, if need be, unsecured bondholders.

Probably the most encouraging policy development in 2012 and 2013 related to ECB operations and the agreement to set up an European Banking Union. Eurozone leaders and the president of the ECB reversed positions vis-à-vis the involvement of the ECB in supporting banks and sovereign debt markets. Eurozone governments probably did this out of desperation in the face of deteriorating sovereign debt markets (that included, in some cases, an associated downgrading of sovereign debt by the credit rating agencies) and the realization that large-scale bank failures were a distinct possibility. For its part, the ECB finally realized that central banks have a lender-of-last-resort role, and it probably felt that the recent agreement by most EU governments (except the Czech Republic and the UK) on a new Fiscal Compact (the Fiscal Stability Treaty, signed on 2 March 2012) gave it significant room for manoeuvre to support sovereign debt markets. Whatever the reasons, the results have been plain to see: massive ECB liquidity support to banks under LTRO 1 and 2 has facilitated their ability to refinance debts and participate (albeit to a limited extent) in sovereign bond markets, nicely reflected in a quite sharp fall in sovereign bond yields.

Of course, sovereign debt reduction is not enough to restore capability: countries need to be put on a growth footing, which means they must be made more competitive. The most important 'reform' in this regard is to reduce relative real wage costs. This could once have been done through the (relatively painless) sleight-of-hand of currency devaluation. But no longer: staying in the eurozone means adjustment by driving down real wages through the threat or fact of unemployment. In some respects, this is probably the greatest remaining challenge for eurozone policymakers because the scale of the likely resulting social disorder (not much in Ireland, rather more in Greece, for example) and whether it can be controlled (yes in Ireland, but the jury is still out on Greece, for example) is so unpredictable. In the short term, real wage cuts also worsen the recession, and governments need to be given some additional room on the fiscal front, if only to be able to provide a minimum social safety net. In turn, this also means that the initial write-off of sovereign debt has to be very large.

The final realization by eurozone leaders that the solution to the crisis involves sovereign debt write-offs, publicly assisted bank recapitalizations, and ECB support for banks and bond markets has been a major impetus for the introduction of a European Banking Union, as discussed in the following section.

EUROPEAN BANKING UNION

Since the 2007–8 banking crisis, financial sector regulators have been trying to introduce a system of regulation that dealt with cross-border and single-market issues more effective. Such policy issues became more pressing with the onset of the eurozone sovereign debt crisis. Moves to Banking Union probably commenced in 2009 with the High-Level Group on Financial Supervision in the EU, chaired by Jacques de Larosiére, publishing a report outlining the proposals for reform of the EU regulatory framework. The so-called de Larosiére Report highlighted the lack of a common regulatory rulebook across EU member states – which led to inconsistencies in crisis management and financial stability oversight. The report recommended the creation of a European Systemic Risk Council (ESRC), chaired by the president of the European Central Bank. The European Commission followed most of the report's recommendations, and a new structure of EU financial sector supervision emerged. In November 2010, the EU Council of Finance (ECOFIN) agreed the creation of the following:

- European Systemic Risk Board (ESRB)
- European System of Financial Supervisors (ESFS) comprising three functional authorities that dealt with banking, insurance, and pensions and securities business. These were the European Banking Authority (EBA), the European Insurance and Occupational Pensions Authority (EIOPA) and the European Securities and Markets Authority (ESMA)

The above system was up and running by the start of 2011. Concerns regarding the eurozone crises and frailty of EU banks led to ongoing discussions, and in September 2012, plans for a European Banking Union were set out, as shown in Box 12.6.

BOX 12.6

Introducing the European Banking Union

Sept. 2012 European Commission presents a 'Roadmap towards a Banking Union', which proposes to set up a Single Supervisory Mechanism within the ECB and amend the European Banking Authority rules in order to strengthen the Economic and Monetary Union. The set of proposals is a first step towards an integrated Banking Union, which includes further components such as a single rulebook, common deposit protection and a single-bank resolution mechanism.

Dec. 2012	The presidents of the European Council, the European Commission, the European Central Bank and the Eurogroup present the report (known as the 'Four Presidents' Report') *Towards a Genuine Economic and Monetary Union*'.
	The report sets out a road map for the creation of a genuine Economic and Monetary Union and builds on the vision presented by Herman Van Rompuy, president of the European Council, in June 2012.
Mar. 2013	The European Parliament and European Council agree on a regulation amending the EBA regulation with regards to the interactions between EBA and ECB within the new Single Supervisory Mechanism (SSM).
July 2013	The European Commission starts a consultation of the ESFS review.
July 2013	The European Commission proposes a Single Resolution Mechanism for the Banking Union. The Single Resolution Mechanism complements the Single Supervisory Mechanism; it is set to centralize key competences and resources for managing the failure of any bank in the euro area and in other member states participating in the Banking Union.
Nov. 2013	Regulation on the Single Supervisory Mechanism comes into force
Jan. 2014	The EC adopts structural measures to improve the resilience of EU credit institutions.
Mar. 2014	The European Parliament and the Council have reach a provisional agreement on the proposed Single Resolution Mechanism for the Banking Union.

The main features of the Banking Union, shown in Figure 12.3, are as follows:

1   Single European banking supervision (Single Supervisory Mechanism – SSM)
2   Common resolution framework (Single Resolution Mechanism – SRM)
3   Common deposit insurance (Single Deposit Guarantee Mechanism – SDM)
4   Single rulebook (common legal framework, EBA single rulebook)

The Single Supervisory Mechanism (SSM) gives to the ECB new supervisory powers aimed at maintaining the stability of euro area banks. Under the SSM, the ECB will directly supervise 'significant' credit institutions and will work closely with the other national regulators. Credit institutions will be classified as 'significant' based on

- the total value of their assets;
- the importance for the economy of the country in which they are located or the EU as a whole;
- the significance of cross-border activities; and
- whether they have requested or received financial assistance from the European Stability Mechanism (ESM) or the European Financial Stability Facility (EFSF).

Typically the ECB only supervises banks deemed as systemically important. This is around 125 to 130 banks that account for 85%+ of eurozone banking sector assets. As part of the ECBs new supervisory role, it undertook an Asset Quality Review and Stress Tests of these banks in October 2014. Supervisory powers commenced on 1 November 2014.

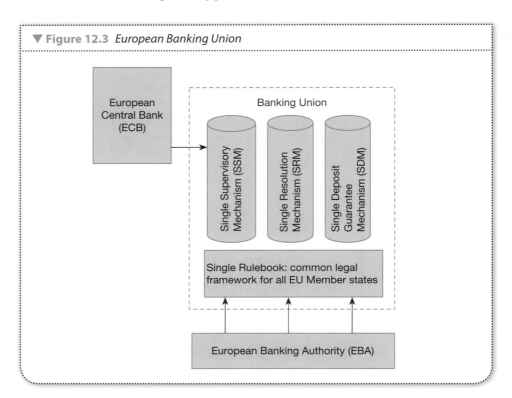

▼ **Figure 12.3** *European Banking Union*

The second pillar of the Banking Union is the introduction of the Single Resolution Mechanism (SRM) – comprising establishing a Single Resolution Board (SRB) and a Single Bank Resolution Fund (SRF). This simply deals with the process of how to deal with banks in trouble, especially large systemic banks. Ideally troubled banks can be closed or restructured in an orderly manner, although if the bank is systemically important, this can be troublesome. The aim of the SRM is to have consistent recovery and resolution rules for dealing with large systemically important banks in the eurozone. A controversial part of the SRM is the creation of a Single Bank Resolution Fund to which all the banks in the participating member states would contribute. The SRM came into force at the start of 2015, whereas bail-in and resolution functions apply from 1 January 2016 onwards,

The two remaining pillars of the Banking Union relate to the introduction of a single-deposit insurance scheme (with wider coverage, no co-insurance, and faster payouts) and a single rule book (regulations covering a variety of issues, particularly the CRD IV (which transposes Basel III capital rules into EU law) and new rules on bank recovery and resolution. Ultimately, the objective is to create a clear rulebook so that banks from different member states are subject to the same regulatory requirements, and depositors are also aware of the support and regulations in place. An ultimate objective of the European Banking Union is to decouple sovereign from banking sector risk. So if a systemically important bank in the eurozone has financial difficulties, then financial support can be provided by the whole EU system, and not just the national authorities. It still remains to be seen whether the new system will be effective in breaking the aforementioned link.

EUROPEAN COMMISSION DIRECTIVES IMPACTING THE FINANCIAL SECTOR

Notwithstanding the problems just covered, a major role of the EC has been to introduce legislation, which is then incorporated into member state law, aimed at creating a single market in financial services. This is part of the much broader aim of creating a single market in capital, goods, services and labour throughout Europe. Table 12.4 highlights the most important legislation affecting the financial sector.

▼ **Table 12.4** *Legislation impacting on the EU financial sector*

1977	*First Banking Directive:* Removed obstacles to the provision of services and establishment of branches across the borders of EU member states. Harmonized rules for bank licensing. Established EU-wide supervisory arrangements.
1988	*Basel Capital Adequacy Regulation (Basel I):* Minimum capital adequacy requirements for banks (8% ratio). Capital definitions: tier 1 (equity), tier 2 (near equity). Risk weightings based on credit risk for bank business.
1988	*Directive on Liberalization of Capital Flows:* Free cross-border capital flows, with safeguards for countries with balance of payments problems.
1989	*Second Banking Directive:* Single EU banking licence. Principles of home country control (home regulators have ultimate supervisory authority for the foreign activity of their banks) and mutual recognition (EU bank regulators recognize equivalence of their regulations). Passed in conjunction with the Own Funds and Solvency Directives, incorporating capital adequacy requirements similar to Basel I into EU law.
2007 onwards	*Capital Requirements Directive (CRD 1):* Updates Basel I and incorporates the measures suggested in the International Convergence of Capital Measurement and Capital Standards (Basel II): • Improved consistency of international capital regulations • Improved risk sensitivity of regulatory capital • Promotion of improved risk management practices among international banks CRD was introduced in 2007 and has been amended (there is a CRD 2, CRD 3 and a CRD 4). The aim of CRD 3 is to improve the quality of firms' capital by establishing clear EU-wide criteria for assessing the eligibility of hybrid capital to be counted as part of a bank's overall capital. It also seeks to improve the management of large exposures by restricting a firm's lending beyond a certain limit to any one party. CRD 3 also aims to improve the risk management of securitization. CRD 4 transposes the 2010 Basel III rules on bank capital into EU law –it has to be implemented by 2019.
2010 onwards	In the light of the credit crisis, the EU set up the European Systemic Risk Board (ESRB). It forms part of the package of measures put in place to reform the ESFS, which creates three authorities to supervise financial activities: • The European Banking Authority (undertaking stress tests on banks) • The European Insurance and Occupational Pensions Authority • The European Securities and Markets Authority The ESRB is responsible for the macro-prudential oversight of the financial system in the EU. One of its main objectives is to prevent and mitigate systemic risks that might prejudice the financial stability of the EU.

(continued)

▼ **Table 12.4** *Legislation impacting on the EU financial sector (continued)*

Sept. 2012	European Commission presents proposals to set up a Single Supervisory Mechanism within the ECB and amend the European Banking Authority rules in order to strengthen the Economic and Monetary Union. The set of proposals is a first step towards an integrated Banking Union.
2013	Capital Requirements Directive (CRD IV); Bank Recovery and Resolution Directive; Deposit Guarantee Scheme Directive Legislation supporting the European Commission's proposal for a European Banking Union. In mid-2013, plans for the Single Resolution Mechanism for the Banking Union were announced. The Single Resolution Mechanism complements the Single Supervisory Mechanism; it is set to centralise key competences and resources for managing the failure of any bank in the euro area and in other member states participating in the Banking Union.

Source: © European Central Bank, Frankfurt am Main, Germany and authors' updates.

One most important move was the introduction of the Financial Services Action Plan (FSAP) in 1999, which set out a 6-year agenda that aimed to harmonize financial services markets within the EU. It was originally scheduled to be completed by the end of 2004 and covered 42 specific legislative areas. The FSAP had four main objectives:

1   Completing a single wholesale market
2   Developing open and secure markets for retail financial services
3   Ensuring the continued stability of EU financial markets
4   Eliminating tax obstacles to financial market integration.

A whole range of initiatives was undertaken as part of the FSAP, and probably the most important resulting legislation was the Markets in Financial Instruments Directive, known as 'MiFID', implemented in 2007 (and updated by MiFID II). Other important legislation covers the Single European Payment Area (SEPA) and the taxation of savings.

The main aim of MiFID is to open up Europe's financial markets by improving transparency and making cross-border trade easier. This will enable banks and investment groups authorized in their home market to offer financial services across the EU without further accreditation. MiFID deals with a host of issues – investment advice, equity market transparency, conflicts of interest, best execution, compliance, consumer protection and record keeping. Along with Basel II and new accountancy standards, the banks to which this applies face considerable development costs. Bob Fuller, head of IT at Dresdner Kleinwort Wasserstein, says MiFID 'is the biggest piece of financial services legislation ever passed in the world'. The most significant change is that investment firms will no longer be required to route orders exclusively through stock exchanges. A report on the economic impact of MiFID published by the EU in March 2009 found that the main effects of the legislation have been to increase competition by reducing securities trading costs and increasing cross-border trading activity. The main beneficiaries have been wholesale traders in securities, with few observable gains for retail investors. London has also benefited through the establishment of alternative trading platforms. A proposed MiFID II was outlined in October 2011 that seeks to introduce further rules aimed at (among other things)

●   improving trade transparency;
●   increasing competition in securities clearing;

- introducing more competition in derivatives trading and tougher rules for OTC derivatives transactions; and
- giving greater powers to the new securities watchdog, the European Securities and Markets Authority.

The aim of SEPA is to make small value payments through the EU from a single bank account and a single universal system. It covers direct debits and credit transfers. Moving money across borders has traditionally been ludicrously expensive – all national payment systems are separate from their cross-border counterparts. SEPA, for example, makes the sale of products like life insurance much easier. Charlie McCreevy, the European commissioner for the internal market and services, believes that savings to users could be in the range of €50–100bn per year. Naturally, the banks who charge high prices for foreign payments will lose revenue and have had to pay an estimated €8bn to develop the system. The Payment Services Directive is an integral part of SEPA and was introduced in 2007; member states were expected to introduce this into their national laws in 2009. Pan-European payment instruments for credit transfers began in January 2008, although those for direct debits and debit cards are only just becoming available. The legislation is expected to increase competition in the provision of EU payments – all national payment operators are expected to be in competition offering such services and many expect substantial consolidation in the sector (to benefit from economies of scale).

In mid-2005, a Savings Tax Directive was passed. EU member states and others must either share information with others about non-resident savings in their country or impose a withholding tax, which initially started at 15%, was increased to 20% from 1 July 2008 and will go up to 35% from 1 July 2011. Austria, Belgium and Switzerland have adopted the Directive but agreed not to share information so their non-resident savers will be subject to the withholding tax. Luxembourg non-resident savers can decide themselves whether they want information disclosed or to be subject to the withholding tax. Surprisingly, some tax havens like the Cayman Islands, British Virgin Islands, Jersey, Guernsey and the Isle of Man have adopted the Directive. It applies to bank deposits, corporate and government bonds and some investment funds, but not to pensions or dividend incomes.

One should also note that substantial legislation has been passed in the context of the introduction of a European Banking Union but this has already been noted earlier in this and the previous section of this chapter.

BANKING TRENDS

The extent to which the European banking industry has become more integrated as a result of the introduction of the euro is questionable. As noted earlier, the most significant barriers to full integration appear to rest within the retail financial sector. Barriers such as differences in legal and tax systems can be regarded as policy induced in that they are erected and maintained by governments, and provide banks with a competitive advantage in their home country. Other differences arising from national economic conditions, culture, language and religion lead to efficiency differentials across countries, making it difficult for banks to offer many types of financial services on a cross-border basis. Such differences also explain why, until recently, there was only a small amount of cross-border merger activity. The introduction of the FSAP in 1999, and the application of many of its proposals, was recognition that the EU banking and financial markets were not fully integrated. The relatively new Takeover Directive has (some say) encouraged cross-border consolidation and linkages across banking systems within the EU and beyond.

Some features of EU banking systems between 1985 and 2013 are highlighted in Table 12.5, and these show some important trends. The number of banks has fallen; the asset share of the top five banks (the five-firm concentration ratio – CR5) has generally increased; and employment in the sector has grown.

The deregulation and integration of European banking markets has had implications for the observed levels of industry concentration. Many banks have been forced to increase in size, either through merger or internally generated growth, in order to compete on a Europe-wide basis. Another major motivation has been to realize potential scale and scope economies and also to reduce employment and other costs in an attempt to eliminate inefficiencies. By the mid-2000s, around two-thirds of financial sector mergers were in the same sector, and one-third were between banks and other types of financial institution. However, cross-industry mergers have become more common as banks have sought to realize scope economies via tie-ups with insurance companies. This has led to the emergence of financial conglomerates in many countries. Due to various barriers, most mergers have taken place within country. However, as opportunities for further growth via mergers have become exhausted within domestic borders, banks have sought out cross-border opportunities. These opportunities have been improved by the removal of many barriers via the FSAP and are likely to be augmented further with the implementation of Basel III through the Capital Adequacy Directive (IV).

As net interest margins have been subjected to increasing competitive pressures, resulting generally in a depression of earnings streams relative to costs, banks have increasingly focused on achieving growth from other, non-interest income sources of earnings. Fees and commissions are one example of an income stream arising from banks diversifying their activities. The growth of banks engaging in insurance, so-called bancassurance, and off-balance sheet operations, like trading and securitization activity, has further fuelled the potential of non-interest income in generating profitability.

The trend in the sources of bank income is clear: a fall in interest margins compensated for by an increase in non-interest-bearing income. As such, much bank growth has been achieved via product diversification by increasing the portions of their revenues coming from non-interest-bearing income from fees, securities trading, services and fiduciary responsibilities. On average, the non-interest-bearing income as a proportion of total income has increased from 28% in 1992 to 43% in 2001, reaching a peak of around 50% at the end of 2007 and falling thereafter. This has led, however, to greater volatility in bank income. Banks have also grown via geographic diversification by increasing their cross-border business. The market shares of foreign banks in many European countries have also increased, leading to increased competition in traditional banking areas.

Up until the onset of the credit crisis, some European banking sectors like the UK were posting record profits and various commentators were heralding a 'new dawn' for European banking business. For many, this buoyant market environment turned sour from the end of 2007, with many banks posting huge losses in 2008 and many struggling in the following years, as noted in Chapter 10.

▼ Table 12.5 Structural indicators for EU15 banking industry 1985–2013

Country	Number of banks				Assets (billion euros)				Number of branches				Employees ('000s)				Concentration (Assets CR$_5$)			
	1985	1995	2005	2013	1985	1995	2005	2013	1985	1995	2005	2013	1985	1995	2005	2013	1985	1995	2005	2013
Austria	1406	1041	880	741	-	396.8	720.5	1089.7	-	4,856	4,300	4,352	-	74	75	76	-	39.0	45.0	36.7
Belgium	120	143	100	116	285.9	589.4	1055.3	960.4	8,207	7,668	4,564	3,738	71	77	69	58	48.1	54.0	85.2	64
Denmark	259	202	197	164	96.3	125.5	722.1	870.4	3,411	2,215	2,114	1,256	52	47	48	36	61.2	72.1	66.3	68.4
Finland	498	381	363	318	-	196.3	234.5	521.7	-	1,612	1,616	1,300	-	31	25	22	-	70.6	83.1	84.1
France	1952	1895	1577	966	1348.8	2513.7	5090.1	6342.9	25,782	26,606	27,075	37,862	449	408	430	416	46.0	41.3	53.5	45.9
Germany	4739	3785	2089	1885	1495.1	3584.1	6826.6	6735.4	39,925	44,012	44,044	36,155	591	724	705	651	-	16.7	21.6	30.6
Greece	41	53	62	62	69.2	94.0	281.1	369.27	1,815	2,417	3,576	3,109	27	54	61	51	80.6	75.7	65.6	94.0
Ireland	42	56	78	554	21.0	45.8	941.9	789.8	-	808	910	1064	-	38	38	32	47.5	44.4	46.0	47.8
Italy	1101	970	792	714	546.8	1070.5	2509.4	2631.3	13,033	20,839	31,498	31,759	319	337	336	306	-	32.4	26.7	39.6
Luxembourg	177	220	155	360	169.8	445.5	792.4	717.9	120	224	155	213	10	19	23	26	26.8	21.2	30.7	33.7
Netherlands	178	102	401	264	226.7	650.0	1697.7	2433.3	6,868	6,729	3,748	2,165	92	111	117	96	72.9	76.1	84.8	83.8
Portugal	226	233	186	162	38.0	116.3	360.2	461.4	1,494	3,401	5,427	5,987	59	60	58	57	61.0	74.0	68.8	70.6
Spain	364	506	348	345	311.3	696.3	2150.7	3488.2	32,503	36,405	41,979	33,713	244	249	253	216	35.1	47.3	42.0	56.2
Sweden	598	249	200	174	-	146.9	653.2	1664.0	-	2,731	1,910	1,974	-	44	46	54	-	59.3	57.3	58.3
UK	772	564	400	390	1293.6	1999.5	8320.2	9294.1	22,224	17,522	13,694	11,381	375	445	483	422	-	28.3	36.3	43.7

Note: The large increase in the number of Irish banks in 2011 was due to a reclassification of credit unions as banks.

Sources: Central Bank Reports (various); ECB and also from ECB Consolidated Banking Data (online resource).

SUMMARY

- The origins of the EU as it is today lie in the *European Coal and Steel Community* in 1952, a pooling of coal and steel resources in Belgium, France, Italy, Luxembourg, the Netherlands and West Germany. These six countries signed the *Treaty of Rome* in 1957 and began the concept of a common market and the *European Economic Community*. The motives were economic and political.

- Enlargement of membership came later with the addition of Denmark, Ireland and the UK in 1973; Greece in 1981; Spain and Portugal in 1986; Austria, Finland and Sweden in 1995; Cyprus, Czech Republic, Estonia, Hungary, Latvia, Lithuania, Malta, Poland, Slovakia, Slovenia in 2004; Bulgaria and Romania in 2007; and Croatia in 2013.

- The *Single European Act* of 1987 (which came into force in January 1993) aimed to eliminate all final barriers to trade within Europe and to establish a genuinely efficient and competitive single market.

- The European Economic Community (EEC) had already been shortened to *European Community* (EC). With the Single European Act, it became the *European Union* (EU).

- The first moves to a single currency and monetary union were suggested in the *Werner Report* of 1970, proposing a single currency by 1980. Upheaval in the 1970s (the collapse of Bretton Woods and oil price inflation) prevented any progress.

- The next move was the *European Monetary System* in 1979. This set up the use of the ECU as a common unit of accountancy, and also the *Exchange Rate Mechanism* (ERM) tying currencies to bands around a target rate against other currencies. The bands were ± 2.25% or ± 6%. By the end of 1990, 11 of Europe's 12 countries were members of the ERM.

- Attacks on currencies in the ERM in 1992 and 1993 led to a revision of the band to ± 15% (except for the guilder/deutschmark rate, which remained at ± 2.25 %).

- In 1989, a report by Jacques Delors, the Commission president, set out steps towards economic and monetary union. The *Maastricht Treaty* laid down convergence conditions, the setting up of a *European Monetary Institute* (EMI) in 1994 to precede the *European Central Bank* and the possibility of the *Economic and Monetary Union* (EMU) beginning in 1999. It was later decided to call the new currency the *euro*.

- Following detailed plans laid down by the EMI, economic and monetary union began on 1 January 1999. Initially, the euro was used for interbank and other wholesale purposes, with notes and coins following on 1 January 2002. In the meantime, the relevant currencies were locked together in fixed exchange rates.

- Eleven countries joined the new system in 1999 – Austria, Belgium, Finland, France, Ireland, Italy, Germany, Luxembourg, the Netherlands, Portugal and Spain. This left Greece, Sweden, the UK and Denmark outside. Greece joined in 2001. Membership expanded to the current 19 countries; Slovenia (joined on 31 December 2006), Cyprus (1 January 2008), Malta (1 January 2008), Slovakia (1 January 2009), Estonia (1 January 2011); Latvia (1 January 2014) and Lithuania (1st January 2015).

- The *European Central Bank* (ECB) began operations in June 1998. It has six executive members who form the executive board. They meet with the 19 governors of the member states to form the governing council. This grouping of the ECB together with the 19 governors is usually called the *European System of Central Banks* (ESCB). However, the ECB has pointed out that legally this includes the governors of the non-EMU states, even though they play no part. It prefers to use the name *Eurosystem*.

- To prevent excessive budget deficits, there is a *Stability and Growth Pact*, which limits budget deficits to a maximum of 3% in relation to GDP, although over time, at least half of the member countries in the eurozone have exceeded the limit. It now has little credibility in light of the eurozone crisis.

- Those countries wishing to join EMU are expected to have spent 2 years in the successor to the ERM, known as *ERM II*.

The EU economy is larger than the US in PPP terms, with a GDP of €12.9 trillion compared to €11.8 trillion, respectively.

- According to IMF figures for 2013, the EU now accounts for 23% of global GDP compared with around 22% for the US. Within the eurozone itself, the market is dominated by Germany, France and Italy, who together account for 66% of the total GDP – Germany alone accounts for 29%. In contrast, China's nominal GDP stood at over $9.5 trillion in 2013, making it the second largest single country economy after the US (nominal GDP of $16.8 trillion).

- The new interbank payment and settlement system for the euro is *TARGET2*.
- The objective of EMU is to produce a range of benefits:
  - Price transparency leading to more competition
  - A logical completion of the move towards a single competitive market
  - A saving in foreign currency transactions
  - A reduction of the cost of capital through more efficient capital markets – bonds, equities and derivatives
  - More integrated retail and wholesale banking systems.
- Critics, however, point to the problems of a 'one size fits all' policy in interest rates and currencies:
  - Differences in business cycles
  - The strains on fiscal policy that will emerge
  - The lack of labour mobility
  - Some weaknesses in the structure of the ECB
  - The fact that full price transparency will not exist due to tax differences and weakness in Europe due to high social costs, inflexible labour markets and a large public sector.
- The major EU country not in EMU is the UK. Prior to the eurozone crisis, those in the UK who wished to join
  - wanted to continue to encourage foreign investment in the UK;
  - wanted to enjoy lower forex costs;
  - wanted greater stability of the currency; and
  - believed that the UK outside would lose influence and the City of London lose ground to Frankfurt.
- Those who disagree believe that
  - the threat to foreign investment is exaggerated;
  - the lower forex costs are modest compared to the total picture;
  - there will still be currency instability against the dollar, yen and Swiss franc;
  - the London dominance in financial markets will not be affected; and
  - the UK will suffer from the 'one size fits all' policy, and they fear greater political integration.
- The *European/eurozone sovereign debt crisis* relates to the financial crisis faced by various countries concerning their inability to finance their spending due to their excessive levels of previous borrowings. The crisis emerged during 2009 as a consequence of the increased debt levels (partly because of banking system bailouts in 2007–8) and also because of the downgrading of various government debt by the rating agencies, which made new borrowing and the financing of existing debt more expensive.

- Countries in the eurozone have been most affected, namely Greece, Ireland and Portugal, and there has been a wave of rescue packages coordinated by the European Commission, ECB and IMF, aimed at stemming the crisis.
- The policies needed to bring an end to the eurozone's sovereign debt crisis have been fairly clear for some time, especially to observers of debt crises in emerging markets and developing economies. These policies are a combination of
  - sovereign debt write-offs;
  - bank recapitalizations;
  - medium-term commitments to fiscal discipline;
  - cuts in labour and other business costs to restore competitiveness; and
  - growth (euphemistically called 'structural reform').
- In September 2012, plans for a European Banking Union were established, the main features of which relate to setting-up a
  - single European banking supervision (Single Supervisory Mechanism – SSM);
  - common resolution framework (Single Resolution Mechanism – SRM);
  - common deposit insurance (Single Deposit Guarantee Mechanism – SDM); and
  - single rulebook (common legal framework, EBA single rulebook).

The Single Supervisory Mechanism (SSM) gives to the ECB new supervisory powers aimed at maintaining the stability of euro area banks. Under the SSM, the ECB will directly supervise 'significant' credit institutions, and it will work closely with the other national regulators. Typically, the ECB will only supervise banks deemed as systemically important, which is around 125 to 130 banks that account for 85%+ of eurozone banking sector assets. As part of the ECBs new supervisory role, it undertook an Asset Quality Review and Stress Tests of these banks in October 2014. Supervisory powers commenced on 1 November 2014.

- The European Commission has pressed on with a series of other initiatives. The *Markets in Financial Instruments Directive* (MiFID 2) and the *single euro payments area* (SEPA) are the most important recent moves in this direction. There is some evidence that London, as Europe's major financial centre, has benefited from MiFID, as it has reduced securities trading costs and boosted cross-border trading in wholesale areas.

REVISION QUESTIONS/ASSIGNMENTS

1 Compare the pros and cons of the EU. Examine the impact it has had on European financial markets and institutions.

2 Examine the main features of the eurozone sovereign debt crisis. Will it lead to the break-up of the monetary union?

3 Discuss the major legislation introduced to improve the competitiveness of European financial systems. Have these reforms had an impact on UK financial firms?

4 Analyse the main features of EU banking systems, and highlight recent trends.

FURTHER READING

Bootle, R. (2014) *The Trouble with Europe*, Nicholas Brealey. Discusses the possible consequences of a break up of the eurozone.

European Council. (2012) 'Towards a Genuine Economic and Monetary Union', Report by President of the European Council Herman Van Rompuy (June 2012), (December 2012).

Heisbourg, F. (2013) *The End of the European Union*, The Foundation for Strategic Research. Argues the case for the eurozone to be broken up to 'save the greater project'.

International Monetary Fund (IMF). (2013) 'European Union: Publication of Financial Sector Assessment Programme Documentation – Technical Note on Deposit Insurance' IMF Country Report 13/66.

Issing, O. (2008) *The Birth of the Euro*, CUP, Cambridge. Authoritative account of the birth and performance of the euro up to 2007 by the former chief economist of the ECB.

Tilly, R., Welfens, P.J., and Heise, M. (eds) (2007) *50 Years of EU Economic Dynamics: Integration, Financial Markets and Innovations*, Springer, Berlin. An edited text with contributions from central bankers and other EU grandees focusing on the institutional evolution of the EU.

Walter, I., and Smith, R.C. (2002) *High Finance in the eurozone: Competing in the New European Capital Market*, FT/Prentice Hall, Upper Saddle River, NJ. Analysis of capital markets and players in the eurozone.

Derivative Products

Traded Options

DERIVATIVE PRODUCTS

Probably the fastest growing sector of the financial markets today is that of derivatives, so named because they derive from another product. The buying of $1m for sterling is the product. The option to buy $1m for sterling later at a price we agree today is the derived product. Borrowing $1m at a floating rate for 5 years is the product. A bank offering (for a fee) to compensate the borrower should rates rise above a given level in the next 5 years is the derived product and so on.

In currency rates, interest rates, bonds, equities and equity indices, there is volatility. Where there is volatility, there are those who believe they know what the next price movement is and back their judgement with money – the 'speculators'. Then there are those who will lose money from a given price movement and seek to protect themselves from this – the 'hedgers'. Both will use the derivative markets for this purpose. The interesting paradox is that one is using them to take risks and the other to reduce risks. Finally, there are those who perceive pricing anomalies and seek to exploit this – the arbitrageurs. Thus, the three types of professional users of derivative products are speculators, hedgers and arbitrageurs.

Additionally, derivatives are increasingly being packaged with retail banking products to provide, for example, fixed rate mortgages or guaranteed investment funds.

Speculators are easy enough to understand, but before we look at hedgers and arbitrageurs, it will be as well to explain one of the derivative products first. The two key products are options and futures. If readers can obtain a good working knowledge of these products, they are well placed to understand others (forward rate agreements, swaps, caps and so on) because those others are simply variations on the options and futures themes. This chapter will discuss options; Chapter 14 covers futures and Chapter 15 the remaining derivative products.

One last point: in Chapter 11, we mentioned that currency options could be purchased on a trading exchange or over the counter (OTC), that is, directly from a bank or trader. Although this was mentioned in the context of currency options, it is generally true that there are exchanges for traded options and financial futures but that these products can also be purchased OTC.

The advantage of a trading exchange is that there is plenty of trading liquidity; there are competing traders to ensure good prices; and there is the implicit protection against default provided by a body called the clearing house. The disadvantage is that the products are standardized and may not suit the user's exact requirements. To take the example, we met in Chapter 10, the cable contract on the Chicago Mercantile Exchange (CME) is based on multiples of £62,500. This means that if the amount required to be bought or sold for dollars is £75,000, then the product offered is not an exact fit.

The big advantage of OTC dealing is its flexibility. The product offered to users can be tailored to their exact needs. On an exchange, however, it may be possible to 'trade' the product later, that is, sell it back to the exchange. Sometimes, OTC products cannot be traded or, if they can, the user is very much in the hands of the seller for a price. Dealers can, however, always back it out with another counterparty, which deals with the price problem but still leaves you with credit risk. OTC markets are often accused of a lack of liquidity when it comes to trading even standardized products at a later stage – although there are exceptions – nobody would accuse the OTC foreign exchange options market of a lack of liquidity in major currency pairs, for instance. Finally, the user must consider the risk of default. If the seller is Deutsche Bank or UBS, we can be quite happy, as the default risk might be considered small, but the Wall Street company Drexel Burnham Lambert crashed in February 1990 and defaulted on many outstanding OTC products, as did Lehman Brothers in 2008. On the other hand, when Baring Bros defaulted on its obligations at the Singapore Monetary Exchange (SIMEX), no futures market counterparties lost any money due to the operation of the clearing house.

In an effort to counteract the flexibility of OTC, some exchanges have introduced more flexible contracts themselves. In 1995, the Philadelphia Stock Exchange (PHLX) introduced the possibility of tailored exercise prices and expiry dates. Similar moves have followed from other exchanges.

Let us turn now to the subject of options.

TRADED OPTIONS: EQUITIES

Calls and Puts

Traded options are standardized exchange-traded options that grant the buyer the right (but not the obligation) to buy or sell financial instruments at standard prices and dates in the future. A premium is charged for this right and is usually paid when the option is bought.

Let us take a simple example. Suppose we look at a hypothetical UK company, XYZ Ltd, and the share price is £1.86. We may be optimistic and believe that the price may well rise to, say, £2.10 in the next 3 months. The option to *buy* a given quantity of XYZ Ltd shares at £1.86 in the next 3 months is very attractive. If we are right and the price goes to £2.10, we can use the option to buy the given quantity of shares at £1.86 and sell them again in the conventional way at £2.10. If we are wrong and the price falls or remains constant, we don't have to do anything as it was only an option, not an obligation. This is clearly a privileged position, and we must pay for it. The price we pay is the premium for the option. This right to *buy* a financial product later is the call option. We buy a call when we wish to gain from an increase in price later.

Alternatively, we may be pessimistic about XYZ Ltd and believe that the price of £1.86 will probably fall to £1.60 in the next 3 months. The option to *sell* a given quantity of XYZ Ltd shares at £1.86 in the next 3 months is very attractive. If we are correct, we can buy them later for £1.60 and use the option to sell them at £1.86. If we are wrong and the price rises or remains constant, we don't have to do anything as it was only an option, not an obligation. Again, we pay a premium for this privilege. The right to *sell* a financial product later is the put option. We buy a put when we wish to gain from a fall in price later.

Let's look at some figures. Suppose the call or put contract is for 1,000 shares and the premium in each case is 10p per share. We'll look at the call and the put in turn.

Call option

Box 13.1 outlines the main features of a call option.

BOX 13.1

Call Options

The right to *buy* a financial product later is a call option.

We have the right to buy 1,000 XYZ Ltd shares within the next 3 months at £1.86 and pay a premium of 10p per share (= £100) up front.

XYZ Ltd share price later:

£1.60?←£1.86→£2.10?

Suppose the price falls to £1.60, and we have come to the end of the 3 months. The right to buy at £1.86 is of no value, as we can buy them at the market price of £1.60. The option will expire. There is no action to take – we just abandon our option. Our loss is the premium of £100 (which we've already paid). Notice that whatever happens, we *can't lose more than the premium*.

Suppose the price rises later to £2.10. Now, we can contact our broker, advise him that we are exercising our option to buy 1,000 shares at £1.86 and ask him to sell them in the usual way for £2.10 (no further capital needs to be paid). We have made 1,000 × (£2.10–£1.86) = 1,000 × 24p = £240. We paid a premium of £100, so the net gain is £140 or 140% (for convenience, dealing costs have been ignored).

The share price rose 24p from £1.86, a rise of about 13%. This rise of 13% generated us a profit of 140%. This effect is called 'gearing', which we met in Chapter 1 (the Americans call it leverage). In general, it's making a given sum of money go further.

In Chapter 1, we looked at balance sheet gearing – making money go further by borrowing other people's money. This is another example. If we had bought 1,000 XYZ Ltd shares, we would have paid £1,860. We backed our view on £1,860 of shares with just £100 premium.

In addition (at least in theory), the remaining £1,760 can be in the bank earning interest. The result, as in the above case, is that a small change in the price of the underlying asset (13%) may lead to a large percentage profit gain (140%). However, gearing cuts both ways. The price didn't need to fall at all for us to lose 100% of the premium, and any fall in price will create larger losses.

Nevertheless, gearing/leverage is a big attraction in derivative products.

Put option

Box 13.2 outlines the main features of a put option.

Option Writers

Who, in the first instance, sells us the XYZ Ltd shares at £1.86 when the market price is £2.10? Who, in the second instance, buys our shares from us at £1.86 when the market

BOX 13.2

Put Options

The right to *sell* a financial product later is a put option

We now have paid for the right to sell 1,000 XYZ Ltd shares within the next 3 months at £1.86, and pay a premium of 10p per share (= £100) up front.

XYZ Ltd share price later:

£1.60?←£1.86 →£2.10?

At this point, the reader might wonder how we can buy the right to sell shares that we don't even own. We shall find that not only is this not a problem, it is part of the beauty of the put option. Suppose the price rises to £2.10, and we have come to the end of the option period. We have the right to sell 1,000 shares at £1.86. If we had the shares (which we don't), we could sell them on the market for £2.10.

Our right is of no value and will expire, losing the premium of £100.

Suppose the price falls later to £1.60. We have the right to sell 1,000 shares at £1.86 but don't actually own any. What we do, of course, is buy 1,000 shares in the conventional way at £1.60 and use the option to sell them at £1.86, making 26p per share, or a net 16p after deducting our cost of 10p per share.

Our profit is £160, or 160%, although the change in share price was only about 14%.

price is £1.60? The answer is the person who sold us the option in the first place, called the option writer, who took our premium and believed that it was a good price for the risk.

Thus, four possibilities exist in the option game. One can buy calls or puts, and one can write calls or puts. The risk profile is quite different for buyers and writers:

	Maximum loss	*Maximum gain*
Option buyer	The premium	Unlimited
Option writer	Unlimited	The premium

Because option writers face unlimited risk, they pay a deposit, called 'margin', to the clearing house. When the deal is opened, they pay initial margin. If the price moves against them, they must pay more margin – variation margin – to cover their losses. If they go into liquidation, the deal is honoured by the clearing house.

Trading Options

In the above cases, we either abandoned our option or exercised it. On a trading exchange, there is the further choice of *trading the option*. Let's illustrate this, and some of the real-life complications, by looking at the prices that might be quoted for XYZ Ltd shares at any one time on London's LIFFE exchange (now owned by Intercontinental Exchange, ICE). The exchange deals in the shares of UK companies and also offers options on the main share index, the FTSE 100 (to be explained later) as well as many other contracts.

The position is more complicated than in our previous example:

- There is a choice of share prices at which calls/puts can be bought/written. They are called exercise or strike prices. There is a choice of dates for expiry of the contract. Three dates are offered to a maximum of 9 months ahead.

- Options must be dealt in set multiples or standard contract sizes (typically 1,000 shares on Liffe, but varying by exchange).
- Options can be traded, that is, sold back to the market for a later premium.
- Having bought an option, it can be exercised at any time prior to the expiry date. This is called an 'American option'. (It's nothing to do with America; most options on European exchanges are American options.)

Let's first look at the matrix of choice and assume that we came to the market on 27 March and looked at options for XYZ Ltd (Table 13.1).

Notice that we have standardized exercise prices of £1.80, £2.00 and £2.20 (in reality there might be several more, but these would tend to be the most liquid). None of them is the market price (£1.86) except by coincidence. We have a further choice of expiry in April, July or October – a maximum of 7 months. Had we come to the market on 1 February, we would still have seen April, July and October, and hence our maximum time horizon of 9 months.

Thus there are nine choices, and for each there is a quoted premium in pence per share. Suppose the premiums for all three exercise prices were the same. Naturally, we would pick the exercise price of £1.80 because we would all like to be able to buy at the cheapest price. It will be no surprise to find that the premium for £1.80 is more expensive than that for £2.00 and much more expensive than that for £2.20. Again, suppose the premiums for all three expiry dates were the same. Naturally, we would pick October to give XYZ Ltd the maximum time to go up in price. For the same reason, the option writer wants a higher premium for October than April.

▼ **Table 13.1** *XYZ Ltd, call options, 27 March*

Market price	Exercise price	Exercise expiry dates		
		April	July	October
	£1.80			
£1.86	£2.00			
	£2.20			

▼ **Table 13.2** *XYZ Ltd, call options, 27 March*

Market Price	Exercise price	April	July	October
			calls (p)	
	£1.80	16	24	32
£1.86	£2.00	7	14	21
	£2.20	3	7	12

Let's look now at the full list of prices in Table 13.2. On 27 March, the right to buy XYZ Ltd shares at £1.80 before an expiry in April costs 16p per share. For the minimum contract of 1,000 shares, this is £160. On 27 March, the right to buy XYZ Ltd shares at £2.00 before an expiry in October costs 21p per share. For the minimum contract, this is £210. Notice the gearing. To *buy* 1,000 XYZ Ltd shares today would cost £1,860.

Which of these nine options do we choose? There is no magic answer. It depends how strongly you feel XYZ Ltd is undervalued, how soon you think the price will rise, and how risk averse you are. You could choose £1.80, already cheaper than the stock market price and October expiry, giving the longest time for XYZ Ltd to go up in price. It looks attractive but at £320 per 1,000 shares is the most expensive. At the other extreme, you could choose £2.20 and expiry in April. This is 34p dearer than the stock market price, and there are perhaps only 4 weeks to the expiry date. It doesn't look attractive, but it's cheap at £30 per 1,000 shares.

Intrinsic Value and Time Value

The £1.80 option is already 6p cheaper than the market price of £1.86. We can argue, therefore, that the premium must be at least 6p. Suppose the premium was 4p. You would buy as many options as you could possibly afford and immediately exercise, buying the shares for £1.80 and selling for £1.86. An obvious profit of 6p for a cost of 4p. No chance. The market calls this 6p the intrinsic value. This occurs when the call exercise price is cheaper than the market price or a put exercise price is dearer than the market price.

The option premium for the April expiry is 16p. We know that it must be at least 6p and can see that 10p has been added to cover the possibility of XYZ Ltd going up in price prior to expiry. We call this the time value in the option. The exercise price of £2 is dearer than the market price, and it has no intrinsic value (we don't use negative intrinsic value).

Breaking the premium down like this, into intrinsic value and time value, let's look at the £1.80 calls for April, July and October and the £2.00 calls for the same expiry dates in Table 13.3. We can see how time value goes up steadily for later expiry dates.

Calculation of the Premium

Where does this time value come from? How are the premiums calculated? Usually, in human activity, if we want to forecast the future, we start with the past: as T.S. Eliot tells us, 'In my beginning is my end.' One way is to look at the previous behaviour of the share price, say, over the last 6 months, and project this forward using statistical techniques and laws of probability. These may suggest that there is a given probability that the XYZ Ltd share price in October will be within a given range. We look at the exercise price, the current market price, one or two other factors we don't need to go into here, and the statistical calculations use the past behaviour to produce a theoretical value, or *fair value*, for the premium. There may then be a question of whether the option writer believes that future price behaviour will be different, and also sheer demand and supply. This way of calculating premium, however, is rather backward looking. Probably a more common way of calculating the premium would be to look at yield differentials in the future (from forward contracts) and their implied volatilities (volatility of forward prices due to market movements) rather than historical performance.

If there are more option buyers than sellers, premiums will rise, and vice versa. Experts compare the market premiums with the fair value premiums and decide whether the premiums look cheap or expensive.

These statistical techniques were developed in May 1973 when Fischer Black and Myron Scholes wrote a paper on the pricing of options in the *Journal of Political Economy*.

▼ **Table 13.3** *£1.80 and £2.00 calls for April, July and October*

Exercise price	Expiry	Intrinsic value (p)		Time value (p)		Premium (p)
£1.80	April	6	+	10	=	16
	July	6	+	18	=	24
	October	6	+	26	=	32
£2.00	April	0	+	7	=	7
	July	0	+	14	=	14
	October	0	+	21	=	21

The Black-Scholes formula, with one or two possible modifications, is still widely used to calculate premiums. Black and Scholes were professors at the University of Chicago, and the timing was apt as the Chicago Board Options Exchange (CBOE) had started trading options in April 1973. A few years later, Professors Cox, Ross and Rubenstein (assisted by Professor Robert Merton) produced a similar formula (one based on a binomial progression for those who understand such things). In October 1997, Scholes and Merton received the Nobel Prize for their work. Black was not included as the prize is never awarded posthumously and, unfortunately, Black had died the previous year. Other areas of probability theory are also used, for example, Monte Carlo simulation. David Gershon, chief executive of SuperDerivatives, promotes alternative formulae for foreign exchange and interest rate options. In late 2005, he made these available on the Internet so that investors could check quoted prices from dealers. The experts argue about the merits of one formula as opposed to another; for the layperson, the results are very similar. (For more technical information, consult the companion website mentioned at the beginning of the book.)

In looking at the past behaviour of two shares, one may be much more volatile than another, although the average price may be similar in each case. The more volatile share may produce higher or lower share prices later than the less volatile one, and thus the premium will be higher (Figure 13.1).

For the option writer, share B is clearly more dangerous and risky than share A, even though the average price over time is much the same. Without knowing anything about statistics, we can accept that the option premiums quoted for share B will be higher than for share A. Those who understand statistics will be aware that this volatility is the standard deviation and a key element in the pricing formula. Experts will analyse market premiums to see the *implied volatility*. They will then decide if they agree with this figure, bearing in mind that future volatility may not be the same as past or *historic volatility*. These are advanced considerations that need not concern us in an introductory text. Be aware, however, that 'volatility' is a big word in the options game. Indeed, in September 2005, the Eurex exchange launched contracts that were based on the implied volatility in the equity index contracts in the German, Swiss and pan-European markets. This enables traders to trade volatility itself.

Volatility is usually quoted as a percentage figure, for example 20%. This would mean that, over one year, there is a 68% chance in the laws of probability that a share price will be either 20% higher or lower than the starting price. Suppose a share price is £1.00 and the volatility is 20%. The premium for a one-year call option, the right to buy the share at £1.00 within the next year, would be 9.9p per share. If the volatility were 40%, the premium would be 17.1p. (This assumes a 10% interest rate and a 5% dividend yield, factors that are also taken into account.)

The Russian crisis of August 1998 is an example of how the volatilities of financial instruments can change. The Hong Kong and Shanghai Banking Corporation (HSBC) estimated the volatility of the UK's FTSE 100 Index in July 1998 at 20%. Two months later, following the Russian crisis, it was 40%. Its range in 1995–96 was just 12–15%. In 2002, after 2 years of dramatic daily movements and large annual falls, the market was estimating the volatility of the FTSE 100 at 25–30%. As option premiums go

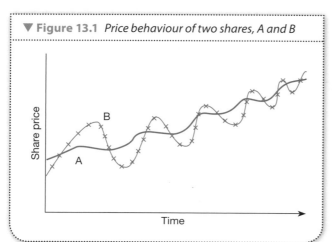

▼ **Figure 13.1** *Price behaviour of two shares, A and B*

up as volatility rises, this means that just as people are looking for protection because the situation has become more uncertain, protection costs a lot more. In its 2009 report on the credit crisis, the BIS noted that implied volatility on a wide range of market indicators increased substantially when Lehman Brothers filed for Chapter 11 bankruptcy protection on 15 September 2008.

Exercise or Trade?

Going back to the XYZ Ltd prices on 27 March, let's assume that we bought a call option with exercise price £1.80 and expiry in July. Let's also assume that it's the minimum of one contract, that is, 1,000 shares. The premium is quoted as 24p, and so we will pay £240 plus broker's commission and a small charge for the costs of the clearing house. (The premiums are actually quoted with a bid/offer spread so that 24p may be a mid-point representing a quote of 23/25p. We will ignore this in the interest of simplicity.)

Let's move on now to 6 June in the same year. We can look at the current call option premiums in Table 13.4. We see that April has gone and been replaced by January, the next month in the series. We also note that the share price has gone up 20p (from £1.86 to £2.06) and the £1.80/July call premium is now quoted as 36p. If we are new to options, this might puzzle us. We could argue that, as the share price has gone up 20p, the right to buy at £1.80 must be 20p more valuable. If the old premium was 24p, it should now be 44p. To understand what is happening to the premium, we must break it down into intrinsic value and time value and compare the positions on 27 March and 6 June. We can see this in Table 13.5.

We can see that intrinsic value has gone up by 20p but time value down by 8p, giving a net increase of 12p. The time value is down simply because, at 6 June, there is less time left to expiry. If we need more time value for more time, as we saw earlier, then we need less time value for less time. It is most important to grasp this. It means that there is an element in the premium, the time value, *which is steadily going down*, regardless of what is happening to the share price. There is an element, intrinsic value, which may be going *up* or *down* – that depends on the share price movement. Because we may *trade* the option, that is, receive the quoted premium, we must understand its behaviour.

Suppose we decide to take profit at this point, We have two choices – exercise the option or trade it. If we *exercise* the option, we buy 1,000 shares at £1.80 and sell them at the market price of £2.06, making 26p per share, ignoring dealing costs. As the option cost is 24p per share, our profit is 2p per share. On the other hand, if we *trade* the option, we sell it back for 36p, today's quoted premium. As the option cost is 24p per share, our profit is 12p per share.

In the first case, we make £20, and in the second, £120. Why was trading more profitable? When we exercise, we buy at the exercise price (£1.80) and sell at the market price (£2.06), this gap being the

▼ **Table 13.4** *XYZ Ltd call options, 6 June*

Market price	Exercise price	July	October	January
			(p)	
	£1.80	36	44	52
£2.06	£2.00	18	28	38
	£2.20	6	13	24

▼ **Table 13.5** *Breaking down premium into intrinsic and time value for the July £1.80 strike call*

Premium date	Market price	Intrinsic value (p)		Time value (p)		Premium (p)
27 March	£1.86	6	+	18	=	24
6 June	£2.06	26	+	10	=	36

intrinsic value. When we exercise, we receive the intrinsic value, in this case 26p. When we trade, we receive the premium, that is, intrinsic value *plus* time value. The premium is 36p because 10p of time value was added to the intrinsic value. In other words, we are gaining from the protection built into the premium by the option writer. In fact, when we trade the option, we *are* an option writer. However, as we previously bought the same option, we are not left with any outstanding position in the market. It follows that, at expiry, there is no time value, and exercising the option or trading it will produce the same result. There is one final point regarding the time value. We have noted that it declines as time passes. However, this decline accelerates as we approach expiry. An option buyer may defer taking profit for several weeks, allowing the share price to rise even further. It may well be, however, that the time value declines faster than the intrinsic value rises, and the total premium falls in value. This will be particularly true with a few weeks of expiry.

Other Terminology

We have noted the term 'intrinsic value', which is used when a call option exercise price is below the market price or a put option exercise price is above it. The option is also described here as *in the money*. If the exercise price is the same as the market price, we say the option is *at the money*. If the call exercise price is dearer than the market or the put exercise price is cheaper, we say the option is *out of the money*. Please note, however, that the use of standard exercise prices means that it is only rarely that one is the same as the market price. As a result, it is common to call the 'at the money' option the one that is *nearest* to the market price.

We described these LIFFE options earlier as American options, that is, they can be exercised at any time prior to the expiry date. The alternative is the 'European option', which can only be exercised at expiry. We will give an example of this shortly. Typically, options on trading exchanges are American options, but European options are quite common in the OTC market. Both options can be traded at any time on trading exchanges.

Options on Indices

Having looked at options on individual shares, we can now consider options on a whole share index, for example, S&P 100, FTSE 100, CAC 40, AEX and so on.

In principle, we can see that the idea has advantages. Now we can back a view on the whole market, not an individual share. Alternatively, we may be a market maker or fund manager owning all the top shares. The index might be a good way of hedging market risk. The practice of index options may be puzzling at first. One can readily envisage exercising an option and buying XYZ Ltd shares. What if we exercise the index option and buy the FTSE 100 Index or the CAC 40? What exactly do we receive?

The contracts are *cash settled*. Because there isn't anything to deliver, the contract is settled by paying cash. The index must be regarded as a price. If a call option on the FTSE 100 is bought at an exercise level of 6,000, then money will be made if the level rises to 6,100 because 'the price' is higher. If the option buyer exercises, buying at 6,000 and selling at 6,100, then 100 points have been gained. To turn this into money, we settle at £10 per point per contract. For one contract, the gain is $100 \times £10 = £1,000$. For 10 contracts, it would be £10,000 and so on. The premium paid would have to be deducted in the usual way to arrive at the net profit. Alternatively, the option could be traded in the way described earlier.

A fund manager with a holding of £30m in shares might be nervous of a fall in the market, but not nervous enough to actually sell the shares. If an assumption is made that their holding of shares will behave in a similar way to the FTSE 100 (the correlation will be measured), then the manager could buy put options on the index contract. If the market falls, the puts will win some money to help compensate for the fall in the value of the portfolio.

How many contracts should the manager buy? Let us say that the index is at a level of 6,000. If the contract is settled at £10 per point per contract, then the whole index is 6,000 × £10 = £60,000. As this is one contract, the total number of contracts needed to cover a portfolio of £30m is

$$£30m/£60,000 = 500$$

The manager buys 500 put options on the index at an exercise level of 6,000 and pays the premium, say, £500 per contract or 500 × £500 = £250,000 in total. (The premiums are also quoted as *index points*, in this case 50 index points. At £10 per point, this gives us a premium of £500.)

If the index falls 10%, to 5,400, the value of the portfolio of £30m is reduced by £3m. However, the manager could exercise the put option, that is, sell at a level of 6,000 and buy at a level of 5,400, making 600 points. Bearing in mind that the manager bought 500 contracts and that they are settled at £10 per point, the gross gain is: 600 points × £10 × 500 contracts = £3m. From this we deduct the premium of £250,000, giving a net gain of £2.75m (ignoring dealing costs). This is a substantial compensation for the fall in the value of the portfolio of £3m. This is a classic hedge.

If the index rises 10%, to 6,600, the put option will expire worthless, with the loss of the premium of £250,000. On the other hand, the value of the portfolio is now £33m not £30m, to help offset this loss. In particular, the manager is pleased that the portfolio was not liquidated due to nervousness about the market.

This is how options on an index are traded everywhere. At Liffe, many index options are traded as well as the FTSE 100 – AEX, CAC 40, BEL 20 and others. The CAC 40, for example, is offered in two contracts, one priced at €1 per point and the other at €10 per point. The CBOE trades the S&P 100 at $100 per point (American). The CME trades the S&P 500 at $250 per point and a mini S&P at $50 per point (both European and American). In the US, the main markets for equity options are the CBOE, NYSE Euronext (which acquired the American Stock Exchange, AMEX, in 2008, and in 2009 it was renamed the NYSE Amex Equities) and the Philadelphia Stock Exchange. Intercontinental Exchange (ICE) acquired the NYSE in late 2013, and so now NYSE and Euronext are divisions of ICE.

In Europe, the main markets for stock index, options and futures are shown in Table 13.6.

There have been big changes in the structure of European derivative exchanges over the last 20 years. In 1993, LTOM merged with the futures exchange LIFFE. Then, in 1998, the German and Swiss exchanges merged to form Eurex and gradually offered derivatives (futures as well as options) over a range of products – indices like the DAX, MDAX, SMI and an index of top European stocks called EURO STOXX 50. Dow Jones invented this, along with sub-indices covering certain market sectors. German Treasury notes and longer dated bonds are offered as well as interest rates – one-month EONIA and 3-month Euribor. Eurex has its own clearing company, Eurex Clearing.

In 2000, the Paris Bourse and the stock exchanges in Amsterdam and Brussels merged to form Euronext, with Lisbon joining in 2002. The Paris Bourse and the Amsterdam and Brussels stock exchanges took over their local derivatives markets (the MONEP merged with the futures market, the MATIF, and became part of the Paris Bourse). In London, the LIFFE was taken over by Euronext, which had merged with the NYSE in 2007; it was

▼ Table 13.6 *Main stock index, options and futures markets in Europe*

Stock/Index Options and Futures Turnover, Year to Date, January 2014

Derivative Exchange	Country	Trading days	Stock options		Single stock futures		Stock index options		Stock index futures	
			Contracts traded	Notional turnover (EUROm)	Contracts traded	Notional turnover (EUROm)	Contracts traded	Notional turnover (EUROm)	Contracts traded	Notional turnover (EUROm)
ATHEX Derivatives Market	Greece	21	1,316	1.3	366,989	175.9	17,690	35.8	259,469	532.2
Spanish Exchanges (BME)	Spain	22	2,905,174	2,631.0	755,334	714.0	827,979	8,243.0	860,522	67,222.0
Borsa Istanbul	Turkey	22	//	//	316	0.4	//	//	//	//
Bucharest Stock Exchange	Romania	0	n/a	n/a	n/a	n/a	n/a	n/a	0	0.0
Budapest Stock Exchange	Hungary	23	0	0.0	45,050	135.7	0	0.0	32,036	19.9
Austrian Derivatives Market	Austria	21	4,834	15.7	0	0.0	1,295	0.6	4,491	228.2
EUREX	Germany/Switzerland	22	18,630,416	67,340.0	4,880,645	25,149.5	32,350,706	1,111,762.5	26,023,464	1,281,617.4
Euronext	Amsterdam, Brussels, London (Liffe), Paris and Portugal	22	6,537,871	16,145.0	0	0.0	1,539,394	61,919.0	4,306,898	213,079.0
ICE Futures Europe	London (previously the International Petroleum Exchange)	22	//	//	//	//	//	//	//	//
NASDAQ OMX Nordic	Denmark/Sweden/Finland/Iceland	22	3,473,174	4,568.0	94,533	109.7	1,689,104	9,602.4	2,634,856	39,464.4
Oslo Børs	Norway	22	624,576	238.0	595,281	226.8	90,889	34.6	288,839	110.0
Warsaw Stock Exchange	Poland	21	n/a	n/a	49,258	102.8	40,949	229.5	669,237	4,014.6
TOTAL			32,177,361	90,939.0	6,787,406	26,614.8	36,558,006	1,191,827.4	35,079,812	1,606,287.7

Created on 07-August-2014 at 12:21

Source: Federation of European Securities Exchanges (2014) European Securities Exchange Statistics, January.

renamed NYSE Liffe, and all the derivative offerings were brought together under this name. Later it was acquired by ICE and the full range of Liffe ICE Futures Europe are shown in Table 14.1. A single electronic trading platform called LIFFE CONNECT is used for all these products. In 2003, LCH.Clearnet Group was formed, following the merger of the London Clearing House and Paris-based Clearnet. As a result of all this, there is now rivalry, as contracts like one-month EONIA, 3-month Euribor and some German government issues can be traded on Eurex and Liffe.

It should, perhaps, be mentioned that MEFF (*Mercado Español de Futuros Financieros*), the Spanish exchange, is still independent and trades options and futures on the IBEX 35 Index of key Spanish shares and government bonds.

Outside Europe and the US, important exchanges exist in Tokyo, Osaka, Singapore, Hong Kong and Sydney. The Singapore Exchange (SIMEX), which started in 1984, has done particularly well and has become the dominant player in Southeast Asia.

TRADED OPTIONS: OTHER OPTIONS

Currencies

So far, we have covered options on equities and equity indices. In Chapter 8, we discussed options on currencies and the ways in which importers and exporters could hedge risk.

Having looked at the mechanics of options, let's return to the 'break forward' option, which we explained in Chapter 8. We showed that a buyer of dollars for sterling in 3 months might be offered a floor rate of $1.88 and a break rate of $1.91. If the spot rate in 3 months was less than $1.88, the importer will buy dollars at $1.88. If the spot rate later was better than $1.91, the importer could buy dollars at the spot rate less 3¢. Thus, if the spot rate later was $1.98, the importer could buy dollars at $1.95 and thus benefit from an improvement in the rate while still gaining substantial protection from any worsening. There is no cost to the importer.

Let us say that the bank has bought a sterling put option at $1.91. If the spot rate later is, say, $1.85, the bank exercises the option to buy dollars at $1.91 and sells them to the client at $1.88, making 3¢. If the spot rate later is, say, $1.98, the option is abandoned. The bank buys the dollars spot at $1.98 and sells them to the client at $1.95, again making 3¢. The 3¢ covers the option premium and a profit margin. The client is happy with the blend of risk protection and profit participation, and the bank makes a profit, a simple example of some of the clever ways in which options can be used.

Bonds

Options are also available on bonds. Many of the major exchanges trading equity options will also trade bonds. Those on Liffe, for example, are shown in Table 14.1. These bond contracts work in a similar way to the options on shares we described earlier. They can be used to speculate or hedge risk.

For example, the option on the German government bond on the Eurex offers standard exercise price levels, such as 108.5, 109, 109.5, 110, 110.5, 111. The contract size is €100,000, and the premiums are expressed as a percentage of the bond's nominal value to two decimal places. Thus, the March call at 110 exercise price may have a premium quoted as 3.25. In money terms, this is 3.25% of €100,000 = €3,250. Each full 1% is €1,000. If the bond price is 112, we can see that an exercise price of 110 has 2% of intrinsic value since it is the right to buy the bond at less than the market price. If the bond price rose to 114, the call buyer could make a profit of 4% = €4,000 *less* the cost of the premium. If there is some time left to expiry, the call option buyer may trade the option and (hopefully) make even more profit. If the market price is 114, the right to buy at 110 has 4.00 intrinsic value plus an element of time value. Since the contract size is €100,000, a bond dealer wishing to hedge a portfolio of €10m will need to deal in 100 contracts. (This explanation has been simplified. At this point, we have ignored the complication that the bond is called *notional* and that the option is an option to have the futures contract. This is explained in Chapter 14.)

Interest Rates

The equity, currency and bond options covered above can *go to delivery*. That is, we can use the option to actually purchase or sell the relevant equities, currencies or bonds.

We also met index options, which cannot go to delivery as there is no real underlying product. These are cash settled. Interest rate options are of this kind. We cannot use the contract to borrow or lend money at a given rate of interest. Just as the index option was settled on the basis of a value per point of index change, so the interest rate option is settled on the basis of a value per 0.01% change in interest rates.

For example, the CME trades 3-month Eurodollar interest rates. The contract size is $1m. Thus, with an underlying sum at risk of $20m, the options user would be dealing in 20 contracts. Each 0.01% of interest rate change will gain or lose $25 per contract. The option user buys a call or a put on a given level of interest rates and pays a premium. If rates change to the profit of the option user by 0.50%, the gain is 50 × $25 = $1,250 per contract.

In the case of index options, the price per point is arbitrary. It is picked to produce a sensible contract size. In the case of the interest rate contract above, the $25 per 0.01% is not arbitrary, but follows logically from the contract size of $1m. If the whole contract, that is, 100%, has a value of $1m, then 0.01% has a value of $100. However, this is a 3-monthly contract, whereas interest rates are typically quoted on an annual basis, so the value is a quarter of this, that is, $25.

So far, the procedure for trading interest rates has seemed quite straightforward. The level of interest rate for 3-month Eurodollars is regarded as a price, like any other, and we either buy cheaper than we sell or face buying dearer than we sell, in which case the option is abandoned. Each 0.01% of gain on the price level wins $25 for each contract traded. We can either use the contract to speculate or hedge interest rate risk.

There is, unfortunately, a complication. This relates to the pricing of the contract. We might expect to see prices like 3.50%, 5.00% or 8.00%. What the market actually does is subtract the desired rate of interest from 100 to arrive at the price level of the contract. Thus an interest rate of 4.00% trades as 96.00 and one of 8.00% trades as 92.00. Let's look at the effect of this pricing:

Interest rate	Contract price
10.00%	100−10% = 90.00
9.00%	100−9% = 91.00
11.00%	100−11% = 89.00

Notice that as the interest rate goes *down* from 10% to 9%, the contract price goes *up* from 90.00 to 91.00. As the interest rate goes *up* from 10% to 11%, the contract price goes *down* from 90.00 to 89.00.

We met this reverse relationship before when we discussed long-dated bonds – interest rates down, bond prices up; interest rates up, bond prices down. The Chicago markets did start trading interest rates in the obvious way (in 1975). After a few weeks, however, the traders preferred to trade the contracts in the way we have just described. It suited bond dealers who were hedging risk, and it suited the psychology of traders. After all, as a generalization, higher interest rates are seen as bad news – equity and bond prices fall. It seemed logical that with higher interest rates, the contract price fell.

This means that the call/put logic we learned earlier must be reversed in the case of interest rate contracts. If you wish to gain from higher interest rates, buy *put* options – the contract price will fall. If you wish to gain from lower interest rates, buy *call* options – the contract price will rise. Other than that, it's quite easy.

Let's take an example. Suppose a US corporate has a $20m loan from the bank at floating rate and reviewed every 3 months. The rate is linked to Eurodollar LIBOR. Let us also suppose that the dates for the CME 3-monthly contracts coincide with the bank's rollover of the loan. The bank has just fixed the rate for 3 months based on Eurodollar LIBOR of 3.75%. The corporate believes that rates are due to rise and seeks a hedge using the CME contract.

As the contract size is $1m and the loan is $20m, the corporate deals in 20 contracts. As it wishes to gain if interest rates go up, it buys 20 *put* options for the next expiry at a level of 3.75%, that is, a contract price level of 100−3.75 = 96.25. The premium is quoted as 0.30 and also must be interpreted at $25 per 0.01 per contract, the way the contract is settled. Thus 0.30 = $750 per contract, and the corporate bought 20 contracts, paying 20 × $750 = $15,000.

Assume that, at the expiry of the contract, the Eurodollar LIBOR rate is 4.75%. The bank notifies the client that the interest charge is 1% higher on the $20m loan for 3 months – an increase of $50,000.

At the CME, the contract price is 100−4.75% = 95.25. The corporate bought 20 put options at 96.25, that is, the right to sell at 96.25. The contract is exercised by selling at 96.25 and buying at 95.25, a profit of 1% for each of 20 contracts. Because 0.01% = $25, the gain is 100 × $25 × 20 contracts = $50,000. Deducting the premium of $15,000, the corporate has $35,000 to help meet the bank's extra interest charge of $50,000.

Suppose interest rates had fallen to 2.75%. The CME contract is not profitable and will be abandoned for the loss of the premium of $15,000. However, the bank notifies the corporate of a reduced interest charge for 3 months of $50,000. The corporate has bought protection from higher rates but can still gain if they fall.

This is the essential character of options to which we referred in Chapter 8. It is worth repeating:

> The option purchase protects against a deterioration in the rate, but the option buyer can still benefit from an improvement in the rate. There is a cost – the premium.

Again, the complication that the CME contract is an option to have the future has been ignored.

OPTION STRATEGIES

The experts in the option market do not content themselves with one position, such as buying a call at a particular exercise price and expiry, but combine several positions in order to carry out complex strategies, as noted in Box 13.3.

BOX
13.3

Option Strategies

For example, in the case of XYZ Ltd in equity options above, we might buy both a call and a put on the exercise price of £1.80 for July expiry.

If the share price rises, we win, and if it falls, we also win – well, in principle at least. The problem is that two premiums have been paid. The call premium is 24, and the put might be 18, that is, 42 in total. Having paid 42 for a £1.80 call, the price must go up to £2.22 (£1.80 + 42) to break even, and that ignores dealing costs. Having paid 42 for a £1.80 put, the price must fall to £1.38 (£1.80–42) to break even.

In other words, this is a strategy for a volatile situation. A sharp share price movement is expected, either up or down. It might be that there is a takeover bid struggle. The bid will either fail and the victim's share price will fall sharply, or the bidder will come back with a higher offer, and the opposite will happen.

The worst case is if the price falls to the strike price of £1.80, yet it is still troublesome for the buyer if the price remains stable at £1.86. The call option will be worth 6p, and the put will expire worthless. The loss is 42–6 = 36: for a single 1,000 share contract, £360 is lost out of the premium of £420.

This has ignored *trading* the option prior to expiry in order to cut the loss and take advantage of the remaining time value in the premium.

This is a well-known strategy called the *straddle*. The straddle buyer expects a volatile situation; the straddle writer thinks they are wrong.

Another strategy might be to buy the July £1.80 calls and write the July £2.20 calls. The premium for the July £1.80 calls is 24p, and for the July £2.20 calls, it is 7p. If the share price goes over £2.20 later, we have bought a call and also sold one at this level, and so no further gain can be made; the purchase and sale will cancel out.

However, we have offset the 24p premium for the £1.80 call by receiving the premium of 7p when we wrote the £2.20 call. Our net cost for a 1,000 share contract is 24–7 = 17p per share, or £170 instead of £240 had we simply bought the £1.80 call alone. We have reduced our possible loss from £240 per contract to £170 per contract and brought the breakeven point down from £1.80 + 24 to £1.80 + 17. What we gave up to achieve this was any profit above a later share price of £2.20.

This strategy is called the '*bull spread*'. We give up some of our unlimited profit potential in order to cut cost and risk. It has become so popular that the Chicago market offers this embedded in the option product. If we are pessimistic about XYZ Ltd, we do the opposite and buy the £1.80 put but write the £1.40 put – a 'bear spread'.

There is no end to the permutations and variations on this theme. There are books on option strategies that list in excess of 50 possible strategies. Often they take their name from the shape of the graph showing the potential profit and loss from future changes in the market price, for example the forked lightning, Mexican hat, Mae West, condor, butterfly and many others.

Look at all the variables there are to play with:

Number of contracts
Calls/puts
Buy/write
Exercise prices
Expiry dates

Apart from trading strategies like these, there are many other variations on the options theme. There is no place in an introductory text like this to mention them all, but we can cover a few just to give the reader an idea of the sheer ingenuity and imagination involved.

Some markets trade 'share ratios', that is, not the share's absolute price and its movement, but how it compares with others. For example, the Australian Stock Exchange offers contracts on leading shares (such as ANZ Bank, Broken Hill, News Corporation) based on the ratio of their price movement compared with the All Ordinaries Index.

'Spread trading' is similar and is based on the difference between two prices. Other spreads are 'calendar spreads', the difference between the option premiums for different expiry dates, for example March and June. We may believe that the difference between the premiums will either get bigger or smaller, and trade accordingly.

There is also a class of options on the OTC market called 'exotic options'; for instance 'barrier options' are popular at the moment. The idea in this case is to cheapen the option premium by attaching some condition. Typically, the option may only be valid if the market price reaches a certain level or barrier (the 'knock in'). Suppose that today's price of a given share is £1.00. We may wish to sell shortly but are prepared to bear a loss down to 90p. We could buy a put option at 90p. A variation is to buy a put option at £1.00, which is only valid if the share price hits 90p – the 'knock in'.

Alternatively, we could buy a put option at £1.00 but agree the option is cancelled if the price ever hits £1.05. If the price hits £1.05, we may accept cancellation of the option on the basis that prices are going up, not down, and accept the risk for a cheaper premium – the 'knock out'. The risk is that having hit £1.05, the price falls later to less than £1.00.

Usually, the option is knocked in or out if the barrier level is reached at any time prior to expiry, and usually the options are European style. A refinement might be that the barrier price only relates to the closing price each day, not the price at any time during the day.

There are also, within the exotics list, 'compound options', that is, options to have another option. At this point, the brain begins to hurt, so let's leave it at that. You get the message. There are many exotics, and teams at banks regularly launch new variations: lookback options, digital (or binary) options, double no-touch options, barrier options, basket options, ladder options, rainbow options and so on. Sometimes these endure and become relatively mainstream (like digital or double no-touch options), whereas others like the lookback have become horribly expensive and have faded away. The Asian option, which is cash settled based on the average price over the option period rather than the price at expiry of the option, is now traded on the London Metal Exchange.

Computers are an essential tool to carry out the necessary calculations, produce the profit/loss graphs and control the total exposure contained in a trader's book of option deals.

Unfortunately, the activities of Nick Leeson, the Baring Bros' derivatives trader who is alleged to have lost £860m and bankrupted the bank, have led many people to believe that derivatives trading is all about gambling. It would, however, be quite wrong to regard it all as simply sophisticated gambling. Risk management is a key topic today, and options make their contribution. Options can be used by banks to hedge risk that yields the banks a profit as well. Another possible tool is the future transaction, and this is covered in Chapter 13.

SUMMARY

- The users of derivative products are *speculators*, *hedgers* and *arbitrageurs*. The key products are *options* and *futures*. All the rest are simply variations on the same theme.
- An option gives the buyer the right, but not the obligation, to buy or sell financial instruments or commodities at an agreed price and at an agreed future date or time period.
- Options can be purchased on a trading exchange or over the counter. The exchange has the advantage of the protection of the *clearing house*, but the OTC market will more easily tailor a product to suit the user's needs.
- Options to buy a given product at a later date are *calls*. Options to sell are *puts*. There are *buyers* and *writers* (sellers) of options.
- The price of the option is the *premium*, and the price of the product at which the option buyer can exercise is the *exercise* or *strike price*. Options can also be *traded*.
- The option buyer cannot lose more than the premium, and the option writer cannot gain more than the premium.
- To protect against default, the clearing house asks option writers for *initial margin* and, each day, *variation margin*.
- If the option to buy or sell is at a price more favourable than the market price, the option is said to have intrinsic value. The balance of the premium is *time value*, which will fall as the expiry date approaches.
- Trading the option will be more profitable than exercising if the option has time value.
- A small percentage change in the price of the underlying asset leads to a large percentage change in the premium. This is *gearing*.
- The premium is based on the past performance of the share price. The more volatile the performance, the higher the premium.
- Options at a price more favourable than the market price are said to be *in the money*. If the price is less favourable than the market, they are *out of the money*, and if the price is the same as the market, they are *at the money*.
- There are options on equities, equity indices, bonds, currencies, interest rates and commodities.
- Combining option positions leads to options strategies such as a *straddle, bull spread* or *butterfly*.
- Other non-standardized options are referred to as *exotic options*, for example barrier options, lookback options, digital options and so on.
- The market in Europe for options and futures has seen an upheaval in Europe's exchanges, such that these products are primarily now handled by just two bodies – Eurex and Euronext (including Liffe).

REVISION QUESTIONS/ASSIGNMENTS

1. Outline the main differences between exchange-traded and OTC options products. Why is the OTC market much larger than the exchange-traded market?
2. Analyse three option products of your choice, highlighting their main features and how they maybe be used for risk management purposes.
3. Explain straddle trading strategies.
4. Examine the terms 'in the money', 'at the money' and 'out of the money'.

FURTHER READING

Chisholm, A. (2004) *Derivatives Demystified: A Step-by-Step Guide to Forwards, Futures and Options*, John Wiley & Sons, New York. Introductory to intermediate guide to derivatives.

Haug, E.G. (2007) *The Complete Guide to Option Pricing Formulas* (2nd edn), McGraw-Hill, New York.

Advanced technical analysis, focusing on option pricing.

Hull, J.C. (2014) *Options, Futures, and Other Derivatives* (9th edn), Prentice Hall, Upper Saddle River, NJ. Classic but advanced text on derivatives products. An industry standard guide.

Financial Futures

FUTURES TRADING

Background

Transactions very similar to options and futures contracts today have existed in commodity markets for hundreds of years. For example, there was the astounding 17th-century Dutch tulip mania. As tulips became more and more fashionable, people bought tulips several months in advance of the harvest. As the price went up, the contracts at the old prices were more valuable and could be sold to other people without waiting to take delivery at harvest time. In the end, the government had to step in when more tulips had been bought than were actually in the ground, and several people made large losses. (For details of this and other amazing financial speculations, see Mackay [1980] *Extraordinary Popular Delusions and the Madness of Crowds.*)

Commodity prices fluctuate, and where there are fluctuations, we find speculators and hedgers. The harvest may be good or bad, and the product is only available once per year anyway. It would be natural to buy or sell ahead of the harvest. As prices went up or down, some of these contracts became more valuable and could be sold on to other people. Metals are not crops, but prices do fluctuate, and it takes some time to receive a consignment from overseas. The London Metal Exchange's 3-month contract came into use after the Suez Canal was opened and metals like copper and zinc could be shipped in 3 months. The largest commodity markets in the world are the Chicago Mercantile Exchange (CME) and the Chicago Board of Trade (CBOT). It was here, too, that modern futures contracts were developed. CBOT opened in 1848, and the CME, in 1874.

Before looking at the mechanism of futures as opposed to options, let's look again at the hedging technique.

Hedgers versus Speculators

A hedger is at risk if a given potential price movement happens. Hedgers seek to create a profit from this price movement in another market in partial compensation for the loss. A sugar dealer may have agreed a fixed price with a customer for a future delivery of sugar. The dealer hasn't yet bought the sugar to meet these contracts. If the price of sugar goes up before the purchase is made, a loss will occur.

Figure 14.1 provides a diagrammatic look at the structure of a hedge.

If a given rise in the price of sugar will lose $X in physical trading, the sugar dealer could buy call options on sugar contracts at the Chicago Coffee, Sugar and Cocoa Exchange. This will create a profit of $Y to at least offset the loss of $X in physical trading. If the price of sugar falls, the dealer will have lost money on the call option but will be delighted because, having sold sugar short, even more profit is made on physical sugar trading. This explains why some traders with large losses may walk off the floor of the futures or options

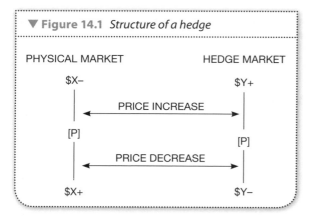

▼ **Figure 14.1** *Structure of a hedge*

exchange and seem to be smiling. They must be hedgers. The price movement they feared hasn't happened. Speculators, of course, will have genuinely lost money.

This is a simple but most important principle, often misunderstood. It's worth repeating:

> If hedgers lose money in the hedge market, they must make money in the market being hedged because the price movement they feared has not happened.

We will find that futures, unlike options, involve unlimited risk. For the reason just explained, hedgers can accept this risk. Indeed, the bigger the loss on the futures hedge, the bigger the offsetting gain in the physical market.

An important issue is this: Who is on the other side of the hedge? It may be another hedger, but one whose position is the opposite – this person will lose money if the price of sugar goes *down*, not up. This means that whatever happens to the price, both will get the hedge they are looking for. The broker will make a living, the exchange will make a profit and everybody goes home happy.

In financial markets, people are quick to claim that it must be a 'zero-sum game', that is, what someone wins, someone else must lose. This is sometimes the case, but by no means always. There are usually plenty of opposite hedgers. Those with loans at floating rate are hoping interest rates will go *down*. Those with investments at floating rate are hoping interest rates will go *up*.

It all seems too good to be true, and it is. The problem is that there won't be the same value of opposite positions except by a miracle. The hedger wants to do a deal but no one wants to say 'yes' – or at least not at a reasonable price. That's where speculators come in. They provide the trading liquidity so that hedgers can reduce the risk and do the deals they want. Often, they are called locals, a term from the Chicago markets, where more than half the membership is locals. Locals work on the floor of the exchange buying and selling for their own account and in the process provide market liquidity. Even the conservative London Metal Exchange, where people cannot be members unless they physically trade metals, agrees in its literature that speculators play an essential role in providing liquidity. It's a new light on a term that most people regard as being totally pejorative.

Commodity Futures

Box 14.1 illustrates the main features of a commodity future.

BOX 14.1

Commodity Futures

A futures transaction provides an alternative to an option as a way of hedging risk.

Its characteristics are different.

A futures contract is a commitment to buy or sell a given quantity of an underlying product by a given date in the future at a price agreed now. Also, a futures transaction is a *commitment*, not an option.

Commodity Futures (*continued*)

If the price moves the wrong way, the option buyer can abandon the contract. As this is a privilege, a premium is paid. A futures contract cannot be abandoned in this way.

Because no privilege is involved, no premium need be paid. For the same reason, a futures contract is riskier. Options had calls, puts, buyers and sellers. Futures contracts only have buyers and sellers. To that extent, they are simpler.

Our sugar trader, worried about the price of sugar going up, could take a futures position in white sugar on the CME (or the exchange in London, now part of ICE Liffe). Let us say that the trader commits to buy 100 tonnes of sugar by the next expiry date, at $250 per tonne. It is clear that if the price of sugar goes up to $280 a tonne, a contract that can buy at $250 a tonne has value and can create profit. This is not difficult to grasp, but what people do find hard to understand is that the above trader hasn't the slightest intention of buying any sugar.

What happens if sugar rises to $280 a tonne? The trader *closes the position* with the opposite contract – the trader commits to *sell* 100 tonnes of sugar by the next expiry date at $280 per tonne. The contracts are not settled in sugar, but on the price difference of $30 a tonne, that is, our trader has gained 100 × $30 = $3,000. This is to offset the trading loss that will result from having sold sugar short and being obliged to buy physical sugar at a higher price.

At this point, people tend to ask: But what happens to the sugar? They have a vision of someone at expiry date trying to handle all the sugar that no one seems to want. Let's realize that no one can contract to buy sugar unless someone contracts to sell. Equally, no one can contract to sell unless someone contracts to buy. If everyone closes his position with the opposite contract later (as we described above), there isn't anybody left at expiry, nor can there be.

If the sugar trader did not close the position, he would indeed buy 100 tonnes of sugar at $250 a tonne. But if the trader did remain open at expiry as a buyer, there must also be a seller with an open position. If there are three buyers left, there must be sellers with a total open position that exactly offsets the total open position of the three buyers. There may (or may not) be three sellers. The sugar is only the means to the end – the hedge or speculation. Either way, with the occasional exception, cash settlement is quite acceptable.

The fact that the contract *can* go to delivery, however, is crucially important. It means that the price of sugar in the futures exchange must relate to the real price of sugar. If it was cheaper, traders would use the futures exchange to buy it and sell it at profit in the cash market – arbitrage.

The contract is not an option, and we see the difference if we assume that sugar were to fall in price to $220 a tonne. If this were an option, the contract would now be abandoned – there is no point in buying sugar at $250 in order to sell it at $220. As a futures contract, the trader is committed to buy at $250 a tonne. The position is closed out by later entering the opposite contract to sell 100 tonnes of sugar at $220 a tonne, losing $3,000.

This loss is not a problem. As the price of sugar has fallen, the short position in the physical sugar market is even more profitable, as sugar can be purchased much more cheaply than it was sold. As we observed earlier, for the hedger a loss in the hedge market must mean a gain in the market being hedged.

Notice the symmetry in the futures contract – a rise in price of $30 a tonne gained $3,000, and a fall in price of $30 a tonne lost $3,000.

Options are not symmetrical because, when the price moves the wrong way, the contract is abandoned.

We now have two terms – forward and futures – which ought to mean the same, but don't:

- *Forward* is buying or selling for actual delivery at a future date at a price set now. Forwards are OTC and can be specified as being physical or cash settled. With forwards being OTC, holders generally have to take on counterparty credit risk. Typically, there are no margin calls on forwards, although it is possible for margin calls to be written into OTC contracts to mitigate credit risk.
- *Futures* are similar to forward, but usually there is no intention to take or make delivery; later, the position will be closed with the opposite contract and settled in cash. Futures are exchange traded and can be cash or physically settled. The credit risk of futures is to the exchange on which they are traded, and there are margin calls to reduce this risk.

Forward is for those who want the physical commodity, futures for those who are speculating or hedging and are happy with cash settlement.

Thus, we need futures exchanges where everyone realizes what the end objective is. There will be formal contract sizes, fixed delivery dates and the guarantee offered by the clearing house. The latter will take margin (deposits) from *both* parties, as both are at risk. All contracts are legally with the clearing house. 'Initial margin' is paid when the position is opened. If the contract moves into loss, extra margin, called 'variation margin', is debited on a daily basis, but if the contract moves into profit, variation margin is credited. The major players will have what is, in effect, a bank account with the clearing house. The locals will arrange to clear with someone who is a full clearing member.

Financial Futures

If options and futures are essentially driven by price volatility, the only surprise is that it took so long to be applied to financial contracts. Looking at interest rates, currency rates, equity prices, equity index levels and bond prices, there is huge volatility and also huge risk for many of the parties involved.

There are four main types of financial contract – bonds, interest rates, currencies and equity indices, as well as commodities and even weather futures. As we will see, exchange traded options are typically options to have the futures contract. Examples of the contracts traded on Liffe ICE Futures Europe are summarized in Table 14.1. Note that Intercontinental Exchange (ICE) acquired Liffe as part of the NYSE Euronext acquisition in 2013. In addition, ICE spun out Euronext in an IPO in 2013 which included the continental European derivatives markets.

Many exchange-traded options are options to buy or sell a particular futures contract. This doesn't make any major difference if the buyer is trading the option, although it can impact pricing, but any exercise is into the futures contract. A key difference between this and a direct option is that in the case of the direct option, having used, say, a call option to purchase the product, it can be sold at the market price. The seller of the option would have to purchase the product. If it is an option to buy the future, the option holder finds himself the buyer of the futures contract (a 'long futures' position). This can be left to go to delivery. The seller of the option is now the seller of the futures contract (a 'short futures' position). However, if she doesn't wish to physically sell the product, she has time to close her position by buying the futures contract and letting someone else go to delivery. In the case of a direct option, she would have no choice. Most option contracts on futures exchanges are options to buy (call) or sell (put) the future.

▼ **Table 14.1** *ICE futures Europe contracts – some examples*

Details of the Liffe contracts that are now listed at ICE Futures Europe here: https://www.theice.com/futures-europe

Interest Rate Derivatives: https://www.theice.com/products/#/Futures-Options/Interest-Rates

Equity Derivatives: https://www.theice.com/products/#/Futures-Options/Equity-Derivatives

Soft commodity derivatives: https://www.theice.com/products/#/Futures-Options/Agriculture

ENERGY	SECTOR
Brent Crude Futures	Crude Oil and Refined Products
CER Futures	Emissions
CFR South China Coal Futures	Coal
CSX Coal Futures	Coal
Dated Brent Future	Crude Oil and Refined Products
Dubai 1st Line Future	Crude Oil and Refined Products
ERCOT North 345KV Real-Time Peak Daily Fixed Price Future	Electricity
ERU Futures	Emissions
Ethane, OPIS Mt. Belvieu Non-TET, Fixed Price Future	Natural Gas Liquids
EUA Futures	Emissions
EUA Futures Options	Emissions
EUA Phase 3 Daily Futures	Emissions
EUAA UK Auction Daily Futures	Emissions
Fuel Oil 180 CST Singapore Future	Crude Oil and Refined Products
Fuel Oil 3.5% FOB Rotterdam Barges Future	Crude Oil and Refined Products
gC Newcastle Coal Futures	Coal
Henry LD1 Fixed Price Future	Natural Gas
Henry Swing Future	Natural Gas
Low Sulphur Gas Oil/Brent Futures Crack	Crude Oil and Refined Products
Low Sulphur Gasoil Futures	Crude Oil and Refined Products
MISO Indiana Hub Day-Ahead Peak Fixed Price Future	Electricity
MISO Indiana Hub Real-Time Peak Fixed Price Future	Electricity
Natural Gasoline, OPIS Mt. Belvieu Non-TET, Fixed Price Future	Natural Gas Liquids

INTEREST RATES

LONG GILT FUTURE	Medium/Long-Term Interest Rates
THREE-MONTH STERLING (SHORT STERLING) FUTURE	Short-Term Interest Rates
Agency DTCC GCF Repo Index®	Short-Term Interest Rates
Eurodollar Futures	Short-Term Interest Rates
Five-Year Mid-Curve Options on Euribor® Futures	Short-Term Interest Rates
Five Year Mid-Curve Options on Short Sterling Futures	Short-Term Interest Rates
FIVE-YEAR $ SWAPNOTE® FUTURE	Swapnotes

▼ Table 14.1 *ICE futures Europe contracts – some examples (continued)*

FIVE-YEAR € SWAPNOTE® FUTURE	Swapnotes
FIVE-YEAR £ SWAPNOTE® FUTURE	Swapnotes
Four-Year Mid-Curve Options on Euribor ® Futures	Short-Term Interest Rates
FOUR YEAR MID-CURVE OPTIONS ON SHORT STERLING FUTURE	Short-Term Interest Rates
LONG BTP FUTURE	Medium/Long-Term Interest Rates
LONG BUND FUTURE	Medium/Long-Term Interest Rates
LONG BUND FUTURE TAS	Medium/Long-Term Interest Rates
LONG GILT FUTURES TAS	Medium/Long-Term Interest Rates
LONG SPANISH GOVERNMENT BOND FUTURE	Medium/Long-Term Interest Rates
LONG SWISS CONFEDERATION BOND FUTURE	Medium/Long-Term Interest Rates
MEDIUM BTP FUTURE	Medium/Long-Term Interest Rates
MEDIUM BUND FUTURES (BOBL)	Medium/Long-Term Interest Rates
MEDIUM BUND FUTURES (BOBL) TAS	Medium/Long-Term Interest Rates
MEDIUM GILT FUTURE	Medium/Long-Term Interest Rates
MEDIUM GILT FUTURES TAS	Medium/Long-Term Interest Rates
MEDIUM SPANISH GOVERNMENT BOND FUTURE	Medium/Long-Term Interest Rates
MEDIUM SWISS CONFEDERATION BOND FUTURE	Medium/Long-Term Interest Rates

AGRICULTURE

Canola Futures	Canola
Cocoa Futures	Cocoa
Coffee C® Futures	Coffee
Cotton No. 2 Futures	Cotton
FCOJ-A Futures	Frozen Orange Juice
Sugar No. 11 Futures	Sugar
Barley Futures	Grains
Barley Options	Grains
Canola 1-month CSO	Canola
Canola Options	Canola
Cocoa Calendar Spread Options	Cocoa
Cocoa Futures TAS	Cocoa
Cocoa Options	Cocoa
Coffee C® Futures TAS	Coffee
Coffee C® Options	Coffee
Coffee C Calendar Spread Options	Coffee
Cotton No. 2 Calendar Spread Options	Cotton
Cotton No. 2 Futures TAS	Cotton
Cotton No. 2 Options	Cotton

▼ **Table 14.1** *ICE futures Europe contracts – some examples (continued)*

Durum Wheat Futures	Grains
Durum Wheat Options	Grains
Euro Cocoa Futures	Cocoa
Euro Cocoa Options	Cocoa
FCOJ-A Futures TAS	Frozen Orange Juice
FCOJ-A Options	Frozen Orange Juice

EQUITY DERIVATIVES

Mini MSCI EAFE Index Future	MSCI Indices
Mini MSCI Emerging Markets Asia (NTR) Index Future	MSCI Indices
Mini MSCI Emerging Markets Index Future	MSCI Indices
Mini MSCI Emerging Markets Latin America Index Future	MSCI Indices
Mini MSCI World Index Future	MSCI Indices
Russell 1000 Growth Index Mini Futures	Russell Indices
Russell 1000 Value Index Mini Futures	Russell Indices
Russell 1000® Index Mini Futures	Russell Indices
Russell 2000 Growth Index Mini Futures	Russell Indices
Russell 2000 Value Index Mini Futures	Russell Indices
Russell 2000® Index Mini Futures	Russell Indices
3I GROUP PLC	Single Stock Options
ABERDEEN ASSET MANAGEMENT PLC	Single Stock Options
Accor	Single Stock Futures
AFREN PLC	Single Stock Options
Ageas NV/SA	Single Stock Futures
AGGREKO PLC	Single Stock Options
Ahold NV, Koninklijke	Single Stock Futures
Air Liquide	Single Stock Futures
Airbus Group	Single Stock Futures
Akzo Nobel NV	Single Stock Futures
Alcatel-Lucent SA	Single Stock Futures
Allianz AG	Single Stock Futures
Alstom SA	Single Stock Futures
AMEC PLC	Single Stock Options
ANGLO AMERICAN PLC	Single Stock Options
AnheuserBusch InBev NV	Single Stock Futures
ANTOFAGASTA PLC	Single Stock Options
ArcelorMittal	Single Stock Futures

Source: Intercontinental Exchange ICE.

From the last remarks, the reader will realize that in some cases, the contracts can go to delivery if the position is not closed out. The gilts contract size is £100,000. A buyer of 20 contracts can let the position go to delivery and buy £2m of gilts at the agreed price. All the NYSE Liffe bond contracts except the Japanese government bond can go to delivery in this way. Prices will be kept close to the futures fair value, which depends on the cash price and cost of carry, or arbitrage will take place.

The FTSE 100 can't go to delivery (as there isn't anything to deliver), and the interest rate contracts can't go to delivery either, so they can't be used to borrow money at an agreed rate of interest. This raises two interesting points. Because the contract can't go to delivery, what happens if a buyer *doesn't* close the position with the opposite sale? For the same reason, how do we know the price will relate to that of the underlying product in the cash market?

Any buyer or seller who doesn't close the position is automatically closed by the clearing house at expiry, as the contract can't go to delivery. If the buyer or seller is letting the contract go to delivery, she don't need to take any action as the position will be closed for her.

The problem of correlation with the market price is solved by the convention that the expiry price is always the market price. The expiry price of the FTSE 100 is called the 'exchange delivery settlement price' (EDSP). At 10.10 a.m. on the expiry day, an auction takes place for each share in the index, and this leads to the EDSP, which is declared at 10.30. The old method of simply averaging the prices in this 20-minute period was abandoned in November 2004 for technical reasons. The expiry price of the short sterling interest rate contract is the average of the sterling LIBOR rate of 16 named banks at 11.00 a.m. on the expiry day, the highest and lowest four values being excluded.

Index Futures

In Chapter 13, we discussed options on share indices – S&P 500, S&P 100, FTSE 100, CAC 40 and similar indices. Futures contracts are also available and make a good starting point, as we've already met options on the indices.

The futures contract is a commitment and there is no premium to pay, only margin to the clearing house.

An insurance company investment manager may be planning to sell £24m of shares in three weeks to meet claims for storm damage. The manager does not wish to sell at the moment as market conditions are poor. The worry about waiting, however, is that the market may fall in the next three weeks and the same quantity of shares raises less than £24m. The answer may be a full hedge using the futures contract on the FTSE 100 contract. This is a way of locking in to today's index level without actually selling the shares.

The first question is: How many contracts? Cash settlement is based on £10 per point. If the index is 6,000, then the whole index is valued at $6,000 \times £10 = £60,000$. Since the value of shares to be hedged is £24m, then the number of contracts is:

$$\frac{£24m}{£60,000} = 400$$

The fund manager sells 400 contracts for the next expiry period. The first complication is that although the stock exchange index is 6,000, the figure in the trading pit may be, say, 6,020 (reflecting supply and demand, market expectations and certain technical factors). So our manager has 400 contracts to 'sell' the index at 6,020.

Three weeks later the market is down 10% at 5,400. The manager sells the shares at this level. For the same quantity of shares that might have been sold three weeks earlier, £21.6m is received, not £24m, a loss of £2.4m.

The position in the exchange is now closed. If the contract in the pit is being traded at a level of, say, 5,430, the position is closed by buying 400 contracts at 5,430. The gain is:

Sell contracts at 6,020
Buy contracts at 5,430
Gain per contract 590 points

The contract is cash settled at £10 per point, a gain of £10 × 590 = £5,900. For 400 contracts, the total gain is 400 × £5,900 = £2.36m. Thus, waiting three weeks lost £2.4m on the share sale but the contract gained £2.36m.

An initial margin was paid of £2,000 per contract and thus £2,000 × 400 contracts = £800,000. However, as this was only a deposit to cover possible loss, this sum is returned. In addition, one can usually negotiate interest on initial margin. There will be brokers' costs to pay and a fee to the clearing house. These might be about £4 per contract or a total of £4 × 400 = £1,600 in this case.

If the index rose in the three-week period, the contract cannot be abandoned, as in the case of options. If the index rose 10%, to 6,600, the futures position is now loss making. If the pit level is 6,610, the position is now closed by buying 400 contracts at 6,610. It is the opposite of the previous case:

Sell contracts at 6,020
Buy contracts at 6,610
Loss per contract 590 points

The total loss is: £10 per contract × 590 points × 400 contracts = £2.36m. We commented before on the essential symmetry of the futures contract. A fall in the index traded of 590 points gains £2.36m but a rise of 590 points loses £2.36m.

Unlike options, the futures contract faces potentially unlimited loss. However, we are not talking here of a speculator but a hedger. When the investment manager sells the shares, the market is up 10% and the shares are sold for £26.4m, not £24m. The gain of £2.4m offsets the loss of £2.36m on the futures contract. This is the point we made earlier in the chapter. For a hedger, a loss on the futures means a gain in the physical market being hedged.

Note one important point: although the manager was protected against loss arising from a market fall, no profit can be made from a rise in the market.

Let's spell out this essential element in futures, as opposed to options:

Futures give the user protection from an adverse price movement but they cannot benefit from a favourable movement. Risk is unlimited but there is no premium to pay.

The manager could give up some of the protection to allow room for a gain should the market rise. Instead of selling 400 contracts, 200 could have been sold. The effect would be that a loss of £2.4m due to a 10% market fall would be offset by a futures gain of only £1.18m. However, it follows that a gain of £2.4m due to a 10% market rise would be offset by a futures loss of only £1.18m. The manager has a range of choices varying from not hedging a position at all right up to an attempted 100% hedge.

One final point: in the above case, there is an implicit assumption that the manager's mix of shares will behave in the same way as the market, that if the market fell 10%, so would the mix of shares the manager is selling. It's not an unreasonable assumption but it won't be left to chance. Using computer techniques and historical share price data, the manager measures the correlation between the returns to the shares in the portfolio and the returns to the FTSE 100 and the relative volatilities of the returns to the shares and the market to calculate what is known as a beta factor for the portfolio of shares. If the shares move in the same way as the index, the beta is 1.0. If the shares move by 90% of an index movement, the beta is 0.9. If the shares move by 110% of an index movement, the beta is 1.1. The number of contracts traded will be adjusted by the beta factor. (Just for the record, the alpha factor refers to the individual behaviour of a share, for example how BP's performance might differ from that of Shell.)

Bond Futures

Box 14.2 shows the key features of bond futures.

BOX 14.2

Bond Futures

The US Treasury bond contract in Chicago, for example, is based on an underlying value of $100,000. The smallest price movement, or tick, is $\frac{1}{32}$. If the contract is £100,000, then 1% = $1,000 and $\frac{1}{32}$ = $31.25. If 10 contracts are sold at a level 10 ticks higher than they were bought, then there is a gain of:
10 ticks × $31.25 × 10 contracts = $3,125.

The contract need not be closed out but left to go to delivery. Certain days are *delivery days*. In the case of the Treasury bond contract and gilts, it's any business day in the delivery month.

In the case of the German government Bund contract, it's the tenth calendar day of the delivery month (if a working day).

The decision as to which day is delivery day is made by the *seller*.

The principle, then, is not difficult but the practice is more complicated.

Most bond futures contracts are based on a *notional* bond, that is, one that doesn't exist.

Newcomers will find the idea of trading in a bond that doesn't exist very strange but the market takes it in its stride. The exchange makes available a list of bonds that can be delivered. The Treasury bond is a 6% coupon bond as the unit of trading. Delivery can be made from a list of actual bonds with 15 years left to maturity. If one of these is an 8% bond, an 8% bond is inherently more attractive than a 6% bond and has a better price. The exchange makes available a *conversion factor*, which calculates the sales value that must be used for delivery purposes.

If the contract is for a 6% bond with $100,000 nominal value, then an 8% bond can deliver $100,000 nominal to meet the contract specification but receive a higher price. There will be one bond in the list that is cheapest to deliver. The price in the trading pit will be based on this *cheapest to deliver* bond, if not, arbitrage between this and the cash market will take place. For example, someone will buy the underlying bonds, sell the futures contract at the current price level and actually deliver the bonds at a profit.

As a result, the list of bonds available for delivery is significant and the exchange will make changes from time to time.

The German Bund contract traded on Eurex, for example, has become the most traded contract in Europe. The underlying basket of deliverable bonds is relatively small compared with these huge volumes. Although far less than 5% of bonds go to delivery, the market is nervous of this position and a possible 'squeeze' if a high percentage went to delivery.

The bond contract is based on a notional coupon of 6%. There are suggestions that it should be lowered to 4% and the list of deliverable bonds raised. These worries are not theoretical. If several dealers don't close out a position but ask for delivery, they may find that one or two other dealers are holding large stocks of the cheapest to deliver bond and may operate what is called a 'squeeze'. The counterparties now asked to make delivery are, in effect, 'held to ransom'.

There were problems in the US in June 2005 with the 10-year Treasury note futures when there was a huge increase in trading volumes.

Interest Rates

Interest rate contracts create valuable opportunities for those at risk from interest rate changes to hedge that risk. Liffe contracts offer short sterling, euro, Eurodollar, euro Swiss franc and Euroyen interest rates. Rival euro interest rate contracts are offered at the other exchanges (MEFF, Eurex and so on), but the Liffe 3-month euro interest rate contract is the biggest in Europe.

Interest rate contracts are cash settled – they cannot go to delivery. At expiry, any open positions are closed by the clearing house at the expiry price, which is always the market price. The pricing of the contract is based on subtracting the implied rate of interest from 100, so that, for example, 10.00% is traded as 90.00.

The normal rule with futures is that the contract is bought in the first instance if a gain is to be made from a price increase. If a gain is to be made from a price fall, the contract is sold in the first instance. If a hedge is involved, then buying the contract is the 'long hedge', and selling the contract is the 'short hedge'.

Once again, interest rate contracts reverse the logic. To gain from a price increase, we *sell* the contract (because, if the price goes up, the contract level will fall). To gain from a price decrease, we *buy* the contract (because if the price goes down, the contract level will go up).

In Chapter 13, we used the example of a corporate with a $20m loan at floating rate related to Eurodollar LIBOR and reviewed every 3 months. To hedge interest rate risk, put option contracts were bought. The effect was that when interest rates went up, the $50,000 extra bank expense was offset by a gain of $35,000 on the option contract. When interest rates went down, the $50,000 fall in bank costs was only offset by the loss of the premium at $15,000. The option buyer still benefited.

Let's look at a futures hedge in the same circumstances in Box 14.3.

BOX 14.3

Futures Hedge

Assume that the interest rate level traded in the pit is the same as current market interest rates (because this was the assumption we made earlier with the interest rate option contract, we need to be consistent).

As the loan is $20m and the contract size on CME is $1m, then the corporate needs to deal in 20 contracts. As they wish to gain from an interest rate rise, they sell 20 contracts for the next expiry at a level of 3.75%, that is, a contract price level of $100 - 3.75 = 96.25$.

No premium is paid, but the initial margin is $500 per contract, so $20 \times \$500 = \$10,000$ is paid to the clearing house. As before, we assume that at the expiry of the contract, the Eurodollar LIBOR rate is 4.75%. The bank notifies the client that the interest charge is 1% higher on the $20m loan for 3 months – an increase of $50,000.

At CME, the contract price is $100 - 4.75\% = 95.25$.

The corporate's position is closed by buying 20 contracts at 95.25. The position is as follows:

Sell 20 contracts at 96.25.
Buy 20 contracts at 95.25.
Gain per contract 1.00.

Each 0.01% is settled at $25, so the gain is $100 \times \$25 \times 20$ contracts = $50,000.

There is no premium to deduct, so the bank's extra $50,000 interest is met by the gain of $50,000 on the CME contract (in the best of all possible worlds). As there was no premium to deduct, the futures contract has so far worked out better.

But what happens if interest rates fall to 2.75%? The bank notifies the corporate of a reduced interest rate charge for 3 months of $50,000. At CME, the contract price is $100 - 2.75\% = 97.25$. The position is closed by buying 20 contracts at 97.25. The position is as follows:

Sell 20 contracts at 96.25.
Buy 20 contracts at 97.25.
Loss per contract 1.00.

The loss is $100 \times \$25 \times 20$ contracts = $50,000. This is, of course, the symmetry in futures.

A rise in interest rates of 1% gains $50,000, a fall in interest rates of 1% loses $50,000. The result is that the corporate does not gain from the fall in interest rates, as the reduced interest rate bill is offset by the loss on the futures contract. Here options gained, as the contract was abandoned when the interest rate fell for the loss of the premium, allowing the corporate a net gain from the interest rate reduction.

Currency Futures

We commented in Chapter 9 on the strength of the OTC market in currency forwards and options. Exchange traded currency options and futures ended in London in 1990, and few are now traded in Europe – most are OTC.

The trading of futures follows the lines we have explained in this chapter. The CME euro contract, for example, is based on €125,000 as the contract size and is quoted at an exchange rate of dollars per euro. A tick is 0.01¢ and is valued at $12.50. A contract might be bought at a dollar/euro exchange rate of $1.0384 and sold at $1.0484, for example – a gain of 100 ticks, or $1,250 per contract traded. Contracts can be left to go to delivery if required.

Some Problems of Futures Exchanges

In general, corporates are not enthusiastic about the use of futures exchanges. The contracts are standard sizes, so a small corporate with a loan of $800,000 finds the interest rate contract size of $1m inconvenient. The expiry dates of the contract are unlikely to coincide with real-life needs. Margin calls upset cash flow calculations, and no interest is paid on variation margin in credit. For interest rate and currency contracts, the banks offer an attractive range of OTC products, some of which we will meet in Chapter 15.

For banks themselves, however, the exchanges have two key advantages – they increase transparency in pricing and also reduce risk via the security of the clearing house. At a time when counterparty risk is a major worry, increasingly this is a key benefit.

For fund managers, too, the index contracts provide secure, liquid trading and the chance to carry out asset allocation smoothly. Suppose a fund has £100m in assets. A decision may be taken to decrease exposure to equities by 2% and increase exposure to gilts by 2%. With one phone call, the fund manager can sell FTSE 100 contracts to the value of £2m and buy gilts contracts to the same value. Over time and at leisure, the manager can progressively sell the equities, buy the gilts and close the futures position.

Open Outcry or Computers?

A major talking point at present is whether traders will continue to buy and sell in trading pits on a floor or whether the market will move to computerized order matching.

The large US markets are based on open outcry trading, but the last European exchange to open on an open outcry basis was the Paris MATIF in 1986. The argument for open outcry is that it's the quickest way to trade high-value standardized contracts. With computerized trading, however, the expensive floor is no longer needed, and a firm audit trail is produced, making fraud more difficult. (In 1989, 47 traders were indicted for fraud in Chicago following an undercover investigation by the FBI.)

The signalling in the pits usually follows the Chicago practice. There are three variables: the number of contracts, buy or sell?, and price. As in foreign exchange, only the last two digits of price will be quoted. If the interest rate contract level is 92.55, the price will be '55'. If the trader is *buying*, the hand begins away from the face and moves back to the forehead. The price is shouted with the hand away from the face and the number of contracts at the forehead. A buyer of 10 contracts at 92.55 will yell: '55 for 10'. If the trader is *selling*, the hand begins at the forehead and moves away, shouting the number of contracts first and the price second: '10 @ 55'. If there are no takers, the price may have to be moved up to 56 or 57 until a counterparty yells 'sold'. The two traders fill in dealing slips, the trades are matched by computer and matched trades are sent electronically to the clearing house.

The Chicago pits are very busy with frenzied shouting and pushing. The classic story is of the trader who died but couldn't fall over because the pit was too busy. Later, other traders who had lost on deals, filled in slips and put them in his pocket, leaving it to his insurer to pay up.

Computer systems are more boring, being based on order matching electronically. There is a CME/Reuters system called 'GLOBEX'. This is being used when the exchanges are closed, enabling them to continue trading and cross time zones with Europe and Japan. The CBOT already operates an evening session and the floor at the Philadelphia Stock Exchange is open 18 hours per day.

London's LIFFE exchange (before it was taken over by Euronext) introduced an electronic trading system, CONNECT, and its success was such that the trading floor closed in early 2000. As was mentioned in Chapter 13, LIFFE CONNECT is now Liffe's trading platform for all derivatives.

In 2003, the CBOT decided to use CONNECT and introduced it in January 2004, at the same time as announcing joint clearing with the CME to help meet competition in the US from Eurex. Some 90% of the trading in US Treasury futures is now electronic. By contrast, 90% of trading in agricultural products is open outcry at the CBOT but electronic trading was introduced in 2006. At the CME, most futures trading has moved to the GLOBEX system. Options are more difficult, but volumes are growing.

Outside financial contracts, the International Petroleum Exchange (IPE) in London trades the Brent oil futures, the industry's benchmark. It went from open outcry to electronic trading in May 2005. The New York Mercantile Exchange (NYMEX), the US rival, opened an office in London in May 2005 in direct competition and used open outcry, hoping to attract disgruntled traders at IPE who were unhappy with the move to electronic trading. NYMEX is the world's largest energy and metal futures exchange, with 134 years of pit trading, but it, too, offered electronic trading in 2006. Its rival, the Intercontinental Exchange (ICE) had already done so. Finally, the London Metal Exchange, one of the world's oldest exchanges, went electronic in 2005.

Another factor affecting exchanges is the increase in decisions to go public. The CME listed in late 2002, the CBOT in October 2005, and NYMEX listed in November 2006. IPE is owned by the Intercontinental Exchange, Atlanta, which floated in November 2005. Following public listing, there has also been significant consolidation in the sector. The CME merged with the CBOT in July 2007, and this group merged with the NYMEX in August 2008. ICE acquired the New York Board of Trade in 2007.

Contract Volumes

The number of contracts traded and/or cleared in the major exchanges in 2013 are shown in Table 14.2. As a guide to size, millions of contracts can, of course, be misleading, since it depends on the size of the contract. The largest derivative exchanges are the CME, ICE and Eurex.

▼ **Table 14.2** *Top 30 derivatives exchanges, 2013*

Top 30 Derivatives Exchages

Ranked by number of contracts traded and/or cleared

Rank	Exchange	Jan-Dec 2013 Volume	Annual % Change	Dec 2013 Open Interest	Annual % Change
1	CME Group	3,161,476,638	9.2%	83,904,116	19.66%
2	Intercontinental Exchange *#	2,807,970,132	14.7%	135,377,377	12.93%
3	Eurex*	2,190,548,148	−4.4%	77,090,544	−2.52%
4	National Stock Exchange of India	2,135,637,457	6.2%	7,786,961	−40.60%
5	BM&FBovespa	1,603,600,651	−2.0%	56,666,689	−11.10%
6	CBOE Holdings*	1,187,642,669	4.7%	351,428	18.86%
7	Nasdaq OMX*	1,142,955,206	2.5%	7,196,312	6.61%
8	Moscow Exchange	1,134,477,258	6.8%	5,233,255	37.80%
9	Korea Exchange	820,664,621	−55.3%	2,683,821	5.11%
10	Multi Commodity Exchange of India	794,001,650	−17.3%	745,474	−68.47%
11	Dalian Commodity Exchange	700,500,777	10.7%	3,153,905	39.23%
12	Shanghai Futures Exchange	642,473,980	75.9%	2,093,921	68.57%
13	Zhengzhou Commodity Exchange	525,299,023	51.3%	1,998,727	74.99%
14	Japan Exchange Group	366,145,920	56.3%	5,436,115	5.65%
15	Hong Kong Exchanges & Clearing	301,128,507	7.7%	8,183,801	13.50%
16	ASX Group	261,790,908	0.7%	13,956,878	−15.16%
17	BSE	254,845,929	4.5%	32,801	−52.02%
18	JSE South Africa	254,514,098	60.2%	17,857,396	32.62%
19	China Financial Futures Exchange	193,549,311	84.2%	123,166	11.58%
20	TMX Group*	155,753,473	−25.6%	4,329,062	2.30%
21	Taiwan Futures Exchange	153,225,238	−2.2%	1,126,754	7.38%
22	BATS Exchange*	151,814,889	16.2%	N/A	N/A
23	Singapore Exchange	112,077,267	39.1%	3,099,510	21.27%
24	Tokyo Financial Exchange	65,527,790	−2.1%	1,066,906	8.53%
25	Tel Aviv Stock Exchange	60,514,431	−9.9%	1,067,027	68.07%
26	Meff	54,694,502	−186%	9,840,349	−3.48%
27	Borsa Istanbul	53,172,365	−14.9%	427,501	54.08%
28	Ronsario Futures Wchange	51,176,700	0.2%	3,149,854	134.50%
29	London Stcok Exchange Group	50,384,211	−26.5%	7,612,192	−2.28%
30	United Stock Exchange of India	44,931,092	406.9%	19,084	67.33%

Open interest for these exchanges does not include options traded in the US and cleared by OCC # Includes NYSE Euronext

Source: Futures Industry Association, *Annual Volume Survey* (2014)

SUMMARY

- Futures trading began with crops, which were only available once per year and whose price fluctuated.
- Buyers and sellers might seek to reduce the risk of an adverse price movement by a *hedge*.
- A *futures contract* is an agreement to buy or sell a product at a set price at a later date. Unlike options, however, it is a commitment. *Speculators*, therefore, are exposed to unlimited risk, but *hedgers* can offset losses with profits on their physical positions.
- Usually, futures contracts do not go to delivery. An opening contract to buy is closed by a later contract to sell; an opening contract to sell is closed by a later contract to buy. The position is *cash settled*. In contracts like equity indices and interest rates, delivery is not possible anyway.
- *Forward* relates to buying or selling for actual delivery at a future date at a price set now. Forwards are OTC and can be specified as being physical or cash settled. With forwards being OTC, holders generally have to take on counterparty credit risk. Typically, there are

no margin calls on forwards, although it is possible for margin calls to be written into OTC contracts to mitigate credit risk.
- *Futures* are similar to forwards, but usually there is no intention to take or make delivery; later, the position will be closed with the opposite contract and settled in cash. Futures are exchange traded and can be cash or physically settled. They are traded on futures exchanges with set contract sizes, set expiry dates and the protection of the clearing house. The credit risk of futures is to the exchange on which they are traded, and there are margin calls to reduce this risk. Futures exist on the same range of products as options, although futures on equities are rare.
- Many options contracts on futures exchanges are *options to have the future*.
- Some exchanges use a trading floor and *open outcry*. Others use systems of order matching by computer. Order matching is now increasing at the expense of open outcry.

REVISION QUESTIONS/ASSIGNMENTS

1 Outline the key differences between forwards and futures. Which type of instrument is the most important globally?
2 Explain how investors can hedge using forward contracts.

3 Examine the advantages of open outcry markets. Are their days numbered?
4 Outline the main features of bond and currency futures.

REFERENCE

Mackay, C. (1980) *Extraordinary Popular Delusions and the Madness of Crowds,* Harmony Books, New York. Early study highlighting behavioural finance issues such as contagion in markets and other herd behaviour in investment and other areas.

FURTHER READING

Chisholm, A. (2004) *Derivatives Demystified: A Step-by-Step Guide to Forwards, Futures and Options*, John Wiley & Sons, New York. Introductory to intermediate guide to derivatives.

Hull, J.C. (2014) *Options, Futures, and Other Derivatives* (9th edn), Prentice Hall, Upper Saddle River, NJ. Classic but advanced text on derivatives products. An industry standard guide.

Dunsby, A., Eckstein, J., Gaspar, J., and Mulholland, S. (2008) *Commodities Investing: Maximizing Returns Through Fundamental Analysis*, John Wiley & Sons, New York. Investor guide focusing on commodity investment and derivative strategies. Intermediate text.

Fabozzi, F.J., Fuss, R., and Kaiser, D.G. (2008) *The Handbook of Commodity Investing*, Frank J. Fabozzi Series, John Wiley & Sons, London. Advanced text outlining various derivative strategies in commodity markets.

Other Derivative Products

INTRODUCTION

All the derivative products we describe in this chapter are essentially options and futures in another guise. They are not, however, traded on exchanges, but are OTC products. In addition, as interest rates, that is, the price of money, lie at the heart of the financial markets, the original products were all about interest rate risk. In recent years, however, credit risk has become more important and led to new products called 'credit derivatives'; these are described later in the chapter.

FORWARD RATE AGREEMENTS

To begin with, we must consider the term forward/forward. This is an arrangement between two counterparties to borrow or lend an agreed sum of money at an agreed rate for an agreed period that will not begin until a future date. For example, A will lend B $1m at 5% for 6 months, commencing in 6 months, called '6 against 12' or simply '6 × 12'.

It may be that a corporate needs a bank loan of $1m in 6 months and is worried about rates going up. It asks the bank to quote a rate of interest now for lending money in 6 months for 6 months. This is rather like an importer asking a bank to quote a rate for buying dollars against euros in 6 months. In foreign exchange, we argued that the bank could avoid risk by buying the dollars today and putting them on deposit for 6 months until needed by the client.

In the interest rate market, if asked to quote forward/forward, the bank could equally borrow money at today's rates and put it on deposit until needed by the client. In the above case, the bank will borrow money for 12 months, deposit it for the first 6 months and then lend it to the client for the remaining 6 months. The rate quoted will depend on

- the bank's cost of borrowing and return from lending;
- the yield curve – if positive, the bank borrowing for longer periods costs more than borrowing for short periods; and
- the reinvestment of the interest it earns on the money in the first 6 months.

This is how such deals were actually handled until the 1980s, when other techniques were developed. The banks are not keen now to quote these forward rates because the borrowing/lending uses up the bank's line of credit with other banks and also the line of credit with its own customers.

The forward rate agreement (FRA) is the bank's answer to the request for the forward/forward deal. The FRA is not about borrowing money, but about a future level of interest rates. The future level is compared to an agreed level, and the agreement is settled on the difference between the two rates. The future level in the London market will be based on the LIBOR rate – in this case, Eurodollar LIBOR.

For example, the corporate arranges with a bank that the 'target rate' of interest for 6 months ahead is 5% on a notional principal of $1m. If, in 6 months, interest rates are 5%, then nothing happens. If rates are 4%, the corporate pays the 0.5% (6 months of a 12-month 1%) of $1m (but will have lower borrowing costs elsewhere). If rates are 6%, however, the bank pays the corporate 0.5% of $1m to help offset its extra borrowing costs (see Figure 15.1). This is 'accounting for differences' and has the advantage of less credit risk. The bank, for example, is not borrowing or lending $1m, only accounting for the difference in rates from a target of 5%.

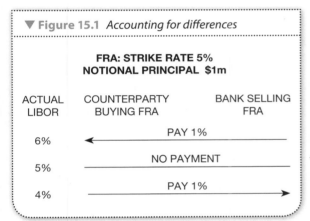

▼ **Figure 15.1** *Accounting for differences*

FRA: STRIKE RATE 5%
NOTIONAL PRINCIPAL $1m

ACTUAL LIBOR	COUNTERPARTY BUYING FRA	BANK SELLING FRA
6%	← PAY 1%	
5%	NO PAYMENT	
4%	PAY 1% →	

The corporate has fixed its rate for borrowing in 6 months in an indirect way. If rates go up, the corporate pays more for the money but is compensated for the extra cost by the FRA. If rates go down, the corporate will not benefit because the lower borrowing costs are offset by a payment under the FRA.

This line of explanation may well sound familiar. It's the same effect that was achieved by the interest rate futures transaction in Chapter 14. In selling the futures at 3.75%, the corporate was agreeing to settle on the difference between 3.75% and market rates at expiry. When rates were 4.75%, the corporate received $50,000 – 1% p.a. for 3 months equals 25 bp (basis points), so they received $20m ´ 0.25% – on the underlying contract value of $20m. When rates were 2.75%, the corporate paid the futures exchange 25 bp on the underlying $20m. The FRA is really an OTC future being arranged with a bank, and not a futures exchange. It has the advantage of flexibility on both dates and amounts of money.

Typical FRA periods are '3 against 6' and '6 against 12'. This is because floating rates on loans and floating rate notes (FRNs) are revised at 3- or 6-month intervals. A bank with a gap in its asset/liability management can thus close the exposure with an FRA. There will be a corporate market, with corporates talking to their commercial banks for deals down to, say, $1m or £1m, and a professional market, the banks between themselves, for typical sums from 50m to 100m and in sterling, yen, Swiss francs and euros.

How does the bank make a profit? The FRA is a product, like any other product, and sold with a bid/offer spread. Just as a market maker buys shares and hopes to sell them at a better rate, so the bank expects to buy FRAs at one rate and sell them at another. It bases the price for future interest rates on the deposit market yield curve or the prices of futures exchange contracts. Suppose that a '3 against 6' dollar FRA is quoted at 5.54/5.50. A bank will sell an FRA based on 5.54% but buy one based on 5.50%. If the rate at the 3-month date is 6%, the bank pays 46 bp on the FRA it sold but receives 50 bp on the one it bought. If rates are 5%, the bank receives 54 bp on the FRA it sold but pays only 50 bp on the one it bought (see Figure 15.2). Four basis points may not seem much for the administrative cost and the risk (*and* capital ratio for the risk) and it isn't. The market is very competitive, and banks need to be totally efficient to make any money. As a result, the trader may choose not to offset the FRA with one in the opposite direction but believe they will receive more money than they will pay. This does, of course, now involve interest rate risk, and risk limits must be set.

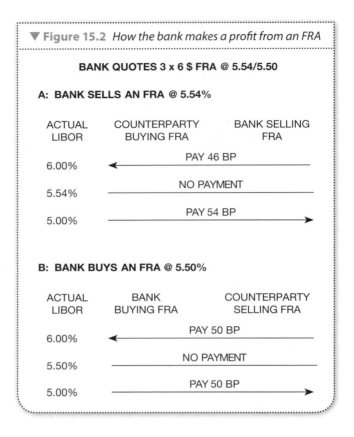

▼ Figure 15.2 *How the bank makes a profit from an FRA*

BANK QUOTES 3 x 6 $ FRA @ 5.54/5.50

A: BANK SELLS AN FRA @ 5.54%

ACTUAL LIBOR	COUNTERPARTY BUYING FRA	BANK SELLING FRA
6.00%	← PAY 46 BP	
5.54%	NO PAYMENT	
5.00%	PAY 54 BP →	

B: BANK BUYS AN FRA @ 5.50%

ACTUAL LIBOR	BANK BUYING FRA	COUNTERPARTY SELLING FRA
6.00%	← PAY 50 BP	
5.50%	NO PAYMENT	
5.00%	PAY 50 BP →	

One technical point: with an FRA that is, say, in 3 months for 3 months, then the payment is made in *advance* of the second 3-month period. As a result, only the net present value is actually paid.

It may be that an FRA buyer is unsure of the direction of interest rates. The FRA will protect against a rise in rates, but no benefit will arise if rates fall. If this is an unacceptable figure, the answer here is to pay for an *option* to have an FRA. If rates rise, the option to have the FRA is exercised. If rates fall, the option is abandoned. The FRA solves the problem of an interest rate risk for one future time, but what about risk over, say, 5 years? For this we turn to swaps.

SWAPS

Comparative Advantage

Interest rate swaps exploit what could be described as 'arbitrage opportunities', and in doing so create a market in which others can hedge or speculate on the movement of interest rates.

It begins with the 19th-century economist David Ricardo (1772–1823) and his 'theory of comparative advantage'. Ricardo argued that two countries could benefit from international trade even where one made all products more productively than the second. Let's

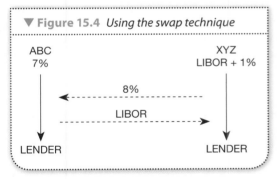

▼ **Figure 15.3** *International trade: Comparative advantage*

	ABC		XYZ
Product A	100	Product A	50
Product B	100	Product B	70

take two countries, ABC and XYZ, and two products, A and B. The product rates per hour for A and B in both countries are shown in Figure 15.3.

Ricardo argued that country ABC should concentrate on producing product A, and country XYZ concentrate on product B, and then trade. This is because although country ABC is superior in both A and B, it has a great *comparative advantage* in A. Country ABC thus produces all product A and exports the surplus to country XYZ. The latter produces all product B and exports the surplus to country ABC. Both countries gain, as ABC exploits to the full its comparative advantage in producing product A. This will become clearer from a study of the corresponding examples from the financial markets (see Figure 15.4 and the accompanying explanation).

We translate this now to borrowing rates instead. The two products become fixed rate finance and floating rate finance. The two countries become two companies, ABC and XYZ. Investors' perception of risk is not the same in the fixed interest rate market as it is in the floating rate market. Thus, company ABC may be able to borrow more cheaply than XYZ at either fixed or floating rate, but the difference is not the same, that is, there is a comparative advantage to be exploited.

Company ABC can raise fixed rate finance at 7% or floating at LIBOR (really wants floating rate funds). Company XYZ has to pay 10% for fixed rate borrowing and LIBOR + 1% for floating rate funds (really prefers fixed rate financing). ABC can borrow cheaper than XYZ in both fixed and floating rate markets but has greater comparative advantage in fixed. Therefore, ABC raises fixed at 7% but agrees to pay LIBOR to XYZ. XYZ borrows floating rate funds at LIBOR + 1% but agrees to pay 8% to ABC (Figure 15.4).

Thus, ABC pays 7% fixed but receives 8% from XYZ. It pays LIBOR to XYZ but in effect is paying LIBOR − 1%, less than if it borrowed at floating rate at LIBOR. XYZ pays LIBOR + 1% but receives only LIBOR from ABC, thus costing XYZ 1%. It pays 8% to ABC, in effect paying 9%, but this is less than if it borrowed fixed at 10%. This is another example of a technique that is not a 'zero-sum game'.

ABC and XYZ are each saving 1% on their cost of borrowing by using the swap technique. This swap opportunity occurs because floating rate lenders do not distinguish between the credit standing of borrowers to the same degree as fixed rate lenders. We might imagine that if one borrower has an AAA credit rating and another BBB, then the difference between the rates of borrowing, whether fixed or floating, would be the same. In fact, this is not the case. If lesser rated credits want to borrow at fixed rate instead of floating, then the rate is not quite as attractive.

▼ **Figure 15.4** *Using the swap technique*

ABC	XYZ
7%	LIBOR + 1%

8% ←- - - - - - - -

- - - - - - - -→ LIBOR

| LENDER | LENDER |

Interest Rate Swaps

In our example above, the difference in rates was a considerable exaggeration on a real-life situation. This was in order to simplify a concept that always seems complex to newcomers. The principle is the same even if the real-life difference is only a matter of a few basis points.

There are, therefore, two aspects to an interest rate swap. One is simply that one party agrees to pay a fixed rate on a notional principal sum of money for a period of time, and the other agrees to pay floating rate. In our FRA example (Figure 15.2), a counterparty bought an FRA at 5.54% from a bank. In effect, they agreed to pay a fixed rate (5.54%) and receive a floating rate (LIBOR) from the bank. Thus, the swap and the FRA are logically the same. Unlike an FRA, which was only for one future time period, a swap is for several time periods ahead, for example 6-monthly rate comparisons for, say, 5 years.

The other element is a possible profit arising from the comparative advantage concept. Even without any 'profit' element, one party with a floating rate commitment may feel happier swapping into a fixed rate commitment.

The elements in the swap are listed here:

- The fixed rate
- The variable rate
- The settlement periods
- The total maturity
- The underlying notional principal

For example, the parties may agree that one pays 5.5% and the other pays Eurodollar LIBOR on a notional underlying principal of $50m. The swap is to last 5 years, and the settlement periods are 6 monthly. That is, every 6 months 5.5% is compared with Eurodollar LIBOR, and a net sum of money is paid over. If the difference was 1%, then 1% of $50m for 6 months is the sum to be paid over – $250,000. The money, however, is not in fact paid over until the end of the 6-monthly period, not at the beginning. This is because interest payments are paid in arrears. A bank, for example, sets the rate on an actual loan for 6 months at 5.5%, but the interest is paid at the end of 6 months, not the beginning.

Making a Market in Swaps

How do these companies, ABC and XYZ, find each other? Obviously, with difficulty. So there is a role for banks to bring the parties together and take a piece of the action. In Figure 14.4, the bank could take 8% from XYZ and only pass on 7.75% to ABC. It could take LIBOR from ABC and only pass on LIBOR – 0.25% to XYZ. ABC and XYZ will still profit from the deal, but the bank now has 0.50% for its trouble.

The market began in 1982, and as it grew, banks became prepared to carry out a swap just for one counterparty, pending finding another counterparty later. This is called a 'warehouse swap'. The bank is prepared to 'warehouse' the swap until a counterparty can be found, in the meantime taking hedging action, as we explain later. It is called an 'unmatched swap'. The swap, therefore, has simply become another product that the banks market with the usual bid/offer rates. The bank may quote a bid/ask spread, for example, 5.80/5.75 for a 5-year dollar swap (Figure 15.5).

If the bank stands in the middle between two counterparties (the matched swap), then the bank has no interest rate risk and a locked-in 5 bp profit. If LIBOR goes up, the bank pays more to counterparty XYZ but receives it from ABC. If rates fall, the bank receives less from ABC but pays less to XYZ. XYZ pays 5.80% to the bank, and the bank pays 5.75% to ABC, keeping 5 bp (Figure 15.6).

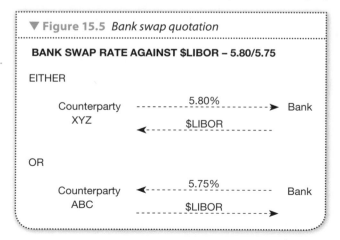

▼ Figure 15.5 *Bank swap quotation*

BANK SWAP RATE AGAINST $LIBOR – 5.80/5.75

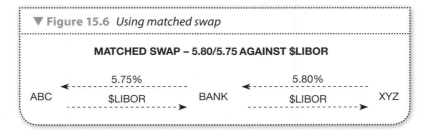

▼ **Figure 15.6** *Using matched swap*

MATCHED SWAP – 5.80/5.75 AGAINST $LIBOR

The bank may have no interest rate risk, but it does have counterparty risk. What if ABC or XYZ goes into liquidation, and the bank is left with an unmatched swap? Under today's rules from regulators, capital must be provided for this risk.

In providing a market in swaps, banks are exposed to risk until they can find someone who wants to do a swap in the opposite direction. In the meantime, they can adopt hedging strategies:

1   If the bank is at risk to a *fall in interest rates* (because it has lent floating and borrowed fixed), then it will buy fixed interest securities, whose price will rise when interest rates fall.
2   If the bank is at risk should *interest rates rise* (because it has borrowed floating and lent fixed), then it can hedge in the *futures* market by selling an interest rate future, giving the right to borrow at prevailing rates of interest. When interest rates rise, this right becomes valuable, and the bank will make a profit on the futures contract.

Notice the language used above. The bank receiving LIBOR and paying 5.75% can be said to have *lent floating* and *borrowed fixed* (and vice versa). Other language used is a reference to the 'payer' and the 'receiver'. This always refers to the fixed rate element.

Actual market rates tend to fall between the rates quoted for an AAA borrower and a single A borrower for borrowing for given periods of time. If dollars, they are usually expressed as a given number of basis points over US Treasury bond rates for the fixed element. If pounds, they are usually expressed as a given number of basis points over the gilts rate. The variable rate is euro or domestic LIBOR.

Users of Swaps

Assuming that a 5-year dollar swap rate is quoted as 5.80/5.75, who are the users of these swaps? We find that the market talks of liability swaps and asset swaps:

* *Liability swaps* are simply swaps for borrowers of money.
* *Asset swaps* are simply swaps for lenders of money.

The treasurer has a bank loan based on dollar LIBOR (see Figure 15.7). Worried that rates will rise, he does a swap, changing the floating rate bank loan into fixed rate by this indirect route.

We can also envisage a situation in which a treasurer with a fixed rate loan could receive 5.75% and pay LIBOR, turning the fixed rate loan into floating rate. A further variation is possible. If the loan is, say, $100m, the treasurer can do the swap for only $50m, leaving half the money at fixed rate and half at floating (quite common).

Using the swap technique, a Eurobond issuer may not only change the fixed rate basis into floating but create a profit margin of 10 bp due to the general comparative advantage concept (see Figure 15.8).

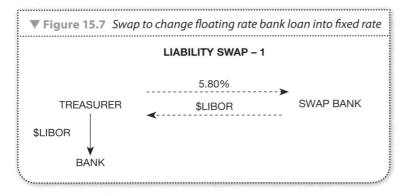

▼ **Figure 15.7** *Swap to change floating rate bank loan into fixed rate*

LIABILITY SWAP – 1

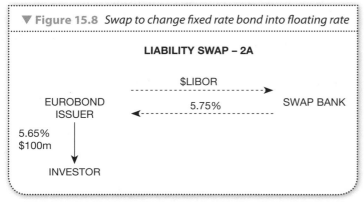

▼ **Figure 15.8** *Swap to change fixed rate bond into floating rate*

LIABILITY SWAP – 2A

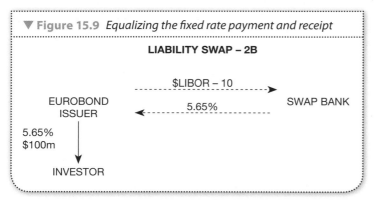

▼ **Figure 15.9** *Equalizing the fixed rate payment and receipt*

LIABILITY SWAP – 2B

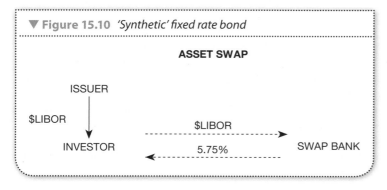

▼ **Figure 15.10** *'Synthetic' fixed rate bond*

ASSET SWAP

What the issuer may well do is equalize the fixed rate payment and receipt and use the profit margin to cut the LIBOR rate (see Figure 15.9). The issuer agrees to receive 5.65% instead of 5.75% and to pay LIBOR − 10 instead of just LIBOR. We say the issuer has achieved 'sub-LIBOR funding'.

The investor is receiving floating rate income based on dollar LIBOR (either from a loan or FRN). Believing that rates will fall, the issuer swaps into a fixed rate return. We say that the investor has changed the FRN into a 'synthetic' fixed rate bond (see Figure 15.10).

Banks often buy fixed rate bonds from lesser rated corporates (that is, higher interest rates) to use for an asset swap to create floating rate income well above LIBOR (see Figure 15.11). In Figure 15.11, the bank receives 6.25% from a bond but only pays 5.75% on the fixed leg of the swap. It also receives LIBOR and thus a total receipt of LIBOR + 50. It will probably 'package' the deal and pass it on to a fund looking for good floating rate income, the bank taking some profit while doing so.

Swaps and Futures

Swaps are really a strip of futures or FRA contracts lasting several years. They are, of course, OTC, with all the flexibility that that involves. When the corporate sold an interest rate future at 3.75%, we saw that the effect was the same as the FRA based on 3.75%. In the same way, selling an interest rate future at 3.75% is choosing to borrow fixed and lend floating (the alternative language we used for swaps). It's a swap (or FRA) for a single time period only. Equally, the buyer of an interest rate future is choosing to borrow floating and lend fixed – the other side of the swap.

Because the language and terminology used in FRAs and swaps is different from that used for futures, newcomers think of them as essentially different

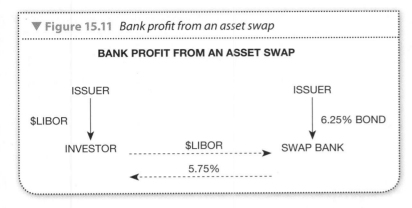

▼ **Figure 15.11** *Bank profit from an asset swap*

products when they are really all variations on the same product. They have the essential characteristic of futures – a hedger can gain protection from an adverse rate movement but will not benefit from a favourable one.

Futures are for 3-month time periods ahead, although we could book all eight quarterly contracts for the next 2 years – called a 'strip' of futures. FRAs are for one time period ahead, but not necessarily 3 months, and again a strip of FRAs could be purchased or sold. For periods of 2 years or more, swaps are more attractive. Most swaps are in the range 2–10 years. However, in the UK, the former Halifax Building Society issued a 25-year bond, which was said to have been swapped into floating rate for 25 years.

Other Swaps

A swap buyer may want a swap but only wish to commence in, say, 6 months' time. This becomes the 'forward swap'. In 6 months' time, the forward swap buyer's view of interest rates may turn out to be incorrect. The buyer is, however, committed to the swap. Another possibility, therefore, is to pay a premium for an option to have the swap later (just like the option to have an FRA). This is called the 'swaption'.

It may be that the notional principal in the swap is not constant but on a 'reducing' basis, for example a swap based on a notional principal of $10m for 5 years, but the amount of the principal is reduced each year. This could apply when the swap backs a loan of which some of the principal is constantly being repaid or a bond for which a sinking fund is being accumulated to redeem the bond. This is called an 'amortizing swap'.

The notional principal at risk might also vary, but up and down rather than on a declining basis. This is the 'roller coaster swap'.

There are swaps in which both parties pay floating rate, but on a different basis. For example, one pays Eurodollar LIBOR and the other pays 3-month US Treasury bill rates. This is the 'basis swap'.

Swapnotes and the Swaps Yield Curve

The list of contracts traded at ICE Futures Europe (previously Liffe) (Table 14.1) included swapnotes. This is potentially confusing in that the contract is actually a bond futures contract, and not a swaps contract as such. The bond is a notional bond with a coupon of 6% p.a. and a payment of principal on final maturity (we met the idea of a notional bond in Chapter 14). You will remember that the net present value of a bond is arrived at by discounting all the future cash flows at the yield curve interest rates. The swapnote contract is similar in that the settlement price is derived in the same way but uses a different yield curve – one known as the 'swaps yield curve'. The normal yield curve is based on government borrowing rates, which is fine if you are using futures to cover the risk on government bonds. What about corporate bonds? The swaps yield curve is based on the appropriate interest rates for top-quality non-government borrowers. Because swaps involve credit risk, the swaps yield curve is studied to ascertain the appropriate interest rates for a swaps contract. For those whose risk is in corporate bonds or mortgage bonds (like *Pfandbriefe*), the swapnote is more appropriate for bond futures than using conventional government bond contracts.

Other users might be swaps traders hedging risk due to possible future changes in the swaps yield curve. The swapnote could also be used to track the spread of these corporate rates over government rates. For example, in a recession, one would expect this spread to increase.

Of course, many corporates are not top quality; indeed, there are many non-investment grade issuers these days. When they issue a bond, the language used is 'issued at X bp above the swaps yield curve'.

CURRENCY SWAPS

As illustrated in Box 15.1, the swaps market began with currency swaps.

BOX 15.1

Currency Swaps

It may be that a US-based issuer wants Swiss francs but is not well known to Swiss franc investors. A Swiss corporate or public body, well known in Switzerland, may want dollars but is not well known to dollar investors.

The US issuer will have to pay a premium to raise Swiss francs, and the Swiss issuer will have to pay a premium to raise dollars. The answer is for the US issuer to raise dollars and the Swiss issuer to raise Swiss francs, and then swap the proceeds. This is the classic 'currency swap'.

The first major case was in 1981, when the World Bank wanted a further Swiss franc issue and was faced with paying a premium to persuade Swiss franc investors to hold even more World Bank paper.

IBM wanted a dollar issue but faced the same problem. Salomon Bros arranged a swap.

The World Bank raised the money in dollars, and IBM raised the money in Swiss francs. Dollar investors were pleased to hold World Bank paper, and Swiss franc investors were pleased to hold IBM paper. The two entities swapped the proceeds. On redemption (in 1986), they arranged to swap back at the same exchange rate. In the meantime, IBM sent dollar interest payments to the World Bank, which sent Swiss franc interest payments to IBM.

Again, as the market grew, banks took on unmatched deals and made a market in currency swaps.

Sometimes, though, the bank can be lucky and match two investors coming to the market at the same time.

In September 1996, the European Investment Bank (EIB) and the Tennessee Valley Authority (TVA) came to the market at the same time. The EIB wanted 10-year deutschmarks, and the TVA wanted 10-year dollars. However, the EIB could borrow in dollars 7 bp less than TVA, but only 4 bp less in deutschmarks. As a result, the EIB borrowed $1bn, the TVA borrowed DM1.5bn and they swapped the proceeds.

It was a classic case of exploiting comparative advantage. In swapping directly, both parties also saved bid/offer spreads and reduced transaction costs.

CAPS, FLOORS AND COLLARS

Sometimes, the user in this market may require protection in one direction only. For example, a corporate may seek protection from interest rates rising, but seek to benefit should they fall. An investor, receiving money at floating rate, may seek protection from rates falling, but seek to benefit should they rise. This end objective can be achieved by interest rate options on trading exchanges. If the rate moves the wrong way for our market position, the option is exercised and compensation obtained. If the rate moves the right way for our borrowing/lending position, the option is abandoned, and we benefit from better rates.

Exchanges, however, have drawbacks, as we have seen. The OTC market has responded with two flexible products to meet the above situations for borrowers and investors – the cap and the floor – see Box 15.2.

> **BOX 15.2**
>
> ## Caps and Floors
>
> ### Caps
>
> The interest rate cap sets a maximum level on a short-term rate interest rate. Buyers are compensated if the interest rate goes above a certain level (the strike level). For example, the arrangement may be based on a 3-month LIBOR and have a term of 3 years. The strike level is 5%, the revision of the rate is quarterly and the notional principal is $10m. Thus, if LIBOR is 6% in 3 months, the seller pays the buyer 1% of $10m for 3 months, say, $25,000 (see Figure 15.12).
>
>
> ▼ Figure 15.12 *The yield curve* 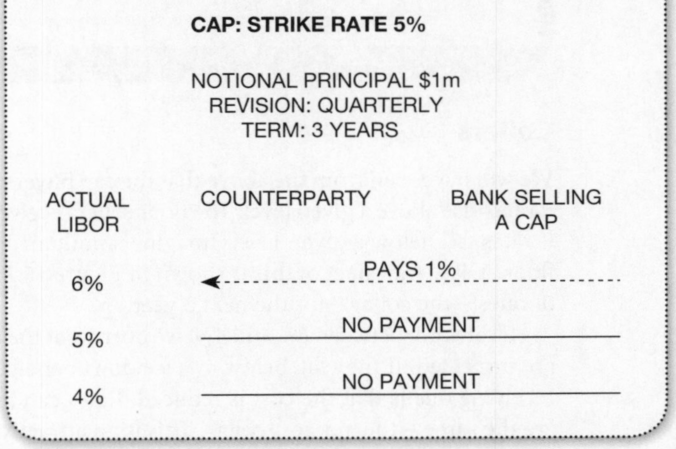
>
> **CAP: STRIKE RATE 5%**
>
> NOTIONAL PRINCIPAL $1m
> REVISION: QUARTERLY
> TERM: 3 YEARS
>
> | ACTUAL LIBOR | COUNTERPARTY | BANK SELLING A CAP |
> |---|---|---|
> | 6% | ◄------- PAYS 1% ------- | |
> | 5% | NO PAYMENT | |
> | 4% | NO PAYMENT | |
>
> If rates are 5% or less, nothing happens, and the cap buyer can benefit from lower borrowing rates. The fee is, of course, the option premium. The OTC cap not only offers the precise dates we require, but it is a continuous arrangement, like a swap, and not just for one time period ahead.

There are the usual variations on the theme that we associate with options. If the buyer is prepared to accept some interest rate risk, the strike rate in the above example could be chosen as 6%. This is 'out of the money' in options terms, and the premium will be cheaper.

Floors

The interest rate 'floor' is simply the opposite product.

An investor, receiving income at floating rate, may buy a floor. This sets a minimum level to a rate of interest. The buyer is compensated if the market goes below this level (see Figure 15.13).

The terms could be exactly as described for the cap, but on the basis that payment is made if rates fall *below* the strike rate. It may be that the user is fairly sure about interest rates for 1 year, but not thereafter. The cap or floor can be arranged to commence in 1 year's time – the forward cap or floor.

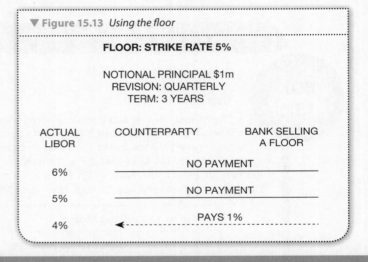

▼ Figure 15.13 *Using the floor*

FLOOR: STRIKE RATE 5%

NOTIONAL PRINCIPAL $1m
REVISION: QUARTERLY
TERM: 3 YEARS

ACTUAL LIBOR	COUNTERPARTY	BANK SELLING A FLOOR
6%	NO PAYMENT	
5%	NO PAYMENT	
4%	◄ PAYS 1%	

Collars

We will have seen from the above that the cap buyer pays a premium and receives payment if rates rise above a given level. The floor seller receives a premium but must make payment if rates fall below a given level. Imagine simultaneously buying a cap at 6% and selling a floor at 4%. The effect of this is shown in Figure 15.14. The net effect is to lock into a band of rates – the collar – for the next 3 years.

If rates are between 6% and 4%, we borrow at the market rate. If rates rise above 6%, we are protected. If they fall below 4%, we don't benefit. The effect of paying a premium and receiving one is that the cost is reduced. Rates can be chosen at which the two premiums are the same – the 'no-cost collar'. This is an attractive device and popular at the moment. All our other devices have turned around a given rate of interest. Here we select a band instead. We have actually met this product before. It was in Chapter 8, and it was the 'cylinder' or 'collar' or 'range forward'. The future buyer of dollars will never have a worse rate than $1.85 per pound but never have a better rate than $1.95. It's just the same logic applied in a different market.

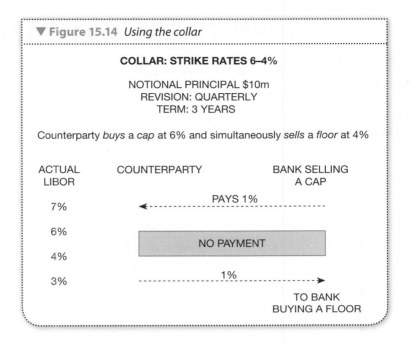

▼ **Figure 15.14** *Using the collar*

Caps, floors and collars are a series of interest rate options over a period of time. At present, 2–5 years is the most popular range.

CREDIT DERIVATIVES

We have become familiar with market risk, such as interest rates, currency rates, equity and bond prices – but what about credit risk? What if your counterparty is a reliable one like Lehman Brothers but suddenly goes into liquidation, as indeed Lehman did in September 2008? What if your bond default risk is insured by AIG, which suddenly looks as if it might do the same? We have seen huge losses from the original LDC crisis in the 1970s and the more recent Southeast Asian and Russian crises and many more losses from the recent credit crisis (see Chapter 10). The original Basel agreement included credit risk, and there is more emphasis in Basel II and Basel III. In addition to this, there is the more general risk to commercial lenders when borrowers can't pay and to investors when bonds default.

Over the past decade or so, a market to lay off risk has exploded. This is the market for credit derivatives – a market that scarcely existed in 2000. We have mentioned banks selling off loan books to others to reduce risk and clear the balance sheet. What has happened with credit derivatives is the possibility of simply selling the risk itself and keeping the loan or bonds.

The basic product is the credit default swap (CDS), as in Box 15.3.

Credit Default Swaps (CDS)

A buyer holding $10m worth of a 5-year bond may ask someone else to take on the risk of default in return for a premium. The premium is paid for 5 years, and if the bond has not defaulted, the seller of the CDS keeps the premiums and has nothing to pay.

If the bond defaults, the buyer of the CDS, the bondholder, hands over the bond in return for its face value. The premium or spread is usually quoted as basis points and relates to the spread of the issuer's bond's yield over the government or risk-free rate. If the spread is 70 bp, the investor holding $10m of the 5-year bond will pay $70,000 p.a. for 5 years to the seller of the CDS (see Figure 15.15).

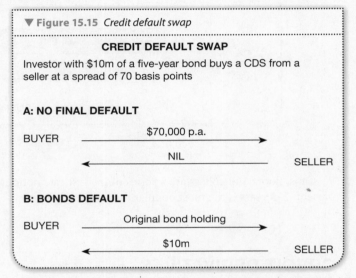

▼ **Figure 15.15** *Credit default swap*

CREDIT DEFAULT SWAP

Investor with $10m of a five-year bond buys a CDS from a seller at a spread of 70 basis points

A: NO FINAL DEFAULT

BUYER ———— $70,000 p.a. ————→

←———— NIL ————— SELLER

B: BONDS DEFAULT

BUYER ———— Original bond holding ————→

←———— $10m ————— SELLER

Let us say that the risk-free rate is 5%, and an investor has a bond paying 5.7% at issue. The spread of 0.7% is the risk element in the bond. The investor is paid 0.7% to take the risk of default.

Why not sell this risk to someone else?

That is exactly what the CDS does. It might be that the spread in the market is only 0.6%. In that case, the investor now has a risk-free return on the bond of 5.1%. However, this will not last long, as arbitrageurs will move in to take advantage and the spreads will soon equalize.

The spread on an AAA bond is likely to be about 20 bp, but non-investment-grade bonds could be several hundred basis points. In the light of the eurozone problems, in March 2012, Italy's 5-year government bonds yielded 3.53%, and its CDS spread was at 366; Spain's debt yielded 3.60% and 395, respectively; and Ireland's stood at 5.28% and 609.

When TDC, the Danish telecommunications group, was taken over by a group of private equity companies with huge leverage, the market was quoting the premium as 253 bp. Thus, to insure against default on €10m of bonds would cost €253,000 p.a.

This is, of course, no different from an individual paying an insurance company $400 p.a. to cover the risk of damage to her car. Indeed, many of the sellers of CDS are insurance companies. What makes it different is that, as you might have guessed, the market complicates it considerably.

Chapter 15 • OTHER DERIVATIVE PRODUCTS

For instance, just as a seller of bond futures may not own the bonds, so a buyer of a CDS may not own the bonds either, but be taking a speculative position. Of course, if there is a default, we could have the embarrassment that there are more bonds traded on CDS contracts than actually exist.

This was the case with Delphi, US motor parts supplier, who filed for bankruptcy on 8 October 2005. The market got together and found a way of cash settlement. An auction determined the price of Delphi bonds, say 30¢ in the dollar. The CDS seller now pays 70¢ in the dollar as settlement. The buyer has 70¢ in the dollar, plus the estimated value of the bond of 30¢ in the dollar, and is compensated for the risk without selling the bonds.

Another complication comes with the creation of default indices, such as those at S&P and Markit. S&P has three indices that track default risk in the US credit default swap market:

1 The US Investment Grade (IG) CDS Index tracks the default risk of 100 equally weighted investment-grade US corporate credits.
2 The S&P US High Yield (HY) CDS Index consists of 80 equally weighted high-yield corporate credits.
3 The S&P 100 CDS Index consist of the 80–90 members of the S&P 100 Equity Index that have CDS with sufficient liquidity.

Markit also offers a range of credit default indices covering multiple sectors. The main indices for North America are listed below:

- Markit CDX North American Investment Grade (125 companies)
- Markit CDX North American Investment Grade High Volatility (30 companies from CDX IG)
- Markit CDX North American High Yield (100 companies)
- Markit CDX North American High Yield High Beta (30 companies)
- North American Emerging Markets (15 companies)
- North American Emerging Markets Diversified (40 companies)

In Europe, probably the best-known index is the Markit iTraxx Europe Index of 125 companies with investment-grade ratings and the iTraxx Europe Crossover Index covering 44 high-yield companies.

The above indices track the credit profile of certain companies. Thus they are a proxy for the credit risk of the corporate bond market at the specific grade being evaluated – typically indices focus on investment grade (like the S&P IG CDS and Markit iTraxx Europe) or high yield (as in the case of the iTraxx Europe Crossover). The compilers usually reset the index every 6 months. Some firms may move from one index to another if their fundamental credit rating changes. Credit events that trigger settlement for individual components are bankruptcy and failure to pay. Credit events are settled via credit event auctions. A default of one name in the index triggers a partial settlement. It works like a single CDS, but for only a fraction of the notional value, for example 1% if there are 100 names in the basket.

The market is not just about the credit on bonds. Banks, in particular, may wish to sell off some risk to improve their capital ratio. In Chapter 6, we covered structured bonds when a whole portfolio of bonds was split into tranches according to risk. This is common in the credit default market. The first tranche, the equity tranche, carries the highest risk of default. The bank usually keeps this. The second tranche, the mezzanine tranche, is a little less risky. Finally, we come to the least risky senior debt tranche. As an example, in December 2005, Citigroup took emerging market credits worth €500m and split them into 100 equally weighted entities. The senior debt tranche was rated AAA and paid 35 bp over EURIBOR; the BB tranche in dollars paid, by contrast, 425 bp over EURIBOR; Citigroup kept the riskiest equity tranche, which represented 6.5% of the portfolio.

The above was structured from bank loans. It could have been structured from bonds or existing CDS. The income is distributed to tranche holders according to risk. We are in the world of the 'synthetic collateralized debt obligation'. Who is buying and selling these risks? Obviously, there are banks and also insurance companies. In addition, there are hedge funds and pension funds. Hedge funds are active players – some have estimated that they may account for 70% of the volume of trading. They move fast and may be in and out of a deal before it can be confirmed on paper. They also often assign the deal to other participants, adding a third party to the deal. All this, and the huge increase in the market, has led to a worry about back office procedures and possible legal problems if there was a crisis. This is not helped by the fact that the market is not transparent, leading many to call for new regulation even before the credit crisis.

No less an authority than Alan Greenspan, former president of the Federal Reserve, had stated in the mid-2000s that the development of such instruments enabling the management of a wide spread of risk was a good thing. On the other hand, Warren Buffett, the 'sage of Omaha', has described credit derivatives as 'time bombs'. In the UK, John Tiner, the former chief executive of the FSA, is on record as saying:

> Credit derivatives bring speculators and hedgers into the market and that means they bring information into the market. I think this makes markets more transparent and that must be good for all players.

We will see later how moves to regulate the CDS business have accelerated since the credit crisis.

As we mentioned above, the plethora of deals being done leads to deals between traders that cancel each other out. The trade, therefore, needs a netting system, exactly like foreign exchange in Chapter 10. TriOptima, a financial technology company, now runs just such a netting service. It collects trade data from dealers and identifies offsetting transactions that can be terminated, leaving dealers with a net exposure to trading partners. Big dealers still buy and sell the bulk of credit derivatives.

Figures for the size of the market are produced by the International Swaps and Derivatives Association. There is a notional value of contracts and a true market value. So in the case of Figure 15.15, the notional value is $10m, but the trade value is 5 × $70,000 = $350,000. The CDS market grew rapidly from 2002–3 onwards, reaching an estimated $62 trillion notional value by the end of 2007. However, the credit crisis had a devastating impact on the market, and it fell in size to $38.6 trillion by the end of 2008. It is important to note that since default has historically been a relatively rare occurrence in most CDS contracts, the only payments being made are the premium payments from buyer to seller. Thus, although the market size data on outstanding notional amounts seem enormous, the actual net cash flows will generally be a small fraction of this total. A good example is the matter of CDS payments in the case of Lehman's bankruptcy on 15 September 2008. Outstanding CDS payments had a notional value of $400bn, but when all payments were made, the total net amount was $5.2bn.

Market concerns about CDS exposure at Lehman's quickly moved, within 1 day, to AIG. The largest general insurer in the US had been selling CDS protection that was not hedged – presumably because it thought credit defaults of any significant scale were unlikely. AIG was holding more than $440bn of notional positions in CDS contracts – often monoline insurance-type transactions. Worries about the spillover effects in the CDS market resulting from the failure of AIG led to a US government support package on 16 September 2008. According to the BIS (2009):

> That package, which would be repeatedly restructured and extended during the following months, prevented the disorderly failure of AIG. It also kept CDS-related risks from being brought back onto clients' balance sheets in an already fragile environment.

Warren Buffett's concerns have come to fruition. Regulators in the US and Europe have moved rapidly to introduce a series of new procedures for the CDS market. In particular, they were concerned that speculators would put greater pressure on banks that may lead to further failures. Remember that holders of CDS are hoping for credit downgrades or defaults to generate returns. The OTC nature of the business also led to a lack of transparency. As such, it has been agreed that new central clearing houses for CDS transactions will be introduced in the US and Europe. Clearing houses act as central counterparties to both sides of a CDS transaction, so they help in reducing the counterparty risk that both buyers and sellers face. The US central clearing operations in the US began in March 2009 operated by the Intercontinental Exchange (ICE). In July, ICE announced that it was extending its clearing to Europe via its ICE Clear Europe arm, just ahead of European banks' self-imposed deadline of 31 July for clearing their credit derivatives trades.

THE MARKET IN DERIVATIVE INSTRUMENTS

The BIS has carried out periodic surveys of the volume and value of derivatives contracts traded both on exchanges and on the much larger OTC market and now carries the updated figures in its quarterly reviews.

The figures in Tables 15.1 and 15.2 illustrate the growth between 2005 and 2011. If we go back to 1985, the growth is even more spectacular. Our OTC total at June 2014 is $691,492bn notional value of outstanding contracts, and the 1985 figure was $47,412bn. The total figure for trading on organized exchanges at June 2014 is $73,400bn. This is an increase compared with June 2009, when trading stood at $69,453bn of notional value of outstanding contracts By far the largest growth over the past 5 years or so has been in OTC activity, as the value of exchange-traded products has not changed a lot since 2009.

The OTC derivatives market has typically grown much faster than exchange traded business, although this is likely to change as the new rules enshrined under the Dodd-Frank in the US and similar EU legislation seeks to make it compulsory to do a much bigger proportion of derivatives transactions via regulated exchanges.

▼ **Table 15.1** *Notional amounts outstanding of OTC derivatives by risk category and instrument in billions of dollars*

Instrument	June 2005	June 2009	June 2011	June 2014
Foreign exchange contracts				
Forwards and forex swaps	24,267	23,107	31,113	35,190
Currency swaps	8,236	15,072	22,228	26,141
Options	6,809	10,596	11,358	13,451
Interest rate contracts				
FRAs and swaps	77,322	388,684	453,207	513,848
Options	27,071	48,513	56,423	49,442
Equity-linked contracts				
Forwards and swaps	176	1,709	2,029	2,433
Options	527	4,910	4,813	4,508
Commodities	1,694	3,729	3,197	2,206
Credit default swaps	10,211	36,046	32,409	19,462
Unallocated	29,086	72,255	46,543	24,810
Grand total	185,399	604,621	707,569	691,492

Note: Unallocated refers to OTC derivative contracts that cannot be classified in the main categories listed.

Source: BIS (2014a).

▼ **Table 15.2** *Derivative instruments traded on organized exchanges, by instrument (notional principal in billions of US dollars)*

Instrument	Sept 2005	June 2009	Dec 2011	June 2014
Foreign exchange futures	110	136	221	242
Foreign exchange options	63	104	88	137
Interest rate futures	19,860	20,096	21,724	27,268
Interest rate options	32,795	42,031	31,581	38,294
Equity index futures	727	951	982	1,587
Equity index options	4,726	6,135	3,733	5,872
Grand total	58,281	69,453	58,332	73,400

Source: BIS (2014b).

Over the last few years, trading in OTC foreign exchange and interest contracts (apart from options) has increased. However, there has been a big fall in the use of commodity derivatives (due to fall in global commodity prices) and also in credit default swaps (credit risk has fallen).

An ongoing debate in the financial world concerns the risks associated with derivatives trading. The outstanding example of the risk in derivative transactions was the collapse in early 1995 of Baring Bros, the UK's oldest merchant bank, alleged to be due to the activities of one trader, Nick Leeson. The bank's controls were woefully inadequate, and management allowed one trader's activities to ruin the bank at a cost of £860m. Other derivatives losses are highlighted in Box 15.4.

BOX 15.4

Major Derivatives Losses

In the US, one trader at Kidder Peabody, Joseph Jett, is alleged to have concealed losses of $350m over a 2-year period.

A rogue trader at Daiwa in New York in 1996 (who lost a similar sum to Nick Leeson) had apparently been concealing his mounting losses for 11 years.

Mr Hamanaka at Sumitomo allegedly used derivatives to corner the world copper market, culminating in losses of around $2.4bn.

Other headline derivative losses are detailed here:

1994: Metallgesellschaft, one of Germany's largest industrial conglomerates, lost $1.5bn on oil futures transactions.

2001: Enron, the seventh largest company in the US and the world's largest energy trader, made massive use of energy and credit derivatives. It became the largest bankruptcy in American history, after systematically attempting to conceal major losses.

2002: Allied Irish Banks lost $750m due to John Rusnak, a US-based rogue trader, who used bogus options contracts to cover losses on spot and forward foreign exchange contracts.

2004: China Aviation lost $550m in speculative derivatives trading in Singapore.

2005: Refco, one of the world's biggest derivatives brokers, went bust.

2006: Amaranth Advisors, a US hedge fund, lost $6bn from trading in natural gas futures.

2008: Société Générale lost €4.9bn in unauthorized futures trading. A rogue trader, Jerome Kerviel, a relatively junior 31-year-old on the futures desk in Paris, whose role was to make 'plain vanilla' hedges on European stock market indices, was the main culprit and architect of the biggest banking fraud to date.

2011: UBS lost an estimated $2.3bn as a result of the activities of an alleged rogue trader, Kweku Adoboli, in the synthetic exchange-traded fund market.

Although these losses are large, they need to be put into context. Most boil down to either excessive risk-taking and/or fraudulent behaviour – the latter often due to weak internal supervision and/or regulatory oversight. The losses that the world's major banks incurred during 2008 put these into context. Isolated losses can have serious repercussions for individual banks and firms, but it is when the derivative interrelationships between banks and other parties are undertaken on a huge scale and in a non-transparent manner that major systemic problems can occur, as in the case of AIG and its CDS business.

It's also unfortunate that the intellectual effort required to gain an understanding of these products leads some people to dismiss it all as 'gambling'. Suppose we have two corporates facing significant interest rate risk over the next 3 years. One buys certainty by doing an interest rate swap and electing to pay fixed. The other does nothing. Who is gambling? Surely, it is the corporate that does nothing and leaves itself open to whatever volatility of interest rates comes along.

The paradox about these products is that the ability to use them to lay off risk means that bankers can take more risk. Insofar as they can take more risk, the more they can offer end users ingenious products that they find beneficial. As the markets grow, there are more opportunities for laying off a growing variety of risks in an ever more efficient way. As a result, more and more end user products are being released, which they find attractive. This is the beneficial aspect of these markets. Of course, there are the gamblers (speculators), and the markets couldn't exist without them, but to dismiss it all as gambling is to make a serious mistake.

We are seeing this in the consumer markets, where individuals can now have fixed rate mortgages for up to 20 years, capped mortgages and an increasing range of exotic variations. These allow the individual to budget with peace of mind. All these new types of mortgage products are created with derivatives structures. Equally, investment products have been launched with a variety of guarantees, typically using options, to ensure that an individual is protected against a market downturn. This, again, allows the person in the street to know that his long-term savings are not exposed to undue risk.

Ongoing major regulatory reforms associated with (the what seems long past) banking crisis of 2007–8 seeks to reduce risk in the OTC derivatives market. While not yet fully implemented, the US Dodd-Frank Act of 2010 and the EU's European Market Infrastructure Regulation (of August 2012) both seek to move a large portion of OTC derivatives business (particularly interest rate swaps) back onto regulated exchanges. Also more information on OTC transactions will be officially monitored (information on trades needs to be given to so-called trade repositories that will keep data and pass to the regulators so they can monitor) so that potential systemic risk problems can be identified early. Details of the EU legislation are shown in Box 15.5.

BOX 15.5

EU Regulation of the OTC Derivatives Market – Pushing It Back on Exchange

Derivatives play an important role in the economy. But they are also associated with certain risks. The financial crisis, including the default of Lehman Brothers and the bail out of AIG, highlighted that these risks were not sufficiently mitigated, particularly in the OTC market, where almost 95% of derivatives are traded. The European Commission committed to deliver, in its Communication on Driving European Recovery of March 2009, appropriate initiatives to increase transparency in the derivatives market and to address financial stability concerns.

In September 2009, at the G-20 Pittsburgh Summit, the leaders of the 19 biggest economies in the world and the European Union agreed that 'all standard OTC derivative contracts should be traded on exchanges or electronic trading platforms, where appropriate, and cleared through central counterparties by end-2012 at the latest'.

Furthermore, they acknowledged that 'OTC derivative contracts should be reported to trade repositories and that non-centrally cleared contracts should be subject to higher capital requirements'.

The Commission's proposal meets the G20 commitments on OTC derivatives markets.

What are the objectives of the new rules?

The new rules objectives are to increase transparency in the OTC derivatives market and to make it safer by reducing counterparty credit risk and operational risk.

- To increase transparency, the new rules require that (i) detailed information on OTC derivative contracts entered into by EU financial and non-financial firms are reported to trade repositories and made accessible to supervisory authorities, and that (ii) trade repositories publish aggregate positions by class of derivatives accessible to all market participants. In the course of the negotiations the scope of the proposal has been widened to cover the reporting of both listed (i.e. non-OTC) and OTC derivatives.
- To reduce counterparty credit risk, the new rules introduce (i) stringent rules on prudential (e.g. how much capital they need hold), organizational (e.g. role of risk committees) and conduct of business standards (e.g. disclosure of prices) for central counterparties (CCPs); (ii) mandatory CCP-clearing for contracts that have been standardised (i.e. they have met predefined eligibility criteria); (iii) risk mitigation standards for contracts not cleared by a CCP (e.g. exchange of collateral).
- To reduce operational risk. Operational risk is the risk of loss resulting from inadequate or failed internal processes, people and systems, or from external events. The proposal requires the use of electronic means for the timely confirmation of the terms of OTC derivatives contracts. This allows counterparties to net the confirmed transaction against other transactions and ensure accurate bookkeeping.

How does the proposal make the derivatives market more transparent?

Currently, there is little reliable information on what is going on in the OTC derivatives market. There are no public prices available, no public information as to who is entering deals with whom, over what period of time, relating to what underlying asset or for which amounts.

Under the final text agreed in the negotiation process, detailed information on each derivatives contract traded by a financial or a non-financial firm will have to be reported to trade repositories. The data in these trade repositories will then be available to regulators, giving them a much better overview of who owes what to whom so they can spot any potential problems early and be in a position to take action if need be. In addition, trade repositories will have to publish aggregate positions by class of derivatives, providing market participants with a clearer view of the derivatives market. However, trade repositories will not publish data at trade level as the type of information is commercially sensitive.

Source: EU. (2012) Regulation on Over-the-Counter Derivatives and Market infrastructures FAQ, Press Release, March.

SUMMARY

- *Forward rate agreements* (FRAs) are a way of fixing a rate of interest for a date in the future and for a given period of time (*forward/forward*).
- The buyer is compensated by the seller if market rates on the given date exceed the given strike rate. The buyer, however, must compensate the seller if market rates fall below the strike rate.
- Borrowers seeking protection will *buy* FRAs, and investors will *sell* them. Banks make a profit through the use of a bid/offer spread.
- Essentially, the FRA is the equivalent of the exchange-traded interest rate futures contract in the OTC market.
- The FRA is for one forward period only. *Swaps* are agreements for many forward periods, for example 1 per year for the next 10 years. Again, the market rate of interest (usually LIBOR) is compared with a given strike rate, leading to a compensatory payment from one party to the other.
- The buyer in the case of the FRA is usually called the *payer* in the swap, that is, the payer of the fixed rate. The seller in the FRA is usually called the *receiver* in a swap, that is, the receiver of the fixed rate.
- The above are interest rate swaps; there are also currency swaps.
- Profit may arise for both parties from the application of the theory of *comparative advantage*. Banks will make a profit through the bid/offer spread.
- Swaps for those borrowing money are *liability swaps*; swaps for investors are *asset swaps*.
- Swaps are essentially a series of FRAs. A swap starting at a future date is a *forward swap*; an option to have a swap is a *swaption* and a swap of two floating rates is a *basis swap*.
- A borrower can be protected from an interest rate rise but still benefit from a fall using an interest rate *cap*; an investor can benefit from an interest rate rise but still be protected from a fall using an interest rate *floor*.
- The combination of a cap and floor leads to a range of interest rates for future transactions called a *collar*. Caps, floors and collars are variations on options.
- The BIS initial estimate of the notional value outstanding of the OTC derivatives market in June 2014 was $691 trillion. The cash flows associated with this activity are much lower as many participants in the market buy and sell contracts to hedge their positions – typical cash flows are around $15 to $20 trillion. The BIS estimates for the notional value outstanding of exchange-traded contracts in June 2014 was $73 trillion.
- Interest rate derivatives accounted for much the largest category for both OTC and exchange-traded derivatives.
- *Credit default swaps* (CDS) are an arrangement by which the risk of default on a bond issue, or a basket of bond issues, is sold for a given premium. This is part of the market for *credit derivatives* generally, which had been the fastest growing sector of the market until the onset of the credit crisis. The rescue of AIG in September 2008 was primarily motivated by regulatory concerns about the collapse of a business that had $440bn of (unhedged) notional outstanding CDS contracts.
- Provisions in the Dodd-Frank Act and similar EU legislation will force a large volume of OTC contracts (particularly interest rate swaps) back onto organized exchanges by the end of the decade.

REVISION QUESTIONS/ASSIGNMENTS

1   Explain the main characteristics of a forward rate agreement (FRA).

2   Analyse the features of the CDS market. Explain how CDS can be used to reduce credit risk exposure.

3   What are caps, collars and floors? Provide practical examples of these.

4   Outline the key features of swaptions. What are they used for?

REFERENCES

Bank for International Settlements (BIS). (2009) *79th Annual Report* (1 April 2008 to 31 March 2009) BIS, Basel. Provides excellent insight into global banking and financial markets, including derivative activity.

Bank for International Settlements (BIS). (2014a) *Semiannual OTC Derivatives Statistics at end-June 2014*, BIS, Basel. BIS statistics on OTC derivatives activity.

Bank for International Settlements (BIS). (2014b) *Statistics on Exchange Traded Derivatives*, September, BIS, Basel. BIS statistics on exchange-traded derivative instruments.

FURTHER READING

Chisholm, A. (2010) *Derivatives Demystified: A Step-by-Step Guide to Forwards, Futures and Options* (2nd edn), John Wiley & Sons, Chichester. Introductory to intermediate guide to derivatives.

Flavell, R. (2010) *Swaps and Other Instruments* (2nd edn), John Wiley & Sons, Chichester. Focuses on the pricing and hedging of swaps, showing how various models work in practice and how they can be built.

Hull, J.C. (2014) *Options, Futures, and Other Derivatives* (9th edn), Prentice Hall, Upper Saddle River, NJ. Classic advanced text on derivatives products. An industry standard guide.

Emerging and Growth-leading Economies (EAGLEs)

INTRODUCTION

The IMF *World Economic Outlook* (2014) highlights the economic prospects for the global economy over the coming years and underscores a general slow-down in both advanced and emerging economies.

The IMF Report reveals

- weaker than expected growth in the US, Japan and euro area. In fact, Italy is expected to shrink; there is no growth in France; and even Germany has had an unexpected fall in output.
- slower growth in Latin America, particularly in Brazil where invest-ment has fallen. Also Russia and the Commonwealth of Independent States (CIS) are experiencing a slowdown due to the general global climate and tensions in the Ukraine.
- that in China, the government has undertaken a variety of measures aimed at boosting the Chinese economy, although growth over 2014 and 2015 is still expected to exceed 7%, compared to about 3% in the US and UK (the fastest growing Western economies).
- that despite the general economic slowdown, China, India, Indonesia, Malaysia, Thailand, Vietnam and others from sub-Saharan Africa are still expected to be the fastest growing economies over the coming years.

There has been much talk of the booming emerging markets and how they will be the drivers of world economy growth in the next few decades. Previous editions of this text focused on China and India, undoubtedly important global economies, but nowadays there is wider discussion of other countries, including the so-called BRIC (Brazil, Russia, India and China) countries, as well as what BBVA Research (2012, 2014) has identified as the EAGLEs (emerging and growth-leading econo-mies). These economies and their financial features are discussed in this chapter.

EAGLES AND NEST COUNTRIES

EAGLEs are particularly interesting as they are defined as economies whose contribution to world economic growth over the next decade or so is expected to exceed the average of the leading industrialized nations, namely the G6 countries (BBVA refers to the G6, by which it means the G7 minus the US, which it excluded from the benchmark because of its size). According to BBVA Research's (2014) annual report, seven countries can be classified as EAGLEs, namely China, India, Indonesia, Russia, Brazil, Turkey and Mexico. (The figures for 2013 upgraded South Korea and Taiwan to developed economies.) They state that all EAGLEs outperform the G6 average threshold of contributing USD490bn to global growth over the next decade. See Box 16.1.

The seven EAGLEs are forecast to contribute 51% of world economic growth between 2013 and 2023, compared to 19% for the slow-growing G7 countries (and 27% for the developed world in total).

There are also the so-called EAGLEs 'nest' countries, a watch list of countries with expected incremental GDP in the next 10 years to be lower than the G6 average (G7 minus the US), but higher than the smallest contributor of that group. The 19 nest countries are

---

BOX 16.1

Rethinking Eagles

The EAGLEs concept was born in 2010 in search of giving transparency, flexibility and dynamism to the identification of the most relevant economies in the emerging world.

Our goal was to identify which emerging economies would be contributing more to world growth in the next 10 years than the largest developed economies, i.e. the G7 countries.

For the EAGLEs threshold, we excluded the US due to its extraordinary size, and we set the G6 member with the smallest contribution, as the Nest.

According to initial criteria, 45 emerging markets were selected as potential candidates to become EAGLEs or belong to the Nest group.

Exclusion of other non-advanced countries was founded on discretionary premises like their consideration as frontier markets or under extremely adverse domestic conditions such as war or international embargoes.

We decided to introduce three adjustments to our methodology. Two of these changes affect the sample of countries included in the analysis, reducing even more discretion and increasing transparency:

- We have adopted the IMF classification to distinguish emerging from developed economies.
- We now include all emerging economies in the sample of potential members of the EAGLEs and Nest groups, dropping the previous discretionary premises mentioned above.
- The third adjustment establishes a new threshold for the Nest group.

In order to avoid sensitivity to forecasts of only one country and to have a more stable threshold, we adopt a broader benchmark: non-G7 developed economies with GDP of over USD100bn PPP-adjusted in 2013.

We consider that these changes do not modify the underlying philosophy of the EAGLEs concept. In fact, we believe that the adjustments reinforce our dynamic approach, improving our metrics and adapting them to a rapidly-changing environment.

Source: BBVA Research (2014).

Egypt, Chile, Thailand, Argentina, Nigeria, Colombia, Poland, Vietnam, Pakistan, Bangladesh, Malaysia, South Africa, the Philippines, Peru, Saudi Arabia, Iraq, Iran, Kazakhstan and Qatar. They are forecast to contribute around 14% of GDP growth over the following decade and may be part of the EAGLEs in the future.

BBVA Research (2014) states that China and India 'play in another league' compared to all other countries, as they are expected to contribute 30% and 11%, respectively, to global growth between 2013 and 2023. Other revealing forecasts suggest that Turkey will contribute more than Germany, and Mexico will add more to global growth than the UK, France and Italy over the aforementioned 10-year time span.

Figure 16.1 shows the contribution to world economic growth forecasts between 2013 and 2023, highlighting the importance of China in particular. Figure 16.2 shows the growth contribution by region, illustrating that Asia (excluding Japan) will create nearly 55% of global GDP growth. North America is second but falls a long way behind, with a 12.5% contribution.

Other interesting findings from BBVA Research's (2014) report are as follows:

- China is in a better position to take further steps to become a substantially wealthier nation, although it should keep an eye on the effects of population aging and excessive leverage.
- Turkey and Mexico share balanced potential growth as well as the challenge to extend trade to faster-growth markets. Macro disequilibria are lower and reform momentum more intense in the case of Mexico, whereas in Turkey there is room to increase female participation rates and reduce the structural current account deficit.
- Brazil's main challenge is improving perceptions of its business climate, correcting macro disequilibria and reducing social inequality.
- Iran and Kazakhstan are sensitive to China's demand and commodity prices. The institutional framework has substantial scope for improvement in Iran as well.
- Prospects for productivity growth are positive in Chile and Malaysia, including a favourable investment climate and institutional framework.
- Russia and Poland face slow growth in trade partners (mainly in the EU) and, like any other country in Emerging Europe except Turkey, a shrinking labour force. However, they differ significantly in other challenges: short-term macro disequilibria are relevant for Poland, but Poland clearly outperforms Russia in terms of its institutional framework and product diversification.
- Argentina could make the best of its growth potential by improving the investment climate and the quality of infrastructure.
- Oil revenues in Qatar and Saudi Arabia keep macro vulnerabilities at low levels, and they have helped to build top-class infrastructure; however, both economies are still highly sensitive to energy prices.
- Colombia and Peru have scope to improve infrastructure quality and, as in the case of Thailand, start increasing technological efforts; the 2 Latin American countries should also aspire to increase product diversification, reduce their external deficits and smooth their uneven income distribution.
- South Africa has good fundamentals to increase productivity, but macro disequilibria and risks of social unrest are considerable due to severe demographic pressures, high unemployment and excessive inequality.
- In all these emerging markets, it is interesting to highlight the extent that foreign bank access differs from country to country. Here are some examples:
  - *China:* limits the share of a single foreign investor in a domestic bank to 20%, and will treat the entire bank as foreign if more than 25% is in non-Chinese hands. This has sparked various complaints from other countries who said

that China did not agree such limits on foreign ownership when it joined the World Trade Organization (WTO) in 2001. In mid-October 2014, the rules for foreign bank licensing were relaxed a little: they now allow foreign banks to open more than one branch at the same time in the same city, and minimum capital requirements for branches are no longer required.

- *India:* Foreign ownership is not allowed to exceed 74% of capital, and individual foreign investors' holdings are capped at 10%.
- *Malaysia:* Foreign bank ownership is capped at 30%.
- *Indonesia:* Foreigners can hold up to 99% of a local bank, although any stakes more than 25% need government approval.

▼ **Figure 16.1** *Contribution to world economic growth and current GDP size 2013 and 2023 (US$ PPP-adjusted, 2013)*

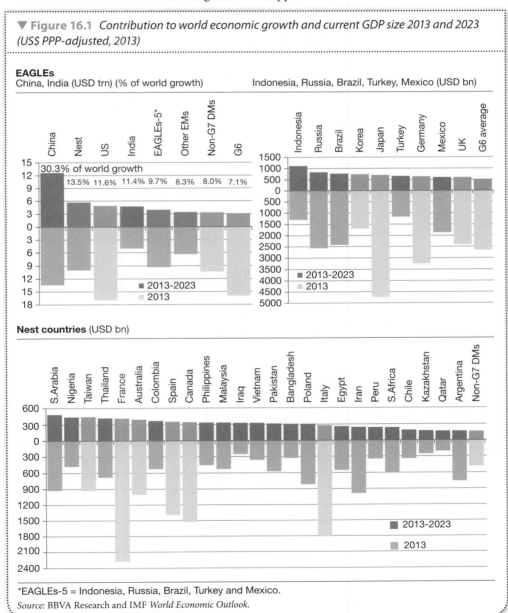

*EAGLEs-5 = Indonesia, Russia, Brazil, Turkey and Mexico.

Source: BBVA Research and IMF *World Economic Outlook.*

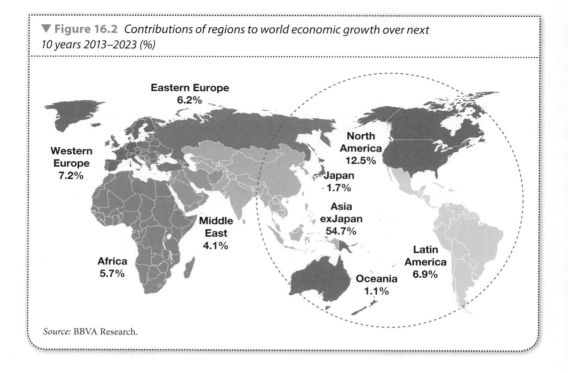

▼ **Figure 16.2** *Contributions of regions to world economic growth over next 10 years 2013–2023 (%)*

Source: BBVA Research.

Other limits to foreign ownership in Asian countries include the following:

- *Pakistan:* Foreign ownership of locally incorporated banks is limited to 49%. Foreign banks whose tier 1 capital exceeds $5bn can operate branches or wholly owned local subsidiaries.
- *Singapore:* Single shareholders need to get permission from the government to increase shareholdings in a local bank at 5%, 12% and 20% thresholds. There is no limit on overall ownership.
- *South Korea:* Foreigners can hold up to 10% stakes in domestic banks, without government approval. Non-financial foreign firms are not allowed to own more than 9%. There is no specific limit imposed on foreigners in holding stakes in banks.
- *Taiwan:* Foreign banks can own up to 100% of local banks, although banks from the Chinese mainland are restricted to a 5% limit.
- *Thailand:* Foreigners can own up to 25% before seeking approval from the central bank. A foreign bank wishing to take a stake between 25% and 49% again needs central bank authority approval. Any stake more than 49% needs Ministry of Finance approval. Single investors need central bank approval if their shareholding exceeds 10% of a local bank.
- *Vietnam:* Foreign ownership in a domestic bank is limited to 30%, with a 15% limit for a strategic investor (can be increased to 20% with government approval). A foreign bank (non-strategic) can own 10%, and a non-bank investor that is not a strategic investor can own 5%. (Note that a strategic investor goes beyond simply investing financial resources into a business, in contrast to a financial investor that just buys company and other investments but has no intention of running the business.)

▼ **Table 16.1** *Stock market capitalization of EAGLEs and nest countries*

Country	Stock market capitalization US $million 2012	Stock market capitalization %
EAGLEs		
Brazil	1,229.8	2.3
China	3,697.4	6.8
India	1,263.3	2.3
Indonesia	396.8	0.7
Mexico	525.1	1.0
Russia	874.7	1.6
Turkey	308.8	0.6
TOTAL		15.4
Nest countries		
Argentina	34.2	0.06
Bangladesh	17.5	0.03
Chile	313.3	0.58
Colombia	262.1	0.49
Egypt	58.0	0.11
Iran	140.8	0.26
Iraq	5	0.01
Kazakhstan	23.5	0.04
Malaysia	476.3	0.88
Nigeria	56.4	0.10
Pakistan	43.7	0.08
Peru	96.9	0.18
Philippines	264.1	0.49
Poland	177.7	0.33
Qatar	126.4	0.23
Saudi Arabia	373.4	0.69
South Africa	612.3	1.13
Thailand	383.0	0.71
Vietnam	32.9	0.06
TOTAL		6.00
World	54,000	100

Source: World Bank (2014) databank at http://data.worldbank.org/indicator/CM.MKT.LCAP.CD and own estimate for Iraq.

Over recent years, foreign access to many emerging markets has been liberalized. There is strong evidence to suggest that foreign banks bring technological and financial know-how to emerging markets; they also force regulators to upskill so as to oversee their foreign banks. Overall, there is a general consensus that foreign banks aid economic and financial development.

Table 16.1 illustrates the size of the stock markets in EAGLEs and nest countries. One can see that the EAGLES typically have larger capital markets than nest countries – the former accounting for seven countries with around 15% of global stock market capitalization. One can see that China, India, and Brazil have the largest markets. Of the nest countries, these have much smaller capital markets, amounting to just 6% of world capitalization, and South Africa has by far the largest market, ahead of Malaysia and Saudi Arabia.

Although the focus so far has been on the EAGLEs, there is no doubt that the two largest emerging economies in this group – China and India – pose massive opportunities to the global economy and financial system. The remainder of this chapter focuses on these economies.

CHINA AND INDIA

Goldman Sachs is on record forecasting that by the year 2050, the world's three top economic powers will be China, India and the US. Although the usual sequence is 'China . . . India', there are those who are putting their bets on India in the long term. Goldman Sachs has also said that, by 2015, India's growth rate will pass that of China. This aspect – China versus India – is examined later.

Some of the reasons for the preoccupation with these two powers will become clearer when we look at some of the facts:

- The population of China is 1.36 billion, and that of India, 1.25 billion.
- The IMF reports that China's nominal GDP was $9.5 trillion for 2013; India's was $1.9 trillion.
- China's economy has been growing by around 9% annually and India's, by 7% over the past decade or so(but the IMF expects 2014 growth to be only 4.6%). The National Bureau of Statistics in China reported growth in 2011 at 8.8%, and this has declined to around 7.5% by the end of 2014.
- China is the world's largest exporter, with $2.2 trillion of goods and services exported during 2013

(more than the whole EU ($2.1trillion) and the US ($1.6 trillion). Export growth has been around 20% annually over the past 5 years but has recently slowed to around 11% in 2014. India is ranked 17th in exporting countries, trading around $313bn.

The US continues to worry about its trade imbalance with China. The US trade gap in 2013 was $703bn. Imports from China amounted to $440bn and exports to China $122bn. Thus, China alone accounts for over 45% ([440 – 122]/703) of the US trade gap, an increase from 36% in 2008. The growth in the US trade deficit with China is estimated to have displaced 2.8 million US jobs between 2001 and 2010 alone, and the most important cause of this increase related to manipulation of the renminbi. This explains US pressure on China to revalue its currency. China's foreign exchange reserves stood at $4.1 trillion at the end of 2013. This amount exceeded the next largest holder of foreign exchange reserves – Japan, with $1.3 trillion of foreign exchange reserves.

China is, of course, far more a manufacturing economy than India; according to the World Bank it accounts for 32% of GDP, as opposed to India's 13%. China is the biggest steel producer in the world, although India's Mittal is the biggest steel company. As a result of all this manufacturing activity, China is a huge importer of raw materials, representing more than 25% of global demand for copper, aluminium, tin and zinc. China is also importing large quantities of components, in particular from Asia. By the end of 2013, China's main imports came from Japan (10%), South Korea (9.3%), other Asian countries (8.1%), the US (8%) and Germany (4.4%).

According to the BP Statistical Review of World Energy (June 2014), China is the second largest importer of oil (after the US), accounting for 12.1% of global oil consumption by 2013 (India accounts for only 4.1%) and has become the world's second largest consumer (after the US).

McKinsey expects China to be the world's biggest car market in 7 years – it is already third after the US and Japan. The expansion is similar to that of the US in the 1930s. China's 17,000 kilometres of motorway in 2000 had more than quadrupled to 85,000 by 2005. China joining the WTO in 2001 has also led to an easing of import barriers. By 2013 China had around 207 million cars registered compared with 259 million in the US.

China's exports are, however, not all low-cost, low-tech goods. According to the *Financial Times* (18 March 2014), China only accounted for a 6.5% share of high tech exports in 2000, but this had surged to a staggering 36.5% by 2013. Official Chinese figures also note that its high-tech exports account for nearly 25% of exports. But it has been noted that these figures are somewhat misleading, as they mainly consist of assembled high-tech products made with imported key parts and components, although the full value of the export is counted as a Chinese high-tech export. One well-cited example is that of the iPhone. In 2009, China exported iPhones worth $4.6bn, although it was estimated that only around 4% was the value added by Chinese workers. A similar figure has also been given for the value added on its PC exports (see Xing, 2011).

India is perhaps better known as an entrepreneurial economy, with services 57% of GDP, as opposed to China's 46% (but growing). Unsurprisingly, retail services are 15% of GDP to China's 10%. Outsourcing is big business, although revenues are still only 1% to 2% of GDP. Some two-thirds of IT services sourced outside the US go to India. Outsourcing is not just call centres but is increasingly getting more sophisticated. The wider term now is 'business process outsourcing' (BPO). This includes high-value services like medical, actuarial and research, sometimes also called 'knowledge process outsourcing'. The increasingly broad based IT sector has grown from virtually nothing 20 years ago to an industry valued at over $100 billion, with major global firms including TCS (Tata Consulting Services), Infosys, Wipro and HCL Technologies.

India's population is young, as opposed to China's with its 'one-child' policy, which is storing up trouble for future years. Around 46% of the population of India is under 25 and has grown up with satellite TV, mobile phones and PCs. India produces more graduates per year than any countries apart from China and the US. An OECD (2012) report forecast that China and India would account for 40% of all the world's graduates by 2020. Ernst &Young forecast that China's middle-class households could rise from 55 million to 500 by 2020; in India it is expected that 200 million individuals could do the same.

Looking at the above facts, we can understand the current pressure for China and India to be admitted to the G8, making it the G10.

Of course, both China and India are poor in world terms, and the growing prosperity of the middle classes contrasts with the great poverty elsewhere. In China, 669 million people live in rural areas, and in India, 850 million. China's GDP per capita was only $8,807 in 2013, and India was even less – $1,499. This compares with the UK GDP per capita of $39,337. Urban average incomes in China are around four times those in rural areas. In 2014, the World Bank set a new measure for the poverty line that amounted to $1.78 per day on a 2011 PPP basis. According to this revised methodology, India had 180 million people below the new poverty line, and China, 138 million. Before closing this section, we should, perhaps, make mention of Hong Kong and Taiwan. Although Hong Kong is clearly part of China, it still has some autonomy, and when people say 'China', they usually mean mainland China. This autonomy has served Hong Kong well in terms of inward investment and a stock market free from mainland restrictions and with more rigorous standards. Chinese companies have been the main issues, two of the biggest are China Mobile and China Construction Bank. However, Hong Kong lost the massive IPO of Alibaba (the world's biggest firm e-commerce company) when it listed on the NYSE in September 2014 raising $25bn – by October the company was valued at $250bn – the biggest company by market valuation in the world. The reason the listing went to New York was because the Hong Kong exchange could not agree on the (relatively complex) listing structure. As foreigners are not allowed to own Chinese firms, the Alibaba issue was actually for equity in a shell company located in the Cayman Islands! Anyway it did not seem to deter investors – it also reflected the conservative nature of the Hong Kong exchange compared to its New York competitor. The position with Taiwan is interesting. Officially, of course, both countries are at loggerheads, and Taiwan is fearful of overdependence on China for trade. Nevertheless, the Taiwanese are enthusiastic investors and exporters into China. Around 42% of Taiwan's $305bn exports go to China. Also, Taiwan has been a major investor in the mainland. As the government officially forbids this, investments are all funnelled via offshore centres like the British Virgin Islands. The Taiwan government tries to restrict this on the grounds of national security – too much dependence on the mainland. One important point to note is that the credit crisis and subsequent economic downturn adversely impacted the export performance of China. Exports fell by nearly 24% between August 2008 and August 2009, and the trade surplus declined 45%, to around $15bn. The largest declines in exports were to Japan, the EU and the US. This helped to reduce pressure on the Chinese currency for a revaluation and was also coupled with a massive fiscal stabilization policy that pumped nearly $600bn into the economy in order to help maintain economic growth targets. Indian exports did not seem to be hit as hard as their Chinese counterparts as a result of the credit crisis. Having said this, exports rebounded, and the World Bank found that average export growth at 8.6% between 2010 and 2014 is higher than in the previous 4 years. According to the IMF, growth for the Indian economy hit

5.6% in 2009 and reached 8.2% in 2010, falling to 7.4% in 2011. The growth rates of both China and India have fallen in 2014 but still remain way above those in major Western systems. Next we will look at the financial markets in these countries – banking and the various capital markets. We then look again at China and India and compare and contrast, analysing strengths and weaknesses. Finally, we close the chapter by looking at a key issue concerning China and India.

FINANCIAL MARKETS

Banking: General

There are broad similarities between the banking systems in China and India. Both operate capital controls and are proud to have missed the financial crises that engulfed so many Asian economies in 1997. In both cases, the sector is dominated by state-owned banks, which, in the case of China, control almost all assets, although the picture is muddied by partial privatizations and the fact that the major banks have started to list in Hong Kong, offering small stakes, such as up to a maximum of 20% for individual foreign stakeholders. According to KPMG (2013) state-owned commercial banks accounted for 44% of banking sector assets in 2013, and foreign banks held less than a 2% market share. The state banks in India control 73% of banking assets (and 83% of branches), with 20% in the private sector and the remainder foreign.

One point of difference is the sheer size of the biggest Chinese banks and the number of their branches. The five biggest Chinese banks have tier 1 capital totalling $737bn, whereas the tier 1 capital of the top four Indian banks totals $52bn. The Industrial and Commercial Bank of China has around 18,000 branches (and a 12% share of the domestic deposit market); the China Construction Bank, around 15,000; and the Bank of China, just over 11,100. The State Bank of India compares with 17,000 branches, but the next biggest in terms of branches is the Punjab National Bank, with 5,800. Of course, much of this can be explained by the totally different historical background of the two countries.

Banking: China

Nationalization as a policy received priority attention in the early years of the People's Republic of China. Banking was controlled totally by the People's Bank of China. Between 1979 and 1987, restructuring took place, leading to the setting up of other institutions; deposits tripled, and there was an enormous increase in bank loans. By 1987, many of the existing dominant banks had been set up, such as the Bank of China, the Agricultural Bank, the China Investment Bank and the China Construction Bank. Also set up was the network of cooperative banks and the People's Insurance Company of China. The People's Bank of China, which had been set up in 1948, was re-established as the central bank in 1983. The governor is Zhou Xiaochuan, who was appointed in January 2003 and reappointed again in March 2013.

China's banking sector has undergone major changes over the last decade or so. By the mid-2000s, the system was dominated by four wholly state-owned policy banks: the Agricultural Bank of China, the Bank of China, China Construction Bank (CCB), and the Industrial and Commercial Bank of China (ICBC). There were several other smaller wholly state-owned policy banks, such as Bank of Communications, China Development Bank (also known as the State Development Bank of China), the Export Import Bank

BOX 16.2

Mission of China's State-owned Policy Banks

The three state-owned banks have a distinct mission:

Agricultural Development Bank of China supports the development of agriculture and rural areas in China.

China Development Bank traditionally was responsible for raising funds for large infrastructure projects, but over the last few years it has begun to diversify its portfolio of investments as part of its transition into a commercial bank.

China Exim Bank provides financial services to promote Chinese exports (particularly of high-tech and new-tech products) and facilitate the import of technologically advanced machinery and equipment.

All three banks have a board of directors and senior officers, appointed by China's cabinet, the State Council. They report directly to the State Council and frequently rely on the State Council's directives in establishing their operational priorities

The policy banks have around 8% of total banking sector assets.

of China (China Exim Bank) and Huaxia Bank. In 2005, China began transforming the wholly state-owned banks into joint-stock corporations, a process it calls 'equitization', that were to operate as commercial banks. Today there are only three fully state-owned banks: the Agricultural Bank of China, China Development Bank and Chian Exim Bank. These three banks have specific objectives, as illustrated in Box 16.2.

The most important group of banks are the five of the previously state-owned policy banks that have been transformed into so-called joint-stock companies, with different categories of shareholders, and operate as commercial banks, although for four of the five equitized banks, the majority of the shares remain non-tradable and are still held by the People's Bank of China (PBOC), the Ministry of Finance (MOF), or other government entities (although some non-tradable stock is owned by foreigners). They are still regarded as state owned (although not 100%), as shown in Table 16.2. These five banks that account

▼ Table 16.2 *Size and ownership of China's equitized commercial banks*

Bank	Market Capital	State Holdings of Outstanding Shares	Major U.S. Holdings of Outstanding Shares
Agricultural Bank of China (ABC)	$1.019 trillion	83.13%	None
Bank of China (BOC)	$1.084 trillion	67.53%	None
Bank of Communications	$398 billion	26.52%	None
China Construction Bank (CCB)	$1.717 trillion	57.0%	Bank of America – 10.9%
Industrial and Commercial Bank of China (ICBC)	$1.810 trillion	70.7%	American Express – 0.2% Goldman Sachs – 4.9%

Source: DBS Research, previously part of DBS Vickers, but now part of DBSBank Limited.

▼ **Table 16.3** *Top 20 Chinese banks by tier 1 capital, 2013*

Bank name	Tier 1 capital $mn
Industrial & Commercial Bank of China (The) – ICBC	207,600
China Construction Bank Corporation	173,980
Bank of China Limited	149,719
Agricultural Bank of China Limited	137,400
Bank of Communications Co. Ltd	68,328
China Merchants Bank Co Ltd	41,687
China CITIC Bank Corporation Limited	37,424
Shanghai Pudong Development Bank	33,956
China Minsheng Banking Corporation	33,230
Industrial Bank Co Ltd	32,962
China Everbright Bank Co Ltd	24,764
Ping An Bank Co Ltd	12,226
Bank of Beijing Co Ltd	12,824
China Guangfa Bank Co Ltd	11,867
Hua Xia Bank Co Ltd	11,362
Bank of Shanghai	9,177
Bank of Jiangsu Co Ltd	7,814
Evergrowing Bank Co Ltd	5,181
Chongqing Rural Commercial Bank	6,027
China Bohai Bank	3,956

Source: Bankscope (July 2014).

for over 50% of the Chinese banking sector are among the largest banks in the world. The largest Chines banks by capital and assets are shown in Tables 16.3 and 16.4, respectively.

Other banks operating in the Chinese banking system include

- 12 joint-stock commercial banks, the second largest group, with 16% of the market; the biggest is China Minsheng Bank.
- 147 city commercial banks (around 8% of banking assets).
- 3,300+ rural financial institutions (11%); holdings of each individual institution are extremely small.
- 44 foreign banks accounting for around 2% market share.

Foreign ownership

There are tight controls over investments by foreign banks. A group of foreign banks may not own more than 25% of a state-owned bank, and no one foreign bank can own more than 20%. Foreign banks can deal in local currency and provide foreign exchange. If they open branches (this needs approval), they can provide much the same service to local clients as Chinese banks. They cannot, however, lend renminbi to corporates except as part of a syndicate of Chinese banks, and they may not underwrite share or bond issues.

▼ **Table 16.4** *Top 20 Chinese banks by total assets, 2013*

Country rank by assets	Bank name	Total assets $ million	Latest accounts date	World rank by assets
1	Industrial & Commercial Bank of China (The) – ICBC	3,100,051	03/2014	2
2	China Construction Bank Corporation	2,517,568	03/2014	3
3	Agricultural Bank of China Limited	2,386,291	03/2014	5
4	Bank of China Limited	2,273,581	06/2014	7
5	China Development Bank Corporation	1,341,642	12/2013	25
6	Bank of Communications Co Ltd	976,818	06/2014	31

▼ **Table 16.4** *Top 20 Chinese banks by total assets, 2013* (*continued*)

7	Postal Savings Bank of China Co Ltd	913,485	12/2013	35
8	CITIC Group	704,588	12/2013	49
9	China Merchants Bank Co Ltd	658,167	03/2014	53
10	Shanghai Pudong Development Bank	603,062	06/2014	58
11	Industrial Bank Co Ltd	602,621	03/2014	60
12	China CITIC Bank Corporation Limited	596,682	03/2014	61
13	China Minsheng Banking Corporation	528,679	12/2013	67
14	Agricultural Development Bank of China	429,779	12/2013	74
15	China Everbright Bank Co Ltd	395,760	03/2014	84
16	Ping An Bank Co Ltd	255,427	03/2013	117
17	China Guangfa Bank Co Ltd	240,864	12/2013	123
18	Hua Xia Bank Co Ltd	236,726	12/2012	126
19	Bank of Beijing Co Ltd	219,055	03/2014	134
20	Bank of Shanghai	160,219	12/2013	160

Source: Bankscope (August 2014).

By 2013, there were 44 foreign banks operating in China, with total assets amounting to some $300bn – around 2% of the banking sector. The most important among these are HSBC, Standard Chartered, Citibank, Goldman Sachs, JPMorgan Chase and Morgan Stanley.

Table 16.5 provides a summary of foreign banking in China. One can see that the number of foreign banks has more than doubled since 2004, although they still only account for fewer than 2% of banking sector assets. Foreign banks are engaged in underwriting and also have access to the retail market in credit cards, mortgages and savings products, particularly for the growing middle classes.

Since the onset of the credit crisis, however, some foreign banks have been reducing exposure to the market. Over the past couple of years or so, RBS, Bank of America and UBS, among others, have reduced their stakes in China's biggest lenders. In April 2009,

▼ **Table 16.5** *Foreign banks in China 2004–12*

	2004	2005	2006	2007	2008	2009	2010	2011	2012
Number of institutions	188	207	224	274	311	338	360	387	412
Total assets in RMB 100 m	5,823	7,155	9,279	12,525	13,448	13,492	17,423	21,535	23,804
As a % of banking sector assets	1.84	1.91	2.11	2.38	2.16	1.71	1.85	1.93	1.82

Source: PricewaterhouseCoopers HK (2014) Foreign Banks in China 2013. January.

Goldman Sachs denied rumours that it was selling its holding in Industrial and Commercial Bank of China. Despite these moves, the market still offers significant opportunities. Oliver Wyman, an international management consultancy, estimated that over the decade to 2015, China would account for 10% of the total increase in global personal financial assets, second only to the US and higher than Germany, Japan and the UK. Retail funds alone are expected to grow from $70bn to $1,000bn. Foreign banks will see little of these spoils without a Chinese partner.

Another interesting feature of the Chinese banking system is the role of underground banks, see Box 16.3.

BOX 16.3

China's Underground/Shadow Banking System

A range of entities operate illegally in China as underground banks, also known as 'shadow banking'.

Some of China's credit guarantee agencies have moved beyond their intended purpose to effectively become banks, taking deposits and providing loans.

Credit Guarantee Agencies

In the 1990s, the Chinese government authorized the creation of credit guarantee agencies. These agencies were created to improve access to credit for small and medium-sized business that had trouble obtaining loans from banks. The idea was that these businesses would be more able to receive approval for their loan applications if the credit guarantee agencies ensured that the bank would be repaid for the loan. China's credit guarantee agencies have grown rapidly, with an estimated 5,000 in operation at the end of 2010. The credit guarantee agencies have also proven to be attractive to foreign investors seeking entry into China's financial markets.

Similarly, some investment brokers and private fund managers in China have used their available capital to provide illegal commercial and personal loans. In addition, some pawn shops are providing illegal banking services to people and businesses unable or unwilling to use the legal banking system.

China's underground banks (or shadow banking system) has emerged for several reasons:

Some people choose to deposit their funds with the underground banks because they offer higher deposit rates than legal banks.

Other people use the underground banks to conceal their wealth from authorities.

Some businesses – particularly small and medium-sized companies – may apply for loans from underground banks because they cannot obtain a loan from legal banks or because the approval process takes too long.

Although the underground banks provide access to credit to individual and businesses with little or no chance of being approved for a loan by a legal bank, the credit comes at a cost.

Interest rates on loans provided by China's underground banks are often 10% per month or higher. As a result, borrowers tend to use the underground banks mainly for short-term loans in order to avoid substantial interest charges.

Another cost of doing business with underground banks is dealing with their sometimes unorthodox methods to obtain overdue loan payments, such as kidnapping family members.

China's Ministry of Finance and the State Administration of Foreign Exchange (SAFE) have been cracking down on underground banks primarily because they are seen as a major conduit for the illegal flow of overseas capital into China.

Since 2002, the Chinese authorities have shut down over 500 underground banks, with over 100 cases involving more than 200 billion yuan ($31 billion) in illegal funds.

Although officially outside of China's banking system, the potential importance of underground banks was made apparent in early October 2011 when the network of private financing in the city of Wenzhou in Zhejiang Province threatened to collapse and possibly precipitate a regional credit crisis. According to one report, a central bank survey of Wenzhou found that about 60% of local businesses and most households had loans with the city's underground banks. Unable to service their debts, a number of private business owners fled the city, leaving behind unpaid workers and outstanding bills. According to some accounts, some of the funding for Wenzhou's underground banks came from commercial loans obtained by local businesses from legitimate commercial banks. The mounting defaults on the underground loans raised the risk that these businesses would be unable to service their loans to the commercial banks.

The Wenzhou underground banking crisis was considered sufficiently important that Premier Wen Jiabao, PBOC Governor Zhou Xiaochuan and Finance Minister Xie Xuren visited the city to assess the situation. Preliminary results indicated that the prevalence of underground financing was unusually high in Wenzhou and that the local credit crisis posed no serious threat to China's banking system. However, following the officials' visit, the CBRC announced that it was looking into ways to curb the use of underground banks

Source: M.F. Martin. (2012) China's Banking System: Issues for Congress, Congressional Research Service Report to Congress, February 20, Washington, DC: Congress.

Foreign exchange

Another key issue surrounding China is the question of foreign exchange. This has received a lot of attention since the mid-2000s, especially with the US expressing anger at China's refusal to strengthen the renminbi rate against the dollar. China (like India) is proud to have shrugged off the currency crises that affected Asian markets in 1997–99. Capital controls have, to a degree, kept the currency stable and insulated from economic problems, although there are some leaks and one or two speculative inflows. The central bank has used T-bill sales to sterilize any excessive inflows in renminbi. There were some small relaxations in capital controls in April 2006, making it easier for individuals and companies to buy foreign currency and invest abroad, but the move fell well short of a complete opening up of China's capital account. Forward purchases of foreign currency are carefully controlled – there must be firm proof that they are based on genuine trade. In May 2005, a new foreign exchange trading system was launched, allowing traders to deal in eight currency pairs, not including the renminbi, such as dollars/pounds. Four pairs involving the renminbi were already permitted. Reuters has set up a platform for this. The official Chinese trading system, set up in 1994, is the China Foreign Exchange Trade System (CFETS), which involves 11 banks. For bonds denominated in foreign currencies, MTS, Europe's electronic bond trading system, has signed a letter of intent with CFETS as part of a move to develop electronic bond trading.

Having pegged the renminbi to the dollar for 10 years, the Chinese moved at last in July 2005 and announced a new system in which the currency would be kept with reference to a basket of currencies, announced later as those of key trading partners – the dollar, euro, yen and South Korean won. Others in the basket, such as the Malaysian ringgit, have a lesser weighting. The initial permitted fluctuation was only 2.1%. This hardly satisfied the Americans, who wanted something much bigger. The Chinese price advantage is such that even a 10% devaluation would make little difference, and there is clearly no chance of that. Interestingly, the Malaysians followed suit at once and announced that the dollar peg would be replaced by a basket of currencies.

When the announcement was made, Zhou Xiaochuan, the central bank governor, said that the move was only an 'initial step'. This led to hopes that it would be followed by further moves to strengthen the currency in the coming months. These hopes were dashed as no further moves took place, and by the early months of 2006, the renminbi had only risen by a further 0.8%. The US was once more banging the revaluation drum when China's trade surplus in May 2006 hit $13bn (£7.8bn), and there have been increasing concerns about trade imbalances and the undervalued currency – the country posted a record trade surplus of $80bn+ in July 2014. China has, of course, huge foreign exchange reserves. The central bank governor announced in January 2006 that it plans for a slower accumulation of reserves. He said that it was committed to encourage consumption and wanted to rebalance the economy away from net exports. The slower accumulation of reserves has not really happened: foreign exchange reserves (minus gold) stood at $1.1 trillion in December 2006, and this has increased to $3.9 trillion by 2014.

Since the mid-1990s, the Chinese authorities have directed banks to lend to a wide range of sectors as part of the development process – some of which has been very successful, but some not too good. This is reflected in the high level of non-performing loans in the system, as shown in Box 16.4.

BOX 16.4

Bank Non-performing Loans in China

Chinese banks' bad loans increased for the ninth straight quarter (by the end of 2013), to the highest level since the 2008 financial crisis, highlighting pressures on asset quality and profit growth as the world's second largest economy slows.

Non-performing loans rose by 28.5 billion **yuan** ($4.7 billion) in the last quarter of 2013, to 592.1 billion yuan, the highest since September 2008, the China Banking Regulatory Commission said in a **statement** on its website yesterday.

Bad loans accounted for 1% of total lending, up from 0.97% 3 months earlier.

Chinese banks are struggling to keep soured loans in check and extend earnings growth as the slowing economy and government efforts to curb shadow financing make it harder for borrowers to repay debt.

Standard & Poor's Ratings Services said this week that loan quality will decline in 2014, as banks remain at risk from debt-laden local government financing vehicles and manufacturers with too much capacity.

'China's economic growth turned downward with the new leadership switching policy focus to reform and risk management from emphasizing stable expansion', said Wang Yichuan, a Wuhan-based analyst at Changjiang Securities Co. 'Naturally the bad loans will increase along with the change. We expect the deterioration to continue for 2 more years'.

Chinese banks added around $15 trillion of assets, mostly through loans, in the past 5 years, equivalent to the entire US banking industry's, CBRC data show. US commercial banks held $14.6 trillion of assets at the end of September, according to the Federal Deposit Insurance Corp.

Source: © Bloomberg L.P., Bloomberg News, 14 February 2014.

Banking: India

The major banks were nationalized in 1949, and the remainder, between 1969 and 1991. The central bank, the Reserve Bank of India (RBI), was set up in 1935. At first a private bank, it, too, was nationalized in 1949. The present governor is Raghuram Rajan (a distinguished University of Chicago economist), who was appointed in September 2013 for a term of 3 years. The top 10 Indian banks, ranked by assets, are shown in Table 16.6.

▼ Table 16.6 *Top 10 Indian banks by assets, 2013*

Bank name	Group	Total assets ($bn)	Return on assets (%)
State Bank of India	State	388	0.88
ICICI Bank Limited	Private	99	1.5
Punjab National Bank	State	91	1.19
Bank of Baroda	State	73	1.24
Bank of India	State	70	0.72
HDFC Bank Limited	Private	67	1.77
Canara Bank	State	61	0.95
IDBI Bank Limited	State	42	0.82
Axis Bank Limited	Private	54	1.68
Union Bank of India	State	13	0.79

Source: The Banker (2014).

Today, the 26 public sector banks and state sector cooperatives control 72.8% of all banking assets. The biggest is the State Bank of India, with assets of $388bn. Of these state banks, the State Bank Group has over 17,000 branches; the Punjab National Bank, 5,800; Bank of Baroda, 4,500; the Bank of India, 4,500; and the Canara Bank, 5,100.

In the 1970s and 1980s, the banking sector was further developed to finance public spending and the investment needs of big companies and to take this financing away from the state itself. A number of banks were not nationalized, and there are 20 of them known as the 'old private sector banks'. Then there are the newer private banks, of which easily the most important are ICICI, the second biggest in India in asset terms ($99bn), and HDFC, the sixth biggest (assets of $66 bn). The whole private sector controls 20% of all banking assets.

Historically, there have always been some foreign banks, such as Standard Chartered (99 branches and over 6,000 employees) and HSBC. Added to these, we now have Citigroup, RBS, Bank of America, BNP Paribas, Bank of Tokyo-Mitsubishi, Deutsche Bank, Calyon Bank (from Crédit Agricole) and many others. These foreign banks control the balance of foreign banking assets. By 2013, there were 41 banks with branch operations in India (plus over 40 representative offices). Foreign owned banks controlled around 7% of banking sector assets. Any foreign ownership of Indian public sector banks is generally restricted to 10%.

Like China, India also has a large, important agricultural economy, which is served by around 2,000 urban cooperative banks and over 100,000 rural cooperative credit institutions. They make loans not only to farmers but also to cottage industries, retail trade, small businesses, professionals and for housing purposes.

For similar reasons, again just as in China, the post office plays a key role and one which could be developed much further. There are 154,000 post offices, 87% outside cities. The post office savings banks have the largest bank network of all in view of the number of branches and number of accounts. These handle various types of savings deposits, a number of national savings certificates, mutual fund sales and money transfers using Western Union Financial Services. Some 800 post offices are designated as head post offices, and a further 1,400 are departmental sub-post offices. These are computerized for counter and back office procedures. Email and Internet facilities have been set up in many villages to give the locals access to these facilities. Finally, many banks, such as ICICI, seeing the value of the network, are working with post offices to help them with IT and giving them the ability to offer a range of the bank's products.

There are also bank financial institutions and non-bank financial institutions for leasing, hire purchase, general loans and investments. These include Citigroup Financial and GE Capital.

By the end of 2012, public sector banks accounted for 67.2% of total banking sector assets, followed by private banks (18.7%) and foreign banks (6.5%). The remainder of the banking sector was taken up by regional rural banks (2.7%), co-operative banks (3.4%) and local area banks (1.5%). There were 26 public sector banks, 20 domestic private and 41 foreign banks. So it can be seen that public sector banks dominate the system. Rural and urban co-operatives banks have a relatively small share in the banking system. However, given their geographic and demographic outreach, they play a key role in providing access to financial services to low- and middle-income households in both rural and urban areas.

According to the World Bank, 65% of individuals older than 15 have no access to a formal financial institution (compared with 36% in China), and only 7% hold debit cards (and 2% credit cards). Those that access financial services tend to be wealthier urban individuals, so the situation is worse in rural areas. There is a huge scope, therefore, for banks to promote financial services and to boost inclusion, although in many cases banks are prevented from charging what they regard as the proper rate for risk. Many villages have no electricity, and those who do experience erratic supplies. To aid weaker sections of the economy, the banks have 'priority lending targets'.

In larger villages and in urban areas, there are, of course, ATMs and Internet connections. Some 80% of cheque clearing is done using magnetic ink character recognition, and there is an electronic funds transfer system covering nearly 200 centres. There are moves to reduce the processing of paper cheques by introducing electronic machines that scan the cheques and payments information being sent electronically from branches to central clearing systems, a process known as 'cheque truncation'. In March 2004, the implementation of a real-time gross settlement system started for interbank transfers. Connectivity was available at over 72,000 branches by 2012.

Credit card usage is increasing rapidly, and by 2012, the number of cardholders approached 143 million. In the mid-2000s, the central bank announced a curb on the aggressive selling of credit cards and raised the risk weighting for capital ratio purposes from 100% to 120%, although this does not appear to have restricted development of the market. A Banking Standards Board has drawn up a banking code of conduct to deal with matters such as aggressive selling and other consumer protection issues.

Foreign ownership

Foreign ownership of Indian banks is restricted, as we have mentioned. Early in 2005, the RBI suggested maximum limits of 5–10% for investment in a state bank. In spite of this, in July 2005, Rabobank was allowed to keep a 20% stake of a new private bank, Yes Bank, which needed extra capital. In the same way, in October 2002, ING acquired a major holding in one of the old private banks, Vysya, because it was in need of restructuring.

Foreign banks can set up in their own right, as we have seen, but licences for new branches are tightly controlled. Foreign ownership of India's private sector banks is not allowed to exceed 74% of paid-up capital, with individual foreign institutional investors' holding capped at 10%. Foreign banks operating in the country must be run as a branch of their headquarters. The central bank has been talking for some time about allowing foreign banks to set up subsidiaries, but this had not happened by the start of 2015. Currently, permission for opening of branches by foreign banks in India is guided by the WTO commitment to allow 12 new branches in a year.

In view of the increasing number of people in the middle classes, the prospects for consumer finance are excellent and foreign banks are champing at the bit. Citigroup's Sanjay Nayar has commented: 'Since our focus is on organic growth, we'd like three times as many branches as we get'. Société Générale has moved in and opened branches in Delhi and Mumbai and has set up private banking for the new high-net-worth individuals.

Although Indian banks do investment banking, generally their expertise is less than the foreign investment banks who see good prospects for underwriting, custodial services, asset management and general non-commercial banking. Credit Suisse First Boston has returned after an absence of 4 years, following an alleged price-fixing scandal. It has started equity and brokerage services but is not looking for a joint venture. HSBC and Standard Chartered have long had a substantial presence in the market for high-net-worth individuals and business. Deutsche Bank has also made substantial inroads in recent years.

Foreign exchange

The Indian currency floats, but there are exchange controls on capital account transactions. Like China, India is proud that it survived the Asian financial crisis of the late 1990s unscathed. The RBI has no target for full convertibility but wants to maintain 'orderly conditions'.

In June 2000, Parliament passed the Foreign Exchange Management Act to promote 'the orderly maintenance of the foreign exchange market in India'. The government manages current account transactions, and the RBI, the capital account. Foreign investors may bring in repatriatable funds, and companies may borrow on international markets subject to RBI approval. Indian residents and firms may not freely convert the rupee in order to acquire assets or lend funds overseas.

High-deficit financing is crowding out the private sector. The combined fiscal deficit of the government and the states is about 8%, and interest payments are 16% of government spending, which limits the room for much needed investment in infrastructure, health and education. The banks have a statutory liquidity ratio, which means they must keep government securities as 25% of net demand and time liabilities. In practice, the figure is believed to be much higher and reflects this excessive government expenditure.

There is poor contract enforcement, weak bankruptcy laws and a much needed credit information database, although this is being set up. To be fair, exactly the same criticisms can be applied to China, if not more so. The end result is that public sector bank managers are conservative when it comes to private sector clients. We have already mentioned the tight grip that moneylenders have over the poor who have no bank accounts. Priya Basu, senior financial economist at the World Bank, comments: 'The banking system has traded efficiency for stability'. Underperforming public banks are being sheltered from the full blast of competition. The system has not changed much over the past few years, and even by 2014, as we noted earlier, around three-quarters of the banking sector still remains under state ownership.

Capital Markets

Equities: China

The main stock exchanges are in Shanghai and Shenzhen. Shares are divided into three main classes:

1 'A' shares are quoted in renminbi and available to domestic investors, but there is restricted access only for 71 'qualified' foreign investors.
2 'B' shares are quoted in hard currencies, mainly in US and Hong Kong dollars.
3 'H' shares are those quoted in Hong Kong.

The stock market regulator is the China Securities Regulatory Commission (CSRC).

Traditionally, the bulk of shares listed on these markets were from state firms. The government has made strong moves to liberalizing their markets by promoting private listing and foreign investment. Over time the purchase of 'A' shares by foreigners was being eased. They must be 'strategic' investors taking a minimum stake of 10% and prepared to hold the shares for three years. The approval of CSRC is still required. There were also strong rumours of a trial programme to merge the status of 'A' and 'B' shares, but no date was given. As a result of this, there was a new feeling of optimism. Another interesting piece of news came in the following month. Air China, already quoted in Hong Kong, was seeking permission to issue new shares on the Shanghai Exchange.

A key feature of Chinese markets is their extreme volatility. In July 2005, a 4-year, 55% decline was arrested by government intervention just as the Shanghai Composite Index was poised to breach the 1,000-point barrier. The market then rose sharply, with the index breaching 6,000 in October 2007 and subsequently falling by 72% by October 2008. Since then, it has hovered between 2,300 and 3,500 – by late 2014, it stood at 2,478. Typically, it is a market characterized by booms and busts apparently unrelated to the country's overall economic performance. Foreign investors are restricted, so the boom-and-bust cycle is pretty much influenced by domestic investors.

This extreme volatility needs to be resolved somehow, particularly as China has a looming pensions crisis and equity and bond assets are needed for investment by pension funds.

Equities: India

India has 22 stock exchanges and a National Stock Exchange (NSE) in Mumbai. The NSE was set up in 1993 as the first debt market exchange for T-bills, government securities and corporate bonds. The Bombay Stock Exchange is really the Mumbai Stock Exchange but is still known as the BSE. It is the dominant equity market, set up in 1875, and is thus the oldest in Asia (Tokyo 1878). Its main share index, the SENSEX 30, is the one that is normally quoted. There is also the Over the Counter Exchange of India for the listing of small and medium-sized companies. The regulator is the Securities and Exchange Board of India, and the market is transparent and well regulated.

The BSE lists over 5,500 companies and has been going through a boom time. The SENSEX Index, which was 3,300 in March 2003, was about 10,400 by late February 2006, although it suffered a fall in May/June 2006 like other world markets. Since then, the SENSEX rose dramatically and touched an all-time peak in January 2008 of 21,078, before falling to 8,800 in February 2009; however, it has risen strongly since, hitting 16,883 in mid-September 2009 and continuing to fluctuate around the 17,500 level. In November 2014, it stood at 28,047. There is a large amount of M&A activity and much foreign investment in private firms. There were record inflows of foreign purchases feeding the increases in recent years, although various commentators believe what is really needed is more *domestic* investment. Securities are held in a dematerialized form, and shares are traded on the BSE using their screen-based system, BOLT. Members may act as either brokers or market makers and settlement is T+2. Debt instruments are also traded on the BSE as well as the NSE. Derivatives are traded and will be covered later.

The Congress Party coalition needs the support of the communists, but they are strongly opposed to the privatization of state enterprises. But for this, the activity of the BSE would be even bigger than it is.

Bonds and money markets: China

The bond markets are dominated by state bonds. They are sold by auction to banks, non-bank financial institutions, insurance companies and corporates. There is secondary trading on the stock exchanges, and both primary and secondary use electronic trading. China's first inflation-linked bond was in 1988, well ahead of the US in 1997. The government also issued a $1.7bn (£1.02bn) Eurobond on the Hong Kong Stock Exchange in mid-2004, split into 5- and 10-year segments. There are also stripped bonds domestically. There are some corporate issues, including convertibles, but the market is small and needs developing as a source of capital for corporates. The Asian Development Bank and the International Finance Corporation became the first foreign issuers of renminbi bonds in 2005. Perhaps inevitably, they have become known as 'panda' bonds.

Following guidelines issued by the central bank, November 2005 saw the start of asset-backed bonds in China. The China Construction Bank issued 3 billion renminbi of residential mortgage-backed securities, organized by Standard Chartered Bank. The China Development Bank followed with a collateralized loan obligation issue. In each case, the collateral offered was scrutinized by the main rating agencies. The bonds were aimed at domestic investors.

There are some corporate bonds, but the market suffers from poor liquidity. They tend to be short term and face a long and difficult approval process.

As regards money markets, there is trading in T-bills, but the markets in certificates of deposit and commercial paper are embryonic. Growth is nevertheless expected. Collins Stewart Tullett entered into a joint venture with the state-controlled Shanghai International Group to launch the country's first interdealer broker together with ICAP, the world's biggest interdealer broker. These moves clearly foresee a growth in the markets for foreign exchange, bonds and commercial paper.

Bonds and money markets: India

As usual, the market is dominated by government issues, with T-bills from 14 days to 12 months, and 5-, 10- and 20-year bonds. Trading is by order matching screens on BSE and NSE. Some bonds have been stripped. There are also bonds issued by the Indian states. In the primary market, the RBI used to take up any bonds not sold at the auctions, but this is dying as a proper system of primary dealers (17) is being set up. Government bond trading dominates the bond sector.

Asset-backed bonds are traded. For example, the Indian Railways Finance Corporation securitized lease receivables with a 10-year issue in April 2005 arranged by Citigroup. Mortgage-backed bonds are also popular. A substantial number of mortgage-backed bonds and other securities have been issued in the Indian market, and securitization techniques are widespread. The market boomed until the onset of the credit crisis – issuance of such instruments has been virtually non-existent since the start of 2008.

In the money markets, there are repos, reverse repos, commercial paper and certificates of deposit. There has been a big increase in the latter, as stamp duty has been withdrawn and the tax is no longer deducted at source. FRAs are used, and the interbank reference rate is MIBOR.

Derivatives: China

Previous losses and scandals have led to the authorities taking an extremely cautious attitude to derivatives trading. For example, in November 2004, China Aviation Oil, an importer of fuel oil, collapsed under the weight of $550m worth of derivative losses. The China Banking Regulatory Commission (CBRC) first issued guidelines in March 2004 that outlined rules regarding derivatives usage by corporations. More recently, the CBRC issued a 'Notice on Further Strengthening the Risk Management of Derivative product Transactions between Banking Financial Institutions and Institutional Clients' on 31 July 2009, which imposed various restrictions on the ability of onshore banks to engage in derivatives transactions with onshore corporate clients, together with various new administrative obligations for both clients and banks. Financial derivative trading has only recently been allowed and includes a variety of contracts including renminbi bond futures, interest rate swaps, FRAs and various options products. In February 2010, the China Securities Regulatory Commission officially approved the Hushen 300 Index futures contracts and business rules on the China Financial Futures Exchange, and Hushen 300 Index futures contracts were first traded on April of the same year. Despite recent developments, Chinese derivatives activity accounts for less than 0.35% of global derivatives business.

Traditionally, the focus has been on commodity derivatives. The nation's three commodity futures exchanges (Zhengzhou, Shanghai and Dalian) traded a record 471 million contracts in 2011 and 69% more than in 2007, according to the China Futures Association.

The People's Bank of China approved a so-called master agreement (in March 2009) to govern derivatives. It is hoped that the standardization of legal documents on which trades are based will help to expand a market currently focused on commodities futures. Rice futures contracts began trading in April 2009 on the Zhengzhou Commodity Exchange. China, the world's biggest grower of rice, has expanded the range of futures contracts to allow producers to hedge against price swings.

Early in 2009, a joint venture between ICAP and China Foreign Exchange Trading System & National Interbank Funding Centre announced that it had started handling foreign exchange derivatives denominated in yuan.

The three main exchanges are in Shanghai, Dalian and Zhengzhou. The Shanghai Futures Exchange operates key contracts for copper, aluminium, rubber and fuel oil. It has over 230 members and 300 distant trading terminals worldwide. It also has an alliance with the CME. Box 16.5 details other recent developments.

Derivatives: India

In India, financial derivative trading is well established, with interest rate options, futures and swaps, mainly OTC. The main exchanges are the NSE and BSE. The BSE offers index futures and options on the SENSEX Index, which began in 2000. There are stock options on the shares of over 100 companies. Having sensed a demand for shorter dated options, weekly stock options were introduced in 2004. Bond futures and options are traded on the NSE. Both exchanges trade electronically, as for equities.

BOX 16.5

Recent Developments in China's Derivatives Market

China's commodity derivative markets are well established.

According to the World Federation of Exchanges, nearly two-thirds of total commodity futures traded globally are on Chinese exchanges, with these exchanges making up three of the largest five commodities derivatives exchanges globally. In addition the Hong Kong RMB denominated derivatives market has also grown rapidly.

The offshore renminbi (or CNH) market (mainly based in Hong Kong) has grown rapidly to the extent that some 146 authorized Hong Kong institutions held some 860.472 billion CNH, or the equivalent of $141.8516 billion USD, in time and demand deposits as of December 2013. CNH spot, swaps, forwards, futures and options market liquidity has improved significantly, with some OTC estimates around CNH average trading volume (ATV) at nearly $30bn combined.

The BIS Triennial Central Bank Survey of FX turnover puts RMB average daily volume (ADV) at $120 billion but does not break out CNH from onshore RMB (known as CNY).

SWIFT estimates that trading in RMB will account for upwards to 5% of the FX spot and derivatives business by 2020, up from the current level of 1.39%.

In January 2014, the Peoples Bank of China published a document establishing the Central Counterparty Interest Rate Swaps Market. In March, the central counterparty service was digitized and became known as the X-Swap.

INSURANCE: CHINA AND INDIA

Emerging markets generally are showing strong growth in insurance, with rates of more than 6% for life business and 8.3% for non-life. The corresponding figures for industrialized nations are 0.3% (Swiss Re, 2014). In China and India, insurance is growing quickly, from modest beginnings. Although growth rates are high, in world terms the market is still small. In 2013, the premium per capita stood at $201 (life and non-life) for China and $52 for India, against a world average of around $652. The total value of premiums is shown in Table 16.7 – $278bn in China and $66bn for India in 2013.

▼ **Table 16.7** *Total premiums for life and non-life insurance, China and India, 2013*

Category	China $mn	India $mn
Life insurance	152,151	52,174
Non-life insurance	125,844	13,401
TOTAL	277,995	65,575

Source: Swiss Re (2014). China is ranked 4th in the world for total insurance premium, compared to India at 15th. (The US at $1,259bn, Japan at $531bn and the UK at $330 bn are the top three.)

In China, the market is controlled by the China Insurance Regulatory Commission (CIRC), set up in 1998. In India, it is the Insurance Regulatory and Development Authority, set up in 1999.

Both markets are emerging from a history of nationalization but are moving towards liberalization. China joined the WTO in 2001 and – as part of this – promised to improve access for foreign insurers who were first admitted in 1992, the first being AIG. Figures from China's CIRC show that 47 foreign-funded insurance organizations from 15 countries and regions have set up 121 operating branches in the country. By the end of 2013, the market share of foreign-funded companies in China's insurance market was around 5% of the life and 2% of the non-life business. The market is dominated by state insurers, of whom the biggest are the People's Insurance Company of China, China Life Insurance and Ping An Insurance, all of which are listed abroad. The top five insurers have 70% of the domestic insurance market. A remaining 60 firms cover the rest. Foreign insurers can own up to 50% of a life insurer in China, but many hold stakes of less than 25%, so the businesses can be classified as domestic insurers, which makes it easier obtaining licenses when entering new provinces or cities. Expanding as a foreigner alone is difficult both because of regulatory barriers and the need to forge new relationships in new markets.

In India, foreign insurers can take a holding in a local insurer of 26%, and there are over 25 joint ventures. The first private Indian life insurer without a foreign partner was Sahara in March 2004. Again, as in China, the state sector dominates, with the Life Insurance Company of India in the life business and New India Insurance, National Insurance, Oriental Insurance and the United India Insurance Companies in the non-life business. In the life business, there are three successful private companies (helped by a foreign joint venture) – ICICI Prudential, Bajaj Allianz and Birla Sun Life. Other foreign companies include Allianz, AIG and Tokyo Marine and Fire in non-life insurance and Allianz, AIG, Aviva and Standard Life in the life business. Lloyd's has also opened an office in India.

Prominent foreign insurers in China are Allianz, Tokio Marine and Fire, Winterthur, Liberty Mutual and RSA in non-life business; and in life, Aegon, AIG, AXA, Generali, Nippon Life, Skandia and Aviva.

Bancassurance (banks selling insurance) is widespread in both markets and accounts for more than 60% of life sales in China and 30% in India.

One problem for both economies is the occurrence of natural catastrophes – both are heavily underinsured. Foreign expertise in underwriting is needed and much strengthening of capital.

Again, both markets have seen the practice of imposing price controls. In China, at least, this seems to be easing following the release of price limits on motor insurance (car usage has gone up so fast that the authorities now wish to cool this market). India still imposes price controls over 75% of the market. China set high price levels to discourage cut-throat competition. India set prices at low levels to protect the consumer, leading to cross-subsidization over different lines of business.

Pensions is another key issue. The one-child policy leaves China with a massive future problem as the population is ageing rapidly. Some 620 million workers are not covered, and there is a growing demand from the better-off for private cover. There is now a new legal framework by which approved institutions can act as custodian, asset manager and fund holder for company schemes. Some tax concessions are available. The first licences were given to 15 investment managers to offer new corporate pension schemes. Four out of the 15 are joint ventures with foreign companies. Pension contributors are to be held in a legally distinct pension fund governed by trust law.

In India, no integral pension or social security schemes exist. The huge agricultural army of farmers and labourers is not covered. For better-off workers, there is an Employee Provident Fund Organisation, and there are civil service pension schemes for central and local government. About 20% of the working population are not covered. New government employees are covered by a defined contribution and fully funded pension scheme. Non-government employees can join on a voluntary basis. The Pension Fund Regulatory and Development Authority was set up in October 2003 to oversee pension reform issues.

Private sector suppliers clearly have a role to play in both markets. Pension products for the better-off are now available. The challenge is the large rural sector and how to reach it. The fact that their incomes are very volatile presents another difficulty.

China and India have great potential for insurance. Standards need to be raised and more emphasis placed on the insurer's asset/liability management skills. Allowing freer foreign access would help.

In order to grow, the business needs a predictable environment, which includes economic stability, legal certainty, stability of institutions and enforcement of property rights.

CHINA AND INDIA: A COMPARISON

China and India are home to almost two-fifths of humanity and are two of the world's fastest growing economies. In terms of GDP, China is three times as big but may not be able to keep up the current rate of growth indefinitely. Some see India moving ahead faster at some point.

In making a comparison, one of the first things that Westerners seize on is that China is a communist state, and India is a democracy. An article in *The Economist* (25 February 2006) noted that India had stability but that 'China's transition to democracy could be traumatic'. It is not clear why it is assumed that China will, in the end, become democratic. Nor is it clear that, in terms of economic development, being a democracy is necessarily an advantage.

Within reason, if the Chinese government decides to do something, it will do it. That's not to say that there may not be some internal dissent at government level. The fact that the share prices of some Chinese companies on the Hong Kong Stock Exchange have gone up has led to criticism that the state's assets are being sold to 'foreigners' too quickly. This has led to a slowdown in approval of some foreign moves into Chinese banks. In addition, there is grave concern among many prominent party members that the rich–poor gap is being closed too slowly. Nevertheless, broadly speaking, the government can make a decision and get on with it. China has 130 airports handling 1 million passengers a year and has another 55 planned by 2020. A major drag on Indian economic development is the poor infrastructure. India's roads are gridlocked, rubbish goes uncollected, sewage pollutes the water and bare power lines run through the slums. The big software houses, India's new 'jewels in the crown' – like Tata, Infosys and Wipro – are planning future expansion elsewhere. Electricity is a key issue for infrastructure. Power supply is often erratic, and only 50% of households have connections to the grid. Both central and state governments have a role here, and government action on this and other issues can be frustrated by lack of action by the states. Apart from electricity, there are problems with roads, airports, phones, rail freight and ports. The World Bank is providing money to assist with a massive road and rail track investment programme. Rail freight costs are said to be two-thirds higher than in China, and airport modernization is badly needed, although a start is being made. The government has awarded various licences for private sector operators to run freight services using railway infrastructure.

This is not to say that everything in the garden is rosy in China. Both countries are enormous and face massive problems with infrastructure. One difference, however, is that India spends some 4–5% of GDP on infrastructure, whereas China spends 8–10%. Where is the money to come from? Central and state government deficits are being cut as it is, and anything spent on infrastructure is not spent on anything else. Drewry Shipping Consultants Ltd estimates that India loses 1.2% of GDP due to poor infrastructure and coalition politics. Other estimates range as high as 3%, so the position is serious.

One area where India scores is graduate education. India produces some 6 million graduates a year, and China, 5 million – both large figures. India, however, has the big advantage in a global world of the use of the English language. In spite of the growing use and teaching of Hindi, even internally the use of English facilitates communications between one part of the country and another. There is also the question of the quality of the graduates. There have been some criticisms of the quality of Chinese graduates because of their receiving what is regarded as 'highly theoretical' training. A McKinsey report concluded that a shortage of well-trained graduates may hinder China's development of service industries, such as IT. A study found that less than 10% of graduates had the skill to work for a foreign company, compared with 25% in India.

Capital markets – equities and bonds – need to be developed much further in both countries. China has laid the foundations for the development of its stock markets, but extreme volatility and speculation by domestic investors are major causes for policy concern. The corporate bond and derivatives markets are underdeveloped. India's stock markets appear less volatile (not difficult) and better developed, but it is foreign, rather than domestic, money that has sustained this. Although there are plenty of private companies, the corporate bond market is not strong and, surprisingly, as a percentage of GDP, is less than China's – although bigger in absolute terms, as GDP is much smaller. In Malaysia, the corporate bond market is 40% of GDP, and in South Korea, over 45%. In China, it is just over 12%, and in India, 1.0%, so there is a long way to go. Finance in both countries comes overwhelmingly from a bank sector dominated by state banks.

India suffers badly from bureaucracy. On average, it takes 89 days to start up a business in India, 41 days in China and 18 days in the UK, according to the *World Bank Group Entrepreneurship Database 2007*. There are widespread demands for registration and licensing as well as restrictive labour laws. Any company with more than 100 employees cannot declare redundancies without approval from local labour boards. The World Bank study ranked countries in terms of ease of doing business. India ranked 116 out of 155 countries, between Indonesia and Albania.

Clearly, China is not free from bureaucracy. For example, a host of prices are state controlled – water, oil, power, cable TV fees, land, education, pharmaceuticals, telecommunications, gold and precious metals, air tickets and even parking fees for cars and bicycles. It is all controlled by the National Development and Reform Commission. The problem is that if you don't ration oil, for example by price, then you get rationing through shortages. This is exactly what has happened as retail prices have been kept artificially well below the world level.

China attracts far more foreign investment than India, but then China is much more a manufacturing economy. Even so, the attitude is different. China seems to realize that foreigners and foreign money can be useful and is prepared to accept them on that basis. In the financial arena, we have seen that foreign firms are allowed bigger shares in banks and brokerages when these firms are in trouble and need recapitalizing. Interestingly, there is an aphorism from the Qing dynasty, which says, 'Make the past serve the present, make the foreign serve China.' Walmart has had a Chinese presence for some time and is estimated to spend $25bn there.

India puts caps on foreign direct investment in aviation, insurance, coal mining and the media, and only franchises are allowed in the important area of retailing. Here, overseas groups can set up wholesale or retail operations for one product range only, for example Louis Vuitton. The entry of firms like Tesco and Walmart was banned until 2007, even though their entry would have created jobs, and much of what they sold would be bought in India. Some 96% of all retailing in India is still done in small stores and bazaars. There are now some 180 shopping 'malls', but this is still small for such a big country.

Poverty is a major issue in both countries and a source of social discontent as the gap between the rural poor and prosperous urban middle classes grows. China has abolished direct agricultural taxes, which have existed for hundreds of years, and announced a 'New Deal' for farming. However, the announcement of further subsidies for unproductive farming communities is itself controversial. Arundhati Roy, the outspoken Indian novelist, says that she sees India as a land where emaciated labourers dig trenches to lay fibreoptic cable by candlelight. The boom has yet to reach the two-thirds of the population who live in the country. The argument that democracy is assisting economic development is also not massively persuasive. The democratic process should facilitate policy actions more in line with public expectations; however, it is far from clear whether democracy leads to decisive government policy making in India. There is new hope in the election in 2014 of Narendra Modi as Prime minister, known as India's 'Margaret Thatcher' for his work in his home province of Gujarat. However, he has now to work within the confines of coalition government, and there is strong resistance to any relaxation of labour protection laws from leftist parties.

In summary, both countries claim to be making reforms to plug weaknesses. India feels that it is tackling bureaucracy, its mass illiteracy and ghastly roads. It claims as plus factors the use of English and managers and technicians who can think for themselves. As China's working population shrinks, India's will be bigger. In the case of China, one key problem for future years is the effect of the one-child policy. The United Nations calculates that today there are 9.1 workers for every pensioner, but in 40 years there will be only 2.1, when China will have 100 million people aged over 80. This will put an enormous demand on resources, and there will come a point when India's working population exceeds that of China. Huge overcapacity, especially in automobiles and steel, is another problem in

China and may lead to a slowing of growth for a time while things stabilize. The Chinese authorities have introduced various financial reforms:

- Scrapping of farm taxes
- A reduction in the rate at which income tax kicks in
- Scrapping the 11-year-old peg against the dollar in favour of a managed float
- The launch of market makers for currency trading and a widening of the market for non-renminbi currency pairs
- The launch of commercial paper and mortgage-backed securities
- Approval for banks to trade currency swaps and forwards
- Establishment of the first money broker
- The first 'panda' bonds for international borrowers in the renminbi
- The start of equity market reorganization
- The agreement to bring its national accounting standards in line with internal rules
- Plans to develop Shanghai as an international financial centre

These reforms are ongoing; nevertheless, major advances still need to be made in a number of areas, including restructuring the public sector, reform of company law (to remove barriers to the entry of new firms), better property rights, proper bankruptcy laws and further development of the financial markets.

It is all for the future, of course, but China is a nation with a reputation for the patient long-term view: 'The journey of a thousand miles begins with one step'. There is also the no doubt apocryphal story of a modern Chinese statesman who, when asked what effect the French Revolution had had on the development of China, replied: 'It is too early to say'. If this view of China was ever true, it certainly seems to have changed now.

CHINA AND INDIA: A THREAT?

The growth of Asia, and China and India, in particular, tends to be seen as a threat. The Americans are particularly paranoid about China in this respect. As well as the fears about the undervalued currency creating major trade and other imbalances, hawks worry about China's military build-up, and there was a considerable overreaction to the attempt by China National Offshore Oil Company (CNOOC), to buy a relatively minor US firm in the same business, Unocol. Congress went into panic mode, seeing Unocol as a 'strategic asset', and the Chinese withdrew. China has also made investments in steel in Brazil, has bought the TV manufacturing business of Thomson, the mobile handset-making side of Alcatel and the PC business of IBM. On the other hand, the bid for the US firm Maytag failed, as did bids for Canada's Norands and Pakistan Telecom. The D'Long conglomerate bought several foreign brands, including Murray lawnmowers and part of bankrupt aircraft maker Fairchild Dornier, before collapsing under the weight of its debts. The idea that China is 'buying the world' looks silly now. For them, it's a way of learning modern business practices – management skills, marketing, brand names and strategic thinking. It's a bit like Japanese buying in the 1980s, such as the Rockefeller Center in New York, and references to unfair trade practices, 'dumping money' – and even a 1991 book with the alarming title *The Coming War with Japan* by George Friedman and Meredith Lebard.

A more optimistic view comes from Roger Bootle, MD of Capital Economics, whose book *Money for Nothing* (2003) has a chapter on this same subject – should we fear Asia?

He prefers to stress the opportunities to sell to Asia and their rising middle classes with an appetite for cars, computers, food, drink, professional services, retail financial products, pharmaceutical products, luxury branded goods and knowledge-based services. In the case of the UK, for example, it is interesting that while exports of goods have at best marked time, our exports of services to Asia have risen by almost 60% since 1997. The new Asian middle classes want retail financial services – loans, mortgages, insurance and pensions. Other opportunities outside finance will also increase. Roger Bootle reminds us of Ricardo's 'theory of comparative advantage'. Even if the Chinese were to prove more efficient at manufacturing everything, we can still concentrate on the areas where the comparative advantage is least. In any case, as prosperity grows over 20–30 years, so the price advantage will reduce.

Although there remain some concerns that the prospects for China, and particularly India are not as bright as we once thought (See *The Economist*, 8 November 2014) their prospects appear better than the other BRICs countries. The article, entitled 'The Dodgiest Duo in the Suspect Six', highlights the problems of the BRICs countries (as well as Thailand and Indonesia). The dodgy duo are identified as Brazil and Russia. All the countries discussed (apart from China) have problems of dual deficits – budget and current account – as well as high inflation. All (apart from China) are also reliant on foreign capital inflows. However the main conclusion is that the prospects for India and China are secure (less so for Brazil and Russia where there currencies are weakening rapidly).

Anyway, the build-up of the aforementioned Asian economic powerhouses means that the west may lose influence, but not prosperity. We must allow workers to transfer from those industries where we cannot compete to those where we can. We should also not forget that over the past 10 years, the prices of clothing, footwear and a host of other consumer items have fallen 40%, giving a boost to real incomes. It's a nice positive note on which to finish.

SUMMARY

- China and India undoubtedly remain important global economies, but nowadays there is greater discussion of other countries, including the so-called BRIC (Brazil, Russia, India and China) countries, as well as what BBVA Research (2012, 2014) has identified as the EAGLEs (*emerging and growth-leading economies*).
- EAGLEs are particularly interesting as they are defined as economies whose contribution to world economic growth over the next decade is expected to exceed the average of the leading industrialized nations (according to BBVA Research, the G7 minus the US).
- Seven countries achieved EAGLE status: namely China, India, Indonesia, Russia, Brazil, Turkey and Mexico.
- The seven EAGLEs are forecast to contribute 51% of world economic growth between 2013 and 2023,

compared to 19% for the slow-growing G7 countries (and 27% for the developed world in total).
- There are also the so-called EAGLEs 'nest' countries, a watch list of countries with expected incremental GDP in the next 10 years to be lower than the G6 average (G7 minus the US), but higher than the smallest contributor of that group. The 19 nest countries are Egypt, Chile, Thailand, Argentina, Nigeria, Colombia, Poland, Vietnam, Pakistan, Bangladesh, Malaysia, South Africa, the Philippines, Peru, Saudi Arabia, Iraq, Iran, Kazakhstan and Qatar. They are forecast to contribute around 14% of GDP growth over the following decade, and may be part of the EAGLEs in the future.
- China and India 'play in another league' compared to all other countries as they are expected to contribute

30% and 11%, respectively, to global growth between 2013 and 2023. Other revealing forecasts suggest that Turkey will contribute more than Germany, and Mexico will add more to global growth than the UK, France and Italy over the aforementioned 10-year time span.

- The population of China is 1.36 billion, and that of India, 1.25 billion.
- The IMF reports that China's nominal GDP was $9.5 trillion for 2013; India's was $1.9 trillion.
- China's economy has been growing by around 9% annually and India's by 7% over the past decade or so, although the IMF is suggesting only 4.6% for 2014. The National Bureau of Statistics in China reported growth in 2011 at 8.8%, but this had declined to around 7.5% by the end of 2014.
- China is the world's largest exporter, with $2.2 trillion of goods and services exported during 2013, more than the whole EU ($2.1trillion) and the US ($1.6 trillion). Export growth has been around 20% annually over the past 5 years but has recently slowed to around 11% in 2014. India is ranked 17th in exporting countries, trading around $313bn.
- China is a large manufacturing economy, and its growth has led to substantial imports of raw materials, including oil and also imports of components from neighbouring Asian economies. Exports are not just of low-cost, low-tech goods, but computers, digital phones and similar products, although the bulk of high-tech exports are assembled from high-tech imports (like iPhones).
- India is an entrepreneurial economy with skilled English-speaking graduates and has a high reputation in the field of IT. It has become a major centre for outsourcing. It is also a young economy. China will face major future problems as a result of its one-child policy.
- Both economies have massive rural populations and face the problem of the contrast between the growing prosperity of the middle classes and the extreme poverty in rural areas.

- Hong Kong retains some autonomy. When people speak of China, they usually mean mainland China.
- Banking in both economies is dominated by state sector banks, and this has led to much wasteful lending to local enterprises. Foreign ownership is carefully controlled. China's state banks are gradually going public, using the Hong Kong Stock Exchange and releasing only a minor percentage of shares for sale.
- There are a large number of rural and urban cooperatives in China and India and also many thousands of post offices, which both countries would like to see playing a larger role in providing banking services.
- The renminbi is kept within a tight band in a basket of currencies, whereas the rupee floats; but both countries impose tight capital controls. The strength of the renminbi has been criticized by the US and the IMF as a key factor in promoting global financial imbalances.
- Capital markets are relatively underdeveloped in both countries. China's stock market is highly volatile, driven by speculative domestic investors. China's top companies float in Hong Kong. India's Mumbai Stock Exchange is more developed, but also subject to wild swings. Bond markets are dominated by state bonds in both economies, and the corporate bond market is weak. Banks are far too dominant as a source of finance, and stronger capital markets are badly needed in China and India.
- Derivative markets in China primarily exist for commodities, although other financial derivatives are emerging. In India, financial derivatives are well established.
- Insurance is growing rapidly in both markets, and many foreign insurers are represented. Financing pensions for the rural poor is a major future challenge for both countries.
- The growth of China and India can be seen as a threat to employment in the US and Europe. At the same time, the influx of low-cost goods reduces inflation and raises living standards. The opportunity is there to sell services, general and financial, to the fast-growing, prosperous middle classes.

REVISION QUESTIONS/ASSIGNMENTS

1 Highlight the key features of the EAGLEs. Which countries are expected to grow the fastest and why?

2 Outline the prospects for derivatives markets in two EAGLEs of your choice.

3 Examine how the economic development of the EAGLEs impacts on the US and Europe.

4 Analyse the main differences between the financial systems of China and India. Which one has the greatest growth potential over the next decade?

REFERENCES

BBVA Research. (2012) *EAGLEs Economic Outlook: Annual Report 2012*, BBVA Research, Madrid. Reports on the prospects for the EAGLEs.

BBVA Research. (2014) *EAGLEs Economic Outlook: Annual Report 2014*, BBVA Research, Madrid. Reports on the prospects for the EAGLEs.

Bootle, R. (2003) *Money for Nothing: Real Wealth, Financial Fantasies and the Economy of the Future*, Nicholas Brealey, London. Predictor of the crash in property and asset prices. Good on the impact of deflation.

Friedman, G., and Lebard, M. (1991) *The Coming War with Japan*, St Martin's Press, New York. Argues that post–Cold War economics and politics will lead to conflict between the US and Japan.

International Monetary Fund (IMF). (2011, 2014) *World Economic Outlook: Slowing Growth, Rising Risks*, IMF, Washington, DC. Short-term forecasts for the global economic and financial system.

KPMG. (2013) *Mainland China Banking Survey*, KPMG, China.

Martin, M.F. (2012) China's Banking System: Issues for Congress Congressional Research Service Report for Congress, February 20, Washington, DC: Congress

PricewaterhouseCoopers. (2014) *Foreign Banks in China 2013*, PwC, HK. Eighth review and survey of foreign banks operating in mainland China.

Swiss Re. (2014) *World Insurance in 2013*, Swiss Re, Zurich. Survey of global insurance markets, with facts and figures on insurance usage country by country.

Xing, Y. (2011) China's High-Tech Exports: Myth and Reality, *National Graduate Institute for Policy Studies (GRIPS) Discussion Paper* No. 11-05, SSRN: http://ssrn.com/abstract=1865013 orhttp://dx.doi.org/10.2139/ssrn.1865013.

FURTHER READING

Avery, M., Zhu, M., and Cai, J. (eds) (2009) *China's Emerging Financial Markets: Challenges and Global Impact*, John Wiley & Sons, Singapore. Analysis of China's banking and financial system by leading bankers, businesspeople and policymakers.

Shah, A., Thomas, A., and Gorham, M. (2008) *India's Financial Markets: An Insider's Guide to How the Markets Work*, Elsevier, Amsterdam. Written by Indian financial market practitioners, it looks at the pros and cons of investing in India.

Trends in the Global Financial Markets

Key Trends

Since the writing of the seventh edition, global financial markets continue to suffer from the aftermath of the 2007–8 credit crises and the related eurozone sovereign debt problems. As a response to these events, regulators have toughened their stance on global banks, introducing higher capital and liquidity requirements, restricting their riskier activities and making wider use of the stress tests (and other financial health checks) to make sure that they have enough resources to withstand future major shocks. The new capital rules, Basel III, aim to be in place by 2019. This new regulatory environment has constrained global bank activity in the financial markets, and the big European banks are reducing their exposure to investment banking business. In addition, concerns about the link between bank stability and sovereign risk in the eurozone has led to the introduction of a European Banking Union where the ECB becomes the main bank regulator.

As big banks have been constrained from lending, this has had a depressing influence on economic growth. As such, the Federal Reserve, Bank of England and Bank of Japan, have engaged in quantitative easing (QE) (buying bank assets), flooding the market with extra-cheap, short-term liquidity, pushing interest rates down to near zero (to historically low) levels. As interest rates have tumbled, this has given a major boost to equity and (in some countries) property markets as individuals and companies with surplus funds have sought areas to place their funds to get higher returns. The Dow and FTSE hit record highs towards the end of 2014, and Japan's stock market boomed in November 2014 when the Bank of Japan decided to reduce QE. In summary, in advanced economies, the picture is of sluggish growth, expansionary non-conventional monetary policy and low interest rates that is boosting equity, property and other securities markets. (The ECB announced a €1 trillion QE program in January 2015 aimed at boosting European growth).

Since the writing of the seventh edition, however, prospects for many emerging economies appears less attractive. As the major Western countries have engaged in expansionary monetary policy and low interest rates, the capital flows into many emerging markets have reversed, and as a result their growth and future economic prospects have slowed. We mentioned in Chapter 16 the dramatically revised prospects for the Brazilian and Russian economies giving the growing budget and current account deficits as well as the big downturn in commodity prices. Over 2013 and 2014, investors have shifted away from emerging markets back into developed markets; oil and other commodity prices have also fallen. Prospects for rapid advancement in the economies and financial markets of much of the emerging and developing world are not as promising as we thought a few years back. Despite optimism in advanced countries' financial and property markets, there are still big worries, too, that Europe may start to resemble Japan in terms of little or no growth if it does not (soon) consider major structural reform – recall that the Japanese economy and financial systems have barely grown since 2000!

In the short time between publishing the sixth edition and the completion of the seventh edition of this text, financial markets have experienced the aforementioned changes; however, many of the trends identified in the previous edition remain important, such as lessons from the crisis, attitudes to risk, deleveraging (particularly of big banks) and regulation of OTC derivatives business. Trends covered in this edition cover the challenges faced by banks and financial markets in dealing with major ongoing regulatory reformism, the creation of the European Banking Union, developments in social, environmental, ethical and trust (SEET) issues; alternative energy investments; the search for yield, including (high) dividend paying stocks; and the prospects for further consolidation in the financial sector.

GLOBAL BANKS, DODD-FRANK, VICKERS AND LIIKANEN

Given the general recognition that banks focused too heavily on high risk non-interest revenue generation – particularly through securities trading and investment banking activity – this has led to a series of major structural proposals or legislation aimed at reducing bank risk and minimizing the likelihood of taxpayer-financed bank bailouts. As discussed in Chapter 6, these include the passing of the US Dodd-Frank Wall Street Reform and Consumer Protection Act in July 2010 (the biggest financial reform in the US since the Great Depression); implementation of the September 2011 Independent Commission on Banking (known as the Vickers Commission after its Chair, Sir John Vickers) into the UK's Banking Reform Act of December 2013; and recommendations made by October 2012 EU High-level Expert Group on Reforming the Structure of the EU Banking Sector, chaired by Erkki Liikanen (otherwise known as the Liikanen Report) – a formal proposal to introduce this into EU legislation was published in January 2014.

In general, the proposals are very similar, although differing in detail. In the UK, the Vickers Report proposes to ring-fence retail and various investment banking activities (these proposals were supported in the Banking Reform Act of December 2013). It also supports recommendations of the US Dodd-Frank Act of 2010 not to allow banks to undertake proprietary trading and to limit their hedge fund and private equity activity; and the EU proposal aim to legally separate various 'risky financial activities from deposit-taking banks within a banking group' (Liikanen, 2012).

However, the reform process (by late 2014) is still ongoing in the US, with full implementation of Dodd-Frank yet to occur (some estimates say that only 40–50% of its rules have implemented so far); the recommendations made by Liikanen (plus the EC's Recovery and Resolution Directive) not yet implemented into EU law; and Vickers (though legally introduced in the Banking Reform Act of December 2013) not yet implemented by any banks. All the aforementioned legislation is targeting the 2019 Basel III (and related EU Capital Requirements Directive IV) deadlines to be fully introduced/implemented. Clearly, the legislation is complex and at different stages of development. It has various interesting features. The US rules stem from a long-standing legal regime, and the provisions in Dodd-Frank are unlikely to be amended. In contrast, the UK rules stemming from Vickers seem to lack details and leave room for substantial arbitrage, especially with regards to defining what parts of the business specifically need to be ring-fenced (or what even ring-fencing specifically means). And it could be argued that the Liikanen Report is even more limited, as it is simply advice from a high-level expert group to an EU Commissioner – not all of its recommendations (so far) have been seriously discussed in terms of legal implementation.

If we compare the Vickers, Liikanen and Dodd-Frank proposals, all recommend either legal separation or ring-fencing the deposit bank from the investment bank or trading arm, with slight variation in detail. All insured banks have to separate deposit and investment banking activity in the US; Liikanen recommends separation only if the activities form a major share of banks activities or pose a systemic stability threat; and Vickers says that ring-fencing should occur only for banks with retail deposits greater than £25 billion. Trading and investment banking activity can be undertaken by a company in the same corporate group as the deposit bank – so long as it does not pose resolution problems (in the case of Vickers and Liikanen), although under the Volcker rule this prohibits propriety trading in any group that contains a deposit bank (and the parent of the bank must be a financial holding company if it is to conduct any investment banking/trading). Deposit banks are also prohibited from an array of securities activities – in the US, for instance, deposit-taking banks are precluded from investing in most securities and entirely from securities dealing (including market-making) and underwriting. Under Dodd-Frank, they will also have to move out of some derivatives and credit default swap (CDS) activities that are currently done in the deposit-taking bank. In the UK legislation, there is a long list of proposed prohibited securities activities (including propriety trading, securities lending, trading, origination, securitization originated outside the ring-fence and so on) – but these can be conducted if they are regarded as 'ancillary' to the main business; Liikanen refers to similar things as well as prohibition of deposit banks' credit exposure to hedge funds and investments in private equity.

The legislation is tougher and more restrictive in the US on the (legal) relationships between deposit banks and investment banks in the same corporate entity, and go far beyond large intra-group exposure rules (this is because of big US corporate finance interest in conflicts and problems that can be caused by things like 'tunnelling' – when funds are 'tunnelled' from, say, a profitable subsidiary to support 'bad' or unprofitable other parts of the bank/firm). In contrast, Liikanen and Vickers are somewhat vague on these issues – the UK has some tentative proposals relating to reducing intra-group guarantees – but it's all rather unclear. Liikanen actually asked the BIS and EC to look at this in more detail. The UK and EC proposals (the latter linked to the European Banking Union) both propose detailed bank resolution regimes, and the Dodd-Frank asks banks themselves to develop their own resolution plans (living wills). In fact, the Fed failed 11 of the country's 'living wills' in August 2014, saying that the banks did not demonstrate that they could deal with a collapse without severely impacting the economy, and so they were asked to go away and write them again! (Thomas Hoenig, second in charge at the FDIC, stated that '… the plans provide credible or clear path through bankruptcy that doesn't require unrealistic assumptions and direct or indirect public support'). Also, the UK and EC legislation propose the use of bail-in debt, whereas this is not the case in the US (although Dodd-Frank may encourage the Fed to ask the biggest banks – systemically important financial institutions, or SIFIs) to hold more contingent capital.

On capital requirements, the EC (and therefore UK) banks are subject to the Capital Requirements Directive 4 (CRD IV) and Capital Requirements Regulation (of 2011). Liikanen has recommended that more capital should be held against trading book exposures and real estate lending; and Vickers suggests more tier 1 capital needs to be held by systemically important banks; the US also has buffers for SIFIs.

The problem for banks is that although the broad features of the aforementioned legislation/reform proposals are similar, they differ in detail. There is also not much legal clarity on many of these issues, and this has led some big banks to state that they may have to create three separate legal entities (or silos/divisions) to deal with different rules going forward. In reality, little reform has yet taken place, although most progress has been unilateral (US, UK) – prospects for effective reform at the EU level look (perhaps) less certain given legislative issues that could be easily held up by the disagreements on the new Banking Union.

EUROPEAN BANKING UNION – ON ITS WAY?

In Chapter 11, we outline the new plans for a European Banking Union aimed at decoupling banking from sovereign risk. In June 2012, the European Council outlined proposals to create the Union as part of a programme aimed to help resolve problems in Europe's financial system, as well as to create a more resilient financial system. The proposals had three key elements. To recap, the responsibility for bank supervision should be at the European level (the ECB), and common mechanisms should be put in place to, secondly, resolve banks and, thirdly, to insure customer deposits. European banking union comprises three main pillars: a Single Supervisory Mechanism (SSM), a European resolution scheme and a pan-European deposit insurance scheme. The first step involves establishing a Single Supervisory System (SSM) with both a European and national dimension. The European level would be given supervisory authority and pre-emptive intervention powers that apply to all banks. The ECB took on responsibility for being the head supervisor in the SSM in November 2014, after it had done an asset quality review and (together with the European Banking Authority) stress-tested 123 of Europe's most systemically important banks. Part of the process of moving towards a SSM involves implementing regulatory reform of the EBA to adapt its role to the new situation, plus the adoption of new rules on capital regulation (the EU's Capital Requirements Regulation) as well as the fourth Capital Requirements Directive (CRD IV). The objective here is to implement a single harmonized supervisory rulebook based on Basel III rather than on divergent national arrangements.

A major concern of the UK authorities, who (along with Sweden) have said they will not participate in the SSM, relates to the potential for differential treatment for euro and non-euro member countries. The arrangements are primarily being put in place to protect the 19 euro members' banking systems, and the remaining 9 non-euro members are being asked whether they will enter into 'close cooperation arrangements' to participate in the SSM. Also, the UK authorities are concerned that the new arrangements will undermine the position of the European Banking Authority (EBA), an independent EU authority established to 'ensure effective and consistent prudential regulation and supervision across the European banking sector. . . The main task of the EBA is to contribute to the creation of the European Single Rulebook in banking, whose objective is to provide a single set of harmonised prudential rules for financial institutions throughout the EU'.

The House of Lords (2012) implies that the SSM is now seeking to establish a set of supervisory rules for euro members at the expense of efforts by the EBA to create a single rulebook across all EU members. The new proposals could lead to conflicts between the EBA and the ECB (that heads the SSM). The argument of differential treatment for euro members and non-members also raises concerns about the role of the European Systemic Risk Board as well as the BIS-based Financial Stability Board (chaired by Mark Carney, the Governor of the Bank of England) in its role in harmonizing regulatory standards across countries. Other issues relate to whether the ECB can attract sufficient supervisory staff to take on the SSM role and what sort of arrangements it will establish to deal with national supervisors – for both euro and non-euro Member states.

The second pillar, a European resolution scheme is to be mainly funded by banks and could provide assistance/support in the application of measures to banks overseen by European supervision. The key objective is to provide a mechanism for the orderly shutdown of non-viable banks, so protecting taxpayer bailouts. Features of the proposed resolution scheme are incorporated in the 2012 Recovery and Resolution Directive that (among other things) applies to all credit institutions and most investment firms, including financial groups; requires firms to have 'living wills'; provides for supervisory early intervention powers; specifies minimum harmonized resolution tools (including the power to sell businesses to third parties, to transfer a business to a State-owned bridge institution or bad assets to a publicly owned asset management firm); bail-in debt where debt converts to equity – institutions would be required to hold a minimum amount of 'bail-inable' liabilities by January 2018); national member states would have to set up pre-funded resolution funds; and national deposit guarantee schemes would be configured for resolution funding purposes.

Many commentators, not least UK policymakers, are sceptical as to whether the EU can establish a credible and effective bank resolution regime. Notwithstanding concerns about different treatment for euro and non-euro members, it is argued that European policymakers and investors have virtually no experience of orderly bank resolution, as most bank failures in the past have been dealt with via nationalization or taxpayer capital injections. Banking systems in Europe, as we noted in Chapter 6, are highly concentrated, and this is true even in the US, where most of the lessons for bank resolution come from (their Prompt Corrective Action legislation of 1991 – aims to deal with the orderly shutting of troubled banks). Also, in Europe, insolvency frameworks are fragmented along national lines which suggest also a major reform of such laws if a single resolution scheme is to be introduced. In principle, an effective resolution regime should reduce banking sector stability and the cost to taxpayers associated with bank rescues; in practice, however, there is little evidence that orderly resolution can be done for major bank failure – sceptics need only point to the US in September 2008 to highlight that their prompt corrective action was totally ineffective in resolving big bank problems!

Finally, the third pillar of the Banking Union is to establish a European deposit insurance scheme, along with the resolution fund, under a common resolution authority. The argument goes that bank deposits must be seen as just as safe in every EU/or euro member country, because if capital is mobile, in the event of banking problems deposits will flee to safe havens. This proposal, however, is also controversial, as it implies a form of debt mutualization within the EU or eurozone whereby deposit protection, say, funded by a member with an orderly banking system, would be used to protect depositors in a country with a failing banking system. Evidence suggests that the German authorities are opposed to such a scheme, and there is even a lukewarm attitude at the ECB:

> Ambassador Boomgaarden made clear Germany's opposition to a single deposit insurance scheme with 'centralised credit lines between national intervention funds'. He stressed that further integration was necessary before a centralised scheme could be considered. More recently, in comments delivered to a German mutual banking event in Frankfurt, the ECB President Mario Draghi indicated that plans for a common deposit scheme may not be revived. (House of Lords, 2012, p. 36)

The proposal for a common deposit protection scheme does not get strong support from Europe's leading economy, so this (many argue) does not augur well for the implementation of a full European Banking Union.

BANK REGULATIONS AND FINANCIAL MARKETS

You may be wondering what all the above regulatory changes have to do with global financial markets. Well, the answer is 'a lot'. Banks are the main providers of credit in economies and the main funders of most companies and nearly all SMES. They are also among the main lenders to households, either mortgages or consumer loans. In addition, the biggest banks dominate trading in foreign exchange and in global investment banking. So when banks (and particularly the world's largest) get into trouble or are constrained, it acts as a drag on the economies and growth slows. Of course, we have seen the emergence of shadow banking that steps in to substitute for traditional banks – we have seen this in the securitization business as well as hedge fund lending to various companies. Hire purchase and other firms also do more household financing. But ultimately, the credit and securities business provided by shadow banks is not enough to replace conventional institutions. So prospects for the economy slow, and so do financial markets.

To try to boost the situation, central banks (as we mentioned above) engage in expansionary (some say lax) monetary policy (QE) by buying bank assets (which banks may have difficulty selling), or they may lend to banks on very attractive terms. All this (known in the 'old days' as printing money) is geared to boosting the economy. Supporters say that such actions have been successful in the US and UK, as growth has improved, inflation remains modest and capital markets are booming. Detractors argue that the cheap money will eventually feed through into spiralling inflation and big problems ahead. Others argue that markets have become addicted to QE – and as soon as it stops, then financial markets and growth will collapse. Let's see. The Fed announced in late October 2014 that it was stopping QE – markets fell a little at the time. It remains to be seen what the long-term implications of this policy action is – but one can be certain that it definitely has had a positive impact on advanced economies financial markets since 2011. And also, as noted above, it has drawn capital away from emerging markets to their economic detriment.

SOCIAL, ENVIRONMENTAL, ETHICAL AND TRUST (SEET) ISSUES

Despite the important functions that banks perform, such as running the payments system, extending credit to households and firms and so on, since the financial crisis of 2007–8, public opinion has increasingly focused on the negative aspects associated with banking/financial markets business. Many questions relating to banking and SEET issues are continually being asked:

- Do banks behave in a socially responsible manner?
- Is it ethical to give massive bonuses to a handful of employees even when banks are making massive losses?
- Can you trust your financial services provider any more?
- Will so-called 'casino capitalism' always mean that ethical behaviour and trust are low on bankers objective functions?
- Are bankers out to make as much for themselves as possible, irrespective of the negative impact a banking sector collapse will have on shareholders, depositors, borrowers, and taxpayers?

- Will banks ever be socially responsible?
- Are banks environmentally responsible?

Although the above questions have yet to be fully or even accurately answered, over the past decade or so, corporate social responsibility (CSR) has developed into an important strategy to enable firms to increase and smooth cash flows through consumer goodwill and loyalty. There have been a number of academic studies investigating the link between CSR and corporate environmental management on organizational performance, but no conclusive result has so far been identified. Nevertheless, it appears that SEET issues are most important in businesses that offer so-called 'credence services'. These industries, such as fund management, insurance and healthcare, provide services whose quality cannot easily be assessed until (often long) after consumption. This is because a judgement about quality requires the consumer to have highly specialized knowledge.

The growing emphasis on CSR has probably had the biggest impact in the investments arena, where there is now an asset class for investors who seek to obtain returns from socially responsible firms. According to the US-based Forum for Sustainable and Responsible Investment (US SIF), sustainable and socially responsible investing (SRI) in the US continues to grow at a faster pace than the broader universe of conventional investment assets under professional management. According to the US Forum for Sustainable and Responsible Investment (http://ussif.org/), typical approaches that investors use in SRI include the following:

- Screening, both positive and negative, where investment portfolios or mutual funds are evaluated on a range of social, environmental and good corporate governance criteria. In constructing, say, an SRI portfolio, investors may look for companies with strong CSR performance, avoiding poor performers. Typically, sustainable and responsible investors seek to own profitable companies that make positive contributions to society. 'Buy' lists may include enterprises with, for example, good employer–employee relations, strong environmental practices, products that are safe and useful, and operations that respect human rights around the world.
- Many sustainable and responsible investors avoid investing in companies whose products and business practices are harmful to individuals, communities or the environment. It is a common mistake to assume that SRI 'screening' is exclusionary or predominantly involves negative screens. In reality, SRI screens are being used more and more frequently to invest in companies that are leaders in adopting clean technologies and exceptional social and governance practices.
- Shareholder advocacy, in which sustainable and responsible investors take an active role as the owners of corporate America. These efforts include talking (or 'dialoguing' via online media) with companies on issues of social, environmental or governance concerns. Shareholder advocacy can involve filing shareholder resolutions on topics such as corporate governance, climate change, political contributions, gender/racial discrimination, pollution, problem labour practices and a host of other issues. This investor pressure can force firms to focus more on SEET issues compared to solely emphasizing profit/shareholder returns maximization motives.
- Community investing which directs capital from investors and lenders to communities that are underserved by traditional financial services institutions. Community investing provides access to credit, equity, capital and basic banking products that these communities would otherwise lack. In the US and around the world,

community investing makes it possible for local organizations to provide financial services to low-income individuals and to supply capital for small businesses and vital community services, such as affordable housing, childcare and health care.

In the US, the value of professionally managed funds that followed SRI amounted to just over $3.7 trillion in 2013, compared with around $640bn in 1995. This is about $1 in every $8 or $9 invested. Globally, around $34 trillion, or 15% of the world's investable assets), in 1,200 investment firms, has been committed to SRI through the United Nations' Principles for Responsible Investing.

Of increasing relevance to the financial sector are a variety of environmental issues. These already influence reinsurance firms via the increased payouts to clients in the aftermath of a series of recent environmental disasters. There is also an ongoing debate as to the extent to which banks are liable to the environmental risks faced by the firms they lend to. More broadly, the growing awareness of climate change issues is emphasized in Lord Nicholas Stern's (2006, p. xv) 700-page review, *The Economics of Climate Change*, which states:

> The scientific evidence is now overwhelming: climate change is a serious global threat, and it demands an urgent global response . . . Using the results of formal economic models, the Review estimates that if we don't act, the overall costs and risks of climate change will be equivalent to losing at least 5% of global GDP each year, now and forever. If a wider range of risks and impacts is taken into account, the estimates of damage could rise to 20% of GDP or more. In contrast, the cost of action – reducing greenhouse gas emissions to avoid the worst impacts of climate change – can be limited to around 1% of GDP each year ... Our actions now and over the coming decades could create [or avoid] risks of major disruption to economic and social activity, on a scale similar to those associated with the great wars and . . . it will be difficult or impossible to reverse these changes.

Stern's report resulted in substantial public interest and has put increasing pressure on governments and businesses to consider climate change as a serious issue. A number of studies have highlighted how banks and other financial firms can embrace climate change, ranging from reductions in energy consumption (eco-efficiency) and carbon emission offsetting to the creation of new products (see Furrer et al., 2009). A more recent reflection of the desire to deal with these issues is highlighted by the announcement at the G20 Summit held in Brisbane, Australia, in November 2014, by the US, Japan and other countries to commit funds (targeting $10bn to $15bn) to the UN Green Climate Fund to help poor nations deal with climate change. Also, the US and China announced big plans to cut carbon emissions over the next decade.

Besides the environment, issues such as poverty, inequality and human rights have also received increasing attention over the past decade. The failure of investors, depositors and supervisors to properly discipline banks has led many to reconsider ethical issues. For instance, the perceived levels of greed and hubris in the financial system moved centre stage on the public agenda. Restoring stability and trust within the financial system will be a long process.

As described in Chapters 6 and 10, governments around the world have responded with a wide range of policies aimed at improving disclosure and transparency and reducing the potential for moral hazard via the safety nets instituted by government agencies. Specific action has been taken, such as

- the extension of the coverage of bank regulations based on economic substance rather than legal form;
- increased capital and liquidity requirements (particularly for systemically important financial institutions);
- countercyclical capital requirements;
- enhanced regulation and supervision of liquidity;
- enhanced supervision of credit rating agencies;
- codes covering executive pay and benefits;
- improved arrangements for the regulation of the activities of cross-border banks;
- reform of accounting disclosure rules; and
- the establishment of consumer protection agencies.

It is hoped that many of these moves will go some way to reinstall trust and more ethical behaviour in the system.

There is a growing body of survey-based research that looks at the issue of trust in both financial and non-financial transactions. Unsurprisingly, the main finding is that if customers have trust in the firms they do business with, they are more likely to repeat purchase or stay longer with the firm or buy more services. When trust weakens, customer relationships weaken, and substitute product and services become more attractive. Obviously, there has been an erosion of trust among

- *banks themselves*, as evidenced by the freeze of the interbank markets in 2008 and 2011/12 during the eurozone crisis;
- *banks and investors*, marked by episodes of market participants short selling shares of financial institutions, as well as the LIBOR and FX price fixing scandals; and
- *banks and their customers*, as evidenced by the depositor runs (such as Northern Rock), and mis-selling of financial services (payments protection insurance, PPI, in the UK) (and again the aforementioned price fixing scandals).

It will be a long time before bankers regain investor and customer trust.

ALTERNATIVE ENERGY INVESTMENTS

In the seventh edition of this text, we talked about the record high price of energy and how this was spurring investors to seek out companies that were engaged in alternative energy projects – such as wind farms, solar energy and wave power. This was the trend as oil prices continued upwards to around $110 a barrel up until mid-2013, but the prices have slumped to $75 by the end of 2014 – and it has fallen to below $50 by the end of 2015! Also, alternative energy investments that promised so much a few years back have been hit with cost overruns, falls in government subsidies and other actions that mean that they have not performed as well as initially expected. Nevertheless, as we note above, there remains a stronger than ever environmental awareness of the need to develop green, alternative energy sources. Investors are increasingly looking to firms that are key in these sectors or key suppliers to these sectors. Google, for instance, has invested $145 million in Sun Edison, a leading global solar technology manufacturer, to develop the US's largest solar plant, based in California.

DIVIDEND-PAYING STOCKS

In the current economic climate, nominal interest rates are at record lows, so savers gain little from holding their funds in the bank. Inflationary pressures are muted, but slowly increasing, as a result of the quantitative easing that has flooded Europe and the US with cheap money, which will further erode the real value of investments – real interest rates are negative in the West. Of course, more inflation is good if you have big debts (like governments), as it reduces real repayment costs. However, it is bad for investors, as the real value of their investments will fall; thus they continue to look to invest in securities that generate good capital growth as well as higher dividends.

Returns on bank deposits and yields on many other assets remain low. Investors however, have rapidly re-entered the stock market since the big losses incurred in early 2009 in the aftermath of the global financial crisis. The figures of stock market performance in the UK and US over the last few years are startling:

	Peak	Peak	Trough	Peak
Dow Jones Industrial Average	Dec. 1999 11,497	Aug. 2007 13,895	Feb. 2009 7,000	Sept. 2014 17,163
FTSE100	Jan. 2000 6,930	Oct. 2007 6,721	Mar. 2009 4,604	Nov. 2014 6,654

Source: FTSE International Limited ('FTSE') © FTSE (2014).

One can see that from its lows in early 2009, the US market has more than doubled, and the UK market is 50% up. The FTSE 100 is still not back at the level it achieved at the peak of the high-tech boom in January 2000, whereas the Dow Jones Industrial average is way above its pre-banking crisis peak. (If you believe that history repeats itself, you can see even from this simple table that the US market tends to peak and bottom out before its UK counterpart – maybe some useful investment advice! Also, the famous financier from the 1980s who liquidated most of his market investments before the 1987 crash said that he had never ever lost money by selling early! Anyway, one can see that there have been substantial opportunities for capital gains in the market since 2009 by just going long. But this does not necessarily reward investors who wish for a good income stream as opposed to capital gain. Hence the continuing desire of investors who require income rather than capital gain to look for higher yields/dividends.

Investing in high-dividend-paying companies can provide opportunities for long-term growth as well as a steady income stream from dividends.

Higher dividend yields can suggest that equities are underpriced or that the company has fallen on hard times, and future dividends will not be as high as previous ones. Similarly, a low dividend yield can be viewed as evidence that the equity is overpriced or that future dividends might be higher. Certain investors find higher yields attractive if they require a decent income stream, although dividends tend to be taxed at income tax rates, which are (generally) higher than capital gains taxes. One should be aware, however, that there is much debate about the link between dividend yields and investment performance. For instance, the low dividend yield of the Dow Jones over the past few years suggests to some investors that the market remains overvalued. In November 2014, of the biggest firms quoted in the US, a number of analysts forecast that Microsoft, Nike, 3M and Home Depot are likely to be the biggest dividend generators over 2015.

MEASURING AND MANAGING RISK

Many are still stunned at the way in which the global banking crisis happened, as well as by the ongoing saga of scandals (LIBOR and FX price fixing, mis-selling of PPI in the UK and so on) that suggest banks cannot even manage their own staff or internal systems effectively. In gauging price movements of financial assets, there are obvious major limitations in risk measurements that rely too slavishly on probability distributions. It has always seemed that risk managers too readily ignore the extremes of distributions: 'This is extremely unlikely, so can be ignored.' Risk managers and their bosses now know that they need to ask: 'Yes, but what if it does happen? Let's feed the consequences into our model.' Did the clever people at Long-Term Capital Management never stop to ask: 'What if Russia defaults?' Equally, those whose assets were insured by AIG never thought to work out at what level of default AIG would simply be unable to pay.

As we noted above, the low-interest-rate environment we are experiencing at present is a consequence of the crisis – governments have undertaken expansionary monetary policy (by cutting official rates) and injecting massive liquidity into the system. Of course, many had little room to manoeuvre as rates were low even before the crisis hit, fanned by financial surpluses, particularly from China and other emerging markets that sought investment opportunities in the West. This excess liquidity prior to the crisis pushed down interest rates and led to a credit frenzy – most noticeably in global property markets. Cheap money financed a bank lending boom, property prices surged, banks and other investors became more leveraged, and the risks were believed to be negligible. So long as property prices kept on increasing, all was okay, collateral values would be strong and this backing helped to support excessive risk-taking. When the value of collateral first started to tumble in the US sub-prime market, the crisis followed. Global markets tumbled, banks and other financial firms collapsed and property markets from Dubai to Las Vegas went into meltdown. Even post-crisis concerns about effective risk measurement and management remain. We are still in a very low-interest-rate environment, securities markets are now booming again as are property markets – particularly in major cities. This could be another boom-and-bust cycle, certainly the 'fizzy' US market is unlikely to keep on powering up – even though oil and other commodity prices have fallen fuelling corporate profits and household spending, particularly in the West. Another worrying signal is that market volatilities remain low – the S&P500 VIX index which measures such things – has been at March 2007 pre-global banking crisis levels from the start of January 2013 up until November 2014. The last time the index was this low for so long with a booming market, we had the 2008 collapse! Maybe we are just being too optimistic – but at least they are issues worth considering.

Clearly, how to measures and manage the risks associated with issues discussed in the last two paragraphs or so are contemporary and important.

We have already outlined how the banks were hit by the crisis and how they will be more heavily regulated in areas spanning capital requirements, liquidity, executive pay, financial innovation and risk management. All this is likely to continue to constrain US and European banks, at least up until the end of the decade when Basel III and its related EU CRD IV legislation is implemented. This, together with Dodd-Frank Act and the ongoing global reform of OTC derivatives markets (shifting much onto more heavily regulated and less risky exchanges), will also constrain banks and their risk management activities. Although shadow banks may step in and take up a bit of the shortfall left by the shrinking global commercial and investment banks, it is unlikely that this somewhat unregulated sector will be able (or allowed) to fully substitute all traditional banking activities. As such, there is likely to be adverse impacts on economic growth that over the longer term will dampen market activity.

Regulating the OTC Derivatives Markets

Of course, if risk can be passed on, we would expect people to be willing to take more risk. The passing on of risk finds expression in the extraordinary market for credit and asset-backed securities, which expanded at breakneck speed and then culminated in a massive collapse. We can begin with a company bond where the holder pays a premium for someone else to accept the credit risk. Then we develop the idea of selling the risk on a pool of bonds. We can make this more sophisticated by splitting the pool into tranches according to risk. As a first cousin to this, we have the collateralized debt obligation (CDO). Here, we sell the risk of a pool of tranched bonds as another bond, but why stop there? Why not take a group of these bonds and pool them – a CDO backed by a portfolio of other CDOs, known as CDO 2? This process can go on and on, with the final holder of the increasingly exotic instrument much detached from the ultimate collateral backing the instrument, for example the credit worthiness of a corporate bond. Exactly the same process occurred in the securitized mortgage market – banks pretty much neglected the credit risk appraisal of mortgage borrowers in the US sub-prime market because they knew the risks would be sold on. And, as noted in Chapter 10, if we hold onto these risks, we can buy credit default swaps (CDS) to insure against default – everything will be fine. The fifth edition (2007, p. 429) foresaw possible problems ahead:

> The easier it is to pass risk on, the more risks people will take, and this is exactly what is happening. In the past, this type of excess has always ended in tears. 'This time it's different,' they say, but then, they always do.

Concerns about the explosion of OTC derivatives contracts – particularly swaps and CDS – have led to the US and the EU to call for much greater regulatory oversight of these instruments and moves to pull them back onto exchanges where activity can be more closely monitored. Excessive exposures and leverage could, in theory at least, be reduced if much of this activity was brought onto exchanges where greater transparency would ensue. The 2010 Dodd-Frank Act and the EU's 2013 EMIR (European Market Infrastructure Regulation) legislation seeks to build a new regulatory infrastructure that pushes a big chunk of this market (which in fact is mainly interest rate swaps and CDS business) onto regulated exchanges where banks have to post more capital (margin calls) if the position of the derivative becomes riskier. Also all information related to these transactions will be held by trade repositories that will track all transactions with data feeds to the regulators, so they can build a picture of bank exposures and network connections – something they had little or no idea about prior to the global banking crisis. Most derivative trading, therefore, will be undertaken through central clearing houses and recognized exchanges and regulators, and the exchanges will determine what should be exchange traded. Exchange-traded derivatives are more transparent than their OTC counterparts, and the credit risks will shift to the exchange.

Gold and Precious Metals

When capital markets falter, investment in precious metals and other alternatives often takes off. Gold prices stood at $500 per troy ounce in 2005, peaked at just over $1,000 in mid-2007, fell back, and then surged from October 2009 onwards, to peak at $1,900 in September 2011. Since then, it has bumped up and down and was around $1,187 in November 2014. According to *The Economist* (8 October 2009), the main cause of the increase in gold was concerns about oil-producing countries replacing the US dollar as the (oil) pricing currency. This put downward pressure on the dollar and encouraged risk-averse investors to acquire gold. Long-term price targets for gold vary dramatically – one forecast expects gold to reach over $3,000 an ounce, based on the view that in a low-interest rate environment (low opportunity cost from holding gold) characterized by substantial uncertainty, major paper currencies (like the dollar) will depreciate, and gold is a good hedge. Pretty much the price of gold tends to boom when expectations of inflation increase, worries about collapse of financial markets heighten and/or there are supply/demand issues relating to mining of the precious metal. Gold has obviously been a poor investment over the last few years, but demand may increase and prices move upwards if financial markets jitter with the end of QE and if inflationary pressures start to heighten. See Cox (2014) for more detail on gold and silver markets.

Other precious metals have followed a similar trend; silver prices rose to a record high above $47 an ounce in April 2011 but had fallen to just over $16 by November 2014; platinum rose to $1,913 per ounce in September 2011 but has also fallen to $1,200 over the same time period. Palladium prices surged to $855 per ounce in February 2011 and have not fallen quite so much – they were at $765 per ounce in November 2014 – this is because car manufacturers are substituting the more expensive platinum used in catalytic converters for the cheaper palladium and also because there have been some supply shortages (major producers being Russia and South Africa). All the base metals, such as lead, zinc and aluminium, have posted similar price trends up to mid-2011 and declined thereafter – to a great extent driven by weakened manufacturing demand from China as well as new supplies coming on stream. In the seventh edition, we talked a lot about investing in rare earth elements/metals – a set of 17 elements in the periodic table, specifically the 15 lanthanides plus scandium and yttrium. They are important for a range of technological products, for example gadolinium is used in the manufacturing of computer memory, and thulium is used in portable X-ray machines. They are also found in jet engines, flat-panel TVs, mobile phones, hybrid and electric vehicles, lasers, a range of medical devices and superconductors. Despite their name, they are not particularly rare, but can be expensive and environmentally costly to extract. China dominates the market and, according to reports in early 2011 by *The Economist* and Bloomberg, had been restricting supply at a time when demand was rapidly increasing. Prices rocketed up until the late summer of 2011, but like gold and silver they have all experienced big falls since then – in fact, so much so that various mineral investment advisors were recommending them as a 'good buy' at the end of 2014.

Islamic Finance

One area of banking business that continues to be of interest and was barely affected by the global credit crisis was Islamic finance. By 2012, sharia-compliant banks held assets amounting to over $1,500bn. Of this, $1.3bn was in banking, $74bn in Islamic mutual funds, $31bn in *takaful* (Islamic insurance) and the remainder in other investments (TheCityUK,

2013). Iran accounts for around 36% of Islamic finance assets, followed by Malaysia (17%), Saudi Arabia (14%), United Arab Emirates (8%), Kuwait (7%) and Bahrain (6%). The UK has a number of full sharia-compliant Islamic banks including Bank of London and The Middle East, European Islamic Investment Bank, Gatehouse Bank, Islamic Bank of Britain, QIB UK and the Abu Dhabi Islamic Bank. Most of the large international banks operating in the UK have Islamic 'windows' through which they undertake Islamic banking and finance business. Islamic banking and financial activity, of course, cover the globe, with all major global commercial banks having Islamic subsidiaries and investment banks arranging and issuing *sukuk* bonds and other sharia-compliant investment services.

Islamic banking, which started on a modest scale in the 1960s, has shown exceptional growth. What started as a small rural banking experiment in the remote villages of Egypt has reached a level where many mega-international banks now offer Islamic banking and financial products. The practice of Islamic banking has spread from East to West – all the way from Indonesia and Malaysia to Europe and the Americas. Forty years ago, Islamic banking was considered not much more than wishful thinking, but now it is a reality. It has been shown to be both feasible and viable and can operate just as efficiently and productively as Western-style financial intermediation. The successful operation of these institutions and the experiences in Pakistan, Iran, Malaysia, Saudi Arabia, Bahrain and throughout the Islamic world demonstrate that it can provide an alternative to Western commercial banking and finance. The fact that many conventional banks also are using Islamic banking and finance techniques is further proof of the viability of the Islamic alternative. Even though Islamic banks emerged in response to the needs of Muslim clients, they are not religious institutions. Like any other type of bank, they are profit-seeking institutions. The big interest in Islamic banks is that they use a different model of financial intermediation, and these features have attracted financiers worldwide as well as the attention of policymakers. In recent years, there has been a new dynamism as this industry has proved increasingly attractive, not only to the world's 1.7 billion Muslims but also to many others who are beginning to understand the unique aspects of Islamic banking and finance. A particular attraction is the more conservative lending practices of Islamic banks as well as the greater emphasis on ethical behaviour in customer relationships.

Despite their rapid growth in recent years, the asset size of the top 500 Islamic banks (in 2013) amounted to an estimated 3% of the total assets of the top 500 Western banks, and the $60bn Islamic *sukuk* (bond) market accounts for around 1% of global debt insurance. The key features of Islamic banking – no charging of interest, profit-and-loss sharing contracts and the emphasis on asset-backed transactions – have meant that Islamic banks have shied away from the complicated securitized asset business that has adversely affected Western institutions. Islamic banks have also relied on abundant Muslim depositors rather than international debt markets to finance their growth, and profits have remained strong. Confidence in the reigning secular financial architecture has also been severely shaken, and an increasing number of commentators continue to look at the success of Islamic banking to see if lessons can be learned in formulating a new and safer operational and regulatory structure for Western banks. There is also widespread interest in the Islamic bond (*sukuk*) issuance. This is dominated by Malaysian issues, although some major project finance deals have been funded by such issues – bond returns for *sukuk* are related to the financial performance of a specific project or business. The UK authorities in 2013 changed bond issuing legislation to encourage such issues as the City of London vying with other major financial centres to be the global capital of Islamic finance. Part of London's Olympic village and the 'Shard' building were financed by Islamic bond (*sukuk*) issuance. Britain became the first country outside the Islamic world to issue sovereign *sukuk* when, in June 2014, it raised £200 million through such an issue. Other non-Islamic countries are considering similar issues.

CONSOLIDATION AND BANKS AS PUBLIC UTLITIES

History tells us that after major financial crises and economic downturn, one can usually expect significant industry restructuring. Surprisingly, in Europe and the US this has not yet happened. It could be that because these financial systems are still heavily dependent on government support, via part-nationalization – still the case in the UK for RBS and Lloyds – that the industry is waiting for a more stable economic environment and lower government involvement before it embarks on a major restructuring. Also, maybe banks believe the competition and other authorities will not sanction major deals for anti-competitive and possible too-big-to fail policy concerns that come with a consolidation wave. However, such an outcome seems a virtual certainty. Having said this, however, the track record of M&As in global banking systems does not always result in positive outcomes. A major motivation for M&A is the desire to boost performance – increased profits and higher market valuation via share price increases. Senior executives engaged in M&A have to convince owners (shareholders) that the deal will boost performance either by increasing revenues or reducing costs. It's unlikely that shareholders will sanction a deal if they believe that the acquisition or merger will reduce performance. And as we noted in Chapter 4, bank CEOs make a big deal about the performance-enhancing features of the acquisitions they aim to put in place. Performance gains from mergers emanate either from efficiency improvements (reduced costs via scale and scope economies) or the ways in which revenues can increase – namely via market power. The latter relates to bigger banks being able to set prices above competitive levels because of market dominance in particular areas.

The point is that if we are to expect a consolidation wave, will this feed through into a more efficient and better run banking system? Extensive literature exists that investigates whether bank M&A leads to performance improvements. Some studies use tests to see whether there are cost and/or profit improvements post-merger. Studies use either accounting ratios or more sophisticated efficiency estimates to compare pre- and post-merger performance. The overall conclusion from the studies that (mainly) examined bank M&A during the 1980s up to the mid-1990s was that cost and profit improvements resulting from bank mergers tended to be elusive, although evidence since then (particularly for European bank M&A) appears to find stronger evidence of performance improvements. Another strand of the literature uses 'event study' methodology to gauge market reactions to M&A announcements. The event study approach aims to evaluate shareholder reactions to merger announcements. The combined effects of the abnormal returns (measured as the difference between the actual stock price and that predicted by a model that extrapolates previous share prices and attempts to indicate what the bank's share price would have been without the M&A announcement) to bidders and targets around the announcement date reflect value creation or destruction for shareholders. This approach is regarded as an indirect measure of the impact of M&A because even if positive abnormal returns are generated, for example combined share prices of the acquirer and acquired banks are higher on the M&A announcement date than predicted by the model, it is not clear whether the positive shareholder reaction is due to perceived improvements in performance resulting from greater market power (higher prices) or improved efficiency. The view that has emerged from the event studies that examined bank M&A in the 1980s and 1990s is that, although target shareholders tend to earn strong positive abnormal returns, bidder shareholders earn marginally negative returns – the combined effects being insignificant.

Up until the early 2000s, the above consensus was that there was no strong evidence that bank M&A was performance enhancing, and so researchers started looking at the so-called 'managerial incentive' literature. This looked at factors such as CEO remuneration, choosing a 'quiet life', and maximizing asset size as alternative explanations for M&A activity. Here, the argument goes that managers engage in M&A in order to maximize their own utility at the expense of shareholders. Managers' utility may relate to growth if their pay and other benefits are linked to firm size. Similarly, managers' utility may also be related to size if they wish for a 'quiet life'. Larger firms may be able to exert greater market power and insulate themselves from various competitive pressures, allowing them to choose a 'quiet life'. Another managerial explanation as to why mergers may destroy value is Richard Roll's hubris hypothesis, which argues that overconfident managers systematically overestimate the benefits of an acquisition, which results in them overbidding (paying too much) for targets, leading to value destruction/no performance improvements. Managerial motives for M&A have mainly been investigated in US banking, and there does seem to be some evidence that CEO compensation increases with changes in asset size due to mergers of large banks. There is also evidence that where CEOs can expect to have large compensation increases from acquisition, they tend to engage in merger programmes, that is, a series of deals. Outside the US, there do not appear to be any recent studies that focus on the managerial motives for bank mergers, probably because recent studies of post-2000 M&A find much greater support for performance-improving bank merger activity.

Looking at previous experiences of successful M&A may help provide a guide for future consolidation activity, not only for private sector banks but also for governments that may wish to reconfigure their beleaguered banking/financial systems. One area that may well be worth investigating relates to the features of actual or potential bank acquisition targets. Studies of domestic bank deals tend to arrive at the same conclusion – poor-performing banks are those most likely to be acquired. They may be less efficient, have lower capital levels, poor risk management processes, lower liquidity and so on. A related literature examining the determinants of cross-border banking also identifies efficiency (as well as country differences in information costs, regulatory, economic and other factors) as being important in influencing overseas expansion. Generally, this literature finds that large efficient banks (from developed financial systems) are more likely to be engaged in overseas expansion; this has also been found to be the case for insurance firm expansion within Europe.

Consolidation can also impact bank customers. Early academic literature typically finds that US bank consolidation in the 1980s resulted in lower deposit rates and higher loan rates in more concentrated markets, although studies that focus on the 1990s tended to indicate weaker relationships between local market concentration and deposit rates. There is also evidence that large banks allocate a smaller proportion of their assets to small business loans compared to small banks, and this effect is more pronounced for merging banks. These adverse effects, however, appear to be counteracted by the increased credit supply to firms by small incumbent banks. In general, the overall impact of bank mergers on both the price and availability of banking services is relatively modest. More recently, greater attention has been paid to looking at how M&A impact small businesses. One study examined the specific case of the merger between two US banks (Fleet and BankBoston) and found that higher spreads were charged for medium-sized mid-market borrowers post merger, although spreads for small mid-market borrowers remained unchanged.

Consolidation is also found to have led to lower credit availability for small borrowers as well as capital constrained firms. Falls in lending to small businesses have been found (in the US at least) to be matched by increased credit from other incumbent banks, as well as increased entry of newly chartered banks. One interesting study found that bank mergers in the US related to higher loan and crime rates.

Mergers can enable banks to acquire proprietary information both to soften lending competition and to grow market share. It has been suggested that as competition increases, the cost of acquiring information about borrowers falls, and this can lead to lower loan rates but also inefficient lending decisions. These findings appear to be partially supported by work on Japanese bank consolidation, which finds that big bank mergers increase their ability to acquire soft information about their corporate borrowers.

Evidence on the impact of consolidation on small business lending in Europe (albeit limited) also appears to present rather mixed findings. Various studies on Italian banking have found that interest rates on loans fall when banks with small shares of local banking markets merge, although in the case of large bank deals, the results are reversed. Italian bank mergers have also been found to have a substantial adverse effect on credit availability that lasts at least 3 years after the merger. Other work looking at German banking has found that the consolidation trend had no impact on small firm credit availability.

Another interesting feature of the pre-crisis M&A trend was the strategic focus on both geographical and product diversification. In the US, the 1999 Gramm-Leach-Bliley Act (the Financial Services Modernization Act) effectively repealed the 1933 Glass-Steagall Act and granted broad-based securities and insurance powers to commercial banks. Also, Japan's so-called 'Big Bang' reforms (completed in 1999) removed the separation of commercial and investment banking, and the earlier 1992 EU single-market programme also legislated for a universal banking system. By 2000, therefore, all major financial systems had removed the major product barriers in the financial services sector, although restrictions still remain and vary according to financial firms involvement with the non-financial sector – otherwise known as 'commerce'. This product sector deregulation followed the earlier removal of national bank branch restrictions in various countries. In addition to banks having the freedom to expand nationally and across product lines, the strategic desire to enter new international markets has also been another key trend. This has led to a substantial work that has sought to identify the impact of these various diversification features.

Diversification (whether geographical or product) was likely to lead to reductions in risk, although these positive benefits could be offset by shifts to higher risk portfolios (income streams) and/or greater operational risks. One approach to investigating the possible impact of diversification is to study the accounting or stock return features of hypothetical bank–non-bank mergers. The handful of these mainly US studies that use this approach tend to find evidence of risk diversification benefits, particularly in the case of hypothetical bank and life assurance company deals.

Another strand of the diversification literature uses stock return event-type studies and these typically reveal mixed findings. Some studies focus on US bank bidder returns and find that significantly higher returns accrue for geographical and product-focused deals. This means that M&A between banks that have a similar business mix and strategies and are based in the same markets tend to do better than diversification-based deals. A number of cross-country European bank merger studies also tend to find that focused mergers do better than diversifying deals in terms of returns to shareholders, although there is also evidence that diversifying deals do better as well – so evidence for Europe is rather mixed.

Recent studies on cross-border mergers involving US and European banks tend to find evidence of no cost efficiency improvements, although there is some evidence of profit efficiency or accounting returns improvements. Other studies that examine diversification focus on a range of issues, including

- potential conflicts of interest associated with commercial bank/investment bank mergers;
- whether banks with securities arms lend more or less to small firms;
- how liquidity shocks and other effects can limit diversification;
- evidence of substantial conglomerate discounts – investors value diversified firms less than focused companies, and so conglomerate or diversified firms are not valued as highly as focused firms; and
- whether the benefits from diversification are generally offset by fee income volatility.

In light of the credit crisis and the barrage of bailouts and other support provided for 'diversified banks', various legislative moves have sought to restrict bank diversification activity, such as the 2010 Dodd-Frank Act in the US.

As banks have become larger and more complex – the largest having thousands of subsidiaries operating in many countries – there is a worry that having big banks and big banking systems poses a major threat to stability and that as such they should be regulated much more like public utilities (Saunders, 2014). Public utilities (like gas, electricity and water companies) have certain economic features that explain why they are typically regulated differently to private companies. Typically these industries have a common network structure: they have extensive distribution systems (piping for gas or cabling for electricity) that involve significant investment (known as large sunk costs) that can be government or privately owned. Quite often utilities are granted legally enforced monopolies over service territories. Activity of utilities can be characterised into production, transmission and distribution. In the case of natural gas, say, production relates to the gas well, transmission (via the web of pipelines) and distribution (the local gas distribution firms – from whom households and firms buy their gas). These three stages can be owned by public or private firms, but usually (even in North America) production is privately owned, whereas transmission or distribution can be either government or private. Banking has similar features – to be a bank and undertake production you need a banking licence, then capital and deposits; transmission is via the payments system (you cannot undertake transactions without means of payment/transfer); and finally distribution is through the branch network and subsidiaries. These stages are typically all privately owned, although in some countries (Brazil and China) state ownership remains important.

There are similarities between the production, transmission and distribution features of public utilities and banks. So perhaps we should regulate banks the same as utilities? The rationale for regulating utilities is threefold:

1 Public utilities are natural monopolies, which means they realize scale economies indefinitely, ultimately leading to one firm in the industry. In natural monopoly, productive efficiency is achieved with one firm. Because utilities tend to be natural monopolies, consumers need to be protected against excessive pricing and other bad treatment, hence the justification for regulating utilities, particularly on their pricing. Banks have a tendency to get very big, with a handful dominating over time. They have features very similar to natural monopolies – that is why so many countries have highly concentrated domestic banking systems.

2 To stop regulators from being captured by producers. The aim here is to protect all producers, and not just the biggest, by making sure utilities do not capture the

regulators and write their own rules. One could argue that in banking this is too late! Big banks for years have helped write the rules for Basel, EU and domestic regulators. The big banks dominate all areas of retail and wholesale activity – they know more than regulators (hence the emergence of shadow banking). Banks also gain from (implicit) safety net benefits that also provide benefits that regulators (unwittingly) provide.

3   Other rationale for regulating utilities relate to the evidence on the economic behaviour of utilities that shows that lowest cost operators are likely to be biggest rent gainers – or to put another way, they can extract monopoly profits; cost-based cross-subsidization is typically widespread; and quasi monopoly rents are likely to be spread among various groups. In banking it's easy to point to examples of previously found monopoly pricing behaviour (SME lending, payments, credit cards); cross-subsidization is widespread (we have seen retail subsidize investment banking in the 1990s at RBS, and the opposite recently at Barclays); and benefits have accrued (some argue) to a few – senior management and shareholders primarily.

In banking there is a definite trend toward natural monopoly, strong evidence of regulatory capture (or at least barriers to capture are low) and rent-seeking by low-cost producers and other parties, and cross-subsidization is also widespread. All these factors justify the regulation of public utilities. So some argue that we need to treat banks as such, regulating their behaviour to limit capture, but also that we need much greater regulatory oversight and policing of their pricing and profitability. Only then will their aggressive risk-taking appetite be effectively curtailed. As a consequence, investors in bank shares should consider benchmarking their performance against utilities as opposed to other types of private firms.

One can see that a relatively mixed and complex array of issues needs to be considered in terms of analysing bank consolidation. It has been argued on a number of occasions that M&A activity should be investigated on a detailed case-by-case study basis, as no deal is the same and all can have different performance/managerial outcomes. In addition, concerns about the build-up of monopoly power and other anti-competitive practices remains a major policy worry. Overseeing the expected bank consolidation process, therefore, presents a challenge for both market operators and governments as their banking and financial systems reconfigure over the coming years.

(STILL) RETHINKING ECONOMIC PARADIGMS

The major events that have occurred over recent years, namely the global financial crisis of 2008–9 and the euro sovereign debt crisis in 2010–11, have generated reams of studies and led many to question the failings of modern economic policy and analysis. In light of massive fiscal stimulus, un-conventional monetary policy and failing economies, probably the most significant 'comeback' has been the reappraisal of John Maynard Keynes (1883–1946), highlighted in the excellent texts by Robert Skidelsky (2009) and Paul Davidson (2009). The Keynesian intellectual framework – a world where pervasive uncertainty leads to persistently inadequate demand – seems to be more relevant today than at any time since the Depression era. There is ongoing debate as to whether Keynesian macroeconomics, which focused on fiscal stimulus (a key feature of recent policy), should redefine or underpin future economic policy or whether it can be viewed as appropriate in crisis situations, but not relevant in more 'normal' environments.

Another interesting insight into Keynesian ideas relates to his views on the use of statistics to gauge the probability of events. According to Skidelsky (2009, p. 22):

> On balance Keynes took the view that the use of statistics was mainly decorative. This corresponded with his rejection of statistical theories of probability. Only under very stringent conditions could the past be used to infer the future.

Clearly, Keynes would not be bowled over by bank risk measurement practices. In addition, there are other unorthodox views on the reasons why financial market experts and other commentators didn't predict the crises. A lot of the discussion hinges on the distinction between risk and uncertainty, as identified by the Chicago economist Frank Knight (1885–1972) in the 1920s. Knight (1921) noted that risk can be quantified and measured, whereas some events are so rare that they are uncertain – so-called 'Knightian uncertainty' – and thus cannot be quantified and measured. Jack Guttentag and Richard Herring's (1986) disaster myopia thesis extends this view to the financial sector. Their thesis is that if potential shocks happen so infrequently, these uncertain events cannot be accurately priced into any risk evaluations, irrespective of the sophistication of the modelling approaches used. Risks associated with uncertain events are not fully reflected in bank loan prices, market prices and conditions. If markets are competitive and banks discount the likelihood of a shock altogether, others are likely to be inclined to follow suit in order to maintain market share:

> In periods of benign financial conditions, disaster myopia is likely to lead to decisions regarding allocations of economic capital, the pricing of credit risk, and the range of borrowers who are deemed creditworthy, that make the financial system increasingly vulnerable to crisis. (Herring, 1999, p. 63)

In the context of the problems faced in the US mortgage market, disaster myopia relates to basing mortgage prices and underwriting rules on the assumption that because property prices had increased over a long period, they would continue to rise. The stalling of property prices sent a shock to both lenders and borrowers, for which neither was prepared. As Guttentag (2007, p. 2) notes:

> Disaster myopia was especially prevalent among aggressive sub-prime lenders, who could make a lot of money in a very short time as long as house prices kept rising. Other sub-prime lenders who might not be disaster-myopic were forced to operate as if they were, to remain competitive. Underwriting requirements in the subprime market are set by the investment banks that buy the loans and package them as securities. While the investment banks may or may not have been disaster-myopic, the ones that were willing to accommodate the more aggressive lenders did more business (as long as house prices were rising) than those who insisted on maintaining more restrictive underwriting rules.

Although Knightian uncertainty, disaster myopia and Keynesian views on the failings of probability analysis help to provide explanations as to why the recent crises arose, they give us little guidance as to how economists, financiers and policymakers should re-engineer to prepare for future crises. As the US, UK and other advanced economies have experienced significant stock market booms from mid-2011 through to the end of 2014, despite ailing economic performance, it could be that investors at the time of writing (November 2014) are collectively experiencing disaster myopia. Maybe the key lesson to learn from recent crises is that uncertain events do occur, accepted economic paradigms can disintegrate, and nothing is ever 'too good to be true'.

CONTINUING CRISIS IN THE EUROZONE

The eurozone continues to lurch along from crisis to crisis, with little real change. 'Greece will leave' has been the common talk since 2011, but it has not happened. 'Only federalism can control a single currency' – but that has not happened either. In May, 2010, a mechanism was finalized to allow the European Financial Stability Facility to issue bonds backed by all eurozone countries, inevitably called (confusingly) Eurobonds – but we haven't seen any. In December, 2011, a new treaty enshrining new budgetary rules failed to get a majority, but the Fiscal Pact signed by almost everyone (not the Czech Republic and the UK) was to make it harder for countries to break budget deficits. However, when we consider the failure of the Stability and Growth Pact (anyone remember that?), no one can be too optimistic about this one.

Mario Draghi (called 'super Mario' after the video games) has calmed international fears with his statement 'I will do what is necessary', but has then proceeded to do very little apart from a few purchases of private bonds. It is a new technique, perhaps called 'management by promises', but he cannot continue forever without doing something.

In the meantime, unemployment generally is 11.5%, and in Italy is 13.2% with youth unemployment a horrifying 41% and not much better in Spain at 25%. It is sad to reflect that the Amsterdam Treaty of 1999 had as one objective the promotion of high employment as a key EU goal. But then, if we are going to look back at earlier hopes for both the EU and the eurozone, 'that way madness lies'.

Political unrest continues – Italy's Five Star movement led by Beppo Grillo; Podemos in Spain; and Marine le Pen in France. However, their influence should not be overemphasized – they are a small percentage in both national and European parliaments. Federalism may not seem to be making much progress, but there is a will for it. The Eurobarometer opinion poll in 2013 reported that 60% want political union, as do all the European leaders. This may horrify the British, but it is a fact.

Whilst Greece, Spain and Italy get all the headlines, perhaps the saddest situation is that of France, once destined to be the powerhouse behind the EU, along with Germany. Now exports have fallen far behind those of Germany, and unemployment is twice that of Germany. There is no real political will to reform the labour market or slim the huge public sector costs.

In December 2014 came the third bailout request from Greece and the final meeting of the year for the European Central Bank. Just before this, the Market Purchasing Manager's Index fell to a 6-month low at 51.1 – any figure under 50 suggests a slide into recession. Even Germany fell to 51.1, and France (no surprise) fell to 47.9.

The ECB meeting dashed the hopes of anyone expecting dramatic action. Indeed, the bank slashed forecasts of growth. Mario Draghi said that he needed more time to study the effects of the oil price collapse. Regarding any quantitative easing, it is clear that there are bitter clashes within the bank, especially with Germany's board member, Sabine Lautenschlager. Draghi said (ominously?) that decisions could be taken by a majority vote, but would he really risk this, even against German opposition? In Germany itself, there is wide talk of judicial opposition on constitutional grounds should this happen. Lautenschlager is on record as saying recently re QE, 'It will do more harm than good at this stage.' In January 2015 the ECB announced a €1 trillion QE program aimed at boosting European growth.

Despite the aforementioned QE announcement we slide into 2015 in the eurozone with the same weary feeling of *'plus ca change'* – the same dismal prophecies and a sclerotic ECB struggling to cope.

REVISION QUESTIONS/ASSIGNMENTS

1 Explain how ethical and environmental factors impact on banks and financial firms.
2 Outline the pros and cons of an investment strategy that focuses on high dividend stocks, giving examples of specific high dividend stock.
3 Analyse the price trends of three precious metals and three energy products (such as oil, gas, coal) over the past 5 years. Which offer the best investment opportunities?
4 Critically appraise the regulatory response to the 2007–8 financial crisis. How effective do you think the regulations will be in preventing another crisis?

REFERENCES

Cox, W. (2014) *Silver to Gold: What You Need to Know About Precious Metal Investing*, Ashwood & Scott Publishing, London.

Davidson, P. (2009) *The Keynes Solution: The Path to Global Economic Prosperity*, Palgrave Macmillan, Basingstoke. Discussion of how we use Keynesian policy to get out of the economic mess caused by the credit crisis.

Furrer, B., Hoffman, V., and Swoboda, M. (2009) *Banking & Climate Change: Opportunities and Risks*, SAM Group Holding, Zurich. Covers an array of financial climate change-linked products and services.

Guttentag, J. (2007) *Shortsighted About the Subprime Disaster*, *Washington Post*, May 26, F02. Explains disaster myopia.

Guttentag, J., and Herring, R.J. (1986) *Disaster Myopia in International Banking*, Essays in International Finance No. 164, Princeton University Press, Princeton, NJ. Insightful and detailed discussion of disaster myopia.

Herring, R.J. (1999) Credit risk and financial instability, *Oxford Review of Economic Policy*, 15: 63–79. Interesting policy study review of credit risk issues in the financial sector.

House of Lords. (2012) *European Banking Union: Key Issues and Challenges*, Report House of Lords (HL) Paper 88, 12 December 2012 HMSO, London.

Knight, F.H. (1921) *Risk, Uncertainty, and Profit*, Hart, Schaffner & Marx/Houghton Mifflin, Boston, MA. Classic study that distinguishes between risk, where a probability can be attached to an outcome, and uncertainty, where it cannot.

Saunders, A. (2014) *Is Basel Turning Banks into Public Utilities*. Available at SSRN: http://ssrn.com/abstract=2475627 or http://dx.doi.org/10.2139/ssrn.2475627

Skidelsky, R. (2009) *Keynes: The Return of the Master*, Penguin Allen Lane, New York. Classic insights into Keynesian views on financial crises by his pre-eminent biographer.

Stern, N. (2006) *The Economics of Climate Change: The Stern Review*, CUP, Cambridge. A report published by the UK government that examines the impact of global warming on the world economy.

TheCityUK. (2013) *Islamic Finance*, TheCityUK, London.

FURTHER READING

DeYoung, R., Evanoff, D.D., and Molyneux, P. (2009) Mergers and acquisitions of financial institutions: A review of the post-2000 literature, *Journal of Financial Services Research*, 36(2): 87–110. Detailed review of the financial sector M&A literature.

Garmaise, M.J., and Moskowitz, T.J. (2006) Bank mergers and crime: the real and social effects of credit market competition, *Journal of Finance*, 61: 495–538. Interesting study that correlates bank M&A activity with increased crime.

Hoepner, A.G., and Wilson, J.O. (2010) Social, environmental, ethical and trust (SEET) issues in banking: An overview. Available at http://papers.ssrn.com/sol3/papers.cfm?abstract_id=1686240. Detailed and interesting review of the SEET literature.

Maloney, M. (2008) *Rich Dad's Advisors: Guide to Investing in Gold and Silver: Protect your Financial Future*, Grand Central Publishing, New York. Guide to investing in gold and silver.

Glossary

accepting Signing a bill of exchange signifying an agreement to pay. Subsequent or alternative signature by a bank virtually guarantees payment.

account For equity settlements, exchanges may have an account period, for example 2 weeks, 1 month and so on, with payment due on 'account' or 'settlement' day. The alternative is a rolling settlement system.

accrued interest The interest accrued so far on a bond and payable by the purchaser. Quoted separately from the 'clean price'.

adverse selection The process whereby 'bad' results occur when buyers and sellers have different information (asymmetric information): 'bad' products or services are more likely to be selected. A bank that sets one price for all its cheque processing accounts runs the risk of being adversely selected against by its low-balance, high-activity (and hence least profitable) customers. Another example relates to the demand for insurance, which increases with risk.

alpha factor The element in a share price that reflects its individual performance as opposed to the market, which is the beta factor.

alternative investment market (AIM) A new market for smaller companies' shares set up in the UK in June 1995.

American depository receipt (ADR) The form in which foreign shares can be traded in the US without a formal listing.

annual yield See *flat yield*.

arbitrage Taking advantage of an anomaly in prices or rates in different markets, for example buying in one and simultaneously selling in the other.

arbitrageurs Those looking for arbitrage opportunities. Applied especially in the US to those trying to exploit takeover possibilities.

Article 65 Article of the Japanese Financial Code that prevented commercial banks from engaging in some investment banking activities (and vice versa); now dismantled.

asset-backed commercial paper (ABCP) Money market paper backed by assets.

asset-backed security (ABS) Securities that have collateral support. The assets may be backed by real or financial assets, for example mortgage-backed securities/bonds.

assets The side of the bank's balance sheet dealing with lending.

assurance The business of life insurance and pensions.

asymmetric information When two parties have different information about contracts or other deals. A depositor knows less about what their deposits are being used for in the bank compared to the bank manager. The bank knows less about how their loans are being used by borrowers.

back office Accounting and settlement procedures.

bad bank A company set up at a time of crisis. Bad loans are moved out of troubled banks into the bad bank that is run by the government.

bank bill A bill of exchange accepted by a bank on the central bank's 'eligible' list. The central bank itself would rediscount a bill of this type. Also called an eligible bill.

Bank for International Settlements (BIS) The central bankers' central bank, based in Basel, Switzerland, established by the Hague agreement of 1930.

Basel Committee   The short form for the Basel Committee on Banking Supervision. Set up by the central bank governors of the G10 countries in 1974, it seeks to improve the supervisory guidelines that central banks or similar regulatory authorities impose on both wholesale and retail banks. It sets banking policy guidelines for both member and non-member countries and resides at the Bank for International Settlements, Basel, Switzerland.

base money   Notes and coins plus bank reserves held at the central bank; also referred to as 'high-powered money'.

basis point (bp)   One-hundredth of 1%.

bearer bond   A bond payable to whoever is in possession, that is, no central register.

beta factor   The effect of overall market movements on a share price (see *alpha factor*).

bid rate   Rate of interest offered for interbank deposits. Generally, the dealer's buying price for equities, bonds, foreign exchange and so on.

Big Bang   Deregulation of the UK stock exchange, 27 October 1986.

bill of exchange   A signed promise to pay by a receiver of goods or services and kept by the supplier. May be sold at a discount.

blue chip   The most highly regarded shares; the metaphor is from gambling casinos.

bond   A certificate issued by a borrower as receipt for a loan longer than 12 months, indicating a rate of interest and date of repayment.

bond stripping   See *coupon stripping*.

bonos   *Bonos del Estado*, Spanish government bonds.

bonus issue   Same as *scrip issue*.

Brady bond   Bonds issued as part of LDC debt reduction under a scheme devised by Nicholas Brady.

Bretton Woods   Meetings at Bretton Woods (US) in 1944 set up the World Bank, IMF and foreign exchange system for the period following the Second World War.

BRICs   A term that refers to the countries of Brazil, Russia, India and China.

broker   An agent for buying/selling securities or intermediary for a loan or sale of foreign exchange (also known as a money broker).

BTAN   *Bons du Trésor à intérêt annuel*, French government 2- and 5-year notes.

BTF   *Bons du Trésor à taux fixe*, French government T-bills.

BTP   *Buoni del Tesoro poliennali*, Italian government bond.

bulldogs   Sterling bonds issued in the UK by foreign organizations.

bullet repayment   The whole of a bond or bank loan is repaid at maturity, instead of staged payments in the last few years.

bund   Short name for the medium-term German government bond contract on Eurex.

Bundesbank   The German central bank.

cable   Shorthand for dollar/sterling rate.

call money   Money lent by banks to other banks or discount houses, which can be recalled as needed.

call option   An option to buy a share/bond/index/interest rate contract later at a price agreed today.

cap   An agreement with a counterparty that sets an upper limit to interest rates for the cap buyer for a stated time period.

capital adequacy   The need to maintain adequate capital to cover counterparty risk and position risk.

capital gain   Profit that results from investments in an asset, such as stocks, bonds, property, art works, precious metals and so on. It is the difference between a higher selling price and a lower purchase price, resulting in a financial gain for the investor. Most countries tax capital gains.

capitalization   Market capitalization of a company is the number of shares multiplied by the current price.

capital markets   The market for medium- and long-term securities.

capital ratio   The ratio of a bank's primary capital to a weighted value of assets (for example cash = 0 weighting).

certificate of deposit (CD)   Issued by banks to raise money – strong secondary market.

CHAPS   Clearing House Automated Payments System, for electronic clearing of payments the same day (UK). Used for sterling and euros.

Chicago Board of Trade (CBOT)   Was established in 1848 and is the world's oldest futures and options exchange. In July 2007, it merged with the Chicago Mercantile Exchange (CME) and in 2008, with the New York Mercantile Exchange (NYMEX) to form the CME Group.

Chicago Mercantile Exchange (CME)   One of the world's largest derivatives exchanges. Initially focused on commodity derivatives but now offers a full spectrum of products. Merged with CBOT in 2007 and the New York Mercantile Exchange (NYMEX) in 2008 to form the CME Group.

CHIPS   Clearing House Interbank Payment System, electronic bank clearing system in New York.

clean price   Price of a bond not including the accrued interest element.

clearing house   Central body guaranteeing contracts in a traded options/futures marketplace.

collar   A combination of a cap and floor. Setting a band within which interest rates will apply, for example 10–12%, for a given period. Also used for currency rates.

collateralized debt obligations (CDOs)   These are a type of asset-backed security whose value and payments are derived from a portfolio of fixed income underlying assets. CDO securities are broken down into various tranches according to risk type. The senior tranches are the lowest risk. Interest payments on the tranches are made according to their seniority, with senior tranches offering lower rates than more risky junior tranches. See *structured finance*.

collateralized mortgage obligation (CMO)   A collateralized mortgage obligation (CMO) is a type of complex debt security that repackages and directs the payments of principal and interest from a collateral pool of a range of mortgage securities to different types and maturities of securities issued by a SPV.

commercial banking   The 'classic' banking business of taking deposits and lending money, either retail or wholesale.

commercial mortgage-backed securities (CMBS)   A form of asset-backed security backed by commercial property mortgages.

commercial paper   A short-term security issued to raise money, usually by corporates.

consolidation   Reorganizing shareholdings so that, for example, 10 shares at 10p nominal are replaced by one at £1 nominal.

convertible   A convertible bond may be converted later into equity, some other bond or even a commodity, for example gold, as an alternative to redemption.

corporate finance   The department of a merchant/investment bank dealing with takeovers, mergers and strategic advice to companies.

counterparty risk   The risk involved if a counterparty fails to settle.

coupon rate   The annual rate of interest on a security noted on coupons issued with bearer bonds.

coupons   Issued with bearer bonds to enable the holder to claim the interest.

coupon stripping   Detaching the coupons from a bond and selling the coupons and the principal as individual zero-coupon bonds.

cover   The amount of dividend paid (net) divided into the amount of profit after tax available for distribution.

covered bonds   A form of asset-backed security where a special purpose vehicle (SPV) is not used.

creation of credit   Banks' ability to lend money, facilitated by the use of notes and coin for a small percentage of transactions only.

credit default swap (CDS)   Selling credit risk for a premium.

credit derivatives   A general market where credit risk is sold for a premium.

credits ratings   For example AAA or Aaa, issued by companies like Standard & Poor's and Moody's to rate the level of risk of a bond or note issue.

crest   The UK paperless equity settlement system, which started in mid-1996.

cross-rates   Rates between two currencies, neither of which is the dollar.

cumulative   Applied to preference shares – if dividend is missed, it is still owed to the holder.

custodian   An organization that will store the original documentation for, say, bonds or equities and will look after settlement.

cylinder   Name used for a collar in currency markets.

debenture   In the UK, a bond secured on assets. In the US and Canada, a bond not secured on assets.

derivatives   Products whose price is derived from the price of an underlying asset, for example if ICI shares are the underlying asset, an option to buy or sell them at a given price is the derivative. Applied to options, futures, swaps and so on.

discounting   Buying/selling a security at less than face value.

disintermediation   Direct market borrowing or lending by companies without going through a bank. A bank is traditionally the 'intermediary' between depositors and borrowers.

dividend   The proportion of corporate earnings paid out to shareholders, usually quarterly. When a company earns profits, this can be put to two main uses. The funds can be reinvested in the business ('retained earnings'), or they can be paid to the owners of the business (shareholders) as dividends. Typically, companies do both and retain some earnings and pay the remainder as dividends.

dividend yield   The annual percentage return on a share price represented by the current dividend – usually gross.

Dodd-Frank Act   Legislation, more formally called the Wall Street Reform and Consumer Protection Act 2010, which established a new regulatory framework for US financial institutions in the light of the banking crisis.

dragon bond   A eurobond issued in Hong Kong or Singapore and targeted for primary distribution to Asian investors.

EAGLEs   Emerging and growth-leading economies, a group of emerging markets whose contribution to global economic growth over the next decade or so is expected to be greater than the average of the leading industrialized nations.

EASDAQ   European Association of Securities Dealers Automated Quotations – a pan-European trading system, which started in late 1996 but was taken over by NASDAQ in 2001.

eligible bills   Bills of exchange eligible for sale to the central bank when acting as lender of last resort.

e-money   Electronic money is a digital equivalent of cash, stored on an electronic device or remotely at a server.

EONIA   Euro Overnight Index Average, average of overnight rates in the eurozone. The Eonia rate is the 1-day interbank interest rate for the Euro zone.

equity   General term for shares.

Eurex   The futures/options exchange, which was established in 1998 by the merger of Germany's Deutsche Terminbörse (DTB) and Switzerland's Swiss Options and Financial Futures Exchange (SOFFEX).

Euribor   Interbank lending rate for the euro in the 17 countries of EMU.

euro   The name of the single currency in Europe's monetary union.

eurobond   A bond issued in a market outside that of the domestic currency.

eurocertificate of deposit   See *certificate of deposit*.

eurocommercial paper   See *commercial paper*.

eurocurrencies   Any currency held by banks, companies or individuals outside its country of origin.

Euro LIBOR   Interbank lending rate for the euro in London.

Euronext   Formed in 2000 by the merger of the Paris Bourse and the Brussels and Amsterdam stock exchanges. Lisbon joined in 2002. Euronext merged with the NYSE Group, in 2007 to form NYSE Euronext. In 2013 Intercontinental Exchange completed the acquisition of NYSE Euronext.

EURONIA   Euro Overnight Index Average, average of overnight euro rates in the London market. It is calculated from the unsecured overnight euro deposit trades originated by money brokers in London.

Euronote   Short-term security denominated in a eurocurrency.

European Banking Union   This was established in November 2014 when the European Central Bank (ECB) took on supervisory responsibility for banks operating in the euro area. The Banking Union has three pillars. Pillar 1 – the ECB will have direct responsibility for supervising the largest banks but will also have the power to deal with small banks if necessary. Pillar 2 there will be a common resolution fund and mechanisms for dealing with failing banks. Pillar 3 relates to the set-up of a common deposit-insurance scheme to prevent bank runs (see Single Supervisory Mechanism and Single Resolution Mechanism)

European Central Bank (ECB)   The European Union's (EU) central bank that administers the monetary policy of the 19 EU eurozone member states. Established by the Treaty of Amsterdam in 1998 and headquartered in Frankfurt, Germany.

European Economic and Monetary Union (EMU)   A single currency area set up for 11 European countries on 1 January 1999. Greece joined later, and notes and coins were included from 1 January 2002. By January 2015, there were 19 member countries.

European Monetary System (EMS)   General agreement on monetary cooperation. Included official use of the ecu, 20% of central banks' reserves held in a European Monetary Cooperation Fund and exchange rates of member countries kept within a stated range, one to another (ERM). Set up in 1979. Replaced by EMU.

European System of Central Banks (ESCB)   The ECB, plus the 19 central banks of the member countries in the eurozone. (Legally, the non-eurozone central banks are included but take no part in decisions on monetary policy.)

Eurosystem   The ECB plus the 19 central banks of the participating countries only, not including those not in the euro area.

exchange delivery settlement price (EDSP)   The price at which certain futures and options contracts expire.

exchange rate mechanism (ERM)   The interim exchange rate system for countries waiting to join EMU.

exchange-traded funds (ETFs)   These are listed securities that mimic the behaviour of an index and can be traded just like an ordinary share.

ex dividend (XD)   If a share or bond is marked 'XD', this means that the purchaser is not entitled to the forthcoming dividend/interest payment, as the cut-off point has passed.

exercise price   The price at which an option can be exercised (also called 'strike price').

ex rights (XR)   In rights issues, if a share is marked 'XR', this means that the purchaser is not entitled to the rights, as the cut-off point has passed.

factoring   Buying trade debts on a regular basis to assist cash flow, usually done by subsidiaries of banks.

fast market   When normal stock market rules are superseded due to chaotic conditions.

FCP   *Fonds communs de placement*, French 'closed-ended' fund.

Fedwire   Electronic payments system between Federal Reserve banks in the US.

Financial Services Authority (FSA)   Regulator of the UK's financial services industry. On 16 June 2010, George Osborne, Chancellor of the Exchequer, announced that the FSA was to be abolished and its responsibilities separated into two new agencies, one to be part of the Bank of England.

Financial Times Stock Exchange (FTSE)   Indices such as FTSE 100.

flat yield   The annual percentage return on a bond taking into account the buying price, for example if £100 nominal worth of an 8% bond is bought for £50, the yield is 16%. Also called 'annual', 'running' and 'interest yield' (see *redemption yield*).

floating rate   A loan with the interest rate varied at agreed intervals, linked to a base rate, for example LIBOR.

floating rate note (FRN)   An issue where the interest is at floating rate.

floor   An agreement with a counterparty that sets a lower limit to interest rates for the floor buyer for a stated time period.

foreign bonds   Bonds in a domestic currency issued by non-residents.

forward contact   A contract to buy or sell a commodity or security for future delivery at a price agreed today.

forward/forward   (1) An agreement to lend money at a future point in time for a given period of time, for example in 6 months for 6 months. (2) A forward foreign exchange deal not dated today, but at a later date.

forward rate   A rate agreed now for a future purchase or sale of a currency. Derived from the difference in interest rates in the two currencies.

forward rate agreement (FRA)   An agreement with a counterparty that agrees on a stated rate of interest to apply to a notional principal sum at a future time to last for a stated time, for example, in 6 months for 6 months.

front office   Dealing room system to facilitate buying and selling.

fundamental analysis   One of the two major approaches used to predict future asset prices. This approaches uses macroeconomic, industry and company analysis to determine future asset price movements (see *also technical analysis*).

futures contract   Similar to a forward contract, but not expected to go to delivery, as the position will be closed out with the opposite contract.

G7, G10   Meetings of international finance ministers – 'Group of 7', 'Group of 10' and so on.

gearing   Carrying out financial transactions on the basis of a deposit or borrowed money (called 'leverage' in the US).

gearing ratio   Ratio of equity and long-term debt.

gilts   Term applied to UK and Irish government bonds. From 'gilt-edged' or virtually guaranteed. In general use for UK government stock from the 1930s onwards.

Glass-Steagall Act   Passed in the US in 1933, prevented commercial banks from engaging in certain investment banking business (and vice versa); now repealed.

global bonds   Designed to be sold in the eurobond market and the US market at the same time.

global depository receipt (GDR)   A form in which foreign shares can be traded outside their domestic markets.

globalization   The movement to integrate world markets regardless of national boundaries.

government-sponsored enterprises (GSEs)   US GSEs, such as Freddie Mac, Fannie Mae, Ginnie Mae, promoted home ownership via their activity in the mortgage-backed securities market.

grey market   The market for sales of a security before the official market opens.

gross dividend yield   See *dividend yield*.

gross redemption yield   See *redemption yield*.

G-SIFI   Global systemically important financial institution. Failure of such an institution may lead to collapse of the global financial system and/or have global consequences or an impact.

haircut   In a stock borrowing/lending agreement, the borrower passes collateral to a value in excess of the market value of the stock (to allow for the price rising). This excess is called a 'haircut'.

hedge fund   An actively managed fund that seeks an absolute return, that is, a return whether markets go up or down.

hedging   A technique for limiting risk. For example, if a price movement would cause loss, a purchase is made of an options or futures contract giving the opposite result; if a rise in interest rates causes loss, a position is taken with interest rate options/futures so that a rise in interest rates will yield a profit.

high-powered money   See *base money*.

hybrid bonds   Bonds that combine features of equity and debt – perpetual, noncumulative and deeply subordinated.

illiquidity   The inability to meet short-term obligations when they fall due.
For example, banks may not be able to meet deposit withdrawals if they do not have cash in their vaults to pay depositors.

indices   Like the S&P 500, the CAC 40, DAX, FTSE 100 and so on.

ineligible bank bills   Bills of exchange accepted by a bank, but one not on the central bank's list (see *bank bill*).

initial margin   Initial deposit required by a clearing house (as opposed to *variation margin*).

initial public offering (IPO)   US term for 'offer for sale'.

insurance   If contrasted with assurance, this is business other than life insurance.

interbank market   Bank lending/borrowing one to another.

interdealer broker (IDB)   Facilitates deals between market makers who can deal in confidence and anonymity.

interest yield   See *flat yield*.

International Monetary Fund (IMF)   Set up in 1946 to help nations in balance of payments difficulties.

intrinsic value   The amount by which a call option exercise price is below the market price (or a put option exercise price is above it), usually called 'in the money'.

introduction   A method of obtaining a stock exchange quotation. No new shares are issued. Usually they are foreign shares seeking a listing on a domestic market.

investment banking   Banking implying a high involvement with securities – new equity issues, rights issues, bond issues, investment management and so on. Also advice to either party for mergers and acquisitions.

investment grade   A credit rating of BBB (Standard & Poor's), Baa (Moody's) or better, that is, a high-quality bond.

investment trust   A company whose whole business is running a wide portfolio of shares. A 'closed-ended' fund.

irredeemable   Same as *perpetual*.

Islamic banking bonds   Issues made to conform to sharia (Islamic) law.

issuing   Offering a security to the market in the first instance.

joint stock   Having shareholders.

junk bonds   Specifically bonds with ratings of BB (S&P), Ba (Moody's) or less. Generally high-risk, high-yield bonds.

kangaroo bond   An Australian dollar bond issued in Australia by a non-resident.

lead manager   Bank(s) taking a key role in a syndicated loan or issue of securities like eurobonds.

lender of last resort (LLR)   An institution that will extend credit when no one else will do so. Mainly used in the context of central banks providing loans to banks so they avoid liquidity problems and maybe bankruptcy. Usually provided to banks viewed as systemically important, or too big to fail.

leverage   American term for gearing or 'making a small amount of capital go a long way'.

liabilities   The side of a bank's balance sheet dealing with borrowing, that is, deposits, formal loans from others. Also share capital.

LIBID   London Interbank Bid Rate, paid by one bank to another for a deposit.

LIBOR   London Interbank Offered Rate, charged by one bank to another for lending money.

LIFFE   London International Financial Futures and Options Exchange, now part of NYSE Euronext.

LIFFE connect   The electronic derivatives trading system at NYSE Liffe.

liquidity   Ability to meet short-term cash obligations when they fall due. These may be predictable liquidity requirements, such as meeting deposit withdrawals, as well as unpredictable requirements, such as large corporates shutting their deposit accounts. Liquidity is held in the form of cash or short-term assets that can be sold quickly to realize cash (T-bills and other money market paper).

liquidity ratio   Usually a percentage relationship between a bank's liquid assets and its eligible liabilities.

locals   Traders dealing for themselves as speculators.

London Metal Exchange (LME)   Deals in six non-ferrous metals.

long   To be 'long' in shares, bonds or foreign exchange is to own more than have been sold.

long-term refinancing operation (LTRO)   Name given to ECB liquidity injection into eurozone interbank markets in December 2011 and February 2012.

loro   Alternative term for *vostro*.

margin   The deposit required by a clearing house.

margin calls   A call from a broker or clearing house demanding the deposit of cash to cover an adverse price movement of a security.

market maker   The dealers in stocks and shares as principals, that is, taking the risk in their own name.

mark to market   Valuing securities or derivatives transactions at the current market price.

matador bond   Peseta bonds issued in Spain by non-residents.

mortgage-backed security (MBS)   An asset-backed security that represents a claim on the cash flows from mortgage loans via a process known as 'securitization'. MBS relates to asset-backed securities backed by mortgages on residential property, and commercial MBS (CMBS) to those backed by commercial property.

medium-term notes   A flexible facility to issue notes of varying maturity, varying currency and either fixed or floating – all within one set of legal documentation.

MEFF   Mercado Español de Futuros Financieros, Spanish futures and options exchange in Madrid and Barcelona.

merchant banks   UK term for investment banks.

mezzanine   Just as a mezzanine floor is a floor in between two others, so mezzanine debt is subordinated debt lying between equity and senior debt.

MONEP   Marché des Options Négociables de Paris, French options exchange, now part of Euronext Paris.

money at call   An interbank short-term loan that may be recalled at any time.

money market   The market for money instruments with a maturity of less than 1 year.

monoline insurers   Special insurance firms that provide services to the capital markets, that is, they provide insurance guaranteeing the timely repayment of bond principal and interest when an issuer defaults. Insured securities include municipal bonds, MBS and CDOs. When bonds are insured, this reduces their risk and can therefore improve their credit rating.

moral hazard   The tendency to take on too many risks when these are not borne by the risk-taker. For instance, a bank that is viewed as 'too big to fail' will take on more risk because if it gets into financial difficulties, the government will save the bank (see *too big to fail*).

multiple option facility (MOF)   A revolving facility from a syndicate of banks permitting the raising of finance with various options – bank loan, banker's acceptance or commercial paper.

mutual   A bank or insurance company that is not a public company, but owned by the members.

mutual funds   General name for pooled funds, such as investment trusts and unit trusts.

NASDAQ OMX   North American Securities Dealers Automated Quotations, computerized dealing system for US OTC trade outside recognized exchanges; merged with the Swedish/European OMX exchange in 2008.

national debt   The total outstanding debt of the central government, especially bonds and national savings.

normal market size (NMS)   This is the classification concept that replaced the three classes, alpha, beta and gamma. It is based on a percentage (currently 2.5%) of an average day's trading. There are 12 bands, and they are used to decide the minimum quote size and the maximum size for immediate publication of trades (UK).

nostro   'Our', the overseas currency account of a bank with a foreign bank or subsidiary.

NYSE Euronext   Stock exchange formed by the US New York Stock Exchange and European Euronext in April 2007.

NYSE LIFFE   The derivatives market of NYSE Euronext.

OATS *Obligations assimilables du Trésor*, French government bonds.

off-balance risk sheets   Risks for bankers other than activities that end up as an asset on the balance sheet. For example, standby loans, standby letters of credit, derivatives generally.

offer for sale   A method of bringing a company to the market. May be at a fixed price or by tender.

offer rate   Rate of interest charged for interbank lending of money. Generally, the dealer's selling price for equities, bonds, foreign exchange and so on. Also called 'ask rate' or price.

open market operations   Involves the central bank buying or selling financial instruments (government bills, bonds, foreign currencies) in order to influence the quantity of money in circulation.

open outcry   Face-to-face trading.

option-dated forward rate   A forward rate (foreign exchange), but the date is more flexible.

options   The right, but not the obligation, to buy/sell equities, bonds, foreign exchange or interest rate contracts at a future date at a price agreed now. 'Traded options' means the options themselves can be bought and sold.

option writer   Term used to describe any option trading strategy that involves selling options. The seller is the writer.

over the counter (OTC)   The OTC market deals outside a trading exchange, for example a currency option purchased from a bank.

Pacman defence   In a takeover situation, when the company that is the subject of a bid turns round and tries to take over the bidder.

panda bond   A bond issued in China by non-residents.

par   The nominal value of a security, for example $1,000 for US Treasury bonds or £100 for UK government bonds.

perpetual   A security without time limit for redemption.

pits   Trading areas in options, futures and commodity exchanges.

placing   A method of bringing a company to the market. The shares are placed with institutional investors and some private investors, that is, not 'offered for sale' generally.

plaza agreement   An example of international cooperation. Following a meeting in October 1975 at the Plaza Hotel, New York, international finance ministers agreed to take measures to reduce the exchange rate for the dollar.

poison pill   A device to frustrate a hostile takeover bid.

preference shares   Dividend is paid as a fixed percentage. They have preference over ordinary shareholders for dividend payment and in case of liquidation. Usually non-voting. ('Preferred stock' in the US.)

price/earnings (P/E) ratio   Ratio of share price to earnings after tax.

primary market   Markets where securities are sold when first issued.

prime broker   A firm (usually an investment bank) that provides a package of services to hedge funds and other professional investors that need the ability to borrow securities and cash for investment purposes. Typically, prime brokers provide a centralized securities clearing facility so that collateral requirements of, say, hedge funds are netted across all deals. The prime broker also extends credit to hedge funds to finance investment activity.

private banking   Specialist banking services for high-net-worth individuals.

private equity   Raising money for venture capital for early stage companies or management buyouts.

private placing   When securities are not offered for open sale, but are 'placed' with institutional investors.

program trading   Bulk sales or purchases of securities triggered by computer programs.

purchasing power parity (PPP)   PPP theory uses the long-term equilibrium exchange rate of two currencies to equalize their purchasing power. For example, if a representative consumption basket costs $3,000 in the US and £2,000 in the UK, the PPP exchange rate would be $1.50/£. If the actual spot rate were $2.00/£, this would indicate that the pound is overvalued by 33%, or equivalently the dollar is undervalued by 25%.

put option   An option to sell a share/bond/index/interest rate contract later at a price agreed today.

quantitative easing (QE)   Process whereby the central bank purchases government bonds on a massive scale to inject liquidity into the financial system/economy. It is used as a form of monetary policy when interest rates are so low they cannot be reduced further.

redemption   Final payment to holders of bonds.

redemption yield   The gross redemption yield takes into account the gain or loss to redemption as well as the flat yield (also called 'yield to maturity').

reinsurance   Laying off the original risk with others. Insurance companies insure their own risks in the reinsurance market.

RELIT   *Règlement livraison de titres*, French stock exchange settlement system.

repo   Sale and repurchase agreement. Securities are sold but must be repurchased later.

reserves   The proportion of bank's assets that are held in a liquid form that has to exceed regulatory requirements (known as 'reserve requirements'). The higher a bank's reserves, the safer, as less has been lent out.

reverse repo   When the buyer of the securities initiates the repo deal.

revolving credit   A commitment to lend on a recurring basis on predefined terms.

rights issue   An offer of shares for cash to existing shareholders in proportion to their existing holdings.

ring-fence   A term used in the UK's Vickers Commission report recommending that high-risk investment banking activity should be distanced/separated in some way from low-risk retail banking.

rolling settlement   For example 'five working days', that is, deal on Tuesday, settle next Tuesday; deal Wednesday, settle next Wednesday, instead of all deals within a given 'account' being settled on a given day.

RONIA   Repurchase Overnight Index Average, the weighted average of all secured sterling overnight cash transactions. It was introduced in June 2011 and is published daily at around 17.00 UK time by the Wholesale Market Brokers' Association. It is the wholesale lending rate for secured overnight transactions.

running yield   See *flat yield*.

Samurai bonds   A yen bond issued in Japan by non-residents.

savings and loans associations (S&Ls)   US institutions similar to UK building societies.

schatze   German short-term Treasury issues.

scrip dividend   Offer of shares instead of a dividend (optional).

scrip issue   A free issue of shares to existing holders.

SEAQ   Stock Exchange Automated Quotations, the system that came in with Big Bang (UK).

secondary markets   The buying and selling of a security after its primary issue.

Securities and Exchange Commission (SEC)   US body controlling regulation of the market.

securitization   The borrowing of money through issue of securities on international markets (in particular) instead of through a bank loan. Also, converting an existing loan into securities, for example mortgage bonds (see *ABS*).

seignorage   The special profit central banks make from printing banknotes whose nominal value is well in excess of their cost to the bank.

series   All options of the same class, exercise price and expiry dates.

settlement day   When the money for a given trade is due to be paid (and the securities handed over).

shadow banking   A group of financial firms, infrastructure and practices that support financial transactions that occur beyond the reach of existing regulation. Includes hedge funds, money market funds and structured investment vehicles. Investment banks were blamed for undertaking a lot of securitization business via the shadow banking system, but they are not shadow banking institutions themselves.

shares   Shareholdings in companies with reward by way of dividend – usually called 'equity'.

sharia   Islamic law.

shell company   A company with few assets, profits nil or in decline, and a very low share price.

short   To be 'short' in shares, bonds or foreign exchange is to have sold more than have been bought.

short selling   An investment strategy based on the price of the security falling. In a typical short sale, stock will be borrowed and sold immediately with a promise to return the stock at a later date. The investor hopes the price will fall, so then it can be purchased and returned to the lender at a profit.

SICAV   *Société d'investissement à capital variable*, French 'open-ended' mutual fund.

Single Supervisory Mechanism (SSM)   The name given to the mechanism whereby the European Central Bank was given responsibility (In November 2014) to supervise banks operating in the euro area (see Single Resolution Mechanism and European Banking Union).

Single Resolution Mechanism (SRM)   The mechanism that will be used by the European Central Bank to deal with failing banks under its role as bank supervisor (see Single Supervisory Mechanism and European Banking Union).

SOFFEX   Swiss Options and Financial Futures Exchange, merged with Deutsche Terminbörse in 1998 to form Eurex.

SONIA   Sterling Overnight Index Average, average of overnight rates.

special purpose vehicle (SPV)   Used for the issue of asset-backed securities.

split   Existing shares are reorganized ('split') into more shares, for example two shares at 25p are exchanged for each one at 50p (nominal values).

spot   Today's rate for settlement in two days.

spread   Difference between bid rate and offer rate. More generally between one rate and another.

stock borrowing/lending   Equity and bond traders may temporarily borrow or lend stock in exchange for collateral – especially useful for a short position. Although called 'borrowing/lending', the stock is legally sold in UK law, but this is not necessarily the case elsewhere.

Stock Exchange Electronic Trading Service (SETS)   UK order-driven electronic trading system implemented in October 1997.

stock index arbitrage   Arbitrage between the options, futures and market price of an index at contract closure.

stocks   Fixed interest securities, for example bonds, debentures, preference shares.

straddle   A traded option strategy – simultaneous purchase/sale of both call option and put option for the same share, exercise price and expiry date.

strategic investor   An investor that goes beyond simply investing financial resources into a business, in contrast to a financial investor that just buys company and other investments, but has no intention of running the business.

strike price   See *exercise price* (alternative term).

structured finance   A general term used to refer to an area of finance that uses relatively complex corporate and/or legal structures to create innovative financial transactions. For example, the creation of special purpose vehicles (SPVs) to hold and issue types of asset-backed securities (ABS).

structured investment vehicle (SIV)   A type of fund set up by banks to invest in long-term assets (typically asset-backed securities including MBS and CDOs). The funds borrowed money by issuing short-term securities (usually commercial paper) at low interest and then used these funds to purchase longer term securities that earned higher interest rates. SIVs were widely used by banks prior to the credit crisis and were often large in size, ranging from $1bn to $30bn. They were considered low risk and did not need capital backing. When the credit crisis hit, the value of the securities held in SIVs became uncertain, and short-term funding disappeared. Banks had to take the SIV investments back onto their balance sheets, incurring massive losses.

subordinated debt   A bond that, in the event of liquidation, can claim only after other senior debts have been met.

sukuk   A bond issued to conform to sharia law.

swap   Exchange of debt obligations between two parties, either exchange of currencies or fixed to floating rate (and vice versa) and sometimes both. The latter applies to a notional principal sum, and the agreement lasts for a stated time period.

swapnote   A contract offered at Euronext. Actually, a bond contract, but the cash flows of the bond are discounted by the swaps yield curve.

swaps yield curve   Based on the appropriate interest rates for top-quality non-government borrowers.

swaption   An option to have a swap at a future point in time.

syndicate   Managers, underwriters and selling agents of a bond or bank loan.

systemically important financial institution (SIFI)   Failure of such an institution may lead to collapse of the financial system.

tap stock   In general, in bond markets, further issues of a previously issued bond.

TARGET   Trans-European Automated Real Time Gross Settlement Express Transfer, the official interbank euro payment system for the eurozone.

technical analysis   One of the two major approaches used to predict future asset prices. This approach uses basic or advanced statistical approaches and mainly past price trends to predict future price movements (see *fundamental analysis*).

tender   A bank loan or new security is offered to dealers who must compete for the business. If settled on a strike price basis, all pay the same price. If offered on a bid price basis, all pay the price they bid.

ticks   Smallest price movement of a contract, for example 0.01, or $^1/32$.

time value   That part of an option premium that is not the intrinsic value.

tombstone   Formal notice in the press of a syndicated loan, bond issue, commercial paper programme and so on.

too big to fail (TBTF)   Banks or other financial institutions are regarded as too big to fail if failure would result in a systemic crisis, and the government would be expected to avoid such a crisis occurring and would therefore save these institutions. This leads to moral hazard.

touch prices   The highest bid price and lowest offer price for a particular stock or share.

trade bill   A bill of exchange not endorsed by a bank and not eligible for rediscount at the central bank.

trade date   The date a trade is agreed, as opposed to settled.

traded options   An option to buy or sell a share/currency/index/interest rate contract later at a price agreed today. This is a standardized market, and the options can themselves be sold.

tranche   A French word meaning 'slice' or 'portion'. In finance, it is usually used to describe a security that can be split up into smaller pieces and subsequently sold to investors. It may also refer to the part of a loan that is drawn down, for example a $200m loan may be lent in 10 $20m tranches over a certain time period.

tranchette   A smaller slice than a tranche (also known as a sub-tranche). For example, there may be a large issue of an existing bond to meet market demands, and this may be followed by a smaller issue.

Treasury bill (T-bill)   Issued by governments to raise money. Typically, 3, 6 or 12 months.

UK Payments Administration   Controls cheque clearing, Bacs and CHAPS in the UK; replaced the Association for Payment Clearing Services in July 2009.

undated   Same as *perpetual*.

underwrite   When a group of financial concerns agree to subscribe for a proportion of a new issue to ensure its full subscription. The other use of the term is in insurance.

underwriter   Anyone offering insurance cover for a premium.

unit trust   A portfolio of holdings in various companies, divided into units that are bought and sold directly. An 'open-ended' fund, for example the French SICAV.

universal bank   A term for a bank that is equally engaged in commercial and investment banking, for example Deutsche Bank, UBS and so on.

Value at Risk (VaR)   VaR analysis uses sophisticated algorithms to evaluate the risk in a bank's positions.

variable rate note (VRN)   A floating rate note where the margin above LIBOR is not fixed, but reset at intervals.

variation margin   Further amounts of deposit (debit or credit) calculated by a clearing house.

vendor placing   In a takeover bid where shares are offered instead of cash, if the victim's shareholders would prefer cash, institutions are found that will buy the shares.

venture capital   Capital provided for high risks that would not normally attract conventional finance.

Vickers Commission   The Independent Commission on Banking, chaired by Sir John Vickers, was set up by the UK government and asked to report on structural and related non-structural reforms to the UK banking sector to promote financial stability and competition. The Final Report was published in September 2011 and recommended, among other things, 'ring-fencing' investment and retail bank activity.

volatility   An important term in options, used to describe the volatility of an asset's price movements – this will affect the premium.

Volcker Rule   A provision in the Dodd-Frank Act that restricts banks proprietary trading activity. Named after the previous governor of the Federal Reserve, Paul Volcker, who had claimed that the crisis was partially due to banks speculative trading activity. There are a number of exemptions to this rule.

vostro   'Your', the domestic currency account of a foreign bank with a domestic bank.

warrant   A certificate attached to a bond or security giving the holder the right to buy equity/bonds later at a set price. May be issued on its own without attachment, for example gilts warrants, currency warrants, CAC 40 warrants, Eurotunnel warrants and so on.

when issued   Grey market trading in government bonds prior to the regular auctions.

white knight   In a takeover situation, a more acceptable bidder may be sought – the white knight.

white squire   Alternatively, key blocks of shares are bought by friendly contacts – the white squire.

wholesale money   The borrowing and lending of large sums of money – usually between banks, large companies and the institutions.

working balance   An accounting term used to explain the surplus cash balances needed by banks to manage their day-to-day cash activities.

world bank   The International Bank for Reconstruction and Development, commonly known as the World Bank. Set up in 1945.

yankee bond   A dollar bond issued in the US by non-residents.

yard   Foreign exchange term for 1,000 million.

yield   See flat yield.

yield curve   A graph showing the relationship between short-term and long-term yields for a given security or type of borrowing. Upward sloping = positive yield curve; downward sloping = negative yield curve.

zero-coupon bond   A bond issued without interest payments, but at a deep discount.

Index